Frommer's®

POSTCARDS

FROM

PARIS

The strollable banks of the Seine. See chapter 6. © Robert Holmes Photography.

Paris's flower markets are a feast for the eyes and the nose. The biggest one is on the Île de la Cité, along the Seine—see chapter 8. © Robert Holmes Photography.

The Seine by night and by boat. See chapter 6 for details on taking a bateau-mouche cruise down the river. Above © Malcolm/Image Bank; opposite © Dave G. Houser Photography.

Cliché or not, the Jardin des Tuileries has long been a favorite spot for lovers. See chapter 7 for a walking tour that will take you through the gardens. © Bryan F. Peterson/The Stock Market.

The ever controversial, inside-out Pompidou Center (known locally as Beaubourg). See chapter 6 for a description of this museum of modern art. © Matthew Weinreb/Image Bank.

The Hôtel de Ville is not a hotel at all, but Paris's City Hall. See chapter 6 for the gruesome history of the building's site. © Catherine Karnow Photography.

If Paris had nothing else to offer, many would still flock here for the food. See chapter 5 for our favorite bakeries, and chapter 8 for our favorite places to buy fresh produce, chocolate, and other foodstuffs. Top © Steven Rothfeld/Tony Stone Images; bottom © Bill Gallery/ Viesti Associates, Inc.; opposite © Robert Holmes Photography.

Notre Dame is at the very center of Paris, geographically and historically. See chapter 6 for the story of the city's most famous church. *Opposite* © *Kevin Galvin. Left* © *Harald Sund/Image Bank; below* © *Herbert Hartmann/ Image Bank.*

Even subway stations can be works of art in Paris. This one is at Port Dauphine. © *Stephen Studd/Tony Stone Images.*

Even if you don't buy anything, Galeries Lafayette department store is worth visiting for its grandiose turn-of-the-century architecture. See chapter 8. © Romilly Lockyer/Image Bank.

The Louvre, with its controversial Pyramid in the middle, lives up to its reputation as one of the world's greatest museums. See chapter 6. Opposite © Kevin Galvin Photography; above © Dave Bartruff Photography.

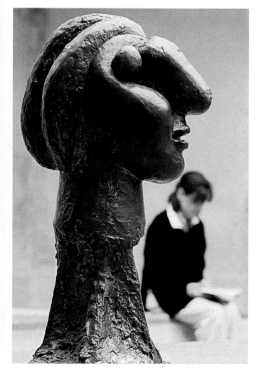

The Picasso Museum offers a more intimate museum experience. See chapter 6. © Catherine Karnow Photography.

The Château of Versailles is a tribute to the folly and opulence of France's grand century. Its Hall of Mirrors (bottom photo) was the setting for the treaty that ended World War I. See chapter 10. Both photos © Robert Holmes Photography.

*Giverny, home of Impressionist
painter Claude Monet, makes for a
lovely and inspiring getaway from the
city. See chapter 10. Above © Robert
Holmes Photography; left © James
Martin/Tony Stone Images.*

Les Deux Magots cafe, in St-Germain-des-Prés, is one of Paris's great literary landmarks. See chapters 5 & 6. © Bob Krist Photography.

Frommer's® 2000

Paris

by Darwin Porter & Danforth Prince

with Online Directory by Michael Shapiro

MACMILLAN • USA

ABOUT THE AUTHORS

Veteran travel writers **Darwin Porter** and **Danforth Prince** have written numerous best-selling Frommer guides, notably to England, France, the Caribbean, Italy, and Germany. Porter, a bureau chief for the Miami Herald at the age of 21, has lived in Paris periodically and written about the city for many years. Prince also has lived in the city for many years as a member of the Paris bureau for the *New York Times*.

MACMILLAN TRAVEL

Macmillan General Reference USA, Inc.
1633 Broadway
New York, NY 10019

Find us online at **www.frommers.com**

Copyright © 2000 by Macmillan General Reference USA, Inc.
Maps copyright © by Macmillan General Reference USA, Inc.

ISBN 0-02-863071-8
ISSN 0899-3203

Editor: David Gibbs
Production Editor: Robyn Burnett
Photo Editor: Richard Fox
Design by Michele Laseau
Staff Cartographers: John Decamillis, Roberta Stockwell
Page Creation by Sean Monkhouse and Linda Quigley
Front cover photo: Eiffel Tower at night.

SPECIAL SALES

Bulk purchases (10+ copies) of Frommer's and selected Macmillan travel guides are available to corporations, organizations, mail-order catalogs, institutions, and charities at special discounts, and can be customized to suit individual needs. For more information write to Special Sales, Macmillan General Reference, 1633 Broadway, New York, NY 10019.

Manufactured in the United States of America

5   4   3   2   1

Contents

List of Maps

AN INVITATION TO THE READER

In researching this book, we discovered many wonderful places—hotels, restaurants, shops, and more. We're sure you'll find others. Please tell us about them, so we can share the information with your fellow travelers in upcoming editions. If you were disappointed with a recommendation, we'd love to know that, too. Please write to:

Frommer's Paris 2000
Macmillan Travel
1633 Broadway
New York, NY 10019

AN ADDITIONAL NOTE

Please be advised that travel information is subject to change at any time—and this is especially true of prices. We therefore suggest that you write or call ahead for confirmation when making your travel plans. The authors, editors, and publisher cannot be held responsible for the experiences of readers while traveling. Your safety is important to us, however, so we encourage you to stay alert and be aware of your surroundings. Keep a close eye on cameras, purses, and wallets, all favorite targets of thieves and pickpockets.

WHAT THE SYMBOLS MEAN

✪ Frommer's Favorites

Our favorite places and experiences—outstanding for quality, value, or both.

The following abbreviations are used for credit cards:

AE	American Express	EURO	Eurocard
CB	Carte Blanche	JCB	Japan Credit Bank
DC	Diners Club	MC	MasterCard
DISC	Discover	V	Visa
ER	enRoute		

FIND FROMMER'S ONLINE

Arthur Frommer's Budget Travel Online (**www.frommers.com**) offers more than 6,000 pages of up-to-the-minute travel information—including the latest bargains and candid, personal articles updated daily by Arthur Frommer himself. No other Web site offers such comprehensive and timely coverage of the world of travel.

The Best of Paris

1

Paris is preparing for an invasion unlike any it has seen before. "We're having a picnic in the year 2000," said Julian Française, a government employee. "We have a better, cleaner, more exciting, and more dynamic city to show the world than we did in the '70s and '80s. 'Ya'll come and see us now,' as they'd say in Texas."

Hoping to put aside its economic woes of the 1990s, Paris is facing the 21st century with a bright face. According to polls, the French people, even the traditionally cynical Parisians, are becoming more optimistic. The city looks better than it has in years, with such monumental projects completed as the cleaning of the Louvre, Opéra, and Notre-Dame. Much of the riverfront has been restored, repaired, and spruced up in anticipation of the millennium. And always the City of Light, Paris will be even more dazzling in 2000, with greater illuminations than ever before.

Paris may not be the most happening city in Europe. London, at least in the opinion of Londoners, still retains that position. But Paris remains queen of the continent, with more museums than ever, greater nighttime diversions, better hotels (many of them also rejuvenated for the millennium), better and more varied shops, and the most talented stable of chefs in the world.

Whether you're heading here for the first or the 50th time, the discovery of the City of Light and the experience of making it your own is and always has been the most compelling reason to visit. Neighborhoods such as Montmartre and Montparnasse, St-Germain and the Marais, are waiting to be explored for the first time or to be rediscovered by a returning visitor. In some ways, they remain the same, as if etched in stone, but after a second look it's obvious that they have changed.

If you're a first-timer, everything in Paris, of course, is new. If you've been away for a while, expect changes: Taxi drivers may no longer correct your fractured French, but address you in English—and that's tantamount to a revolution. More Parisians have a rudimentary knowledge of English, and the country, at least at first glance, seems less hysterically xenophobic than in past years. Part of this derives from Parisians' interest in music, videos, and films from foreign countries, and part from France's growing awareness of its role within a united Europe.

Yet France has never been more concerned about the loss of its identity, as it continues to attract an increasing number of immigrants from

Paris at a Glance

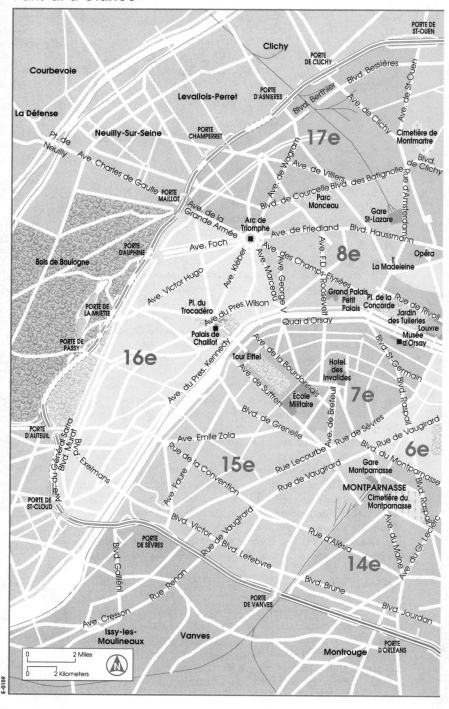

Courbevoie

Clichy

PORTE DE ST-OUEN

PORTE DE CLICHY

Levallois-Perret

PORTE D'ASNIERES

La Défense

Blvd. Berthier

Blvd. Bessières

Ave. de St-Ouen

Pt. de Neuilly

Neuilly-Sur-Seine

PORTE CHAMPERRET

Blvd. Berthier

Ave. de Clichy

Cimetière de Montmartre

Ave. Charles de Gaulle

PORTE MAILLOT

17e

Blvd. de Clichy

Ave. de Wagram

Ave. de Villiers

Rue d'Amsterdam

Ave. de la Grande Armée

Blvd. de Courcelle Blvd. des Batignolle

Parc Monceau

Gare St-Lazare

PORTE DAUPHINE

Arc de Triomphe

Ave. de Friedland

Blvd. Haussmann

Bois de Boulogne

Ave. Foch

Ave. des Champs-Elysées

8e

Opéra

La Madeleine

Ave. Victor Hugo

Ave. Kléber

Ave. Marceau

Ave. George V

Ave. F.D. Roosevelt

Grand Palais

Petit Palais

Pl. de la Concorde

Rue de Rivoli

Jardin des Tuileries

PORTE DE LA MUETTE

Pl. du Trocadéro

Ave. du Pres. Wilson

Quai d'Orsay

Louvre Musée d'Orsay

PORTE DE PASSY

Palais de Chaillot

16e

Ave. du Pres. Kennedy

Tour Eiffel

Ave. de la Bourdonnais

Ave. de Suffren

École Militaire

Hotel des Invalides

7e

Blvd. St-Germain

Blvd. Raspail

PORTE D'AUTEUIL

Ave. du Général Sarra

Blvd. Murat

Blvd. Exelmans

Blvd. de Grenelle

Ave. de Breteuil

Rue de Sèvres

6e

Ave. Emile Zola

Rue de la Convention

Ave. Faure

15e

Rue Lecourbe

Rue de Vaugirard

Blvd. du Montparnasse

Blvd. Raspail

PORTE DE ST-CLOUD

Gare Montparnasse

MONTPARNASSE

Cimetière du Montparnasse

PORTE DE SÈVRES

Blvd. Victor de Vaugirard

Rue de Blvd. Lefebvre

Rue d'Alésia

Ave. du Maine

Ave. du Leclerc

Blvd. Galliéni

14e

Rue Renan

PORTE DE VANVES

Blvd. Brune

Blvd. Jourdan

Ave. Cresson

Issy-les-Moulineaux

Vanves

Montrouge

PORTE D'ORLEANS

0   2 Miles

0   2 Kilometers

E-0159

2

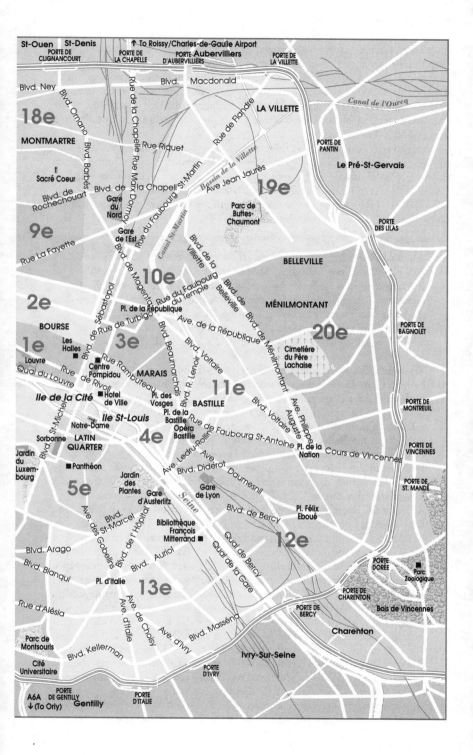

its former colonies. Many have expressed concern that France will lose the battle to keep its language strong, distinct, and unadulterated by foreign slang or catchwords. But as the country approaches the millennium, foreign tourists spending much-needed cash are no longer perceived as foes or antagonists. *Au contraire:* The rancor of France's collective xenophobia has been increasingly redirected toward the many immigrants seeking better lives in Paris, where the infrastructure has nearly been stretched to its limits.

Though Paris is clearly a city in flux culturally and socially, it still lures travelers for the same reasons it always has. Grand indestructible sights such as the Tour Eiffel are still here, as is the spruced-up Champs-Elysées—and both are as crowded as ever. The beauty of Paris is still overwhelming, especially in the illumination of night. The City of Light, one of the premier tourist destinations in the world, always puts on a memorable show.

1 Frommer's Favorite Paris Experiences

- **A Walk Along the Faubourg St-Honoré.** In the 1700s, the wealthiest of Parisians resided in the Faubourg St-Honoré; today the quarter is home to stores that cater to the rich. Even if you don't buy anything, it's great to window-shop the big names: Hermès, Larouche, Courrèges, Cardin, Saint Laurent.
- **An Afternoon of Cafe-Sitting.** The cafe is integral to life in Paris. Whether you have one small coffee or the most expensive cognac in the house, nobody will hurry you.
- **Afternoon Tea at Angélina.** Drinking tea in London has its charm, but the Parisian salon de thé is unique. Skip over those cucumber-and-watercress sandwiches and delve into a rich, luscious dessert such as Mont Blanc, a creamy puree of sweetened chestnuts once beloved by the Aga Khan. Try the grandest Parisian tea salon of them all, Angélina, 226 rue de Rivoli, 1er (Métro: Concorde).
- **A Night at the Ballet.** Renoir may have detested the Opéra Garnier, place de l'Opéra, for an opulence he felt bordered on vulgarity, but it has been the center for ballet in Paris ever since its opening. An evening here takes you back to the Second Empire world of marble and gilt and grand staircases, all sheltered under a controversial ceiling by Chagall. Dress with pomp and circumstance.
- **A Day at the Races.** Paris has eight tracks for horse racing. The most famous and the classiest is Longchamp, in the Bois de Boulogne, 16e. It's the site of the Prix de l'Arc de Triomphe and the Grand Prix. These and other top races are major social events, so you'll have to dress up, of course. Take the Métro to Porte d'Auteuil, then a special bus from there to the track. *Paris Turf,* a racing newspaper, and other weekly entertainment magazines have details about racing times.
- **A Stroll Along the Seine.** Painters such as Sisley, Turner, and Monet have fallen under the River Seine's spell. Lovers still walk hand in hand alongside it, and anglers still cast their lines here. Clochards still seek a home for the night under its bridges, and on its banks the bouquinistes still peddle their mix of postcards, 100-year-old pornography, and tattered editions of old histories of Indochina. Some athletic visitors walk the full 7-mile stretch of the river through the city, but it is enough to confine your stroll to central Paris. For a spectacular view of the Louvre, cross the Pont des Arts. The first iron bridge in the city, it is one of only four pedestrian bridges in Paris. The Pont-Neuf is the oldest and most famous bridge in Paris. (In the Middle Ages, Parisians came here to have their teeth pulled.) From here you have an excellent view of the Palais de Justice and Sainte-Chapelle on Ile de la Cité.

- **The Flower Market.** A fine finish to any day spent meandering with the river would include a stroll through the *marché aux fleurs,* on the Ile de la Cité. Here you can purchase rare flowers, the gems of the French Riviera, bouquets that have inspired artists throughout the centuries. Next door is the famed *marché aux oiseaux,* where you can admire rare birds from around the world.

- **An Ice Cream at Bertillion.** A landmark on Ile St-Louis, Bertillion is said to offer the world's best selection of ice creams. Try rhubarb, fresh melon, kumquat, black currant, or any exotic fresh fruit in season—more than 50 flavors to choose from and nothing artificial. Parisians have flocked to this place in such numbers that gendarmes have been called out to direct the traffic of ice-cream aficionados.

- **An Evening at the Folies-Bergère.** Often attacked and denounced, this Parisian showcase has been pleasing audiences since 1868, even though classic acts like Chevalier, Mistinguett, and Josephine Baker, who performed her famous banana dance here, vanished long ago. The Tour Eiffel cancan is a bit corny, and the show has become less daring. But those ladies in their sequins, feathers, and pom-poms still evoke an older Paris, immortalized on a Manet canvas, and the show, tacky or not, seems to go on forever.

- **An Evening of Opera.** The Opéra Bastille was inaugurated in July 1989 to compete with the grande dame of the Paris musical scene, the Opéra Garnier. With 2,700 seats in its main hall, the Bastille is the largest opera house in France, and features opera and symphony performances in four different concert halls. Wear your most elegant evening clothes and soak up the glorious music in an opulent atmosphere that is very, very cultured and very, very French.

- **Discovering Hidden Montmartre.** This district has earned a reputation as the most touristy part of Paris. It's true that buses swarm the area surrounding Sacré-Coeur; yet, far removed from here, another neighborhood unfolds—that of the true Montmartrois. To discover it, drift onto the back streets away from the souvenir shops. Many Parisian families have lived in the neighborhood for generations; actors, producers, journalists, and directors are restoring other homes. Arm yourself with a good map and seek out such streets as rue Lepic (refresh yourself at the Lux Bar at no. 12); rue Constance; rue Tholozé (with its view over the rooftops of Paris); the lively rue des Abbesses, or rue Germain-Pilon. None of these streets are famous or celebrated, but each has buildings whose detailing shows the pride and care that permeates Paris's architecture. Flank out from these, and discover dozens of other streets on your own. At dusk, sit on the top steps of the church with the square Willette in front of you and watch as nighttime Paris begins to come alive. First a twinkle like a firefly—then all the lights go on like magic.

- **Checking Out the Marchés.** A daily Parisian ritual is to amble through one of the open-air markets to purchase fresh food—a ripe and properly creamy Camembert, or a pumpkin-gold cantaloupe—to be consumed before sundown. Even if you're staying in a room without a kitchen, you can take part in this time-honored French tradition and prepare for a picnic in one of the city's parks. Like artists, the food vendors arrange their wares into a mosaic of vibrant colors. Sanguine, an Italian citrus whose juice is the color of a brilliant orange sunset; ruby-red peppers; golden yellow bananas from Martinique—all dazzle the eye. Our favorite market is the one on rue Montorgeuil, beginning at rue Rambuteau, 1er (Métro: Les Halles). On mornings at this grubby little cluster of food stalls, we've spotted some of France's finest chefs stocking up for the day.

- **Cocktails at Willi's.** Back in the early 1970s, the first-time visitor to Paris might arrive with a copy of Hemingway's *A Moveable Feast* and, taking the author's endorsement to heart, head first for Harry's Bar at "Sank roo doe Noo." Harry's is still here and now draws an older, conservative clientele. Today's chic younger expats head for Willi's Wine Bar, 13 rue des Petits-Champs, 1er (Métro: Bourse, Louvre, or Palais-Royal). The young, long-haired bartenders are mostly English, as are the waitresses, dressed in Laura Ashley garb. The place, which gained popularity through word of mouth, is like an informal club for Brits, Australians, and Yanks, especially in the afternoon. Some 300 wines await your selection.

- **Calling on the Dead.** You don't have to be a ghoul to be thrilled by an afternoon at the most famous cemetery in Europe: Père-Lachaise. Chances are, one of your idols will be resting here, and you can pay your respects to all the gang—Gertrude Stein and Alice B. Toklas, Jim Morrison, Oscar Wilde, Yves Montand (temporarily dug up for a DNA test in a paternity suit), Edith Piaf, Isadora Duncan, Abélard and Héloïse, Frédéric Chopin, Marcel Proust, and Eugène Delacroix. And it's not just the residents who provide fascination; the tomb designs themselves are eerie and intriguing. Laid out in 1803 on the slopes of a hill in Ménilmontant, the cemetery offers a surprise a minute with its elaborate, often bizarre monuments, unexpected views, and ornate sculpture.

- **A Day at Fauchon.** "I'd much rather spend a day at Fauchon than a night at the Comédie-Française," a Frenchman confided to us. Perhaps he's right. An exotic world of food, Fauchon has a vast array of treasures. More than 20,000 products from the far corners of the globe are sold here. It's been called a "supermarket for millionaires," but it democratically maintains a reasonably priced self-service cafeteria for those who aren't. Everything you never knew you were missing is here in aisle after aisle of coffees, spices, pastries, fruits, vegetables, and rare Armagnacs. Take your pick: Toganese mangoes, smoked Scottish salmon, preserved cocks' combs, rose petal jelly from Romania, blue-red pomegranates from India, golden brown dates from Tunisia (only from the most famous oasis, of course), larks stuffed with foie gras, dark morels from France's rich earth, reindeer's tongue from Finland, century-old eggs from China, and a Creole punch from Martinique that's reputed to be the best on earth.

- **Free Concerts.** In the summer, free concerts—one of the joys of Paris—are held all over the city, in parks and churches. Pick up an entertainment weekly for details. Some of the best concerts are held at the **American Church in Paris,** 65 quai d'Orsay, 7e (☎ **01-40-62-05-00;** Métro: Alma-Marceau; RER: Pont de l'Alma). **St-Merri,** 76 rue de la Verrerie, 4e (☎ **01-42-71-40-75;** Métro: Châtelet), is also known for its free concerts, which are regularly featured during September and July at 9pm on Saturday and 4pm on Sunday.

- **Sneaking Away from It All.** When the glory and pomp of Paris overcome us, we slip away to St-Germain-en-Laye, 13 miles to the northwest. Take the RER (Réseau Express Régional) train, line A1. The suburb was once the residence of the kings of France, from François I to Louis XIV (the "Sun King"), who was born here. Visitors often overlook this area, but Parisians adore it and often come here to escape the summer heat. You can visit the Château Vieux, where Louis XIV lived, but mostly you'll want to wander around, inspecting the streets, parks, and gardens. A meal at the Pavillon Henri IV, a hotel with a restaurant, brings a summer day to perfection. It's named for the king, who in the 1500s built a home on this site for his illegitimate children. Dumas wrote *The Three Musketeers* at the pavillon in 1843, and earlier, the Sun King romped here with his mistress, Madame de Montespan. Whatever your main dish, you'll want to order it with béarnaise sauce, which is said to have been invented here.

2 Best Hotel Bets

- **Best Newcomer:** Hot, hot, hot, **Hôtel de Vendôme** (☎ **01-42-60-32-84**) enjoys one of the world's most prestigious addresses. Housed in the former Embassy of Texas (yes, there was one when that state was a nation), the hotel has been vastly restored and redesigned for opulent living. Media darlings check in for a touch of Right Bank elegance and glamor.

- **Best for Business Travelers:** Corporate types from all over the world converge at the **Hôtel Balzac,** 6 rue Balzac, 8e (☎ **01-44-35-18-05**), a belle-epoque town house with a good business center 2 blocks from many of the business offices along the Champs-Elysées. Its restaurant serves some of the best food in town and is suitable for entertaining clients.

- **Best for Families:** A good and affordable Left Bank choice is **Hôtel de Fleurie,** 32 rue Gregoire-de-Tours, 6e (☎ **01-53-73-70-00**), in the heart of St-Germain-des-Prés. Accommodations are thoughtfully appointed, and many are sold as family rooms, a pair of connecting rooms with two large beds. Children under 12 stay free with their parents.

- **Best Value:** Not far from the Champs-Elysées, the **Résidence Lord Byron,** 5 rue de Chateaubriand, 8e (☎ **01-43-59-89-98**), is a classy little getaway that is far from opulent, but is clean, comfortable, and a good buy. Unlike so many of the grander places surrounding it in the 8th, it's totally lacking in pretension. Also, set in one of the most evocative neighborhoods of Old Paris (the Ile St. Louis) the **Hôtel de Lutèce,** 65 rue St-Louis-en-l'Ile, 4e (☎ **01-43-26-23-52**), resembles a Breton country house, and has flourished despite forever refusing to raise its prices. Its tasteful bedrooms, decorated with antiques and fine reproductions, provide an affordable elegance.

- **Best Location:** **Le Pavillon de la Reine,** 28 place des Vosges, 3e (☎ **01-40-29-19-19**), is a chic, elegant 17th-century mansion. It not only has a garden courtyard, but also opens onto the most harmonious and beautiful square of Paris, the place des Vosges of Victor Hugo fame.

- **Best View:** Of the 32 bedrooms at **Hôtel du Quai-Voltaire** (☎ **01-42-61-50-91**), 28 open onto views of the Seine. If you stay here, you'll be following in the footsteps of Wilde, Baudelaire, and Wagner. This former 17th-century abbey was transformed into a hotel back in 1856, and it's been welcoming discerning guests ever since—those who appreciate its tattered charms.

- **Best for Nostalgia:** If you yearn for a Left Bank "literary" address, make it **Odéon-Hôtel** (☎ **01-43-25-90-67**), set in the heart of the 6th arrondissement, filled with memories of André Gide, Hemingway, Fitzgerald, James Joyce, and Ms. Stein & Alice. Evoking a Norman country inn, this hotel of considerable charm lures with its high crooked ceilings, exposed beams, and memories of yesterday.

- **Best Stargazing:** Those California tycoons, legendary stars, and platinum mistresses of yesterday—Douglas Fairbanks and Mary Pickford, William Randolph Hearst and Marion Davies—knew where to stay back then. Tom Cruise and his ilk know it's still true today. **Hôtel de Crillon,** 10 Place de la Concorde, 8e (☎ **01-44-71-15-00**), is the address of Paris. If you want its grandest suite and have a discriminating taste for the macabre, ask for the Marie Antoinette Apartment; it exhibits classic Antoinette-style elegance, and its namesake was beheaded practically at the doorstep of this deluxe citadel.

- **Best for Opulence:** **Le Ritz,** 15 place Vendôme, 1er (☎ **01-43-16-30-30**), has dripped with wealth, luxury, and decadence since César Ritz opened it in 1898. Barbara Hutton, Coco Chanel, and Marcel Proust are just a few names inscribed in its glorious guest book. Join the parade of Saudi oil princes, Milanese divas, and movie legends.

- **Best-Kept Secret:** Constructed in 1913 and long in a seedy state, the fully restored **Terrass Hôtel,** 12-14 rue Joseph-de-Maistre, 18e (☎ 01-46-06-72-85), is now the only four-star choice in Montmartre, an area not known for luxury accommodations. Its rooms take in far-ranging views of the Eiffel Tower, Arc de Triomphe, and the Paris Opéra.

- **Best Historic Hotel:** Inaugurated by Napoléon III in 1855, the **Hôtel du Louvre,** Place André Malraux, 1e (☎ 01-44-58-38-38), was once described by a French journalist as "a palace of the people, rising adjacent to the palace of kings." Today, the hotel offers luxurious accommodations and panoramic views down the avenue de l'Opéra.

- **Best for Romance:** Until the 1970s, **L'Hôtel,** 13 rue des Beaux-Arts, 6e (☎ 01-44-41-99-00), was a fleabag filled with drunks and addicts. Millions of francs of renovations later, rooms that were cramped and claustrophobic are now ravishingly romantic, wrought like small jewel boxes.

- **Best Trendy Hotel:** A converted town house, **Costes** (☎ 01-42-44-50-50) evokes the imperial heyday of Napoléon III. Fashion headliners especially like it—it's the choice of many a lanky model, as the Paris editorial offices of *Harper's Bazaar* are close at hand. If you're into heavy swags, patterned fabrics, jewel-tone colors, and lavish accessories, this can be your gilded-age address.

- **Best Service:** Although no one can fault the **Plaza Athénée,** 23-27 av. Montaigne 8e (☎ 01-53-67-66-65), for its flawless decor, the billionaires check in because they get the royal treatment from the jaded but indulgent and ever-so-polite staff. Nestled in an upscale neighborhood between the Seine and the Champs-Elysées, the Plaza Athénée offers service that is, quite simply, impeccable.

3 Best Dining Bets

- **Best All-Around: Taillevent,** 15 rue Lamennais, 8e (☎ 01-45-95-15-01), named for a chef of the 14th century who wrote one of the oldest known books on French cookery, is the most outstanding all-around restaurant in Paris.

- **Best Chef:** Can there be any doubt? **Alain Ducasse,** 59 av. Raymond Poincaré, 16e (☎ 01-47-27-12-27), has taken Paris by storm, assuming the throne of Joël Robuchon. He artfully combines produce from every region of the country in a cuisine that is contemporary but not quite new, embracing the Mediterranean without abandoning France.

- **Best Decor:** Declared a French national treasure, the belle-epoque **Le Train Bleu** in the Gare de Lyon, 12e (☎ 01-43-43-09-06), evokes the heyday of the gilded age. Completely restored, the restaurant is draped with heavy purple velvet hangings, boxes sprinkled with green plants, Napoléon III antiques, gleaming brass, and a glare of lighting fixtures made of bronze and Bohemia opaline-shaped glass cups—all in perfect harmony.

- **Best View: La Tour d'Argent,** 15-17 quai de la Tournelle, 5e (☎ 01-43-54-23-31), is a penthouse restaurant owned by shrewd ex-playboy Claude Terrail, who pays part of Notre-Dame's electric bill to illuminate the cathedral at night for his diners' pleasure.

- **Best for Stargazing:** No, it's not Taillevent or even Alain Ducasse. On the see-and-be-seen circuit, it's the **Buddha Bar,** 8 rue Boissy d'Anglas, 8e (☎ 01-53-05-90-00). Clients don't actually come for the cuisine, although its fusion of

French and Pacific Rim is exceedingly well executed. If Madonna's in town and calls you up for a date, this is where you should take her.

- **Best Unkept Secret:** Deep in the heart of the Latin Quarter, **Perraudin,** 157 rue St-Jacques, 5e (☎ **01-46-33-15-75**), duplicates the allure of a turn-of-the-century bistro. You get the feeling Émile Zola could walk in the door at any minute. It offers great food and great value, with old-fashioned dining that is too rapidly disappearing from the city.

- **Best Newcomer:** Although every escaped kitchen-scullion claims to be the "new Robuchon," you are likely to find his dead ringer at **L'Astor,** in the Hôtel Astor, 11 rue d'Astorg, 8e (☎ **01-53-05-05-20**), where Eric Lecerf reigns. As a kind of Richelieu to Lecerf's Louis XIII, Robuchon still drops in two to three times a week, and though some of his dishes are served, the menu has become Lecerf's.

- **Best Brasserie:** Head for the Left Bank and the **Brasserie Balzar,** 49 rue des Ecoles, 5e (☎ **01-43-54-13-67**), established in 1898. If you dine here on the good and familiar French food, you'll be following in the footsteps of such former patrons as Sartre and Camus. You can even have a complete dinner in the middle of the afternoon.

- **Best Baby Bistro:** Near place de l'Etoile, **La Rôtisserie d'Armaillé,** 6 rue d'Armaillé, 17e (☎ **01-42-27-19-20**), is a side show created by one of France's grandest chefs, Jacques Cagna. Unlike his citadel devoted to haute cuisine, the food here is democratically priced. Cagna, along with other great French chefs, realized that the average visitor can't afford haute cuisine, so they created these baby bistros to serve "food like our mothers fed us." If that claim was sincere, we suspect Cagna must have been a fat, happy baby.

- **Best Underappreciated Restaurant:** Once hailed by some as the best restaurant in Paris, **Le Vivarois,** 192-194 av. Victor Hugo, 16e (☎ **01-45-04-04-31**) no longer enjoys such acclaim. Yet we think the cuisine is better than ever. It's not flashy, inventive, or pretentious, just classic fare that Escoffier would have blessed.

- **Best Seafood:** The fattest lobsters and prawns in the Rungis market emerge on platters at **Goumard,** 9 rue Duphot, 1er (☎ **01-42-60-36-07**), which is so chic that even the toilets are classified as a historical monument by the French government. Nothing is allowed to interfere with the taste of the sea here: You'll have to fly to the Riviera to find a better bouillabaisse.

- **Best Cuisine Bourgeoise (Comfort Food):** If today Joyce, Verlaine, Valéry, and Hemingway rose from the grave and strode into the **Crémerie-Restaurant Polidor,** 41 rue Monsieur-le-Prince, 6e (☎ **01-43-26-95-34**), they wouldn't notice any difference, not even on the menu, but would calmly ask for their napkins locked in a cabinet in back with their names on them.

- **Best Atmosphere:** A favorite of Colette and Cocteau, the world-famous **Le Grand Véfour,** 17 rue de Beaujolais, 1er (☎ **01-42-96-56-27**), at the Palais-Royal, has an interior that's classified as a historical monument. It serves some of the most refined cuisine in Paris.

- **Best Opulence:** Although "Pierre Cardin's place," as it is called, has an ever-growing list of detractors, **Maxim's,** 3 rue Royale, 8e (☎ **01-42-65-27-94**), is still the ultimate choice in art nouveau grandeur, just as it was decades ago when Leslie Caron dined here in *Gigi.*

- **Best Kosher Food:** If corned beef, pastrami, schmaltz herring, and dill pickles thrill you, then head to **rue des Rosiers** in the 4th arrondissement (Métro: St-Paul). This street is in one of the most colorful neighborhoods of Paris. John Russel wrote that rue des Rosiers is the "last sanctuary of certain ways of life;

what you see there in miniature is Warsaw before the ghetto was razed." North African overtones also reflect the arrival, long ago, of Jews from Morocco, Tunisia, and especially Algeria. The best time to go is Sunday morning, when many parts of Paris are still sleeping. You can wander the streets eating as you go—apple strudel, Jewish rye bread, pickled lemons, smoked salmon, and merguez, a spicy smoked sausage from Algeria. Many spots offer proper sit-down meals, including **Chez Jo Goldenberg,** 7 rue des Rosiers, 4e (☎ 01-48-87-20-16), where the *carpe farcie* (stuffed carp) is outstanding and the beef goulash a fine runner-up.

- **Best American Cuisine: Joe Allen,** 30 rue Pierre-Lescot, 1er (☎ 01-42-36-70-13), is a Yankee outpost in Les Halles. The burgers are the finest in the city. Desserts include real New York cheesecake, pecan pie with fresh pecans imported from the United States, and the inspired cultural fusion of American brownies made with French chocolate.

- **Best Vegetarian Cuisine: Aquarius,** 54 rue Ste-Croix-de-la-Bretonnerie, 4e (☎ 01-48-87-48-71), is one of the best-known veggie restaurants in the Marais. Choose from their array of soups and salads, or have a galette of wheat served with raw vegetables, or a mushroom tart. In this rustic 17th-century setting you can expect flavorful, wholesome, and generous meals.

- **Best Place to Experiment:** Tripe is a delicacy at **Pharamond,** 24 rue de la Grande-Truanderie, 1er (☎ 01-42-33-06-72). If you're at all experimental, you'll find no better introduction to it than here in Les Halles.

- **Best Wine Cellar:** At the elegant **Lasserre,** 17 av. Franklin D. Roosevelt, 8e (☎ 01-43-59-53-43), you'll find one of the great wine cellars of France, with some 180,000 bottles.

- **Best Cheese:** Cheese is king at **Androuët,** 6 rue Arsène Houssaye, 8e (☎ 01-42-89-95-00). Many cheese lovers opt for a bottle of wine, a green salad, and all-you-can-eat choices from the most sophisticated *dégustation de fromages* in the world.

- **Best on the Champs-Elysées:** The specialties of Denmark are served with flair at the **Copenhague/Flora Danica,** 142 av. des Champs-Elysées, 8e (☎ 01-44-13-86-26). In summer you can dine on the terrace of this "Maison du Danemark."

- **Best Late-Night Dining:** Nowhere else in Paris can you be more assured of getting a good meal at 3am than at **Au Pied de Cochon,** 6 rue Coquillière, 1er (☎ 01-40-13-77-00). Although everyone lauds its grilled pig's feet served with béarnaise sauce, few have noticed that you can also purchase some of the freshest oysters in town here.

- **Best Wine Bar: Willi's Wine Bar,** 13 rue des Petit-Champs, 1er (☎ 01-42-61-05-09; Métro: Bourse, Louvre, or Palais-Royal), named after owner Mark Williamson, is as close as Paris gets to a typical London wine bar. Excellent-quality wines are available by the glass. Meet that strange creature here, the tweedy Frenchman. See chapter 9.

- **Best Breakfast:** At **Les Ambassadeurs,** 10 place de la Concorde, 8e (☎ 01-44-71-15-00; Métro: Concorde), you can enjoy breakfast along with the diplomatic elite amid the marble and crystal of the Hôtel de Crillon. See chapter 4.

- **Best Brunch:** From May to November, the **Hôtel Méridien Etoile,** 81 bd. Gouvion-St-Cyr, 17e (☎ 01-40-68-34-34; Métro: Porte Maillot), hosts "Le Sunday Jazz Brunch," where jazz artists play as you gorge yourself on smoked salmon and succulent roasts.

- **Best Tea:** Try **Angélina,** 226 rue de Rivoli, 1er (☎ **01-42-60-82-00**), for a view of haute couture's lionesses having their tea. The house specialty, which goes exquisitely with a cup of tea, is the **Mont Blanc,** a combination of chestnut cream and meringue and much favored as the signature sweet.
- **Best Picnic Fare:** For the most elegant picnic fixings in town, go to **Fauchon,** 26 place de la Madeleine, 8e (☎ **01-47-42-60-11;** Métro: Madeleine). Here you'll find a complete charcuterie and famous pastry shop. It's said to offer 20,000 kinds of imported fruits, vegetables, and other exotic delicacies, snacks, salads, and canapés, all packed to take out. (See "Food" in chapter 8.)
- **Best Champagne Julep:** While you wait for a table at the **Closerie des Lilas,** 171 bd. du Montparnasse, 6e (☎ **01-40-51-34-50**), savor the best champagne julep in the world at the bar.
- **Best Ice Cream:** Try **Bertillion,** 31 rue St-Louis-en-l'Ile, 4e (☎ **01-43-54-31-61;** Métro: Pont-Marie), a salon de thé that after three dozen years in the business still sells 30 of the most delectable ice-cream flavors ever concocted. It's open Wednesday to Sunday from 10am to 8pm.
- **Best Pizza:** The **Chicago Pizza Pie Factory,** 5 rue de Berri, 8e (☎ **01-45-62-50-23**), is devoted to the almighty pizza pie. The chef creates endless delicious variations on eight different themes.
- **Best People Watching:** Spend an afternoon on the terrace of **Café de la Paix,** place de l'Opéra, 9e (☎ **01-40-07-30-20**), and watch the world go by. See and be seen or settle into anonymity while enjoying the vast variety of faces in this international mingling joint.

2 Planning a Trip to Paris

This chapter provides most of the nuts-and-bolts information you'll need before setting off for Paris. We've put everything from information sources to the major airlines at your fingertips. Also see "Frommer's Online Directory" at the back of this book for resources on the Web.

1 Visitor Information

BEFORE YOU GO

Your best source of information before you go is the **French Government Tourist Office,** which can be reached at the following addresses.

In the United States   444 Madison Ave., 16th Floor, New York, NY 10022 (☎ 212/838-7800); 676 N. Michigan Ave., Suite 3360, Chicago, IL 60611-2819 (☎ 312/751-7800); or 9454 Wilshire Blvd., Suite 715, Beverly Hills, CA 90212-2967 (☎ 310/271-6665). To request information, you can call **France on Call** at ☎ **202/659-7779.** The Internet address is www.francetourism.com.

In Canada   Write or phone the Maison de la France/French Government Tourist Office, 1981 av. McGill College, Suite 490, Montréal H3A 2W9 (☎ **514/288-4264**).

In the United Kingdom   Write or phone the Maison de la France/French Government Tourist Office, 178 Piccadilly, London W1V 0AL (☎ **0891/244-123;** fax 0171/493-6594).

In Australia   Write or phone the French Tourist Bureau, BNP Building, 12th Floor, 12 Castlereagh St., Sydney NSW 2000 (☎ **02/9231-5244;** fax 02/9221-8682).

In New Zealand   There's no representative in New Zealand, so citizens should contact the Consular Section of the French Embassy, 1 Willeston St., Wellington (☎ **64/4-4720-200**).

In South Africa   Write or phone the French Government Tourist Office, P.O. Box 41022, Craig Hall 2024, South Africa (☎ **011/880-8062**).

In Ireland   Write or phone the Maison de la France/French Government Tourist Office, 10 Suffolk St., Dublin 2, Ireland (☎ **01/679-0813**).

IN PARIS

See chapter 3, "Visitor Information," under "Orientation."

2 Entry Requirements & Customs Regulations

PASSPORT/VISAS

All foreign (non-French) nationals need a valid passport to enter France (check its expiration date). The French government no longer requires visas for **U.S. citizens,** providing they're staying in France for less than 90 days. For longer stays, U.S. visitors must apply for a long-term visa, residence card, or temporary-stay visa. Each requires proof of income or a viable means of support in France and a legitimate purpose for remaining in the country. Applications are available from the **Consulate Section of the French Embassy,** 4101 Reservoir Rd. NW, Washington, DC 20007 (☎ **202/ 944-6000**), or from the **Visa Section of the French Consulate** at 10 E. 74th St., New York, NY 10021 (☎ **212/606-3689**). Visas are required for students planning to study in France even if the stay is for less than 90 days.

At the moment, citizens of Australia, Canada, New Zealand, Switzerland, Japan, and European Community countries do not need visas.

South Africans need a visa to enter France. They're available from the French Consulate, 2 Dean St. (next to Queen Victoria St.), Cape Town 8001 (☎ **021/23-15-75;** fax 021/24-84-70).

CUSTOMS

WHAT YOU CAN BRING INTO FRANCE

Customs restrictions differ for citizens of the European Community (EC) and for citizens of non-EC countries. **Non-EC nationals** can bring in duty-free 200 cigarettes, 100 cigarillos, 50 cigars, or 250 grams of smoking tobacco. This amount is doubled if you live outside Europe. You can also bring in 2 liters of wine and either 1 liter of alcohol over 22 proof or 2 liters of wine under 22 proof. In addition, you can bring in 50 grams (1.75 ounces) of perfume, one-quarter liter (250ml) of eau de toilette, 500 grams (1 pound) of coffee, and 200 grams (one-half pound) of tea. Visitors 15 years of age and over may also bring in other goods totaling 300 F ($51); the allowance for those 14 and under is 150 F ($25.50). (Customs officials tend to be lenient about general merchandise, realizing that the limits are unrealistically low.)

Visitors from **European Union (EU)** countries can bring in 300 cigarettes or 150 cigarillos or 75 cigars or 400 grams of smoking tobacco. You can also bring in 2 liters of wine and either 1 liter of alcohol over 38.80 proof or 2 liters of wine under 38.80 proof. In addition, visitors can bring in 75 grams of perfume, three-eighths of a liter of toilet water, 1,000 grams of coffee, and 80 grams of tea. Passengers 15 and over can bring in 2,400 F ($408) worth of merchandise duty-free; those 14 and under can bring in 620 F ($105.40) worth.

IMPORT RESTRICTIONS

Returning **U.S. citizens** who have been away for 48 hours or more are allowed to bring back, once every 30 days, $400 worth of merchandise duty-free. You'll be charged a flat rate of 10% duty on the next $1,000 worth of purchases. Be sure to have your receipts handy. On gifts, the duty-free limit is $100. You cannot bring fresh foodstuffs into the United States; tinned foods, however, are allowed. For more information, contact the **U.S. Customs Service,** 1301 Constitution Ave. (P.O. Box 7407), Washington, DC 20044 (☎ **202/927-6724**), and request the free pamphlet **Know Before You Go.** It's also available on the Web at www.customs.ustreas.gov/travel/ kbygo.htm.

Citizens of the U.K. will go through a separate Customs exit (called the "Blue Exit") especially for EC travelers. In essence, there is no limit on what you can bring back from an EC country, as long as the items are for personal use (this includes gifts), and you have already paid the necessary duty and tax. However, customs law sets out guidance levels. If you bring in more than these levels, you may be asked to prove that the goods are for your own use. Guidance levels on goods bought in the EC for your own use are 800 cigarettes, 200 cigars, 1kg smoking tobacco, 10 liters of spirits, 90 liters of wine (of this not more than 60 liters can be sparkling wine), and 110 liters of beer. For more information, contact **HM Customs & Excise,** Passenger Enquiry Point, 2nd Floor, Wayfarer House, Great South West Rd., Feltham, Middlesex TW14 8NP (☎ **0181/910-3744;** from outside the U.K., ☎ 44/181-910-3744), or consult their Web site at www.open.gov.uk.

For a clear summary of **Canadian** rules, write for the booklet *I Declare,* issued by **Revenue Canada,** 2265 St. Laurent Blvd., Ottawa K1G 4KE (☎ **613/993-0534**). Canada allows its citizens a $500 exemption, and you're allowed to bring back duty-free 200 cigarettes, 2.2 pounds of tobacco, 40 imperial ounces of liquor, and 50 cigars. In addition, you're allowed to mail gifts to Canada from abroad at the rate of Can$60 a day, provided they're unsolicited and don't contain alcohol or tobacco (write on the package "Unsolicited gift, under $60 value"). All valuables should be declared on the Y-38 form before departure from Canada, including serial numbers of valuables you already own, such as expensive foreign cameras. *Note:* The $500 exemption can only be used once a year and only after an absence of 7 days.

The duty-free allowance in **Australia** is A$400 or, for those under 18, A$200. Personal property mailed back from England should be marked "Australian goods returned" to avoid payment of duty. Upon returning to Australia, citizens can bring in 250 cigarettes or 250 grams of loose tobacco, and 1,125ml of alcohol. If you're returning with valuable goods you already own, such as foreign-made cameras, you should file form B263. A helpful brochure, available from Australian consulates or Customs offices, is *Know Before You Go.* For more information, contact **Australian Customs Services,** GPO Box 8, Sydney NSW 2001 (☎ **02/9213-2000**).

The duty-free allowance for **New Zealand** is NZ$700. Citizens over 17 can bring in 200 cigarettes, or 50 cigars, or 250 grams of tobacco (or a mixture of all three if their combined weight doesn't exceed 250 grams); plus 4.5 liters of wine and beer, or 1.125 liters of liquor. New Zealand currency does not carry import or export restrictions. Fill out a certificate of export, listing the valuables you are taking out of the country; that way, you can bring them back without paying duty. Most questions are answered in a free pamphlet available at New Zealand consulates and Customs offices: *New Zealand Customs Guide for Travellers, Notice no. 4.* For more information, contact New Zealand Customs, 50 Anzac Ave., P.O. Box 29, Auckland (☎ **09/359-6655**).

3 Money

CURRENCY French currency is based on the franc (F), which consists of 100 centimes (c). Coins come in units of 5, 10, 20, and 50 centimes; and 1, 2, 5, and 10 francs. Notes come in denominations of 20, 50, 100, 200, 500, and 1,000 francs. The front of the 200-franc note honors Gustave Eiffel, creator of the Eiffel Tower, father of experimental aerodynamics, and part-designer of New York's Statue of Liberty.

All banks are equipped for foreign exchange, and you will find exchange offices at the airports and airline terminals. Banks are open from 9am to noon and 2 to 4pm Monday through Friday. Major bank branches also open their exchange departments on Saturday between 9am and noon.

When converting your home currency into French francs, be aware that rates vary. Your hotel will probably offer the worst rate of exchange. In general, banks offer the best rate, but even banks charge a commission for the service, often $3, depending on

The French Franc, the U.S. Dollar, the British Pound & the Euro

Because exchange rates fluctuate, this table should be used only as a general guide.
For American Readers   At this writing, $1 = approximately 5.88 F (or 1 F = 17¢).
This was the rate of exchange used to calculate the dollar values given in this book.
For British Readers   At this writing, £1 = approximately 9 F (or 1 F = 11
pence), the rate of exchange used to calculate the pound values in the table below.
The Euro   As a rough guideline, subject to multiple revisions as the currency
increases in viability and visibility, one Euro equals approximately $1.17 U.S.,
6.60 French francs, or 76 pence.

FF	U.S.$	U.K.£	Euro	FF	U.S.$	U.K.£	Euro
1	0.17	0.11	0.15	75.00	12.75	8.25	11.25
2	0.34	0.22	0.30	100.00	17.00	11.00	15.00
3	0.51	0.33	0.45	125.00	21.25	13.75	18.75
4	0.68	0.44	0.60	150.00	25.50	16.50	22.50
5	0.85	0.55	0.75	175.00	29.75	19.25	26.25
6	1.02	0.66	0.90	200.00	34.00	22.00	30.00
7	1.19	0.77	1.05	225.00	38.25	24.75	33.75
8	1.36	0.88	1.20	250.00	42.50	27.50	37.50
9	1.53	0.99	1.35	275.00	46.75	30.25	41.25
10	1.70	1.10	1.50	300.00	51.00	33.00	45.00
15	2.55	1.65	2.25	350.00	59.50	38.50	52.50
20	3.40	2.20	3.00	400.00	68.00	44.00	60.00
25	4.25	2.75	3.75	500.00	85.00	55.00	75.00
50	8.50	5.50	7.50	1000.00	170.00	110.00	150.00

the transaction. Whenever you can, stick to the big banks of Paris, like Crédit Lyonnais, which usually offer the best exchange rates and charge the least commission. Always make sure you have enough francs for the weekend.

If you need a check denominated in French francs before your trip, say, to pay a deposit on a hotel room, you can contact **Ruesch International,** 700 11th St. NW, 4th Floor, Washington, DC 20001-4507 (☎ **800/424-2923**). Ruesch performs a wide variety of conversion-related services, usually for $3 per transaction. You can also inquire at a local bank.

THE EURO   The euro, the new single European currency, became the official currency of France and 10 other countries on January 1, 1999, but the French franc will remain the only currency for cash transactions until December 21, 2001. At that time, euro banknotes and coins will be introduced, and French franc banknotes and coins will be withdrawn from circulation during a maximum 6-month transition period. The symbol of the euro is a stylized **E,** which actually looks like an uppercase C with a horizontal double bar through the middle; its official abbreviation is EUR.

TRAVELER'S CHECKS   Traveler's checks are something of an anachronism from the days before the ATM (automated teller machine) made cash accessible at any time. The only sound alternative to traveling with dangerously large amounts of cash, traveler's checks were as reliable as currency, unlike personal checks, but could be replaced if lost or stolen, unlike cash.

What Things Cost in Paris	U.S. $
Taxi from Charles de Gaulle Airport to the city center	42.50
Taxi from Orly Airport to the city center	28.90
Public transportation for a trip within the city with a Métro carnet (packet) of 10	.80
Local telephone call	.35
Double room at the Ritz (very expensive)	612.00
Double room at Lord Byron (moderate)	147.90
Double room at Hôtel Opal (inexpensive)	100.30
Lunch for one, without wine, at Chez Georges (moderate)	54.40
Lunch for one, without wine, at Crémerie-Restaurant Polidor (inexpensive)	18.00
Dinner for one, without wine, at Le Grand Véfour (very expensive)	135.00
Dinner for one, without wine, at Laudurée (moderate)	51.00
Dinner for one, without wine, at Aux Charpentiers (inexpensive)	30.00
Glass of wine	3.60
Coca-Cola	3.85
Cup of coffee	3.60
Roll of ASA 100 film, 36 exposures	7.00
Admission to the Louvre	7.65
Movie ticket	8.00
Theater ticket (at the Comédie-Française)	11.90–32.30

These days, traveler's checks seem less necessary because most cities have 24-hour ATMs that allow travelers to withdraw small amounts of cash as needed—and thus avoid the risk of carrying a fortune around an unfamiliar environment. Many banks, however, impose a fee every time a card is used at an ATM in a different city or bank. If you're withdrawing money every day, you might be better off with traveler's checks—provided that you don't mind showing identification every time you want to cash a check.

You can get traveler's checks at almost any bank. **American Express** offers denominations of $10, $20, $50, $100, $500, and $1,000. You'll pay a service charge ranging from 1% to 4%. You can also get American Express traveler's checks over the phone by calling ☎ 800/221-7282; by using this number, Amex gold and platinum cardholders are exempt from the 1% fee. AAA members can obtain checks without a fee at most AAA offices.

Visa offers traveler's checks at Citibank locations nationwide, as well as several other banks. The service charge ranges between 1.5% and 2%; checks come in denominations of $20, $50, $100, $500, and $1,000. **MasterCard** also offers traveler's checks. Call ☎ 800/223-9920 for a location near you.

ATMs　ATMs are linked to a national network that most likely includes your bank at home. **Cirrus** (☎ 800/424-7787; www.mastercard.com/atm/) and **Plus** (☎ 800/843-7587; www.visa.com/atms) are the two most popular networks; check the back of your ATM card to see which network your bank belongs to. Use the 800 numbers to locate ATMs in your destination (Cirrus only). Be sure to check the daily withdrawal limit before you depart, and ask whether you need a new personal ID number.

CREDIT CARDS   Credit cards are invaluable when traveling. They are a safe way to carry money and provide a convenient record of all your expenses. You can also withdraw cash advances from your credit cards at any bank (though you'll start paying hefty interest on the advance the moment you receive the cash, and you won't receive frequent-flyer miles on an airline credit card). At most banks, you don't even need to go to a teller; you can get a cash advance at the ATM if you know your PIN number. If you've forgotten your PIN number or didn't even know you had one, call the phone number on the back of your credit card and ask the bank to send it to you. It usually takes 5 to 7 business days, though some banks will provide the number over the phone if you tell them your mother's maiden name or pass some other security clearance.

THEFT   Almost every credit card company has an emergency 800 number that you can call if your wallet or purse is stolen. They may be able to wire you a cash advance off your credit card immediately, and in many places, they can deliver an emergency credit card in a day or two. The issuing bank's 800 number is usually on the back of the credit card—though of course that doesn't help you much if the card was stolen. Citicorp Visa's U.S. emergency number is ☎ **0800-90-2033** (toll-free); 410-581-3836 (collect). American Express cardholders and traveler's check holders should call ☎ **47-77-70-00** for all money emergencies. MasterCard holders should call ☎ **0800-90-1387** (toll-free).

If you opt to carry traveler's checks, be sure to keep a record of their serial numbers, separately from the checks of course, so you're ensured a refund in case of an emergency.

Odds are that if your wallet is gone, the police won't be able to recover it for you. However, after you realize that it's gone and you cancel your credit cards, it is still worth informing them. Your credit-card company or insurer may require a police report number.

4 When to Go

In August, Parisians traditionally leave for their annual holiday and put the city on a skeleton staff to serve visitors. July has also become a popular vacation month, with many a restaurateur shuttering up for a monthlong respite.

Hotels, especially first-class and deluxe, are easy to come by in July and August. Budget hotels, on the other hand, are likely to be full during these months of student invasion. You might also try to avoid the first 2 weeks in October, when the annual auto show attracts thousands of automobile enthusiasts.

THE CLIMATE   Balmy weather in Paris has prompted more popular songs and love ballads than weather conditions in any other city in the world. But the weather here is actually quite fickle. Rain is much more common than snow throughout the winter, prompting many longtime residents to complain about the occasional bone-chilling dampness.

In recent years, Paris has had only about 15 snow days a year, and there are only a few oppressively hot days (that is, over 86°F) in midsummer. What will most likely chill a Parisian heart, however, are blasts of rapidly moving air—wind tunnels sweep along the city's long boulevards, channeled by bordering buildings of uniform height. Other than the occasional winds and rain (which add an undeniable drama to many of the city's panoramas), Paris offers some of the most pleasant weather of any capital in Europe, with a highly tolerable average temperature of 53°F.

Paris's Average Daytime Temperature & Rainfall

	Jan	Feb	Mar	Apr	May	June	July	Aug	Sept	Oct	Nov	Dec
Temp (°F)	38	39	46	51	58	64	66	66	61	53	54	40
Rain (inches)	3.2	2.9	2.7	3.2	3.5	3.3	3.7	3.3	3.3	3.0	3.5	3.1

HOLIDAYS   Holidays in France are known as *jours feriés.* Shops and banks are closed, as well as many (but not all) restaurants and museums. Major holidays include January 1, Easter, Ascension Day (40 days after Easter), Pentecost (seventh Sunday after Easter), May 1, May 8 (V-E Day), July 14 (Bastille Day), August 15 (Assumption of the Virgin Mary), November 1 (All Saints' Day), November 11 (Armistice Day), and December 25 (Christmas).

Paris Calendar of Events

Check the Paris Tourist Office Web site (**www.paris-touristoffice.com**) and other Web sites listed above for up-to-the-minute details on these and other events.

January
- **International Ready-to-Wear Fashion Shows** (Le Salon International de Prêt-à-Porter), Parc des Expositions, Porte de Versailles, Paris, 15e (☎ **01-44-94-70-00;** Métro: Porte de Versailles). Hundreds of designers, from the giants to the virtually unknown, unveil their visions (some say hallucinations) about what the public should be wearing 6 months down the road. Technically, the event within the massive convention facilities of the Porte de Versailles is geared to wholesalers, retailers, buyers, journalists, and industry professionals, but for the entrance fee of 130 F ($22.10), the rules are usually bent to accommodate the merely fashion-conscious. Much more exclusive are the *défilés* (fashion shows) held around the same time at the headquarters of individual designers like Lanvin, Courrèges, and Valentino. Mid-January to mid-February.

February
- **Special Exhibitions, Special Concerts:** During Paris's grayest month, look for a splash of temporary expositions and concerts designed to perk up the city. Concerts and theaters spring up at such diverse sites as the **Salle Pleyel,** 252 Faubourg St-Honoré, 8e (☎ **01-45-61-53-00;** Métro: Ternes); the **Théâtre des Champs-Elysées,** 15 av. Montaigne, 8e (☎ **01-49-52-50-50;** Métro: Alma-Marceau); and the **Maison Radio-France,** 116 av. du Président-Kennedy, 16e (☎ **01-42-30-15-16;** Métro: Passy-Ranelagh). Also look for openings of new operas at the **Opéra National de Paris Bastille,** 2 place de la Bastille, 4e (☎ **08-36-39-78-68;** Métro: Bastille); concerts beneath the most famous glass pyramid in Europe, **Pyramide du Louvre,** 1er (☎ **01-40-20-52-29;** Métro: Musée du Louvre); and the **Salle Cortot,** 78 rue Cardinet, 17e (☎ **01-47-63-85-72;** Métro: Malesherbes). A copy of *Pariscope* or *L'Officiel des Spectacles,* available at any news kiosk, is the best source of information during a month in which much is happening, but not necessarily within the framework of any particular festival.

March
- **Foire du Trône,** on the lawns of the Pelouse de Reuilly, in the Bois de Vincennes, 12e (☎ **01-46-27-52-29;** Métro: Porte Dorée). A mammoth amusement park that its fans promote as the largest country fair in France, the Foire du Trône's origins date from the year 957, when merchants met with farmers on a nearby site to exchange grain and wine. This high-tech continuation of that tradition incorporates a high-flying Ferris wheel, carrousels, acrobats, jugglers, fire-eaters,

and amusements and diversions that seem like a Gallic version of Coney Island. It operates from the end of March to late May, Sunday through Thursday from 2pm to midnight, Friday and Saturday from 2pm to 1am.

April

- **International Marathon of Paris.** Beginning at the Champs-Elysées at 9am, runners take over many of the boulevards of Paris in a televised race that brings in competitors from around the world. Depending on their speed and endurance, participants arrive at the finishing point on Avenue Foch, 16e, beginning 2½ hours later. If you haven't felt like jogging lately, this event might inspire you to begin. First weekend in April. For more information, call ☎ **01-41-33-15-68.**
- **Les Grandes Eaux Musicales.** These musical events are intended to re-create the atmosphere of the ancien régime at Versailles. These are some of the rare occasions when the fountains of the parks around the palace are all turned on, with special emphasis on the Fountain of Neptune, which sits squarely in front of the best view of the château. Visitors can promenade in the garden and listen to the drifting music of French-born composers (Couperin, Charpentier, Lully) and others (Mozart and Haydn) whose careers thrived in the years of the palace's construction. The music is generally recorded. Concerts take place every Sunday afternoon between 11:15am and 3:30pm. From April to early October.

May

- **VE Day.** The celebration commemorating the capitulation of the Nazis on May 7, 1945, lasts from May 5 to 8 in Paris, with a parade along the Champs-Elysées and additional ceremonies in Reims. Pro-American sentiments are probably higher during this festival than at any other time of the Parisian calendar.
- **Grand Steeplechase de Paris.** This is a counterpoint to the horse races conducted at Chantilly (see below). It takes place at the Auteuil and Longchamp racetracks in the Bois de Boulogne on May 30. Call ☎ **01-49-10-20-30** for more information. Métro: Porte d'Auteuil.
- **French Open Tennis Championship,** Stade Roland-Garros, 16e (Métro: Porte d'Auteuil). The Open features 10 days of Grand Slam men's and women's tennis. European and South American players traditionally dominate on the hot, red, slow, dusty courts. Call ☎ **01-47-43-48-00** for more information. Late May to mid-June.

June

- **Le Prix du Jockey Club** (June 6 at 2pm) and the Prix Diane-Hermès (June 8 at 2pm), Hippodrome de Chantilly. Thoroughbreds from as far away as Kentucky and Brunei, as well as mounts sponsored by the old and new fortunes of Europe, compete in a very civil format that's broadcast around France and talked about in horsey circles around the world. On race days, as many as 30 trains depart from Paris's Gare du Nord for Chantilly, where they are met with free shuttle buses to the track. Alternatively, buses depart on race days from Place de la République and Porte de St-Cloud, on a schedule that coincides with the beginning and end of the races. Call ☎ **01-49-10-20-30** for information on this and on all other equine events in this calendar.
- **Paris Air Show.** This is where the military-industrial complex of France shows off enough high-tech hardware to make anyone think twice about invading La Patrie. Fans, competitors, and industrial spies mob the exhibition halls of Le Bourget Airport for a taste of what Gallic technocrats have wrought. Mid-June in alternate years only. The 2000 dates are June 14 to 18. For information, call ☎ **01-53-23-33-33.**

- **Festival Chopin.** Hear all you ever wanted to hear from the Polish exile who lived most of his life in Paris. Piano recitals take place in Versaille's Orangerie du Parc de Bagatelle. For information, call ☎ **01-45-00-22-19.** June 19 to July 14.
- **Fête de la Musique.** This citywide celebration at the summer solstice is the one day that noise laws don't apply in Paris. You can make music (legally) with anything, even if it means banging two garbage cans together or driving around the city blowing your car horn (illegal otherwise). Musicians, or wannabes, pour out into the streets. You might hear anything from newly arrived Russians on the balalaikas to Cubans playing salsa rhythms. There are musical parties in virtually all the open spaces of Paris, with more organized concerts at the place de la Bastille, place de la République, La Villette, and the Latin Quarter. For more information about this event, call ☎ **01-40-03-94-70.** June 21.
- **Gay Pride Parade.** A week of expositions and parties climaxes in a massive parade patterned after those in New York and San Francisco. It begins at place de l'Odéon and proceeds to place de la Bastille. The parade is followed by a dance at the Palais de Bercy, a major convention hall/sports arena. For more information, contact the **Centre Gai et Lesbien,** 3 rue Keller, 75011 Paris (☎ **01-43-57-21-47**). June 24, 2000.
- **La Villette Jazz Festival.** One of the Paris region's most dynamic homages to the art of jazz incorporates 50 concerts in churches, auditoriums, and concert halls in all neighborhoods of the Paris suburb of La Villette. Past festivals have included Herbie Hancock, Shirley Horn, Michel Portal, and other artists from around Europe and the world. The festival runs from late June through the first week in July. For information, call ☎ **08-03-30-63-06.**

July

⊗ **Bastille Day.** On July 14, the accepted birth date of modern-day France, festivities reach their peak in Paris with street fairs, pageants, fireworks, and feasts. The day begins with a parade down the Champs-Elysées and ends with fireworks at Montmartre. Wherever you are, before the end of the day you'll hear Piaf warbling "La Foule" ("The Crowd"), the song that celebrated her passion for the stranger whom she met and later lost in a crowd on Bastille Day. Get in the spirit by humming the "Marseillaise," outfitting yourself with a beret, a pack of Gauloises, and a bottle of cheap wine, and stamping madly around the city.

- **Festival de St-Denis.** This series presents 4 days of artfully contrived music in the burial place of the French kings, a grim early Gothic monument in Paris's industrialized northern suburb of St-Denis. Call ☎ **01-48-13-06-07** for information; Métro: St-Denis-Basilique. July 2 to 4.
- **Paris Quartier d'Été.** For a 4-week period, the Arènes de Lutèce, or the "Cour d'Honneur" at the Sorbonne, both within the Latin Quarter, host pop orchestral concerts in a village green setting. The dozen or so concerts are usually grander than the outdoors setting would imply, and include performances by the Orchestre de Paris, the Orchestre National de France, and the Baroque Orchestra of the European Union. On the fringes one can find plays, jazz concerts, parades choreographed in the Tuileries Gardens for the pleasure of children and their guardians, and a scattering of jazz. For information, call ☎ **01-44-94-98-00** or fax 01-44-94-98-01. July 15 to August 15.
- **Tour de France.** Europe's most visible, most highly contested, and most overabundantly televised bicycle race pits crews of wind-tunnel-tested athletes along an itinerary that traces the six sides of the French "hexagon," and includes detours deep into the Massif Central and across the Alps of francophone Switzerland.

The race is decided at a finish line drawn across the Champs-Elysées. July 3 to 21. For information, call ☎ **01-41-33-15-00.**

August

- **Music at the Carrousel du Louvre.** The ornate courtyards of the Louvre are the midsummer setting for concerts by Austrian, English, and French chamber orchestras. The series lasts 5 consecutive days and includes music by Schumann, Schubert, Britten, Janácek, and Stravinsky. For tickets and information, call ☎ **01-43-16-47-47** or 01-44-70-24-69. August 23 to 27.

September

- **Festival Musique en l'Ile.** A series of concerts, most dignified masses composed between the 17th and late 19th centuries, are given within medieval churches in the 4th, 5th, and 6th arrondissements. Sites include St-Louis-en-l'Ile, St-Severin, and St-Germain-des-Prés. Call ☎ **01-44-94-28-50** for more information. September 5 to October 17.

- **Festival d'Automne.** Paris welcomes the return of its residents from their August holidays with an ongoing and eclectic festival of modern music, ballet, theater, and modern art. Venues include art galleries, churches, concert halls, auditoriums, and parks throughout Paris. There's a great emphasis on experimental works, which the festival's promoters scatter judiciously between more traditional productions. Depending on the event, tickets cost from 100 F to 300 F ($18 to $54). For details, write to the **Festival d'Automne,** 156 rue de Rivoli, 75001 Paris (☎ **01-53-45-17-00;** fax 01-53-45-17-01). Late September to mid-December.

- **International Ready-to-Wear Fashion Shows** (Le Salon International de Prêt-à-Porter), Parc des Expositions, Porte de Versailles, Paris, 15e (Métro: Porte de Versailles). More of what took place at the fashion shows in January, with a stress on what *le beau monde* will be wearing the next spring. Early September.

October

- ✪ **Paris Auto Show.** Glistening metal, glitzy attendees, lots of hype, and the latest models from world auto makers form a showcase for European car design. The auto show takes place at the Parc des Expositions, near the Porte de Versailles in western Paris, for a 10-day period in early October. In addition, a permanent exhibition on French auto design at the Cité des Sciences et de l'Industrie is upgraded and enriched during all of October. Call ☎ **01-53-23-07-40** for information on either venue.

- **Prix de l'Arc de Triomphe.** France's answer to England's Ascot is the country's most prestigious horse race, culminating the equine season in Europe. Hippodrome de Longchamp, 16e (☎ **01-49-10-20-30;** Métro: Porte d'Auteuil). Early October.

November

- **Armistice Day.** The signing of the controversial document that ended World War I is celebrated with a military parade from the Arc de Triomphe to the Hôtel des Invalides. November 11.

- **City of Paris Festival of Sacred Art.** A dignified series of classical concerts is held in five of the oldest and most recognizable churches of Paris. End of November through early December. For information, call **01-44-70-64-10.**

December

- **Boat Fair** (Le Salon International de la Navigation de Plaisance). Europe's most visible exposition of what's afloat and of interest to wholesalers, retailers, individual boat owners (or wannabes), and anyone involved in the business of

Paris at the Millennium

In the spirit of a new century, Paris will launch major exhibitions, and dozens of celebrations will be announced in the year 2000. Paris isn't celebrating the millennium with a grand monument, as it did with the Eiffel Tower or Britain is doing with its Greenwich Millennium Dome. Instead, the city will launch a series of smaller-scale projects, exhibits, and cultural festivals. A "planetary garden" is being carved out of a large space at La Villette. A sundial is to be installed at the Place de la Concorde. Major exhibitions will be announced at the newly renovated Georges Pompidou Center (Beaubourg). And a series of exhibits called Visions of the Future is planned at the Grand Palais for the year 2000. A spectacular "message for peace" is to be installed at the Trocadero across from the Eiffel Tower, in the form of a wailing wall like the one in Jerusalem—visitors can leave their peace messages in the cracks in the wall, taking a message left by another. And in the same spirit, a monumental sculpture representing the world's children hand in hand will be erected in front of UNESCO's headquarters. Concerts, sporting events, and parades are also in the works, with festivities expected to reach their peak on the national holiday of July 14, 2000. And the largest balloon in the world (104 feet) will let passengers view Paris from an altitude of 975 feet.

Check with the tourist offices listed under "Visitor Information" above or the Web sites listed in the back of this book to find out exactly what millennial celebrations will be taking place at the time of your visit. Better yet, visit France's official millennial Web site at **www.celebration2000.gouv.fr**.

---

waterborne holiday-making. Parc des Expositions, Porte de Versailles, Paris, 15e (☎ **01-41-90-47-10;** fax 01-41-90-47-00; Métro: Porte de Versailles). The Fair lasts for 8 days in early December.

- **Fête de St-Sylvestre** (New Year's Eve). It's most boisterously celebrated in the quartier latin around the Sorbonne. At midnight, the city explodes. Strangers kiss strangers, and boulevard St-Michel becomes a virtual pedestrian mall, as does the Champs-Elysées. December 31.

5 Health & Insurance

WHAT TO DO IF YOU GET SICK AWAY FROM HOME

It can be hard to find a doctor you can trust when you're in an unfamiliar place. Try to take proper precautions the week before you depart, to avoid falling ill while you're away from home. Amid the last-minute frenzy that often precedes a vacation break, make an extra effort to eat and sleep well—especially if you feel an illness coming on.

If you worry about getting sick away from home, you may want to consider **medical travel insurance** (see the section on travel insurance later in this chapter). In most cases, however, your existing health plan will provide all the coverage you need. Be sure to carry your identification card in your wallet.

If you suffer from a chronic illness, consult your doctor before your departure. For conditions like epilepsy, diabetes, or heart problems, wear a **Medic Alert Identification Tag** (☎ **800/825-3785;** www.medicalert.org), which will immediately alert doctors to your condition and give them access to your records through Medic Alert's 24-hour hot line. Membership is $35, plus a $15 annual fee.

Pack prescription medications in your carry-on luggage. Carry written prescriptions in generic, not brand-name, form, and dispense all prescription medications from their original labeled vials. Also bring along copies of your prescriptions in case you lose your pills or run out.

If you wear contact lenses, pack an extra pair in case you lose one.

Contact the **International Association for Medical Assistance to Travelers (IAMAT)** (☎ **716/754-4883** or 416/652-0137; www.sentex.net/~iamat). This organization offers tips on travel and health concerns in the countries you'll be visiting, and lists many local English-speaking doctors.

INSURANCE

There are three kinds of travel insurance: trip cancellation, medical, and lost luggage coverage. **Trip cancellation insurance** is a good idea if you have paid a large portion of your vacation expenses up front. The other two types of insurance, however, don't make sense for most travelers. *Note:* Check your existing policies before you buy any additional coverage.

Your existing health insurance should cover you if you get sick while on vacation (though if you belong to an HMO, you should check to see whether you are fully covered when away from home). If you need hospital treatment, most health insurance plans and HMOs will cover out-of-country hospital visits and procedures, at least to some extent. However, most make you pay the bills up front at the time of care, and you'll get a refund after you've returned and filed all the paperwork. Members of **Blue Cross/Blue Shield** can now use their cards at select hospitals in most major cities worldwide (☎ **800/810-BLUE** or www.bluecares.com/blue/bluecard/wwn for a list of hospitals). For independent travel health-insurance providers, see below.

Your homeowner's insurance should cover **stolen luggage.** The airlines are responsible for upto $1,250 on domestic flights if they lose your luggage; if you plan to carry anything more valuable than that, keep it in your carry-on bag.

The differences between travel assistance and insurance are often blurred, but in general the former offers on-the-spot assistance and 24-hour hot lines (mostly oriented toward medical problems), while the latter reimburses you for travel problems (medical, travel, or otherwise) after you have filed the paperwork. The coverage you should consider will depend on how much protection is already contained in your existing health insurance or other policies. Some credit- and charge-card companies may insure you against travel accidents if you buy plane, train, or bus tickets with their cards. Before purchasing additional insurance, read your policies and agreements over carefully. Call your insurers or credit/charge-card companies if you have any questions.

Some credit cards (American Express and certain gold and platinum Visa and MasterCards, for example) offer automatic flight insurance against death or dismemberment in case of an airplane crash.

If you do require additional insurance, try one of the companies listed below. But don't pay for more than you need. For example, if you need only trip cancellation insurance, don't purchase coverage for lost or stolen property. Trip cancellation insurance costs approximately 6% to 8% of the total value of your vacation.

Among the reputable issuers of travel insurance are:

Access America, 6600 W. Broad St., Richmond, VA 23230 (☎ **800/284-8300**)

Travel Guard International, 1145 Clark St., Stevens Point, WI 54481 (☎ **800/826-1300**)

Travel Insured International, Inc., P.O. Box 280568, East Hartford, CT 06128 (☎ **800/243-3174**)

Columbus Travel Insurance, 279 High St., Croydon CR0 1QH (☎ **0171/375-0011** in London; www2.columbusdirect.com/columbusdirect)

International SOS Assistance, P.O. Box 11568, Philadelphia, PA 11916 (☎ **800/523-8930** or 215/244-1500), strictly an assistance company

Travelex Insurance Services, P.O. Box 9408, Garden City, NY 11530-9408 (☎ **800/228-9792**)

Medicare only covers U.S. citizens traveling in Mexico and Canada. For Blue Cross/Blue Shield coverage abroad, see above. Companies specializing in accident and medical care include:

MEDEX International, P.O. Box 5375, Timonium, MD 21094-5375 (☎ **888/ MEDEX-00** or 410/453-6300; fax 410/453-6301; www.medexassist.com)

Travel Assistance International (Worldwide Assistance Services, Inc.), 1133 15th St. NW, Suite 400, Washington, DC 20005 (☎ **800/821-2828** or 202/828-5894; fax 202/828-5896)

6 Tips for Travelers with Special Needs

TRAVELERS WITH DISABILITIES

A disability shouldn't stop anyone from traveling. There are more resources out there than ever before. *A World of Options,* a 658-page book of resources for disabled travelers, covers everything from biking trips to scuba outfitters. It costs $35 ($30 for members) and is available from **Mobility International USA,** P.O. Box 10767, Eugene, OR 97440 (☎ **541/343-1284,** voice and TDD; www.miusa.org). Annual membership for Mobility International is $35, which includes their quarterly newsletter, *Over the Rainbow.* In addition, **Twin Peaks Press,** P.O. Box 129, Vancouver, WA 98666 (☎ **360/694-2462**), publishes travel-related books for people with disabilities.

The **Moss Rehab Hospital** (☎ **215/456-9600**) has been providing friendly and helpful phone advice and referrals to disabled travelers for years through its **Travel Information Service** (☎ **215/456-9603;** www.mossresourcenet.org).

You can join the **Society for the Advancement of Travel for the Handicapped (SATH),** 347 Fifth Ave., Suite 610, New York, NY 10016 (☎ **212/447-7284;** fax 212-725-8253; www.sath.org), for $45 annually, $30 for seniors and students, to gain access to their vast network of connections in the travel industry. They provide information sheets on travel destinations and referrals to tour operators that specialize in traveling with disabilities. Their quarterly magazine, *Open World for Disability and Mature Travel,* is full of good information and resources. A year's subscription is $13 ($21 outside the U.S.).

You can obtain a copy of *Air Transportation of Handicapped Persons* by writing to Free Advisory Circular No. AC12032, Distribution Unit, U.S. Department of Transportation, Publications Division, M-4332, Washington, DC 20590.

Vision-impaired travelers should contact the **American Foundation for the Blind,** 11 Penn Plaza, Suite 300, New York, NY 10001 (☎ **800/232-5463**), for information on traveling with Seeing Eye dogs.

Facilities in Paris for travelers with disabilities are certainly better than you'll find in most cities. Every year the French government does more and more to help ease life for persons with disabilities in the public facilities of the country.

Nearly all modern hotels in France now have rooms designed especially for persons with disabilities in mind. Older hotels, unless renovated, may not provide such important features as elevators, special toilet facilities, or ramps for wheelchair accessibility. For a list of hotels in Paris offering facilities for persons with disabilities, contact the **APF Evasion** (Association des Paralysés de France), 17 bd. Auguste Blanqui, 75013 Paris (☎ **01-40-78-69-00**).

Most high-speed trains in France can deal with wheelchairs. Guide dogs ride free. Older trains have special compartments built for wheelchair boarding. On the Paris Métro, persons with disabilities can sit in wider seats provided for their comfort. Some stations don't have escalators or elevators, however, and this may present problems.

GAY & LESBIAN TRAVELERS

Before going to France, both lesbians and gay men might want to pick up a copy of Frommer's brand-new *Gay & Lesbian Europe.*

"Gay Paree" has one of the world's largest gay populations, with dozens of gay clubs, restaurants, organizations, and services. Other than publications (see below), one of the best sources of information on gay and lesbian activities is the **Centre Gai and Lesbien,** 3 rue Keller, 75011 (☎ **01-43-57-21-47;** Métro: Bastille). Well equipped to dispense information and to coordinate the activities and meetings of gay people from virtually everywhere, it's open daily from 2 to 6pm only. On Sunday, **Le Café Positif** at the Center features music, cabaret, and information about AIDS and sexually transmitted diseases.

SOS Écoute Gay (☎ **01-44-93-01-02**) is a gay hot line, theoretically designed as a way to creatively counsel persons with gay-related problems. The phone is answered by volunteers, some of whom are not as skilled and helpful as others. A phone counselor responds to calls Monday through Thursday from 8 to 10pm and Friday from 6 to 10pm. **SOS Homophobie** (☎ **01-48-06-42-41**) is a separate hot line specifically intended for victims of homophobia or gay-related discrimination; calls are received by a panel of French-trained lawyers and legal experts who offer advice every Monday through Friday from 8 to 10pm.

Another helpful source is **La Maison des Femmes,** 163 rue de Charenton, 12e (☎ **01-43-43-41-13;** Métro: Reuilly-Diderot), offering information about Paris for lesbians and bisexual women and sometimes sponsoring informal dinners and get-togethers. Call any Wednesday from 4 to 7pm or Saturday from 3 to 5pm for further information.

Gai Pied's publication *Guide Gai* (revised annually) is the best source of information on gay and lesbian clubs, hotels, restaurants, organizations, and services in the capital. Lesbian or bisexual women might also like to pick up a copy of *Lesbia,* if only to check out the ads. These publications and others are available at Paris's largest and best-stocked gay bookstore, **Les Mots à la Bouche,** 6 rue Ste-Croix-de-la-Bretonnerie, 4e (☎ **01-42-78-88-30**). Hours are Monday through Saturday from 11am to 11pm, Sunday from 2 to 8pm. Both French- and English-language publications are available.

France is one of the world's most tolerant countries toward gays and lesbians, and there are no special laws that discriminate against them. Technically, sexual relations are legal for consenting partners age 16 and over. However, one doesn't come of legal age in France until 18, so under the murkiness of French law, parents could bring a lawsuit claiming that their son or daughter was seduced or coerced into having sex, even though he or she in theory consented. Therefore, sex with anyone 17 and under, consent or not, poses a certain legal danger. Paris, of course, is the center of gay life in France, although gay and lesbian establishments exist through the provinces as well.

Where to Stay & Play

See chapter 4 for a list of gay-friendly hotels, and chapter 9 for gay and lesbian nightlife.

SENIORS

Don't be shy about asking for discounts, but always carry some kind of identification, such as a driver's license, that shows your date of birth. Also, mention the fact that you're a senior citizen when you first make your travel reservations. For example, many hotels offer seniors discounts. In most cities, people over age 60 qualify for reduced admission to theaters, museums, and other attractions, and discounted fares on public transportation.

Members of the **American Association of Retired Persons (AARP),** 601 E St. NW, Washington, DC 20049 (☎ 800/424-3410 or 202/434-2277), get discounts not only on hotels but on airfares and car rentals, too. AARP offers members a wide range of special benefits, including *Modern Maturity* magazine and a monthly newsletter.

The **National Council of Senior Citizens,** 8403 Colesville Rd., Suite 1200, Silver Spring, MD 20910 (☎ 301/578-8800), a nonprofit organization, offers a newsletter six times a year (partly devoted to travel tips) and discounts on hotel and auto rentals; annual dues are $13 per person or couple.

Mature Outlook, P.O. Box 9390, Des Moines, IA 50306 (☎ 800/336-6330), began as a travel organization for people over 50, though it now caters to people of all ages. Members receive discounts on hotels and receive a bimonthly magazine. Annual membership is $19.95, which entitles members to discounts and, often, free coupons for discounted merchandise from Sears.

Golden Companions, P.O. Box 5249, Reno, NV 89513 (☎ 702/324-2227), helps travelers 45-plus find compatible companions through a personal voice-mail service. Contact them for more information.

Mature Traveler, a monthly 12-page newsletter on senior citizen travel, is a valuable resource. It is available by subscription ($30 a year) from GEM Publishing Group, Box 50400, Reno, NV 89513-0400. GEM also publishes *The Book of Deals,* a collection of more than 1,000 senior discounts on airlines, lodging, tours, and attractions around the country; it's available for $9.95 by calling ☎ 800/460-6676. Another helpful publication is *101 Tips for the Mature Traveler,* available from Grand Circle Travel, 347 Congress St., Suite 3A, Boston, MA 02210 (☎ 800/221-2610 or 617/350-7500; fax 617/346-6700).

Grand Circle Travel is also one of the hundreds of travel agencies specializing in vacations for seniors (347 Congress St., Suite 3A, Boston, MA 02210; ☎ 800/221-2610 or 617/350-7500). Many of these packages, however, are of the tour-bus variety, with free trips thrown in for those who organize groups of 10 or more. Seniors seeking more independent travel should probably consult a regular travel agent. **SAGA International Holidays,** 222 Berkeley St., Boston, MA 02116 (☎ 800/343-0273), offers inclusive tours and cruises for those 50 and older. SAGA also sponsors the more substantial **Road Scholar Tours** (☎ 800/621-2151).

If you want something more than the average vacation or guided tour, try **Elderhostel** (☎ 877/426-8056; www.elderhos☎org) or the University of New Hampshire's **Interhostel** (☎ 800/733-9753), both variations on the same theme: educational travel for senior citizens. On these escorted tours, the days are packed with seminars, lectures, and field trips, and the sightseeing is all led by academic experts. **Elderhostel,** 75 Federal St., Boston, MA 02110-1941 (☎ 877/426-8056; www.elderhostel.org), arranges study programs for those age 55 and over (and a spouse or companion of any age) in the United States and in 77 countries around the world, including France. Most courses last about 3 weeks and many include airfare, accommodations in student dormitories or modest inns, meals, and tuition. Write or call for a free catalog that lists upcoming courses and destinations. **Interhostel** takes travelers 50 and over (with companions over 40) and offers 2- and 3-week trips, mostly international. The courses in both these programs are ungraded, involve no homework, and often focus on the liberal arts. They're not luxury vacations, but they're fun and fulfilling.

FAMILIES

Several books on the market offer tips to help you travel with kids. Most concentrate on the United States, but two, *Family Travel* (Lanier Publishing International) and *How to Take Great Trips with Your Kids* (The Harvard Common Press), are full of good general advice that can apply to travel anywhere. Another reliable tome, with a worldwide focus, is *Adventuring with Children* (Foghorn Press).

Family Travel Times is published 6 times a year by TWYCH (Travel with Your Children; ☎ **888/822-4388** or 212/477-5524), and includes a weekly call-in service for subscribers. Subscriptions are $40 a year for quarterly editions. A free publication list and a sample issue are available by calling or sending a request to the above address.

Families Welcome!, 92 N. Main St., Ashland, OR 97520 (☎ **800/326-0724** or 541/482-6121), a travel company specializing in worry-free vacations for families, offers "City Kids" packages to certain European cities, including Paris.

STUDENTS

Paris offers student discounts on nearly everything, from museums to movies. The best resource for students is the **Council on International Educational Exchange (CIEE).** They can set you up with an ID card (see below), and their travel branch, **Council Travel Service** (☎ **800/226-8624;** www.ciee.com), is the biggest student travel agency operation in the world. It can get you discounts on plane tickets, rail passes, and the like. Ask them for a list of CTS offices in major cities so you can keep the discounts flowing (and aid lines open) as you travel.

From CIEE you can obtain the student traveler's best friend, the $18 **International Student Identity Card (ISIC).** It's the only officially acceptable form of student identification, good for cut rates on rail passes, plane tickets, and other discounts. It also provides you with basic health and life insurance and a 24-hour help line. If you're no longer a student but are still under 26, you can get a GO 25 card from the same people, which will get you the insurance and some of the discounts.

In Canada, **Travel CUTS,** 200 Ronson St., Ste. 320, Toronto, ONT M9W 5Z9 (☎ **800/667-2887** or 416/614-2887; www.travelcuts.com), offers similar services. **Campus Travel,** 52 Grosvenor Gardens, London SW1W 0AG (☎ **0171/730-3402;** www.campustravel.co.uk), opposite Victoria Station, is Britain's leading specialist in student and youth travel.

WOMEN TRAVELERS

Several Web sites offer women advice on how to travel safely and happily. The **Executive Woman's Travel Network** (www.delta-air.com/womenexecs/) is the official woman's travel site of Delta airlines and offers women tips on staying fit while traveling, eating well, finding special airfares, and dealing with many other feminine travel issues. **WomanTraveler** (www.womantraveler.com) is an excellent guide that suggests places where women can stay and eat in various destinations. The site is authored by women and includes listings of women-owned businesses such as hotels, hostels, etc.

SINGLE TRAVELERS

Many people prefer traveling alone, but booking a single room usually costs well over half the price of a double. **Travel Companion** (☎ **516/454-0880**) is one of the nation's oldest roommate finders for single travelers. Register with them and find a trustworthy travel mate who will split the cost of the room with you and be around as little, or as often, as you like during the day.

Several tour organizers cater to solo travelers as well. **Experience Plus** (☎ **800/685-4565;** fax 907/484-8489) offers an interesting selection of single-only trips, and **Travel Buddies** (☎ **800/998-9099** or 604/533-2483) runs single-friendly tours with no singles supplement.

7 Getting There

BY PLANE
FROM NORTH AMERICA

The flying time to Paris from New York is about 7 hours; from Chicago, 9 hours; from Los Angeles, 11 hours; from Atlanta, about 8 hours; and from Washington, D.C., about 7½ hours.

One of the best choices for passengers flying to Paris from both the southeastern United States and the Midwest is **Delta Airlines** (☎ **800/241-4141;** www.delta-air. com), whose network greatly expanded after its acquisition of some of the former Pan Am routes. From such cities as New Orleans, Phoenix, Columbia (South Carolina), and Nashville, Delta flies to Atlanta, connecting every evening with a nonstop flight to Charles de Gaulle Airport in Paris. Delta also operates daily nonstop flights to Charles de Gaulle from Cincinnati and New York's JFK. All of these flights depart late enough in the day to permit easy transfers from much of Delta's vast North American network.

Another excellent choice for Paris-bound passengers is **United Airlines** (☎ **800/ 538-2929;** www.ual.com), with nonstop flights from Chicago, Washington, D.C. (Dulles), and San Francisco to Paris's Charles de Gaulle Airport. United also offers discounted fares in the low and shoulder seasons to London's Heathrow from five major North American hubs. From London, it's an easy train and Hovercraft or Chunnel connection to Paris, a fact that tempts many passengers to spend a weekend in London either before or after their visit to Paris.

Another good option is **Continental Airlines** (☎ **800/231-0856;** www. flycontinental.com), which services the Northeast and much of the Southwest through its busy hubs in Newark and Houston. From both of those cities, Continental provides nonstop flights to Charles de Gaulle Airport. Flights from Newark depart daily, while flights from Houston depart between four and seven times a week, depending on the season.

TWA (☎ **800/221-2000;** www.twa.com), operates daily nonstop service to Charles de Gaulle Airport from New York's JFK, and, in summer, several flights a week from Boston and Washington, D.C.'s Dulles airport. In summer, TWA also flies to Paris from St. Louis several times a week nonstop, and to Paris from Los Angeles three times a week, with connections in St. Louis or New York's JFK. In winter, flights from Los Angeles and Washington, D.C., are suspended, and flights from St. Louis are routed with brief touchdowns en route to Paris in New York or Boston.

The French flag carrier, **Air France** (☎ **800/237-2747;** www.airfrance.com), offers daily or several-times-a-week flights between Paris's Charles de Gaulle and Newark, New Jersey; Washington, D.C.'s Dulles; Miami; Chicago; New York's JFK; Houston; San Francisco; Los Angeles; Boston; Cincinnati; Atlanta; Montréal; Toronto; and Mexico City.

American Airlines (☎ **800/433-7300;** www.american.air.com), provides daily nonstop flights to Paris (Orly) from Dallas/Fort Worth, Chicago, Miami, Boston, and New York's JFK.

US Airways (☎ **800/428-4322;** www.usairways.com), offers daily nonstop service from Philadelphia International Airport to Paris's Charles de Gaulle Airport.

Canadians usually choose **Air Canada** (☎ 800/776-3000 from the U.S. and Canada; www.aircanada.ca) for flights to Paris from Toronto and Montréal. Nonstop flights from Montréal and Toronto depart every evening for Paris. Two of the nonstop flights from Toronto are shared with Air France and feature Air France aircraft.

FROM THE UNITED KINGDOM

From London, **Air France** (☎ 0181/742-6600) and **British Airways** (☎ 0345/222111 in the U.K. only) fly frequently to Paris, with a trip time of only 1 hour. These airlines alone operate up to 17 flights daily from Heathrow, one of the busiest air routes in Europe. Many commercial travelers also use regular flights originating from the London City Airport in the Docklands. Direct flights to Paris also exist from major cities such as Manchester, Edinburgh, and Southampton. Contact Air France, British Airways, British Midland (☎ 332/854-854), or Air UK (☎ 099/074074) for details.

There are no hard-and-fast rules about getting the best deals for European flights. Daily papers often carry advertisements for companies offering cheap flights; highly recommended companies include **Trailfinders** (☎ 0171/938-3999), which sells discounted fares, and **Avro Tours** (☎ 0181/715-0000), which operates charters. In London, there are many ticket consolidators (who buy inventories of tickets from airlines and then resell them) in the neighborhood of Earl's Court and Victoria Station that offer cheap fares. For your own protection, make sure that the company you deal with is a member of the IATA, ABTA, or ATOL. CEEFAX, a British television information service (received by many private homes and hotels), presents details of package holidays and flights to Europe and beyond.

FROM AUSTRALIA

Getting to Paris from Australia is rather difficult, as Air France has discontinued all its flights to and from the country. However, the French-based airline **A.O.M.** (☎ 01/4979-1000; triel.info.unicaen.fr/aom) flies twice weekly from Sydney to Paris. **British Airways** (☎ 02/8904-8844; www.british-airways.com) flies daily from both Sydney and Melbourne to London for a connecting flight to either Charles de Gaulle or Orly airports. **Qantas** (☎ 13-12-11; www.qantas.com) does not fly to Paris, but goes to London, where plentiful connections exist for the hop across the channel.

FROM SOUTH AFRICA

Air France (☎ 021/418-8180 in Cape Town or 011/880-8052 in Johannesburg; www.airfrance.com) has a daily flight to Charles de Gaulle from Johannesburg and Cape Town. **British Airways** (☎ 011/441-8600; www.british-airways.com) flies daily from Johannesburg to London for a connecting flight to either Charles de Gaulle or Orly airports. Six flights weekly depart Cape Town for London and then to Paris. **South African Airways** (☎ 021/936-2662 in Cape Town or 011/978-1111 in Johannesburg; www.saa.co.za) has three weekly flights from Johannesburg to Charles de Gaulle in Paris.

PARIS AIRPORTS

Paris has two major international airports: **Orly** (☎ 01-49-75-15-15), 8½ miles south, and **Charles de Gaulle,** or **Roissy** (☎ 01-48-62-22-80), 14¼ miles northeast of the city. A shuttle operates between the two airports about every 30 minutes, taking 50 to 75 minutes. Tickets are 75 F ($12.75).

CHARLES DE GAULLE AIRPORT (ROISSY)   At Charles de Gaulle Airport, foreign carriers use Aérogare 1, and Air France uses Aérogare 2. From Aérogare 1, you

Flying for Less: Tips for Getting the Best Airfares

Passengers within the same airplane cabin rarely pay the same fare for their seats. Business travelers who need to purchase tickets at the last minute, change their itinerary at a moment's notice, or get home before the weekend pay the premium rate, known as the full fare. Passengers who can book their ticket long in advance, who don't mind staying over Saturday night, or who are willing to travel on a Tuesday, Wednesday, or Thursday after 7pm, will pay a fraction of the full fare. On most flights, even the shortest hops, the full fare is close to $1,000 or more, but a 7-day or 14-day advance purchase ticket is closer to $200 to $300. Here are a few other easy ways to save:

1. Periodically airlines lower prices on their most popular routes. Check your newspaper for advertised discounts or call the airlines directly and ask if any **promotional rates** or special fares are available. You'll almost never see a sale during the peak summer vacation months of July and August, or during the Thanksgiving or Christmas seasons, only in periods of low-volume travel. If your schedule is flexible, ask if you can secure a cheaper fare by staying an extra day or by flying midweek. (Many airlines won't volunteer this information.) If you already hold a ticket when a sale breaks, it may even pay to exchange your ticket, which usually incurs a $50 to $75 charge.

   Note, however, that the lowest-priced fares are often nonrefundable, require advance purchase of 1 to 3 weeks and a certain length of stay, and carry penalties for changing dates of travel.

2. **Consolidators,** also known as bucket shops, are a good place to find low fares. Consolidators buy seats in bulk from the airlines and then sell them back to the public at prices below even the airlines' discounted rates. Their small boxed ads usually run in the Sunday travel section at the bottom of the page. Before you pay a consolidator, however, ask for a record locator number and confirm your seat with the airline itself. Be prepared to book your ticket with a different consolidator—there are many to choose from—if the airline can't confirm your reservation. Also be aware that bucket shop tickets are usually nonrefundable or rigged with stiff cancellation penalties, often as high as 50% to 75% of the ticket price.

   Council Travel (☎ 800/226-8624; www.counciltravel.com) and **STA Travel** (☎ 800/781-4040; www.sta.travel.com) cater especially to young travelers, but their bargain basement prices are available to people of all ages. **Travel Bargains** (☎ 800/AIR-FARE; www.1800airfare.com) was formerly owned by TWA but now offers the deepest discounts on many other airlines, with a 4-day advance purchase. Other reliable consolidators include **1-800-FLY-CHEAP**

---

take a moving walkway to the passport checkpoint and the Customs area. The two terminals are linked by a shuttle bus *(navette).*

The free shuttle bus connecting Aérogare 1 with Aérogare 2 also transports passengers to the Roissy rail station, from which fast **RER trains** leave every 15 minutes for such Métro stations as Gare du Nord, Châtelet, Luxembourg, Port-Royal, and Denfert-Rochereau. The train fare from Roissy to any point within central Paris is 69 F ($11.75) in first class or 47 F ($8) in second class. You can also take an **Air France shuttle bus** to central Paris for 60 F ($10.20). It stops at the Palais des Congrès (Port Maillot), then continues on to the place del'Etoile, where underground lines can carry you farther along to (www.1800flycheap.com); **TFI Tours International** (☎ **800/745-8000** or 212/736-1140), which serves as a clearinghouse for unused seats; or "rebators" such as **Travel Avenue** (☎ **800/333-3335** or 312/876-1116) and the **Smart Traveller** (☎ **800/448-3338** in the U.S. or 305/448-3338; www.smart-traveller@juno.com), which rebate part of their commissions to you.

3. Search the **Internet** for cheap fares—though it's still best to compare your findings with the research of a dedicated travel agent, if you're lucky enough to have one, especially when you're booking more than just a flight. See the online directory at the end of this book for Web sites devoted to finding low fares on the Internet and information on the airlines' **E-savers** programs.

4. Book a seat on a **charter flight.** Discounted fares have pared the number available, but they can still be found. Most charter operators advertise and sell their seats through travel agents, thus making these local professionals your best source of information for available flights. Before deciding to take a charter flight, however, check the restrictions on the ticket: You may be asked to purchase a tour package, to pay in advance, to be amenable if the day of departure is changed, to pay a service charge, to fly on an airline you're not familiar with (this usually is not the case), and to pay harsh penalties if you cancel—but be understanding if the charter doesn't fill up and is canceled up to 10 days before departure. Summer charters fill up more quickly than others and are almost sure to fly, but if you decide on a charter flight, seriously consider cancellation and baggage insurance.

5. Look into **courier flights.** Companies that hire couriers use your luggage allowance for their business baggage; in return, you get a deeply discounted ticket. Flights are often offered at the last minute, and you may have to arrange a pretrip interview to make sure you're right for the job. **Now Voyager,** open Monday through Friday from 10am to 5:30pm and Saturday from noon to 4:30pm (☎ **212/431-1616**), flies from New York and sometimes has flights to San Francisco for as little as $199 round-trip. Now Voyager also offers non-courier discounted fares, so call the company even if you don't want to fly as a courier.

6. Join a travel club such as **Moment's Notice** (☎ **718/234-6295**) or **Sears Discount Travel Club** (☎ **800/433-9383,** or 800/255-1487 to join), which supply unsold tickets at discounted prices. You pay an annual membership fee to get the club's hot line number. Of course, you're limited to what's available, so you have to be flexible.

any other point within Paris. Depending on traffic, the ride takes between 45 and 55 minutes. The shuttle departs about every 12 minutes between 5:40am and 11pm.

Another option, the **Roissybus** (☎ **01-48-04-18-24**), departs from a point near the corner of the rue Scribe and the place de l'Opéra every 15 minutes from 5:45am to 11pm. The cost for the 45- to 50-minute bus ride is 45 F ($7.65).

Taxis from Roissy into the city will run about 250 F ($42.50) on the meter. At night (from 8pm to 7am), fares are about 40% higher. Long queues of both taxis and passengers form outside each of the airport's terminals in a surprisingly orderly fashion.

Caution

Don't take a meterless taxi from Orly Sud or Orly Ouest—it's much safer (and usually cheaper) to hire a metered cab from the taxi queues, which are under the scrutiny of a police officer.

ORLY AIRPORT Orly has two terminals: Orly Sud (south) for international flights and Orly Ouest (west) for domestic flights. A free shuttle bus links them together.

Air France buses leave exit E of Orly Ouest, and from exit F, Platform 5 of Orly Sud, every 12 minutes between 5:45am and 11pm, heading for Gare des Invalides in central Paris at a cost of 45 F ($7.65) one-way. Other buses depart for the place Denfert-Rochereau in the south of Paris. Passage on any of these buses costs 30 F ($5.10).

An alternative method for reaching central Paris involves taking a free shuttle bus that leaves both of Orly's terminals at intervals of approximately every 15 minutes for the nearby **RER train station** (Pont-de-Rungis/Aéroport-d'Orly), from which RER trains take 30 minutes to reach the city center. A trip to Les Invalides, for example, costs 35 F ($5.95).

A **taxi** from Orly to the center of Paris costs about 170 F ($28.90) and is higher at night and on weekends. Returning to the airport, **buses** to Orly Airport leave from the Invalides terminal to either Orly Sud or Orly Ouest every 15 minutes, taking about 30 minutes.

BY TRAIN

If you're already in Europe, you might decide to travel to Paris by train, especially if you have a Eurailpass. Even if you don't, the cost is relatively low. For example, the one-way fare from London to Paris by Eurostar ranges from $179 to $299 in first class and $109 to $149 in second class. Rail passes or individual rail tickets within Europe are available at most travel agencies, at any office of **Rail Europe** (☎ **800/4-EURAIL** in the U.S.; www.raileurope.com) or **Eurostar** (☎ **800/EUROSTAR** in the U.S.).

In London, an especially convenient place to buy railway tickets to virtually anywhere is just opposite Platform 2 in Victoria Station, London SW1V 1JZ, where Wasteels, Ltd. (☎ **0171/834-6744**) provides railway-related services and discusses the pros and cons of various types of fares and rail passes. Occasionally, Wasteels charges a £5 ($8.25) fee for its services, but its information warrants the fee and the company's staff spends a generous amount of time planning itineraries with each client. Some of the most popular passes, including Inter-Rail and EuroYouth, are available only to those under 26 years of age for unlimited second-class travel in 26 European countries.

PARIS TRAIN STATIONS

There are six major train stations in Paris: **Gare d'Austerlitz,** 55 quai d'Austerlitz, 13e (serving the southwest, with trains from the Loire Valley, the Bordeaux country, and the Pyrénées); **Gare de l'Est,** place du 11 Novembre 1918, 10e (serving the east, with trains from Strasbourg, Nancy, Reims, and beyond to Zurich, Basel, Luxembourg, and Austria); **Gare de Lyon,** 20 bd. Diderot, 12e (serving the southeast with trains from the Côte d'Azur, Provence, and beyond to Geneva, Lausanne, and Italy); **Gare Montparnasse,** 17 bd. Vaugirard, 15e (serving the west, with trains from Brittany); **Gare du Nord,** 18 rue de Dunkerque, 15e (serving the north, with trains from Holland, Denmark, Belgium, and northern Germany); and **Gare St-Lazare,** 13 rue d'Amsterdam, 8e (serving the northwest, with trains from Normandy).

For general train information and to make reservations, call ☎ **08-36-35-35-39** from 7am to 8pm daily. Buses operate between rail stations. Each of these stations has a Métro stop, making the whole city easily accessible. Taxis are also available at designated stands at every station. Look for the sign that says TÊTE DE STATION. Be alert in train stations, especially at night.

BY BUS

Bus travel to Paris is available from London and many other cities throughout the Continent. In the early 1990s, the French government established strong incentives for long-haul buses not to drive into the center of Paris. The arrival and departure point for Europe's largest bus operators, **Eurolines France,** is a 35-minute Métro ride from central Paris, at the terminus of Métro line 3 (Métro: Gallieni), in the eastern suburb of Bagnolet. Despite this inconvenience, many people prefer bus travel. Eurolines France is located at 28 av. du Général-de-Gaulle, 93541 Bagnolet (☎ **08-36-69-52-52**).

Long-haul buses are equipped with toilets and stop at mealtimes for rest and refreshment. The price of a round-trip ticket between Paris and London (a 7-hour trip) is 450 F ($76.50) for passengers 26 or over, and 410 F ($69.70) for passengers under 26.

A round-trip ticket from Rome to Paris (a trip time of 22½ hours) costs 910 F ($154.70) for passengers 26 or over, 820 F ($139.40) for passengers under 26. The price of a round-trip ticket from Stockholm to Paris (a trip time of almost 28 hours) costs 1,450 F ($246.50) for passengers 26 or over, 1,340 F ($227.80) for passengers under 26.

Because Eurolines does not have a U.S.-based sales agent, most people wait until they reach Europe to buy their tickets. Any European travel agent can arrange these purchases. If you're traveling to Paris from London, you can contact **Eurolines (U.K.) Ltd.,** 52 Grosvenor Gardens, Victoria, London SW1, or call ☎ **0990/143219** for information or for credit-card sales.

BY CAR

Driving in Paris is definitely not recommended, unless you have nerves of steel, lots of experience with European traffic patterns, and lots of time and money. Parking is difficult, traffic is dense, and networks of one-way streets make navigation, even with the best of maps, a problem. If you do drive, remember that Paris is encircled by a ring road called the *périphérique.* Always obtain detailed directions to your destination, including the name of the exit on the périphérique you're looking for (exits are not numbered). Avoid rush hours.

Few hotels, except the luxury ones, have garages, but the staff will usually be able to direct you to one nearby.

The **major highways** into Paris are the A1 from the north (Great Britain and Benelux); the A13 from Rouen, Normandy, and other points of northwest France; the A10 from Bordeaux, the Pyrénées, France's southwest, and Spain; the A6 from Lyon, the French Alps, the Riviera, and Italy; and the A4 from Metz, Nancy, and Strasbourg in eastern France.

BY FERRY FROM ENGLAND

In spite of competiton from the Chunnel, services aboard ferryboats and hydrofoils operate day and night, in all seasons, with the exception of last-minute cancellations during particularly fierce storms. Many channel crossings are carefully timed to coincide with the arrival/departure of major trains (especially those between London and Paris). Trains let you off a short walk from the piers. Most ferries carry cars, trucks, and massive amounts of freight, but some hydrofoils take passengers only. The major routes include at least 12 trips a day between Dover or Folkestone and Calais or

Boulogne. Hovercraft and hydrofoils make the trip from Dover to Calais, the shortest distance across the channel, in just 40 minutes during good weather, whereas the slower-moving ferries might take several hours, depending on weather conditions and tides. If you're bringing a car, it's important to make reservations, as space below decks is usually crowded. Timetables can vary depending on weather conditions and many other factors.

The leading operator of ferryboats across the channel is **P&O Stena Lines** (call BritRail for reservations at ☎ **800/677-8585** within North America or 0870/600-0600 in England). It operates car and passenger ferries between Portsmouth, England, and Cherbourg, France (three departures a day; $4^1/4$ hours each way during daylight hours, 7 hours each way at night); between Portsmouth and Le Havre, France (three a day; $5^1/2$ hours each way). Most popular of all are the routes it operates between Dover and Calais, France (25 sailings a day; 75 minutes each way), costing £24 ($39.60) one-way for adults or £12 ($19.80) for children.

The shortest and by far the most popular route across the channel is between Calais and Dover. **Hoverspeed** operates at least 12 hovercraft crossings daily; the trip takes 35 minutes. It also runs a SeaCat (a catamaran propelled by jet engines) that takes slightly longer to make the crossing between Boulogne and Folkestone; the SeaCats depart about four times a day on the 55-minute voyage. For reservations and information, call Hoverspeed (☎ **800/677-8585** for reservations in North America or 08705/240-241 in England). Typical one-way fares are £25 ($41.25) per person.

If you plan to transport a rental car between England and France, check in advance with the rental company about license and insurance requirements and additional drop-off charges. And be aware that many car-rental companies, for insurance reasons, forbid transport of one of their vehicles over the water between England and France. Transport of a car each way begins at £75 ($123.75).

UNDER THE CHANNEL

Queen Elizabeth and the late French president François Mitterrand officially opened the Channel Tunnel in 1994, and the *Eurostar Express* now has daily passenger service from London to both Paris and Brussels. The $15 billion tunnel, one of the great engineering feats of our time, is the first link between Britain and the Continent since the Ice Age. The 31-mile journey takes 35 minutes, although the actual time spent in the Chunnel is only 19 minutes.

Eurostar tickets, for train service between London and Paris or Brussels, are available through **Rail Europe** (☎ **800/4-EURAIL;** www.raileurope.com). A one-way first-class nonrefundable ticket costs $179 ($219 if refundable). In second class, a nonrefundable one-way ticket goes for $109 ($149 if refundable). In London, make reservations for Eurostar at ☎ **0990/300003** (accessible in the United Kingdom only); in Paris, at ☎ **01-44-51-06-02;** and in the United States, at ☎ **800/EUROSTAR.** Chunnel train traffic is roughly competitive with air travel, if you calculate door-to-door travel time. Trains leave from London's Waterloo Station and arrive in Paris at the Gare du Nord.

The tunnel also accommodates passenger cars, charter buses, taxis, and motorcycles, transporting them under the English Channel from Folkestone, England, to Calais, France. It operates 24 hours a day, 365 days a year, running every 15 minutes during peak travel times, and at least once an hour at night. Tickets may be purchased at the toll booth at the tunnel's entrance. With "Le Shuttle," gone are the days of weather-related delays, seasickness, and advance reservations.

Before boarding Le Shuttle, motorists stop at a toll booth and then pass through British and French immigration services at the same time. They then drive onto a

| **A Weekend Trip to London** |

For a look at package deals with the Chunnel, turn to "A Weekend Trip to London" in chapter 10.

half-mile-long train and travel through an underground tunnel built beneath t he seabed through a layer of impervious chalk marl and sealed with a reinforced-concrete lining. During the ride, motorists stay in bright, air-conditioned carriages, remaining inside their cars or stepping outside to stretch their legs. When the trip is completed, they simply drive off toward their destinations. Total travel time between the French and English highway systems is about 1 hour. Once on French soil, British drivers must remember to drive on the right-hand side of the road.

Stores selling duty-free goods, restaurants, and service stations are available to travelers on both sides of the channel. A bilingual staff is on hand to assist travelers at both the French and British terminals.

PACKAGE TOURS

Package tours are not the same thing as escorted tours. They are simply a way to buy airfare and accommodations at the same time. For popular destinations like Paris, they are a smart way to go because they save you a lot of money. In many cases, a package that includes airfare, hotel, and transportation to and from the airport will cost you less than just the hotel alone would have, had you booked it yourself. That's because packages are sold in bulk to tour operators—who resell them to the public at a cost that drastically undercuts standard rates.

Packages, however, vary widely. Some offer a better class of hotels than others. Some offer the same hotels for lower prices. Some offer flights on scheduled airlines, while others book charters. In some packages, your choice of accommodations and travel days may be limited. Some packages let you choose between escorted vacations and independent vacations; others will allow you to add on just a few excursions or escorted day trips (also at lower prices than you could locate on your own) without booking an entirely escorted tour. Each destination usually has one or two packagers that are cheaper than the rest because they buy in even greater bulk. If you spend the time to shop around, you will save in the long run.

Finding a Package Deal   The best place to start your search is the travel section of your local Sunday newspaper. Also check the ads in the back of national travel magazines like *Travel & Leisure, National Geographic Traveler,* and *Conde Nast Traveler.* **Liberty Travel** (☎ 888/271-1584 to be connected with the agent closest to you; www.libertytravel.com), one of the biggest packagers in the Northeast, often runs a full-page ad in the Sunday papers. You won't get much in the way of service, but you will get a good deal. **American Express Vacations** (☎ 800/241-1700; www.leisureweb.com) is another option. Check out its **Last Minute Travel Bargains** site, offered in conjunction with **Continental Airlines** (www6.americanexpress.com/travel/lastminutetravel/default.asp), with deeply discounted vacation packages and reduced airline fares that differ from the E-savers bargains that Continental e-mails weekly to subscribers. **Northwest Airlines** offers a similar service. Posted on Northwest's Web site every Wednesday, its **Cyber Saver Bargain Alerts** offer special hotel rates, package deals, and discounted airline fares.

Another good resource is the airlines themselves, which often package their flights together with accommodations. Fly-by-night packagers are uncommon, but they do exist; when you buy your package through the airline, however, you can be pretty sure that the company will still be in business when your departure date arrives. Among the airline packagers, your options include **American Airlines FlyAway Vacations** (☎ 800/321-2121), **Delta Dream Vacations** (☎ 800/872-7786), and **US Airways Vacations** (☎ 800/455-0123). Pick the airline that services your hometown most often.

Delta Dream Vacations offers a full package called Jolie France, lasting 10 nights and costing $4,097 for two people, taking in not only Paris, but some of the regional highlights of France, including Tours, Bordeaux, Carcassonne, Nice, Nimes, Dijon, and back to Paris. All hotels, tours, and breakfasts are included, plus four dinners.

The **French Experience,** 370 Lexington Ave., Room 812, New York, NY 10017 (☎ **212/986-1115;** fax 212/986-3808), offers inexpensive airline tickets to Paris on most scheduled airlines. They arrange tours and stays in various types and categories of country inns, hotels, private châteaux, and bed-and-breakfasts. They take reservations for about 30 small hotels in Paris and arrange short-term apartment rentals in the city or farmhouse rentals in the countryside. They also offer all-inclusive packages in Paris as well as prearranged package tours of various regions of France. Any tour can be adapted to suit individual needs.

3

Getting to Know Paris

Ernest Hemingway referred to the many splendors of Paris as a "moveable feast" and wrote, "There is never any ending to Paris, and the memory of each person who has lived in it differs from that of any other." It is this aura of personal discovery that has always been the most compelling reason to come to Paris. And perhaps that's why France has been called *le deuxième pays de tout le monde,* "everybody's second country."

The Seine not only divides Paris into a Right Bank and a Left Bank, but it also seems to split the city into two vastly different sections and ways of life. Depending on your time, interest, and budget, you may quickly decide which section of Paris suits you best.

1 Orientation

VISITOR INFORMATION

The main Paris tourist information office is at 127 av. des Champs-Elysées, 8e (☎ **01-49-52-53-54**), where you can obtain information about both Paris and the provinces. The office is open daily from 9am to 8pm from April through October, with an annual closing May 1. Between November and March, the office is open daily from 11am to 6pm, with an annual closing December 25. There are additional branches in the base of the Eiffel Tower (open only May through October, Monday to Saturday from 8am to 8pm), and in the arrivals hall of the Gare de Lyon (open year-round, Monday to Saturday from 8am to 8pm). Any of these tourist offices will give you free copies of 50-page English-language leaflets entitled *Time Out* and *Paris User's Guide.*

CITY LAYOUT

Paris is surprisingly compact. Occupying 432 square miles (6 more than San Francisco), it is home to more than 10 million people. The River Seine divides Paris into the **Right Bank** *(Rive Droite)* to the north and the **Left Bank** *(Rive Gauche)* to the south. These designations make sense when you stand on a bridge and face downstream, watching the waters flow out toward the sea—to your right is the north bank, to your left the south. Thirty-two bridges link the banks of the Seine, some providing access to the two small islands at the heart of the city, **Ile de la Cité,** the city's birthplace and site of Notre-Dame, and **Ile St-Louis,** a moat-guarded oasis of sober 17th-century mansions. These islands can cause some confusion to walkers who think they've just crossed a bridge from one bank to the other, only to find themselves caught up in an almost medieval maze of narrow streets and old buildings.

MAIN ARTERIES & STREETS   Between 1860 and 1870, Baron Haussmann forever changed the look of Paris by creating the legendary boulevards: St-Michel, St-Germain, Haussmann, Malesherbes, Sébastopol, Magenta, Voltaire, and Strasbourg.

The "main street" on the Right Bank is, of course, the **Champs-Elysées,** beginning at the Arc de Triomphe and running to place de la Concorde. Haussmann also created avenue de l'Opéra (as well as the Opéra), and the 12 avenues that radiate starlike from the Arc de Triomphe, giving it its original name, place de l'Etoile (renamed place Charles-de-Gaulle following the general's death). Today it is often referred to as place **Charles-de-Gaulle-Etoile.**

Haussmann also cleared Ile de la Cité of its medieval buildings, transforming it into a showcase for Notre-Dame. Finally, he laid out the two elegant parks on the western and southeastern fringes of the city: the **Bois de Boulogne** and the **Bois de Vincennes.**

FINDING AN ADDRESS   Paris is divided into 20 municipal wards called *arrondissements,* each with its own mayor, city hall, police station, and central post office. Some even have remnants of market squares. Most city maps are divided by arrondissement, and all addresses include the arrondissement number (written in Roman or Arabic numerals and followed by *e* or *er*). Arrondissements are the last two digits in a zip code (the first three are 750-).

Numbers on buildings running parallel to the River Seine usually follow the course of the river—that is, east to west. On north–south streets, numbering begins at the river.

STREET MAPS   If you're staying more than 2 or 3 days, purchase an inexpensive pocket-size book that includes the plan de Paris by arrondissement, available at all major newsstands and bookshops. If you can find it, the little forest green *Paris Classique— L'indispensable* is a thorough, well-indexed, and accurate guide to the city and its suburbs. Most map guides provide you with a Métro map, a foldout map of the city, and indexed maps of each arrondissement, with all streets listed and keyed. Also, check out the free full-color foldout map in the back of this guide.

The Arrondissements in Brief

Each of Paris's 20 arrondissements possesses a unique style and flavor. You will want to decide which district appeals most to you and then find accommodations there. Later on, try to visit as many areas as you can.

1st Arr. (Musée du Louvre/Les Halles)   "I never knew what a palace was until I had a glimpse of the Louvre," wrote Nathaniel Hawthorne. Perhaps the world's greatest art museum, the **Louvre,** a former royal residence, still lures all visitors to Paris to the 1st arrondissement. Walk through the **Jardin des Tuileries,** the most formal garden of Paris (originally laid out by Le Nôtre, gardener to Louis XIV). Pause to take in the classic beauty of the **place Vendôme,** the opulent, wealthy home of the Ritz Hotel. Zola's "belly of Paris" (Les Halles) is no longer the food and meat market of Paris (traders moved to the new, more accessible suburb of Rungis)—today the **Forum des Halles** is a center of shopping, entertainment, and culture.

2nd Arr. (La Bourse)   Home to the **Bourse** (stock exchange), this Right Bank district lies mainly between the Grands Boulevards and the rue Etienne Marcel. From Monday to Friday, the shouts of brokers—J'ai! (I have it!) or Je prends! (I'll take it!)—echo across the place de la Bourse until it's time to break for lunch, when the movers and shakers of French capitalism channel their hysteria into the restaurants of the district. Much of the eastern end of the arrondissement **(Le Sentier)** is devoted to wholesale outlets of the Paris garment district, where thousands of garments are sold (usually in bulk) to buyers from clothing stores throughout Europe. "Everything that exists elsewhere exists in Paris," wrote Victor Hugo in *Les Misérables,* and this district provides ample evidence of that.

3rd Arr. (Le Marais)   This district embraces much of Le Marais (the swamp), one of the best loved of the old Right Bank neighborhoods. (It extends into the 4th as well.) After decades of seedy decay, Le Marais recently made a comeback, although it may never again enjoy the prosperity of its 17th-century aristocratic heyday. One of the district's chief attractions today is **Musée Picasso,** a kind of pirate's ransom of painting and sculpture that the Picasso estate had to turn over to the French government in lieu of the artist's astronomical death duties. Forced donation or not, it's one of the world's great repositories of 20th-century art.

4th Arr. (Ile de la Cité/Ile St-Louis & Beaubourg)   At times it seems as if the 4th has it all: not only Notre-Dame on Ile de la Cité, but Ile St-Louis and its aristocratic town houses, courtyards, and antique shops. **Ile St-Louis,** a former cow pasture and dueling ground, is home to dozens of 17th-century mansions and 6,000 lucky louisiens, its permanent residents. Seek out Ile de la Cité's two glorious Gothic churches, **La Sainte-Chapelle** and **Notre-Dame,** a majestic and dignified structure that, according to the poet e.e. cummings, doesn't budge an inch for all the idiocies of this world.

In the 4th, you not only get France's finest bird and flower markets, but the nation's law courts, which Balzac described as a "cathedral of chicanery." It was here that Marie Antoinette was sentenced to death in 1793. The 4th is also home to the **Centre Georges Pompidou,** one of the top three tourist attractions of France. (Sadly, Centre Pompidou will be partially closed for renovations until the millennium tolls on December 31, 1999.) After all this pomp and glory, you can retreat to the **place des Vosges,** a square of perfect harmony and beauty where Victor Hugo lived from 1832 to 1848 and penned many of his famous masterpieces. (His house is now a museum— see "Literary Landmarks" in chapter 6.)

5th Arr. (Latin Quarter)   The Quartier Latin is the intellectual heart and soul of Paris. Bookstores, schools, churches, smoky jazz clubs, student dives, Roman ruins, publishing houses, and, yes, expensive and chic boutiques, characterize the district. Discussions of Artaud or Molière over long cups of coffee may be rarer than in the past, but they aren't at all out of place here. Beginning with the founding of the **Sorbonne** in 1253, the quarter was called Latin because all students and professors spoke the scholarly language.

You'll follow in the footsteps of Descartes, Verlaine, Camus, Sartre, James Thurber, Elliot Paul, and Hemingway as you explore this historic district. Changing times have brought Greek, Moroccan, and Vietnamese immigrants, among others, hustling everything from couscous to fiery-hot spring rolls and souvlaki. The 5th borders the Seine, and you'll want to stroll along quai de Montebello, inspecting the inventories of the bouquin-istes who sell everything from antique Daumier prints to yellowing copies of Balzac's *Père Goriot* in the shadow of Notre-Dame. The 5th also has the **Panthéon,** which was con-structed by a grateful Louis XV after he'd recovered from the gout and wanted to do some-thing nice for Ste-Geneviève, Paris's patron saint. It's the dank, dark resting place of Rousseau, Gambetta, Émile Zola, Louis Braille, Victor Hugo, Voltaire, and Jean Moulin, the World War II Resistance leader whom the Gestapo tortured to death.

6th Arr. (St-Germain/Luxembourg)   This is the heartland of Paris publishing and, for some, the most colorful quarter of the Left Bank, where waves of earnest young artists still emerge from the famous **Ecole des Beaux-Arts.** The secret of the district lies in discovering its narrow streets, hidden squares, and magnificent gardens. To be really authentic, you'll stroll these streets with an unwrapped loaf of country sour-dough bread from the wood-fired ovens of **Poilâne,** the world's most famous baker, at 8 rue du Cherche-Midi.

Everywhere you turn in the district, you encounter famous historical and literary associations, none more so than on **rue Jacob.** At #7, Racine lived with his uncle as a teenager; Richard Wagner resided at #14 from 1841 to 1842; Ingres once lived at #27 (now it's the offices of the French publishing house Editions du Seuil); and Hemingway once occupied a tiny upstairs room at #44. Today's big name is likely to be filmmaker Spike Lee checking into his favorite hotel, **La Villa,** 29 rue Jacob. The 6th takes in the **Jardin du Luxembourg,** a 60-acre playground where Isadora Duncan went dancing in the predawn hours and a destitute writer, Ernest Hemingway, went looking for pigeons for lunch, carrying them in a baby carriage back to his humble flat for cooking.

7th Arr. (Eiffel Tower/Musée d'Orsay)   Paris's most famous symbol, the **Eiffel Tower,** dominates Paris and especially the 7th, a Left Bank district of respectable residences and government offices. The tower is now one of the most recognizable landmarks in the world, despite the fact that many Parisians (especially its nearest neighbors) hated it when it was unveiled in 1889. Many of Paris's most imposing monuments are in the 7th, including the **Hôtel des Invalides,** which contains both Napoléon's Tomb and the Musée de l'Armée. But there is much hidden charm here as well.

Rue du Bac was home to the swashbuckling heroes of Dumas's *The Three Muske-teers,* and to James McNeill Whistler, who moved to #110 after selling his *Mother.* Auguste Rodin lived at what is now the **Musée Rodin,** 77 rue de Varenne, until his death in 1917.

Even visitors with little time should rush to the **Musée d'Orsay,** the world's premier showcase of 19th-century French art and culture. The museum is housed in the old Gare d'Orsay, which Orson Welles used in 1962 as a setting for his film *The Trial,* based on the book by Franz Kafka.

8th Arr. (Champs-Elysées/Madeleine)   The prime showcase of the 8th is the **Champs-Elysées,** which stretches grandly from the **Arc de Triomphe** to the purloined Egyptian obelisk on **place de la Concorde.** Here you'll find the fashion houses, the most elegant hotels, expensive restaurants and shops, and the most fashionably attired Parisians. By the 1980s, the Champs-Elysées had become a garish strip, with too much traffic, too many fast-food joints, and too many panhandlers. In the 1990s, Jacques Chirac, then the Gaullist mayor of Paris, launched a massive cleanup, broadening side-walks and planting new rows of trees.

Everything in the 8th is the city's "best, grandest, and most impressive": It has the best restaurant in Paris (**Taillevent**); the sexiest strip joint (**Crazy Horse Saloon**); the most splendid square in all of France (**place de la Concorde**); the best rooftop cafe (**La Samaritaine**); the grandest hotel in France (**The Crillon**); the most impressive triumphal arch on the planet (**L'Arc de Triomphe**); the world's most expensive residential street (**avenue Montaigne**); the world's oldest subway station (**Franklin-D-Roosevelt**); and the most ancient monument in Paris (the 3,300-year-old **Obelisk of Luxor**).

9th Arr. (Opéra Garnier/Pigalle)   From the Quartier de l'Opéra to the strip joints of Pigalle (the infamous "Pig Alley" for World War II GIs), the 9th endures, even if fickle fashion prefers other addresses. Over the decades, the 9th has been celebrated in literature and song for the music halls that brought gaiety to the city. The building at 17 bd. de la Madeleine was the death site of Marie Duplessis, who gained fame as the heroine Marguerite Gautier in Alexandre Dumas the younger's *La Dame aux camélias*. (Greta Garbo later redoubled Marie's legend by playing her in the film *Camille*.)

At **place Pigalle,** gone is the cafe La Nouvelle Athènes, where Degas, Pissarro, and Manet used to meet. Today, you're more likely to encounter nightclubs in the area. Other major attractions include the **Folies Bergère,** where cancan dancers have been high-kicking it since 1868. More than anything, it was the **Opéra Garnier** (Paris Opera House) that made the 9th the last hurrah of Second Empire opulence. Renoir hated it, but several generations later, Chagall did the ceilings. Pavlova danced *Swan Lake* here, and Nijinsky took the night off to go cruising.

10th Arr. (Gare du Nord/Gare de l'Est)   The Gare du Nord and the Gare de l'Est, along with porno houses and dreary commercial zones, make the 10th one of the least desirable arrondissements for living, dining, or sightseeing in Paris. We always try to avoid the 10th, except for two longtime favorite restaurants: **Brasserie Flo,** 7 cour des Petites-Ecuries, best known for its formidable choucroute, a heap of sauerkraut garnished with everything; and **Julien,** 16 rue du Faubourg St-Denis, called the poor man's Maxim's for its belle-epoque interiors and moderate prices.

11th Arr. (Opéra Bastille)   For many years, this quarter seemed to sink lower and lower into poverty and decay, overcrowded by working-class immigrants from the far reaches of the former French Empire. The opening of the **Opéra Bastille,** however, has given the 11th new hope and new life. The facility, called the "people's opera house," stands on the landmark place de la Bastille, where on July 14, 1789, 633 Parisians stormed the fortress and seized the ammunition depot, as the French Revolution swept across the city. Over the years, the prison held Voltaire, the Marquis de Sade, and the mysterious "Man in the Iron Mask."

The 11th has its charms, but they exist only for those who seek them out. **Le Marché** at place d'Aligre, for example, is surrounded by a Middle Eastern food market and is a good place to hunt for secondhand bargains: Everything is cheap, and although you must search hard for treasures, they often appear.

12th Arr. (Bois de Vincennes/Gare de Lyon)   Very few out-of-towners came here until a French chef opened a restaurant called **Au Trou Gascon** (see chapter 5). The 12th's major attraction remains the **Bois de Vincennes,** a sprawling park on the eastern periphery of Paris. It's been a longtime favorite of French families, who enjoy its zoos and museums, its royal château and boating lakes, and most definitely, the

---

Impressions

In Paris they simply stared when I spoke to them in French; I never did succeed in making those idiots understand their language.

—Mark Twain, *Wisdom and Ignorance*

Decoding Postal Codes

If you know the postal code of a hotel, restaurant, or attraction in Paris, you know what arrondissement it's in: The arrondissement is always the last two digits. So a hotel whose postal code is 75008 is in the 8th arrondissement; 75016 indicates an address in the 16th arrondissement. These can also be represented as 8e and 16e respectively.

Parc Floral de Paris, a celebrated flower garden whose springtime rhododendrons and autumn dahlias are among the major lures of the city. Venture into the dreary **Gare de Lyon** for **Le Train Bleu,** a restaurant whose ceiling frescoes and art nouveau decor are classified as national artistic treasures. The food's good, too.

The 12th arrondissement, once a depressing urban wasteland, has been singled out for budgetary resuscitation, and is beginning to sport new housing, shops, gardens, and restaurants. Many of these new structures will occupy the site of the former Reuilly railroad tracks.

13th Arr. (Gare d'Austerlitz)   Centered around the grimy Gare d'Austerlitz, the 13th might have its devotees, but we've yet to meet one. British snobs who flitted in and out of the train station were among the first of the district's foreign visitors, and in essence wrote the 13th off as a dreary working-class counterpart of London's East End. The 13th is also home to Paris's **Chinatown,** stretching for 13 square blocks around the Métro stop of Tolbiac. It emerged out of the refugee crisis at the end of the Vietnam War, taking over a neighborhood that had been mostly Arab-speaking peoples. Today, recognizing the overcrowding that's now endemic within the district, the Paris civic authorities are imposing new, not particularly welcome, restrictions on population densities. The neighborhood is home to several thousand Vietnamese, Laotian, Cambodian, and Chinese residents, and to a much lesser extent Korean and Japanese immigrants.

14th Arr. (Montparnasse)   The northern end of this large arrondissement is devoted to **Montparnasse,** home of the "lost generation" and former stamping ground of Stein, Toklas, Hemingway, and other American expatriates of the 1920s. After World War II, it ceased to be the center of intellectual life in Paris, but the memory lingers in its cafes. One of the monuments that sets the tone of the neighborhood is **Rodin's statue of Balzac** at the junction of boulevard Montparnasse and boulevard Raspail. At this corner are some of the world's most famous **literary cafes,** including La Rotonde, Le Select, La Dôme, and La Coupole. Though Gertrude Stein avoided them (she loathed cafes), all the other American expatriates, including Hemingway and Fitzgerald, had no qualms about enjoying a drink here (or quite a few of them, for that matter). Stein stayed at home (27 rue de Fleurus) with Alice B. Toklas, collecting paintings, including those of Picasso, and entertaining the likes of Max Jacob, Apollinaire, T. S. Eliot, and Matisse.

15th Arr. (Gare Montparnasse/Institut Pasteur)   A mostly residential district beginning at Gare Montparnasse, the 15th stretches all the way to the Seine. In size and population, it's the largest quarter of Paris, but it attracts few tourists and has few attractions, except for the **Parc des Expositions,** the **Cimetière du Montparnasse,** and the **Institut Pasteur.** In the early 20th century, many artists—Chagall, Léger, and Modigliani—lived in this arrondissement in a shared atelier known as "The Beehive."

16th Arr. (Trocadéro/Bois de Boulogne)   Originally the village of Passy, where Benjamin Franklin lived during most of his time in Paris, this district is still reminiscent of Proust's world. Highlights include the **Bois de Boulogne;** the **Jardin du Trocadéro;** the **Maison de Balzac;** the **Musée Guimet** (famous for its Asian collections); and the **Cimetière de Passy,** resting place of Manet, Talleyrand, Giraudoux, and Debussy. One of the largest of the city's arrondissements, it's known today for its well-heeled bourgeoisie, its upscale rents, and some rather posh (and, according to its critics, rather smug) residential boulevards. The arrondissement also has the best vantage of the Eiffel Tower, the **place du Trocadéro.**

17th Arr. (Parc Monceau/Place Clichy)   Flanking the northern periphery of Paris, the 17th incorporates neighborhoods of conservative bourgeois respectability (in its western end) and less affluent neighborhoods in its eastern end. It boasts two of the greatest restaurants of Paris, **Guy Savoy** and **Michel Rostang** (see chapter 5).

18th Arr. (Montmartre)   The 18th is the most famous outer quartier of Paris, containing **Montmartre,** the **Moulin Rouge,** the **Basilica of Sacré-Coeur,** and the **place du Tertre.** Utrillo was its native son, Renoir lived here, and Toulouse-Lautrec adopted the area as his own. The most famous enclave of artists in Paris's history, the **Bateau-Lavoir,** of Picasso fame, gathered here. Max Jacob, Matisse, and Braque were all frequent visitors. Today, place Blanche is known for its prostitutes, and Montmartre is filled with honky-tonks, too many souvenir shops, and terrible restaurants. You can still find pockets of quiet beauty, though. The city's most famous flea market, the **Marché aux Puces de Clignancourt,** is another landmark.

19th Arr. (La Villette)   Today, visitors come to what was once the village of La Villette to see the angular, much-publicized **Cité des Sciences et de l'Industrie,** a spectacular science museum and park built on a site that for years was devoted to the city's slaughterhouses. Mostly residential, and not at all upscale, the district is one of the most ethnically diverse in Paris, the home of people from all parts of the former French Empire. A highlight is **Les Buttes Chaumont,** a park where kids can enjoy puppet shows and donkey rides.

20th Arr. (Père-Lachaise Cemetery)   The 20th's greatest landmark is **Père-Lachaise Cemetery,** the resting place of Edith Piaf, Marcel Proust, Oscar Wilde, Isadora Duncan, Sarah Bernhardt, Gertrude Stein, Colette, and many, many others. Otherwise, the 20th arrondissement is a dreary and sometimes volatile melting pot comprising residents from France's former colonies. Although nostalgia buffs sometimes head here to visit Piaf's former neighborhood, **Ménilmontant-Belleville,** it has been almost totally bulldozed and rebuilt since the bad old days when she grew up here.

2 Getting Around

Paris is a city for strollers whose greatest joy in life is rambling through unexpected alleyways and squares. Only when you're dead tired and can't walk another step, or have to go all the way across town in a hurry, should you consider using the swift and dull means of urban transport.

BY PUBLIC TRANSPORTATION

Discount Passes   You can purchase a **Paris-Visite pass,** a tourist pass valid for 1 to 5 days on the public transportation system, including the Métro, city buses, RER (regional express) trains within Paris city limits, and even the funicular ride to the top of Montmartre. (The RER has both first- and second-class compartments, and the pass lets you travel in first class.) The cost is 55 F ($9.35) for 1 day, 90 F ($15.30) for 2 days, 120 F ($20.40) for 3 days, or 175 F ($29.75) for 5 days. The card is available at **RATP** (Régie Autonome des Transports Parisiens; ☎ **08-36-69-77-14**), tourist offices, or at the main Métro stations; call ☎ **01-44-68-20-20** for information.

Another pass available to temporary visitors is **Carte Mobilis,** allowing unlimited travel on all bus, subway, and RER lines in Paris during a 1-day period for 30 F to 70 F ($5.10 to $11.90), depending on the zone. The pass can be purchased at any Métro station.

BY SUBWAY/RER

The **Métro** (☎ **08-36-68-77-14** for information) is the easiest and most efficient way to get around Paris. Most stations display a map of the system at the entrance; you'll find a copy of this map on the inside cover of this book. Within Paris, you can transfer between the subway and the RER regional trains for no additional cost. To make sure you catch the right train, find your destination, then visually follow the line it's on to the end of the route and note its name. This is the sign you look for in the stations and the name you'll see on the train. Transfer stations are known as *correspondances.* (Note that some require long walks—Châtelet/Les Halles is the most notorious.)

Few trips will require more than one transfer. Some stations have maps with push-button indicators that will help you plot your route by lighting up automatically when you press the button for your destination. A ride on the urban lines costs 8 F ($1.35) to any point within the 20 arrondissements of Paris, as well as to many of its near suburbs. A bulk purchase of 10 tickets (which are bound together into what the French refer to as a *carnet*) costs 52 F ($8.85). Métro fares to far-flung, outlying suburbs on the Sceaux, the Noissy-St-Léger, and St-Germain-en-Laye lines cost more, and are sold on an individual basis depending on the distance you travel.

At the entrance to the Métro station, insert your ticket into the turnstile and pass through. Take the ticket back, since it may be checked by uniformed police officers when you leave the subway. There are also occasional ticket checks on the trains, platforms, and passageways.

If you are changing trains, get out and determine which direction (final destination) on the next line you want, and follow the bright orange CORRESPONDANCE signs until you reach the proper platform. Don't follow a SORTIE sign, which means "exit." If you exit, you'll have to pay another fare to resume your journey.

The Paris Métro runs daily from 5:30am to around 1:15am, at which time all underground trains reach their final terminus at the end of each of their respective lines. Be alert that the last train may pass through central Paris as much as an hour before that time. The subways are reasonably safe at any hour, but beware of pickpockets.

New Subway Line

The latest news from the bowels of Paris is that the city has a new subway line for a new century. After 6 years of construction, line #14 (Météor) opened in the autumn of 1998, running from rue de Tolbiac near the François Mitterand Library on the Left Bank to the Madeleine stop, with connections to parallel Métro and R.E.R. rapid-transit lines at Gare de Lyon and Châtelet. Completed at a cost of $1 billion, the Météor moves at a speed one-third faster than conventional subway trains. Trains are run from a central control—no conductors. Unlike the art nouveau designs at the turn of the century, the new Météor stations look more like monorails at Frankfurt. Eventually, perhaps by 2003, tunneling will extend this line.

BY BUS

Bus travel is much slower than the subway. Most buses run from 7am to 8:30pm (a few operate until 12:30am, and 10 operate during the early morning hours). Service is limited on Sunday and holidays. Bus and Métro fares are the same and you can use the same carnet tickets on both.

At certain bus stops, signs list the destinations and numbers of the buses serving that point. Destinations are usually listed north to south and east to west. Most stops along the way are also posted on the sides of the buses. To catch a bus, wait in line at the bus stop. Signal the driver to stop the bus and board.

Most bus rides (including any that begin and end within the 20 arrondissements of Paris) require one ticket, but there are some destinations in the suburbs that require up to, but never more than, two. If you intend to use the buses a lot, pick up an **RATP bus map** at their office on place de la Madeleine, 8e, at any tourist information office, or at RATP headquarters, 52-54 quai de la Rapée, 12e (☎ **01-44-68-20-20**). For detailed information on bus and Métro routes, call **08-36-68-41-14.**

The same entity that maintains Paris's network of Métros and buses, the **RATP** (☎ **08-36-68-77-14** for information), has initiated a motorized mode of transport designed exclusively as a means of appreciating the city's visual grandeur. Known as the **Balabus,** it's a fleet of big-windowed, orange-and-white motor coaches whose most visible drawback is their limited hours—they run only on Sunday and national holidays from noon to 9pm, from April 15 to September 30.

The coaches journey in both directions between the Gare de Lyon and the Grande Arche de La Défense, encompassing some of the city's most monumental vistas, and making regular stops. Presentation of either three Métro tickets (24 F/$4.10), a valid Carte Mobilis (see above), or a valid Paris-Visite card (see above) will carry you along the entire route. You'll recognize the bus and the route it follows by the "Bb" symbol emblazoned on each bus's side and on signs posted beside the route it follows.

BY CAR

Again, don't even think about driving in Paris. The streets are narrow, with confusing one-way designations, and parking is next to impossible. Besides, most visitors don't have the ruthlessness required to survive in Parisian traffic.

BY TAXI

It's nearly impossible to get a taxi at rush hour. Taxi drivers are organized into an effective lobby to keep their number limited to 14,300.

Watch out for the common ripoffs. Always check the meter to make sure you're not paying the previous passenger's fare. Beware of cabs without meters, which often try to snare tipsy patrons outside nightclubs—always settle the tab in advance. Regular cabs can be hailed on the street when their signs read LIBRE. Taxis are easier to find at the many stands near Métro stations.

The flag drops at 14 F ($2.40), and you pay 3.36 F (55¢) per kilometer. At night, expect to pay 5.45 F (95¢) per kilometer. On airport trips you're not required to pay for the driver's empty return ride. You're allowed several small pieces of luggage free if they're transported inside and don't weigh more than 5kg (11 pounds). Heavier suitcases carried in the trunk cost 6 F ($1) apiece. Tip 12% to 15%—the latter usually elicits a *merci.* To radio cabs, call ☎ **01-45-85-85-85, 01-42-70-41-41,** or **01-42-70-00-42**—note that you'll be charged from the point where the taxi begins the drive to pick you up.

BY BICYCLE

To ride a bicycle through the streets and parks of Paris, perhaps with a baguette tucked under your arm, might have been a fantasy of yours since you saw your first

Maurice Chevalier film. If the idea appeals to you, you won't be alone: The city in recent years has added many miles of right-hand lanes specifically designated for cyclists, and hundreds of bike racks. (When these aren't available, many Parisians simply chain their bike to the nearest fence or lamppost.) Cycling is especially popular in Paris's larger parks and gardens.

Paris-Vélos, 2 rue du Fer-à-Moulin, 5e (☎ 01-43-37-59-22; Métro: Censier-Daubenton), rents by the day, weekend, or week, charging from 100 F to 160 F ($17 to $27.20) per weekday, from 160 F to 220 F ($27.20 to $37.40) Saturday and Sunday, and from 450 F to 600 F ($76.50 to $102) for a week. Deposits of 1,000 F to 2,500 F ($170 to $425) must be posted. Bikes are rented Monday through Saturday from 10am to 12:30pm and 2 to 7pm.

BY BOAT

The **Batobus** (☎ 01-44-11-33-44), a series of 150-passenger ferryboats with big windows suitable for viewing the passing riverfronts, operates at 15-minute intervals from 10am to 7pm every day between April and mid-October. Boats chug along between the quays at the base of the Eiffel Tower and the quays at the base of the Louvre, stopping at the Musée d'Orsay, St-Germain-des-Prés, Notre-Dame, and the Hôtel de Ville. Transit between each stop costs 20 F ($3.40), although most participants opt to pay a flat rate (good all day) of 60 F ($10.20) per adult, 30 F ($5.10) for children under 12, and then settle back and watch the monuments from a prime seat on one of the most historically evocative rivers in Europe. Camera opportunities are endless aboard this leisurely but intensely panoramic "floating observation platform."

Fast Facts: Paris

American Express   The largest travel service in the world operates a 24-hour-a-day hot line from its administrative headquarters in the Paris suburb of Reuil-Malmaison (☎ 01-47-77-70-00). Day-to-day services, such as tours and money exchange, are available at 11 rue Scribe, 9e (☎ 01-47-77-47-61; Métro: Opéra), or the smaller branch at 38 Av. Wagram, 8e (☎ 01-42-27-58-80; Métro: Ternes). Both of the branches are open Monday through Friday from 9am to 5pm, with money-changing services ending at 4pm. The rue Scribe office is open Saturday from 9am to 5:30pm (no mail pickup).

Area Code   There isn't one. The area code for Paris and Ile-de-France, 1, ceased to exist in 1996. Instead, the prefix 01- should be added to all existing 8-digit numbers in Paris and Ile-de-France. Areas of mainland France outside of the Paris region use any of four other area codes (02, 03, 04, or 05, according to their location within France). The international access code from France is now 00.

Banks   American Express may be able to meet most of your banking needs. If not, banks in Paris are open from 9am to 4:30pm Monday through Friday. A few are open on Saturday. Ask at your hotel for the location of the bank nearest you. Shops and most hotels will cash your traveler's checks, but not at the advantageous rate a bank or foreign-exchange office will give you, so make sure you've allowed enough funds for the weekend.

Business Hours   Opening hours in France are erratic, as befits a nation of individualists. Most museums close 1 day a week (often Tuesday) and on national holidays; hours tend to be from 9:30am to 5pm. Some museums, particularly the smaller ones, close for lunch from noon to 2pm. Most French museums are open

Saturday, but many close Sunday morning and reopen in the afternoon. (See chapter 6 for specific times.) Generally, offices are open Monday through Friday from 9am to 5pm, but don't count on it. Always call first. Large stores and chain stores are open from 9 or 9:30am (often 10am) to 6 or 7pm without a break for lunch. Some shops, particularly those operated by foreigners, open at 8am and close at 8 or 9pm. In some small stores, the lunch break can last 3 hours, beginning at 1pm.

Car Rentals   See "Getting Around," above.

Climate   See "When to Go" in chapter 2.

Currency   See "Money" in chapter 2.

Currency Exchange   See "Money" in chapter 2.

Dentists   For emergency dental service, call S.O.S. Dentaire (☎ **01-43-37-51-00**) Monday through Friday from 8pm to midnight, Saturday and Sunday from 9:30am to midnight. You can also call or visit the **American Hospital,** 63 bd. Victor Hugo, Neuilly (☎ **01-46-41-25-43**). A 24-hour English/French dental clinic is on the premises. Métro: Pont de Levallois or Pont de Neuilly. Bus: 82.

Doctors   See "Hospitals," below.

Documents Required   See "Entry Requirements & Customs Regulations" in chapter 2.

Driving Rules   See "Getting Around," above.

Drugstores (Late-Night)   After regular hours, ask at your hotel where the nearest 24-hour *pharmacie* is. You'll also find the address posted on the doors or windows of other drugstores in the neighborhood. One all-night drugstore is the **Pharmacy les Champs,** in La Galerie Les Champs, 84 av. des Champs-Elysées, 8e (☎ **01-45-62-02-41;** Métro: George V).

Electricity   In general, expect 200 volts AC (60 cycles), although you'll encounter 110 and 115 volts in some older establishments. Adapters are needed to fit sockets. Many hotels have two-pin (in some cases, three-pin) sockets for electric razors. It's best to ask at your hotel before plugging in any electrical appliance.

Embassies/Consulates   If you have a passport, immigration, legal, or other problem, contact your consulate. Call before you go, as they often keep strange hours and observe both French and home-country holidays.

The Embassy of the **United States,** at 2 av. Gabriel, 8e (☎ **01-43-12-22-22;** Métro: Concorde), is open Monday through Friday from 9am to 6pm. Passports are issued at its consulate at 2 rue St-Florentin (☎ **01-43-12-22-22;** Métro: Concorde). Getting a passport replaced costs $55.

The Embassy of **Canada** is at 35 av. Montaigne, 8e (☎ **01-44-43-29-00;** Métro: F.-D.-Roosevelt or Alma-Marceau), open Monday through Friday from 9am to noon and 2 to 5pm. The Canadian consulate is at the embassy.

The Embassy of the **United Kingdom** is at 35 rue Faubourg St-Honoré, 8e (☎ **01-44-51-31-00;** Métro: Concorde or Madeleine), open Monday through Friday from 9:30am to 1pm and 2:30 to 5pm. The consulate is at 16 rue d'Anjou, 8e (☎ **01-44-66-29-79**), and is open Monday through Friday from 9:30am to 12:30pm and 2:30 to 5pm.

The Embassy of **Australia** is at 4 rue Jean-Rey, 15e (☎ **01-40-59-33-00;** Métro:Bir-Hakeim), open Monday through Friday from 9:15am to noon and 2:30 to 4:30pm. The embassy of **New Zealand** is at 7 ter rue Léonard-de-Vinci,

75116 Paris (☎ **01-45-00-24-11;** Métro: Victor Hugo), open Monday through Friday from 9am to 1pm and 2:30 to 6pm.

The Embassy of **Ireland** is at 12 ave. Foch, 16e, 75116 Paris (☎ **01-44-17-67-00;** Métro: Argentine). Hours are Monday through Friday from 9:30am to noon.

The **Embassy of South Africa** is at 59 quai d'Orsay (☎ **01-53-59-23-23;** Métro: Invalides). Hours are Monday through Friday from 8:45 to 11am.

Emergencies   For the police, call ☎ **17;** to report a fire, call ☎ **18.** For an ambulance, call the fire department at ☎ **01-45-78-74-52;** a fire vehicle rushes patients to the nearest emergency room. For **S.A.M.U.,** an independently operated, privately owned ambulance company, call ☎ **15.** For less urgent matters, you can reach the police at 9 bd. du Palais, 4e (☎ **01-53-71-53-71** or 01-53-73-53-73; Métro: Cité).

Holidays   See "When to Go" in chapter 2.

Hospitals   **Central Médical Europe,** 44 rue d'Amsterdam, 9e (☎ **01-42-81-93-33;** Métro: Liège), maintains contacts with medical and dental practitioners in all fields. Appointments are recommended. Open Monday through Saturday from 8:30am to 7pm. Another choice is the **American Hospital of Paris,** 63 bd. Victor-Hugo, Neuilly (☎ **01-46-41-25-43;** Métro: Pont-de-Levallois or Pont-de-Neuilly; Bus: 82), which operates 24-hour medical and dental service. An additional clinic is the **Centre Figuier,** 2 rue du Figuier (☎ **01-42-78-55-53;** Métro: St-Paul). Call before visiting.

Information   See "Visitor Information" and "Entry Requirements & Customs Regulations" in chapter 2.

Internet Access   A centrally located cybercafe, in the Latin Quarter, is **Cyber-café Latino,** 13 rue de l'Ecole Polytechnique, 5e (☎ **01-40-51-86-94;** www.cybercafelinto.com/). Métro: Maubert-Mutualité. See also Le Web Bar, under "Bars, Pubs & Clubs" in chapter 9.

Legal Aid   This may be hard to come by in Paris. The French government advises foreigners to consult their embassy or consulate (see "Embassies/Consulates," above) in case of a dire emergency, such as an arrest. Even if a consulate or embassy declines to offer financial or legal help, they will generally offer advice as to how you can obtain help locally. For example, they can furnish a list of attorneys. Most visitor arrests are for illegal possession of drugs, and the U.S. embassy and consulate officials cannot interfere with the French judicial system in any way on your behalf. A consulate can only advise you of your rights.

Liquor Laws   Visitors will find it easier to buy wine, beer, or spirits in France than in England or other countries. Supermarkets, smaller grocery stores, and cafes all sell alcoholic beverages. The legal drinking age is 16, but persons under that age can be served an alcoholic drink in a bar or restaurant if accompanied by a parent or legal guardian. Wine and liquor are sold every day of the week, year-round.

Hours of cafes vary. Some open at 6am, serving drinks until 3am; others are open 24 hours a day. Bars and nightclubs may stay open as late as they wish.

The Breathalyzer test is in use in France, and a motorist is considered "legally intoxicated" with 0.5 grams of alcohol per liter of blood (the more liberal U.S. law is 1 gram per liter). If convicted, a motorist faces a stiff fine and a possible prison term of 2 months to 2 years. If bodily injury results, sentences can range from 2 years to life.

Mail/Post Offices   Most post offices in Paris are open Monday through Friday from 8am to 7pm and Saturday from 8am to noon. The **main post office (PTT)** for Paris is at 52 rue du Louvre, 75001 Paris (☎ **01-40-28-20-00;** Métro: Louvre). It's open 24 hours a day for the sale of stamps, phone calls, and expedition of faxes and telegrams, with more limited hours—8am to 5pm Monday through Friday and 8am to noon on Saturday—for more esoteric financial services that include the sale of money orders. Stamps can also usually be purchased at your hotel reception desk and at *café-tabacs* (tobacconists). You can send faxes at the main post office in each arrondissement.

Airmail letters within Europe cost 3 F (50¢); to the United States and Canada, 4.40 F (75¢); and to Australia and New Zealand, 5.10 F (85¢).

You can have mail sent to you *poste restante* (general delivery) at the main post office for a small fee. Take an ID, such as a passport, if you plan to pick up mail. American Express (see above) also offers a *poste restante* service, but you may be asked to show an American Express card or traveler's checks.

Maps   See "Getting Around," above.

Medical Emergencies   Seek assistance first at your hotel desk if language is a problem. If you are ill and need medicine at night or on Sunday, the local *commissariat de police* can tell you the location of the nearest doctor on duty. The police or fire department will also summon an ambulance if you need to be rushed to a hospital. See also "Drugstores" and "Hospitals," above.

Money   See "Money" in chapter 2.

Newspapers/Magazines   English-language newspapers are available at nearly every kiosk in Paris. Published Monday through Saturday, the *International Herald-Tribune* is the most popular paper with visiting Americans and Canadians; the *Guardian* provides a British point of view. For those who read in French, the leading domestic newspapers are *Le Monde, Le Figaro,* and *Libération;* the top magazines are *L'Express, Le Point,* and *Le Nouvel Observateur.* Kiosks are generally open daily from 8am to 9pm.

Pets   If you have certificates from a vet and proof of antirabies vaccination, you can bring most house pets into France.

Police   Call ☎ **17** for emergencies. The principal Prefecture is at 9 boulevard du Palais, 4e (☎ **01-53-71-53-71;** Métro: Cité).

Rest Rooms   If you are in dire need, duck into a cafe or brasserie to use the lavatory. It's customary to make some small purchase if you do so. In the street, the domed self-cleaning lavatories are a decent option if you have small change; Métro stations and underground garages usually have public lavatories, but the degree of cleanliness varies.

Safety   In Paris, be especially aware of child pickpockets. They roam the French capital, preying on tourists around attractions such as the Louvre, Eiffel Tower, and Notre-Dame, and they also often strike in the Métro, sometimes blocking a victim from the escalator. A band of these young thieves can clean your pockets even while you try to fend them off. Their method is to get very close to a target, ask for a handout (sometimes), and deftly help themselves to your money or passport.

Although public safety is not as much a problem in Paris as it is in large American cities, concerns are growing. Robbery at gun- or knifepoint is uncommon here, but not unknown. Be careful.

Taxes   See "The Shopping Scene," in chapter 8 for an explanation of the Value-Added Tax refund.

Taxis   See "Getting Around," above.

Telephone   Public phones are found in cafes, restaurants, Métro stations, post offices, airports, train stations, and occasionally on the streets. Finding a coin-operated telephone in France is an arduous task. A simpler and more widely accepted method of payment is the *télécarte,* a prepaid calling card available at kiosks, post offices, and Métro stations. These debit cards are priced at 41 F to 98 F ($6.95 to $16.65), for 50 and 120 units respectively. A local call costs 1 unit, which provides you with 6 to 18 minutes of conversation, depending on the rate. Avoid making calls from your hotel, which might double or triple the charges.

To call **long distance within France,** dial the 10-digit number (9-digit in some cases outside Paris) of the person or place you're calling. To make a **direct international call,** first dial 00, listen for the tone, then slowly dial the country code, the area code, and the local number. The country code for the **USA and Canada** is 1; **Great Britain,** 44; **Ireland,** 353; **Australia,** 61; **New Zealand,** 64; **South Africa,** 27.

An easy and relatively inexpensive way to call home is **USA Direct/AT&T WorldConnect.** From within France, dial any of the following numbers: ☎ **0800/99-0011, -1011, -1111, -1211.** Then follow the prompt, which will ask you to punch in the number of either your AT&T credit card or a Master-Card or Visa. Along with the **USA,** the countries that participate in the system—referred to as WorldConnect—include **Canada,** the **UK, Ireland, Australia, New Zealand,** and **South Africa.** By punching in the number of the party you want in any of these countries, you'll avoid the surcharges imposed by the hotel operator. An AT&T operator will be available to help you with complications arising during the process.

Time   France is usually 6 hours ahead of eastern standard time in the United States. French daylight saving time lasts from around April to September, when clocks are set 1 hour ahead of the standard time.

Tipping   By law, all bills show *service compris,* which means the tip is included; additional gratuities are customarily given as follows:

For **hotel staff,** tip the porter 6 F to 10 F ($1.10 to $1.80) per item of baggage and 10 F ($1.80) per day for the chambermaid. You're not obligated to tip the concierge, doorman, or anyone else, unless you use his or her services. In **cafes and restaurants,** waiter service is usually included, although you can leave a couple of francs. Tip **taxi drivers** 10% to 15% of the amount on the meter. In **theaters and restaurants,** give cloakroom attendants at least 5 F (90¢) per item. Give **rest room attendants** in nightclubs and such places about 2 F (35¢). Give **cinema and theater ushers** about 2 F (35¢). Tip the **hairdresser** about 15%, and don't forget to tip the person who gives you a shampoo or a manicure 10 F

Calling Paris from Abroad

To call Paris from abroad, first dial the **international prefix,** then France's **country code (33),** then the local number minus the initial 0 (zero). From the United States or Canada, the international prefix is **011,** from Australia **0011,** from Great Britain, Ireland, or New Zealand **00,** and from South Africa **09.** Thus, to call **Notre-Dame** (☎ **01-42-34-56-10**) from the U.S., you would dial ☎ **011-33-1-42-34-56-10.**

($1.80). For **guides** for group visits to museums and monuments, 5 F to 10 F (90¢ to $1.80) is a reasonable tip.

Transit Info   For information on the city's public transportation, call ☎ **08-36-68-77-14.**

Useful Telephone Numbers   Police, ☎ **17;** fire, ☎ **18;** emergency medical assistance, ☎ **15;** directory assistance, ☎ **12.**

Visas   See "Visitor Information" and "Entry Requirements & Customs Regulations" in chapter 2.

Water   Drinking water is generally safe, although it has been known to cause diarrhea in some unaccustomed stomachs. If you ask for water in a restaurant, it will be bottled water (for which you'll pay), unless you specifically request tap water *(l'eau du robinet).*

Yellow Pages   Your hotel will almost certainly have a copy, but you'll need the help of a French-speaking resident before tackling them.

4 Accommodations

Immediately, the river that divides Paris geographically and culturally demands that you make a choice. Do you prefer a hotel deep in the heart of St-Germain, sleeping in a room where Jean-Paul Sartre and Simone de Beauvoir might have spent the night? Or are you more Right Bank, preferring to sleep in sumptuous quarters at the Crillon Hotel? Would you rather look for that special curio in a dusty shop on the Left Bank's rue Jacob, or inspect the latest haute couture of Karl Lagerfeld, Jean Patou, or Guy Laroche in a Right Bank boutique along the avenue Montaigne? Neighborhoods in Paris are each very different, and your experiences and memory of Paris will likely be formed by where you choose to stay.

It is estimated that Paris has some 2,000 hotels—with about 80,000 rooms—spread across its 20 arrondissements. They range from the Ritz to dives so repellent that even George Orwell, author of *Down and Out in Paris and London,* wouldn't have considered checking in. (Of course, none of those are in this guide!) We've included deluxe places for those who want to live like the Sultan of Brunei and a wide range of moderate and inexpensive choices. See chapter 1 for our favorites.

Most visitors, at least those from North America, come in July and August. Since many French are on vacation then and trade fairs and conventions come to a halt, there are usually plenty of rooms, even though these months have traditionally been the peak season for European travel. In most hotels, February is just as busy as April or September because of the volume of business travelers and the increasing number of tourists who've learned to take advantage of off-season discount airfares.

Since hot weather never lasts long in Paris, few hotels, except the deluxe ones, provide air-conditioning. If you're trapped in a garret on a hot summer night, you'll have to sweat it out. You can open your window to get some cooler air, but open windows admit a major nuisance: noise pollution. To avoid this, you may wish to request a room in the back when making a reservation. Almost all hotels, except for those in the Inexpensive category, have hair dryers in the rooms.

Hotel breakfasts are fairly uniform and include your choice of coffee, tea, or hot chocolate, a freshly baked croissant and roll, plus limited quantities of butter and jam or jelly. It can be at your door moments after you call for it, and is served at almost any hour requested. (When we mention breakfast charges in our listings, we

---

How to Read Government Ratings

The government of France grades hotels with a star system, ranging from one star for a simple inn to four stars for a deluxe hotel. Moderately priced hotels usually get two or three stars. This system is based on a complicated formula of room sizes, facilities, state of the plumbing, and dozens of other factors, including elevators, floor plans, dining options, and renovations. In a one-star hotel, bathrooms are often shared and facilities are extremely limited. Breakfast is often the only meal served. You may or may not have a phone in the room. In the two- or three-star hotels, there is usually elevator service, a private bath in each room, a room phone, and even a private TV. In the four-star hotels, you get the works, with all the amenities plus facilities and services such as room service, a 24-hour concierge, elevators, perhaps a health club. The system is a bit misleading. For tax reasons, a four-star hotel might deliberately elect to have a three-star rating, which, with the hotel's permission, is granted by the government. The government will not add a star where it's not merited, but with the hotel's request will remove a star.

---

refer to continental breakfasts only.) Breakfasts with eggs, bacon, ham, or other items must be ordered from the à la carte menu. For a charge, larger hotels serve the full or "English" breakfast, but smaller hotels typically serve only the continental variety.

CHOOSING WHERE TO STAY

The first decision to make after choosing between lodgings in central Paris or an outlying district is simple: Right Bank or Left Bank?

If you desire chic surroundings, choose a **Right Bank** hotel. That puts you near all the most elegant shops and within walking distance of important sights such as the Arc de Triomphe, the place de la Concorde, the Tuileries Gardens, and the Louvre. Afterward, every glittering cafe along the Champs-Elysées is an oasis for a coffee during the day or for an aperitif at night.

The best Right Bank hotels are near the Arc de Triomphe in the 8th arrondissement, though many first-class lodgings cluster near the Trocadéro and Bois du Boulogne in the 16th, or near the Palais des Congrès in the 17th. If you'd like to be near the place Vendôme, try for a hotel in the 1st.

Other Right Bank hotel sections include the increasingly fashionable Marais and Bastille districts in the 3rd and 4th arrondissements, and Les Halles/Beaubourg, home of the Centre Pompidou and Les Halles shopping mall, which are stationed in the 3rd arrondissement.

If you want less formality and tiny bohemian streets, head for the **Left Bank,** where prices are traditionally lower. Hotels that cater to students are found in the 5th and 6th arrondissements, best known for the Sorbonne, cafe life, and bookstores. The 7th provides a touch of avant-garde St-Germain.

A NOTE ON PRICE CATEGORIES

Classifying Paris hotels by price is a long day's journey into night. It's possible many times to find a moderately priced room in an otherwise "very expensive" hotel or an "expensive" room in an otherwise "inexpensive" property. That's because most hotel rooms, at least in the older properties, are not standard; therefore, the range of rooms goes from superdeluxe suites to the "maid's pantry," now converted into a small bedroom. At some hotels, in fact, you'll find rooms that are "moderate," "expensive," and "very expensive," all under one roof.

The following price categories are only for a quick general reference. When we've classified a hotel as "moderate," it means that the average room is moderately priced, not necessarily all the rooms. It should also be noted that Paris is one of the most expensive cities in the world for hotels.

1 Right Bank

We'll begin with the most centrally located arrondissements on the Right Bank, then work our way through the more outlying neighborhoods.

1ST ARRONDISSEMENT (LOUVRE/LES HALLES)
VERY EXPENSIVE

✪ **Costes.** 239 rue St-Honoré, 75001 Paris. ☎ **01-42-44-50-50**. Fax 01-42-44-50-01. 83 units. A/C MINIBAR TV TEL. 2,250–3,500 F ($382.50–$595) double; 5,250–5,500 F ($892.50– $935) suite. AE, DC, MC, V. Métro: Tuileries or Concorde.

Grand style and a location close to the headquarters of some of the most upscale shops in Paris seem to attract goodly numbers of high-style fashion types, some of whom work within the nearby editorial offices of *Harper's Bazaar.* The five-story, town house–style premises functioned as a maison bourgeoise for many generations, presenting a severely dignified facade to the prestigious neighborhood around it. In 1996, it was richly adorned with the jewel-toned colors, heavy swag curtains, and lavish accessories of the late 19th century (the Napoléon III style). Today, everything about it evokes the rich days of France's Gilded Age, especially the bedrooms. Although small, they're cozy and ornate, with a CD player and fax machine. Units contain one or two large beds, each with a sumptuous mattress. Bathrooms are fairly spacious, with makeup mirrors, deluxe toiletries, thick towels, and a tub and shower combination.

Dining: Four dining rooms, each with a different decorative theme, and each overlooking the building's Italianate-style inner courtyard, are chock-a-block with chinoiserie, dried and framed flowers, and 19th-century art. Open daily from noon to 1am, they feature delectable dishes such as grilled scallops and a grilled version of steak tartare with all the spicy ingredients of its original (raw) version.

Amenities: Car-rental desk, concierge, room service, dry cleaning, laundry service, baby-sitting, and a gym with a steam room, indoor pool, and masseurs/masseuses.

✪ **Hôtel de Vendôme.** 1 Place Vendôme, 75001 Paris. ☎ 01-42-60-32-84. Fax 01-49-27-97-89. E-mail: reservations@hoteldevendome.com. 30 units. A/C MINIBAR TV TEL. 2,800–3,200 F ($476–$544) double; 4,500–5,500 F ($765–$935) suite. AE, DC, MC, V. Métro: Concorde or Opéra.

Once the home of the Embassy of Texas when that state was a nation, this is a jewel box of a hotel that opened in the summer of 1998 at one of the world's most prestigious addresses. Although the sumptuous bedrooms are only moderate in size, you live in opulent comfort here. Most of the bedrooms are decorated in a classic Second Empire style with luxurious beds and mattresses, tasteful fabrics, and well-upholstered, hand-carved furnishings. Bathrooms are equally sumptuous, with a tub and shower combination, robes, thick towels, and Guerlain toiletries. The security is fantastic, with TV intercoms. This new version of the hotel replaces a lackluster one that stood here for a century. Both its facade and roof are classified as historic monuments by the French government. The building dates from 1723, when it was the home of the secretary to Louis XIV.

Dining: The hotel restaurant, **Café de Vedôme,** is directed by Gérard Sallé, who has worked at some of the premier addresses of Paris, including the Bristol and the Plaza Athénée. The cuisine is imaginative, the setting rather austere but elegant.

Amenities: Room service, laundry, concierge.

Hôtel du Louvre. Place André Malraux, 75001 Paris. ☎ **800/888-4747** in the U.S. and Canada, or 01-44-58-38-38. Fax 01-44-58-38-01. www.hoteldulouvre.com. 195 units. A/C MINIBAR TV TEL. 1,850–2,500 F ($314.50–$425) double; from 3,000 F ($510) suite. AE, DC, MC, V. Ask about midwinter discounts. Parking 100 F ($17). Métro: Palais-Royal.

When Napoléon III inaugurated this hotel in 1855, French journalists described it as "a palace of the people, rising adjacent to the palace of kings." In 1897, Camille Pissarro moved into a room with a view that inspired many of his Parisian landscapes. Set between the Musée du Louvre and the Palais Royal, the hotel has a decor of soaring marble, bronze, and gilt. The rooms are quintessentially Parisian—cozy, soundproof, and filled with souvenirs of the belle epoque. Most were renovated between 1996 and 1998. Some of the bedrooms are small, but most of them are medium in size—with elegant fabrics and upholstery, excellent wool carpeting, double-glazed windows, plush and comfortable beds with fine linens and quality mattresses, and traditional wood furniture. Bathrooms are medium in size. Extras include robes and trouser presses. The newer rooms have shower stalls, but the older rooms are fitted with large bathtubs.

Dining: Le Bar "Defender" is a cozy hideaway, with mahogany trim, Scottish overtones, and a collection of single-malt whiskies; a pianist plays after dusk. There's also the **French Empire Brasserie du Louvre,** whose tables extend to the terrace in fine weather.

Amenities: Concierge, room service (24 hours), baby-sitting, laundry, dry cleaning, valet, business center.

Hôtel Regina. 2 place des Pyramides, 75001 Paris. ☎ **01-42-60-31-10.** Fax 01-40-15-95-16. tel.comtel.comwww.regina-hotel.com. E-mail: reservation@regina-hotel.com. 135 units. A/C MINIBAR TV TEL. 1,990–2,300 F ($338.30–$391) double; 2,800–4,100 F ($476–$697) suite. AE, DC, MC, V. Parking 85 F ($14.45). Métro: Pyramides or Tuileries.

Until a radical renovation upgraded its old-fashioned grandeur in 1995, this hotel slumbered in central Paris, adjacent to rue de Rivoli's equestrian statue of Joan of Arc. The management has poured lots of money into the renovation, retaining the patina and beeswax of the art nouveau interior and making historically appropriate improvements. The rooms that overlook the Tuileries enjoy panoramic views as far away as the Eiffel Tower. The public areas have every period of Louis furniture imaginable, Oriental carpets, 18th-century paintings, and bowls of flowers. Fountains play in a flagstone-covered courtyard, site of alfresco cafe tables and an extension of the hotel's restaurant. Bedrooms are richly decorated, all with comfortable mattresses.

Dining: In the well-managed **Le Pluvinel,** conservative French cuisine is served in an art deco atmosphere. Pluvinel is closed on weekends, when there's only a less appealing but more affordable bistro-style snack bar.

Amenities: Concierge, 24-hour room service, twice-daily maid service, baby-sitting, laundry/dry cleaning, valet, secretarial service, in-room massage, conference room; visits to a nearby health club can be arranged upon request.

✪ **Le Ritz.** 15 place Vendôme, 75001 Paris. ☎ **800/223-6800** in the U.S. and Canada, or 01-43-16-30-30. Fax 01-43-16-31-78. E-mail: resa@ritzparis.com. 187 units. A/C MINIBAR TV TEL. 3,600–4,400 F ($612–$748) double; from 6,200 F ($1,054) suite. AE, DC, MC, V. Parking 220 F ($37.40). Métro: Opéra.

The Ritz is Europe's greatest hotel. This enduring symbol of elegance stands on one of Paris's most beautiful and historic squares. César Ritz, the "little shepherd boy from Niederwald," converted the private Hôtel de Lazun into a luxury hotel that he opened in 1898. With the help of the culinary master Escoffier, he made the Ritz a miracle of luxury living.

Hotels in the Heart of the Right Bank

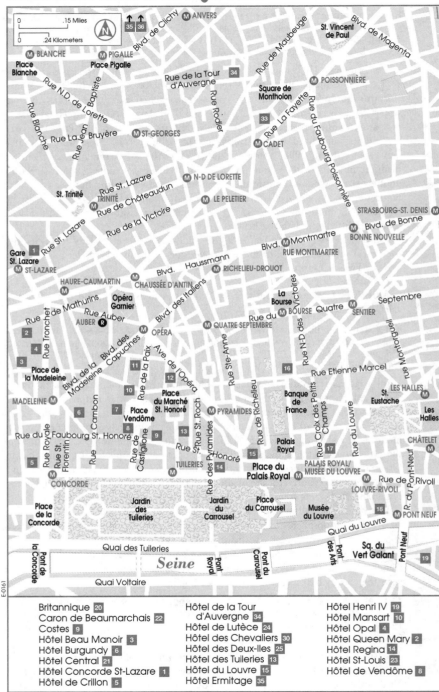

Britannique 20
Caron de Beaumarchais 22
Costes 9
Hôtel Beau Manoir 3
Hôtel Burgundy 6
Hôtel Central 21
Hôtel Concorde St-Lazare 1
Hôtel de Crillon 5

Hôtel de la Tour d'Auvergne 34
Hôtel de Lutèce 24
Hôtel des Chevaliers 30
Hôtel des Deux-Iles 25
Hôtel des Tuileries 13
Hôtel du Louvre 15
Hôtel Ermitage 35

Hôtel Henri IV 19
Hôtel Mansart 10
Hôtel Opal 4
Hôtel Queen Mary 2
Hôtel Regina 14
Hôtel St-Louis 23
Hôtel de Vendôme 8

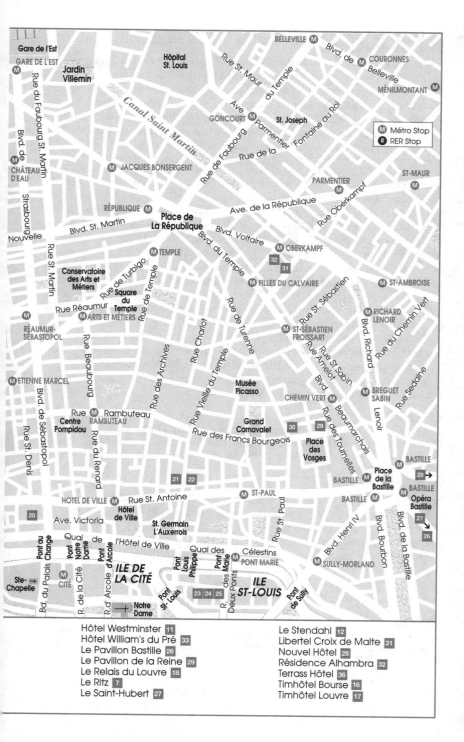

Hôtel Westminster **11**
Hôtel William's du Pré **33**
Le Pavillon Bastille **26**
Le Pavillon de la Reine **29**
Le Relais du Louvre **18**
Le Ritz **7**
Le Saint-Hubert **27**

Le Stendahl **12**
Libertel Croix de Malte **31**
Nouvel Hôtel **28**
Résidence Alhambra **32**
Terrass Hôtel **36**
Timhôtel Bourse **16**
Timhôtel Louvre **17**

A Hotel Tale

During Paris's occupation, on August 25, 1944, Ernest Hemingway "liberated" the Ritz. Armed with machine guns, "Papa" and a group of Allied soldiers pulled up to the hotel in a Jeep, intent on capturing Nazis and freeing, if only symbolically, the landmark. After a sweep from the cellars to the roof, the group discovered that the Nazis had already fled. Hemingway led his team to the Ritz bar to order a round of dry martinis. In commemoration of the 50th anniversary of the liberation, the renovated Bar Hemingway reopened on August 25, 1994.

In 1979, the Ritz family sold the hotel to the Egyptian businessman Mohamed Al Fayed (Dodi's father), who refurbished it and added a cooking school. (Dodi Al Fayed and Princess Diana were staying here when they set out on their fateful drive through Paris.) Two town houses were annexed, joined by a long arcade lined with miniature display cases representing 125 of the leading boutiques of Paris. The salons are furnished with museum-caliber antiques. The spacious marble bathrooms are among the city's most luxurious, filled with deluxe toiletries, scales, a private phone, cords to summon maids and valets, fluffy towels and robes, full-length and makeup mirrors, and dual basins. Ever since Edward VII got stuck in a too-narrow bathtub with his lover of the evening, bathtubs at the Ritz have been deep and big. The hotel has its own workshop to repair and reproduce the plumbing.

Dining/Diversions: The **Espadon** grill room is one of the finest in Paris. The **Ritz Supper Club** includes a bar, a salon with a fireplace, a restaurant, and a dance floor. You can order drinks in either the **Bar Vendôme** or the **Bar Hemingway.**

Amenities: Concierge, 24-hour room service, laundry, valet, health club with pool and massage parlor, florist, shops, squash court.

EXPENSIVE

Hôtel des Tuileries. 10 rue St-Hyacinthe, 75001 Paris. ☎ **01-42-61-04-17.** Fax 01-49-27-91-56. www.members.aol.com/htuileri/. E-mail: htuileri.aol.com. 26 units. A/C MINIBAR TV TEL. 890–1,400 F ($151.30–$238) double. AE, DC, MC, V. Parking 100 F ($17). Métro: Tuileries or Pyramides.

On a narrow, quiet street, this hotel occupies a 17th-century town house that's remembered as the minipalace Marie Antoinette used when she left Versailles for an unofficial visit to Paris. Don't expect mementos of the queen, as all the frippery of her era was long ago stripped away. But in honor of royal antecedents, the hotel's public areas and guest rooms are filled with copies of Louis XV furniture—a bit dowdy but still comfortable. The baths contain whirlpool tubs, separate toilets, and touches of marble. Rooms provide safe, comfortable, cozy getaways from the urban congestion in this busy neighborhood—a welcome and comfortable refuge.

Amenities: Room service 7am to 11pm, newspaper delivery upon request.

MODERATE

Hôtel Britannique. 20 av. Victoria, 75001 Paris. ☎ **01-42-33-74-59.** Fax 01-42-33-82-65. www.hotel-britannique.fr. E-mail: mailbox@hotel-britannique.fr. 40 units. MINIBAR TV TEL. 697–998 F ($118.50–$169.65) double. AE, DC, MC, V. Parking 100 F ($17). Métro: Châtelet.

Cozy, conservatively modern, and plush-looking, this much-renovated 19th-century hotel was re-rated with three stars after a complete renovation in the mid-1980s. The place is not only British in name but seems also to have cultivated an English style of graciousness. It's in the heart of Paris, near Les Halles, the Pompidou Centre, and Notre-Dame. The rooms may be small, but they're spick-and-span, comfortable, and soundproof, with comfortable beds and a safe-deposit box. A satellite receiver gets U.S. and U.K. TV shows. The reading room is a cozy retreat.

⚪ **Hôtel Burgundy.** 8 rue Duphot, 75001 Paris. ☎ **01-42-60-34-12.** Fax 01-47-03-95-20. www.perso.wanadoo.fr/hotel.burgundy. E-mail: hotel.burgundy@iname.com. 89 units. MINIBAR TV TEL. 960 F ($163.20) double; 1,600 F ($272) suite. AE, DC, MC, V. Métro: Madeleine.

The Burgundy is one of the best values in an outrageously expensive neighborhood. This frequently renovated building is a former pension, where Baudelaire wrote some of his eerie poetry in the 1860s. What you'll see today was conceived as two side-by-side town houses in the 1830s. One flourished as a bordello before they were linked by British-born managers, who insisted on using the English name. Radically renovated in 1992, the hotel often hosts many North and South Americans. It features conservatively decorated and very comfortable rooms with cozy-looking decor; efficient, modestly sized bathrooms; and comfortable beds. The **Charles Baudelaire** restaurant is open for lunch and dinner Monday through Friday. There's no bar, but drinks are served in the lobby during restaurant hours. Amenities include limited concierge services, room service from 6:30am to 9:30pm, laundry/dry cleaning, and a conference room.

Hôtel Mansart. 5 rue des Capucines, 75001 Paris. ☎ **01-42-61-50-28.** Fax 01-49-27-97-44. www.hotels.eslprit.de.france.com. E-mail: espranc@micronet.fr. 57 units. MINIBAR TV TEL. 600–900 F ($102–$153) double; 1,600 F ($272) suite. AE, DC, MC, V. Métro: Opéra or Madeleine.

After operating as a glorious wreck for many decades, this hotel—designed by its namesake—was radically renovated in 1991 and now offers some of the lowest rates in this pricey neighborhood. The public areas contain Louis-inspired reproductions and startling floor-to-ceiling geometric designs inspired by inlaid marble floors (or formal gardens) of the French Renaissance. The small- to medium-size guest rooms are subtly formal and comfortable, though only half a dozen of the suites and most expensive rooms actually overlook the famous square. Twenty of the rooms are air-conditioned; all have beds with firm mattresses. The compact bathrooms have a shower stall. Breakfast, the only meal offered, is served one floor above lobby level.

Relais du Louvre. 19 rue des Prêtres, 75001 Paris. ☎ **01-40-41-96-42.** Fax 01-40-41-96-44. 20 units. MINIBAR TV TEL. 850–980 F ($144.50–$166.60) double; 1,300–2,200 F ($221–$374) suite. AE, MC, V. Parking 70 F ($11.90). Métro: Louvre or Pont-Neuf.

One of the neighborhood's most up-to-date hotels opened in 1991, midway between the wings at the eastern end of the Musée du Louvre. The Relais has a lot more atmosphere and glamor than its major competitor, the Britannique. Between 1800 and 1941, its upper floors contained the printing presses that recorded the goings-on in Paris's House of Representatives. Its street level held the Café Momus, favored by Voltaire, Hugo, and intellectuals of the day, and where Puccini set one of the pivotal scenes of *La Bohème.* The guest rooms are painted in bold colors, with modern conveniences, soundproof windows, reproductions of antique furniture, and elegant grace notes such as French doors opening in some cases onto tiny balconies. Recent renovations upgraded the mattresses and upholsteries. Many rooms are a bit small, but others contain roomy sitting areas.

INEXPENSIVE

Hôtel Henri IV. 25 place Dauphine, 75001 Paris. ☎ **01-43-54-44-53.** 21 units (3 with shower). 185–205 F ($31.45–$34.85) double without shower; 240–265 F ($40.80–$45.05) double with shower. Rates include breakfast. No credit cards. Métro: Pont-Neuf.

Four hundred years ago, this narrow, decrepit building housed the printing presses used for the edicts of Henri IV. Today one of the most famous and most consistently crowded budget hotels in Europe sits in a dramatic location at the westernmost tip of the Ile de la Cité, beside a formal and unexpected park lined with orderly rows of trees. The clientele is mostly bargain-conscious academics, journalists, and francophiles, many of whom reserve rooms as early as 2 months in advance. The low-ceilinged lobby, a flight above street level, is cramped and bleak; the creaky stairway leading to the bedrooms is almost impossibly narrow. Rooms are considered romantically threadbare by many, and run-down and substandard by others. Each contains a sink, but not even the trio of rooms with showers have toilets.

Timhôtel Louvre. 4 rue Croix des Petits-Champs, 75001 Paris. ☎ **01-42-60-34-86.** Fax 01-42-60-10-39. 56 units. TV TEL. 580 F ($98.60) double. AE, DC, MC, V. Métro: Palais-Royal.

This hotel and its sibling, Timhôtel Palais-Royal, are mirror images of each other, at least inside; they're part of a new breed of two-star business-oriented hotels that are cropping up around France. These Timhôtels share the same manager and the same temperament, and though the rooms at Timhôtel Palais-Royal are a bit larger than the ones here, the Louvre branch is so close to the museum as to be almost irresistible. The ambience is bland and standardized, but modern and comfortable, with tiled baths, monochromatic guest rooms, and wall-to-wall carpeting that was upgraded and renovated in 1998. The beds are good, with firm mattresses, but the bathrooms are a bit cramped. Breakfasts are served rather anonymously from self-service cafeterias.

Timhôtel Palais-Royal is at 3 rue de la Banque, 75002 Paris (☎ **01-42-61-53-90;** fax 01-42-60-05-39; Métro: Bourse); it has 46 rooms and charges the same price as above.

2ND ARRONDISSEMENT (LA BOURSE)
VERY EXPENSIVE

Hôtel Westminster. 13 rue de la Paix, 75002 Paris. ☎ **800/203-3232** or 01-42-61-57-46. Fax 01-42-60-30-66. E-mail: resa.westminster@warwickhotels.com. 102 units. A/C MINIBAR TV TEL. 2,400–2,700 F ($408–$459) double; from 6,600 F ($1,122) suite. AE, DC, MC, V. Métro: Opéra.

Set in a desirably central neighborhood midway between the Opéra and the place Vendôme, the Westminster was built during Baron Haussmann's redesigning of Paris in 1846, and incorporated a deconsecrated convent within its walls. Around 1900, it was bought by a gilded-age entrepreneur, Monsieur Bruchon, who installed a famous collection of clocks. Between 1996 and 1999, the owners painted the bedrooms and installed new fabrics, carpeting, air-conditioning, and telephone systems throughout the hotel, while carefully maintaining its 19th-century design and allure. The Westminster is well groomed, maintaining a certain charm and character. A heavily British clientele patronizes this very British hotel. Bedrooms are generally spacious, with private safes and king-size beds fitted with quality mattresses. The marble bathrooms are first-class, with deluxe toiletries and thick towels.

Dining: The hotel restaurant, **Le Céladon,** is one of the finest hotel dining rooms in Paris. It's not only noted for its celadon porcelain on display but for serving light traditional dishes on an imaginative menu. Less formal are bistro meals within Les Chenets, site of an evening piano bar.

Amenities: Room service, laundry, valet.

EXPENSIVE

Le Stendhal. 22 rue Danielle Casanova, 75002 Paris. ☎ **01-44-58-52-52.** Fax 01-44-58-52-00. 20 units. A/C MINIBAR TV TEL. 1,440–1,630 F ($244.80–$277.10) double; from 1,800 F ($306) suite. AE, DC, MC, V. Parking 100 F ($17). Métro: Opéra.

Established in 1992, this hotel mixes a young and hip style with a sense of tradition. Its location, close to the glamorous jewelry stores on the place Vendôme, couldn't be grander. Overall, the effect is that of a small, boutique-style *hôtel de luxe* that in some ways seems like an urban and very Parisian version of an upscale English B&B. Bedrooms, accessible via a tiny elevator, have vivid color schemes. Most bedrooms are small but not without their charm; each comes with fine linen and a quality mattress, plus a tidily maintained and elegant private bath. The red-and-black Stendhal Suite pays homage to the author, who made this his private home for many years and died here in 1842.

Dining: Breakfast is served in a stone cellar with a vaulted ceiling. A small bar adjoins the lobby, but offers little in size or allure. Simple meals can be ordered and are served in the bedrooms or at the bar, 24 hours a day.

Amenities: A receptionist/concierge is able to arrange baby-sitting, dry cleaning, secretarial services, and car rentals.

3RD ARRONDISSEMENT (LE MARAIS)
VERY EXPENSIVE

✪ **Pavillon de la Reine.** 28 place des Vosges, 75003 Paris. ☎ **01-40-29-19-19.** Fax 01-40-29-19-20. E-mail: pavillon@clubinternet.fr. 55 units. A/C MINIBAR TV TEL. 1,900–2,100 F ($323–$357) double; 2,050–2,500 F ($348.50–$425) duplex; 2,550–3,900 F ($433.50–$663) suite. AE, DC, MC, V. Free parking. Métro: Bastille.

Built in 1986, this cream-colored neoclassical villa blends in seamlessly with the rest of the square. You enter through an arcade that opens onto a small formal garden. The Louis XIII decor evokes the heyday of the place des Vosges, and wing chairs with flame-stitched upholstery combine with iron-banded Spanish antiques to create a rustic feel. Each guest room is unique; some are duplexes with sleeping lofts above cozy salons. All have a warm decor of weathered beams, reproductions of famous oil paintings, and roomy marble baths with thick towels. Most rooms are of good size. The better rooms come with private safes. The preferred rooms are on the upper floors opening onto the romantic square. Quality mattresses and fine linens are used on all the excellent French beds.

Dining: The hotel has an "honesty bar" and a limited 24-hour room-service menu.

Amenities: A receptionist/concierge can arrange massage, dry cleaning, car rentals, and tickets for shows, concerts, and the theater.

MODERATE

Hôtel des Chevaliers. 30 rue de Turenne, 75003 Paris. ☎ **01-42-72-73-47.** Fax 01-42-72-54-10. 24 units. MINIBAR TV TEL. 640–680 F ($108.80–$115.60) double; 854 F ($145.20) triple. Métro: Chemin-Vert or St-Paul.

Half a block from the northwestern edge of the place des Vosges, this carefully renovated hotel occupies a dramatic corner building whose 17th-century vestiges have been elevated into high art. These include the remnants of a stone-sided well in the cellar, a sweeping stone barrel vault that covers the breakfast area, half-timbering that's artfully exposed in the stairwell, and Louis XIII accessories that'll remind you of the hotel's origins. Each room is comfortable and well maintained. Bathrooms are compact, with just a shower stall.

4TH ARRONDISSEMENT (ILE DE LA CITÉ/ILE ST- LOUIS & BEAUBOURG)
MODERATE

✪ **Hôtel Caron de Beaumarchais.** 12 rue Vieille-du-Temple, 75004 Paris. ☎ **01-42-72-34-12.** Fax 01-42-72-34-63. www.carondebeaumarchais.com. 19 units. A/C MINIBAR TV TEL. 730–810 F ($124.10–$137.70) double. AE, DC, MC, V. Métro: St-Paul or Hôtel-de-Ville.

ⓘ Family-Friendly Hotels

Timhôtel Louvre *(see p. 60)* This is an especially convenient choice because it offers some rooms with four beds for the price of a double. The location near the Louvre is irresistible.

Résidence Lord Byron *(see p. 66)* The Byron is not only a good value and an unusually family-oriented place for the swanky 8th arrondissement, but is only a 10-minute walk from many of the city's major monuments.

Hôtel Saint-Louis *(see p. 63)* The family atmosphere cultivated by proprietor Guy Record and his wife, Andreé, is a precious commodity in Paris these days. This 17th-century town house is set fashionably on the historic Ile Saint-Louis and priced with families in mind.

Hôtel de Fleurie *(see p. 76)* In the heart of St-Germain-des-Prés, this has long been a Left Bank family favorite. The hotel is known for its *chambres familiales*— two connecting rooms with a pair of large beds in each room. Children under 12 stay free with their parents.

Built in the 18th century and gracefully renovated and upgraded in 1998, this good-value choice features floors of artfully worn gray stone, antique reproductions, and elaborate fabrics based on antique patterns. Most of the rooms retain their original ceiling beams, and though they're compact, they're comfortable and soundproof. Hotelier Alain Bigeard likes his primrose-colored rooms to evoke the taste of 18th-century French gentry when the Marais was the scene of high society dances or even duels. The smallest units overlook the interior courtyard, and the top floor rooms are also tiny, but they have panoramic balcony views across the Right Bank. Rooms on the lower five levels are more spacious, but contain balconies only on the second and fifth floors. Bathrooms are exceedingly compact but well maintained, most often with a tub and shower combination.

✪ **Hôtel de Lutèce.** 65 rue St-Louis-en-l'Ile, 75004 Paris. ☎ **01-43-26-23-52.** Fax 01-43-29-60-25. www.france-hotel-guide.com/h75004lutece.htm. 23 units. A/C TV TEL. 860 F ($146.20) double; 1,100 F ($187) triple. AE, MC, V. Parking 80 F ($13.60). Métro: Pont-Marie or Cité.

This hotel feels like a country house in Brittany. The lounge, with its old fireplace, is graciously furnished with antiques and contemporary paintings. Each of the individualized guest rooms boasts antiques, adding to a refined atmosphere that attracts celebrities, like the duke and duchess of Bedford. Many of the accommodations, ranging in size from small to medium, were renovated in 1998, with new mattresses added. Each room is well maintained, traditional, and comfortable, with wool carpeting and upholstered chairs. Bathrooms are small but tidy. The hotel is comparable in style and amenities to the Deux-Iles (see below), under the same ownership.

Hôtel des Deux-Iles. 59 rue St-Louis-en-l'Ile, 75004 Paris. ☎ **01-43-26-13-35.** Fax 01-43-29-60-25. 17 units. TV TEL. 860 F ($146.20) double. AE, MC, V. Métro: Pont-Marie.

This much-restored 17th-century town house was an inexpensive hotel until 1976, when an elaborate decor with lots of bamboo and reed furniture and French provincial touches was added. The result is an unpretentious but charming hotel with a great location. Bedrooms and bathrooms are on the small side. A garden of plants and flowers off the lobby leads to a basement breakfast room with a fireplace. Amenities include room service from 7:30am to 8pm and laundry/dry cleaning.

۞ Hôtel Saint-Louis. 75 rue St-Louis-en-l'Ile, 75004 Paris. ☎ **01-46-34-04-80.** Fax 01-46-34-02-13. hotel.www.paris-hotel.tm.fr/saint-louis-marais. 21 units. TEL. 775–875 F ($131.75–$148.75) double. MC, V. Métro: Pont-Marie.

Proprietor Guy Record and his wife, Andrée, maintain a charming family atmosphere (which is becoming harder and harder to find in Paris) at this antique-filled small hotel in a 17th-century town house. Despite a full renovation completed in 1998, it still represents an incredible value considering its prime location on the highly desirable, crowded island of Saint-Louis. With mansard roofs and old-fashioned moldings, top-floor rooms sport a tiny balcony with sweeping views over the rooftops of Paris. Expect cozy, slightly cramped rooms. All the bathrooms were renovated in 1998. The break-fast room is in the cellar, whose stone vaulting dates from the 17th century.

8TH ARRONDISSEMENT (CHAMPS-ELYSÉES/MADELEINE)
VERY EXPENSIVE

۞ Hôtel Balzac. 6 rue Balzac, 75008 Paris. ☎ **800/457-4000** in the U.S. and Canada, or 01-44-35-18-00. Fax 01-44-35-18-05. E-mail: hotelbalzac@wanadoo.fr. 70 units. A/C MINIBAR TV TEL. 2,200 F ($374) double; from 3,300 F ($561) suite. AE, DC, MC, V. Parking 150 F ($25.50). Métro: George-V.

If the Crillon or the Ritz is a Rolls-Royce, the Balzac is a Bentley. Elegant and discreet, it boasts a well-trained formal staff and comfortable accommodations with modern furniture. The subtle opulence is unmatched by other hotels in the neighborhood. The hotel opened in 1986 in a belle-epoque mansion, then was redecorated in 1994 by the famed English designer Nina Campbell. Each room is sound proof and conceived as a comfortable, well-upholstered hideaway. Most rooms are medium to spacious in size, with double glazing, private safes, mirrored closets, and king-size beds. Bathrooms are clad in marble with thick towels, robes, and deluxe toiletries.

Dining: In November 1996 a prominent spot near the hotel's elegant lobby was rented to the **Restaurant Pierre Gagnaire.** Its namesake is a promising culinary new-comer to Paris whose three-star cuisine has impressed critics throughout France.

Amenities: Concierge, 24-hour room service, dry cleaning, express laundry.

۞ Hôtel de Crillon. 10 place de la Concorde, 75008 Paris. ☎ **800/241-3333** in the U.S. and Canada, or 01-44-71-15-00. Fax 01-44-71-15-04. www.crillon-paris.com. E-mail: crillon@crillon-paris.com. 163 units. A/C MINIBAR TV TEL. 3,500–4,300 F ($595–$731) double; from 4,950 F ($841.50) suite. AE, DC, MC, V. Parking 150 F ($25.50). Métro: Concorde.

One of Europe's greatest hotels, the Crillon sits across from the U.S. Embassy. The 200-year-old building, once the palace of the duc de Crillon, has been a hotel since the early 1900s and is now owned by Jean Taittinger of the champagne family. Inside are many preserved architectural details as well as museum-quality antiques and repro-ductions. The salons boast 17th- and 18th-century tapestries, gilt-and-brocade furni-ture, chandeliers, fine sculpture, and Louis XVI chests and chairs. Guest rooms are large and luxurious. Some of the accommodations are spectacular, such as the Leonard Bernstein Suite, which has one of the maestro's pianos and one of the grandest views of any hotel room in Paris. Baths are sumptuous as well, with deluxe toiletries, marble, dual sinks, robes, thick towels, and, in some, thermal taps.

Dining: You can dine at the elegant **Les Ambassadeurs** or the more informal **L'Obélisque,** where menu choices are less experimental. Les Ambassadeurs offers a businessperson's lunch Monday through Friday only. A menu dégustation is served at lunch on weekends and every evening. We've ranked Les Ambassadeur's breakfast menu a Best Bet in chapter 1.

Amenities: 24-hour room service, secretarial/translation service, laundry, valet, meeting and conference rooms, garden-style courtyard with restaurant service, shops.

Hôtel Plaza Athénée. 27 av. Montaigne, 75008 Paris. ☎ **800/223-6800** in the U.S. and Canada, or 01-53-67-66-65. Fax 01-53-67-66-66. E-mail: email@hotel-plaza-athenee-fr. 185 units. A/C MINIBAR TV TEL. 3,500–4,000 F ($595–$680) double; 7,600–13,000 F ($1,292–$2,210) suite. AE, MC, V. Parking 150 F ($25.50). Métro: F. D. Roosevelt or Alma Marceau.

Plaza Athénée, a grand art nouveau marvel from 1889, is a landmark of discretion and style. About half the celebrities visiting Paris have been pampered here; in the old days, Mata Hari used to frequent the place. Decors throughout are sumptuous. The finest public room is the Montaigne Salon, paneled in grained wood and dominated by a marble fireplace. The quietest guest rooms overlook a courtyard with awnings and parasol-shaded tables; they have ample closet space, and their large tiled baths have double basins and a tub and shower. Some rooms overlooking the Avenue Montaigne have views of the Eiffel Tower. In 1999, the hotel completed a radical overhaul, creating larger rooms out of some of the smaller, less desirable rooms.

Dining/Diversions: **La Régence** offers superb food—try the lobster soufflé. For lunch, **Grill Relais Plaza** is the meeting place of dress designers and personalities from the worlds of publishing, cinema, and art. The **Bar Anglais** is a favorite spot for a late-night drink.

Amenities: Concierge, 24-hour room service, laundry, conference rooms, beauty salon, massage, fitness club.

Le Bristol. 112 rue du Faubourg St-Honoré, 75008 Paris. ☎ **01-53-43-43-00.** Fax 01-53-43-43-26. www.hotel-bristol.com. E-mail: resa@hotel-bristol.com. 3,250–4,000 F ($552.50–$680) double; 4,600–36,000 F ($782–$6,120) suite. AE, DC, MC, V. Free parking. Métro: Miromesnil.

This medium-size palace is near the Palais d'Elysée (home of the French president), on the shopping street that runs parallel to the Champs-Elysées. Personalized old-world service is rigidly and meticulously maintained in a venue that some guests find stiff and forbidding, and others absolutely adore. The classic 18th-century Parisian facade has a glass-and-wrought-iron entryway, where guests are greeted by uniformed English-speaking attendants. Hippolyte Jammet founded the Bristol in 1924, installing many valuable antiques and furnishings from the Louis XV and Louis XVI eras. Bedrooms are opulently furnished, either with antiques or well-made reproductions, inlaid wood, bronze, and crystal, Oriental carpets, and original oil paintings. Each room is renovated and freshened every 3 years.

Dining/Diversions: The Restaurant d'Été (Summer Restaurant), set within a greenhouse-style room overlooking the garden, is open from April through October, and the richly paneled Restaurant d'Hiver (Winter Restaurant) is open the rest of the year. Tea and drinks are served either at the hushed and sometimes irritatingly reverent Bristol Bar or in the garden.

Amenities: 24-hour room service, business center with translation services, hair-dressing salon, massage parlor, sauna, conference rooms, lobby bar and cocktail lounge, heated indoor swimming pool, rooftop solarium with a view of Sacré Coeur (open daily from 6:30am to 10:30pm.)

EXPENSIVE

Hôtel Beau Manoir. 6 rue de l'Arcade, 75008 Paris. ☎ **800/528-1234** in the U.S. and Canada, or 01-42-66-03-07. Fax 01-42-68-03-00. www.paris-hotels-charm.com. E-mail: bm@paris-hotels-charm.com. 32 units. A/C MINIBAR TV TEL. 1,200 F ($204) double; 1,600 F ($272) suite. Rates include breakfast. AE, DC, MC, V. Métro: Madeleine.

Open since 1994, this four-star hotel has a 19th-century feel. The lobby is like a private living room, with walnut reproductions of 18th- and 19th-century antiques, Aubusson tapestries, and fresh flowers. Breakfast is served beneath the chiseled vaults

Hotels near Place Charles-de-Gaulle

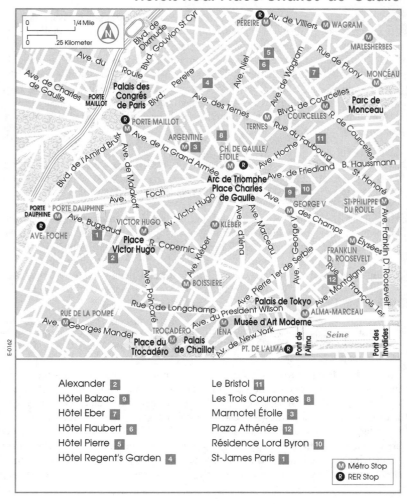

Alexander 2
Hôtel Balzac 9
Hôtel Eber 7
Hôtel Flaubert 6
Hôtel Pierre 5
Hôtel Regent's Garden 4

Le Bristol 11
Les Trois Couronnes 8
Marmotel Étoile 3
Plaza Athénée 12
Résidence Lord Byron 10
St-James Paris 1

M Métro Stop
R RER Stop

of a very old stone cellar. The guest rooms are charming and well accessorized, ranging in size from small to spacious. Each is soundproof, with a safe for valuables. Baths are in marble, with thick towels. The suites often have exposed beams or sloping garret-style ceilings.

Amenities: Limited room service from 7am to 7pm. A receptionist/concierge can arrange most things within reason.

Hôtel Concorde St-Lazare. 108 rue St-Lazare, 75008 Paris. ☎ **800/888-4747** in the U.S. outside New York State and Canada, 212/752-3900 in New York State, 0171/630-1704 in London, or 01-40-08-44-44. Fax 01-42-93-01-20. www.concordestlazare-paris.com. E-mail: stlazare@concordestlazare-paris.com. 300 units. A/C MINIBAR TV TEL. 1,450–2,500 F ($246.50–$425) double; 2,800–6,000 F ($476–$1,020) suite. AE, DC, MC, V. Parking 150 F ($25.50). Métro: St-Lazare.

Across from the St-Lazare rail station, this hotel—the best in the area—was built in 1889 as lodging for the visitors who flocked to the Universal Exposition. During the late 1990s, each of the guest rooms was elevated to modern standards of comfort and redecorated. Many rooms (medium-size to quite large) have high ceilings, especially those on the lower floors, which also have double-glazed windows to cut down on the noise. Beds are plush and comfortable.

Dining/Diversions: The hotel has a room devoted to French billiards—the only room of its kind in any Paris hotel. There's an American bar, **Le Golden Black;** the **Café Terminus,** with daily brasserie service from noon to 11pm; and the **Bistrot 108,** which serves provincial dishes and great vintages you can order by the glass.

Amenities: Concierge, 24-hour room service, baby-sitting, laundry, valet, currency exchange.

MODERATE

Hôtel Queen Mary. 9 rue Greffulhe, 75008 Paris. ☎ **01-42-66-40-50.** Fax 01-42-66-94-92. E-mail: hotelqueenmary@wanadoo.fr 36 units. A/C MINIBAR TV TEL. 755–975 F ($128.35–$165.75) double; 1,350 F ($229.50) suite. AE, DC, MC, V. Parking 80 F ($13.60). Métro: Madeleine or Havre-Caumartin.

Meticulously renovated both inside and out, this hotel was built around the turn of the century. It's graced with an iron-and-glass canopy, ornate wrought iron, and the kind of detailing normally reserved for more expensive hotels. The public rooms have touches of greenery and reproductions of mid-19th-century antiques; each guest room has an upholstered headboard, comfortable beds, and mahogany furnishings, plus a carafe of sherry. All the rooms, ranging from small to medium in size, were fully renovated in 1998. Bathrooms have a tub and shower combination.

✪ **Résidence Lord Byron.** 5 rue de Chateaubriand, 75008 Paris. ☎ **01-43-59-89-98.** Fax 01-42-89-46-04. www.leisureplan.com. 31 units. MINIBAR TV TEL. 870–970 F ($147.90–$164.90) double; from 1,340 F ($227.80) suite. AE, DC, MC, V. Parking 75 F ($12.75). Métro: George V. RER: Etoile.

Just off the Champs-Elysées on a curving street of handsome buildings, Lord Byron may not be as grand as other hotels in the neighborhood, but it is affordable. Correct, unassuming, and a bit staid, it's exactly what repeat clients want and expect: a sense of luxury, solitude, and understatement. It remains a good value for the upscale 8th arrondissement, and is a fine choice for families. Some of the city's major monuments are only a 10-minute walk away. Rooms are small to medium in size. Bathrooms are small, with a tub and shower combination (or else only shower). If you choose to have breakfast at the hotel, you can order it in the dining room or in a shaded inner garden.

INEXPENSIVE

Hôtel Opal. 19 rue Tronchet, 75008 Paris. ☎ **01-42-65-77-97.** Fax 01-49-24-06-58. www.hotels.fr/opal. E-mail: h_opal@club-internet.fr. 36 units. A/C MINIBAR TV TEL. 590–730 F ($100.30–$124.10) double. Extra bed 100 F ($18). AE, DC, V. Parking 120 F ($20.40) nearby. Métro: Madeleine.

This rejuvenated hotel is a real find in the heart of Paris, behind the Madeleine and near the Opéra Garnier. The guest rooms are somewhat cramped but very clean and comfortable, and many of them are air-conditioned. Those on the top floor are reached by a narrow staircase; some have skylights. Most rooms have twin brass beds with decent mattresses. Compact bathrooms have shower stalls and hair dryers. Reception will make arrangements for parking at a nearby garage.

9TH & 10TH ARRONDISSEMENTS (OPÉRA GARNIER/ GARE DU NORD)
INEXPENSIVE

Hôtel de la Tour d'Auvergne. 10 rue de la Tour d'Auvergne. 75009 Paris. ☎ **01-48-78-61-60.** Fax 01-49-95-99-00. 24 units. TV TEL. 550–750 F ($93.50–$127.50) double. AE, DC, MC, V. Parking 100 F ($17). Métro: Cadet or Gare du Nord.

You wouldn't know it from the exterior, but the building that contains this hotel was erected before Baron Haussmann reconfigured the avenues of Paris around 1870. Later, Modigliani rented a room here for 6 months, and the staff will tell you that both Victor Hugo and Rodin lived on this street for brief periods before moving on to greater glory. The interior was long ago modernized into a glossy internationalism, with touches of paneling and marble. The comfortable bedrooms are meticulously coordinated, though the small decorative canopies over the headboards make them feel cluttered, particularly after you put down all your luggage and travel gear. Although the views over the courtyard in back are uninspired, even gloomy, some clients request a rear-view room for its relative quiet. Every year five rooms are renovated, so the comfort level is kept at a high standard. The small bathrooms have a tub and shower combination and a hair dryer.

Hôtel William's du Pré. 3 rue Mayran, 75009 Paris. ☎ **01-48-78-68-35.** Fax 01-45-26-08-70. 30 units. TV TEL. 480–515 F ($81.60–$87.55) double. AE, MC, V. Parking 60 F ($10.20). Métro: Cadet.

Front bedrooms overlook one of the arrondissement's largest public gardens, a verdant oasis in an otherwise highly congested and commercial neighborhood. Set behind a severe, dignified, six-story facade, this 19th-century building was bought by a citywide chain of unpretentious hotels and renovated in 1992. Bedrooms are simple, clean, and uncomplicated, although the decor is a bit cold and uninspired. Each is soundproof thanks to double window glazing, and each has a safe and hair dryer. Rooms that open onto the fifth and second floors have small wrought-iron balconies. The hotel offers breakfast in a cellar room that shows vestiges of the original masonry.

11TH & 12TH ARRONDISSEMENTS (OPÉRA BASTILLE/ BOIS DE VINCENNES)
MODERATE

Le Pavillon Bastille. 65 rue de Lyon, 75012 Paris. ☎ **01-43-43-65-65.** Fax 01-43-43-96-52. www.france-paris.com. E-mail: hotel-pavillon@akamail.com. 24 units. A/C MINIBAR TV TEL. 815–955 F ($138.55–$162.35) double; 1,375 F ($233.75) suite. AE, DC, V. Parking 85 F ($14.45). Métro: Bastille.

For those who want to stay in this increasingly fashionable district, this is the finest choice. Hardly your cozy little backstreet Paris digs, it's a bold, brassy, and innovative hotel. The 1991-vintage town house is situated across from the Bastille Opera House and about a block south of place de la Bastille. A 17th-century fountain graces the courtyard between the hotel and the street. The rooms provide twin or double beds with firm mattresses, partially mirrored walls, and comfortable, contemporary built-in furniture. The English-speaking staff is friendly and efficient, offering room service, baby-sitting, and laundry and valet service. Breakfast is served below the ceiling vaults of the cellar. Partly because of its location near Paris's hottest new classical music venue and partly because it emphasizes middle-bracket comfort and practicality, the hotel derives at least 70% of its business from foreign visitors, especially Americans, Australians, and Japanese. If you're looking for a bargain, the cheapest rooms at 815 F ($138.55) have the same size and configuration as the more expensive *chambres privilegées,* priced at 955 F ($162.35). The extra cost gets you added amenities such as slippers, better cosmetics in the bathrooms, fruit baskets, and a complimentary bottle of wine upon arrival. Nice extras, but not at that price. Bathrooms are efficiently organized and well equipped.

INEXPENSIVE

Libertel Croix de Malte. 5 rue de Malte, 75011 Paris. ☎ **01-48-05-09-36.** Fax 01-43-57-02-54. 29 units. TV TEL. 570 F ($96.90) double. AE, MC, V. Métro: Oberkampf.

A member of a nationwide chain of mostly two-star hotels, this is a clean, well-maintained choice. Business here has been increasing thanks to a radical overhaul in 1992 and its proximity to both the Opéra de la Bastille and the Marais. The hotel consists of buildings of two and three floors, one of which is accessible through a shared breakfast room. There's a landscaped courtyard in back with access to a lobby bar. The cozy bedrooms have brightly painted modern furniture accented with vivid green, blue, and pink patterns that flash back to the psychedelia of the 1960s. Rooms are small with reasonably good mattresses. Bathrooms are cramped but tidily maintained.

Nouvel Hôtel. 24 av. du Bel-Air, 75012 Paris. ☎ **01-43-43-01-81.** Fax 01-43-44-64-13. 28 units. TV TEL. 450–600 F ($76.50–$102) double. AE, DC, MC, V. Métro: Nation.

This hotel evokes the French provinces far more than the urban landscapes of Paris. Surrounded by greenery, and set within a neighborhood that's rarely visited by tourists, the hotel conjures a calmer day, when parts of Paris still seemed like small country towns. The beauty of the place is most visible from the inside courtyard, site of warm-weather breakfasts, the only meal served here. Winding hallways lead to small bedrooms that overlook either the courtyard or, less appealingly, the street. Each contains flowered fabrics and old-fashioned furniture. Bathrooms are small.

Résidence Alhambra. 11 bis, 13 rue de Malte, 75011 Paris. ☎ **01-47-00-35-52.** Fax 01-43-57-98-75. www.hotelalhambra.fr. E-mail: serviceclient@hotelalhambra.fr. 58 units. TV TEL. 320–350 F ($54.40–$59.50) double; 450–490 F ($76.50–$83.30) triple. AE, DC, MC, V. Métro: Oberkampf.

Named for the famous cabaret and vaudeville theater that once stood nearby, the Alhambra was built in the 1800s. A radical renovation in 1989 plus additional upgrades in the late 1990s gave the hotel its comfortable, contemporary format. The hotel rises five stories (10 rooms per floor). In the rear garden, its two-story chalet offers eight additional bedrooms. The thrifty and rather small accommodations are bland but comfortable, each outfitted in a monochromatic pastel scheme that differs from floor to floor. All the bedrooms have been recently renovated, with new beds and firm mattresses, plus refurbished baths with a tub and shower combination and hair dryers. Although they only serve breakfast, a wide array of restaurants lies within the vicinity of the nearby place de la République and the place de la Bastille.

16TH ARRONDISSEMENT (TROCADÉRO/BOIS DE BOULOGNE)
VERY EXPENSIVE

Saint-James Paris. 43 av. Bugeaud, 75016 Paris. ☎ **800/525-4800** in the U.S. and Canada, or 01-44-05-81-81. Fax 01-44-05-81-82. stjames@club-internet.fr. 48 units. A/C MINIBAR TV TEL. 2,000 F ($340) double; from 2,250 F ($382.50) suite. AE, DC, MC, V. Métro: Porte Dauphine. RER: Avenue Foch.

In an 1892 stone building inspired by a château in the French countryside, the Saint James is as grand as any of the very expensive hotels within the more visible (and more central) neighborhoods of Paris. Set among the staid and aggressively luxurious residences of the 16th arrondissement, staying in the hotel gives you access to the otherwise private restaurant, bar, and fitness center, which you'll share with the aristocratic Parisian members. You're likely to find it intimate, discreet, and warm, even if exclusivity (and snobbery) are part of its image. Rooms are spacious, the older ones featuring art deco detailing, the more newly renovated ones with sleek contemporary styling. Rooms have private safes. Baths are equipped with bidets, a shower and tub combination, and thick towels.

Finding Your Way

For a map of 16th- and 17th- arrondissement hotels, turn to the "Hotels Near Place Charles-de-Gaulle" page 65.

Dining: The hotel has a restaurant open daily for lunch, serving classic French cuisine. The bar contains a polished-oak library with some 10,000 leather-bound books.

Amenities: 24-hour room service, health club with Jacuzzi and sauna, billiard room.

EXPENSIVE

Alexander. 102 av. Victor Hugo, 75116 Paris. ☎ **800/888-4747** or 212/752-3900 in the U.S. and Canada, or 01-45-53-64-65. Fax 01-45-53-12-51. 62 units. MINIBAR TV TEL. 890–1,490 F ($151.30–$253.30) double; 1,800–2,200 F ($306–$374) suite. AE, DC, MC, V. Parking 100 F ($17) across the street. Métro: Victor Hugo.

Though it functioned as a simple pension throughout the 1950s, the hotel was radically upgraded in the 1970s and became the four-star property you'll see today. Rich paneling in the reception hall immediately assures guests they will be met with luxury, and bedrooms cement the deal with fabric stretched over the walls for added ambience, warmth, and soundproofing. Half of the rooms face a well-planted, quiet courtyard. About a dozen bedrooms are renovated every year, and comfort is of a very high standard. Most beds are twins. Bathrooms are beautifully maintained, with thick towels and a tub and shower combination.

Dining/Diversions: A hotel bar open daily from 7am to 9:30pm serves sandwiches and light snacks. Room service is available from 7am to 10pm.

Amenities: One-day laundry service. A receptionist/concierge can help meet most needs.

17TH ARRONDISSEMENT (PARC MONCEAU)
MODERATE

Hôtel Eber. 18 rue Léon Jost, 75017 Paris. ☎ **01-46-22-60-70.** Fax 01-47-63-01-01. 18 units. A/C TV TEL. 660–710 F ($112.20–$120.70) double; 1,150–1,460 F ($195.50–$248.20) suite. AE, DC, MC, V. Parking 100 F ($17). Métro: Courcelles.

Hidden on a quiet side street, this turn-of-the-century three-star hotel is comfortably rustic, with exposed stone and wood paneling, paneled ceilings, and a Renaissance-style fireplace. Bedrooms are comfortable, and most have an armchair for reading. The courtyard provides a quiet oasis for breakfast and afternoon tea.

Hôtel Regent's Garden. 6 rue Pierre D emours, 75017 Paris. ☎ **01-45-74-07-30.** Fax 01-40-55-01-42. TEL. www.bestwestern.com. E-mail: hotel.regents.garden@wonadoo.fr. 39 units. A/C MINIBAR TV TEL. 810–1,600 F ($137.70–$272) double. AE, DC, MC, V. Parking 55 F ($9.35). Métro: Ternes or Charles-de-Gaulle-Etoile.

The Regent's Garden has a proud heritage: Napoléon III built the stately château for his physician. It's near the convention center and minutes from the Arc de Triomphe. There are two gardens, one with ivy-covered walls and umbrella tables—a perfect place to meet other guests. The interior resembles a classically and comfortably decorated country house. Fluted columns mark the entryway, which leads to a casual mixture of comfortable furniture in the lobby. The rooms have flower prints on the walls; bedspreads; traditional French furniture; tall soundproof windows with light, airy curtains; and reasonably comfortable furniture and beds. Baths are compact with tidy maintenance and adequate shelf space.

INEXPENSIVE

Hôtel Flaubert. 19 rue Rennequin, 75017 Paris. ☎ **01-46-22-44-35.** Fax 01-43-80-32-34. 36 units. MINIBAR TV TEL. 480–550 F ($81.60–$93.50) double. AE, DC, V. Métro: Ternes or Charles-de-Gaulle-Etoile.

Rooms here are appealing, clean, and well maintained, and the staff grew accustomed long ago to handling whatever problems their international guests were able to create. Though the lush climbing plants in the courtyard overshadow the rooms, they are nonetheless comfortable and, particularly for those beneath the mansard's eaves, cozy. Terra-cotta tiles and bentwood furniture in the public areas make for an efficient if not lushly comfortable setting for breakfast. Bedrooms are small to medium in size, with comfortable beds—most often twins. Bathrooms are small but tidy, with a shower stall.

Les Trois Couronnes. 30 rue de l'Arc de Triomphe, 75017 Paris. ☎ **01-43-80-46-81.** Fax 01-46-22-53-96. www.easynet.fr/hotel3s/hotel.htm. E-mail: hotel3s@easynet.fr. 20 units. MINIBAR TV TEL. 455–695 F ($77.35–$118.15) double. AE, DC, MC, V. Parking 100 F ($17). Métro: Charles-de-Gaulle-Etoile.

This prestigious older hotel in the business hub of Paris is within easy access to the Métro and many of the city's attractions. With its blend of art deco and art nouveau, it was radically redecorated and upgraded in 1995 and is under an enthusiastic new management. The cheerful rooms, small and old-fashioned but comfortable, take in the surrounding area. Baths are a little cramped but have adequate shelf space. There is a small bar and a restaurant adjacent to the lobby. Laundry service is available.

Marmotel Étoile. 34 av. de la Grande Armée, 75017 Paris. ☎ **01-47-63-57-26.** Fax 01-45-74-25-27. 23 units. MINIBAR TV TEL. 460–480 F ($78.20–$81.60) double. AE, MC, V. Métro: Argentine.

This hotel is set on a relatively inconvenient side of the place de l'Etoile, and you have to ford a roaring river of traffic to get to the nearby Champs-Elysées. Rooms are clean and simple—small but comfortable. The ones overlooking the carefully landscaped, flagstone-covered courtyard benefit from an unexpected oasis of calm; those fronting the avenue's traffic are less peaceful. Bathrooms are cramped but still have adequate shelf space.

18TH ARRONDISSEMENT (MONTMARTRE)
VERY EXPENSIVE

✪ **Terrass Hôtel.** 12-14 rue Joseph de Maistre, 75018 Paris. ☎ **800/344-1212** in the U.S. and Canada, or 01-46-06-72-85. Fax 01-42-52-29-11. E-mail: terrass@francenet.fr. 101 units. MINIBAR TV TEL. 1,320–1,470 F ($224.40–$249.90) double; 1,710 F ($290.70) suite. Rates include breakfast. AE, DC, MC, V. Métro: Place de Clichy or Blanche.

Built in 1913, and richly renovated into a plush but traditional style in 1991, this is the only four-star hotel on the Butte Montmartre. In an area filled with some of the seediest hotels in Paris, this place is easily in a class of its own. Its main advantage is its location amid Montmartre's bohemian atmosphere (or what's left of it). Staffed with English-speaking employees, it has a large marble-floored lobby ringed with blond oak paneling and accented with 18th-century antiques and even older tapestries. The bedrooms are high-ceilinged, cozy, and well upholstered, and often have views.

Dining/Diversions: An elegant street-level restaurant and a seventh-floor summer-only garden terrace with bar and food service and sweeping views of many of Paris's most important monuments. In colder weather, the hotel's **Lobby Bar** offers live piano music and a working fireplace.

Amenities: Foreign exchange, car rentals, tour desk, laundry/dry cleaning, conference facilities.

INEXPENSIVE

Hôtel Ermitage. 24 rue Lamarck, 75018 Paris. ☎ **01-42-64-79-22.** Fax 01-42-64-10-33. 12 units. TEL. 440–500 F ($74.80–$85) double. No credit cards. Parking 60 F ($10.20). Métro: Lamarck-Caulaincourt.

Erected in 1870 of chiseled limestone in the Napoléon III style, this hotel's facade might remind you of a perfectly proportioned, small-scale villa. It's set in a calm and quiet area—just a brief uphill stroll from the Basilica of Sacré-Coeur—where all the neighbors seem to have known each other for generations. Views extend out over Paris, and there's a verdant garden in the back courtyard. The small bedrooms evoke a countryside auberge with exposed ceiling beams, flowered wallpaper, and casement windows that open onto the garden or onto a street seemingly airlifted from the respectable provinces. Mattresses are reasonably comfortable. Only breakfast is served.

2 Left Bank

We'll begin with the most centrally located arrondissements on the Left Bank, then work our way through the more outlying neighborhoods.

5TH ARRONDISSEMENT (LATIN QUARTER)
MODERATE

Grand Hôtel St-Michel. 19 rue Cujas, 75005 Paris. ☎ **01-46-33-33-02.** Fax 01-40-46-96-33. www.123france.com. E-mail: grand.hotel.st.michel@wanadoo.fr. 45 units. MINIBAR TV TEL. 890 F ($151.30) double; 1,400 F ($238) suite. AE, DC, MC, V. Métro: Cluny-La Sorbonne. RER: Luxembourg or St-Michel.

Built in the 19th century, this hotel is larger and more businesslike than many of the smaller town house–style inns nearby. It basks in the reflected glow of the Brazilian dissident Georges Amado, whose memoirs (released in 1996) recorded his 2-year literary sojourn in one of the rooms. In 1997, the hotel completed a renovation and moved from two- to three-star status. The changes enlarged some rooms, lowering their ceilings and adding such modern amenities as minibars, but retained old-fashioned touches like wrought-iron balconies (fifth floor only). Public rooms are particularly lavish and tasteful, outfitted with oil portraits, rich upholsteries, and a sense of early- 19th-century grandeur. Rooms on the sixth (uppermost) floor have interesting views over the rooftops. Bedrooms have been overhauled and fitted with new mattresses. The bathrooms are as small as ever, but are tidily maintained.

Hôtel Abbatial St-Germain. 46 bd. St-Germain. 75005 Paris. ☎ **01-46-34-02-12.** Fax 01-43-25-47-73. www.abbatial.com. E-mail: abbatial@hotellerie.net. 43 units. A/C MINIBAR TV TEL. 750–850 F ($127.50–$144.50) double. AE, MC, V. Parking 100 F ($17). Métro: Maubert-Mutualité.

The origins of this hotel run deep: Interior renovations have revealed such 17th-century touches as dovecotes and massive oak beams. In the early 1990s, a radical restoration brought the six stories of rooms up to modern and smallish but comfortable standards. The public areas are especially appealing. The guest rooms are furnished in faux Louis XVI. Bathrooms are small. All windows are double glazed, and the fifth- and sixth-floor rooms enjoy views over Notre-Dame. Breakfast is served beneath the vaulted ceilings of the stone-sided cellar.

Hôtel Agora St-Germain. 42 rue des Bernardins, 75005 Paris. ☎ **01-46-34-13-00.** Fax 01-46-34-75-05. 39 units. A/C MINIBAR TV TEL. 720–820 F ($122.40–$139.40) double; 960 F ($163.20) triple. AE, DC, MC, V. Parking 120 F ($20.40). Métro: Maubert-Mutualité.

Hotels in the Heart of the Left Bank

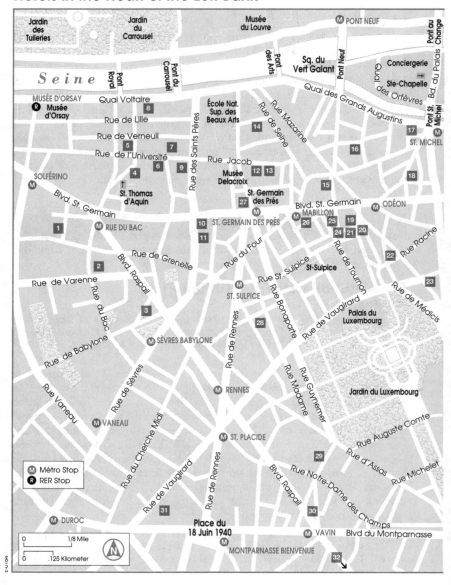

One of the best of the neighborhood's moderately priced choices, this hotel occupies a building constructed in the early 1600s, probably to house a group of guardsmen protecting the brother of the king at his lodgings nearby. It's in the heart of the artistic and historic section of Paris and offers compact, soundproof guest rooms, each comfortably, although not particularly fashionably, furnished. Towels are relatively small and thin, and mattresses are adequately comfortable. Room service is provided daily from 7:30 to 10:30am.

Hôtel des Arènes. 51 rue Monge, 75005 Paris. ☎ **01-43-25-09-26.** Fax 01-43-25-79-56. 52 units. MINIBAR TV TEL. 450–700 F ($76.50–$119) double. AE, MC, V. Parking 80 F ($13.60). Métro: Monge or Cardinal-Lemoine.

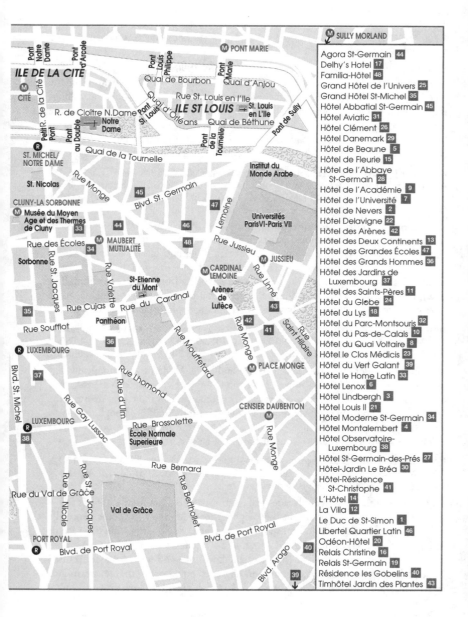

Set within a 19th-century structure whose chiseled stone facade evokes fine old traditions, this hotel offers well-maintained modern bedrooms. Many in back overlook the tree-dotted ruins of Paris's ancient Roman arena, unearthed in 1865 during the construction of the surrounding labyrinth of streets. Breakfast is served in a simple, windowless room in the hotel's cellar. The staff is overworked and somewhat distracted, and the place a bit anonymous, but the location is appealing, and the rooms are practical and comfortable. Bedrooms range from small to medium in size. Each unit has a compact private bath with a shower stall and adequate shelf space.

Hôtel des Grands Hommes. 17 place du Panthéon, 75005 Paris. ☎ **01-46-34-19-60.** Fax 01-43-26-67-32. 32 units. A/C MINIBAR TV TEL. 700–600 F ($119–$102) double;

1,200 F ($204) suite. AE, DC, MC, V. Parking 80 F ($13.60). Métro: Cardinal-Lemoine or Luxembourg.

Built in the 18th century and renovated in the early 1990s, this six-story hotel offers direct profile views (from many rooms) of the Panthéon. All but a handful of the accommodations have exposed ceiling beams and pleasantly old-fashioned furnishings that sometimes include brass beds. The rooms on the second and fifth floors have small balconies; those on the fifth and sixth floors have the best views; and those with the most space are on the ground floor. Towels are small and thin, and mattresses are comfortable but not plush. The welcome is charming, and the staff speaks English.

Hôtel des Jardins du Luxembourg. 5 impasse Royer-Collard, 75005 Paris. ☎ **01-40-46-08-88.** Fax 01-40-46-02-28. www.globe-market.com/w/75005jardlux.htm. 25 units. A/C MINIBAR TV TEL. 795–840 F ($135.15–$142.80) double. AE, DC, MC, V. Parking 85 F ($14.45). Métro: Cluny-La Sorbonne. RER: Luxembourg.

Built during Baron Haussmann's 19th-century overhaul of Paris, this hotel boasts an imposing facade of honey-colored stone accented with ornate iron balconies. The interior is outfitted in strong, clean lines, often with groupings of vintage art deco furnishings. The high-ceilinged guest rooms, some with Provençal tiles and ornate moldings, are well maintained, the size in general ranging from small to medium. Best of all, they overlook a quiet dead-end alley, ensuring relatively peaceful nights. Some have balconies overlooking the rooftops. Mattresses are comfortable but not plush.

Hôtel Moderne St-Germain. 33 rue des Ecoles, 75005 Paris. ☎ **01-43-54-37-78.** Fax 01-43-29-91-31. 45 units. TV TEL. 590–840 F ($100.30–$142.80) double; 750–1,050 F ($127.50–$178.50) triple. AE, DC, MC, V. Parking 150 F ($25.50). Métro: Maubert-Mutualité.

Built in the heart of the Latin Quarter, the Grand Hôtel Moderne was completely renovated in 1998. Its charming owner, Madame Gibon, welcomes guests warmly. The comfortably furnished bedrooms are spotlessly maintained. In the rooms fronting the rue des Ecoles, double-glazed aluminum windows hush the traffic. Though the rooms are small, this is still one of the better three-star hotels in the neighborhood. Clients enjoy access to the sauna and Jacuzzi at the Hotel Sully next door.

Hôtel Observatoire-Luxembourg. 107 bd. St-Michel. 75005 Paris. ☎ **01-46-34-10-12.** Fax 01-46-33-73-86. 37 units. TV TEL. 780–935 F ($132.60–$158.95) double. AE, DC, V. Métro: Cluny-La Sorbonne. RER: Luxembourg.

The hotel's simple art nouveau facade—tall, narrow, and built around 1900—is something of an architectural oddity in this neighborhood. Many of its rooms, especially those on the fifth and sixth floors, overlook either the Luxembourg Gardens, which lie just across the street, or the nearby Church of St. Jacques. (Room 507, although not the largest, boasts the best view, encompassing both trees and medieval architecture.) Inside, a highly successful 1992 renovation upgraded public areas; they're streamlined and angular but softened by bright colors. Mattresses are a bit older than you might have hoped for, but are nonetheless comfortable.

Bathrooms sport slabs of glossy marble, but the towels are thin. Breakfast is served in the cellar-level dining room.

Hôtel-Résidence St-Christophe. 17 rue Lacépède, 75005 Paris. ☎ **01-43-31-81-54.** Fax 01-43-31-12-54. E-mail: hotelstchristophe@compuserve.com. 31 units. MINIBAR TV TEL. 600 F ($102) double. AE, DC, MC, V. Parking 100 F ($17). Métro: Place-Monge.

This hotel, in one of the Latin Quarter's undiscovered but charming districts, has a gracious English-speaking staff. It was created in 1987 when a derelict hotel was connected to a butcher shop. All the small- to medium-size rooms were successfully renovated in 1998. Millions of francs later, the St-Christophe is inviting and comfortable, with Louis XV–style furniture, wall-to-wall carpeting, and comfortably firm mattresses. The compact bathrooms have adequate shelf space. Breakfast is the only meal served, but the staff offers advice about neighborhood bistros.

INEXPENSIVE

✪ **Familia-Hôtel.** 11 rue des Ecoles, 75005. ☎ **01-43-54-55-27.** Fax 01-43-29-61-77. 30 units. MINIBAR TV TEL. 380–580 F ($64.60–$98.60) double. AE, DC, MC, V. Métro: Jussieu or Maubert-Mutualité.

As the name implies, this is a hotel that has been family run for decades. Many personal touches make the place unique, and it was lavishly renovated in 1998. The walls of 14 rooms are graced with finely executed sepia-colored frescoes of Parisian scenes. Eight rooms have restored stone walls and seven rooms have balconies with delightful views over the Latin Quarter. All rooms have cable TV (with CNN), hair dryers, and high-quality mattresses, making the hotel more comfortable than most in this price category.

Hotel des Grandes Écoles. 75 rue de Cardinal Lemoine, 75005 Paris. ☎ **01-43-26-79-23.** Fax 01-43-25-28-15. 51 units. TEL. 490–670 F ($83.30–$113.90) double. MC, V. Parking 100 F ($17). Metro: Cardinal-Lemoine, Monge.

Few other hotels in the neighborhood offer so much low-key charm at such reasonable prices. It's composed of a trio of high-ceilinged buildings, each interconnected via a sheltered courtyard where singing birds provide a worthy substitute for the TVs deliberately missing from the rooms. Rooms are artfully old-fashioned, with feminine touches that include Laura Ashley–inspired flowered upholsteries and ruffles. Many offer views of a bucolic-looking garden whose trellises and flower beds evoke the countryside. Bathrooms are small but exceedingly well organized, with adequate shelf space, shower stalls, and hair dryers. Thanks to dozens of restaurants in the surrounding rue Mouffetard neighborhood, no one seems to mind the hotel's lack of a restaurant, and when the weather cooperates, breakfast is served in the garden.

✪ **Hôtel Le Home Latin.** 15-17 rue du Sommerard, 75005 Paris. ☎ **01-43-26-25-21.** Fax 01-43-29-87-04. 55 units. TV TEL. 550–650 F ($93.50–$110.50) double. AE, V. Parking 85 F ($14.45). Métro: St-Michel or Maubert-Mutualité.

This is one of the most famous budget hotels in Paris, known since the 1970s for clean and simple lodgings. The blandly functional rooms—streamlined without a lot of frills—were renovated in 1999; some of them have small balconies overlooking the street. The rooms facing the courtyard are quieter than those fronting the street. The elevator doesn't reach beyond the fifth floor, but to make up for the stair climb, the sixth floor's *chambres mansardées* offer a romantic location under the eaves and panoramic views over the rooftops. Bathrooms are sterile-looking and efficient, with thin towels.

Timhôtel Jardin des Plantes. 5 rue Linné, 75005 Paris. ☎ **01-47-07-06-20.** Fax 01-47-07-62-74. www.timhotel.fr. 33 units. TV TEL. 580–650 F ($98.60–$110.50) double. AE, DC, MC, V. Parking 80 F ($13.60). Métro: Jussieu. Bus: 67 or 89.

Opened in 1986 and renovated in 1997, the two-star Timhôtel Jardin des Plantes lies across from the Jardin des Plantes, the botanical gardens created by order of Louis XIII's doctors in 1626 (there are still some 15,000 medicinal herbs in the gardens). Some of the small but well-equipped rooms open onto flowered, sunny terraces. Each has a hair dryer and a relatively comfortable mattress. A vaulted lounge in the basement, a sauna, and ironing facilities are provided. Equipped with an elevator, the hotel has a small roof terrace and a brasserie/snack bar where breakfast is served.

6TH ARRONDISSEMENT (ST-GERMAIN/LUXEMBOURG)
VERY EXPENSIVE
Relais Christine. 3 rue Christine, 75006 Paris. ☎ **01-40-51-60-80.** Fax 01-40-51-60-81. E-mail: relaisch@club-internet.fr. 51 units. A/C MINIBAR TV TEL. 1,800–2,300 F ($306–$391) double; 2,400–4,200 F ($408–$714) duplex or suite. AE, DC, MC, V. Free parking. Métro: Odéon.

Relais Christine welcomes you into what was a 16th-century Augustinian cloister. You enter from a narrow cobblestone street into first a symmetrical courtyard and then an elegant reception area with baroque sculpture and Renaissance antiques. Each guest room is uniquely decorated with wooden beams and Louis XIII–style furnishings. The rooms come in a wide range of styles and shapes, and some are among the most spacious on the Left Bank, with such extras as mirrored closets, plush carpets, thermostats, and in some cases balconies facing the outer courtyard. The least attractive, smallest, and dimmest rooms are those in the interior.

Dining: Off the reception area is a paneled sitting room/bar area ringed with 19th-century portraits and comfortable leather chairs. The breakfast room is in a vaulted cellar; the ancient well and massive central stone column are part of the cloister's former kitchen.

Amenities: 24-hour room service, laundry, baby-sitting.

EXPENSIVE

✪ **Hôtel de Fleurie.** 32-34 rue Grégoire-de-Tours, 75006 Paris. ☎ **01-53-73-70-00.** Fax 01-53-73-70-20. www.hotel-de-fleurie.tm.fr. E-mail: bonjour@hotel-de-fleurie.tm.fr. 29 units. A/C MINIBAR TV TEL. 930–1,200 F ($158.10–$204.00) double; 1,550–1,650 F ($263.50–$280.50) family room. Children 12 and under stay free in parents' room. AE, DC, MC, V. Métro: Odéon.

Just off boulevard St-Germain on a colorful little street, the Fleurie is one of the best of the "new" old hotels. About half the rooms and bathrooms were renovated in 1999. The hotel has a facade that's studded with spotlit statuary, recapturing a 17th-century elegance. The stone walls have been exposed in the reception salon, where you check in at a refectory desk. An elevator takes you to well-furnished bedrooms, each with a comfortable bed and a safe. Many of them have elaborate curtains, reproductions of antiques, and a sense of late- 19th-century charm. This hotel has long been a family favorite because of the interconnecting doors that open between certain pairs of its rooms, thereby creating safe havens the hotel refers to as *chambres familiales.*

Dining: Only breakfast is served, although there is a small bar.

Amenities: Car rentals arranged, room service, dry cleaning, laundry.

✪ **Hôtel de l'Abbaye St-Germain.** 10 rue Cassette, 75006 Paris. ☎ **01-45-44-38-11.** Fax 01-45-48-07-86. www.hotel-abbaye.com. E-mail: hotel.abbaye@wanadoo.fr. 46 units. A/C TV TEL. 1,080–1,600 F ($183.60–$272) double; 1,950–2,000 F ($331.50–$340) suite. Rates include continental breakfast. AE, MC, V. Métro: St-Sulpice.

Built early in the 18th century as a convent for the Eglise St-Germain, this place later became a cheap youth hostel. It's since been transformed into a charming boutique hotel whose brightly colored rooms have traditional furniture like you'd find in a private club, and touches of sophisticated flair. In front is a small garden, and in back is a verdant courtyard featuring a fountain, raised flower beds, and masses of ivy and climbing vines. If you don't mind the expense, one of the most charming rooms has a terrace overlooking the upper floors of neighboring buildings.

Dining: Only breakfast is served, but the public areas include a trio of salons and a bar.

Amenities: Car rentals arranged, concierge, room service, dry cleaning, laundry.

La Villa. 29 rue Jacob, 75006 Paris. ☎ **01-43-26-60-00.** Fax 01-46-34-63-63. 32 units. A/C MINIBAR TV TEL. 1,250–1,800 F ($212.50–$306) double; from 2,000 F ($340) suite. AE, MC, V. Métro: St-Germain-des-Prés.

The Centre Pompidou of small hotels. From the outside, the five-story facade of this hotel resembles those of many of the other buildings in the neighborhood. Inside, however, the decor is a stripped-down, ultramodern, minimalist creation that thoroughly rejects all traditional tenets of French aesthetics. Public areas and bedrooms contain Bauhaus-like furniture; angular lines in the lobby are somewhat softened with bouquets of leaves and flowers. Most unusual are the bathrooms, whose shimmering stainless steel, pink, black, or beige marble, and chrome surfaces are either post-Sputnik or postmodern, depending on your frame of reference. Mattresses are firm and comfortable.

Diversions: The cellar-level jazz club offers live music nightly Monday through Saturday.

Amenities: 24-hour room service, laundry/dry cleaning.

✪ **L'Hôtel.** 13 rue des Beaux-Arts, 75006 Paris. ☎ **01-44-41-99-00.** Fax 01-43-25-64-81. www.l-hotel.com. E-mail: reservation@l-hotel.com. 26 units. A/C MINIBAR TV TEL. 800–2,800 F ($136–$476) double; from 3,000 F ($510) suite. AE, DC, MC, V. Métro: St-Germain-des-Prés.

This boutique hotel was once a 19th-century fleabag called the Hôtel d'Alsace, whose major distinction was that Oscar Wilde died here, broke and in despair. But today's guests aren't anywhere near poverty row: Show-business and fashion celebrities march through the lobby. L'Hôtel was the creation of the late French actor Guy-Louis Duboucheron, who established an atmosphere of supersophistication. You'll feel like a movie star while bathing in your rosy-pink marble tub. An eclectic collection of antiques pops up throughout the hotel. The spacious 2,800 F ($476) room contains the original furnishings and memorabilia of Mistinguette, France's legendary stage star, a frequent performer with Maurice Chevalier and his on-again, off-again lover. Her pedestal bed is set in the middle of the room, surrounded everywhere by mirrors, as she liked to see how she looked or "performed" at all times of the day and night! Rooms vary widely in size, style, and price, from quite small to deluxe. (Elizabeth Taylor found all the rooms too small for her trunks.) All rooms have nonworking fireplaces, private safes, and fabric-covered walls. The relatively small marble baths are well equipped, with thick towels and a bidet; however, about half of them are tiny tubless nooks.

Dining: Other than breakfast, afternoon tea, and room service, there's no conventional dining within the hotel. Breakfast and tea are served in a greenhouse-style room loaded with plants.

Amenities: Concierge, room service daily from 6:30am to 11pm, baby-sitting, laundry, and valet services.

Odéon-Hôtel. 3 rue de l'Odéon, 75006 Paris. ☎ **01-43-25-90-67.** Fax 01-43-25-55-98. 33 units. A/C TV TEL. 800–1,412 F ($136–$240.05) double. AE, DC, MC, V. Parking 80 F ($13.60). Métro: Odéon.

Reminiscent of a modernized Norman country inn, the Odéon offers charming rustic touches such as exposed beams, rough stone walls, high crooked ceilings, and tapestries mixed with contemporary fabrics, mirrored ceilings, and black leather furnishings. Conveniently located near both the Théâtre de l'Odéon and boulevard St-Germain, the Odéon stands on the first street in Paris to have pavements (1779) and gutters. By the turn of the century, this area, which had drawn the original Shakespeare & Co. bookshop to no. 12 rue de l'Odéon, began attracting such writers as Gertrude Stein and her coterie. Rooms are small to medium size, with comfortable mattresses.

Relais St-Germain. 9 carrefour de l'Odéon, 75006 Paris. ☎ **01-43-29-12-05.** Fax 01-46-33-45-30. 22 units. A/C MINIBAR TV TEL. 1,600–1,850 F ($272–$314.50) double; 2,100 F ($357) suite. Rates include breakfast. AE, DC, MC, V. Métro: Odéon.

Adapted from a 17th-century building, St-Germain is an oasis of charm and comfort. It's comparable to the Relais Christine, its nearest competitor, but with a more accommodating staff. The decor is a medley of traditional and modern, the cozy interior evoking a charming provincial house. All the necessary amenities have been tucked in under the beams, including safes and soundproofing. Four rooms feature a kitchenette, and two of the suites come with a terrace. Mattresses were replaced in 1998.

Dining: The **Comptoir du Relais,** a bistro/wine bar, is a cozy, well-managed retreat where you can order such dishes as potted goose pâté, pork-and-pistachio sausage, and any number of sandwiches with traditional French bread.

Amenities: Limited concierge services, dry cleaning/laundry, newspaper delivery upon request, twice-daily maid service.

MODERATE

Grand Hôtel de l'Univers. 6 rue Grégoire-de-Tours, 75006 Paris. ☎ **01-43-29-37-00.** Fax 01-40-51-06-45. 34 units. A/C MINIBAR TV TEL. 890–900 F ($151.30–$153) double. AE, DC, MC, V. Métro: Odéon.

In the 1400s, this was home to a family of the emergent bourgeoisie. The hotel's main competitor—on the same street near the Luxembourg Palace—is the Hôtel de Fleurie, which has a slight edge. But de l'Univers still exudes charm and tranquillity. The pleasantly renovated rooms are cramped but well maintained. Some of them provide a panoramic view over the crooked rooftops of the surrounding neighborhood. La Bonbonnière (the Candy Box) is a red-and-white confection of a bedroom. All rooms have satellite TV reception and private safe. Amenities include room service from 7 to 11am and newspaper delivery upon request. Breakfast is served in the cellar beneath the 500-year-old stone vaults. There is also a small and not particularly impressive bar that serves guests only. For reasons known only to them, Michelin consistently ignores this worthy hotel.

Hôtel Aviatic. 105 rue de Vaugirard, 75006 Paris. ☎ **01-45-44-38-21.** Fax 01-45-49-35-83. www.aviatic.fr. E-mail: parishotel@aol.com. 43 units. A/C MINIBAR TV TEL. 680–1,180 F ($115.60–$200.60) double. AE, DC, MC, V. Parking 140 F ($23.80). Métro: Montparnasse-Bienvenue.

This is a bit of old Paris, with a modest inner courtyard and a vine-covered lattice on the walls. It has been a family-run hotel for a century. The reception lounge, with marble columns, brass chandeliers, antiques, and a petit salon, provides an attractive setting. It doesn't have the decorative flair of some of the other 6th arrondissement hotels we've listed, but it offers good comfort and a warm ambience. Completely remodeled, it's in an interesting section of Montparnasse, surrounded by cafes frequented by artists, writers, and jazz musicians. Rooms were renovated in stages throughout the 1990s, and each has a safe and comfortable beds. The staff speaks English.

Hôtel Danemark. 21 rue Vavin, 75006 Paris. ☎ **01-43-26-93-78.** Fax 01-46-34-66-06. 15 units. MINIBAR TV TEL. 640–850 F ($108.80–$144.50) double. AE, DC, MC, V. Métro: Vavin or Notre-Dame-des-Champs. RER: Port-Royal.

Anyone who traveled in Paris during the 1960s might remember this place as a battered hostel, but it was taken over by a hardworking family and has since become a three-star hotel. Overall, the effect is both economical and pleasing. Bedrooms, all renovated within the past few years, are small but cozy, some with sloped ceilings. Some rooms are windowless and illuminated only with small skylights. The best views are of nearby walls (ask for a room with a view anyway). Bathrooms are trimmed in Italian marble. The staff is young and usually perky and well intentioned.

Hôtel des Deux Continents. 25 rue Jacob, 75006 Paris. ☎ **01-43-26-72-46.** Fax 01-43-25-67-80. 41 units. TV TEL. 785–835 F ($133.45–$141.95) double; 1,040 F ($176.80) triple. MC, V. Métro: St-Germain-des-Prés.

Built from three antique, interconnected buildings, each between three and six stories high, this hotel is a solid and reliable choice with a sense of Latin Quarter style. The carefully coordinated bedrooms, each renovated between 1992 and 1998, range in size from small to medium, and include reproductions of antique furnishings, soundproof upholstered walls, and marble-trimmed bathrooms.

Hôtel des Saints-Pères. 65 rue des Sts-Pères, 75006 Paris. ☎ **01-45-44-50-00.** Fax 01-45-44-90-83. www.hotelsts.peres@wanadoo.fr. 39 units. MINIBAR TV TEL. 650–1,150 F ($110.50–$195.50) double; 1,700 F ($289) suite. AE, MC, V. Métro: St-Germain-des-Prés or Sèvres-Babylone.

This hotel just off boulevard St-Germain is comparable to the Odéon, attracting people who love Paris or, more specifically, love traditional Left Bank hotels. There is no better recommendation for this old favorite than the long list of guests who return again and again. The late Edna St. Vincent Millay enjoyed the camellia-trimmed garden. The hotel, designed in the 17th century by Louis XIV's architect Jacques Gabriel, is decorated in part with antique paintings, tapestries, and mirrors. Many of the bedrooms face a quiet courtyard accented in summer with potted plants. The most sought-after room is the *chambre à la fresque,* which has a 17th-century painted ceiling. The hotel has installed new plumbing and has replastered and repainted the rooms. Whenever weather permits, breakfast is served in the courtyard.

Hôtel du Pas-de-Calais. 59 rue des Sts-Pères, 75006 Paris. ☎ **01-45-48-78-74.** Fax 01-45-44-94-57. E-mail: lepasdecalais@horeca.tm.fr. 41 units. A/C TV TEL. 920 F ($156.40) double. AE, DC, MC, V. Parking 200 F ($34). Métro: St-Germain-des-Prés or Sèvres-Babylone.

The five-story Pas-de-Calais was built in the 17th century by the Lavalette family. Its elegant facade, complete with massive wooden doors, has been retained. The romantic novelist Chateaubriand lived here from 1811 to 1814. Its most famous guest was Jean-Paul Sartre, who struggled with the play *Les Mains Sales (The Red Gloves)* in room 41 during the hotel's prerestoration days. The hotel is a bit weak on style, but as one long-time guest confided, in spite of the updates and renovations, "we still stay here for the memories." Rooms are modern with large baths. Each has been renovated, with new mattresses added, in the past few years. Inner rooms surround a modest courtyard with two garden tables and several trellises. All rooms have TVs and safe-deposit boxes. Off the lobby is a comfortable, carpeted sitting room.

Hôtel-Jardin "Le Bréa." 14 rue Bréa. 75006 Paris. ☎ **01-43-25-44-41.** Fax 01-44-07-19-25. 23 units. TV TEL. 750–880 F ($127.50–$149.60) double; 880 F ($149.60) triple. AE, DC, MC, V. Métro: Vavin.

Although the building that contains this hotel originally had a garden in back, it was long ago covered with a roof and assimilated into the floor plan. Today, bright colors deck the public rooms, which lead to plain, small, efficiently decorated bedrooms that were partially renovated in 1997. To balance the lack of space, you can expect a polite welcome, and the neighborhood is convenient to the shops, cinemas, and the razzle-dazzle of Montparnasse.

Hôtel Le Clos Médicis. 56 rue Monsieur-le-Prince, 75006 Paris. ☎ **01-43-29-10-80.** Fax 01-43-54-26-90. E-mail: clos_medicis@compuserve.com. 38 units. A/C MINIBAR TV TEL. 790–1,200 F ($134.30–$204) double; 1,400 F ($238) duplex suite. AE, DC, MC, V. Métro: Odéon. RER: Luxembourg.

The location of this relatively new hotel, adjacent to the Jardin du Luxembourg, is a major advantage. You'll find a verdant garden with lattices and exposed stone walls, a lobby with modern spotlights and simple furniture, and a multilingual staff. The warmly colored guest rooms, small to medium in size, are comfortable, with medium-quality mattresses. Breakfast is the only meal served.

Hôtel Louis II. 2 rue St-Sulpice, 75006 Paris. ☎ **01-46-33-13-80.** Fax 01-46-33-17-29. 22 units. A/C MINIBAR TV TEL. 620–920 F ($105.40–$156.40) double; 1,100 F ($187) triple. AE, DC, MC, V. Métro: Odéon.

Housed in a formerly neglected 18th-century building, this hotel has bedrooms decorated in rustic French tones. Afternoon drinks and morning coffee are served in the reception salon, where gilt-framed mirrors, fresh flowers, and well-oiled antiques radiate a provincial aura, like something out of Proust. Upstairs, generally small, soundproof rooms with exposed beams and lace bedding complete the impression. Many visitors ask for the romantic attic rooms. The compact bathrooms have adequate shelf space, and most have a tub and shower combination. TVs are available upon request.

Hôtel St-Germain-des-Prés. 36 rue Bonaparte, 75006 Paris. ☎ **01-43-26-00-19.** Fax 01-40-46-83-63. 30 units. MINIBAR TV TEL. 980–1,350 F ($166.60–$229.50) double; from 1,700 F ($289) suite. Rates include breakfast. MC, V. Métro: St-Germain-des-Prés.

Most of this hotel's attraction comes from its enviable location in the Latin Quarter—behind a well-known Left Bank street near many shops. Janet Flanner, the legendary correspondent for the *New Yorker* in the 1920s, lived here for a while. Each room is small but charming, with antique ceiling beams, a safe, and reasonably comfortable beds. Each has been renovated within the past few years. The public areas are severely elegant. Air-conditioning is available in most of the rooms.

Libertel Quartier Latin. 9 rue des Écoles, 75006 Paris. ☎ **800/949-7562** in the U.S., or 01-44-27-06-45. Fax 01-43-25-36-70. 29 units. MINIBAR TV TEL. 975–1,050 F ($165.75–$178.50) double; 1,050–1,200 F ($178.50–$204) suite. AE, DC, MC, V. Parking 100 F ($17) nearby. Métro: Jussieu.

Set within a century-old six-story hotel in a neighborhood that's crowded with *quartier latin* color, this hotel was radically upgraded in 1997, with each of the bedrooms transformed into a temple to French literature. Expect a hardworking and articulate staff, book-lined public rooms that evoke a cozy studiousness, and small bedrooms where comfortable furniture is offset with framed portraits of such authors as Colette, André Gide, and Jacques Prévert. Bathrooms are small but efficiently organized, with adequate shelf space. Breakfast is the only meal served here, but no one seems to mind because of the many restaurants that lie within the surrounding neighborhood.

INEXPENSIVE

Delhy's Hotel. 22 rue de l'Hirondelle, 75006 Paris. ☎ **01-43-26-58-25.** Fax 01-43-26-51-06. 21 units, 7 with private bathroom (shower only). TV TEL. 356 F ($60.50) double without bathroom, 446 F ($75.80) double with shower; 586 F ($99.60) triple with shower. Rates include breakfast. AE, DC, MC, V. Métro: St-Michel.

This building was built around 1400 and later acquired by François I as a home for one of his mistresses. It's on a narrow and crooked alley in the heart of the densest part of the Latin Quarter. Don't expect luxury, but look for certain touches of charm that help compensate for the lack of an elevator. If you get a room without a shower, you'll have to go down to the ground floor for access to the public facilities. The building's staircase is listed as a national relic, and most of the compact rooms still have the original, almost fossilized, timbers and beams. Rooms were for the most part renovated in the late 1990s. Mattresses are reasonably comfortable; bath linens are acceptable but not plush.

Hôtel Clément. 6 rue Clément, 75006 Paris. ☎ **01-43-26-53-60.** Fax 01-44-07-06-83. E-mail: hotelment@worldnet.fr. 31 units. A/C TV TEL. 530–580 F ($90.10–$98.60) double; 750 F ($127.50) suite. AE, DC, V. Métro: Mabillon.

This hotel sits on a quiet, narrow street, within sight of the twin towers of the Église St-Sulpice. Built in the 1700s, the six-story structure that houses the hotel was stripped down and renovated several years ago into a bright, uncomplicated design. Don't expect deluxe bedrooms; they're simple and small, in some cases not much bigger than the beds they contain. Mattresses are medium quality, but not luxurious, and towels are thin. On the premises is a simple bistro with specialties from the Auvergne.

Hôtel Delavigne. 1 rue Casimir-Delavigne, 75006 Paris. ☎ **01-43-29-31-50.** Fax 01-43-29-78-56. E-mail: lavigne@micronet.fr. 34 units. TV TEL. 610–680 F ($103.70–$115.60) double. MC, V. Métro: Odéon.

Despite this hotel's radical modernization, you can still get a sense of the building's 18th-century origins. The public areas feature an attractively rustic use of chiseled stone, some of which is original. The high-ceilinged guest rooms are tasteful, sometimes with wooden furniture, often with upholstered headboards, and sometimes with Spanish-style wrought iron. Don't expect voluptuous comfort; the venue is sparse and spare, with medium-grade mattresses and thin towels. Breakfast is the only meal served.

Hôtel du Globe. 15 rue des Quatre-Vents, 75006 Paris. ☎ **01-46-33-62-69.** Fax 01-46-33-62-69. E-mail: hotelglobe@post.club-internet.fr. 15 units. TV TEL. 450–530 F ($76.50–$90.10) double. MC, V. Closed 3 weeks in Aug. Métro: Mabillon, Odéon, or St-Sulpice.

This 17th-century building occupies an evocative street in one of Paris's oldest neighborhoods. Inside, you'll find most of the original stonework and dozens of original timbers and beams. Each room is decorated with individual old-fashioned flair. There's no elevator (you have to lug your suitcases up a very narrow, antique staircase) and no breakfast area (trays are brought to your room). *One tip:* The rooms with a tub are almost twice as large as those with a shower stall, so for the extra expense you'll get a lot more than just better plumbing. The largest and most desirable rooms are nos. 1, 12 (with a baldaquin-style bed), 14, 15, and 16. The room without a bath is a single at 270 F ($45.90). Mattresses were each custom-made for this hotel, and configured to fit the hotel's inventory of odd-sized but comfortable beds. Towels are relatively thin.

Hôtel du Lys. 23 rue Serpente, 75006 Paris. ☎ **01-43-26-97-57.** Fax 01-44-07-34-90. 22 units. TV TEL. 520 F ($88.40) double; 620 F ($105.40) triple. Rates include breakfast. MC, V. Métro: Cluny-La Sorbonne.

With tall casement windows and high ceilings dating from its 17th-century construction, this establishment has functioned as a hotel since the turn of the century. It's a cozy place where all rooms have different patterns of curtains and wallpaper. About a quarter of them were renovated in 1998. Mattresses are about average in quality, and bathroom linens are functional but not great. Don't expect attentive service; this place is like an upscale dormitory, with residents pursuing a wide array of interests and activities in the surrounding Latin Quarter. Few spend any time within the hotel's limited public areas. There's no elevator, a fact that guarantees you'll make frequent use of the historic 17th-century staircase that stretches four floors above ground level. Breakfast, included in the price, can be served in your room.

7TH ARRONDISSEMENT (EIFFEL TOWER/MUSÉE D'ORSAY)
VERY EXPENSIVE

✪ **Hôtel Montalembert**. 3 rue de Montalembert, 75007 Paris. ☎ **800/447-7462** in the U.S. and Canada, or 01-45-49-68-68. Fax 01-45-49-69-49. www.montalembert.com. E-mail: welcome@hotel-montalembert.fr. 56 units. A/C MINIBAR TV TEL. 1,750–2,300 F ($297.50–$391) double; 2,850 F ($484.50) junior suite; 4,400 F ($748) suite. AE, DC, MC, V. Parking 120 F ($20.40). Métro: Rue-du-Bac.

Unusually elegant for the Left Bank, the Montalembert was built in 1926 in beaux arts style. It was restored between 1989 and 1992 and was hailed as a smashing success, borrowing sophisticated elements of Bauhaus and postmodern design in honey beiges, creams, and golds. Bedrooms are spacious, except for some standard doubles, which are quite small unless you're a very thin model. All rooms have VCRs and safes. Embroidered linens and quality mattresses adorn the large beds, and the bathrooms are elegant, with marble vanities, generous shelf space, and thick towels.

Dining/Diversions: Le Montalembert is favored by area artists, writers, publishers, and antique dealers. The stylish dining room provides excellent service and exceptionally good food based on market-fresh ingredients. Dishes include traditional veal chops slathered with wild mushrooms, along with more inventive fare from the relatively young kitchen staff. Expect crowds for weekday lunches; it thins out at other times. In summer, dining is offered on the terrace. The hotel also has a full-fledged bar and 24-hour room service.

Amenities: The concierge can arrange for practically anything under the sun. Hotel clients receive privileges at a nearby health club.

EXPENSIVE

Hôtel de l'Université. 22 rue de l'Université, 75007 Paris. ☎ **01-42-61-09-39**. Fax 01-42-60-40-84. www.paris-hotel.tm.fr/fr/saintgermain.04/universite.html. 27 units. A/C TV TEL. 850–1,300 F ($144.50–$221) double. AE, MC, V. Métro: St-Germain-des-Prés.

Long favored by well-heeled parents of North American students studying in Paris, this 300-year-old town house filled with fine antiques enjoys a location in a discreetly upscale neighborhood. Number 54 is a favorite room, with a rattan bed, period pieces, and a marble bath. Another charmer is no. 35, opening onto a courtyard and with a fireplace. The most expensive accommodation, at 1,300F ($234), has a small terrace overlooking the surrounding rooftops. Most of the compact bathrooms have a tub and shower combination and adequate shelf space. The bistro-style breakfast room opens onto a courtyard with a fountain.

Le Duc de Saint-Simon. 14 rue de St-Simon, 75007 Paris. ☎ **01-44-39-20-20**. Fax 01-45-48-68-25. 34 units. TEL. 1,050–1,450 F ($178.50–$246.50) double; from 1,900 F ($323) suite. AE, MC, V. Métro: Rue-du-Bac.

Set on a quiet residential street on the Left Bank, this is the only hotel in the 7th arrondissement to pose a serious challenge to the Montalembert. Two immortal cafes, Les Deux Magots and Le Flore, are a few steps away. The small villa has a tiny front garden and an 1830s decor with *faux-marbre* trompe-l'oeil panels, a frescoed elevator, and climbing wisteria gracing the courtyard. Each bedroom is unique and sure to include at least one antique. A few of the rooms are ridiculously small, but most offer adequate space. Baths are tiny, with just shower stalls, but have adequate shelf space. The service reflects the owner's extensive training in the art of pampering guests.

Dining: Room service is offered daily from 7am to 10:30pm.

Amenities: The concierge can arrange for just about anything, discreetly; and the hotel supplies televisions for clients who request them.

Hotels near the Eiffel Tower & Invalides

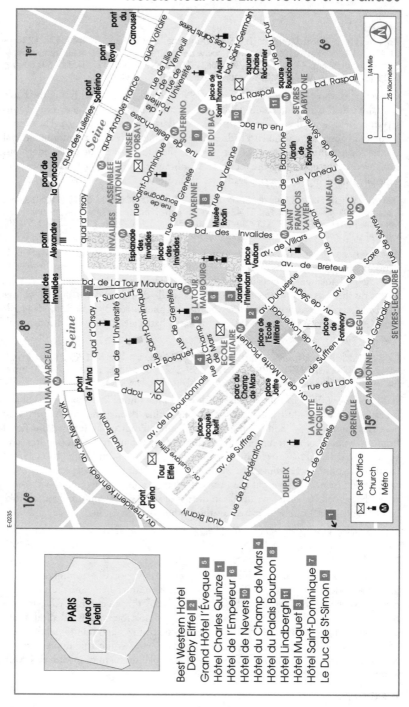

PARIS
Area of Detail

Best Western Hotel
Derby Eiffel 2
Grand Hôtel l'Évêque 5
Hôtel Charles Quinze 1
Hôtel de l'Empereur 6
Hôtel de Nevers 10
Hôtel du Champ de Mars 4
Hôtel du Palais Bourbon 8
Hôtel Lindbergh 11
Hôtel Muguet 3
Hôtel Saint-Dominique 7
Le Duc de St-Simon 9

MODERATE

Best Western Hotel Derby Eiffel. 5 av. Duquesne, 75007 Paris. ☎ **800/528-1234** or
01-47-05-12-05. Fax 01-47-05-43-43. www.derbyeiffelhotel.com. E-mail: reservation@
derbyeiffelhotel.com. 43 units. A/C MINIBAR TV TEL. 690–750 F ($117.30–$127.50) double;
900 F ($153) suite. AE, DC, MC, V. Métro: Ecole Militaire.

Converted to three-star status in the early 1990s, this six-story hotel facing the Ecole
Militaire contains airy and comfortable public areas. Our favorite is a glass-roofed con-
servatory in back filled year-round with plants and used as a breakfast area. The soundproof and conservatively modern bedrooms employ thick fabrics and soothing neutral
colors. Most front-facing rooms offer views of the Eiffel Tower. In 1998, enormous
sums were spent upgrading the rooms and bathrooms, changing the mattresses, and
generally improving the interior aesthetics of the hotel.

Hôtel de l'Académie. 32 rue des Sts-Pères, 75007 Paris. ☎ **800/246-0041** in the U.S. and
Canada, or 01-45-49-80-00. Fax 01-45-49-80-10. E-mail: academie@aol.com. 34 units. A/C
MINIBAR TV TEL. 690–990 F ($117.30–$168.30) double; 1,290–1,590 F ($219.30– $270.30)
suite. AE, DC, MC, V. Parking 150 F ($25.50). Métro: St-Germain-des-Prés.

The exterior walls and old ceiling beams are all that remain of this 17th-century residence of the private guards of the duc de Rohan. In 1999, the hotel was completely
renovated to include an elegant reception area. The up-to-date guest rooms have
duvets on the beds and comfortable mattresses, an Ile-de-France decor, and views over
the 18th- and 19th-century buildings of the neighborhood. By American standards
the rooms are small, but they're average for Paris. Baths are attractive and functional.
The staff speaks English.

✪ Hôtel du Quai-Voltaire. 19 quai Voltaire, 75007 Paris. ☎ **01-42-61-50-91.** Fax 01-42-
61-62-26. 33 units. TV TEL. 670–720 F ($113.90–$122.40) double; 850 F ($144.50) triple.
AE, DC, MC, V. Parking 110 F ($18.70) nearby. Métro: Musée d'Orsay.

Built in the 1600s as an abbey, then transformed into a hotel in 1856, Quai-Voltaire
is best known for its illustrious guests, including Wilde, Baudelaire, and Wagner, who
occupied rooms 47, 56, and 55, respectively. Camille Pissarro painted Le Pont Royal
from the window of his room on the 4th floor. Many rooms in this modest inn have
been renovated, and most overlook the bookstalls and boats of the Seine. In 1999, the
facade of the hotel was painted, as were most of the bedrooms. Mattresses are comfortable and firm, with rarely, if ever, any complaints from the guests, and bathrooms
are well designed. You can have drinks in the bar or small salon, and simple meals (like
omelets and salads) can be prepared for those who prefer to eat in.

Hôtel Lenox. 9 rue de l'Université, 75007 Paris. ☎ **01-42-96-10-95.** Fax 01-42-61-52-83.
34 units. TV TEL. 740–1,100 F ($125.80–$187) double; 1,500 F ($255) duplex suite. AE, DC,
MC, V. Métro: Rue-du-Bac.

The Lenox is a favorite for those seeking reasonably priced accommodations in
St-Germain-des-Prés. In 1910, T. S. Eliot spent a summer here "on the old man's
money" when the hotel was just a basic pension. Today this much-improved establishment offers a helpful staff and cramped but comfortable rooms. Radically and
expensively upgraded in 1996, the rooms evoke the chintzes and traditional furniture
of an English country house. Many returning guests request the attic duplex with its
tiny balcony and skylight. Most of the rooms are small to medium in size, each with
a firm mattress. Bathrooms are tiny but have adequate shelf space.

INEXPENSIVE

Grand Hôtel L'Évêque. 29 rue Cler, 75007 Paris. ☎ **01-47-05-49-15.** Fax 01-45-50-49-
36. www.interresa.ca/hotel/leveque/fr. E-mail: leveque@hotellerie.net. 50 units. TV TEL.
380–400 F ($64.60–$68) double. AE, MC, V. Métro: Ecole Militaire.

Built in the 1930s, with pastel-colored bedrooms that retain a vague art deco inspiration, this five-story hotel is loaded with English-speaking clients, many of whom appreciate its proximity to the Eiffel Tower. Each bedroom contains a hair dryer, a small lockbox for valuables, just enough space to be comfortable, and double-insulated windows that overlook either a courtyard in back or the street in front. In 1998, the hotel's interior was completely renovated and repainted, although the older, very comfortable mattresses were left in place. Clients rarely, if ever, complain about them. There's an elevator.

Hôtel de Beaune. 29 rue de Beaune, 75007 Paris. ☎ **01-42-61-24-89.** Fax 01-49-27-02-12. 19 units. MINIBAR TV TEL. 450–530 F ($76.50–$90.10) double. AE, DC, MC, V. Métro: Rue du Bac.

This white seven-story 19th-century building is a stone's throw from several upscale antiques stores. Bedrooms are small and efficiently furnished, but lack imagination. Each, however, is fitted with a firm mattress and good linen. Bathrooms are small, often with a tub and shower combination, but each has adequate shelf space and a hair dryer. The hotel is convenient to many nearby attractions, especially the Musée d'Orsay. A renovation was completed in 1998.

Hôtel de l'Empereur. 2 rue Chevert, 75007 Paris. ☎ **01-45-55-88-02.** Fax 01-45-51-88-54. www.franc.hotel.guide.com/h75007empereur.htm. E-mail: globeman@easynet.fr. 38 units. MINIBAR TV TEL. 470–530 F ($79.90–$90.10) double. AE, DC, MC, V. Parking 110–150 F ($18.70–$25.50) across the street. Métro: Latour-Maubourg.

This inexpensive and convenient six-story hotel was built in the early 1700s and enjoys a loyal group of repeat visitors. There's an elevator inside to haul you and your luggage to one of the smallish but attractively decorated bedrooms. In 1998, the two top floors were renovated. There's no restaurant or bar, but a nearby restaurant will send up platters of food upon request.

Hôtel de Nevers. 83 rue du Bac, 75007 Paris. ☎ **01-45-44-61-30.** Fax 01-42-22-29-47. 11 units. MINIBAR TV TEL. 415–520 F ($70.55–$88.40) double. No credit cards. Métro: Rue-du-Bac.

This is one of the most historic choices in the neighborhood. It was a convent from 1627 to 1790, when it was disbanded by the Revolution. The building is *classé,* which means that any restoration must respect the original architecture. That precludes an elevator, so you'll have to use the beautiful but never-ending white staircase. The cozy and pleasant rooms contain a combination of antique and reproduced furniture. Rooms 10 and 11 are especially sought after for terraces overlooking either a corner of rue du Bac or a rear courtyard. Bathrooms are small but worthy retreats, each with a tub and shower combination or a shower stall, and suitable shelf space.

Hôtel du Champ de Mars. 7 rue du Champ de Mars, 75007 Paris. ☎ **01-45-51-52-30.** Fax 01-45-51-64-36. www.hotel-du-champ-de-mars.com. 25 units. TV TEL. 410 F ($69.70) double. AE, DC, MC, V. Parking 100–150 F ($17–$25.50) in nearby public parking lot. Métro: Ecole Militaire.

Favored by families, this hotel rises five floors close to the park that flanks the base of the Eiffel Tower. It offers clean and simple bedrooms that are frilly and pretty enough to be referred to as "coquettish" by the manager. In 1998, most of the bedrooms were renovated and redecorated, retaining their charm and rather cramped dimensions. Most of the mattresses were changed. Baths are efficiently scaled and modern looking. The most memorable of the public areas is a stone-sided breakfast room, which features the only meal served at the hotel.

Hotel du Palais Bourbon. 49 rue de Bourgogne, 75007 Paris. ☎ **01-44-11-30-70.** Fax 01-45-55-20-21. www.globe-market.com/h75007palaisbourbon.htm. E-mail: htlbourbon@

aol.com. 32 units. MINIBAR TV TEL. 600 F ($102) double; 700 F ($119) triple. MC, V. Métro: Varenne.

The solid stone walls of this five-story 18th-century building are not nearly as grand as those of the embassies and stately private homes nearby. But don't be put off by the cramped entrance hall and rather dark hallways: Though bedrooms on the upper floors are larger, all rooms are comfortable and pleasantly decorated, with carefully crafted built-in furniture. The small, ultramodern bathrooms feature shower stalls and good shelf space. The staff is well informed and can direct you to all the nearby monuments and attractions.

Hôtel Lindbergh. 5 rue Chomel, 75007 Paris. ☎ **01-45-48-35-53.** Fax 01-45-49-31-48. www.hotellindbergh.com. E-mail: linhotel@club-internet.fr. 26 units. TV TEL. 460–670 F ($78.20–$113.90) double; 600–830 F ($102–$141.10) triple or quad. AE, DC, MC, V. Parking 70 F ($11.90). Métro: Sèvres-Babylone or St-Sulpice.

This hotel has streamlined and simple medium-size rooms, about a 3-minute walk from St-Germain-des-Prés. Mattresses and beds are comfortable and not overly soft, and each bathroom has a hair dryer. Breakfast is the only meal served, but the staff will point out worthy restaurants nearby—an inexpensive, well-managed bistro, **Le Cigale,** is a few buildings away. Room service is available daily from 7am to 7pm.

Hôtel Muguet. 11 rue Chevert, 75007 Paris. ☎ **01-47-05-05-93.** Fax 01-45-50-25-37. 45 units. E-mail: muguet@wanadoo.fr. A/C TV TEL. 540–580 F ($91.80–$98.60) double. AE, DC, MC, V. Parking 130–150 F ($22.10–$25.50) nearby. Métro: Latour-Maubourg.

Adjacent to the Hôtel de l'Empereur, which has just a few more grace notes, this simple two-star hotel benefits from an elevator and a location near Les Invalides. Six stories high and capped with a Mansard-style roof, the Muguet is comfortable and practical, but not at all luxurious. Some sought-after rooms on the sixth floor sport views over Napoléon's nearby gilded dome. Bedrooms are conservative, tasteful, and dignified, with wooden headboards and comfortable mattresses. There's no on-site restaurant, but many lie within the neighborhood, and there's a garden in back, where breakfast is served during warm weather.

Hôtel Saint-Dominique. 62 rue Saint-Dominique, 75007 Paris. ☎ **01-47-05-51-44.** Fax 01-47-05-81-28. 34 units. MINIBAR TV TEL. 500–580 F ($85–$98.60) double. AE, DC, MC, V. Métro: Latour-Maubourg or Invalides.

Part of the charm of this establishment derives from its division into three separate buildings interconnected through an open-air courtyard. The most visible of these was a convent in the 18th century; you can still see its battered ceiling beams and structural timbers in the reception area. The rooms aren't large, but each is warm, simply decorated, and comfortable. Many have patterned wallpaper in nostalgic patterns. Beds usually have wooden headboards and comfortable mattresses. Bathrooms are cramped, but they have hair dryers.

13TH & 14TH ARRONDISSEMENTS (GARE D'AUSTERLITZ/MONTPARNASSE)
INEXPENSIVE

Hôtel du Parc-Montsouris. 4 rue du Parc de Montsouris, 75014 Paris. ☎ **01-45-89-09-72.** Fax 01-45-80-92-72. 35 units. TV TEL. 340–450 F ($57.80–$76.50) double; 520 F ($88.40) suite. AE, DC, MC, V. Métro: Porte d'Orléans. RER: Cité Universitaire.

The staff is a bit absentminded, and the decor doesn't even pretend to be stylish, but prices are reasonable enough that this two-star hotel (a simple six-story structure built in the 1930s) attracts a loyal crowd of repeat clients. Your fellow guests might include parents of students studying at the nearby Cité Universitaire, or provincial clothiers attending fashion shows at the nearby Porte de Versailles. The residential neighborhood is far removed from the bustle of central Paris. Bedrooms are low-key, unpretentious, and quiet. Each was renovated in the late 1990s, and most of the mattresses were replaced with newer, firmer models. Bathrooms are compact and efficient. There's nothing wildly exciting about this hotel, but many visitors find it convenient.

Hôtel du Vert Galant. 41 rue Croulebarbe, 75013 Paris. ☎ **01-44-08-83-50.** Fax 01-44-08-83-69. 15 units. MINIBAR TV TEL. 450–500 F ($76.50–$85) double. Parking 35 F ($5.95). AE, DC, MC, V. Métro: Corvisart or Gobelins.

Verdant climbing plants and shrubs make this hotel feel like an auberge deep within the French countryside. Bedrooms have either tiled or carpeted floors, comfortable and unfussy furniture, enough space to stretch out in, and in most cases, green views of either the garden or the public park across the street. Bedrooms are small, but considering the price, this is a very good value for Paris. The compact bathrooms have shower stalls only. One of the best aspects of the place is the well-known Basque inn next door, the **Auberge Etchegorry,** which shares the same management. Clients of the hotel receive a discount, enjoying set-price menus for 100 F ($17) each.

Résidence les Gobelins. 9 rue des Gobelins, 75013 Paris. ☎ **01-47-07-26-90.** Fax 01-43-31-44-05. 32 units. TV TEL. 425–445 F ($72.25–$75.65) double; 535 F ($90.95) triple; 635 F ($107.95) quad. AE, MC, V. Métro: Gobelins.

There's nothing particularly glamorous about this hotel, and the location—far south of the Latin Quarter—rarely attracts tourists. But thanks to ongoing renovations, the accommodations are clean, plain, and well maintained, and cost much less than at equivalent hotels more centrally located. Bathrooms are cramped but efficient. Though the staff isn't terribly helpful, if you're just looking for a cheap room to crash in, this isn't a bad choice. There's an elevator on-site and cable TV in the rooms. The breakfast room overlooks a small plant-filled courtyard.

15TH ARRONDISSEMENT (GARE MONTPARNASSE/ INSTITUT PASTEUR)
INEXPENSIVE

Hôtel Charles Quinze. 36 rue Rouelle, 75015 Paris. ☎ **01-45-79-64-15.** Fax 01-45-77-21-11. 30 units. MINIBAR TV TEL. 520–560 F ($88.40–$95.20) double. AE, DC, MC, V. Métro: Dupleix or Charles Michels.

This is a modern, clean, and uncluttered place with no particular history. Built in 1988, the hotel scatters bedrooms over three upstairs floors, each with conservatively modern furnishings. Although you'll be able to crane your neck upward for views of the nearby Eiffel Tower from the street outside, the landmark isn't visible from any of the bedrooms. Beds are comfortable and upscale, with high-quality mattresses. A small cafe serves breakfasts as well as snacks throughout the day.

3 Near the Airports
ORLY

Hilton International Orly. Aéroport Orly, 267 Orly Sud, 94544 Val-de-Marne. ☎ **800/ 445-8667** in the U.S. and Canada, or 01-45-12-45-12. Fax 01-45-12-45-00. www.hilton.com. 356 units. A/C MINIBAR TV TEL. 1,020–1,510 F ($173.40–$256.70) double; 1,570–2,290 F ($266.90–$389.30) suite. AE, DC, MC, V. Parking 88 F ($14.95). Free shuttle bus between the hotel and both Orly terminals; 40-minute taxi ride from central Paris, except during rush hours.

Boxy and bland, the Hilton International at Orly remains a solid and well-maintained, but not particularly imaginative, hotel that business travelers appreciate for its convenience. Try as they might, incoming jets can't penetrate the bedrooms' sound barriers, guaranteeing you a decent shot at a night's sleep. (And unlike the 24-hour Charles de Gaulle Airport, Orly is closed to arriving flights between midnight and 6am.) Bedrooms are standard chain-hotel, with most of the mattresses replaced in 1998.

Dining: The hotel has two restaurants: an upscale restaurant open Monday through Friday for lunch and dinner, and a less expensive bistro that serves lunch and dinner 7 days a week.

Amenities: 24-hour room service, laundry, exercise room and sauna, nearby tennis courts.

ROISSY/CHARLES DE GAULLE

Hôtel Sofitel Paris Aéroport CDG. Aéroport Charles de Gaulle, Zone Central, B.P. 20248, 95713 Roissy. ☎ **800/221-4542** in the U.S. and Canada, or 01-49-19-29-29. Fax 01-49-19-29-00. www.accor.com. 352 units. A/C MINIBAR TV TEL. 980–1,550 F ($166.60–$263.50) double; from 1,900 F ($323) suite. AE, DC, MC, V. Parking 160 F ($27.20). Free shuttle bus service to and from the airport.

Many international travelers shuttle happily through this bustling but somewhat anonymous member of the nationwide French chain. Rising nine floors above a gray, industrial landscape, it employs a multilingual staff that's accustomed to accommodating constantly arriving and departing international business travelers. The monochromatic, conservatively international bedrooms are soundproof havens against the all-night roar of jets. Each was renovated in 1998, and many of the older mattresses were replaced with newer models. Bathrooms have oversized mirrors.

Dining: International food with a French slant is served at a comfortable restaurant and a bar on the hotel's ground floor.

Amenities: 24-hour room service, business center, video movies in several different languages, swimming pool and sauna.

4 Gay-Friendly Hotels

Virtually any hotel receptionist in Paris will register a same-sex couple as a matter of course, and perform the required paperwork with the courtesy and nonchalance for which the French are famous. So, although any hotel recommended in this guidebook is considered at least tolerant of same-sex couples, the hotels that follow are especially welcoming of gay guests.

Hôtel Central. 33 rue Vieille-du-Temple, 75004 Paris. ☎ **01-48-87-99-33.** Fax 01-42-77-06-27. 8 units (1 with private bathroom). TEL. 535 F ($90.95) double with shared bathroom; 650 F ($110.50) double with bathroom. MC, V. Métro: Hôtel de Ville.

This is the most famous gay hotel in Paris. The bedrooms lie on the second, third, and fourth floors of an 18th-century building. If you arrive between 8:30am and 3pm, you'll find a registration staff one floor above street level; otherwise, you'll have to retrieve your room keys and register at the street-level bar, **Le Central.** Frankly, many visitors prefer the bar over the bedrooms, but if you want a hotel that will really put you smack in the middle of the gay scene, this is it. Bedrooms are simple and serviceable, but show evidence of much wear and tear. With a single exception, one private bath is shared for each two rooms. Women are welcome, but rare. The bar is open Monday through Friday from 4pm to 2am, Saturday and Sunday from 2pm to 2am.

Hôtel Pierre. 25 rue Théodore-de-Banville, 75017 Paris. ☎ **01-47-63-76-69.** Fax 01-43-80-63-96. 50 units. MINIBAR TV TEL. 690–2,200 F ($117.30–$374) double. AE, DC, MC, V. Parking 100 F ($17). Métro: Péreire.

The Pierre was named as a facetious comparison to a favorite North American hotel, the Pierre in New York City. The owners combined three five-story 19th-century buildings into a clean, modern hotel with art deco styling. Opened in 1986, it sits at the end of a residential street a short walk from the Arc de Triomphe. The stylish accommodations each have a TV with video movies and a safe with a combination lock. Most are outfitted with conservative modern furnishings. There's no restaurant or bar, but room service is available from 7am to 10:30pm Monday through Friday. At the time of this writing, the hotel had been torn apart for a complete and radical overhaul of each of its accommodations and bathrooms, a process whose end was envisioned for sometime late in 1999.

Le Saint-Hubert. 27 rue Traversière, 75012 Paris. ☎ **01-43-43-39-16.** Fax 01-43-43-35-32. 15 units. TV TEL. 315–345 F ($53.55–$58.65) double. MC, V. Métro: Gare de Lyon.

Renovated in 1996, this hotel occupies a five-story 19th-century town house on a quiet but unremarkable residential street. The small but immaculately clean bedrooms have blue, brown, or salmon-colored walls and simple accessories. Bathrooms are small, compact boxes. Because there is no elevator, rooms on the fourth and fifth floors are cheaper than those closer to the street-level reception area and breakfast room.

5 Dining

Welcome to the city that prides itself on being the culinary capital of the world. Only in Paris can you turn onto the nearest side street, enter the first place you see, sit down at the bare and wobbly table, glance at an illegibly hand-scrawled menu, and get a memorable meal. If you're not feeling that adventuresome, see chapter 1 for a list of our favorite restaurants in Paris.

1 Today's Restaurant Scene

If Paris has a king chef today—the equivalent of Escoffier of yesterday—it is none other than Alain Ducasse, who has become the first chef to garner six stars in a single year from the Michelin guide. Three were awarded to **Alain Ducasse** in Paris and three to his other establishment, the swanky **Louis XV** in the Hôtel de Paris in Monte Carlo. Monsieur Ducasse commutes regularly between Paris and Monaco.

Now the "six-star" chef has opened a second place in the City of Light. His new restaurant, **Spoon, Food and Wine,** serves everything but the exquisite cuisine that earned him his galaxy of stars. Here at his new bistro he offers macaroni and cheese with gravy (you heard that right), along with barbecued ribs, and blackened chicken breast. And, yes, that's Philadelphia Cream Cheese you spot on the cheese tray.

Ten years ago, it would have been unthinkable, maybe even laughable, but a British restaurant entrepreneur, Sir Terence Conran of design fame, has bravely and boldly expanded his London dining empire to Paris. He's opened the **Alcazar Bar & Restaurant** in the 5th arrondissement, a bright, airy, brasserie-type place seating 200. Wisely, Conran has chosen Guillaume Lutard, formerly of the three-star Taillevent, to man the stoves of his glassed-in kitchen. Whether Paris will embrace this U.K. invasion remains to be seen.

Although these new restaurants made the news in 1999, the famous old favorites are hardly standing by idle. Take the legendary Le Grand Véfour, in the gardens of the Palais Royale. Its chef, Guy Martin, has been named chef of the year by the *Gault Millau* guidebook. Martin's cookery is based primarily on traditional recipes from the French alpine regions, mixing classic with modern recipes.

Paris always has a surplus of restaurants. Temples of gastronomy include **Alain Senderens,** the legendary **Taillevent, Lasserre,** and **La Tour d'Argent,** still dispensing ever-changing cuisine to the faithful. Belle-epoque **Maxim's,** arguably the most famous restaurant in the world, is still going strong, as overrated and overpriced as ever.

Mystifying Menu?

For a glossary of French-language menu terms, please turn to Appendix B.

Savvy diners confine their trips to luxe establishments to special occasions. An array of other choices awaits, including simpler restaurants dispensing cuisines from every province of France and from former colonies such as Morocco and Algeria. Paris now has hundreds of restaurants serving exotic **international fare,** reflecting the changing complexion of Paris itself and the city's increasing appreciation for food from other cultures. Your most memorable meal in Paris may turn out to be Vietnamese or West African.

Hundreds of **bistros, brasseries,** and **cafes** await you. Many bistros can be chic and elegant, sometimes heavily Mediterranean in style, but others dispense gutsy fare, including the *pot-au-feu* that the chef's grandmother prepared for him as a kid. Brasseries are often open 24 hours, including Alsatian establishments that serve sauerkraut with an array of pork products. Cafes, too, are not just places for an aperitif, a café au lait, or a croissant; many serve rib-sticking fare as well, certainly entrecôte with french fries, but often such classics as blanquette of veal.

More attention in the 1990s has focused on the **wine bar,** a host of which we recommend in chapter 9. Originally, wine bars concentrated on their lists of wines, featuring many esoteric choices and ignoring the food except for some *charcuterie* (cold cuts) and cheeses. Today, you are likely to be offered various daily specials, ranging from homemade foie gras to *boeuf à la mode* (marinated beef braised with red wine and served with vegetables, almost like a pot roast).

One often-asked question is, "Can you dine badly in Paris?" The answer is an emphatic yes, and increasingly so. Our mailbox fills with complaints from visitors who encountered haughty service and paid outrageous prices for what turned out to be swill.

Often these complaints are directed at restaurants that cater almost solely to tourists. To avoid them, survey our assessments, make new discoveries, and do as the Parisians do: Take your choice of a restaurant seriously. Considering the cost of a meal in Paris, view the culinary pursuit as an investment. While the tourists claw each other for a tacky table along the Champs-Elysées, you can enjoy finer fare at a distant, well-recommended choice—truffle-studded foie gras served on Limoges china at **Le Grand Véfour** or the eponymous pig's feet at **Pied de Cochon** where the chefs follow a recipe unaltered since 1946.

Although Paris prices seem extravagant to visitors from other parts of the world, there has been an emergence of informal, moderately priced restaurants here, and we'll recommend several of these.

A final trend that has hit the dining scene is the **baby bistro,** a reasonably priced spin-off from an ultradeluxe restaurant. We've covered the best of them.

DINING SAVOIR-FAIRE

- Three-star dining remains extremely expensive in Paris, with appetizers sometimes priced at $50 and dinners easily costing $200 per person in the top Michelin-starred dining rooms of celebrated chefs. But you can get around that high price tag in many places by ordering a fixed-price menu or opting for the cheaper lunch menus.
- In France, **lunch** (as well as dinner) tends to be a full-course meal with meat, vegetables, salad, bread, cheese, dessert, wine, and coffee. It may be difficult to find a restaurant that serves the type of light lunch that North Americans usually eat. Cafes, however, offer sandwiches, soup, and salads in a relaxed setting.

Ducasse Lite

If you're traveling on a lean budget, you can still get a peek into the celestial world of Alain Ducasse by dropping into the bar at his avenue. Raymond Poincaré restaurant and ordering one of the best arrays of tapas in town. Of course, you'll have to put up with a lot of fashionable cigar smoke.

- Establishments are still required by law to post menus outside, so review them carefully. The **prix-fixe** (fixed-price) menu is an admirable choice if you want a general idea of what the bill will be when the waiter presents it. In terms of **tips,** in simple bistros, the small change is left on the table; in luxe or first-class establishments, patrons often add another 5% to the bill.
- Average visitors will head, as always, for the old-fashioned, family-run **bistro,** and we've ferreted out the best of these. In today's Paris, tradition and nostalgia, along with affordable prices, make these bistros busier than ever, especially since so many of them are being forced out of existence because of rising rents.
- **Coffee,** in France, is served after the meal and carries an extra charge. The French consider it barbaric to drink coffee during the meal, and, unless you specifically order it with milk (au lait), the coffee will be served black. In more conscientious establishments, it is prepared as the traditional filtre, a slow but rewarding java draw.
- In years gone by, no one would consider dining out, even at the neighborhood bistro, without a suit and a tie for men or a smart dress for women. That **dress code** is more relaxed now, except in first-class and luxe establishments. Relaxed doesn't mean sloppy jeans and jogging attire, however. Parisians still value style, even when dressing informally.

2 Restaurants by Cuisine

ALGERIAN
Au Clair de Lune (2e, *I*)
Wally Le Saharien (9e, *M*)

ALSATIAN
Bofinger (4e, *M*)
Brasserie de l'Ile St-Louis (4e, *I*)

AMERICAN
Chicago Pizza Pie Factory (8e, *I*)
Hard Rock Cafe (9e, *I*)
Joe Allen (1er, *I*)
Planet Hollywood (8e, *I*)

AUVERGNAT
L'Ambassade d'Auvergne (3e, *I*)
Restaurant Bleu (14e, *I*)

BASQUE
Auberge Etchegorry (13e, *M*)
Chez l'Ami Jean (7e, *I*)

BRETON
Chez Michel (10e, *I*)

BURGUNDIAN
Chez Pauline (1er, *M*)

CAFES
Brasserie Lipp (6e, *M*)
Café Beaubourg (4e, *I*)
Café Cosmos (6e, *I*)
Café de Flore (6e, *M*)
Cafe de la Musique (19e, *I*)
Café de la Paix (9e, *I*)
Café de l'Industrie (11e, *I*)
Café des Hauteurs (7e, *I*)
Café Marly (1er, *M*)
Café/Restaurant/Salon de Thé
   Bernardaud (8em, *M*)
Fouquet's (8e, *M*)
La Coupole (14e, *M*)

Key to Abbreviations: *VE* =Very Expensive; *E* = Expensive; *M* = Moderate; *I* = Inexpensive

La Rotonde (6e, *M*)
La Samaritaine (*e, I*)
Le Café Zephyr (9e, *I*)
Le Gutenberg (1er, *I*)
Le Rouquet (7e, *I*)
Les Deux-Magots (6e, *I*)
Lizard Lounge (4e, *I*)

CANTONESE
Chez Vong (1er, *I*)

CENTRAL EUROPEAN
Chez Jo Goldenberg (4e, *I*)
La Cagouille (14e, *M*)

CHINESE
Le Canton (6e, *I*)

CREOLE
Babylone (2e, *I*)

DANISH
Copenhague/Flora Danica (8e, *E*)

FRENCH—MODERN
Alain Ducasse (16e, *VE*)
Alcazar Bar & Restaurant (5e, *M*)
Androuët (8e, *M*)
Bofinger (4e, *M*)
Buddha Bar (8e, *E*)
Carré des Feuillants (1er, *VE*)
Chez Diane (6e, *I*)
Chez Jean (9e, *E*)
Jacques Cagna (6e, *VE*)
Julien (10e, *I*)
L'Ambroisie (4e, *VE*)
L'Arpège (7e, *VE*)
Lasserre (8e, *VE*)
L'Astor (8e, *VE*)
La Tour d'Argent (5e, *VE*)
Le Bistro d'à Côté Flaubert
   (17e, *E*)
Le Brise-Miche (4e, *I*)
Le Violon d'Ingres (7e, *E*)
Le Vivarois (16e, *VE*)
Lucas-Carton (Alain Senderens)
   (8e, *VE*)
Marc-Annibal de Coconnas (4e, *M*)
Michel Rostang (17e, *VE*)
Pierre Gagnaire (8e, *VE*)
Restaurant d'Eric Frechon (19e, *M*)
Restaurant Opéra (9e, *E*)
Taillevent (8e, *VE*)

FRENCH—TRADITIONAL
Alain Ducasse (16e, *VE*)
Androuët (8e, *M*)
Astier (11e, *M*)
Au Clair de Lune (2e, *I*)
Au Gourmet de l'Ile (4e, *I*)
Au Pied de Cochon (1er, *M*)
Au Pied de Fouet (7e, *I*)
Au Rendezvous des Camionneurs
   (1er, *I*)
Aux Charpentiers (6e, *I*)
Bistro de la Grille (6e, *I*)
Bofinger (4e, *M*)
Brasserie Balzar (5e, *M*)
Brasserie de l'Ile St-Louis (4e, *I*)
Chartier (9e, *I*)
Chez Diane (6e, *I*)
Chez Georges (17e, *M*)
Chez Georges (2e, *M*)
Chez Gramond (5e, *M*)
Chez Jean (9e, *E*)
Chez Pauline (1er, *M*)
Chez René (5e, *M*)
Closerie des Lilas (6e, *E*)
Crémerie-Restaurant Polidor (6e, *I*)
Dame Tartine (4e, *I*)
Faugeron (16e, *VE*)
Guy Savoy (17e, *VE*)
Jacques Cagna (6e, *VE*)
Jamin (16e, *VE*)
Julien (10e, *I*)
La Butte Chaillot (16e, *M*)
La Cagouille (14e, *M*)
La Clementine (2e, *I*)
L'Affriolé (7e, *E*)
La Fontaine de Mars (7e, *I*)
La Grille (10e, *M*)
L'Ambassade d'Auvergne (3e, *I*)
L'Ambroisie (4e, *VE*)
L'Ami Louis (3e, *E*)
La Petite Chaise (7e, *M*)
La Petite Hostellerie (5e, *I*)
La Poule au Pot (1er, *I*)
La Rose de France (1er, *I*)
La Rôtisserie d'Armaillé (17e, *M*)
La Rôtisserie d'en Face (6e, *M*)
Lasserre (8e, *VE*)
L'Astor (8e, *VE*)
La Tour d'Argent (5e, *VE*)
La Tour de Monthléry (Chez Denise)
   (1er, *I*)

Laudurée (8e, *M*)
L'Ébauchoir (12e, *I*)
Le Berry's (8e, *I*)
Le Bistro d'à Côté Flaubert (17e, *E*)
Le Bistro de l'Étoile (16e, *I*)
Le Grand Véfour (1er, *VE*)
Le Grand Zinc (9e, *I*)
Le Procope (6e, *M*)
Lescure (1er, *I*)
Les Gourmets des Ternes (8e, *I*)
Le 30 (Chez Fauchon) (8e, *E*)
Le Train Bleu (12e, *M*)
Le Vaudeville (2e, *M*)
Le Vieux Bistro (4e, *M*)
Le Violon d'Ingres (7e, *E*)
Le Vivarois (16e, *VE*)
Marc-Annibal de Coconnas (4e, *M*)
Marie-Louise (18e, *I*)
Maxim's (8e, *VE*)
Michel Rostang (17e, *VE*)
Perraudin (5e, *I*)
Pharamond (1er, *M*)
Pub Saint-Germain-des-Prés (6e, *I*)
Restaurant d'Eric Frechon (19e, *M*)
Restaurant des Beaux-Arts (6e, *I*)
Restaurant Opéra (9e, *E*)
Taillevent (8e, *VE*)
Trumilou (4e, *I*)

GASCONY
Au Trou Gascon (12e, *E*)

INDIAN
Yugaraj (6e, *M*)

INDOCHINESE
Café Indochine (8e, *I*)

INTERNATIONAL
Le Fumoir (1er, *M*)
Spoon, Food & Wine (8e, *E*)

ITALIAN
Il Cortile (1er, *M*)

JAPANESE
Isama (4e, *M*)

JEWISH
Chez Jo Goldenberg (4e, *I*)

KOREAN
Shing-Jung (8e, *I*)

LANDES
Chez Dumonet (Chez Joséphine) (6e, *I*)
Restaurant du Marché (15e, *M*)

LATE-NIGHT
Au Pied de Cochon (1er, *M*)
Babylone (2e, *I*)
La Poule au Pot (1er, *I*)
La Tour de Monthléry (Chez Denise) (1er, *I*)
Le Vaudeville (2e, *M*)
Pub Saint-Germain-des-Prés (6e, *I*)

LEBANESE
Al Dar (5e, *I*)

LIGHT FARE
Angélina (1er, *I*)

LOIRE VALLEY (ANJOU)
Au Petit Riche (9e, *M*)

MEDITERRANEAN
Il Ortile (1er, *M*)

MOROCCAN
Mansouria (11e, *I*)

NORMAND
Pharamond (1er, *M*)

NORTHERN FRENCH
Le Bambouche (7e, *M*)

PACIFIC RIM
Buddha Bar (8e, *E*)

PIZZA
Chicago Pizza Pie Factory (8e, *I*)

PROVENÇAL
Campagne et Provence (5e, *I*)
Chez Janou (3e, *I*)
La Bastide Odéon (6e, *I*)

PYRENÉE
La Fontaine de Mars (7e, *I*)

SEAFOOD
Goumard (1er, *VE*)
Keryado (13e, *I*)
La Grille (10e, *M*)
Paul Minchelli (7e, *E*)

SENEGALESE

Le Dogon (10e, *I*)
Le Manguier (11e, *I*)
Paris-Dakar (10e, *I*)

SOUTHWESTERN FRENCH

Chez l'Ami Jean (7e, *I*)
Chez Lulu (14e, *M*)
La Fermette du Sud-Ouest (1er, *I*)
La Fontaine de Mars (7e, *I*)
La Régalade (14e, *M*)

TEA

Angélina (1er, *I*)

THAI

Blue Elephant (11e, *E*)

VEGETARIAN

Aquarius (4e, *I*)
Le Grain de Folie (17e, *I*)

VIETNAMESE

Le Canton (6e, *I*)

3   Right Bank

We'll begin with the most centrally located arrondissements on the Right Bank, then work our way through the more outlying neighborhoods.

1ST ARRONDISSEMENT (MUSÉE DU LOUVRE/LES HALLES)
VERY EXPENSIVE

Carré des Feuillants. 14 rue de Castiglione (near place Vendôme and the Tuileries), 1er. ☎ **01-42-86-82-82.** Fax 01-42-86-07-71. Reservations required. Main courses 240–280 F ($40.80–$47.60); fixed-price menu 295 F ($50.15) at lunch, 780 F ($132.60) at dinner. AE, DC, MC, V. Mon–Fri noon–2:30pm; Mon–Sat 7:30–10:30pm. Closed first 3 weeks in Aug. Métro: Tuileries, Concorde, Opéra, or Madeleine. FRENCH.

When leading chef Alain Dutournier converted this 17th-century convent into a restaurant, it was an overnight success. The interior is like a turn-of-the-century bourgeois house with several small salons opening onto a skylit courtyard, across from which is a glass-enclosed kitchen. Much of the inspiration here derives from a sophisticated reinterpretation of cuisine from France's southwest, using seasonally fresh ingredients and lots of know-how. Examples include roasted veal kidneys cooked in their own fat; grilled wood pigeon served with chutney and polenta; filet of rabbit in a bitter chocolate sauce with quince; and roasted leg of suckling lamb from the Pyrénées with autumn vegetables. Lighter dishes include scallops in a crispy coat of parsley-infused puff pastry served with cabbage and truffles, and mullet-studded risotto with lettuce. Dessert might include a slice of something many grandmothers in the southwest of France remember from their childhoods: pistachio cream cake with candied tangerines.

Goumard. 9 rue Duphot, 1er. ☎ **01-42-60-36-07.** Fax 01-42-60-04-54. Reservations recommended. Main courses 190–380 F ($32.30–$64.60); fixed-price lunch 390 F ($66.30); *menu gastronomique* (tasting menu) 780 F ($132.60). AE, DC, MC, V. Tues–Sat 12:30–2:30pm and 7:30–10:30pm. Closed 2 weeks in Aug. Métro: Madeleine or Concorde. SEAFOOD.

Opened in 1872, this landmark is one of the leading seafood restaurants in Paris. It's so devoted to the fine art of preparing fish that other food is strictly banned from the menu, although if someone who dislikes fish wanders in by accident, a limited roster of meat dishes will be orally presented by the cooperative staff. The decor consists of an unusual collection of Lalique crystal fish displayed in artificial aquariums lining the walls. Even more unusual are the men's and women's rest rooms, now classified as historical monuments by the French government. The commodes were designed by the art nouveau master cabinetmaker Majorelle around the turn of the century.

Much of the seafood is flown in direct from Brittany every day. Examples include a craquant of crayfish in its own herb salad; lobster soup with coconut; a *parmentier* of crabmeat served with a mousseline of potatoes; fillet of grilled seawolf served with a fricassée of artichokes and Provençal *pistou;* and a salad of grilled turbot on a bed of artichokes with tarragon. Especially appealing is poached turbot with hollandaise sauce, served with leeks in vinaigrette. In all these dishes nothing (no excess butter, spices, or salt) is allowed to interfere with the natural flavor of the sea. Be prepared for some very unusual food—the staff will help translate the menu items for you.

✪ **Le Grand Véfour.** 17 rue de Beaujolais, 1er. ☎ **01-42-96-56-27.** Fax 01-42-86-80-71. Reservations required. Main courses 230–380 F ($39.10–$64.60); fixed-price menu 360–780 F ($61.20–$132.60) at lunch, 780 F ($132.60) at dinner. AE, DC, MC, V. Mon–Fri 12:30–2pm and 7:30–10:15pm. Métro: Louvre. FRENCH.

This restaurant has been around since the reign of Louis XV, though not under the same name. Napoléon, Danton, Hugo, Colette, and Cocteau have dined here—as the brass plaques on the tables testify—and it's still a great gastronomic experience. Guy Martin, chef here for the past 8 years, bases many dishes on recipes from the French Alps. His best dish is roast lamb in a juice of herbs. And have you ever had cabbage sorbet in a dark chocolate sauce? Other specialties include noisettes of lamb with star anise and Breton lobster. The desserts are often grand, like the gourmandises au chocolat, a richness of chocolate served with chocolate sorbet.

MODERATE

✪ **Au Pied de Cochon.** 6 rue Coquillière, 1er. ☎ **01-40-13-77-00.** Reservations recommended for conventional lunch and dinner hours. Main courses 86–148 F ($14.60–$25.15). AE, DC, MC, V. Daily 24 hours. Métro: Les Halles. FRENCH/LATE-NIGHT.

Although the great market that used to surround this restaurant has moved to Rungis, by the distant expanses of Orly, traditions die hard. Au Pied de Cochon's famous onion soup still lures visitors, and besides, where else in Paris can you be assured of getting a good meal at 3am? The house specialty is the restaurant's namesake: pig's feet grilled and served with béarnaise sauce. Both dishes are as good—or, in the view of some, as bad—as they always were. Along the same lines is the *tentation* ("temptation") platter, including a grilled version of pig's tail, pig's snout, and a half pig's foot served with béarnaise sauce and *frites.* (The French get all nostalgic about this dish, which reminds them of their childhood.) A*ndouillette* (chitterling sausages) with béarnaise sauce is another speciality. Two particularly flavorful dishes that North Americans might prefer include a *jarret* of pork, caramelized in honey and served on a bed of sauerkraut; and grilled pork ribs served with sage sauce.

On the street outside, you can buy some of the freshest oysters in town. The attendants will give you slices of lemons to accompany them, and you can down them on the spot.

Chez Pauline. 5 rue Villedo, 1er. ☎ **01-42-96-20-70.** Reservations recommended. Main courses 190–400 F ($32.30–$68); fixed-price menu 220 F ($37.40). AE, DC, MC, V. Mon–Fri 12:15–2:30pm and 7:30–10:30pm; Sat 7:30–10:30pm. Closed Sat–Sun between May and early Sept. Métro: Palais-Royal. BURGUNDIAN/FRENCH.

Loyal fans say that this "bistrot de luxe" is a less expensive, less majestic version of Le Grand Véfour. The early- 20th-century setting is grand enough to impress a business client and lighthearted enough to attract an impressive roster of VIPs. You'll be ushered to a table on one of two levels, amid polished mirrors, red leather banquettes, and the memorabilia of long-ago Paris. The emphasis is on the cuisine of central France, especially Burgundy, as shown by the liberal use of wines in time-honored favorites like cassoulet of Burgundian snails with bacon and tomatoes; a terrine of parslied ham; sweetbreads in puff pastry; filet of wild duckling with seasonal berries; old-fashioned beef bourguignonne with tagliatelle; salmon steak with green peppercorns; and a ragout of wild hare in an aspic of Pouilly. If you're at all in doubt about the composition of any of these, you'll do well with the roasted Bresse chicken with dauphinois potatoes, or any of the stews that swim with savory morsels of duck, wild boar, and venison. Dessert might include a clafoutis of apricots and raspberries lightly sautéed in sugar, or a caramelized version of rice pudding. Owner and chef André Genin is a noteworthy author of children's books, some of them instructional volumes for children on the value and techniques of French cuisine.

Il Cortile. In the Hotel Castille, 37 rue Cambon, 1e. ☎ **01-44-58-45-67.** Reservations recommended. Main courses 100–150 F ($17–$25.50). AE, DC, MC, V. Mon–Fri noon–2:30pm and 7:30–10:30pm. Métro: Concorde or Madeleine. ITALIAN/MEDITERRANEAN.

Flanking the verdant courtyard of a small, discreetly elegant hotel, this much-talked-about restaurant has the best Italian food in Paris. During warm weather, tables are set up within an enclosed patio—a welcome luxury within this congested neighborhood.

The cuisine is fresh, inventive, and seasonal. Dishes are from throughout Italy, with emphasis on the north, as shown by a special promotion of wines of Tuscany and the Piedmont. Look for items that include *farfalle* pasta with squid ink and fresh shellfish; fettuccine with pistou; and an award-winning version of guinea fowl. Spit-roasted and served with artfully shaped slices of the bird's gizzard, heart, and liver, it comes with polenta. Service is virtually flawless: The Italian-speaking staff is diplomatic and good humored.

If you really want a view of what's cooking, ask for a seat with a view of the open rotisserie, where spit-roasted hens and guinea fowl slowly spin.

Le Fumoir. 6 rue de l'Amiral Coligny, 1er. ☎ **01-42-92-00-24.** Reservations recommended. Main courses 105–120 F ($17.85–$20.40). Daily for salads, pastries, and snacks 11am–1am; complete menu daily noon–3pm and 7–11:30pm. AE, DC, MC, V. Métro: Louvre. INTERNATIONAL.

Stylish and breezy, and set in an antique building a few steps from the Louvre, this is an upscale brasserie with ample opportunities for watching the denizens of Paris's arts scene come and go. Currently, it is the most fashionable place in Paris to be seen eating or drinking. In a high-ceilinged ambience of warm but somber browns and indirect lighting, you can order salads, pastries, and drinks during off-hours, and platters of more substantial food during conventional mealtimes. Examples include fillet of codfish with onions and herbs; sliced rack of veal simmered in its own juices with tarragon; calf's liver with onions; a combination platter of lamb chops with grilled tuna steak; and herring in a mustard-flavored cream sauce.

✪ Pharamond. 24 rue de la Grande-Truanderie, 1er. ☎ **01-42-33-06-72.** Reservations required. Main courses 90–150 F ($15.30–$25.50); fixed-price menu 200 F ($34) at lunch (with wine), 310 F ($52.70) at dinner (with wine). AE, DC, MC, V. Tues–Sat noon–2:30pm; Mon–Sat 7:30–10:45pm. Métro: Les Halles or Châtelet. FRENCH/NORMAN.

Part of an 1832 neo-Norman structure that's classified as a national landmark, Pharamond sits on a Les Halles street once frequented by the vagabonds of Paris. For an appetizer, work your way through half a dozen Breton oysters (October to April). But the dish to order is *tripes à la mode de Caen,* served over a charcoal burner. Tripe is a delicacy, and if you're at all experimental, you'll find no better introduction to it. Try the *coquilles St-Jacques au cidre* (scallops in cider) if you're not up to tripe.

INEXPENSIVE

✪ Angélina. 226 rue de Rivoli, 1er. ☎ **01-42-60-82-00.** Reservations accepted for lunch, not for teatime. Pot of tea for one 34–36 F ($5.80–$6.10); sandwiches and salads 58–98 F

Restaurants in the Heart of the Right Bank

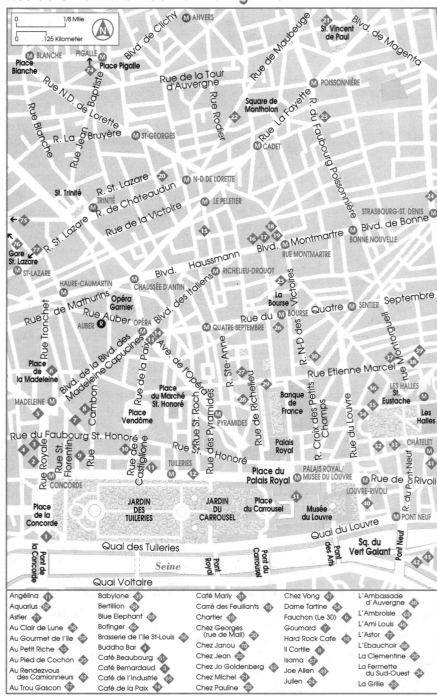

Angélina	Babylone	Café Marly	Chez Vong	L'Ambassade d'Auvergne
Aquarius	Bertillion	Carré des Feuillants	Dame Tartine	L'Ambroisie
Astier	Blue Elephant	Chartier	Fauchon (Le 30)	L'Ami Louis
Au Clair de Lune	Bofinger	Chez Georges (rue de Mail)	Goumard	L'Astor
Au Gourmet de l'Île	Brasserie de l'Île St-Louis		Hard Rock Cafe	L'Ebauchoir
Au Petit Riche	Buddha Bar	Chez Janou	Il Cortile	La Clementine
Au Pied de Cochon	Café Beaubourg	Chez Jean	Isama	La Fermette du Sud-Ouest
Au Rendezvous des Camionneurs	Café Bernardaud	Chez Jo Goldenberg	Joe Allen	
Au Trou Gascon	Café de l'Industrie	Chez Michel	Julien	La Grille
	Café de la Paix	Chez Pauline		

98

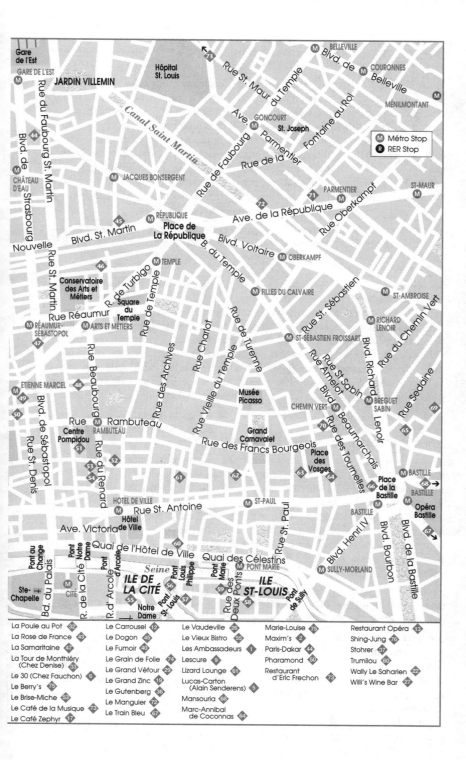

Gare de l'Est
GARE DE L'EST
Ⓜ
JARDIN VILLEMIN

Hôpital St. Louis

Rue du Faubourg St. Martin

Ⓜ 44
Blvd. de
Ⓜ CHÂTEAU D'EAU
Rue St. Martin

BELLEVILLE
Ⓜ
Blvd. de
Ⓜ COURONNES
Belleville

MÉNILMONTANT
Ⓜ

Canal Saint Martin

Rue St. Maur du Temple

Ⓜ JACQUES BONSERGENT

Ave. GONCOURT
Ⓜ St. Joseph
Parmentier

Rue de Faubourg

Rue de la

Fontaine au Roi

PARMENTIER
ST-MAUR
Ⓜ

Rue Oberkampf

Ⓜ 71

Ave. de la République
22

Ⓜ Métro Stop
Ⓡ RER Stop

Nouvelle

Rue St. Martin

Ⓜ 45
Ⓜ RÉPUBLIQUE
Place de La République
Blvd. St. Martin

Blvd. Voltaire
B. du Temple

Ⓜ OBERKAMPF

46
Ⓜ TEMPLE

Conservatoire des Arts et Métiers

R. de Turbigo

Square du Temple

Rue de Temple

Ⓜ FILLES DU CALVAIRE

Ⓜ ST-AMBROISE

Rue du Chemin Vert

Ⓜ RICHARD LENOIR

Rue Réaumur
Ⓜ RÉAUMUR-SÉBASTOPOL
Ⓜ 17 ARTS ET MÉTIERS

Rue Beaubourg

Rue des Archives

Rue Charlot

Rue Vieille du Temple

Rue de Turenne

Rue St. Sébastien
Ⓜ ST-SÉBASTIEN FROISSART

Rue St. Sabin
Rue Amelot
Blvd. Beaumarchais
Blvd. Richard Lenoir
Rue Sedaine

Ⓜ 49 ÉTIENNE MARCEL
48
50

Blvd. de Sébastopol
Rue St. Denis

Rue Rambuteau
Rambuteau
Ⓜ RAMBUTEAU
Centre Pompidou
51
Rue du Renard
52
53
54

Musée Picasso

Grand Camavalet
Rue des Francs Bourgeois

Place des Vosges
63
64

BREGUET SABIN
65
69

CHEMIN VERT
Ⓜ
70
Rue des Tournelles

Ⓜ BASTILLE
68 →
BASTILLE

61
62
66
Place de la Bastille
Ⓜ BASTILLE
Opéra Bastille
67 →

HOTEL DE VILLE
Ⓜ
Rue St. Antoine
Ⓜ ST-PAUL

Hôtel de Ville
Ave. Victoria

Rue St. Paul
BASTILLE
Blvd. Henri IV
Blvd. Bourbon
Blvd. de la Bastille

Quai de l'Hôtel de Ville
60
Quai des Célestins
PONT MARIE
Ⓜ SULLY-MORLAND

Pont au Change
Pont Notre Dame
Pont d'Arcole
Seine
Pont Louis Philippe
Pont Marie

ILE DE LA CITÉ
ILE ST-LOUIS

Bd. du Palais
Ste-Chapelle
Ⓜ CITÉ
R. de la Cité
R. d'Arcole
55
56
Pont St. Louis
57
Rue des Deux Ponts
58
59
Pont de Sully
Notre Dame

La Poule au Pot **32**	Le Carrousel **12**	Le Vaudeville **26**	Marie-Louise **75**	Restaurant Opéra **13**
La Rose de France **43**	Le Dogon **45**	Le Vieux Bistro **55**	Maxim's **2**	Shing-Jung **76**
La Samaritaine **41**	Le Fumoir **40**	Les Ambassadeurs **1**	Paris-Dakar **44**	Stohrer **37**
La Tour de Monthléry (Chez Denise) **33**	Le Grain de Folie **74**	Lescure **9**	Pharamond **50**	Trumilou **60**
Le 30 (Chez Fauchon) **6**	Le Grand Véfour **23**	Lizard Lounge **61**	Restaurant d'Éric Frechon **73**	Wally Le Saharien **22**
Le Berry's **75**	Le Grand Zinc **19**	Lucas-Carton (Alain Senderens) **5**		Willi's Wine Bar **27**
Le Brise-Miche **53**	Le Gutenberg **36**	Mansouria **88**		
Le Café de la Musique **73**	Le Manguier **72**	Marc-Annibal de Coconnas **64**		
Le Café Zephyr **17**	Le Train Bleu **67**			

99

($9.85–$16.65); main courses 68–135 F ($11.55–$22.95). AE, V. Daily 9am–7pm (lunch served 11:45am–3pm). Métro: Tuileries. TEA/LIGHT FARE.

In the high-rent district near the Hôtel Inter-Continental, this *salon de thé* combines fashion-industry glitter and bourgeois respectability. The carpets are plush, the ceilings are high, and the gilded accessories have the right amount of patina. For a view (over tea and delicate sandwiches) of the lionesses of haute couture, this place has no equal. Overwrought waitresses bear silver trays with light platters, pastries, drinks, and tea or coffee to tiny marbletop tables. Lunch usually offers a salad and a plat du jour like chicken salad, steak tartare, sole meunière, or poached salmon. The house specialty, designed to go well with a cup of tea, is a Mont Blanc, a combination of chestnut cream and meringue. There are two drawbacks: The tearoom is in a section of rue de Rivoli that's getting scuzzy, and the service tends to be a bit snooty.

Au Rendezvous des Camionneurs. 72 quai des Orfèvres, 1er. ☎ **01-43-54-88-74.** Reservations recommended on weekends. Main courses 88–98 F ($14.95–$16.65); fixed-price menu 78–138 F ($13.25–$23.45). AE, MC, V. Daily noon–2:30pm and 7–11:30pm (last order). Métro: Pont-Neuf. FRENCH.

Set adjacent to the Pont-Neuf on the Ile de la Cité, this restaurant that draws a gay crowd has the look, feel, and service of a traditional Lyonnais bistro. It was founded in 1870, and many of its original mirrors and banquettes remain, even the burgundy, olive, and khaki color scheme. Its traditional fare is reasonably priced and well prepared. Dishes include terrine of rabbit, *crottin de chevignol* (a traditional appetizer layered with goat's cheese), noisettes of lamb with tarragon, snails with garlic cream sauce, and a ragout of mussels and shrimp on a bed of leeks. Particularly delicious is St-Jacques with Dieppoise sauce—a stew of scallops garnished with mussels, shrimp, white wine, herbs, and cream. The staff is intelligent and charming.

Chez Vong. 10 rue de la Grande-Truanderie, 1er. ☎ **01-40-26-09-36.** Reservations recommended. Main courses 100–185 F ($17–$31.45). AE, DC, MC, V. Mon–Sat noon–2:30pm and 7pm–midnight. Métro: Etienne-Marcel. CANTONESE.

This is the kind of Les Halles restaurant you head for when you've had your fill of grand French cuisine and grander culinary pretensions. The decor is a soothing mixture of green and browns, steeped in a Chinese colonial ambience that evokes turn-of-the-century Shanghai. Menu items feature shrimp and scallops served as spicy as you like, including a superheated version with garlic and red peppers; "joyous beef" that mingles sliced filet with pepper sauce; chicken in puff pastry with ginger; and a tempting array of fresh fish dishes. No run-of-the-mill setting, the whims of fashion have decreed this as one of the hipster-restaurants-of-the-moment, and, as such, it's full of folk from the worlds of entertainment and the arts.

✪ **Joe Allen.** 30 rue Pierre-Lescot, 1er. ☎ **01-42-36-70-13.** Reservations recommended for dinner. Fixed-price menu 112–140 F ($19.05–$23.80). Main courses 75–140 F ($14–$25). AE, MC, V. Daily noon–1am. Métro: Etienne-Marcel. AMERICAN.

Joe Allen long ago invaded Les Halles with his hamburger. Though the New York restaurateur admits "it's a silly idea," it works, and it's easily the best burger in Paris. While listening to the jukebox, you can order savory black-bean soup, spicy chili, juicy sirloin steak, barbecued spareribs, or apple pie. Joe Allen is getting more sophisticated, catering to modern tastes with dishes like grilled salmon with coconut rice and sun-dried tomatoes.

Joe claims that his saloon is the only place in Paris that serves authentic New York cheesecake or real pecan pie. Thanks to French chocolate, he feels that his brownies are better than those in the States. Giving the brownies tough competition are the California chocolate-mousse pie, strawberries Romanoff, and coconut-cream pie. On a

La Gastronomie 101

In a nation devoted to the pursuit of gastronomic excellence, you'll find a wide array of chefs (skilled and otherwise) eager to impart a few of their culinary insights—for a fee. A knowledge of at least rudimentary French is a good idea before you enroll, although a visual demonstration of any culinary technique is often more valuable than reading or hearing about it. The cooking schools listed below will send you information in English or French if you write to them in advance; their courses might be attended by professional chefs and serious or competitive connoisseurs.

Ritz-Escoffier Ecole de Gastronomie Française, 15 place Vendôme, 75001 Paris (☎ **800/966-5758** in the United States, or 01-43-16-30-50). Famed for his titanic rages in the kitchens of the French and English aristocrats who engaged him to prepare their banquets, and also for his well-publicized culinary codifications, Georges-Auguste Escoffier (1846–1935) taught the Edwardian Age how to eat. Today, the Ritz Hotel, site of many of Escoffier's meals, maintains a school that offers daily demonstration classes of the master's techniques. Ritz-Escoffier demonstrations are held Monday and Thursday from 3 to 5:30pm and cost 275 F ($46.75). Classes (taught in French or English) in specific techniques, such as baking, pastry, fish preparation, or French cooking, cost from 5,700 to 6,000 F ($969 to $1,020) for 1 week. The 12-week Ritz-Escoffier course, priced at 74,000 F ($12,580), is designed to present an overview of most aspects of the repertoire of French cuisine, and as such, is heavily patronized by passionate amateurs and ambitious professional chefs.

Le Cordon Bleu, 8 rue Léon Delhomme, 75015 Paris (☎ **800/457-CHEF** in the U.S., or 01-53-68-22-50). Originally established in 1895, this is the most famous French cooking school. Cordon Bleu's most prestigious and sought-after courses are 9-month curriculums that expose the participant to every aspect of the French culinary process. At graduation, certificates of competence are issued—highly prized within the restaurant world. Many gourmet enthusiasts prefer a less intense immersion into the rituals of French cuisine and opt for either a 4-day workshop or a 3-hour demonstration class. Enrollment in either of these is on a first-come, first-served basis; the cost is 220 F ($37.40) for a demonstration that shows every aspect of how to prepare at least one (and sometimes two or three) complicated culinary specialty from start to finish. A 4-day culinary workshop covering most of the major categories of food preparation (soup, terrines, meats, fish, and desserts) costs 5,070 F ($861.90). Also of interest to professional chefs (or wannabes) is a 5-week course in catering; it's offered twice a year and attracts avid business hopefuls. Any of these programs, even the 3-hour quickies, offer unexpected insights into the culinary subculture of Paris.

regular night, if you haven't made a reservation for dinner, expect to wait at the New York bar for at least 30 minutes.

La Fermette du Sud-Ouest. 31 rue Coquillière, 1er. ☎ **01-42-36-73-55.** Reservations recommended. Main courses 70–105 F ($11.90–$17.85); fixed-price menu (served at lunch and before 9pm at dinner) 90–145 F ($15.30–$24.65). MC, V. Mon–Sat noon–2:30pm and 7:30–10:30pm. Métro: Les Halles. SOUTHWESTERN FRENCH.

Set in the heart of one of the most ancient neighborhoods of Paris, a stone's throw from the Church of Ste-Eustache, this restaurant occupies the site of what was built as a convent during the 1500s. After the French Revolution, the convent was converted into a coaching inn that preserved the original's stonework and massive beams. La Fermette prepares rich, savory stews and confits that celebrate agrarian France, serving them on the ground floor and on a mezzanine resembling a medieval choir loft. Menu items include an age-old but ever-popular version of magret of duckling with flap mushrooms; *andouilletes* (chitterling sausages); and a sometimes startling array of *cochonailles* (pork products and by-products) that you probably need to be French to appreciate. Cassoulet is an enduring specialty that continues year after year.

La Poule au Pot. 9 rue Vauvilliers, 1er. ☎ **01-42-36-32-96.** Reservations recommended before 10pm, otherwise not necessary. Main courses 100–150 F ($17–$25.50); fixed-price menu 160 F ($27.20). MC, V. Tues–Sun 7pm–6am. Métro: Louvre or Les Halles. FRENCH/LATE-NIGHT.

This all-night bistro welcomes late-night carousers and show-biz personalities looking for a meal after a performance. (Past aficionados have included members of the Rolling Stones, the artist formerly known as Prince, and Johnny Hallyday.) The decor is authentically art deco, the ambience nurturing, permissive, and warm-hearted. The time-tested and savory menu items include a salad of warm goat cheese on toast, pan-fried stingray with capers, burgundy-style snails, country pâté on a bed of onion marmalade, and a succulent and very large version of the restaurant's namesake, chicken served in a pot with slices of pâté and fresh vegetables. In summer, this savory house specialty can be served cold, on a bed of lettuce, with a vinaigrette sauce, as an antidote to the summer heat.

La Rose de France. 24 place Dauphine, 1er. ☎ **01-43-54-10-12.** Reservations recommended. Main courses 80–100 F ($13.60–$17); menu du jour 140 F ($23.80). AE, V. Mon–Fri noon–2pm and 7–10pm. Closed last 3 weeks in Aug and 15 days at end of Dec. Métro: Cité or Pont-Neuf. FRENCH.

This restaurant is located in the old section of Ile de la Cité near Notre-Dame, just around the corner from the old Pont-Neuf. You'll dine with a crowd of young Parisians who know they can expect a good meal here at reasonable prices. Founded more than 30 years ago by its present owner, Mr. Cointepas, this place can be relied on for fresh food at affordable prices served in a warm and friendly atmosphere. In warm weather the sidewalk tables overlooking the Palais de Justice are most popular.

Main dishes include sweetbreads, veal chop flambéed with Calvados and served with apples, filet of beef en croûte, and lamb chops seasoned with the herbs of Provence and served with gratin of potatoes. For dessert, try the fruit tart of the day or the sorbet of the month.

La Tour de Monthléry (Chez Denise). 5 rue des Prouvaires, 1er. ☎ **01-42-36-21-82.** Reservations not necessary. Main courses 65–135 F ($11.05–$22.95). V. Open continuously from Mon at 7am to Sat at 7am. Métro: Louvre or Les Halles. FRENCH/LATE-NIGHT.

This restaurant manages to be both workaday and stylish at the same time—no small feat considering the fact that its gregarious owner, Denise Bénariac, has maintained her reign over this place for more than 30 years. The name derives from the establishment's position at the end of one of France's first rail spurs. Produce and passengers from Monthléry, near Lyons, were carried to a point near this restaurant for generations before the line's eventual shutdown. Amid a decor that has changed little since 1900 (note the long nickel-plated bar near the entrance), you can order hearty, unfussy cuisine. The food tastes best late at night after a long night of carousing. Menu items include grilled pig's trotters, mutton stew, steaks with peppercorns, stuffed cabbage, and a golden-velvety pâté of chicken livers. Wine goes with this kind of food beautifully, and the restaurant complies by recommending several worthy but unpretentious vintages.

☻ **Lescure.** 7 rue de Mondovi, 1er. ☎ **01-42-60-18-91.** Reservations not accepted. Main courses 26–84 F ($4.40–$14.30); 4-course fixed-price menu 105 F ($17.85). V. Mon–Fri noon–2:15pm and 7–11pm. Closed 3 weeks in Aug. Métro: Concorde. FRENCH.

This minibistro is a major find—it's one of the few reasonably priced restaurants near place de la Concorde. It's animated, fun, irreverent, and very appealing. You'll get a lot for your franc here. The tables on the sidewalk are tiny and there isn't much room inside, but what this place does have is rustic charm. The kitchen is wide open, and the aroma of drying bay leaves, salami, and garlic pigtails hanging from the ceiling fills the room. Expect *cuisine bourgeoise*—nothing that innovative, just substantial, hearty fare. Perhaps begin with *pâté en croûte* (pâté encased in pastry). Main-course house specialties include *confit de canard* (duckling) and cabbage stuffed with salmon. The chef's fruit tarts are a favorite dessert. In autumn and winter, expect a savory repertoire of game dishes such as venison and pheasant.

2ND ARRONDISSEMENT (LA BOURSE)
MODERATE

Chez Georges. 1 rue du Mail, 2e. ☎ **01-42-60-07-11.** Reservations required. Main courses 140–160 F ($23.80–$27.20). AE, MC, V. Mon–Sat noon–2:15pm and 7–9:45pm. Closed 3 weeks in Aug. Métro: Bourse. FRENCH.

This bistro is something of a local landmark, opened in 1964 near the Bourse, and run by three generations of the same family. Naturally, at lunch it's packed with stock-exchange members. The owners serve what they call *la cuisine bourgeoise,* or comfort food. Waiters bring around bowls of appetizers, such as celery rémoulade, to get you started. You can follow with sweetbreads with morels, duck breast with cèpe mushrooms, a classic cassoulet, or a pot-au-feu (beef simmered with vegetables). A delight is fillet of sole with a sauce made from Pouilly wine and crème fraîche. Beaujolais goes great with this hearty food.

Le Vaudeville. 29 rue Vivienne, 2e. ☎ **01-40-20-04-62.** Reservations recommended in the evenings. Main courses 90–180 F ($15.30–$30.60); fixed-price menu 132 F ($22.45) at lunch, 132–179 F ($22.45–$30.45) at dinner. AE, DC, V. Daily noon–3:30pm and 7pm–2am. Métro: Bourse. FRENCH/LATE-NIGHT.

Adjacent to the stock exchange (La Bourse), this bistro has retained its original marble walls and art deco carvings since 1918. It has the same nostalgic atmosphere as the fabled La Coupole on the Left Bank, but is smaller and more convivial. In summer, tables dot a terrace amid banks of geraniums. Any time of year, the place is boisterous and informal, often welcoming groups of six or eight diners at a time to its closely spaced tables. A bar near the entrance provides a perch if your reservation is delayed.

The bountiful roster of platters includes snails in garlic butter, platters of shellfish, smoked salmon, sauerkraut, and several kinds of grilled meats. Three dishes in particular reign as enduring favorites: the fresh codfish served with mashed potatoes and truffle juice, the fresh escalope of warm foie gras served with grapes, and breast of duck with acacia honey. Le Vaudeville serves the type of fare French bistro-goers expect, which means it's rarely innovative, and not every dish is inspirational—the main value here is the fixed-price menu.

INEXPENSIVE

Au Clair de Lune. 13 rue Française, 2e. ☎ **01-42-33-59-10.** Main courses 54–70 F ($9.20–$11.90); fixed-price menu 68 F ($11.55). DC, MC, V. Daily noon–2:30pm and 7:30–11pm. Métro: Etienne-Marcel or Sentier. ALGERIAN/FRENCH.

This neighborhood staple has flourished in the heart of Paris's wholesale garment district since the 1930s, when Algeria was a distinct part of the French-speaking world. Today you'll dine in a long, narrow room whose walls are hung with colorful Berber carpets and whose patrons are likely to include many shop workers from the nearby wholesale clothiers. There's always the Algerian staple of couscous on the menu, as well as an array of such oft-changing daily specials as veal stew, shoulder or rack of lamb, grilled fish, and roast chicken. The portions are so large you should take along a ravenous appetite. The wines are from throughout France and North Africa.

Babylone. 34 rue Tiquetonne, 2e. ☎ **01-42-33-48-35.** Main courses 75–125 F ($12.75–$21.25). V. Daily 8pm–7am. Métro: Etienne-Marcel or Sentier. CREOLE/LATE-NIGHT.

This place honors the French Caribbean island of Guadeloupe with culinary special-ties of accras of codfish and Creole *boudin* (blood sausage), which usually preface such main courses as fricassee of shrimp or chicken or a *colombo* (stew) of baby goat. Look for African masks, touches of zebra skin, and photos of the divas and celebrities (like Stevie Wonder and Jesse Jackson) who have dined here. Some (Diana Ross) you might know; others are celebrated French sports stars and fashion models. Don't think of coming before dark. After 2am or so, the focus shifts away from the hearty Caribbean soul food toward reggae, jazz, and cocktails.

La Clementine. 5 rue St-Marc, 2e. ☎ **01-42-36-91-72.** Reservations required. Main courses 80–105 F ($13.60–$17.85); fixed-price menu 135 F ($22.95). AE, MC, V. Mon–Fri noon–2:30pm and 8–10:30pm. Métro: Bourse or Rue Montmartre. FRENCH.

Set in an antique building adjacent to the Musée Grévin, this well-managed bistro serves time-honored food with an occasional individualistic flair. Among turn-of-the-century panels, polished brass, and mirrors, you can order pepper steak, codfish steak studded with lard, veal braised in the oven and served in its own juices, and an unusual preparation of chicken breast with goat cheese. The *fondant au chocolat* (chocolate candy) seems to be an assiduously guarded, long-cherished family recipe. Since the site includes room for barely 25 diners, advance reservations are important.

3RD ARRONDISSEMENT (LE MARAIS)
EXPENSIVE

L'Ami Louis. 32 rue du Vertbois, 3e. ☎ **01-48-87-77-48.** Reservations required. Main courses 195–320 F ($33.15–$54.40). AE, DC, MC, V. Wed–Sun noon–2pm and 8–11pm. Closed July 19–Aug 25. Métro: Temple. FRENCH.

L'Ami Louis is in one of the least fashionable neighborhoods of central Paris, far removed from the part of the Marais that has become chic, and its facade has seen better days. Nonetheless, this bistro preserves something magical from the prewar years. It's always luring in politicians and moguls, who could be accused of slumming if it were any cheaper.

L'Ami Louis became one of the most famous brasseries in all of Paris in the 1930s, thanks to excellent food served in copious portions and its ostentatiously old-fashioned décor. Its traditions are fervently maintained today. Amid a "brown gravy" decor (the walls retain a smoky patina from the old days), dishes such as roasted suckling lamb, pheasant, venison, confit of duckling, and endless slices of foie gras may commune atop your marble table. Though some whisper that the restaurant's ingredients aren't as select as they were in its heyday, its sauces are as thick as they were between the wars. Don't save room for dessert, which isn't very good.

INEXPENSIVE

Chez Janou. 2 rue Roger-Verlomme, 3e. ☎ **01-42-72-28-41.** Reservations recommended. Main courses 68–98 F ($11.55–$16.65). No credit cards. Daily noon–3pm and 7:30pm–midnight. Métro: Chemin-Vert. PROVENÇAL.

On one of the narrow 17th-century streets behind place des Vosges, this unpretentious bistro operates from a pair of cramped but cozy dining rooms filled with memorabilia from Provence. Service is brusque and sometimes hectic. The menu items include such dishes as large shrimp with pastis sauce, *brouillade des pleurotes* (baked eggs with oyster mushrooms), *velouté* of frogs' legs, fondue of ratatouille, a gratin of mussels, and a simple but savory version of *daube provençale,* which is sometimes compared to pot roast. There's a covered terrace.

L'Ambassade d'Auvergne. 22 rue de Grenier St-Lazare, 3e. ☎ **01-42-72-31-22.** Reservations recommended. Main courses 88–120 F ($14.95–$20.40); fixed-price menu 170 F ($28.90). AE, MC, V. Daily noon–2pm and 7:30–10pm. Métro: Rambuteau. AUVERGNAT/ FRENCH.

You enter this rustic tavern through a busy bar, with heavy oak beams, hanging hams, and ceramic plates. More than any other Paris restaurant, this favorite showcases the culinary generosity of France's most isolated and slow-to-change region, the Auvergne, whose pork products are celebrated throughout France. Examples include a chicory salad with apples and pieces of country ham; pork braised with cabbage, turnips, and white beans; grilled tripe sausages with mashed potatoes and cantal cheese with garlic; and pork jowls with green lentils. Nonpork specialties include pan-fried duck liver with gingerbread; fillets of perch steamed in verbena tea; and roasted rack of lamb with wild mushrooms. Dessert might consist of a poached pear with crispy almonds and caramel sauce, or a wine-flavored sorbet.

4TH ARRONDISSEMENT (ILE DE LA CITÉ/ ILE ST-LOUIS & BEAUBOURG)
VERY EXPENSIVE

✪ **L'Ambroisie.** 9 place des Vosges, 4e. ☎ **01-42-78-51-45.** Reservations required. Main courses 350–530 F ($59.50–$90.10). AE, MC, V. Tues–Sat noon–1:30pm and 8–9:30pm. Métro: St-Paul. FRENCH.

One of the most talented chefs in Paris, Bernard Pacaud has drawn world attention with his vivid flavors and expert culinary skill. He trained at the prestigious Le Vivarois before striking out on his own, first on the Left Bank and now at this early 17th-century town house in Le Marais, a former goldsmith's shop converted into two high-ceilinged salons with a decor that vaguely recalls an Italian palazzo. In summer, there's outdoor seating as well.

Pacaud's tables are nearly always filled with satisfied diners who come back again and again to see where his imagination will take him next. The dishes change with the seasons. From time to time, they'll include a fricassee of Breton lobster with a civet/ red wine sauce served with a puree of peas; or a fillet of turbot braised with celery, served with a julienne of black truffles; or one of our favorite dishes in all of Paris, *poulard de Bresse demi-deuil hommage à la Mère Brazier*—chicken roasted with black truffles and truffled vegetables in a style invented by a Lyonnais matron (La Mère Brazier) after World War II. An award-winning dessert is a *tarte fine sablée* served with bitter chocolate and vanilla-flavored ice cream.

MODERATE

✪ **Bofinger.** 5-7 rue de la Bastille, 4e. ☎ **01-42-72-87-82.** Reservations recommended. Main courses 86–144 F ($14.60–$24.50); fixed-price menu 178 F ($30.25). AE, DC, MC, V. Mon–Fri noon–3pm and 6:30pm–1am, Sat–Sun noon–1am. Métro: Bastille. ALSATIAN/FRENCH.

Founded in the 1860s, Bofinger is the oldest Alsatian brasserie in town and certainly one of the best. It's a belle-epoque dining palace, resplendent with shiny brass and stained glass. If you prefer, you can dine on an outdoor terrace, weather permitting.

Affiliated today with La Coupole, Julien, and the Brasserie Flo, the restaurant has updated its menu, retaining only the most popular of its traditional dishes, such as sauerkraut and a well-prepared version of sole meunière. Recent additions have included such stylish platters as roasted leg of lamb with a fondant of artichoke hearts and a puree of parsley; grilled turbot served with a brandade of fennel; and fillet of stingray with chives and a burnt butter sauce. Shellfish, including an abundance of fresh oysters and lobster, is almost always available in season.

Isama. 4 quai d'Orleans, 4e. ☎ **01-40-46-06-97.** Reservations recommended. Sushi and sashimi, 10–35 F ($1.70–$5.95) per piece; meals 75–225 F ($12.75–$38.25), depending on the fish and how many pieces ordered. Tues–Sat noon–2pm and 7:30–10pm. Métro: Pont-Marie. JAPANESE.

Sitting down in this place is guaranteed to evoke a sense of cultural dislocation, as the staff is mostly from Japan, and few speak very much French or English. That, however, is part of the place's allure for its loyal, usually diet-conscious clients, many of whom work in the arts. The staff is quick to tell you that only authentic Japanese versions of sushi and sashimi are served, with absolutely none of what they define as the California/Japanese cuisine you might have expected. Begin a meal here with miso soup or some pickled vegetables, as a prelude for the wide array of fish (tuna, salmon, whitefish, fluke, snapper, bluefish, oysters, clams, shrimp, and more) that forms this restaurant's backbone. Everything goes quickly here, including the meal—lingering is not encouraged.

Le Vieux Bistro. 14 rue du Cloître-Notre-Dame, 4e. ☎ **01-43-54-18-95.** Main courses 90–165 F ($15.30–$28.05). MC, V. Daily noon–2pm and 7:30–11pm. Métro: Cité. FRENCH.

Few other restaurants offer so close-up, and so forbidding, a view of the massive and somber walls of Paris's largest cathedral, visible through lacy curtains from the windows of the front dining room. To reach it, you'll bypass a dozen souvenir stands, then settle into one of two old-time dining rooms for a flavorful meal of standard French staples. In a pair of rooms flanked with mirrors and a jutting zinc-plated bar, you can order snails with garlic butter, filet mignon roasted in a bag and served with marrow sauce, filets of veal, and a dessert that every French child is exposed to early in life, a *tarte Tatin,* studded with apples and sugar, drenched with Calvados, and capped with fresh cream.

Marc-Annibal de Coconnas. 2 bis place des Vosges, 4e. ☎ **01-42-78-58-16.** Reservations required. Main dishes 90–110 F ($15.30–$18.70); fixed-price menu 135 F ($22.95). AE, DC, MC, V. Wed–Sun noon–2:30pm and 8–10:30pm. Métro: Bastille or St-Paul. FRENCH.

Chef Claude Terrail (owner of La Tour d'Argent) serves superb cuisine in this restaurant named after the legendary rake whose peccadillos scandalized the place des Vosges. The restaurant features a Louis XIII decor of high-backed chairs and elegantly rustic accessories. Menu items change frequently, but present a cost-conscious alternative to the grand cuisine featured by the other restaurants within the chain. Look for items you'd expect in an upscale bistro, such as foie gras maison; baked goat's cheese that's been dunked in white wine; a roasted half-duckling with mashed potatoes; coq au vin; and such desserts as a crème brûlée. None of these items sets off fireworks, but the ingredients are fresh and harmonious, and the prices are fair for the quality.

INEXPENSIVE

✪ **Aquarius.** 54 rue Ste-Croix-de-la-Bretonnerie, 4e. ☎ **01-48-87-48-71.** Reservations not required. Main courses 50–64 F ($8.50–$10.90); fixed-price menu 64–94 F ($10.90–$16) at lunch, 94 F ($16) at dinner. MC, V. Mon–Sat noon–10:15pm. Métro: Hôtel-de-Ville. RER: Châtelet–Les Halles. VEGETARIAN.

In a 17th-century building whose original stonework forms part of the rustic, earthy decor, this is one of the best-known vegetarian restaurants of the Marais. The owners serve only a limited array of (strictly organic) wine, and smoking is expressly forbidden. Their flavorful meals are healthfully prepared and come in generous portions. Choose from an array of soups and salads; a galette of wheat served with crudités and mushroom tarts; or a country plate composed of fried mushrooms and potatoes, garlic, and goat cheese, served with a salad.

✪ **Au Gourmet de l'Ile.** 42 rue St-Louis-en-l'Ile, 4e. ☎ **01-43-26-79-27.** Reservations required. Main courses 70–95 F ($11.90–$16.15); fixed-price menu 100–140 F ($17–$23.80). AE, MC, V. Wed–Sun noon–2pm and 7–10:30pm. Métro: Pont-Marie. FRENCH.

Local regulars swear by the cuisine at Au Gourmet de l'Ile, whose fixed-price meals are among the best bargains in Paris. The setting is beautiful, with a beamed ceiling, walls dating from the 1400s, and candlelit tables. Many Parisian restaurants have attained this level of decor, but they cannot approach the food on this "Gourmet Island."

In the window you'll see a sign emblazoned with five As, which, roughly translated, stand for the Amiable Association of Amateurs of the Authentic Andouillette. These chitterling sausages are soul food to the French. Popular and tasty, too, are *la charbonnée de l'Ile*, a savory pork with onions, and the stuffed mussels in shallot butter. The fixed-price menu includes a choice of 15 appetizers, 15 main courses, salad or cheese, and a choice of 15 desserts.

Brasserie de l'Ile St-Louis. 55 quai de Bourbon, 4e. ☎ **01-43-54-02-59.** Reservations recommended. Main courses 85–130 F ($14.45–$22.10). MC, V. Thurs–Tues noon–midnight. Métro: Pont-Marie. ALSATIAN/FRENCH.

This is the kind of retro-chic brasserie where the likes of Mitterrand, Bardot, Elizabeth Taylor, Grace Jones, and filmmaker John Frankenheimer have always scheduled informal meals and rendezvous. Little about the establishment's patina and paneled decor has changed since the 1880s, giving it an aura modern competitors can only imitate. The menu is conservative and well prepared, including an always-popular version of Alsatian sauerkraut; cassoulet in the old-fashioned style of Toulouse; calf's liver; and a succulent version of jarret of pork with warm apple marmalade.

✪ **Chez Jo Goldenberg.** 7 rue des Rosiers, 4e. ☎ **01-48-87-20-16.** Reservations recommended. Main courses 75–110 F ($12.75–$18.70). AE, DC, MC, V. Daily noon–1am. Métro: St-Paul. JEWISH/CENTRAL EUROPEAN.

This is the best-known restaurant on the "Street of the Rose Bushes." Albert Goldenberg, the doyen of Jewish restaurateurs in Paris, long ago moved to choicer surroundings (at 69 av. de Wagram, 17e), but his brother, Joseph, has remained here. Dining is on two levels, one for nonsmokers. Look for the collection of samovars and the white fantail pigeon in a wicker cage. Interesting paintings and strolling musicians add to the ambience. The *carpe farcie* (stuffed carp) is a preferred selection, but the beef goulash is also good. We like the eggplant moussaka and the pastrami. The menu also offers Israeli wines, but Monsieur Goldenberg admits that they're not as good as French wine. Live Israeli music is presented every night beginning at 9pm, and during Jewish holidays, such as Pesach, Rosh Hashana, and Yom Kippur, special menus are presented in honor of the event— but reservations are a must.

Dame Tartine. 2 rue Brise-Miche, 4e. ☎ **01-42-77-32-22.** Reservations not necessary. Platters 31–45 F ($5.25–$7.65). MC, V. Daily noon–midnight. Métro: Rambuteau. FRENCH.

This place is a restaurant, but it feels like a busy cafe. Don't expect either intimacy or haute gastronomy: It's hectic, with streams of clients on their way to and from the nearby Centre Pompidou and students counting their francs. You can expect simple but generous platters that include salads, chicken with curries or cinnamon sauce, salmon with coconut and curry sauce, ham steak, and fried fillet of fish with tartar sauce. Most are served with bread, so you can create your own made-to-order open-faced sandwich. Most of the artwork on the wall is for sale.

Le Brise-Miche. 10 rue Brise-Miche, 4e. ☎ **01-42-78-44-11.** Reservations recommended. Main courses 55–85 F ($9.35–$14.45); fixed-price menu 75 F ($12.75) until 9pm. AE, DC, MC, V. Apr–Sept daily 8am–midnight, with full menu available daily noon–11pm (last order); Oct–Mar Mon–Fri 10am–5pm (last order), Sat–Sun 10am–10:30pm (last order). Métro: Rambuteau, Hôtel-de-Ville, or Châtelet–Les Halles. FRENCH.

Whimsical and sometimes chaotic, this appealing restaurant shares something of the avant-garde aesthetic of its neighbor, the Centre Pompidou. Named after the bread rations that were issued here during World War II, it occupies an enviable location beside the medieval church of St-Merri and the neighborhood's most charming fountain. In fair weather, tables and chairs overlook a spinning, spitting, and bobbing fountain, beautifully sculpted by Jean Tingueley and Niki de Saint-Phalle. You might begin with a beef (or shark!) carpaccio with green salad, then follow with a noisette of lamb flavored with whisky and fresh thyme, or perhaps a fricassee of poultry with morels. Finish with an orange and kiwi salad in a vanilla-flavored wine sauce.

Trumilou. 84 quai de l'Hôtel-de-Ville, 4e. ☎ **01-42-77-63-98.** Reservations recommended on Sat–Sun. Main courses 75–100 F ($12.75–$17); fixed-price menu 80–98 F ($13.60–$16.65). MC, V. Daily noon–3pm and 7–11pm. Métro: Hôtel-de-Ville. FRENCH.

This is one of the most popular of the many restaurants surrounding Paris's Hôtel de Ville, and, as such, has welcomed most of France's politicians, including George Pompidou, who came here frequently before he was elected president of France. ("As soon as they become president, they opt for grander restaurants," say the good-natured owners, the Drumond family.) The countrified decor includes a collection of farm implements and family memorabilia, amidst a clutch of tables. Most diners remain on the street level, although additional seating is available in the cellar. The menu rarely changes, nor does it need to. Examples include chicken Provençal, sweetbreads "in the style of our grandmother," duckling with plums, stuffed cabbage, and the inevitable blanquette de veau, or veal in white sauce.

8TH ARRONDISSEMENT (CHAMPS-ELYSÉES/MADELEINE)
VERY EXPENSIVE

✪ **Lasserre.** 17 av. Franklin D. Roosevelt, 8e. ☎ **01-43-59-53-43.** Fax 01-45-63-72-23. Reservations required. Main courses 150–270 F ($25.50–$45.90) at lunch, 240–340 F ($40.80–$57.80) at dinner. AE, MC, V. Tues–Sat 12:30–2:30pm; Mon–Sat 7:30–10:30pm. Closed Aug. Métro: F. D. Roosevelt. FRENCH.

This elegant restaurant was a simple bistro before World War II, but it's since become a legend that attracts gourmands from around the world. The main salon stretches two stories high, with a mezzanine on each side. Tall arched windows draped with silk frame tables set with fine porcelain, crystal glasses edged in gold, and silver candelabras. Overhead, the ceiling is painted with lamb-white clouds and a cerulean sky, but in good weather the staff slides back the roof to reveal the real sky, letting moonlight or sunshine pour into the room.

Food is a combination of classicism and originality, and count on imagination and high drama in the presentation. Michelin awards this restaurant only two stars, as opposed to three for Lucas-Carton or Taillevent, but we've never understood why.

The appetizers are among the finest in Paris, including a salad of truffles, a three-meat terrine, or Belon oysters flavored with Chablis. The signature main course is fillets of sole *Club de la Casserole*, poached fillets served in puff pastry with asparagus tips and asparagus-flavored cream sauce. When you taste the meat and poultry dishes, such as veal kidneys flambé or pigeon André Malraux, you'd swear Escoffier were still alive. The spectacular desserts include a soufflé Grand Marnier or a selection of three freshly made sorbets of the season. The cellar, with some 180,000 bottles of wine, is among the most remarkable in Paris.

✪ **L'Astor.** In the Hotel Astor, 11 rue d'Astorg, 8e. ☎ 01-53-05-05-20. Fax 01-53-05-05-30. Reservations recommended. Main courses 110–240 F ($18.70–$40.80); fixed-price menu 298–520 F ($50.65–$88.40). AE, DC, MC, V. Mon–Fri noon–2pm and 7:30–10pm. Métro: St-Augustin. FRENCH.

What happens to great French chefs after they retire? If they're lucky enough, they maintain their role by defining themselves as "culinary consultants" and dropping in to keep an eye on what's happening two or three times a week. That's what happened when guru Joël Robuchon retired from his citadel on avenue Raymond Poincaré in favor of a quieter life. His replacement is well-respected Eric Lecerf, a formidable chef who knows better than anyone else how to match the tours-de-force of the master. The setting, established early in 1996, is a gray-and-white enclave sheltered by an etched-glass art deco ceiling with discreetly luxurious touches inspired by the 1930s and 1940s.

If you dine here, expect an almost religious devotion to Robuchon's specialties, and a less overwhelming emphasis on newer dishes created and fostered by his replacement. Examples of "classic Robuchon" include caramelized sea urchins in aspic with a fennel-flavored cream sauce; cannellonis stuffed with eggplant with fillets of tuna and olive oil; and spit-roasted Bresse chicken roasted with flap mushrooms. Items created by Lecerf include carpaccio of Breton lobster with olive oil and confit of tomatoes; roasted and braised rack of lamb; and supreme of pigeon with cabbage and foie gras. The old Robuchon standbys have stood the test of time, although to an increasing degree they're viewed as one would vintage Chanel or Dior, and priced accordingly.

✪ **Lucas-Carton (Alain Senderens).** 9 place de la Madeleine, 8e. ☎ **01-42-65-22-90.** Fax 01-42-65-06-23. Reservations required several days ahead for lunch and several weeks ahead for dinner. Main courses 240–700 F ($40.80–$119); fixed-price lunch 395 F ($67.15). AE, DC, MC, V. Tues–Fri noon–2:30pm; Mon–Sat 8–10:15pm. Closed 3 weeks in Aug. Métro: Madeleine. FRENCH.

When Alain Senderens took over this landmark belle-epoque restaurant, he added some welcome modern touches, along with a brilliantly realized culinary repertoire. The dining rooms downstairs and private rooms upstairs are decorated with mirrors, fragrant bouquets of flowers, and wood paneling that has been polished every week since its installation in 1900.

Every dish here is influenced by Senderens's creative flair. Menu items, which change with the seasons, include polenta with black truffles, duckling Apicius (roasted with honey and spices), a pastillade of rabbit, and sweetbreads with acidified carrot juice. The puree of chestnuts is a perfect choice to end the meal. Senderens is constantly creating and experimenting, so, by the time you visit, there will probably be a fresh addition to his innovative menu. His latest sensations include lobster roasted with vanilla, and *poularde demi-deuil,* a Bresse hen whose flesh has been scored with black truffles. (The resulting black-and-white flesh is supposed to be "in partial mourning.") It's accompanied by saffron-flavored rice.

Maxim's. 3 rue Royale, 8e. ☎ **01-42-65-27-94.** Fax 01-40-17-02-91. Reservations required. Main courses 225–330 F ($38.25–$56.10) at lunch, 300–470 F ($51–$79.90) at dinner. AE, DC, MC, V. Mon–Sat 12:30–2:30pm and 7:30–10:30pm. Métro: Concorde. FRENCH.

Maxim's is the world's most legendary restaurant. The Michelin guide no longer even bothers to recommend it, much less give it stars, but Maxim's carries on in its overpriced way. And with the almost shameless exploitation by its present owners, satellite branches, each with a replica of the original's belle-epoque decor, have popped up in New York, Beijing, Tokyo, Moscow, and Shanghai. Each branch trades on the nostalgic—and partially faded—glamor of the Rue Royale original, which aggressively orchestrates it all.

The restaurant was a favorite of Edward VII, prince of Wales, and Louis Jourdan—at that time considered "the handsomest man in the world"—took Leslie Caron to dine here in the musical *Gigi*. Today, rich tourists from around the world occupy fabled tables where Onassis wooed Callas. Clothing-industry giant Pierre Cardin took over the restaurant in 1981. Although not always available, billiby soup—made with mussels, white wine, cream (of course), chopped onions, celery, parsley, and coarsely ground pepper—is a classic opener. Another favorite, the sole Albert, named after the late maître d'hôtel, is flavored with chopped herbs and bread crumbs, plus a large glass of vermouth. Other specialties include filet of beef cooked with truffles, noisettes of lamb with foie gras, and Bresse chicken with tarragon sauce. For dessert, try the tarte Tatin.

✪ **Pierre Gagnaire.** 6 rue Balzac, 8e. ☎ **01-44-35-18-25.** Fax 01-44-35-18-37. Reservations are imperative and difficult to make. Main courses 290–450 F ($49.30–$76.50); fixed-price menu 500–900 F ($85–$153) at lunch, 900 F ($153) at dinner. AE, DC, MC, V. Mon–Fri 12:30–2:15pm; Sun–Fri 7–10pm. Métro: George V. FRENCH.

Although the PR here may be the worst in Paris, if you are able to make a reservation, it's worth the effort. Menus are seasonally adjusted to take advantage of France's rich bounty. The chef has a dazzling way of blending flavors and textures. Every dish is cooked to order, and Pierre Gagnaire, the famous owner, demands perfection before the plate is served. One critic wrote, "Picasso stretched the limits of painting; Gagnaire does it with cooking." Try anything from a menu that changes every 2 months: Examples of the creative panache include freshwater crayfish cooked tempura style with thin-sliced flash-seared vegetables and a sweet-and-sour sauce, or turbot cooked in a bag and served with fennel and Provençal lemons. Chicken with truffles is part of a two-tiered service: first, featuring the breast in a wine-based aspic, and second, featuring the thighs chopped into roughly textured pieces. Dessert might be a chocolate soufflé served with a frozen parfait and Sicilian pistachios.

✪ **Taillevent.** 15 rue Lamennais, 8e. ☎ **01-44-95-15-01.** Fax 01-42-25-95-18. Reservations required weeks, even months, in advance for both lunch and dinner. Main courses 295–500 F ($50.15–$85). AE, DC, MC, V. Mon–Fri noon–2:30pm and 7–10pm. Closed Aug. Métro: George V. FRENCH.

Taillevent dates from 1946 and has since climbed steadily in the ranks of excellence. Today it's recognized as the most outstanding all-around restaurant in Paris, challenged only by Lucas-Carton, Pierre Gagnaire, and Lassere in this highly competitive arrondissement.

The setting is a grand 19th-century town house off the Champs-Elysées, with paneled rooms and crystal chandeliers. The restaurant is named after a famous chef of the 14th century (Guillaume Tirel Taillevent) who wrote one of the oldest known books on French cookery. The place is small, as the owner wishes, since it permits him to give personal attention to every facet of the operation and maintain a discreet club atmosphere. You might begin with a *boudin* (sausage) of Breton lobster à la Nage; cream of watercress soup with Sevruga caviar; or duck liver with spice bread and ginger. Main courses include red snapper with black olives; Scottish salmon cooked in sea salt with a sauce of olive oil and lemons; or a cassolette of crayfish from Brittany. Dessert might be a nougatine glacé with pears. The wine list is among the best in Paris.

Although Monsieur Vrinat likes Americans, it isn't always easy for visitors from the States and other countries to book a table, since the owner prefers about 60% of his clients to be French.

Restaurants near Place Charles-de-Gaulle

Alain Ducasse ◆ 2
Androuët ◆ 16
Café Indochine ◆ 13
Chez Georges ◆ 7
Chicago Pizza Pie Factory ◆ 19
Copenhague/Flora Danica ◆ 23
Faugeron ◆ 3
Fouquet's ◆ 22
Guy Savoy ◆ 9

Jamin ◆ 5
La Butte Chaillot ◆ 4
La Rôtisserie d'Armaillé ◆ 4
Lasserre ◆ 14
Ladurée ◆ 21
Le Bistro d'à
  Côté Flaubert ◆ 11
Le Bistro de l'Étoile ◆ 6
Le Vivarois ◆ 1

Les Gourmets
  des Ternes ◆ 12
Michel Rostang ◆ 10
Pierre Gagnaire ◆ 17
Planet Hollywood ◆ 20
Spoon, Food & Wine ◆ 15
Taillevent ◆ 18

Ⓜ Métro Stop
Ⓡ RER Stop

EXPENSIVE

✪ **Buddha Bar.** 8 rue Boissy d'Anglas, 8e. ☎ **01-53-05-90-00.** Reservations recommended. Main courses 115–260 F ($19.55–$44.20). AE, MC, V. Mon–Fri noon–3pm; daily 6pm–2am. Métro: Concorde. FRENCH/PACIFIC RIM.

This place is hot, hot, hot—truly the restaurant of the moment in Paris. A location on a chic street near the Champs-Elysées, and allegiance to a fashionable fusion of French, Asian, and Californian cuisine, almost guarantees a clientele devoted to the whims of fashion and trend. That might actually enhance your appreciation of a cutting-edge culinary theme that combines Japanese sashimi, Vietnamese spring rolls, lacquered duck, sautéed shrimp with black bean sauce, grilled chicken skewers with orange sauce, sweet-and-sour spareribs, and crackling squab à l'orange. Many come here just for a drink in the carefully lacquered, hip-looking bar, upstairs from the street-level dining room.

✪ **Copenhague/Flora Danica.** 142 av. des Champs-Elysées, 8e. ☎ **01-44-13-86-26.** Reservations recommended. Main courses 70–180 F ($11.90–$30.60); fixed-price menu

175–260 F ($29.75–$44.20). AE, DC, MC, V. Restaurant Copenhague: Mon–Fri noon–2:30pm; Mon–Sat 7–10:30pm; closed Aug and Jan 1–7. Flora Danica: daily noon–2:30pm and 7–11pm. Métro: George V. DANISH.

The specialties of Denmark are served with flair at the "Maison du Danemark," which functions as a quasi-official Danish goodwill ambassador. In many ways, it's the best restaurant along the Champs-Elysées, with an outside terrace for midsummer dining. There are two dining areas to choose from: the Flora Danica, on the street level, and the somewhat more formal Restaurant Copenhague, upstairs.

To be thoroughly Danish, order an aperitif of aquavit and ignore the wine list in favor of Carlsberg. Menu items include a terrine of reindeer, foie gras, smoked salmon, fresh shrimp, or an elegant array of open-faced sandwiches. The house specialty is a platter of Scandinavian delicacies drawn from the many seafood and dairy specialties that the Danes prepare exceptionally well. Our preferred dish is grilled Norwegian salmon cooked on one side only. The cookery is forever competent here, not "forever boring," as one critic suggested.

Le 30 (Chez Fauchon). 30 place de la Madeleine, 8e. ☎ **01-47-42-56-58.** Reservations recommended, especially for lunch. Main courses 150–310 F ($25.50–$52.70). AE, DC, MC, V. Mon–Sat 12:15–2:30pm and 7:30–10:30pm. Métro: Madeleine. FRENCH.

In 1990, Fauchon, one of Europe's most legendary delicatessens (see "Food" in chapter 8), transformed one of its upper rooms into an airy pastel-colored showplace that caught on immediately as a lunch spot for local bankers, stockbrokers, and merchants. Menu selections employ the freshest ingredients available downstairs, and might include crayfish tails roasted with sweet spices; foie gras with pepper and champagne sauce; warm oysters with a purée of cauliflower and parsley; crayfish roasted with fennel, smoke-flavored salt, and saffron-flavored vinegar; and strips of sole poached in a vanilla-flavored coffee sauce.

Spoon, Food & Wine. In the Marignan-Elysée Hotel, 14 rue Marignan, 8e. ☎ **01-40-76-34-44.** Reservations recommended. Appetizers, main courses, vegetable side dishes each 65–180 F ($11.05–$30.60). Mon–Fri noon–2:30pm and 7–11:30pm. AE, DC, MC, V. Métro: F. D. Roosevelt. INTERNATIONAL.

The newest venture of *wunderkind* chef Alain Ducasse, opened in December 1998, has been both hailed as a "restaurant for the millennium" and condemned by some Parisian food critics. Surreal and a bit absurd, the venue is hypermodern, with a claustrophobic dining room that evokes both stylish Paris and stylish California. The cuisine roams the world for inspiration, with such middlebrow offerings as classic but rather bland American macaroni and cheese, a BLT, barbecued ribs, chicken wings, and pastrami. Other dishes evoke Italy, Latin America, Asia, and India. (Sometimes the wait staff didn't know the national origin of a dish—youm loumg, for example, which is squid and shellfish in a spicy bouillon.) The steamed lobster with mango chutney is a winner. For a "vegetable garden," you can mix and match among 15 ingredients, including iceberg lettuce. Pasta comes with a selection of five different sauces. Although a first glance at the menu makes the restaurant seem moderate in price, tabs zoom up very quickly, especially when wine, service, and VAT are added in.

MODERATE

Laudurée. 75 av. des Champs-Elysées, 8e. ☎ **01-40-75-08-75.** Reservations needed for the restaurant, not for the cafe. Main courses 150–250 F ($25.50–$42.50); pastries from 25 F ($4.25). AE, DC, MC, V. Daily 8am–1am. FRENCH.

Laudurée, acclaimed since 1862 as one of the grand cafes of Paris (in a location near the Madeleine), has invaded the Champs-Elysées, adding an extra touch of class to the neighborhood. This offshoot of one of the city's best-loved tea salons was expanded in 1999 and caters to an international set attired in everything from Givenchy to GAP.

Le Grand Fromage

Cheese is king at ✪ **Androuët,** 6 rue Arsène Houssaye, 8e (☎ **01-42-89-95-00**). True, it's a novelty restaurant, but if you're devoted to cheese, there is nothing like it in Europe. Established in 1909 by Monsieur Androuët, who frequently asked friends over to sample cheese and wine, the restaurant is now an institution. To accommodate continued and growing popularity, it moved to new headquarters in 1997. Most of the dishes are concocted with a cheese base. A savory and impressive array of wines, well-prepared green salads, and ultrafresh bread is available to accompany whatever you order. Examples include a fondue of three cheeses, beef filet with Roquefort sauce flambéed with Calvados, and *magret de canard* (duckling). Many cheese lovers, however, opt for just a bottle of wine, a green salad, and all-you-can-eat choices from the most sophisticated *dégustation de fromages* (cheese tasting) in the world. Six platters, each loaded with a different category of cheese (one with goat cheeses, another with triple crèmes, and so on), are brought to your table, allowing you to select random samples. Reservations are required. Main courses are 110 to 280 F ($18.70 to $47.60); set-price meals are 250 to 300 F ($42.50 to $51); and the dégustation des fromages is 300 F ($51). AE, DC, MC, V are accepted. Androuët is open Monday through Friday from noon to 2:30pm and Monday through Saturday from 7:30 to 10pm. Métro: Etoile.

The ornate belle-epoque decor is an ideal setting for sampling the magnificent macaroons for which Ladurée has long been celebrated—not the sticky coconut version familiar to Americans, but actually two almond meringue cookies, flavored with vanilla, coffee, strawberry, or pistachio, and stuck together with buttercream.

Noting all the fast-food neighbors along the Champs-Elysées, the talented young chef here, Pierre Hermé, claims that the opening of Ladurée is a "return to civility" for the boulevard. Many come here for breakfast, others preferring a late-night dinner. There are no real main dish specialties, as the menu is constantly adjusted to take advantage of the freshest ingredients on any day. Although service is not always efficient, the food is competently prepared and tasty regardless of the hour served. Menu items include a crisp and tender filet of pork accompanied with a potato-and-parsley purée, and marinated fillets of red mullet on a salad of cold ratatouille. And if you're interested in a midafternoon pick-me-up to accompany your cups of tea, consider a dish of ice cream scented with rose petals and fresh raspberries.

INEXPENSIVE

Café Indochine. 195 rue du Faubourg St-Honoré, 8e. ☎ **01-53-75-15-63.** Reservations recommended. Main courses 80–118 F ($13.60–$20.05); fixed-price menu 175 F ($29.75). AE, MC, V. Mon–Fri noon–2:30pm; Mon–Sat 7–11:30pm. Métro: Etoile or Ternes. INDOCHINESE.

The setting here evokes the French Colonial Empire at its peak, and includes art objects from Laos, Cambodia, and Thailand, artfully outdated maps, and antique photographs of the region and its people. In any of the street-level dining rooms, you can enjoy a cross section of the cuisines of at least four different nations. Caramelized pork or chicken, cooked with coconut milk, accents an array of shrimp, scallops, and beef dishes prepared with red or green curry, and fiery-hot soups. For a novelty, try the shrimp and scallops with calamari and pepper-flavored basil sauce; steamed fish wrapped in a banana leaf; or a Thai version of Provençal bouillabaisse. Equally appealing are the grilled meats, seared over flames and served with a spicy sauce that goes especially well with wine or, even better, any of the restaurant's medley of international beers.

✪ **Chicago Pizza Pie Factory.** 5 rue de Berri, 8e. ☎ **01-45-62-50-23.** Reservations accepted only on weekdays for groups of 8 or more. Pizza for two 88–149 F ($14.95–$25.35); pizza for four 129–195 F ($21.95–$33.15); fixed-price lunch 51–71 F ($8.65–$12.05). AE, DC, MC, V. Daily 11:30am–1am. Métro: George V. AMERICAN/PIZZA.

On a side street of the Champs-Elysées, you'll find a busy tribute to the city of Chicago in a former garage. The bar is outfitted with anything and everything to do with Chicago: photos, sports banners, and all manner of kitsch. The dining room is as large and raucous as the Windy City itself. Come here for the best pizza in Paris, prepared in endless variations on eight basic themes. They also offer cheesecake, mud pie, and marvelous-tasting high-fat brownies. The management proudly refuses, except under dire circumstances, to serve burgers of any kind. No one will mind if you bypass the food altogether in favor of a drink at the bar. Happy hour in the restaurant is from 4 to 7pm, and at the bar from 6 to 8pm. During these times some drinks (but not beer) are reduced in price.

Le Berry's. 46 rue de Naples, 8e. ☎ **01-40-75-01-56.** Reservations recommended. Main courses 56–92 F ($9.50–$15.65); fixed-price menu 100 F ($17). MC, V. Mon–Fri noon–2:30pm; Mon–Sat 7pm–1am. Métro: Villiers. FRENCH.

This restaurant was conceived as an inexpensive bistro to complement one of the district's grandest restaurants, Le Grenadin. Its platters emerge from the same kitchen and are infused with the same kind of zeal as those presented next door for three times the price. Don't expect cutting-edge experimentation, but do look for honest dishes from France's agrarian heartland and a refreshing lack of pretension. The unfussy dishes are listed on a chalkboard in a setting that celebrates the game of rugby. Items include a fricassee of chicken prepared with Sancerre white wine; thin-sliced smoked ham from Sancerre; filet of veal with red wine sauce; raw pike with cabbage; and a traditional Berry pear tart.

Les Gourmets des Ternes. 87 bd. de Courcelles, 8e. ☎ **01-42-27-43-04.** Main courses 85–135 F ($14.45–$22.95). AE, MC, V. Mon–Fri noon–2:30pm and 7–10pm. Métro: Ternes. FRENCH.

Les Gourmets des Ternes is brusque in a way that betrays success, catering as it does to hordes of clients who appreciate affordable prices and lack of pretension. Satisfied clients have included the mayor of Atlanta, who wrote the bistro a thank-you letter, as well as hundreds of ordinary folks from this residential neighborhood. Thriving in this spot since it was established in 1892, the place retains a turn-of-the-century paneled decor, with some additions from the 1950s, including bordeaux-colored banquettes, mirrors, wooden panels, touches of brass, and paper tablecloths. The finely grilled signature dishes include rib steak with marrow sauce and french fries; country pâtés and sausages; sole, turbot, and monkfish; and simple, satisfying desserts that include peach Melba and *baba au Rhum* (rum cake with raisins).

Planet Hollywood. 78 av. des Champs-Elysées, 8e. ☎ **01-53-83-78-27.** Reservations not accepted. Burgers 72–85 F ($12.25–$14.45); salads 49–89 F ($8.35–$15.15); main courses 75–114 F ($12.75–$19.40). AE, MC, V. Daily 11:30am–1am. Métro: George V or F. D. Roosevelt. AMERICAN.

It would have been a distressing gaffe to deny Paris one of the nearly 50 Planet Hollywoods in the world, so in 1995, Hollywood's grit-and-glitter *kulturmeisters* (Bruce and Demi, Sly and Arnold, plus two less visible partners) opened a branch smack bang in the heart of the Champs-Elysées. Your experience here will be overwhelmingly American, with dishes such as boeuf bourguignonne set uncomfortably next to fajitas, pizza, and a thousand types of burgers, both meat and vegetarian. They don't even think of accepting reservations, so your journey into blockbuster consciousness begins the moment you line up at the bar to wait for a table. (While you wait, enjoy such high-octane libations as a Beetle Juice, an Indecent Proposal, or a Terminator, or such alcohol-free substitutes as a Home Alone.) You won't lack for entertainment: The sound system is better than at many discos, and a vast and endlessly perky gift shop does a hot trade in American trinkets destined for garage sales the world over.

Shing-Jung. 7 rue Clapeyron, 8e. ☎ **01-45-22-21-06.** Reservations recommended for dinner. Main courses 80–110 F ($13.60–$18.70); fixed-price menu 65–75 F ($11.05–$12.75) at lunch, 100–200 F ($17–$34) at dinner. Mon–Sat noon–2:30pm and 7–10:30pm. Métro: Rome. KOREAN.

Of the 30 or so Korean restaurants in all of Paris, Shing-Jung is best known for low prices and generous portions. Its sashimi is comparable to Japanese versions, although the portions of the fresh tuna, salmon, or duarade tend to be more generous. A specialty is the Korean barbecue called *bulgoogi,* which seems more authentic thanks to a clever decor that juxtaposes Korean chests and paintings.

9TH ARRONDISSEMENT (OPÉRA GARNIER/PIGALLE)
EXPENSIVE

Chez Jean. 8 rue St-Lazare, 9e. ☎ **01-48-78-62-73.** Reservations recommended. Main courses 175–200 F ($29.75–$34); fixed-price menu 185 F ($31.45). MC, V. Daily noon–2:30pm and 7–11pm. Métro: Notre-Dame de Lorette, Opéra, or Cadet. FRENCH.

There's been a brasserie of one sort or another on this site since around 1900, and some specialties remain intact from the days of Clemenceau. You'll dine amid well-oiled pinewood panels and carefully polished copper, on menu items that include some of grandmother's favorites. More modern dishes include risotto with lobster and squid ink; scallops with a fricassee of endive; a "nougat" of oxtails with a balsamic-flavored vinaigrette; lamb roasted with basil; and a pavé of duckling served with honey sauce and a fricassee of exotic mushrooms. The ever-changing menu attracts fans who consider the food a lot more sophisticated than the efforts of other brasseries. Part of this is the result of chefs who gained their prior experience in some surprisingly upscale restaurants.

Restaurant Opéra. In Le Grand Hôtel Inter-Continental, place de l'Opéra, 9e. ☎ **01-40-07-30-10.** Reservations recommended. Main courses 180–340 F ($30.60–$57.80); fixed-price menu 245–585 F ($41.65–$99.45). AE, DC, MC, V. Mon–Fri noon–2pm and 7:30–10:30pm. Métro: Opéra. FRENCH.

This elegant and prestigious restaurant is situated in the historic Grand Hôtel Inter-Continental, which has played an important role in Parisian history since its construction in 1860. If you dine here, you'll join the roll of patrons such as Salvador Dalí, Harry Truman, Josephine Baker, Marlene Dietrich, Maurice Chevalier, Maria Callas, and Marc Chagall, who often came here while working on the famous ceiling of the nearby Opéra. On August 25, 1944, Charles de Gaulle placed this famous restaurant's first food order in a newly freed Paris: a cold plate to go. One of the best things about this place is the way that, despite a formidable elegance, the staff doesn't take itself too seriously. The bons vivants who dined here long ago established a sense of fun that's still going strong.

Today you can enjoy an aperitif in a lavishly ornate bar before heading for a table in the gilded jewel box of a dining room. The menu is not a prisoner of the past, but is seasonal and fairly inventive, reaching out to the provinces of France and to the world. Start with a sautéed veal head and foot ravioli. Follow with the perfectly prepared fillet of John Dory (a delicately fleshed fish not unlike turbot or sole in flavor) with celery, or else sweetbreads fried with pistachios, lemon, and licorice. *Tout chocolat* is the perfect dessert for die-hard chocoholics.

MODERATE

Au Petit Riche. 25 rue Le Peletier, 9e. ☎ **01-47-70-68-68.** Reservations recommended. Main courses 94–130 F ($16–$22.10); fixed-price menu 165 F ($28.05) at lunch, 140–180 F ($23.80–$30.60) at dinner. AE, MC, V. Mon–Sat noon–2:15pm and 7pm–midnight. Métro: Le Peletier or Richelieu-Drouot. LOIRE VALLEY (ANJOU).

When it opened in 1865, this bistro was conceived as the food outlet for a grandly ornate cafe (Café Riche) that stood next door. Today, you'll find yesterday's grandeur and simple, well-prepared food here. You'll be ushered to one of five different areas, each crafted for maximum intimacy, with red velour banquettes, ceilings painted with allegorical themes, and accents of brass and frosted glass. The wine list favors Loire Valley vintages that go well with such dishes as *rillettes* and *rillons* (potted fish or meat, especially pork) in an aspic of Vouvray wine; a platter of poached fish served with a buttery white wine sauce; old-fashioned blanquette of chicken; and seasonal game dishes that include a civet of rabbit.

Wally Le Saharien. 36 rue Rodier, 9e. ☎ **01-42-85-51-90.** Reservations recommended. Main courses 150 F ($25.50); fixed price dinner menu 240 F ($40.80). MC, V. Tues–Sat noon–2pm; Mon–Sat 7–10pm. Métro: Anvers. ALGERIAN.

Head here for an insight into the spicy, slow-cooked cuisine that fueled the Colonial expansion of France into North Africa. The inspiration is southern Algerian, served within a dining room lined with photographs of the desert and tribal artifacts crafted from ceramics, wood, and weavings. The set-price menu that's featured every evening begins with a trio of starters that includes a spicy soup, stuffed and grilled sardines, and a savory *pastilla* of pigeon in puff pastry. This can be followed by any of several kinds of couscous, or a succulent *méchouia* (slow-cooked tart) of lamb dusted with an optional coating of sugar, according to your taste. *Merguez,* the cumin-laden spicy sausage of the North African world, factors importantly into any meal, as does homemade (usually honey-infused) pastries. End your meal with a traditional cup of mint-flavored tea.

INEXPENSIVE

Chartier. 7 rue de Faubourg Montmartre, 9e. ☎ **01-47-70-86-29.** Main courses 38–54 F ($6.45–$9.20). MC, V. Daily 11:30am–3pm and 6–10pm. Métro: Rue Montmartre. FRENCH.

Established in 1896, this unpretentious *fin-de-siècle* restaurant is now an official monument. Chartier has long been a favorite budget restaurant offering good value in surroundings that feature a whimsical mural with trees, a flowering staircase, and an early depiction of an airplane. It was painted in 1929 by a penniless artist who executed his work in exchange for food. Menu items follow conservative brasserie-style traditions, including dishes few foreigners dare to eat—boiled veal's head, tripe, tongue, sweetbreads, chitterling sausages, and lamb's brains—as well as some old-time tempters. The waiter will steer you through dishes such as beef bourguignonne, *pot-au-feu* (one of the best-sellers, combining beef, turnips, cabbage, and carrots into a savory platter), pavé of rump steak, and at least five kinds of fish. Prices are low, even for a three-course meal, a fact that as many as 320 diners appreciate at a time.

Hard Rock Cafe. 14 bd. Montmartre, 9e. ☎ **01-53-24-60-00.** Sandwiches, salads, and platters 65–110 F ($11.05–$18.70). AE, MC, V. Daily 11:30am–2am. Métro: Grand Boulevards or Richelieu-Drouot. AMERICAN.

Like its counterparts, which now stretch from Hong Kong to Reykjavík, the Hard Rock Cafe offers a collection of musical memorabilia as well as musical selections from

35 years of rock-and-roll classics. You'll be able to identify the place by the vintage Cadillac suspended over the sidewalk and the music pouring out into the street (at fairly reasonable levels during lunch and fairly unreasonable levels in the evening). The crowd appreciates the juicy steaks, hamburgers, veggie burgers, salads, and heaping platters of informal French-inspired food. As you dine, scan the high-ceilinged room for such venerated objects as the stage tuxedo worn by Buddy Holly, Jim Morrison's leather jacket, Jimi Hendrix's psychedelic vest, and a black-and-gold bustier sported by Madonna during one of her concerts in Paris.

✪ **Le Grand Zinc.** 5 Faubourg Montmartre, 9e. ☎ **01-47-70-88-64.** Reservations not required. Main courses 55–142 F ($9.35–$24.15); fixed-price menu 99 F ($16.85). AE, DC, MC, V. Mon–Sat noon–midnight. Métro: Rue Montmartre. FRENCH.

The Paris of the 1880s lives on here. You make your way into the restaurant past baskets of *bélons* (brown-fleshed oysters) from Brittany, a year-round favorite. The specialties of the house are *coq au vin* (chicken in white wine) and savory, old-fashioned staples like rack of lamb, rump steak, veal chops with morels—even a simple form of Provençal bouillabaisse. Nothing ever changes—certainly not the time-tested recipes.

10TH ARRONDISSEMENT (GARE DU NORD/GARE DE L'EST)
MODERATE

La Grille. 80 rue du Faubourg-Poissonière, 10e. ☎ **01-47-70-89-73.** Reservations required. Main courses 100–170 F ($17–$28.90). AE, DC, MC, V. Mon–Fri noon–2:30pm and 7:15–10pm. Métro: Poissonière. FRENCH/SEAFOOD.

Few other restaurants within this price category are as hotly pursued by Parisians as this nine-table holdover from another age. For at least a century after the French Revolution, fishermen from the coastal town of Dieppe used this place as a springboard for carousing and cabaret-watching after delivering their cartloads of fish to the food markets at Les Halles. When patrons from grander neighborhoods show up, it's usually because of a particular dish that has been perfected since its development 3 decades ago. The holy grail at La Grille is an entire turbot, cooked whole, and prepared tableside with a slightly foamy, emulsified white butter sauce. If the turbot doesn't appeal, consider other dishes such as seafood terrine; old-fashioned beef bourguignonne; marinated sardine fillets; and such high-calorie, high-satisfaction desserts as chocolate mousse or vanilla custard. Incidentally, don't think that this establishment's name derives from a grill used for cooking. The 200-year-old wrought-iron grills in front are classified as national treasures, among the best examples of their kind in Paris.

INEXPENSIVE

✪ **Chez Michel.** 10 rue de Belzunce, 10e. ☎ **01-44-53-06-20.** Reservations recommended. Fixed-price menu 180 F ($30.60). MC, V. Tues–Sat noon–2pm and 7pm–midnight. Métro: Gare du Nord. BRETON.

Consciously adapting itself to the tastes and income level of a loyal crowd, this restaurant near the Gare du Nord serves well-prepared Normand and Breton dishes in generous portions. At least part of this food derives from the northwestern origins of the owner and chef Thierry Breton. (The name never lies.) In a pair of dining rooms accented in exposed wood, you'll enjoy the fruits of the fields and seacoast. Dishes are savory, densely flavored, and traditional, and include veal chops fried in butter, served with gratin of potatoes enriched with bits of calf's foot gelatin; and codfish fillets served on beds of tomatoes and onions and a tapenade of black olives. The appropriate conclusion to a meal here is a snifter of Calvados, the apple-based brandy of the northern French coast, a potent pick-me-up that sneaks its way into everything from apple tarts to roasted loins of pork.

Julien. 16 rue du Faubourg St-Denis, 10e. ☎ **01-47-70-12-06.** Reservations required. Main courses 80–130 F ($13.60–$22.10); fixed-price menu 198 F ($33.65). AE, DC, MC, V. Daily noon–3pm and 7pm–1:30am. Métro: Strasbourg–St-Denis. FRENCH.

"The poor man's Maxim's," Julien offers an opportunity to dine in one of the most sumptuous belle-epoque interiors in Paris. It began life at the turn of the century as an elegant and acclaimed restaurant but became tawdry, grimy, and unappreciated after World War II. Renovation returned Julien to its former elegance, vivifying the magnificent dining room. Of special interest are four murals representing the four seasons, and a sometimes very fashionable clientele.

The food served here is in the style of cuisine bourgeoise, but without the heavy sauces. The sumptuous starter courses include eggplant caviar and wild mushroom salad. Among the main courses are a Gascony cassoulet, sliced foie gras with lentils, fresh salmon with sorrel, and chateaubriand béarnaise. The wine list is extensive and reasonably priced.

Le Dogon. 30 rue René Boulanger, 10e. ☎ **01-42-41-95-85.** Reservations recommended. Main courses 70–95 F ($11.90–$16.15). AE, MC, V. Mon–Fri noon–3pm; daily 6:30pm–1am. Métro: République. SENEGALESE.

Amid animal pelts and carved masks from Mali, the place offers well-seasoned exotica that the curious French view as culinary oddities but nonetheless return to from time to time. Examples include *maffé,* a spicy concoction that mixes peanuts with chicken, herbs, and rice; grilled fish with cumin and rice; vegetarian platters seasoned with onions and lemons; and North African couscous. You can opt for conventional wines or beers, but truly adventurous diners sometimes ask for either date-palm wine or fermented coconut juice.

Paris-Dakar. 95 rue du Faubourg St-Martin, 10e. ☎ **01-42-08-16-64.** Reservations recommended. Main courses 73–99 F ($12.40–$16.85); fixed-price menu 59–149 F ($10.05–$25.35) at lunch, 129–149 F ($21.95–$25.35) at dinner. MC, V. Tues–Thurs and Fri–Sat noon–3pm; Tues–Sun 7pm–midnight. Métro: Gare de l'Est. SENEGALESE.

Named after the famous rally that carries vehicles across the toughest terrain in the world, this restaurant celebrates the culinary traditions of France's former colonies in West Africa. After receiving a genuine welcome, you'll have the option of sampling such Senegalese dishes as *yassa* (chicken braised with limes and onions); *maffé* (beef fried with peanuts, onions, and spice); and the national dish of Senegal, tiep *bou dieone* (fish sautéed with rice, fresh vegetables, and dollops of fiery-hot chile peppers). The lunch menu is attractively priced. If you're adventurous, ask for a glass of the palm wine, fermented from coconuts in a style that's common in West Africa.

11TH & 12TH ARRONDISSEMENTS (OPÉRA BASTILLE/ BOIS DE VINCENNES)
EXPENSIVE

✪ **Au Trou Gascon.** 40 rue Taine, 12e. ☎ **01-43-44-34-26.** Reservations required. Main courses 145–165 F ($24.65–$28.05); fixed-price menu 200 F ($34) at lunch, 320 F ($54.40) at dinner. AE, DC, MC, V. Mon–Fri noon–2pm; Mon–Sat 7:30–10pm. Closed Aug. Métro: Daumesnil. GASCONY.

One of the most acclaimed chefs in Paris today, Alain Dutournier launched his cooking career in the Gascony region of southwest France. His parents mortgaged their own inn to allow Dutournier to open a turn-of-the-century bistro in an unfashionable part of the 12th arrondissement. At first he got little business, but word soon spread of a savant in the kitchen who knew and practiced authentic cuisine moderne. His wife, Nicole, is the welcoming hostess, and the wine steward has distinguished himself for his exciting cave containing several little-known wines along with a fabulous collection of Armagnacs. It is estimated that the wine cellar has some 800 varieties.

You can enjoy the true and authentic cuisine of Gascony. Start with fresh duck foie gras cooked in a terrine, or Gascony cured ham cut from the bone. Main courses include fresh tuna with braised cabbage and the best cassoulet in town. Try the chicken from the Chalosse region of Landes, which Dutournier roasts and serves in its own drippings. We'd compare these hens to the finest birds of Bresse for good quality and flavor.

Blue Elephant. 43 rue de la Roquette, 11e. ☎**01-47-00-42-00.** Reservations recommended. Main courses 85–160 F ($14.45–$27.20); fixed-price menu 150 F ($25.50) Mon–Fri at lunch, 275 F ($46.75) at dinner. AE, DC, MC, V. Sun–Fri noon–2:30pm; daily 7pm–midnight (Sun until 11pm). Métro: Bastille. THAI.

This is the Paris branch of an international chain of stylish Thai restaurants. The decor evokes an artful version of the jungles of Southeast Asia, interspersed with Thai sculptures and paintings. Menu items are savory, succulent, and infused with lemongrass, curries, and the aromas that make Thai cuisine so distinctive. Examples include a salad made with *pomelo*, a Thai fruit that's larger and more tart than a grapefruit, studded with shrimp and herbs. Other specialties include salmon soufflé served in banana leaves, chicken in green curry sauce, and a delectable grilled fish served with passion fruit.

MODERATE

Astier. 44 rue Jean-Pierre-Timbaud, 11e. ☎ **01-43-57-16-35.** Reservations recommended. Fixed-price menu 120–145 F ($20.40–$24.65). V. Mon–Fri noon–2pm and 8–11pm. Métro: Oberkampf. FRENCH.

Nobody could accuse this place of being glamorous; they understand that hearty, well-prepared food has its own allure. The mandatory set menu is a good value, with at least 10 different choices for each of four courses. Examples include roasted rabbit with mustard sauce; *racasse* (scorpionfish) with fresh spinach; grilled steaks and chops of all kinds; and breast of duckling served with a foie-gras cream sauce. There's also a superbly varied cheese platter, and desserts such as crème caramel or chocolate mousse.

✪ **Le Train Bleu.** In the Gare de Lyon, 12e. ☎ 01-43-43-09-06. Reservations recommended. Main courses 100–185 F ($17–$31.45); fixed-price menu 250 F ($42.50), including wine. AE, DC, MC, V. Daily 11:30am–3pm and 7–11pm. Métro: Gare de Lyon. FRENCH.

To reach this restaurant, climb the ornate double staircase that faces the grimy platforms of the Gare de Lyon. Both restaurant and station were built simultaneously with the Grand Palais, the Pont Alexandre III, and the Petit Palais, for the World Exhibition of 1900. As a fitting end to a traveler's long trip, the station's architects designed a restaurant whose decor is classified as a national artistic treasure. Inaugurated by the French president in 1901 and renovated and cleaned at great expense in 1992, the restaurant displays an army of bronze statues, a lavishly frescoed ceiling, mosaics, mirrors, old-fashioned banquettes, and 41 belle-epoque murals. Each of these celebrates the distant corners of the French-speaking world, which join Paris via its rail network.

Service is fast, attentive, and efficient, in case you're about to catch a train. A formally dressed staff will bring steaming platters of soufflé of brill, escargots in Chablis sauce, steak tartare, loin of lamb Provençal, veal kidneys in mustard sauce, rib of beef for two, and rum cake with raisins. The cuisine is well prepared in a classic French Escoffier manner.

INEXPENSIVE

L'Ébauchoir. 43 rue de Cîteaux, 12e. ☎ **01-43-42-49-31.** Reservations recommended for dinner. Main courses 75–110 F ($12.75–$18.70); fixed-price lunch 68 F ($11.55). MC, V. Mon–Sat noon–2:30pm and 8–10:30pm. Métro: Faidherbe-Chaligny. FRENCH.

Tucked into a neighborhood rarely visited by foreign tourists, and decorated with a 1950s decor that, to the surprise of its staff, has suddenly become fashionable again, this bistro attracts neighborhood carpenters, plumbers, and electricians, as well as an occasional journalist and screenwriter. Framed with buffed aluminum trim, and plaster and stucco walls tinted dark orange-yellow and blue, the place might remind you of a canteen in an automobile factory. You can order generous, surprisingly well-prepared versions of stuffed sardines, fillet of snapper with olive oil and garlic, crab-meat soup, fried calf's liver with coriander and honey, and a dish that combines rack of lamb with saddle of lamb on the same platter.

Le Manguier. 67 avenue Parmentier, 11e. ☎ **01-48-07-03-27.** Reservations recommended. Main courses 70–95 F ($11.90–$16.15). AE, MC, V. Mon–Fri 11am–3pm; Mon–Sat 7pm–2am. Métro: Parmentier. SENEGALESE.

Many of the clients who dine here don't know much about the cuisine of Senegal, but thanks to a charming and friendly welcome, and live music that presents African jazz at its most compelling, they tend to come back. The decor evokes a West African fishing village. You can order zesty fare like roast chicken marinated with lime and served with onions. Other choices include smoked shark meat and the national dish of Senegal, *thiebkoudiene,* a delectable blend of fish, rice, and fresh vegetables. The medley is perked up tableside with a selection of fiery sauces that you apply yourself. The drinks of choice are beer, a rum-based cocktail *(Le Dakar),* and, to a lesser degree, wine.

Mansouria. 11 rue Faidherbe, 11e. ☎ **01-43-71-00-16.** Reservations recommended. Main courses 100–150 F ($17–$25.50). MC, V. Daily noon–2pm and 7:30–11pm. Métro: Faidherbe-Chaligny. MOROCCAN.

One of the most charming and best-managed Moroccan restaurants in Paris occupies a much-restored building midway between place de la Bastille and place de la Nation. The decor combines a minimalist version of futuristic French architecture with bare white walls accented only with several sets of antique doors and portals imported from Morocco's sub-Sahara. Menu items are artfully prepared and served with the dignity of ancient traditions. Look for a half-dozen kinds of couscous, including versions made with chicken, with brochettes of beef, and one prepared "in the style of the imperial city of Fez," with lamb, onions, and almonds. Tagines are succulent versions of chicken or fish, prepared with aromatic herbs and slow cooked in clay pots, which are carried directly to your table.

16TH ARRONDISSEMENT (TROCADÉRO/BOIS DE BOULOGNE)
VERY EXPENSIVE

✪ **Alain Ducasse.** In the Le Parc Hotel, 59 av. Raymond Poincaré, 16e. ☎ **01-47-27-12-27.** Fax 01-47-27-31-22. Reservations required 6 weeks in advance. Main courses 385–590 F ($65.45–$100.30); fixed-price menu 480 F ($81.60) at lunch, 920–1,490 F ($156.40–$253.30) at dinner. AE, DC, MC, V. Mon–Fri noon–2pm and 7:45–10pm. Métro: Trocadéro. FRENCH.

The celebrated Monte Carlo chef has taken Paris by storm since taking over the reins from the great Joël Robuchon (now semiretired). This six-star Michelin chef divides his time between Paris and Monaco, although he insists that he does not repeat himself in the Paris restaurant. In this restored four-story mansion he seeds his dishes with produce from every corner of France. He serves rare local vegetables, fish from the country's coasts, and dishes incorporating cardoons, turnips, celery, turbot, cuttlefish, and Bresse fowl. His French cuisine is contemporary and Mediterranean, though not new. Although many dishes are light, Ducasse isn't afraid of lard, as he proves by his thick, fatty, oozing slabs of pork grilled to a crisp. He's kept a single Robuchon dish on the menu as a tribute: the famed caviar in aspic with cauliflower cream. The food remains sober in presentation—true, precise, and authentic.

The wine list is based on the fine cellar left by Robuchon; it's noted for its classic composition, extensiveness, and high quality. Ducasse has added many new acquisitions from France's vineyards, but he has also opened his cellar doors to young wine growers of his generation, including those from Germany, Switzerland, Spain, and Italy.

Faugeron. 52 rue de Longchamp, 16e. ☎ **01-47-04-24-53.** Fax 01-47-55-62-90. Reservations required. Main courses 250–360 F ($42.50–$61.20); fixed-price menu 320–700 F ($54.40–$119) at lunch, 550–700 F ($93.50–$119) at dinner. AE, MC, V. Mon–Fri noon–2pm and 7–10pm (Oct–Apr dinner only, Sat 7–10pm). Closed Aug. Métro: Trocadéro. FRENCH.

Henri Faugeron is an inspired chef who many years ago established this restaurant as an elegant yet unobtrusive backdrop for his superb cuisine, which he calls "revolutionary." The interior of this turn-of-the-century building now glitters with discreet touches of gilt and has a sun motif emblazoned on the ceiling. Even so, the food outshines its surroundings. Much of the zesty cuisine depends on the season and the market, since Faugeron only chooses the freshest ingredients. In winter your taste for truffles can be indulged by one of the many dishes expertly prepared in the bustling kitchen. Examples include a brunoise of truffles with asparagus and olive oil and ravioli stuffed with truffles and foie gras. Roasted leg of milk-fed veal and lamb and crispy-skinned quail are also succulent choices. And if you want something really esoteric, consider the *vol-au-vent* of lobster, sweetbreads, and morels.

✪ **Jamin.** 32 rue de Longchamp, 16e. ☎ **01-45-53-00-07.** Fax 01-45-53-00-15. Reservations required. Main courses 185–230 F ($31.45–$39.10); fixed-price menu 280–375 F ($47.60–$63.75) at lunch, 375 F ($63.75) at dinner. AE, DC, MC, V. Mon–Fri 12:30–2pm and 7:30–10pm. Métro: Trocadéro. FRENCH.

In the 1980s, Joël Robuchon, the great French chef, became a sensation at this very spot, and all Paris made its way to his door. Now Benoit Guichard, his longtime second in command, is in charge. He's clearly inspired by his master, but is an imaginative and inventive chef in his own right. Guichard has chosen pale green panels and pink banquettes—referred to as "Italo–New Yorkaise"—for a soothing backdrop to his brief but well-chosen menu. Lunches can be relatively simple affairs, although each dish, such as a beautifully seasoned salmon tartare, is done to perfection. Classic technique and a homage to tradition characterize the cuisine, which is filled with such offerings as John Dory with celery and fresh ginger, or a pigeon sausage with foie gras, pistachios, and mâche lettuce. His beef shoulder was so tender it had obviously been braising for hours. This grand chef makes delectable what is normally thrown away. A particularly earthy dish celebrates various parts of the sow that are usually rejected by most upscale diners, blending the tail and cheeks of the sow on a platter with walnuts and fresh herbs. Finish off with an apple tarte Tatin.

Le Vivarois. 192-194 av. Victor Hugo, 16e. ☎ **01-45-04-04-31.** Reservations required. Main courses 240–300 F ($40.80–$51); fixed-price lunch 355 F ($60.35). AE, DC, MC, V. Mon–Fri noon–2pm and 8–9:45pm. Closed Aug. Métro: Rue de la Pompe. FRENCH.

Food critics have called Le Vivarois "a revelation." *Gourmet* magazine once hailed it as "a restaurant of our time . . . the most exciting, audacious, and important restaurant in Paris today." Le Vivarois still maintains its standards, but it no longer occupies such a lofty position.

Chef Claude Peyrot's menu is constantly changing. His warm oysters with curry sauce or his braised red snapper with olives are considered masterpieces, but to many, his most

---

ⓘ Family-Friendly Restaurants

Meals at the grand restaurants of Paris are rarely suitable for young children. Nevertheless, many parents drag their children along, often to the annoyance of other diners. You may have to make some compromises, such as dining earlier than most Parisians. **Hotel dining rooms** can be another good choice for family dining. They usually have children's menus, or at least one or two *plats du jour* cooked for children, such as spaghetti with meat sauce.

If you take your child to a moderate or inexpensive restaurant, ask if the restaurant will serve a child's plate. If not, order a *plat du jour* or *plat garni,* which will be suitable for most children, particularly if a dessert is to follow.

Most **cafes** welcome children throughout the day and early evening. At a cafe, children always seem to like the sandwiches (try a *croque-monsieur*), the omelets, and especially the *pommes frites* (crispy french fries). Although this chapter lists a number of cafes (see "The Best Cafes," below), one that particularly appeals to children is **La Samaritaine,** 75 rue de Rivoli (☎ 01-40-41-20-20; Métro: Pont-Neuf). The snack bar down below doesn't have a panoramic view, but the restaurant on the fifth floor does. You can take children to the top and order ice cream for them at teatime daily from 3:30 to 6pm.

Les Drug Stores (149 bd. St-Germain-des-Prés, 6e, and at Publicis Champs-Elysées, 133 av. des Champs-Elysées, 8e)—like American drug stores but with sections for upscale gift items and food service—also welcome children, especially in the early evening, as do most **tearooms,** and you can tide the kids over with pastries and ice cream if dinner will be late. You could also try a **picnic** in the park, or try the many fast-food chains, such as **Pizza Hut** and **McDonald's,** all over the city.

- **Le Brise-Miche** *(see p. 108)*   The ideal choice when visiting Beaubourg, with a captivating view of the most playful fountain in Paris from its terrace.
- **Chicago Pizza Pie Factory** *(see p. 114)*   There are no frogs' legs or snails to gross out little minds and stomachs at Chicago Pizza Pie Factory, just the City of Light's best pizza followed by a kid-pleasing cheesecake.
- **Androuët** *(see p. 113)*   If your kids love cheese, they'll get the fill of a lifetime here, where cheese enters all the dishes. Especially delectable is the ravioli stuffed with goat cheese.
- **Joe Allen** *(see p. 100)*   This American restaurant in Les Halles delivers everything from chili to chocolate mousse pie to the best hamburgers in Paris.
- **Crémerie-Restaurant Polidor** *(see p. 132)*   One of the most popular restaurants on the Left Bank, this reasonably priced dining room is so family-friendly it calls its food *cuisine familiale.* This might be the best place to introduce your child to bistro food.

---

winning dish is an upscale version of *coq au vin* that's flavored with a red Burgundy wine known as Pommard. Dessert might be an esoteric version of chestnut ice cream.

MODERATE

La Butte Chaillot. 110 bis av. Kleber. 16e. ☎ **01-47-27-88-88.** Reservations recommended. Main courses 98–116 F ($16.65–$19.70); fixed-price menu 150–195 F

In case you want to see the world.

At American Express, we're here to make your journey a smooth one. So we have over 1,700 travel service locations in over 130 countries ready to help. What else would you expect from the world's largest travel agency?

do more

Travel

Call 1 800 AXP-3429 or visit
www.americanexpress.com/travel

In case you want to be welcomed there.

We're here to see that you're always welcomed at establishments everywhere. That's why millions of people carry the American Express® Card – for peace of mind, confidence, and security, around the world or just around the corner.

do more

Cards

And in case you'd rather be safe than sorry.

We're here with American Express® Travelers Cheques. They're the safe way to carry money on your vacation, because if they're ever lost or stolen you can get a refund, practically anywhere or anytime. To find the nearest place to buy Travelers Cheques, call 1 800 495-1153. Another way we help you do more.

do more

Travelers Cheques

($25.50–$33.15). AE, MC, V. Daily noon–2:30pm and 7pm–midnight. Métro: Trocadéro. FRENCH.

First conceived as the headquarters for a bank, this site was converted into a baby bistro to showcase culinary high priest Guy Savoy. As such, it draws a busy clientele from the affluent neighborhood's many corporate headquarters. Diners congregate within posh but congested areas tinted in salmon and dark yellow. Menu items change weekly (and sometimes daily), depending on what is in season, and betray a strange sense of mass production not unlike that found in a luxury cruise line's dining room. Examples include a sophisticated medley of terrines; a "low-fat" version of chunky mushroom soup; a salad of snails and herbed potatoes; a succulent rack of lamb; and roasted rabbit with sage, with a compôte of onions, bacon, and mushrooms. A starkly contemporary stainless-steel staircase leads to supplemental seating in the cellar.

INEXPENSIVE

Le Bistro de L'Étoile. 19 rue Lauriston, 16e. ☎ **01-40-67-11-16.** Reservations recommended. Main courses 96–115 F ($16.30–$19.55); fixed-price lunch 135–165 F ($22.95–$28.05). AE, DC, MC, V. Mon–Fri noon–2:30pm; Mon–Sat 7:30pm–midnight. Métro: Etoile. FRENCH.

This is the most interesting of three separate baby bistros, each with the same name, clustered around place de l'Etoile. They're affordable versions of the grand cuisine featured in superstar Guy Savoy's nearby two-star restaurant (see below). The setting is a warmly contemporary dining room outfitted in shades of butterscotch and caramel. Menu items include a *mijotée*—a dish of pork and sage cooked over low heat for hours, coming out *extremely* tender (almost mushy)—and codfish studded with dabs of lard and prepared with a coconut-lime sauce. A particularly interesting sampler involves three of Savoy's creations on a platter, including a cup of lentil cream soup, a fondant of celery, and a panfried slice of foie gras. Equally appealing are fillets of red snapper with caramelized endive and exotic mushrooms. Expect some odd terms on the dessert menu, which only a professional chef can fully describe. An example is spice bread baked in the fashion of *pain perdu* (lost bread) garnished with banana sorbet and pineapple sauce.

17TH & 18TH ARRONDISSEMENTS (PARC MONCEAU/MONTMARTRE)
VERY EXPENSIVE

✪ **Guy Savoy.** 18 rue Troyon, 17e. ☎ **01-43-80-40-61.** Fax 01-46-22-43-09. Reservations required 1 week in advance. Main courses 250–700 F ($42.50–$119); menu dégustation (tasting menu) 950 F ($161.50). AE, MC, V. Mon–Fri noon–2pm; Mon–Sat 7:30–10:30pm. Métro: Charles-de-Gaulle–Etoile. FRENCH.

Guy Savoy serves the kind of food that he himself likes to eat, and it is prepared with consummate skill. He's consistently named one of the five or six hottest chefs in Europe, and deservedly so. We think he has a slight edge over his nearest rival, Michel Rostang (see below). Though the food is superb and meals comprise as many as nine courses, the portions are small; you won't necessarily be satiated before the meal has run its course.

The menu changes with the seasons, but might, at the time of your visit, include a light cream soup of lentils and crayfish, foie gras of duckling with aspic and gray salt, and red snapper with a liver and spinach sauce served with crusty potatoes. If you visit in the right season, you may have a chance to order such masterfully prepared game as mallard or venison. Savoy is fascinated with mushrooms, and has been known to serve a dozen different types, especially in the autumn.

☺ **Michel Rostang.** 20 rue Rennequin, 17e. ☎ **01-47-63-40-77.** Fax 01-47-63-82-75. Reservations required. Main courses 198–385 F ($33.65–$65.45); fixed-price menu 345–640 F ($58.65–$108.80) at lunch, 640–860 F ($108.80–$146.20) at dinner. AE, MC, V. Mon–Fri 12:30–2:30pm; Mon–Sat 8–10:30pm. Closed 2 weeks in Aug. Métro: Ternes. FRENCH.

Monsieur Rostang is one of the most creative chefs in Paris, and he's the fifth generation of one of the most distinguished French "cooking families." The restaurant is composed of four different dining rooms, each paneled in mahogany, cherry, or pearwood, and, in some cases, accented with frosted panels of Lalique crystal. The menu changes every 2 months, and features modern improvements on France's cuisine bourgeoise. In midwinter, truffles are the dish of choice; in spring, you'll find racks of suckling lamb from the salt marshes of France's western seacoasts; and in game season, look for sophisticated preparations of pheasant and venison. Three year-round staples include quail eggs with a coque of sea urchins, a fricassee of sole, or a young chicken from Bresse (the finest in France) served with a crusty mushroom purée and a salad composed of the chicken's thighs.

EXPENSIVE

Le Bistro d'à Côté Flaubert. 10 rue Flaubert, 17e. ☎ **01-42-67-05-81.** Reservations recommended. Main courses 98–145 F ($16.65–$24.65); fixed-price lunch 150 F ($25.50). AE, MC, V. Daily 12:30–2pm and 7:30–11pm. Métro: Ternes. FRENCH.

This is one of four branches of Michel Rostang's baby bistro, each of which feature a pared-down version of his haute gastronomy (see above). We feel this branch is the most interesting because it's just next door to the source. You'll enter a nostalgically decorated dining area ringed with unusual porcelain and antique copies of Michelin guides, some of which date from around 1900. The venue is breezy, stylishly informal, and chic, with a simple menu enhanced by daily specials written on a blackboard. Tantalizing items include ravioli stuffed with pulverized lobster; an upscale version of macaroni that's laced with Serrano ham; and a *rable de lievre* (rabbit stew) en cocotte.

MODERATE

Chez Georges. 273 bd. Pereire, 17e. ☎ **01-45-74-31-00.** Reservations recommended. Main courses 100–145 F ($17–$24.65). V. Daily noon–2:30pm and 7pm–midnight. Métro: Porte-Maillot. FRENCH.

Not to be confused with a bistro with the same name in the 2nd arrondissement, this worthy choice has flourished since 1926, despite an obscure location. The setting has changed little—cheerfully harassed waiters barge through a dining room sheathed with old-fashioned paneling and etched glass, and savory odors emerge from a hysterically busy kitchen. Two enduring specialties are the leg of lamb with white kidney beans, and standing rib roast served with herbs (especially thyme) in its own juices with a gratin of potatoes. Preceding these are Baltic herring in cream sauce, cheese ravioli, cabbage soup, or a wide selection of sausages and pork products that taste best when consumed with bread, butter, and sour pickles. The adventurous French love the calf's head and the braised veal trotters, both served cold, in vinaigrette.

☺ **La Rôtisserie d'Armaillé.** 6 rue d'Armaillé, 17e. ☎ **01-42-27-19-20.** Reservations recommended. Fixed-price menu 165 F ($28.05) at lunch, 165 F or 218 F ($28.05 or $37.05) at dinner. AE, DC, MC, V. Mon–Fri noon–2:30pm; Mon–Sat 7:30–11pm. Métro: Etoile. FRENCH.

The impresario behind this attractive baby bistro is Jacques Cagna, who established his role as a gastronomic star long ago from his headquarters in the Latin Quarter. The chic place bristles with business lunches and dinners, as well as well-shod residents and shoppers from the very grand surrounding neighborhood. It's ringed with light-colored wood paneling and banquettes with patterns of pink and green. At lunch, the menu

Finding Your Way

For a map of 16th- and 17th- arrondissement restaurants, turn to "Restaurants near place Charles-de-Gaulle," page 111.

includes a main course and either a starter or dessert. The pricier of the dinner meals includes a starter, main course, and dessert. Either way, you'll have many choices within each category. Examples include a flan of wild mushrooms with a red wine sauce; a salad of sweetbreads and crayfish; and a rack of lamb accented with parsley and sage. The artwork features bucolic depictions of the cows, pigs, and lambs that are likely to figure among the grilled steaks and chops featured on the menu.

INEXPENSIVE

Le Grain de Folie. 24 rue de la Vieuville, 18e. ☎ **01-42-58-15-57.** Reservations recommended. Main courses 50–70 F ($8.50–$11.90); fixed-price menu 48–95 F ($8.15–$16.15). No credit cards. Mon–Fri 12:30–2:30pm and 7:30–10:30pm; Sat–Sun noon–11:30pm. Métro: Abbesses. VEGETARIAN.

Simple, wholesome, and unpretentious, the cuisine at this vegetarian restaurant has been inspired by France, Greece, California, and India. The menu includes an array of salads, cereals, tarts, terrines, and casseroles. Dessert selections might include an old-fashioned tart or a fruit salad. The decor includes potted plants, exposed stone, and a gathering of masks from around the world. You can choose one of an array of wines or a frothy glass of vegetable juice to accompany your meal.

Marie-Louise. 52 rue Championnet, 18e. ☎ **01-46-06-86-55.** Reservations recommended. Main courses 80–125 F ($13.60–$21.25); fixed-price menu 130 F ($22.10). DC, V. Tues–Sat noon–2pm and 7:30–10pm. Closed Aug. Métro: Simplon or Porte-de-Clignancourt. FRENCH.

Established in a decidedly unfashionable neighborhood in 1957, and named after the matriarch who first owned it, this bistro offers views of Paris rarely experienced by visitors who gravitate toward the Seine. The decor evokes old-time France with allusions to the establishment's birth in the age of Sputnik. Staff members will be less effusive and smooth than at, say, the Hard Rock Cafe, but that should appeal to anyone looking for an escape from the usual places. Opt for a table on the busy main floor, or on the quieter floor above street level. The item that longtime fans of this place order again and again is *boeuf à la ficelle* (poached filet of beef tied together with string and served in its natural juices). Also popular are the large and unpretentious platters of sautéed monkfish with pasta; coq au vin; chicken "Marie-Louise" (with rice and a paprika cream sauce); and grilled sirloin steak with pepper or béarnaise sauce.

19TH ARRONDISSEMENT (BUTTES CHAUMONT)
MODERATE

Restaurant d'Eric Frechon. 10 rue Général Brunet, 19e. ☎ **01-40-40-03-30.** Reservations required. Fixed-price menu 200 F ($34). MC, V. Tues–Sat noon–2:30 and 7–11pm. Métro: Botzaris. FRENCH.

With perfect justification, this place calls itself a "bistro gastronomique," and, as such, attracts a remarkably stylish crowd to the city's calm and rarely visited northern periphery within the Buttes Chaumont district. Frechon learned his craft at some of the grandest restaurants of Paris, including the spectacularly expensive restaurants at the Hotel de Crillon. Don't expect an impressive decor, just a monochromatic brown and beige that the staff refers to as "1970s retro."

Menu items include roasted chicken stuffed with foie gras, celery, and artichoke hearts; a seasoned tartare of salmon and oysters floating on a bed of creamy horseradish sauce; lasagna of celery and scallops; and a bouillon of pot-au-feu garnished with ravioli stuffed with foie gras. Note that if you're hoping for a table here on a Friday or Saturday, it's wise to reserve several days in advance.

4 Left Bank

We'll begin with the most centrally located arrondissements on the Left Bank and then survey the outlying neighborhoods.

5TH ARRONDISSEMENT (LATIN QUARTER)
VERY EXPENSIVE

✪ **La Tour d'Argent.** 15-17 quai de la Tournelle, 5e. ☎ **01-43-54-23-31.** Fax 01-44-07-12-04. Reservations required. Main courses 200–400 F ($34–$68); fixed-price lunch 350 F ($59.50). AE, DC, MC, V. Tues–Sun noon–2:30pm and 7:30–10:30pm. Métro: Maubert-Mutualité or Cardinal-LeMoine. FRENCH.

La Tour d'Argent is a national institution. From this penthouse restaurant, the view over the Seine and of the apse of Notre-Dame is panoramic. Although this restaurant's long-established reputation as "the best" in Paris has been eclipsed, to dine here remains unsurpassed as a theatrical event.

A restaurant of some sort has stood on this site since at least 1582. Madame de Sévigné refers to a cafe here in her celebrated letters, and Dumas used it as a setting for one of his novels. The fame of La Tour d'Argent spread during its ownership by Frédéric Delair, who bought the fabled wine cellar of Café Anglais to supply his restaurant. It was Delair who started the practice of issuing certificates to diners who ordered the house specialty: *caneton* (pressed duckling). The birds are numbered: The first one was served to Edward VII in 1890, and now they're up to nearly one million.

Under the sharp eye of its current owner, Claude Terrail, the cooking is superb, and the service impeccable. Limoges china adorns each table. Although a good part of the menu is devoted to duck, we assure you that the kitchen does know how to prepare other dishes. We especially recommend the ravioli with foie gras, salmon and turbot *à la Sully*, and, to begin your meal, either the pheasant consommé or the quenelles of pike-perch André Terrail.

MODERATE

Brasserie Balzar. 49 rue des Ecoles, 5e. ☎ **01-43-54-13-67.** Reservations strongly recommended. Main courses 75–124 F ($12.75–$21.10). AE, MC, V. Daily noon–midnight. Métro: Odeon or Cluny–La Sorbonne. FRENCH.

Established in 1898, Brasserie Balzar is battered but cheerful, with some of the friendliest waiters in Paris. The menu makes almost no concessions to nouvelle cuisine, and includes pepper steak, sole meunière, sauerkraut garnished with ham and sausage, pig's feet, and calf's liver fried and served without garnish. The food is decently prepared, and it's clear these dishes still keep people happy. Be warned that if you just want coffee or a drink, you probably won't get a table during meal hours. But the staff will be happy to serve you if you want to have a full dinner in the midafternoon, accustomed as they are to the odd hours of their many clients. You'll be in good company here: Former patrons have included both Sartre and Camus (who often got in arguments), James Thurber, countless professors from the nearby Sorbonne, and a bevy of English and American journalists.

Chez René. 14 bd. St-Germain, 5e. ☎ **01-43-54-30-23.** Reservations recommended. Main courses 80–170 F ($13.60–$28.90); fixed-price lunch 170 F ($28.90). V. Mon–Fri 12:15–2:15pm; Mon–Sat 7:45–11pm. Métro: Maubert-Mutualité. FRENCH.

Restaurants like this used to be widespread, particularly on the Left Bank, but many became pizzerias. Established in 1957, Chez René maintains its allegiance to the tenets of French cuisine. The staff is often overwhelmed, and the seating is cramped as only a bistro can be. The dining room isn't fancy, but its clients return loyally, often several nights a week, for the steady and reliable stream of food and the frequently changing plats du jour. For an appetizer, try fresh wild mushrooms laced with butter and garlic or a platter of country-style sausages. You'll find such reliable old-time French fare as beef bourguignonne or veal in white sauce. Enjoy it all with a bottle of Beaujolais.

INEXPENSIVE

Al Dar. 8 rue Frédéric Sauton, 5e. ☎**01-43-25-17-15.** Reservations recommended. Main courses 85–92 F ($14.45–$15.65). AE, DC, MC, V. Daily noon–midnight. Métro: Maubert-Mutualité. LEBANESE.

This is a well-respected restaurant that works hard to popularize the savory cuisine of Lebanon. You'll dine on dishes that might include *taboulé,* a refreshing combination of finely chopped parsley, mint, milk, tomatoes, onions, lemon juice, olive oil, and salt; *baba ganoush,* pulverized and seasoned eggplant; and *hummus,* pulverized chick-peas with herbs. Any of these can be followed with savory roasted chicken; tender minced lamb prepared with mint, cumin, and Mediterranean herbs; and any of several kinds of delectable tangines and couscous.

Campagne et Provence. 25 quai de la Tournelle, 5e. ☎ **01-43-54-05-17.** Reservations recommended. Fixed-price lunch 120 F ($20.40); 2-course fixed-price dinner 170 F ($28.90); 3-course fixed-price dinner 198 F ($33.65). V. Tues–Fri noon–2pm; Mon–Sat 7:30–11pm. Métro: Maubert-Mutualité. PROVENÇAL.

This modestly priced restaurant is across from the Ile de la Cité beside a quay. Bouquets of dried flowers garnish pale blue walls, and the upholstery hints of Provence's blue sky. The waiters are likely to speak with the modulated accents of southern France. The savory foods served here include a salad of wild Provençal mesclun garnished with Parmesan; a *pissaladière* (Provençal tart) flavored with onions or a combination of sardines and red mullet; and grilled fish served with risotto. A particularly tasty dessert is the anise-flavored crème brûlée.

La Petite Hostellerie. 35 rue de la Harpe (just east of bd. St-Michel), 5e. ☎ **01-43-54-47-12.** Fixed-price menu 45–89 F ($7.65–$15.15). Tues–Sat noon–2pm; Mon–Sat 7–11pm. AE, DC, MC, V. Métro: St-Michel or Cluny–La Sorbonne. FRENCH.

This place dating from 1902 has a ground-floor dining room that's usually crowded and a larger one upstairs (seating 100) with attractive 18th-century woodwork. People come for the cozy ambience and decor, decent French country cooking, polite service, and excellent prices. The fixed-price dinner menu might feature favorites like coq au vin, duckling à l'orange, or steak with mustard sauce. Start with onion soup or stuffed mussels and finish with cheese or salad and peach Melba or apple tart. Rue de la Harpe is a side street north of boulevard St-Germain.

✪ **Perraudin.** 157 rue St-Jacques, 5e. ☎ **01-46-33-15-75.** Reservations not accepted. Main courses 59 F ($10.05); fixed-price menu 63 F ($10.70) at lunch, 150 F ($25.50) at dinner. No credit cards. Tues–Fri noon–2:15pm; Mon–Sat 7:30–10:15pm. Métro: Cluny–La Sorbonne. RER: Luxembourg. FRENCH.

Everything about this place—decor, cuisine, price, and service—attempts to duplicate the bustling allure of the turn-of-the-century bistro. This one was built in 1870 as an outlet for coal and wine (both sold as remedies against the cold). Eventually, the site evolved into the old-fashioned, wood-paneled bistro you see today, where very

Restaurants in the Heart of the Left Bank

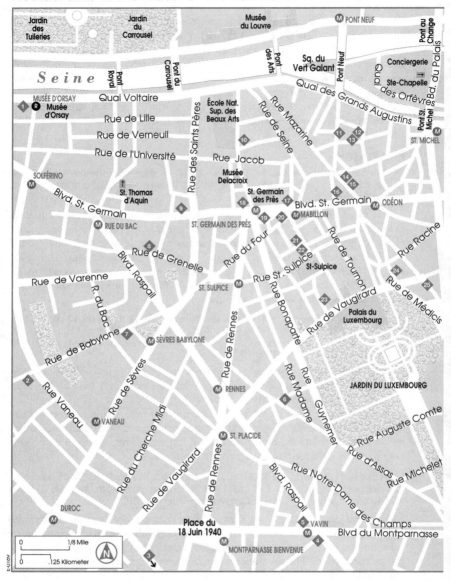

little has changed since Émile Zola was buried nearby in the Pantheon. Walls look like they've been marinated in tea; the marbletop tables, old mirrors, and posters of Parisian vaudeville have likely been here forever.

Reservations aren't made in advance: Instead, clients usually drink a glass of kir at the zinc-topped bar as they wait. (Tables turn over quickly.) The old-fashioned dishes include roast leg of lamb served with dauphinois potatoes, beef bourguignonne, or navarin of lamb and grilled salmon with sage sauce. An onion tart, pumpkin soup, snails, or any of several pâtés and terrines precede the main course.

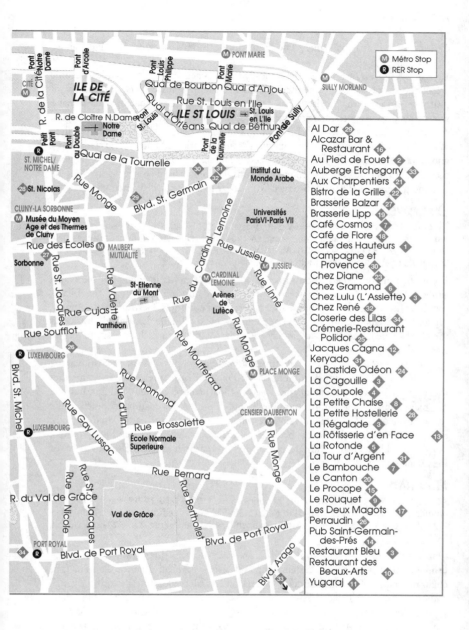

M Métro Stop
R RER Stop

Al Dar 29
Alcazar Bar & Restaurant 16
Au Pied de Fouet 2
Auberge Etchegorry 33
Aux Charpentiers 21
Bistro de la Grille 22
Brasserie Balzar 27
Brasserie Lipp 19
Café Cosmos 7
Café de Flore 18
Café des Hauteurs 1
Campagne et Provence 30
Chez Diane 23
Chez Gramond 6
Chez Lulu (L'Assiette) 3
Chez René 32
Closerie des Lilas 34
Crémerie-Restaurant Polidor 25
Jacques Cagna 12
Keryado 31
La Bastide Odéon 24
La Cagouille 3
La Coupole 4
La Petite Chaise 8
La Petite Hostellerie 28
La Régalade 3
La Rôtisserie d'en Face 13
La Rotonde 5
La Tour d'Argent 31
Le Bambouche 7
Le Canton 20
Le Procope 15
Le Rouquet 9
Les Deux Magots 17
Perraudin 26
Pub Saint-Germain-des-Prés 14
Restaurant Bleu 3
Restaurant des Beaux-Arts 10
Yugaraj 11

6TH ARRONDISSEMENT (ST-GERMAIN/LUXEMBOURG)
VERY EXPENSIVE

✪ **Jacques Cagna**. 14 rue des Grands-Augustins, 6e. ☎ **01-43-26-49-39.** Fax 01-43-54-54-48. Reservations required. Main courses 180–350 F ($30.60–$59.50); fixed-price menu 260–470 F ($44.20–$79.90) at lunch, 470 F ($79.90) at dinner. AE, DC, MC, V. Tues–Fri noon–2pm; Mon–Sat 7:30–10:30pm. Closed 3 weeks in Aug. Métro: St-Michel. FRENCH.

St. Germain knows no finer dining than at Jacques Cagna, a sophisticated restaurant set in a 17th-century town house with massive timbers, burnished paneling, and

17th-century Dutch paintings. The main dining room is located one flight above street level.

Jacques Cagna is one of the best classically trained chefs in Paris, though he's become a half-apostle to the cuisine moderne. This is evident in his delectable carpaccio of pearly sea bream with a caviar-lavished *céleric rémoulade* (celery root in a mayonnaise sauce tinged with capers, parsley, gherkins, spring onions, chervil, chopped tarragon, and anchovy essence). Other dishes, such as rack of suckling veal with ginger and lime sauce, Challons duckling in a red burgundy sauce, or fried scallops served with celery and potatoes in a truffle sauce, are equally sublime. The menu is forever changing, according to the season and momentary inspirations, but if you're lucky, he'll be offering his line-caught sea bass served with caviar in a potato shell when you visit.

EXPENSIVE

✪ **Closerie des Lilas.** 171 bd. du Montparnasse, 6e. ☎ 01-40-51-34-50. Reservations recommended (restaurant only). Main courses 190–280 F ($32.30–$47.60); brasserie main courses 90–180 F ($15.30–$30.60). AE, DC, V. Restaurant daily noon–3pm and 7:30–11pm. Brasserie daily 11:30am–1am. Métro: Port-Royal or Vavin. FRENCH.

Established in 1847, the Closerie was long a social and culinary magnet for the avant-garde. The famous people who have sat in the "Pleasure Garden of the Lilacs" watching the leaves blow along the streets are almost countless: Gertrude Stein, Ingres, Henry James, Chateaubriand, Picasso, Hemingway, Apollinaire, Lenin and Trotsky (at the chess board), and Whistler. Today the crowd is likely to include a sprinkling of stars and the starstruck.

The place resounds with the sometimes rather loud sounds of a jazz pianist, making the cramped interior seem even more claustrophobic than it already is. It's sometimes tough to get a seat in what is called the *bateau* (boat) section of the restaurant, but you can make the wait a lot more enjoyable by ordering the best champagne julep in the world at the bar. It's possible just to have coffee or a drink at the bar if you don't want to eat here, although the food is better than it was when the place was highly touted. Try the veal kidneys with mustard or ribs of veal in a cider sauce, the steak tartare, or the quenelles of pike-perch.

MODERATE

Alcazar Bar & Restaurant. 62 rue Mazarine, 6e. ☎ **01-53-10-19-99.** Reservations recommended. Main courses 90–190 F ($15.30–$32.30); fixed-price lunch 140–180 F ($23.80–$30.60). AE, DC, MC, V. Daily noon–5:30pm and 7pm–1am. Métro: Odéon. FRENCH.

One of Paris's newest high-profile, stylish *brasseries de luxe* is this artfully hi-tech establishment funded by British restaurateur and *wunderkind* Sir Terence Conran. (His chain of well-publicized restaurants in London has succeeded in captivating a tough audience of terminally jaded European foodies.) Set within what functioned for many years as the headquarters of a publishing house, it features an all-white futuristic decor within a large street-level dining room, a busy and hyperstylish bar one floor above street level, and a menu that stresses the establishment's role as an upscale bistro and brasserie. Examples of justifiably popular dishes include grilled entrecôte with béarnaise sauce and fried potatoes; Charolais duckling with honey and spices; sashimi and sushi with lime; fillet of monkfish with saffron in puff pastry; and a comprehensive collection of shellfish and oysters from the waters of Brittany. Wines are as stylish and diverse as you'd expect, and the trendy clientele tends to wear a lot of black.

Chez Gramond. 5 rue de Fleurus, 6e. ☎ **01-42-33-28-89.** Reservations recommended. Main courses 130–219 F ($22.10–$37.25). MC, V. Mon–Sat noon–2:30pm and 7–10pm. Closed in Aug. Métro: Notre-Dame-des-Champs. FRENCH.

Aficionados of the way France used to be tend to seek this restaurant out, preferring it to its trendier, more modern competitors nearby. And if you're looking for the kind of cuisine that used to satisfy the *grands intellectuels* of the Latin Quarter during the 1960s, and which sustained even François Mitterand before he was elected president, you might find the place very appealing. It seats only 20 people at a time, each of whom are treated to the old-time savoir-faire of Auvergne-born Jean-Claude Gramond and his charming wife, Jeannine. Menu items are listed the old-fashioned way, in purple ink that's duplicated on an old-timey mimeograph machine in back. Examples include roasted partridge in wine sauce; suckling lamb with sorrel sauce; terrines of foie gras; seared scallops served with butter sauce on a bed of leeks; and a succulent version of lamb stew served with white beans. Try the *soufflé Grand Marnier* for dessert. The wine list is carefully balanced and fairly priced.

La Rôtisserie d'en Face. 2 rue Christine, 6e. ☎ **01-43-26-40-98.** Reservations recommended. Fixed-price menu 100–159 F ($17–$27.05) at lunch, 210 F ($35.70) at dinner. AE, MC, V. Mon–Fri noon–2:30pm; Mon–Sat 7–11pm. Métro: St-Michel. FRENCH.

This is the most frequented "baby bistro" in Paris. It's operated by Jacques Cagna, whose vastly expensive restaurant (see above) is across the street. The simply prepared food is very good and uses high-quality ingredients. The busy, informal place features a postmodern decor with high-tech lighting and black lacquer chairs. Dishes include several types of ravioli, a pâté of duckling en croûte with foie gras, a *friture d'éperlans* (tiny fried freshwater fish), and smoked Scottish salmon with spinach. Monsieur Cagna has added pork cheeks to the menu, based on an old-fashioned family recipe. His Barbary duckling in red wine sauce is incomparable.

Le Procope. 13 rue de l'Ancienne-Comédie, 6e. ☎ **01-40-46-79-00.** Reservations recommended. Main courses 80–160 F ($13.60–$27.20); fixed-price menu 178 F ($30.25). AE, DC, MC, V. Daily 11am–1am. Métro: Odeon. FRENCH.

The food may not be the best—typical brasserie fare—and the service may be lacking, but few places can match the nostalgia of this old and venerated place. Opened in 1686 by a Sicilian named Francesco Procopio dei Coltelli, Le Procope is the oldest cafe in Paris. Now more restaurant than cafe, it is sumptuously decorated with gilt-framed mirrors, antique portraits of former illustrious clients, crystal chandeliers, banquettes of bordeaux-colored leather, and marbletop tables.

Voltaire, Benjamin Franklin, Rousseau, Anatole France, Robespierre, Danton, Marat, a youthful Bonaparte, Balzac (who drank endless cups of very strong coffee), and Verlaine (who preferred absinthe, now illegal) all came here in their day. There are two levels for dining, with two rooms downstairs and five rooms upstairs. Fresh oysters and shellfish are served from a chilled display. A well-chosen selection of classic French dishes is presented, including baby duckling with spices and "green coffee," filet of beef with peppercorns, and "drunken chicken." The major drawback of the place is that it's too famous—everybody wants to venerate it at once.

Yugaraj. 14 rue Dauphine, 6e. ☎ **01-43-26-44-91.** Reservations recommended. Main courses 98–165 F ($16.65–$28.05); fixed-price menu 130–280 F ($22.10–$47.60) at lunch, 180–280 F ($30.60–$47.60) at dinner. AE, DC, MC, V. Tues–Sun noon–2:15pm; daily 7–11pm. Métro: Odeon. INDIAN.

Set within two floors of an old building in the Latin Quarter, this restaurant serves flavorful, moderately priced food based on the recipes of northern and, to a lesser degree, southern India. In rooms outfitted in vivid shades of "Indian pink," with formally dressed staff and lots of intricately carved Kashmiri panels and statues, you can sample the spicy, aromatic tandoori dishes that are becoming all the rage in France. Seafood specialties are usually concocted from warm-water fish imported from the Seychelles, including species

such as thiof, capitaine, and bourgeois, prepared as they would be in Calcutta, with tomatoes, onions, cumin, coriander, ginger, and garlic. Flavors are spicy and earthy, rich with
mint and touches of yogurt. Curried lamb with coriander is a particular favorite.

INEXPENSIVE

Aux Charpentiers. 10 rue Mabillon, 6e. ☎ **01-43-26-30-05.** Reservations required. Main
courses 90–125 F ($15.30–$21.25); fixed-price menu 120 F ($20.40) at lunch, 158 F ($26.85)
at dinner. AE, DC, MC, V. Daily noon–3pm and 7:30–11:30pm. Métro: Mabillon. FRENCH.

This bistro, established more than 130 years ago, was once the rendezvous of the
master carpenters, whose guild was next door. Nowadays it's where young men take
their dates. Although the food is not especially imaginative, it is well prepared in the
best tradition of cuisine bourgeoise: hearty but not refined. Appetizers include pâté of
duck and rabbit terrine. Especially recommended as a main course is the roast duck
with olives. The plats du jour recall French home cooking: salt pork with lentils, pot-
au-feu, or stuffed cabbage. The wine list has a large selection of Bordeaux direct from
the châteaus, including Château Gaussens.

Bistro de la Grille. 14 rue Mabillon, 6e. ☎ **01-43-54-16-87.** Reservations recommended.
Main courses 70–110 F ($11.90–$18.70); fixed-price menu 105 F ($17.85) at lunch, 155 F
($26.35) at dinner. MC, V. Daily noon–midnight. Limited menu available 3:30–7pm. Métro:
Mabillon. FRENCH.

Many of your fellow diners at this arts-conscious bistro are likely to own, or work in,
nearby boutiques. The bistro's popularity has survived since the French Revolution,
when plots and counterplots were hatched among its clients, many of whom eventually ended up on the guillotine themselves. If you're alone, you might opt to dine at
the bar near the entrance, surrounded by photos of film stars from the early years of
the French-based Pathé cinema. Tables upstairs are moderately more sedate than those
on the bustling street level. Menu items arrive in generous portions, but are rarely
daring. Examples include platters of fresh shellfish, as well as traditional versions of
bone marrow spread over roughly textured bread, sautéed salmon with wild mushrooms, and the old-fashioned but ever-popular (at least in France) veal's head with
capers and a mayonnaise and mustard sauce. Desserts include traditional favorites such
as tarte Tatin and mousse au chocolat.

✪ **Chez Diane.** 25 rue Servandoni, 6e. ☎ **01-46-33-12-06.** Reservations recommended
for groups of 4 or more. Main courses 100–140 F ($17–$23.80); fixed-price menu 160 F
($27.20). V. Mon–Fri noon–2pm; Mon–Sat 8–11:30pm. Métro: St-Sulpice. FRENCH.

Fashionable restaurant food at simple bistro prices. Designed to accommodate only
40 diners at a time, this place is illuminated with Venetian glass chandeliers and paved
with old-fashioned floor tiles. Inside, deep ochres and terra-cottas are redolent of the
landscapes and villas of Provence. Chez Diane's offerings acknowledge the seasons, per-
ishable ingredients, and their owners' inspirations. Recently we enjoyed sweetbreads in
a sauce of flap mushrooms; nuggets of wild boar in honey sauce; minced salmon prepared as a terrine with green peppercorns; and a modern, light-textured adaptation of
hachis Parmentier, an elegant meat loaf lightened with parsley, chopped onions, and
herbs.

✪ **Crémerie-Restaurant Polidor.** 41 rue Monsieur-le-Prince, 6e. ☎ **01-43-26-95-34.**
Reservations not accepted. Main courses 40–76 F ($6.80–$12.90); fixed-price menu (Mon–Fri)
55 F ($9.35) at lunch, 100 F ($17) at dinner. No credit cards. Daily noon–2:30pm; Mon–Sat
7pm–12:30am, Sun 7–11pm. Métro: Odéon. FRENCH.

Crémerie Polidor is the most traditional bistro in the Odeon area, serving *cuisine familiale*. Its name dates from the early part of the century, when the restaurant specialized
in frosted cream desserts, but the restaurant itself can trace its history back to 1845.

The Crémerie is one of the Left Bank's oldest and most established literary bistros. It was André Gide's favorite, and Hemingway, Valéry, Artaud, Joyce, and Kerouac also dined here. The place is still frequented largely by students and artists, who head for the rear. Peer beyond the lace curtains and polished brass hat racks to see drawers in the back where repeat customers lock up their cloth napkins. Smiling, overworked waitresses with frilly aprons and T-shirts bearing the likeness of old mère Polidor serve a 19th-century cuisine. Try the old-fashioned pumpkin soup followed by hearty portions of beef bourguignonne or veal in white sauce. Equally satisfying is the Basque-style chicken. For dessert, get a chocolate, raspberry, or lemon tart—the best in all of Paris.

La Bastide Odéon. 7 rue Corneille, 6e. ☎ **01-43-26-03-65.** Reservations recommended. Fixed-price menu 150–190 F ($25.50–$32.30). MC, V. Tues–Sat 12:30–2pm and 7:30–11pm. Métro: Odeon. RER: Luxembourg. PROVENÇAL.

Those who can't rush off to southern France can alleviate some of their yearnings with a visit to a brasserie that's become a star amid the city's inexpensive restaurants. The sunny climes of Provence come through in pale yellow walls, heavy oaken tables, and artfully arranged bouquets of wheat and dried roses. Chef Gilles Ajuelos, formerly employed in some very grand Parisian restaurants, prepares a market-based Provençal cuisine that varies according to the freshness and availability of ingredients. His simplest first courses are the most satisfying, including a platter of sardines and seared sweet peppers with olive oil and pine nuts; grilled eggplant layered with herbs and oil; and roasted rabbit stuffed with eggplant and served with olive toast and balsamic vinegar. Main courses include wild duckling with pepper sauce and such exotica as lamb's feet and giblets prepared in the immemorial style of Provence. A winner among desserts is warm almond pie served with prune and Armagnac ice cream.

Le Canton. 5 rue Gozlin, 6e. ☎ **01-43-26-51-86.** Main courses 40–59 F ($6.80–$10.05); fixed-price menu 55–69 F ($9.35–$11.75) at lunch, 75–90 F ($12.75–$15.30) at dinner. MC, V. Mon–Sat noon–2:30pm and 7–11pm. Métro: St-Germain-des-Prés. CHINESE/VIETNAMESE.

The cuisine at Le Canton is exotic, especially the Vietnamese dishes, and the setting is relaxing and evocative of Asia. Best of all, the food is affordable and much more savory than at the nearby fast-food joints. Begin a meal with any of several versions of *nem* (Vietnamese ravioli) stuffed with shrimp and vegetables. Delicate dim sum are available, as well as such main courses as salt-and-pepper shrimp, Szechuan-style chicken, and one of the best-selling dishes in the house, the Yorkson shrimp quick-fried with garlic, peppers, and onions. Soups here are succulent and tasty, and throughout the repertoire, the chefs rely on ample use of basil, the smell of which permeates the establishment's two dining rooms.

Pub Saint-Germain-des-Prés. 17 rue de l'Ancienne-Comédie, 6e. ☎ **01-43-29-38-70.** Reservations not required. Bottle of beer 28–70 F ($4.75–$11.90); menu items 70–200 F ($11.90–$34). AE, DC, MC, V. Daily 24 hours. Métro: Odéon. FRENCH/LATE-NIGHT.

For late-night drinking and snacking, this is one of the most popular spots on the Left Bank. The pub offers one of the best beer selections in France, with 26 varieties on tap and 500 international beers by the bottle. There are nine different rooms and 600 seats, making it the largest pub in France. Sit in one of the leather booths and enjoy such late-night fare as steak tartare or beef strips simmered with herbs in beer. Bands play every night from 10:30pm to at least 4am.

Restaurant des Beaux-Arts. 11 rue Bonaparte, 6e. ☎ **01-43-26-92-64.** Reservations recommended. Main courses 65–115 F ($11.05–$19.55); fixed-price menu 95 F ($16.15). MC, V. Daily noon–2:15pm and 7–10:45pm. Métro: St-Germain-des-Prés. FRENCH.

Located across from Paris's School of Fine Arts, this is the most famous budget restaurant in Paris. Does it please everyone? Hardly. Are there complaints about bad food and service? Some. Is it packed every day with hungry patrons? Inevitably. That means it must please thousands of diners every year, drawn to its cheap prices, large portions, and stick-to-the-ribs dishes, all featured on a set menu. The place still captivates the starving students of the Latin Quarter.

The best tables are upstairs, but on the main floor you can see the steaming pots in the open kitchen. This is what a provincial French family might cook at home—*bourguignon navarin d'agneau* (lamb chops cooked with carrots, onions, and tomatoes), grilled pig's foot, trout with saffron sauce, rabbit leg with mustard sauce, and codfish fillet with garlic sauce.

7TH ARRONDISSEMENT (EIFFEL TOWER/MUSÉE D'ORSAY)
VERY EXPENSIVE

L'Arpège. 84 rue de Varenne, 7e. ☎ **01-47-05-09-06.** Fax. 01-44-18-98-39. Reservations required. Main courses 320–560 F ($54.40–$95.20); fixed-price lunch 390 F ($66.30); menu dégustation (tasting menu) 1,200 F ($204). AE, DC, V. Mon–Fri 12:30–2pm and 7:30–10pm. Métro: Varenne. FRENCH.

One of the least expensive of Paris's three-star restaurants, L'Arpège is best known for Alain Passard's adventurous and divine specialties. No restaurant in the 7th serves better food. Set across from the Rodin Museum in a prosperous residential neighborhood, L'Arpège has claimed the site of what for years was the world-famous L'Archestrate, where Passard worked in the kitchens.

Amid an intensely cultivated modern decor of etched glass, burnished steel, monochromatic oil paintings, and pearwood paneling, you can enjoy specialties heralded as among the most innovative to emerge in recent culinary history. Some of Passard's latest creations include Breton lobster in a sweet-and-sour rosemary sauce, scallops prepared with cauliflower and a lime-flavored grape sauce, and panfried duck with juniper and lime sauce, followed by the signature dessert, a candied tomato stuffed with 12 kinds of dried and fresh fruit and served with anise-flavored ice cream.

EXPENSIVE

L'Affriolé. 17 rue Malar, 7e. ☎ **01-44-18-31-33.** Reservations required. Fixed-price menu 120–190 F ($20.40–$32.30). MC, V. Mon–Sat noon–2:30pm and 7:30–11:30pm. Métro: Invalides. FRENCH.

Fine food, reasonable prices, and simplicity have guaranteed this upscale bistro's burgeoning business. Loyal clients line up by the dozen for a table within a long and narrow, deliberately old-fashioned art deco dining room. The house staple is the fixed-price menu—they refer to it as a "menu-carte." It includes an "amuse-bouche" (a kind of preappetizer), a starter (often concocted with some derivation of foie gras), a main course (worthy choices include a jarret of glazed and roasted pork or scallops with lime juice), a cheese, a "predessert" (pear tarte, caramelized banana), and a dessert (crêpes stuffed with quince marmalade, chocolate soup, or clafoutis with grapes were all available during our recent visit). For most of these courses, seven options are available, each changing at frequent intervals. The vast majority opt for the six-course medley, but if you're not feeling particularly hungry, you can order a two-course menu (starter and main course) for 120 F ($22).

✪ Le Violon d'Ingres. 135 rue St-Dominique, 7e. ☎ **01-45-55-15-05.** Fax 01-45-55-48-42. Reservations required. Main courses 130–190 F ($22.10–$32.30); fixed-price menu 240–400 F ($40.80–$68) lunch, 400 F ($68) at dinner. AE, MC, V. Tues–Sat noon–2:30pm and 7–10:30pm. Métro: Ecole Militaire. FRENCH.

This restaurant is quickly becoming Paris's pièce de résistance. For a chance to experience chef/owner Christian Constant's gastronomic masterpieces, you have to reserve a table a minimum of 3 to 4 days in advance. There is talk that Monsieur Constant will

Restaurants near the Eiffel Tower & Invalides

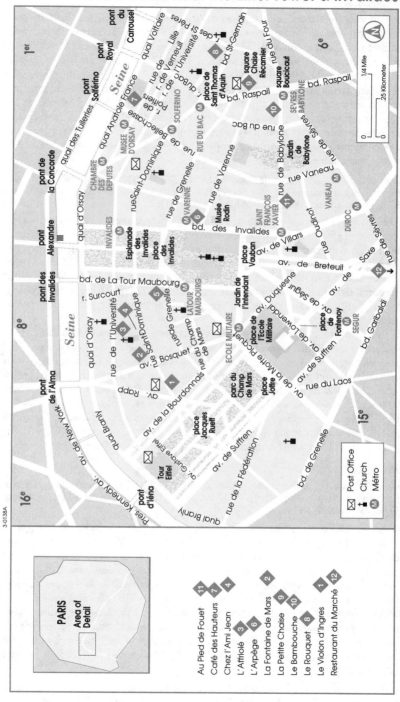

Au Pied de Fouet — 11
Café des Hauteurs — 7
Chez l'Ami Jean — 3
L'Affriolé — 4
L'Arpège — 6
La Fontaine de Mars — 2
La Petite Chaise — 9
Le Bambouche — 10
Le Rouquet — 8
Le Violon d'Ingres — 1
Restaurant du Marché — 12

☒ Post Office
✝■ Church
Ⓜ Métro

PARIS
Area of Detail

3-0138A

135

be "the new Robuchon," although many Parisian chefs are vying for that lofty position. Those who are fortunate enough to dine in the Violin's warm atmosphere of rose-colored wood, soft cream walls, and elegant chintz fabrics patterned with old English tea roses always rave about the cleverly artistic dishes. They range from a starter of pan-fried foie gras with gingerbread and spinach salad to more elegant main courses such as lobster ravioli with crushed vine-ripened tomatoes, roasted veal in a light and creamy milk sauce served with tender spring vegetables, or even a selection from the popular rôtisserie, like spit-roasted leg of lamb rubbed with fresh garlic and thyme. Even his familiar dishes seem new at each tasting. Chef Constant keeps a copious and well-chosen selection of wine to accompany his overwhelmingly satisfying meals. The service is charming and discreet.

Paul Minchelli. 54 bd. de la Tour-Maubourg, 7e. ☎ **01-47-05-89-86.** Reservations required. Main courses 160–490 F ($27.20–$83.30). MC, V. Tues–Sat noon–3pm and 8–11pm. Closed Aug. Métro: La Tour Maubourg. SEAFOOD.

This restaurant had an immediate and powerful impact on the Paris dining scene upon its arrival in 1994. Much of its appeal derives from its deliberate earthiness, its refusal to indulge in the gratuitous rituals of some of its competitors. Its founder is Marseille-born Paul Minchelli, whose cuisine is described even by his financial backers as "marginal," having rejected this city's culinary conventions in favor of an old-fashioned Provençal technique. He is said to have reinvented fish (or at least the way we cook it) by stripping away extra sauces and conflicting flavors to reveal the true "taste of the sea."

In a dining room lined with Norwegian birchwood that's been stained to a distinctive yellow and outfitted with modern furniture and round seascapes evocative of the portholes on a ship, you can order such dishes as raw saltwater fish served only with olive oil, salt, and pepper; an old-fashioned recipe known as merlan Colbert; grilled John Dory; and fillet of sea bass steamed in seaweed. Other popular dishes include lobster cooked with honey and spices and one of the best versions of herring salad in Paris. Some of the shellfish is so fresh it might have been scooped from an aquarium just moments before it was cooked.

Be warned: There aren't many alternatives for those who dislike fish.

MODERATE

La Petite Chaise. 36-38 rue de Grenelle, 7e. ☎ **01-42-22-13-35.** Reservations required. Fixed-price menu 125–190 F ($21.25–$32.30). AE, V. Daily noon–2pm and 7–11pm. Métro: Sèvres-Babylone. FRENCH.

This is the oldest restaurant in Paris, established as an inn in 1680 by the Baron de la Chaise at the edge of what was a large hunting preserve. (According to popular lore, the baron used the upstairs bedrooms for midafternoon dalliances, between fox and pheasant hunts.) Very Parisian, the "Little Chair" invites you into a world of cramped but attractive tables, very old wood paneling, and ornate wall sconces. Guests choose from a four-course set menu with a large choice of dishes in each category.

A vigorous chef has brought renewed taste and flavor to this longtime favorite. Samplings from the menu might include salad with strips of duck breast on a bed of fresh lettuce; a seafood and scallop ragout with saffron; filet of beef prepared with green peppercorns; and poached fish with steamed vegetables served in a sauce of fish and vegetable stock and cream.

Le Bambouche. 15 rue de Babylone, 7e. ☎ **01-45-49-14-40.** Reservations recommended. Main courses 110–190 F ($18.70–$32.30); fixed-price menu 190 F ($32.30). AE, MC, V. Mon–Fri noon–2:30pm and 8–11pm. Métro: Sèvres-Babylone. NORTHERN FRENCH.

Still struggling to gain a niche, Le Bambouche has prices that are more reasonable than you'd expect for cuisine with this degree of finesse. Meals are served in a pair of dining rooms painted in the colors of ancient Pompeii or Renaissance Tuscany (dark ochre and burnt orange) depending on your point of view. Menu items change with the season, but are likely to include roasted foie gras wrapped in glazed Parma ham, served with fresh asparagus; cream of cauliflower soup with truffles and essence of lobster; sea bass braised with fresh vegetables and anise; and veal chops from Corrèze caramelized and served with tea sauce. Dessert might include a chocolate mousse served with dried fruit and herb-flavored ice cream.

INEXPENSIVE

Au Pied de Fouet. 45 rue de Babylone, 7e. ☎ **01-47-05-12-27.** Reservations not necessary. Main courses 50–70 F ($8.50–$11.90). No credit cards. Mon–Sat noon–2:30pm; Mon–Fri 7–9:30pm. Closed Aug. Métro: Vaneau. FRENCH.

Au Pied de Fouet is one of the smallest, oldest, and most reasonably priced restaurants in the neighborhood. In the 1700s, it was a stopover for carriages en route to Paris from other parts of Europe, offering wine, food, and stables. Don't expect a leisurely or attentive meal: Food and drink will disappear quickly from your table, under the gaze of others waiting their turn. Dishes are solid and unpretentious, and include veal in white sauce, *petit salé* (a savory stew made from pork and vegetables), and such fish dishes as sole meunière, a warhorse of French cuisine but always good.

Chez l'Ami Jean. 27 rue Malar, 7e. ☎ **01-47-05-86-89.** Reservations recommended. Main courses 75–105 F ($12.75–$17.85). V. Mon–Sat noon–3pm and 7–10:30pm. Métro: Invalides. BASQUE/SOUTHWESTERN FRENCH.

Its ardent fans claim that its Basque cuisine and setting are the most authentic and uncompromising on the Left Bank. Established by a Basque nationalist in 1931, details include wood panels, memorabilia from pelote (a Basque game much like jai alai) and soccer, and red and white woven tablecloths like the ones sold in Bayonne, along with a bent bargoer or two sporting the Basque nation's headwarmer of choice, the beret. Menu items include cured Bayonne ham; earthy and herb-laden Béarn-influenced vegetable soups; a succulent omelet with peppers, tomatoes, and onions; squid stewed in its own ink and served with tomatoes and herbs; and the poultry dish of the Basque world, *poulet basquaise,* cooked with spicy sausage, onions, peppers, and very strong red wine. In springtime, look for a truly esoteric specialty rarely available from nearby competitors: *saumon de l'Adour* (Adour river salmon) served with béarnaise sauce.

La Fontaine de Mars. 129 rue St-Dominique, 7e. ☎ **01-47-05-46-44.** Reservations recommended. Main courses 75–140 F ($12.75–$23.80). AE, MC, V. Daily noon–2:30pm and 7:30–11pm. Métro: Ecole-Militaire. PYRÉNéE/SOUTHWESTERN FRANCE.

The name of this restaurant doesn't derive from its location near the Champ de Mars, but from the ornate, historic stone fountain that sits on its tree-lined terrace. You'll find an animated, sometimes boisterous dining room on the street level, plus two cozier and calmer upstairs rooms whose round tables and wooden floors make you feel like you're in a private home. An additional 70 or so seats become available by the fountain whenever weather permits. Much of the cuisine here derives from the Pyrénées and southwestern France, bearing rich, heady flavors that go well with robust red wines. Examples include a confit of duckling with parsley potatoes; a cassoulet inspired by the traditions of Toulouse; veal chops with morels; fillets of red mullet or monkfish with herb-flavored butter; and other typical Parisian bistro food. Our favorite dessert is a thin tart filled with a sugared purée of apples, capped with more apple, and garnished with Calvados and cream.

13TH ARRONDISSEMENT (GOBELINS/PORTE D'IVRY)
MODERATE
Auberge Etchegorry. 41 rue Croulebarbe, 13e. ☎ **01-44-08-83-51.** Reservations recommended. Main courses 90–100 F ($15.30–$17); fixed-price menu 145–220 F ($24.65–$37.40). AE, DC, V. Mon–Sat noon–2:30pm and 7:30–10:30pm. Métro: Gobelins or Corvisart. BASQUE.

Its windows overlook a verdant patch of lawn that's so green you might for a moment imagine that you've entered a rustic inn deep within the countryside. Dark paneling, deep colors, hanging hams and pigtails of garlic, and lacy curtains emulate the Basque country, the corner of southwestern France adjacent to Spain, prized for its succulent cuisine. Victor Hugo and Chateaubriand ate here in centuries past. Cramped tables are a drawback, but not much of one in this rich atmosphere. The menu includes a roster of Basque or southwestern French specialties, including cassoulet, magret of duckling, filet of beef with peppercorns, peppery omelet known as piperades, cocottes of mussels, and terrines or panfried slices of foie gras. There's a comfortable and unpretentious three-star hotel (Le Vert Galant) associated with the restaurant.

INEXPENSIVE
Keryado. 32 rue de Regnault, 13e. ☎ **01-45-83-87-58.** Reservations recommended. Main courses 85–145 F ($14.45–$24.65); fixed-price menu 110–150 F ($18.70–$25.50). MC, V. Mon–Sat noon–2:30pm; Tues–Sat 7:30–10:30pm. Métro: Porte d'Ivry. SEAFOOD.

Since it was taken over by a sophisticated management in 1992, this all-blue-and-white seafood bistro has specialized in a dish only the most dedicated or arrogant chef would try at home: bouillabaisse. Bouillabaisse has led to more lost reputations, crackups, and suicides than any other dish in the history of French cuisine. Fortunately, Keryado's version is as rich, savory, and satisfying as what you'd get in some of the best restaurants of Provence. And it's priced at a relatively modest 145 F ($24.65) per person, much less than at grander restaurants. If bouillabaisse isn't your cup of soup, consider such other fish dishes as a *chaudrée de poissons aïoli,* a stew pot of fillets from six different types of fish, laced with a rich garlicky broth. Slightly more experimental is a stingray with green cabbage and curry.

14TH & 15TH ARRONDISSEMENTS (GARE MONTPARNASSE/ DENFERT-ROCHEREAU)
MODERATE
Chez Lulu (L'Assiette). 181 rue du Château, 14e. ☎ **01-43-22-64-86.** Reservations recommended. Main courses 150–200 F ($25.50–$34). AE, MC, V. Wed–Sun noon–2:30pm and 8–10:30pm. Closed Aug. Métro: Gaité. SOUTHWESTERN FRENCH.

Everything about this place seems to appeal to a nostalgic clientele seeking down-to-earth prices and flavorful food. You'll recognize it by the bordeaux-colored facade and potted plants in the windows. Mitterrand used to drop in with his cronies for his favorite platters of oysters, crayfish, sea urchins, and clams. The place was a *charcuterie* (pork butcher's shop) in the 1930s, and today it maintains some of its old accessories. Dishes are unashamedly inspired by Paris's long tradition of bistro cuisine, with a few twists. Examples include a salad of chanterelle mushrooms; *rillettes* (a roughly textured pâté) of mackerel; roasted guinea fowl; and desserts made on the premises, including a crumbly version of apple cake served with fresh North African figs. Particularly delicious is a *petit salé* (stew with vegetables) of duckling with wine from the Poitou region of west-central France.

La Cagouille. 10-12 place Brancusi, 14e. ☎ **01-43-22-09-01.** Reservations recommended. Main courses 120–180 F ($20.40–$30.60); fixed–price menu 150–250 F ($25.50–$42.50). AE, V. Daily noon–2pm and 5:30–10:30pm. Métro: Gaité. FRENCH/CENTRAL EUROPEAN.

Don't expect to find meat at this temple of seafood. The burly and genteel owner, Gérard Allamandou, refuses to feature it on his menu. Everything about La Cagouille is a testimonial to a modern version of the culinary arts of La Charente, the sandy, flat district that hugs the Atlantic south of Bordeaux. In a trio of deliberately simple, oak-sheathed dining rooms with marbletop tables and a minimum of accessories, you'll sample seafood that's prepared as simply and naturally as possible. You get no fancy sauces or elaborate cooking techniques here. The beauty is in the cooking's utter simplicity and a strict allegiance to fresh ingredients, many arriving only a few hours before they are cooked. Allamandou's preferred fish is red mullet, which might appear sautéed in a bland oil, or baked in rock salt from the Ile de Ré. The all-natural dishes are served with the same lack of pretension as the methods used to cook them. The name of the place derives from the regional symbol of La Charnte: the sea snail, whose preparation here is elevated to a fine culinary art. Look for a vast assemblage of all-French, mostly white wines, and at least 150 types of cognac.

La Régalade. 49 av. Jean-Moulin, 14e. ☎ **01-45-45-68-58.** Reservations recommended. Fixed-price menu 185 F ($31.45). Tues–Fri noon–2:15pm and 7pm–midnight; Sat 7pm–midnight. Closed mid-July to mid-Aug. Métro: Alésia. SOUTHWESTERN FRENCH.

The setting is that of a crowded, convivial bistro with banquettes the color of aged Bordeaux wine, congenially harassed service, and unexpectedly good food. Priced at an unchanging rate, the obligatory set menu presents a choice of at least 10 starters, 10 main courses, and either one of about a dozen freshly made desserts or selections from a cheese tray. The inspiration is Yves Camdeborde's, known for his training at the frighteningly posh Hotel de Crillon. The menu changes with the seasons, but is likely to include filet of wild boar prepared with red wine sauce; a savory mixture of potatoes with blood sausage; and an always-popular platter of fried goose liver served on toasted slices of spice bread.

Restaurant du Marché. 57-59 rue de Dantzig, 15e. ☎ **01-48-28-31-55.** Reservations recommended. Main courses 140–170 F ($23.80–$28.90); fixed-price menu 190 F ($32.30). AE, DC, V. Mon–Fri noon–2:30pm; Mon–Sat 7–11pm. Métro: Porte-de-Versailles. LANDES.

Although very little about the decor of this place has changed since the 1930s, its wood panels are waxed and shined constantly, and bouquets of fresh flowers are frequently replenished. Menu items derive from dishes popular in and around Bordeaux, and include an impressive roster of wines from that region to accompany the heaping platters of traditional foie gras; deboned hare stuffed with foie gras and braised in red wine and brandy; and hen stewed with vegetables and Armagnac. Incidentally, the restaurant's name derives from the fact that many of its fresh, unusual ingredients are supplied directly by producers in the Landes district, near Bordeaux.

INEXPENSIVE

Restaurant Bleu. 46 rue Didot, 14e. ☎ **01-45-43-70-56.** Reservations recommended. Fixed-price menu 98–165 F ($16.65–$28.05) at lunch, 120–165 F ($20.40–$28.05) at dinner. MC, V. Tues–Sat noon–2:30pm and 7:30–10:15pm. Closed Aug. Métro: Alésia. AUVERGNAT.

Why is this restaurant named blue? The answer is no secret—it's in honor of the eyes of the chef and owner, Simon Christian, who has been entertaining Paris diners for the last 5 years. The decor will remind you of a market town's inn, with dark paneling, farm implements, paintings of barnyard animals (especially sheep), and souvenirs of another time. The hostess, who speaks English, recommends a house specialty *(truffade des bergers)* to anyone who doesn't know a saucisson from a saucisse. Made with potatoes, goose fat, Auvergnat cheese, and parsley, it's a worthy opener for such main courses as grilled Charolais beefsteak served with a sauce made from the heady red wine of Cahors; grilled blood sausage; and braised shoulder of pork. For something different, try a cassoulet of fish. Prune tarts make a flavorful ending. There are only about 40 spots here, so advance reservations are important.

5 The Best Cafes

Parisians use cafes as combination club/tavern/snack bars, almost as extensions of their living rooms. They are spots where you can read your newspaper or meet a friend, do your homework or write your memoirs, nibble at a hard-boiled egg or drink yourself into oblivion. At cafes you meet your dates to go on to a show or to stay and talk. Above all, cafes are for people watching.

Their single common denominator is the encouragement of leisurely sitting. Regardless of whether you have one small coffee or the most expensive cognac in the house, nobody badgers, pressures, or hurries you. If you wish to sit here until the place closes, that's your affair. For the cafe is one of the few truly democratic institutions— a solitary soda buys you the same view and sedentary pleasure as an oyster dinner.

Coffee, of course, is the chief drink. It comes black in a small cup, unless you specifically order it *au lait* (with milk). Tea (*thé,* pronounced tay) is also fairly popular, but is generally not of a high quality.

If you prefer beer, we advise you to pay a bit more for the imported German, Dutch, or Danish brands, which are much better than the local brew. If you insist on a French beer, at least order it *à pression* (draft), which is superior. There is also a vast variety of fruit drinks, as well as Coca-Cola, which can be rather expensive.

French chocolate drinks—either hot or iced—are absolutely superb and on par with the finest Dutch brands. They're made from ground chocolate, not a chemical compound.

Cafes keep flexible hours, depending on the season, the traffic, and the part of town they're in. Nearly all of them stay open until 1 or 2am, and a few are open all night.

Now just a few words on cafe etiquette. You don't pay when you get your order— only when you intend to leave. Payment indicates that you've had all you want. *Service compris* means the tip is included in your bill, so it technically isn't necessary to tip extra; still, most people leave an extra franc or so.

You'll hear the locals call for the "garçon," but as a foreigner it would be more polite to say "monsieur." All waitresses, on the other hand, are addressed as "mademoiselle," regardless of age or marital status.

In the smaller cafes, you may have to share your table. In that case, even if you haven't exchanged a word with your table companion, when you leave it is customary to bid them good-bye.

Brasserie Lipp. 151 bd. St-Germain, 6e. ☎ **01-45-48-53-91.** Full meals average 280 F ($47.60); café au lait 18 F ($3.05). Daily 9am–2am; restaurant service 11am–1am. Métro: St-Germain-des-Prés.

On the day of Paris's liberation in 1944, former owner Roger Cazes (now deceased) spotted Hemingway, the first man to drop in for a drink. Then as now, famous people often drop by the Lipp for its beer, wine, and conversation. Cazes's nephew, Michel-Jacques Perrochon, now runs this quintessential Parisian brasserie. The food is secondary, yet quite good, providing you can get a seat (an hour and a half waiting time is customary if you're not familiar to the management). The specialty is *choucroute garni,* the best sauerkraut in Paris. You not only get sauerkraut, but a thick layer of ham and braised pork as well, which can all be downed with the house Riesling (a white wine) or beer. Even if you don't go inside for a drink, you can sit at a sidewalk cafe table to enjoy a cognac and people-watch.

Café Beaubourg. 100 rue St-Martin, 4e. ☎ **01-48-87-63-96.** Glass of wine 23–40 F ($3.90–$6.80); beer 26–45 F ($4.40–$7.65); American breakfast 110 F ($18.70); sandwiches and platters 30–120 F ($5.10–$20.40). Sun–Thurs 8am–1am, Fri–Sat 8am–2am. Métro: Rambuteau or Hôtel-de-Ville.

Located next to the all-pedestrian plaza of the Centre Pompidou, this is a trendy, avant-garde cafe with soaring concrete columns and a minimalist decor. Many of the regulars work in the neighborhood's eclectic shops and galleries. In warm weather, tables are set up on the sprawling outdoor terrace, providing a great place to watch the young and the restless go by.

Café Cosmos. 101 bd. du Montparnasse, 6e. ☎ **01-43-26-74-36.** Métro: Vavin. Café Espresso 25 F ($4.25); platters 42-85 F ($7.15–$14.45); set price lunch 69 F ($11.75). MC, V. Daily 8AM–3AM. Métro: Vavin.

Does today's generation have a cafe to equal the Lost Generation's Select or Coupole? Perhaps it's the ultramodern Cosmos. Today you might rub elbows with a French film star or executive ("no one writes novels anymore"). The cafe features wooden tables, black leather chairs, and black clothing in winter—the perfect backdrop for smoked salmon with toast.

Café de Flore. 172 bd. St-Germain, 6e. ☎ **01-45-48-55-26.** Café espresso 23 F ($3.90); glass of beer 39–41 F ($6.65–$6.95). Daily 7am–2am. Métro: St-Germain-des-Prés.

Sartre—the granddaddy of existentialism, a key figure in the Resistance movement, and a renowned cafe-sitter—often came here during World War II. Wearing a leather jacket and beret, he sat at his table and wrote his trilogy, *Les Chemins de la Liberté (The Roads to Freedom)*. Camus, Picasso, and Apollinaire also frequented the Flore. The cafe is still going strong, although the famous patrons have moved on, and tourists have taken up all the tables.

Le Café de la Musique. 212 ave. Jean-Jaurès, 19e. ☎ **01-48-03-15-91.** Plats du jour 55–110 F ($9.35–$18.70). Daily 8am–2am (full menu daily 11am–midnight). Métro: Porte-de-Pantin.

Its location within the Cité de la Musique—one of the grandest of Mitterand's *grands travaux*—guarantees the presence of a clientele that's passionately devoted to music. Consequently, the recorded sounds that play in the background here are likely to be more diverse, and more eclectic, than at any other cafe in Paris. The red- and green-velour setting might remind you of a modern opera house. Windows overlook the nearby place de la Fontaine. Every Wednesday, between 10pm and 1am, there's a program of live jazz.

✪ **Café de la Paix.** Place de l'Opéra, 9e. ☎ **01-40-07-30-20.** Café espresso 19 F ($3.25); fixed-price menu 139 F ($23.65) for 2 courses, 180 F ($30.60) for 3 courses; daily specials from 105 F ($17.85). Daily noon–midnight. Métro: Opéra.

This hub of the tourist world rules the place de l'Opéra, and the legend goes that if you sit here long enough, you'll see someone you know passing by. Huge, grandiose, frighteningly fashionable, and sometimes brusque and anonymous, it harbors not only Parisians, but, at one time or another, nearly every visiting American—a tradition dating from the end of World War I. Once Émile Zola sat on the terrace; later,

Factoid

You'll pay substantially less in a cafe if you stand at the counter, since there's no service charge.

Hemingway and Fitzgerald frequented it. The best news for tourists who stop in for a bite is that prices have recently been lowered because of stiff competition in the area.

Café de l'Industrie. 16 rue St-Sabin, 11e. ☎ **01-47-00-13-53.** Reservations not accepted. Glass of wine 16–26 F ($2.70–$4.40); main courses 50–80 F ($8.50–$13.60). MC, V. Sun–Fri 10am–2am. Métro: Bastille or Breguier-Sabin.

Founded just before the outbreak of World War II, this cafe received a vital new lease on life, and new floods of business, after the nearby opening of the Opéra de la Bastille. Today, amid three dining rooms and a decor that manages to evoke aspects of both the tropics and faux-baroque Europe, it combines generous platters of food with green plants and lots of original oil paintings by long-term clients. Known for decanting obscure vintages from the Touraine and the region around Beaujolais, it appeals to photographers and lesser-known characters within French-speaking show biz. If you're hungry, consider any of the plats du jour, which arrive in generous portions and are based on long-term staples of the French brasserie tradition. Examples include leeks steeped in vinaigrette, beef bourguignonne, fried haddock, and such pasta dishes as tagliatelle flavored with salmon, chives, and cream sauce.

Café des Hauteurs. In the Musée d'Orsay, 1 rue de Bellechasse, 7e. ☎ **01-45-49-47-03.** Reservations not accepted. "Suggestions du Jour" 30–65 F ($5.10–$11.05). AE, MC, V. Tues–Wed and Fri–Sun 10am–5pm, Thurs 10am–9pm. Métro: Solférino. RER: Musée d'Orsay. FRENCH.

The designers of the Musée d'Orsay recognized the crushing fatigue that can sometimes come with a museum visit. That's why this fifth-floor cafe is something midway between a bar and a short-term rest home, where you can recuperate in front of a sweeping view that stretches as far as Notre-Dame and Sacré-Coeur, and looks over the glass-encased mechanism of a clock resembling London's Big Ben. In addition to the usual doses of caffeine and alcohol, you can order platters that are more substantial than a snack, but less filling than the main course of a conventional meal. Examples include smoked salmon with shrimp salad and rye bread, or a platter of assorted cheeses.

Café Marly. Cour Napoléon du Louvre, 93 rue de Rivoli, 1er. ☎ **01-49-26-06-60.** Reservations recommended. Main courses 110–150 F ($18.70–$25.50). AE, DC, MC, V. Daily 8am–2am (meals 11:30am–1am). Métro: Palais-Royal or Musée-du-Louvre.

In 1994, the French government gave the green light for a cafe and restaurant to open in one of the most historic courtyards of the Louvre. It's accessible only from a point close to the famous glass pyramid that rises above the Cour Marly, and has become a favorite refuge for Parisians trying to escape the roar of traffic on the rue de Rivoli. Anyone is welcome to sit down for a café au lait between 8am and 2am daily. But more substantial fare is the norm here, served in one of three different dining rooms, each outfitted in tones of burgundy, black, and gilt. Menu items include club sandwiches, fresh fish, pepper steak, and an array of upscale, bistro-inspired food. In summer, outdoor tables overlook the celebrated courtyard.

Café/Restaurant/Salon de Thé Bernardaud. 11 rue Royale, 8e. ☎ **01-42-66-22-55.** Reservations recommended at lunch, not necessary for breakfast or afternoon tea. Continental breakfast 60 F ($10.20); lunch main courses 80–120 F ($13.60–$20.40); cup of afternoon tea with a pastry 75 F ($12.75). MC, V. Mon–Fri 8am–7pm, Sat noon–7pm. Métro: Concorde. FRENCH.

Few other cafes and tearooms in Paris mingle salesmanship with culinary pizzazz as effectively as this one. It was established in 1995 by a venerable Limoges-based manufacturer of porcelain—Bernardaud—and the staggeringly beautiful stuff is on display everywhere. Set squarely within some of the most expensive commercial real estate in Europe, it occupies a medium-green, aggressively upscale art deco–style space. Lunchtime is flooded with employees of the nearby offices, and no one minds if you opt just for a salad or something more substantial, such as a medley of fresh fish in herb sauce with vegetables. Afternoon teas add a new, not terribly discreet commercial twist: A staff member will present a choice of five different porcelain patterns in which your tea will be served, and if you finish your Earl Grey with an absolute fixation on the particular pattern you've chosen, you'll be directed into the adjacent showroom to place your order.

Fouquet's. 99 av. des Champs-Elysées, 8e. ☎ **01-47-23-70-60.** Glass of wine from 42 F ($7.15); sandwiches 45–70 F ($7.65–$11.90); main courses 160–270 F ($27.20–$45.90); fixed-price menu 265 F ($45.05). Daily 9am–2am. Restaurant noon–3pm and 7pm–1am; bar 9am–2am. Métro: George V.

Fouquet's has been collecting anecdotes and a patina since it was founded in 1901. A celebrity favorite, it has attracted Chaplin, Chevalier, Dietrich, Churchill, Roosevelt, and Jackie O. The premier cafe on the Champs-Elysées sits behind a barricade of potted flowers at the edge of the sidewalk. You can choose a table in the sunshine or retreat to the glassed-in elegance of the leather banquettes and rattan furniture of the street-level grill room. Although Fouquet's is a full-fledged restaurant, with a beautiful, very formal dining room on the second floor, most visitors come by just for a glass of wine, coffee, or a sandwich.

La Coupole. 102 bd. du Montparnasse, 14e. ☎ **01-43-20-14-20.** Breakfast buffet 89 F ($15.15); main courses 89–188 F ($15.15–$31.95) at lunch, 109–188 F ($18.55–$31.95) at dinner; fixed-price menu 132–169 F ($22.45–$28.75) at lunch, 169 F ($28.75) at dinner before 10:30pm, 132–169 F ($22.45–$28.75) after 10:30pm. Daily 7:30am–2am (breakfast buffet Mon–Fri 7:30–10:30am). Métro: Vavin.

Once a leading center of artistic life, La Coupole is now a bastion of the grand Paris brasserie style in Montparnasse. It was born in 1927 at the height of the city's jazz age. Former patrons included Josephine Baker, Henry Miller, Dalí, Calder, Hemingway, Dos Passos, Fitzgerald, and Picasso. The big, attractive cafe has grown more cosmopolitan through the years, attracting fewer locals and art-school waifs, but some of the city's most interesting foreigners show up.

The sweeping outdoor terrace is among the finest in Paris. At one of its sidewalk tables, you can sit and watch the passing scene and order a coffee or a cognac VSOP. The food is quite good, despite the fact that the dining room resembles an enormous railway station waiting room. Try such main dishes as sole meunière, cassoulet, and some of the best pepper steak in Paris. The fresh oysters and shellfish are especially popular. The waiters are as rude and inattentive as ever, and aficionados of the place wouldn't have it any other way.

La Rotonde. 105 bd. du Montparnasse, 6e. ☎ **01-43-26-68-84.** Glass of wine 20 F ($3.40); fixed-price menu 75 F ($12.75) at lunch, 180 F ($30.60) at dinner. Cafe daily 7am–2am, food service daily noon–2am. Métro: Vavin.

Once patronized by Hemingway, the original Rotonde faded into history but is immortalized in the pages of *The Sun Also Rises,* in which Papa wrote, "No matter what cafe in Montparnasse you ask a taxi driver to bring you to from the right bank of the river, they always take you to the Rotonde." Lavishly upgraded, its reincarnation has a paneled art deco elegance, and shares the once-hallowed site with a motion-picture theater. If you stand at the bar, prices are lower.

Le Café Zephyr. 12 bd. Montmartre, 9e. ☎ **01-47-70-80-14.** Reservations not accepted. Café au lait 22 F ($3.75); plats du jour 65–92 F ($11.05–$15.65). MC, V. Mon–Sat 8am–2am, Sun 8am–10pm. Métro: Rue Montmartre.

The patrons of this cafe like it for the quiet refuge it provides in the midst of a bustling, heavily commercialized neighborhood. Understated and sedate, it holds

In Pursuit of the Perfect Parisian Pastry

Could it be true, as rumor has it, that more eggs, sugar, cream, and butter per capita are consumed in Paris than any other city in the world, with the possible exception of Vienna? From the modern-day Proust sampling the madeleine to the child munching into a chocolate-filled croissant, everybody in Paris seems to be looking for two things: the perfect lover and the perfect pastry, not necessarily in that order. As a Parisian food critic once said, "A day without a pastry is a day in hell!"

Who would think of beginning a morning in Paris without a **croissant**—not the prepackaged kind made with leadlike dough, but flaky and freshly baked, light as a feather and made with real butter, preferably from Norman cows.

The Greeks may have invented pastry making, but the French perfected it. Some French pastries have made a greater impact on the world than others. **Brioche,** a sweet, yeasty breakfast bread, is baked around the world today, as is the fabled **chocolate éclair,** a cream-filled choux pastry. Another pastry you should sample on its home turf (you'll never get it quite right in your own kitchen) is the **Napolitain.** Made with cake flour and almonds, its layers are spread with a fruit puree. The term is not to be confused with **Neapolitan,** referring to sweets and cakes made with layers of two or more colors, each layer being flavored differently. Very much in vogue in Paris is the **mille-feuille,** or "thousand leaves," made by arranging thin layers of flaky pastry one on top of the other, along with layers of cream or some other filling such as thick fruit purees or jams.

To get you going, here are some of our favorite *pâtisseries.* **Stohrer,** 51 rue Montorgueil, 2e (☎ **01-42-33-38-20**), has been going strong ever since it was opened by Louis XV's pastry chef in 1730. With a day's notice, you can order an 18th-century specialty, *un pithivier,* a.k.a. *une galette des rois.* Available at any time is one of the most succulent desserts in Paris, baba au rhum, or its even richer cousin, un Ali Baba, which also incorporates cream-based rum and raisin filling. Stohrer boasts an interior decor that's classified as a national historic treasure, with frescoes of damsels in 18th-century costume bearing flowers and, what else, pastries.

firmly to its roots in an increasingly modern and international area of Paris. Stop by here for a leisurely café au lait or a light snack, but don't expect any culinary masterpieces—you're more likely to enjoy the atmosphere than the food.

Le Gutenberg. 64 rue Jean-Jacques Rousseau, 1er. ☎ **01-42-36-14-90.** Reservations not accepted. Café au lait 10 F ($1.70); sandwiches 14 F ($2.40); plats du jour 47 F ($8). No credit cards. Sun–Fri 8am–7pm, Sat noon–3:30pm. Métro: Louvre-Rivoli.

Set behind the largest post office in France, and named in honor of the printing presses that used to operate nearby, this is the most evocative and authentic of the cafes close to the Louvre. There's a zinc-top bar, and two inner rooms loaded with antique mirrors and uniformed staff members. No one can agree on whether the place is 150 or 225 years old.

Le Rouquet. 188 bd. St-Germain, 7e. ☎ **01-45-48-06-93.** Reservations not accepted. Café au lait 13–23 F ($2.20–$3.90); plats du jour 55 F ($9.35). MC, V. Mon–Sat 7am–9pm. Métro: St-Germain-des-Prés.

Despite conventional food and high prices, Le Rouquet enjoys an enviable cachet and sense of chic, partly because it competes on a less flamboyant scale with the nearby

Opened in 1862, a few steps from the Madeleine, **Ladurée Royale,** 16 rue Royale, 8e (☎ **01-42-60-21-79;** Métro: Madeleine), is the dowager tearoom of Paris. A hot young pastry chef, Pierre Hermé, is the new "star of the **macaroon,**" a pastry for which this establishment is celebrated. Karl Lagerfeld still comes here and raves about them, as did the late Pamela Harriman. The macaroon here is not the sticky coconut version known to many, but two almond meringue cookies, flavored with chocolate, vanilla, pistachio, coffee, or other flavors. You may also want to try one of Hermé's latest creations—Coeur du Faubourg, a luscious and dense chocolate cake with layers of caramel and soft apricots.

In business since Napoléon was in power, **Dalloyau,** 101 rue Faubourg St-Honoré, 8e (☎ **01-42-99-90-00;** Métro: St-Philippe-du-Roule), has a name instantly recognizable throughout Paris; they supply pastries to the Elysée Palace (the French White House) and many Rothschild mansions nearby. Its specialties include **Le Dalloyau,** a praline cake filled with almond meringue that's marvelously light textured, and the famous **Mogador** (chocolate cake, chocolate mousse, and a fine layer of raspberry jam). Unlike Stohrer, Dalloyau has a tearoom (open 7 days a week from 8:30am to 7pm) one floor above street level, where ladies who lunch can drop in for a slice of pastry that Dalloyau warns is "too fragile to transport, or to mail, over long distances."

The best way to end your pastry tour of Paris is to sample a **madeleine,** a tea cake shaped like tiny scallop shells, at **Lerch,** 4 rue Cardinal-Lemoine, 5e (☎ **01-43-26-15-80;** Métro: Cardinal-Lemoine). Founded in 1971 by the Alsatian-born Lerch family, this pastry shop sells goods to such luminaries as Martha Stewart, along with the dozens of Proust fans who come here hoping the madeleine will "invade the senses with exquisite pleasure," as it did for the narrator of *Remembrance of Things Past.* Ideally the madeleine is dipped into tea, preferably the slightly lime-flavored tilleuil.

Café de Flore and Deux Magots, and partly because the decor hasn't changed since a remodeling in 1954. Less than 60 yards from the Church of St-Germain, you can sit for as long as you want, watching a clientele composed of stylish Italians and Americans performing shopping and people-watching rituals barely altered since Le Roquet's founding in 1922.

Les Deux-Magots. 6 place St-Germain-des-Prés, 6e. ☎ **01-45-48-55-25.** Café au lait 25 F ($4.25); whisky soda 70 F ($11.90); plats du jour 90–140 F ($15.30–$23.80). Daily 7:30am–1:30am. Métro: St-Germain-des-Prés.

This legendary hangout for the sophisticated residents of St-Germain-des-Prés becomes a tourist favorite in summer. Visitors monopolize the few sidewalk tables as waiters rush about, seemingly oblivious to anyone's needs. Regulars from around the neighborhood reclaim it in the off-season. Deux-Magots was once a gathering place of the intellectual elite, including Sartre, Simone de Beauvoir, and Jean Giraudoux. Inside are two large statues of Confucian wise men *(magots)* that give the cafe its name. The crystal chandeliers are too brightly lit, but the regulars seem to be accustomed to the glare. After all, some of them even read their daily newspapers here.

Lizard Lounge. 18 rue du Bourg-Tibourg, 4e. ☎ **01-42-72-81-34.** Reservations not accepted. Cocktails 32–48 F ($5.45–$8.15); sandwiches, salads, and plats du jour 38–70 F ($6.45–$11.90); Sun brunch 50–95 F ($8.50–$16.15). MC, V. Daily 11:30am–2am (food service noon–10:30pm; Sat–Sun brunch 11:30am–4pm). Métro: Hôtel de Ville.

Founded by Los Angeles escapee Phil Morgan in 1994, this place resembles an Amsterdam or New York City cocktail lounge. It's an indulgently heterosexual enclave in an increasingly gay neighborhood. A rectangular space with a high ceiling, wood paneling, and bars on three different levels, it doubles as a restaurant. Looking to strike up a friendship? Order one of the margaritas, the house beer (a Dutch brew known as "Cheap Blond"), or the drink nobody can seem to get enough of, a cream-and-Kahlúa-based "Screaming Orgasm." If you're hungry, try a New York–style deli sandwich (turkey with bacon is the best-seller), a Lizard Salad garnished with Cheddar cheese and tikka slow-cooked chicken, or any of the French-inspired plats du jour. Sunday brunch features an all-you-can-eat vegetarian buffet whose offerings are augmented with such garnishes as omelets with Canadian bacon or American-style ham and sausage.

Exploring Paris 6

Paris is one of those cities where taking in the street life should claim as much of your time as sightseeing in churches or museums. A gourmet picnic in the Bois de Boulogne, a sunrise pilgrimage to the Seine, an afternoon of bartering at the flea market—Paris bewitches you with these kinds of experiences. For all the Louvre's beauty, you'll probably remember the Latin Quarter's crooked alleyways better than the 370th oil painting of your visit.

Suggested Itineraries for the First-Timer

These itineraries are obviously intended for the first-time visitor, but even those making their 30th trip to Paris will want to revisit such attractions as the Louvre, where you could spend every day of your life and always see something you missed before. Use these tips as a guide, but not a bible. Paris rewards travelers with guts and independence of mind, those who will pull open the doors to a chapel or an antiquarian's shop not because they're listed on a souvenir map, but because they look intrinsically interesting. In Paris, they usually are.

If You Have 1 Day

Far too little time, but you'll have to make the most of it. Get up early and begin walking the streets in the neighborhood of your hotel. The streets of Paris are live theater. Find a little cafe; chances are there will be one on every block. Go in and order a typical Parisian breakfast of coffee and croissants. If you're a museum and monument junkie, and you don't dare return home without seeing the "must" sights, know that the two most popular museums are the **Louvre** and the **Musée d'Orsay.** The three most enduring monuments are the **Eiffel Tower,** the **Arc de Triomphe,** and **Notre-Dame** (which can be seen later in the day). If it's a toss-up between the Louvre and the d'Orsay, we'd make it the Louvre if you're a first-timer because it holds a greater variety of works. If you feel the need to choose between monuments, we'd make it the Eiffel Tower just for the panoramic view of the city. If you feel your day is too short to visit museums or wait in lines for the tower, we'd suggest that instead you spend most of your time strolling the streets of Paris. The most impressive neighborhood is the **Ile St-Louis,** which we believe is the most elegant place for a walk in Paris. After exploring this island and its mansions, wander at will through such Left Bank districts as **St-Germain-des-Prés** or the area around **place St-Michel,** the heart of the student quarter. As the

The Major Attractions

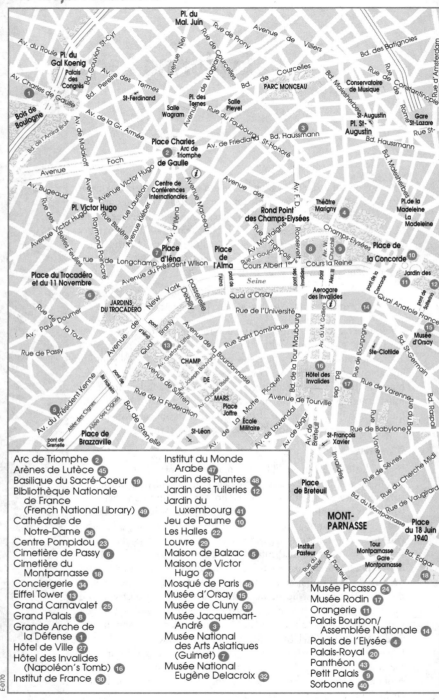

E-0170

148

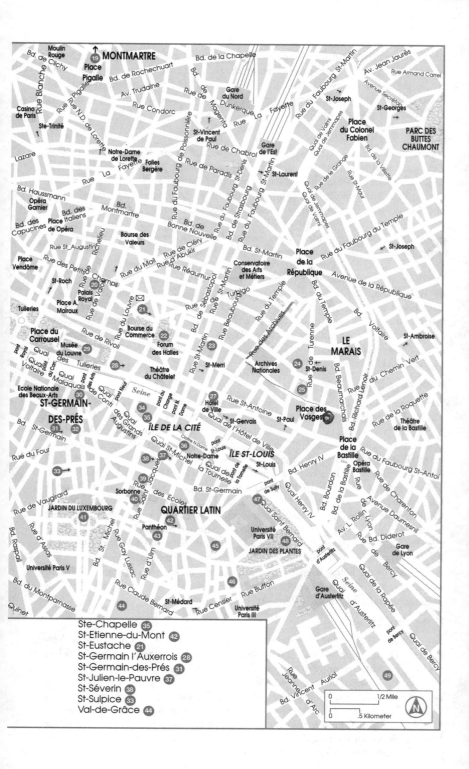

St Chapelle 35
St-Etienne-du-Mont 42
St-Eustache 21
St-Germain l'Auxerrois 28
St-Germain-des-Prés 31
St-Julien-le-Pauvre 37
St-Séverin 38
St-Sulpice 33
Val-de-Grâce 44

sun sets over Paris, head for Notre-Dame, which stands majestically along the banks of the Seine. This is a good place to watch shadows fall over Paris as the lights come on for the night. Afterward, walk along the banks of the Seine, where vendors sell books and souvenir prints. Promise yourself a return visit and have dinner in the Left Bank bistro of your choice.

If You Have 2 Days

Follow the itinerary for day 1 above. Since you've paid so much attention to the Left Bank on your first day, spend most of this day taking in the glories of the Right Bank. Begin at the Arc de Triomphe and stroll down the **Champs-Elysées,** the main boulevard of Paris, until you reach the Egyptian obelisk at the place de la Concorde. This grand promenade is one of the most famous walks in the world. The place de la Concorde affords terrific views of the Madeleine, the Palais-Bourbon, the Arc de Triomphe, and the Louvre. This is where some of France's most notable figures lost their heads on the guillotine. A nearby square, **place Vendôme,** is worth a visit, too, as it represents the Right Bank at its most elegant, with such addresses as the Ritz, and Paris's top jewelry stores. After all this walking, we'd suggest a rest stop in the **Jardin de Tuileries,** directly west and adjacent to the Louvre. After a long lunch in a Right Bank bistro, for a total contrast to monumental Paris, go for a walk in the **Marais.** Our favorite stroll is along the rue des Rosiers, a narrow street that's the heart of the Jewish community. And don't miss the **place des Vosges.** After a rest at your hotel, select one of the restaurants down in **Montparnasse,** following in Hemingway's footsteps. This area is far livelier at night.

If You Have 3 Days

Spend days 1 and 2 as above. As you've already gotten a look at the Left Bank and the Right Bank, this day should be about following your special interests. If you're a Monet fan, you might head for the **Musée Marmottan-Claude Monet.** Or perhaps you'd rather wander the sculpture garden of the **Musée National Auguste-Rodin.** If it's the **Picasso Museum** you select, you can use part of the morning to explore a few of the art galleries of the Marais. Following in the trail of Descartes and Madame de Sévigné, select a cafe or restaurant here for lunch. Reserve the afternoon for **Ile de la Cité,** where you'll not only get to see Notre-Dame again, but you can visit the **Conciergerie** where Marie Antoinette and others were held captive before they were beheaded. See also the stunning stained glass of **Sainte-Chapelle** in the Palais de Justice. For dinner that night, we'd suggest a Right Bank bistro in Le Marais. Afterward, if your energy holds, you can sample Paris's nightlife—whatever you fancy, the dancers at the **Lido** or the **Folies-Bergère** or a smoky Left Bank jazz club. If you'd just like to sit and have a drink, Paris has some of the most elegant hotel bars in the world at such places as the **Hôtel Crillon** or **Plaza-Athenée.**

If You Have 4 Days

For your first 3 days, follow the itinerary above. On your fourth day, head to **Versailles,** 13 miles south of Paris, and the greatest attraction in the Ile de France. When Louis XIV decided to move to the suburbs, he created a spectacle unlike anything the world had ever seen. The good news is that most of the palace remains intact, in all its opulence and glitter. A full day here almost feels like too little time. After you return to Paris for the night, take a good rest and spend the evening wandering around the Left Bank's **Latin Quarter,** enjoying the student cafes and bars and selecting your bistro of choice for the evening. Some of the livelier streets for wandering include rue de la Huchette and rue Monsieur-le-Prince.

If You Have 5 Days

Spend days 1 to 4 as recommended above. On your fifth day, devote at least a morning to an area heretofore neglected, **Montmartre,** the community formerly known for its artists perched atop the highest of Paris's seven hills. It's like a village encircled by sprawling Paris. Although the starving artists who made it the embodiment of *la vie de bohème* have long since departed, there is much to charm and enchant you, especially if you wander the back streets. Here, away from the tacky shops and sleazy clubs, you'll see the picture-postcard lanes and staircases known to Picasso, Toulouse-Lautrec, and Utrillo. Of course, it's virtually mandatory to visit the **Basilica of Sacré-Coeur,** for the view if nothing else. Since it's your last night in Paris, let your own interests take over here. Lovers traditionally spend it clasping hands in a farewell along the Seine; less goggle-eyed visitors can still find a full agenda. We'd suggest a final evening at **Willi's Wine Bar** (see chapter 9), with more than 250 vintages and good food to go along with it. For a nightcap, we always head for the **Hemingway Bar** at the Ritz, where Garbo, Noel Coward, and F. Scott Fitzgerald once lifted their glasses. If that's too elegant, head for **Closerie des Lilas** in the 6th arrondissement, where you can rub shoulders with the movers and shakers of the film industry and fashion's "playthings." Even if you've been saving money up until now, our final suggestion is that you go all out for one really grand French meal at a fabulous restaurant. It's a memory you'll probably treasure long after you've recovered from paying the tab.

1 Sights & Attractions by Arrondissement

See neighborhood maps throughout this chapter.

THE RIGHT BANK
1ST ARR. (MUSÉE DU LOUVRE/ LES HALLES)

Arc de Triomphe du Carrousel (p. 154)
Conciergerie (p. 179)
Galerie Nationale du Jeu de Paume (p. 163)
Grande Promenade Walking Tour (p. 217)
✪ Jardin de Tuileries (p. 220)
Les Halles (p. 185)
Musée des Arts Décoratifs (p. 194)
✪ Musée du Louvre (The Louvre) (p. 159)
Musée du Parfum (p. 201)
Palais-Royal (p. 182)
Place Vendôme (p. 221)
Pont-Neuf (p. 185)
Sainte-Chapelle (p. 176)
✪ St-Eustache (p. 178)
St-Germain l'Auxerrois (p. 178)
Square du Vert Galant (p. 185)

2ND ARR. (LA BOURSE)

Harry's New York Bar (p. 211)

3RD ARR. (LE MARAIS)

Hôtel de Rohan (p. 232)
Hôtel des Ambassadeurs de Hollande (p. 232)
Hôtel Le-Peletier-de-St-Fargeau (p. 231)
Marais Walking Tour (p. 228)
Musée Carnavalet (p. 198)
Musée Cognacq-Jay (p. 192)
Musée d'Art et d'Histoire du Judaïsm (p. 198)
Musée de la Chasse (Hunting Museum) (p. 200)
Musée de l'Histoire de France (p. 199)
✪ Musée Picasso (p. 168)
Passage de Retz (p. 232)

4TH ARR. (ILE DE LA CITÉ/ ILE ST-LOUIS/BEAUBOURG)

Atelier (workshop) of Constantin Brancusi (p. 164)
✪ Cathédrale de Notre-Dame (p. 155)
Centre Pompidou (p. 164)
Colonne de Juillet (July Column) (p. 230)
Galerie Sud (p. 164)

THE LEFT BANK
5TH ARR. (LATIN QUARTER)

Arènes de Lutèce (p. 179)
Church of the Sorbonne (p. 227)
Institut du Monde Arabe (p. 198)
Latin Quarter Walking Tour (p. 225)
Mosquée de Paris (p. 174)
Musée National d'Histoire Naturelle (Museum of Natural History) (p. 210)
Musée National du Moyen Age/Thermes de Cluny (Musée de Cluny) (p. 167)
The Panthéon (p. 183)
Roman Baths (p. 167)
Rue de la Huchette (p. 226)
Rue du Chat-qui-Pêche (p. 226)
St-Etienne-du-Mont (p. 176)
St-Julien-le-Pauvre (p. 226)
St-Séverin (p. 226)
Shakespeare and Company (p. 212)
Sorbonne (p. 227)
Val-de-Grâce (p. 178)

6TH ARR. (ST-GERMAIN/ LUXEMBOURG)

Deux-Magots (p. 211)
Institut de France (p. 182)
Jardin du Luxembourg (p. 201)
La Rotonde (p. 212)
Le Procope (p. 212)
Musée National Eugène Delacroix (p. 168)
Musée Zadkine (p. 195)
Rue Monsieur-le-Prince (p. 211)
Rue Visconti (p. 188)
St-Germain-des-Prés (p. 175)
St-Sulpice (p. 175)
27 rue de Fleurus (p. 188)

7TH ARR. (EIFFEL TOWER/ MUSÉE D'ORSAY)

American Church (p. 215)
Champ-de-Mars (p. 158)
Eglise du Dôme (Church of the Dome) (p. 159)
✪ Eiffel Tower (p. 156)
Hôtel des Invalides (Napoléon's Tomb) (p. 158)
Institut Neerlandais (p. 215)
Les Egouts (The Sewers of Paris) (p. 213)
Musée de l'Armée (p. 158)
Musée des Plans-Reliefs (p. 159)
✪ Musée d'Orsay (p. 162)
Musée Rodin (p. 170)
Palais Bourbon/Assemblée Nationale (p. 182)

13TH ARR. (GARE D'AUSTERLITZ)

Bibliothèque Nationale de France (French National Library) (p. 179)
Manufacture Nationale des Gobelins (p. 196)

14TH ARR. (MONTPARNASSE)

Cimetière du Montparnasse (p. 205)
Les Catacombs (p. 213)

15TH ARR. (GARE MONTPARNASSE/ INSTITUTE PASTEUR)

Musée Bourdelle (p. 191)
La Grande Arche de La Défense (Puteaux) (p. 182)
Manufacture Nationale de Sèvres (Sèvres) (p. 195)
Musée National de Céramique de Sèvres (Sèvres) (p. 196)

2 The Top Attractions

In this city of hidden faces and brazen charms, wandering through contorted lanes and down vast boulevards is something every traveler should take the time to do. We've outlined our four favorite walks in chapter 7. The first spans Paris's **Grand Promenade,** the Champs-Elysées, which has witnessed some of France's proudest and most painful moments. The second takes you to hilly **Montmartre,** home of windmills, gleaming white Sacré-Coeur, cabarets, circus freaks, and prostitutes. The **Latin Quarter** is the site of our third walk, a warren of cafe-strewn streets where students meet and fall in love over café-crème and croissants. Our last walk presents the **Marais,**

Memorial to a Princess

Place de l'Alma (Métro: Alma-Marceau) has been turned into a tribute to the late Diana, princess of Wales, who was killed in an auto accident August 31, 1997, in the nearby underpass. The bronze flame in the center is a replication of the flame in the Statue of Liberty and was a 1987 gift by the *International Herald Tribune* to honor Franco-American friendship. Many bouquets and messages are still placed around the flame, which seems to have come to represent the princess. By the time of your visit, Paris may also have opened a memorial garden to Princess Diana in the Marais, at 21 rue des Blancs-Manteaux.

---

which has swung the pendulum stroke from an aristocratic haven to a site of industrial tenements, and which is on a fashionable upswing again.

☼ Arc de Triomphe. Place Charles-de-Gaulle-Etoile, 8e. ☎ **01-55-37-73-77.** Admission 40 F ($6.80) adults, 25 F ($4.25) ages 12–25, free for children 11 and under. Apr–Sept daily 9:30am–11pm; Oct–Mar daily 10am–10:30pm. Métro: Charles-de-Gaulle-Etoile.

At the western end of the Champs-Elysées, the Arc de Triomphe suggests one of those ancient Roman arches, only it's larger. Actually, it's the biggest triumphal arch in the world, about 163 feet high and 147 feet wide. To reach it, don't try to cross the square, the busiest traffic hub in Paris. With a dozen streets radiating from the "Star," the roundabout was called by one writer "vehicular roulette with more balls than numbers" (death is certain!). Take the underground passage and live a little longer.

After the death of Charles de Gaulle, the French government—despite protests from anti-Gaullists—voted to change the name of this site from place de l'Etoile to place Charles-de-Gaulle.

The arch has witnessed some of France's proudest moments, and some of its more shameful and humiliating defeats, notably those of 1871 and 1940. The memory of German troops marching under the arch that had come to symbolize France's glory and prestige is still painful to the French. Who could ever forget the 1940 newsreel of the Frenchman standing on the Champs-Elysées openly weeping as the Nazi storm troopers goose-stepped through Paris?

Commissioned by Napoléon in 1806 to commemorate his victories, the arch wasn't ready for the entrance of his new empress, Marie-Louise, in 1810. It served its ceremonial purpose anyway, and, in fact, wasn't completed until 1836, under the reign of Louis-Philippe. Four years later, the remains of Napoléon, brought from his grave at St. Helena, passed under the arch on the journey to his tomb at the Invalides. Since that time it has become the focal point for state funerals. It is also the site of the permanent tomb of the unknown soldier, in whose honor an eternal flame is kept burning.

The greatest state funeral was that of Victor Hugo in 1885; his coffin was placed under the center of the arch, and much of Paris turned out to pay tribute to the author. Another notable funeral was that of Ferdinand Foch, the supreme commander of the Allied forces in World War I, who died in 1929. The Arc's happiest moment occurred in 1944, when the liberation of Paris parade passed through. That same year, Eisenhower paid a visit to the tomb of France's unknown soldier, a new tradition among leaders of state and important figures.

Of the sculptures on the monument, the best-known is Rude's *Marseillaise,* also called *The Departure of the Volunteers.* The *Triumph of Napoléon in 1810,* by J. P. Cortot, and the *Resistance of 1814* and the *Peace of 1815,* both by Etex, also adorn the facade. The monument is engraved with the names of hundreds of generals (those underlined died in battle) who commanded French troops in Napoleonic victories.

It's a big world.

And we've got the network to cover it.

Global
connection
with the AT&T
Network

AT&T
direct
service

Enjoy going to the corners of the earth? We're with you. With the world's most powerful network, **AT&T Direct** Service gives you fast, clear connections from more countries than anyone,* and the option of an English-speaking operator. All it takes is your AT&T Calling Card or credit card.† And the planet is yours. FOR A LIST OF **AT&T ACCESS NUMBERS**, TAKE THE ATTACHED WALLET GUIDE.

For Travelers
who want more than
the Official Line

Macmillan Publishing USA

Also Available:

You can take an elevator or climb the stairway to the top, where there is an exhibition hall with lithographs and photos depicting the Arc throughout its history. From the observation deck, you have the finest view of the Champs-Elysées and of such landmarks as the Louvre, the Eiffel Tower, Sacré-Coeur, and the new district of La Défense.

✪ **Cathédrale de Notre-Dame.** 6 place du parvis Notre-Dame, 4e. ☎ **01-42-34-56-10.** www.paris.org/Monuments/NDame. Free admission to the cathedral; towers and crypt 32 F ($5.45) adults, 21 F ($3.55) ages 12–25 and over 60, free for children under 12; museum and treasury 15 F ($2.55) adults, 5 F (85¢) ages 12–25 and over 60, free for children under 12. Cathedral daily 8am–6:45pm year-round. Towers and crypt Apr–Sept daily 9:30am–6pm, Oct–Mar daily 10am–4:15pm. Museum Wed and Sat–Sun 2:30–6pm. Treasury Mon–Sat 9:30–11:30am and 1–5:45pm. Métro: Cité or St-Michel. RER: St-Michel.

Notre-Dame is the heart of Paris, even of France; distances from Paris to all parts of France are calculated from its center.

Although many disagree, Notre-Dame is, in our opinion, more interesting outside than in. You'll want to walk around the entire structure to fully appreciate this "vast symphony of stone." Better yet, cross over the bridge to the Left Bank and view it from the quay.

Its setting on the banks of the Seine has always been memorable. Founded in the 12th century by Maurice de Sully, bishop of Paris, Notre-Dame grew and grew. Over the years, the cathedral has changed as Paris has, often falling victim to whims of decorative taste. Its famous flying buttresses (the external side supports, which give the massive interior a sense of weightlessness) were rebuilt in 1330.

The history of Paris and that of Notre-Dame are inseparable. Many prayed here before going off to fight in the Crusades. "Our Lady of Paris" was not spared by the revolutionaries, who destroyed the Galerie des Rois and converted the building into a secular temple. Later, Napoléon was crowned emperor here, yanking the crown out of Pius VII's hands and placing it on his own head. But carelessness, vandalism, embellishments, and wars of religion had already demolished much of the previously existing structure.

The cathedral was once scheduled for demolition, but, partly because of the popularity of Victor Hugo's *Hunchback of Notre Dame* and the revival of interest in the Gothic, a movement mushroomed to restore the cathedral to its original glory. The task was completed under Viollet-le-Duc, an architectural genius.

The houses of old Paris used to crowd in on Notre-Dame, but Haussmann ordered them torn down to show the cathedral to its best advantage from the square, known as the *parvis.* This is the best vantage for seeing the three sculpted 13th-century portals.

On the left, the **portal of the Virgin** depicts the signs of the zodiac and the coronation of the Virgin, an association found in dozens of medieval churches. The restored central **portal of the Last Judgment** depicts three levels: The first shows Vices and Virtues; the second, Christ and his Apostles; and above that, Christ in triumph after the Resurrection. The portal is a close illustration of the Gospel according to Matthew. Over this portal is a remarkable rose window, 31 feet wide, forming a showcase for a statue of the Virgin and Child. On the far right is the **portal of St. Anne,** depicting such scenes as the Virgin enthroned with Child. It is the best preserved and the most perfect piece of sculpture in Notre-Dame.

Equally interesting (although often missed by the scurrying visitor) is the **portal of the cloisters** (around on the left), with its dour-faced 13th-century Virgin, a survivor among the figures that originally adorned the facade. (Unfortunately, the Child she is holding is decapitated.) Finally, on the Seine side of Notre-Dame, the portal of St. Stephen traces that saint's martyrdom.

If possible, come to see Notre-Dame at sunset. Inside, of the three giant medallions that warm the austere cathedral, the **north rose window** in the transept, dating from the mid–13th century, is best. The main body of the church is typically Gothic, with slender, graceful columns. In the **choir,** a stone-carved screen from the early 14th century depicts such biblical scenes as the Last Supper. Near the altar stands the 14th-century *Virgin and Child,* highly venerated among Paris's faithful.

In the treasury are displayed vestments and gold objects, including crowns. Exhibited are a cross presented to Haile Selassie, the former emperor of Ethiopia, and a reliquary given by Napoléon. Notre-Dame is especially proud of its relic of the True Cross and the Crown of Thorns.

Finally, to visit those grimy gargoyles immortalized by Hugo, you have to scale steps leading to the twin square **towers** that rise to a height of 225 feet. Once here, you can closely inspect the devils (some giving you the raspberry), hobgoblins, and birds of prey. Look carefully and you may see the hunchback Quasimodo.

Approached through a garden behind Notre-Dame is the **Deportation Memorial,** jutting out on the very tip of the Ile de la Cité. Here, birds chirp and the Seine flows gently by, but the memories are far from pleasant. It commemorates the French citizens who were deported to such camps as Auschwitz and Buchenwald during World War II. Carved into stone in blood red are the words (in French): "Forgive, but don't forget." The memorial is open Monday through Friday from 8:30am to 9:45pm, and Saturday and Sunday from 9am to 9:45pm. Admission is free.

✪ **Eiffel Tower (La Tour Eiffel).** Champ-de-Mars, 7e. ☎ **01-44-11-23-23.** www.paris. org/Monuments/Eiffel. Admission to first landing 21 F ($3.55), second landing 43 F ($7.30), third landing 60 F ($10.20). Stairs to second floor 15 F ($2.55). Sept–May daily 9:30am–11pm; June–Aug daily 9am–midnight. In fall and winter, the stairs are open only until 6:30pm. Métro: Trocadéro, Ecole Militaire, or Bir-Hakeim. RER: Champ-de-Mars–Tour Eiffel.

This is without a doubt the single most recognizable structure in the world. Weighing 7,000 tons but exerting about the same pressure on the ground as an average-size person sitting in a chair, the tower was never meant to be permanent. It was built for the Exhibition of 1889 by Gustave Alexandre Eiffel, the French engineer whose fame rested mainly on his iron bridges. (Incidentally, he also designed the framework for the Statue of Liberty.)

The tower, including its 55-foot television antenna, is 1,056 feet high. On a clear day you can see it some 40 miles away. An open-framework construction, the tower unlocked the almost unlimited possibilities of steel construction, paving the way for the skyscrapers of the 20th century. Skeptics said it couldn't be built, and Eiffel actually wanted to make it soar higher than it did. For years it remained the tallest man-made structure on earth, until such skyscrapers as the Empire State Building surpassed it.

We could fill an entire page with Eiffel Tower statistics. (Its plans spanned 6,000 square yards of paper, and it contains 2½ million rivets.) But forget the numbers. Just stand underneath the tower and look straight up. It's like a rocket of steel lacework shooting into the sky.

Initially, artists and writers vehemently denounced the tower, although later generations sang its praise. People were fond of calling it names: "a giraffe," "the world's greatest lamppost," "the iron monster." Others suggested, "Let's keep art nouveau grounded."

Ile de la Cité

After visiting Notre-Dame, try to take some time to explore Ile de la Cité and its other main attractions, the infamous **Conciergerie** (see page 179) and the lovely **Sainte-Chapelle** (see page 176), best seen in radiant sunlight.

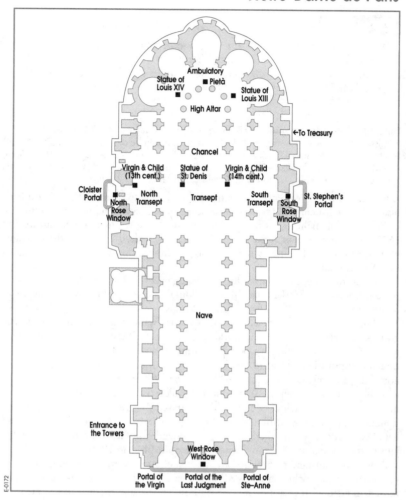

Ambulatory
Statue of Louis XIV
Pietà
Statue of Louis XIII
High Altar
←To Treasury
Chancel
Virgin & Child (13th cent.)
Statue of St. Denis
Virgin & Child (14th cent.)
Cloister Portal
North Rose Window
North Transept
Transept
South Transept
South Rose Window
St. Stephen's Portal
Nave
Entrance to the Towers
West Rose Window
Portal of the Virgin
Portal of the Last Judgment
Portal of Ste-Anne

E-0172

Nature lovers feared it would interfere with the flight patterns of birds over Paris.

In the early 1890s, the tower escaped destruction when it found a new practical use: The French government installed antennae on it, thus enabling wireless communications throughout the city.

Everyone visits the landmark that has become the symbol of Paris. To see it best, however, don't sprint—approach it gradually. You can visit the tower in three stages. Taking the elevator to the **first landing,** you have a view over the rooftops of Paris. On the first level there's a cinema museum that shows films, restaurants, and a bar open year-round. The **second landing** provides a panoramic look at the city. The **third and final stage** gives the most spectacular view. On the ground level, in the eastern and western pillars, you can visit the 1899 lift machinery when the tower is open. Eiffel's office has been re-created on the third level; wax figures depict the engineer receiving Thomas Edison.

Of course, it's the view that most people come for, and this extends for 42 miles, theoretically. In practice, weather conditions tend to limit it. Nevertheless, it's fabulous, and the best time for visibility is about an hour before sunset.

Time-Out

When visiting the Eiffel Tower, try to leave some time for the **Champ-de-Mars,** 7e (Métro: Trocadéro, Ecole Militaire, or Bir-Hakeim), the gardens between the Tower and the Military School. Laid out around 1770, these gardens were the World's Fair grounds and the scene of many military parades.

Hôtel des Invalides (Napoléon's Tomb). Place des Invalides, 7e. ☎ **01-44-42-37-72.** Admission to Musée de l'Armée, Napoléon's Tomb, and Musée des Plans-Reliefs 37 F ($6.30) adults, 27 F ($4.60) ages 12–18, free for children 11 and under. Oct–Mar daily 10am–5pm; Apr–May and Sept daily 10am–6pm; June–Aug daily 10am–7pm. Closed Jan 1, May 1, Nov 1, and Dec 25. Métro: Latour-Maubourg, Varenne, or Invalides.

It was the Sun King who decided to build this "hotel" to house soldiers who'd been disabled. It wasn't entirely a benevolent gesture, since they had been injured, crippled, or blinded while fighting his battles. The massive building program was launched in 1670; when it was completed (Louis XIV was long dead by then), the corridors stretched for miles. Eventually the building was crowned by a gilded dome designed by Jules Hardouin-Mansart.

It is best to approach the Invalides by crossing over the Right Bank via the turn-of-the-century Alexander III Bridge. In the building's cobblestone forecourt, a display of massive cannons makes for a formidable welcome.

Before rushing on to Napoléon's tomb, you may want to take the time to visit the greatest military museum in the world, the **Musée de l'Armée.** In 1794, a French inspector started collecting weapons, uniforms, and equipment, and with the continued accumulation of war material over the centuries, the museum has become a horrifying documentary of man's self-destruction. Viking swords, Burgundian battle axes, blunderbusses from the 14th century, Balkan khandjars, American Browning machine guns, war pitchforks, salamander-engraved Renaissance serpentines, "Haute Epoque" armor, a 1528 Griffon, musketoons, grenadiers . . . if it can kill, it's enshrined here. As a sardonic touch, there's even the wooden leg of General Daumesnil. Oblivious to the irony of the act, the Germans looted the place in 1940.

Among the outstanding acquisitions are suits of armor worn by the kings and dignitaries of France, including Louis XIV, the best of which lie in the new Arsenal. The most famous one, the "armor suit of the lion," was made for François I. Henri II ordered his suit engraved with the monogram of his mistress, Diane de Poitiers, and, perhaps reluctantly, that of his wife, Catherine de Médicis. The showcases of swords are among the finest in the world.

The mementos of World War I, including those of American and Canadian soldiers, are especially interesting. Included is the Armistice Bugle, which sounded the cease-fire on November 7, 1918, before the general cease-fire on November 11, 1918.

And then there's that little Corsican general who became France's greatest soldier. Here you can see the plaster death mask Antommarchi made of him, as well as an oil by Delaroche, painted at the time of Napoléon's first banishment (April 1814), which depicted him as he probably looked, paunch and all. The First Empire exhibit displays Napoléon's field bed with his tent. In the room devoted to the Restoration, the 100 Days, and Waterloo, you can see Napoléon's reconstituted bedroom at the time of his death at St. Helena. On the more personal side, you can view Vizir, a horse he owned (now stuffed), as well as a saddle he used mainly for state ceremonies. The Turenne Salon contains other souvenirs, including the hat Napoléon wore at Eylau, his sword from his victory at Austerlitz, and his "Flag of Farewell," which he kissed before departing for Elba.

The Salle Orientale in the west wing shows arms of the Eastern world, including Asia and the Muslim countries of the Mideast, from the 16th to the 19th centuries. Turkish armor (look for Bajazet's helmet) and weaponry, and Chinese and Japanese armor and swords, are on display. The west wing also houses exhibits on World Wars I and II.

You can gain access to the **Musée des Plans-Reliefs** through the west wing. This collection shows French towns and monuments done in scale models.

A walk across the Court of Honor delivers you to the **Eglise du Dôme** (Church of the Dome), designed by Hardouin-Mansart for Louis XIV. The great architect began work on the church in 1677, although he died before its completion. The dome is the second-tallest monument in Paris. The hearse used at the emperor's funeral on May 9, 1821, is in the Napoléon Chapel.

To accommodate the Tomb of Napoléon, the architect Visconti had to redesign the high altar in 1842. First buried at St. Helena, Napoléon's remains were returned to Paris in 1840, as Louis-Philippe had demanded of England. The triumphal funeral procession passed under the Arc de Triomphe, down the Champs-Elysées, en route to the Invalides, as snow swirled through the air.

The tomb is made of red Finnish porphyry, the base from green granite. Napoléon's remains were locked inside six coffins. Legends have abounded that some of his body parts went missing, notably his penis and his heart. According to Napoleonic scholars, the two doctors who dissected the emperor placed all his body parts in an urn positioned between his legs. Scholars deny the truth of these legends about the missing parts, although one wealthy gentleman in Connecticut frequently exhibits a penis preserved in alcohol, claiming it was once attached to the emperor. Surrounding the tomb are a dozen amazonlike figures representing his victories. Almost lampooning the smallness of the man, everything is done on a gargantuan scale. You'd think a real giant was buried here, not a symbolic one. In his coronation robes, the statue of Napoléon stands 8½ feet high. The grave of Napoléon's son, "the King of Rome," lies at his feet.

Napoléon's tomb is surrounded by those of his brother, Joseph Bonaparte; the great Vauban; Foch, the Allied commander in World War I; Turenne; and La Tour d'Auvergne, the first grenadier of the republic (actually, only his heart is entombed here).

✪ **The Louvre (Musée du Louvre).** 34-36 quai du Louvre, 1er. Main entrance in the glass pyramid, Cour du Louvre. ☎ **01-40-20-53-17** (01-40-20-51-51 recorded message, 01-49-87-54-54 advance credit-card sales). www.louvre.fr. Admission 45 F ($7.65) before 3pm, 26 F ($4.40) after 3pm and on Sun; free for age 17 and under; free first Sun of every month. Mon and Wed 9am–9:45pm (Mon, short tour only), Thurs–Sun 9am–6pm. (Parts of the museum begin to close at 5:30pm.) 1½-hour English-language tours leave Mon and Wed–Sat various times of the day for 17 F ($2.90), free for children 12 and under with museum ticket. Métro: Palais-Royal–Musée-du-Louvre.

From far and wide they come—from North Dakota to Pakistan, from Nova Scotia to Japan—all bent on seeing the legendary Louvre. People on one of those "Paris-in-a-day" tours try to break track records to get a glimpse of the two most famous ladies of the Louvre: the *Mona Lisa* and the armless *Venus de Milo*. (The scene in front of the *Mona Lisa* is best described as a circus. Viewers push and shove in front of the lady's bulletproof glass as the staff looks idly on, and flashbulbs, which are forbidden, go off like popcorn on a hot stove. In all this fracas, it's hard to contemplate—or share in— her inimitable smile.) The herd then dashes on a 5-minute stampede in pursuit of *Winged Victory*, that headless statue discovered at Samothrace and dating from about 200 B.C. In defiance of the assembly-line theory of art, we head instead for David's *Portrait of Madame Récamier*, depicting Napoléon's opponent at age 23. On her comfortable sofa, she reclines agelessly in the style of classical antiquity.

Then a big question looms: Which of the rest of the 30,000 works on display would you like to see?

The Louvre suffers from an embarrassment of riches. Here, the casual visitor often passes masterpieces blindly, simply because there are too many to behold. The Louvre is the world's largest palace and the world's largest museum (some say the greatest). As a palace, it leaves us cold, except for its old section, the **Cour Carrée.** As a museum, it's one of the greatest art collections in the world.

Between the Seine and the rue de Rivoli (Métro to Palais-Royal or Louvre, the latter the most elegant subway stop in the world), the Palace of the Louvre stretches for almost half a mile. In the days of Charles V, it was a fortress, but François I, a patron of Leonardo da Vinci, had it torn down and rebuilt as a royal residence. Less than a month after Marie Antoinette's head and body parted company, the Revolutionary Committee decided that the king's collection of paintings and sculpture should be opened to the public. At the lowest point in its history, in the 18th century, the Louvre was home for anybody who wanted to set up housekeeping there. Laundry hung out the windows, corners were literally pigpens, and familys built fires to cook their meals during the long winters. Napoléon ended that, chasing out the squatters and restoring the palace. In fact, he chose the Louvre for the site of his wedding to Marie-Louise.

So where did all these paintings come from? The kings of France, notably François I and Louis XIV, acquired many of them. Others have been willed to or purchased by the state. Many contributed by Napoléon were taken from reluctant donors: The church was one especially heavy and unwilling giver. Much of Napoléon's plunder had to be returned, although France hasn't seen its way clear to giving back all the booty.

To enter the Louvre, you'll pass through a controversial 71-foot-high **glass pyramid** in the courtyard. Commissioned by French president François Mitterrand and completed in 1989, it has received mixed reviews. Designed by I. M. Pei to allow sunlight to shine on an underground reception area, it shelters a complex of shops and restaurants. Automatic ticket machines help relieve the long lines of yesteryear.

The collections are divided into seven departments: Egyptian Antiquities; Oriental Antiquities; Greek, Etruscan, and Roman Antiquities; Sculpture; Painting; Decorative Arts; and Graphic Arts. A number of new galleries, devoted to Italian paintings, Roman glass and bronzes, Oriental antiquities, and Egyptian antiquities, were opened in 1997 and 1998. If you don't have to do Paris in a day, perhaps you can come here several times, concentrating on different collections or schools of painting. Those with little time should go on one of the **guided tours** (in English), which lasts about 1½ hours.

Da Vinci's much-traveled *La Gioconda* **(Mona Lisa),** has been the source of legend and lore for centuries. It was acquired by François I to hang above his bath. Note the guard and bulletproof glass: The world's most famous painting was stolen in the summer of 1911 and found in Florence in the winter of 1913. At first, both the poet Guillaume Apollinaire and Picasso were suspected as the thieves, but it was discovered in the possession of a former Louvre employee, who had apparently carried it out of the museum under his overcoat. Less well known (but to us even more enchanting) are Da Vinci's *Virgin and Child with St. Anne* and the *Virgin of the Rocks.*

After paying your respects to the enigmatically "Smiling One," allow time to see some French works stretching from the Richelieu wing through the entire **Sully wing** and even overflowing into part of the **Denon wing.** It's all here: Antoine Watteau's *Gilles* with the mysterious boy in a clown suit staring back at you; Jean-Honoré Fragonard's and François Boucher's rococo renderings of the aristocracy; and the greatest masterpieces of Jacques-Louis David, including his stellar 1785 work, *The Oath of the Horatii,* and the vast and vivid *Coronation of Napoléon.* Only the Uffizi in

The Louvre

The Pyramid

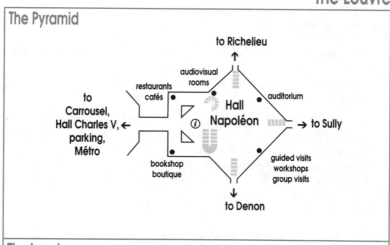

to Richelieu

audiovisual
rooms

restaurants
cafés

to
Carrousel,
Hall Charles V, ←
parking,
Métro

Hall
Napoléon

auditorium

→ to Sully

bookshop
boutique

guided visits
workshops
group visits

to Denon

The Levels

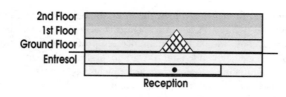

2nd Floor
1st Floor
Ground Floor
Entresol

Reception

The Wings

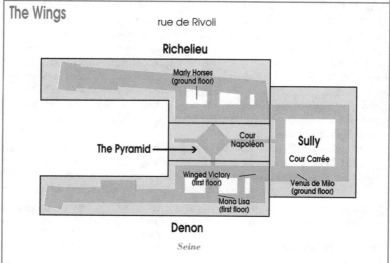

rue de Rivoli

Richelieu

Marly Horses
(ground floor)

The Pyramid →

Cour
Napoléon

Sully

Cour Carrée

Winged Victory
(first floor)

Venus de Milo
(ground floor)

Mona Lisa
(first floor)

Denon

Seine

E-0171

Some Louvre Tips

Long waiting lines outside the Louvre's pyramid entrance are notorious, but there are some tricks for avoiding them.

• Enter via the underground shopping mall, the Carrousel du Louvre, at 99 rue de Rivoli.

• Enter directly from the Palais-Royal–Musée du Louvre Métro station.

• Buy *Le Pass-Musée* (Museum and Monuments Pass) allowing direct entry through the priority entrance at the Passage Richelieu, 93 rue de Rivoli.

• Order tickets by phone at ☎ 01-49-87-54-54, have them charged to your Visa or MasterCard, then pick them up at any FNAC store. This also gives you direct entry through the Passage Richelieu.

Florence rivals the Denon wing for its Italian Renaissance collection—everything from Raphael's *Portrait of Balthazar Castiglione* to Titian's *Man with a Glove.* Paolo Veronese's gigantic *Wedding Feast at Cana* occupies an entire wall. This painting is a delight, a romp of high Viennese society of the 1500s. (That's Paolo himself playing the cello.)

Of the Greek and Roman antiquities, the most notable collections, aside from the *Venus de Milo* and *Winged Victory,* are fragments of a frieze from the Parthenon (located in the Denon wing). In Renaissance sculpture, you'll see two slaves by Michelangelo, originally intended for the tomb of Julius II but sold into other bondage. The Denon wing houses masterpieces including Ingres's *The Turkish Bath;* the Botticelli frescoes from the Villa Lemmi; Raphael's *La Belle Jardinière;* and Titian's *Open Air Concert.* The Sully wing is also filled with old masters, including Boucher's *Diana Resting after Her Bath* and Fragonard's *Bathers.*

The **Richelieu wing,** inaugurated in 1993, houses the museum's collection of northern European and French paintings, along with decorative arts, French sculpture, Oriental antiquities (a rich collection of Islamic art), and the salons of Napoléon III. First built from 1852 to 1857, the Richelieu wing was expanded to add some 230,000 square feet of exhibition space, and now shelters 12,000 works of art in 165 rooms and three covered courtyards. One of its galleries displays 21 works that Rubens painted in a space of only 2 years for Marie de Médicis's Luxembourg Palace. This wing stacks masterpiece upon masterpiece: Dürer's *Self-Portrait,* Anthony Van Dyck's *Portrait of Charles I of England,* and Holbein the Younger's *Portrait of Erasmus of Rotterdam,* with a wealth of surrounding art that includes Sumerian and Babylonian treasures, Assyrian winged bulls, and Persian friezes.

When you get tired, consider a pick-me-up at **Café Marly** in the Richelieu wing (see chapter 5). In three grandiose rooms with high ceilings and lavish adornments, the cafe overlooks the museum's glass pyramid and offers a selection of coffees, pastries (by Paris's most legendary pastry-maker, Lenôtre), salads, sandwiches, and simple platters.

✪ **Musée d'Orsay.** 1 rue de Bellechasse or 62 rue de Lille, 7e. ☎ **01-40-49-48-14.** www.paris.org/Musees/Orsay. Admission 40 F ($6.80) adults, 30 F ($5.10) ages 18–24 and seniors, free for children 17 and under. Tues–Wed and Fri–Sat 10am–6pm, Thurs 10am–9:45pm, Sun 9am–6pm. June 20–Sept 20, museum opens 9am. Métro: Solférino. RER: Musée d'Orsay.

In the middle of Paris, architects transformed a defunct rail station, the handsome neo-classical Gare d'Orsay, into one of the greatest museums in the world. Don't skip the Louvre, but come here even if you have to miss all the other art museums of Paris. It contains one of the world's most important collections devoted to the watershed years between 1848 and 1914. Standing across the Seine from the Louvre and the Tuileries, it has a treasure trove of van Gogh, Manet, Monet, Degas, and Renoir, but of all the less-known groups as well: the Symbolists, Pointillists, Nabis, Realists, and late Romantics.

The thousands of pieces of sculpture and painting housed here are spread across 80 different galleries, which also include belle-epoque furniture, photographs, objets d'art, and architectural models. There's even a cinema that shows classic films.

A monument to the Industrial Revolution, the Orsay station, once called "the elephant," is covered by an arching glass roof, which floods the museum with light. The museum displays works ranging from the creations of academic and historic painters such as Ingres to Romanticists such as Delacroix, to neo-Realists such as Courbet and Daumier. The Impressionists and Post-Impressionists, including Cézanne, van Gogh, and the Fauves, share space with Matisse, the Cubists, and the Expressionists in a setting once used by Orson Welles to film a nightmarish scene in *The Trial,* based on Kafka's unfinished novel. You'll find Millet's sunny wheat fields, Barbizon landscapes, the mists of Corot, and parti-colored Tahitian Gauguins all in the same hall.

But it's the Impressionists who keep the crowds lining up. When the Louvre tripped over its traditional toes and chose not to display their works, it gave birth to a great rival. Led by Manet, Renoir, and the blessedly myopic Monet, the Impressionists shunned ecclesiastical and mythological set-pieces for a light-bathed Seine, faint figures strolling in the Tuileries, pale-faced women in hazy bars, even vulgar rail stations such as the Gare St-Lazare. And the Impressionists were the first to paint that most characteristic feature of Parisian life: the sidewalk cafe, especially in the artists' quarter of Montmartre.

The most famous painting from this era is Manet's 1863 *Déjeuner sur l'herbe (Picnic on the Grass),* whose forest setting with a nude woman and two fully clothed men sent shock waves through respectable society when it was first exhibited. Two years later, Manet's *Olympia,* also here, created another scandal. It depicts a woman lounging on her bed and wearing nothing but a flower in her hair and high-heeled shoes; she is attended by an African maid in the background. Zola called Manet "a man among eunuchs."

One of Renoir's brightest, most joyous paintings is also here: the *Moulin de la Galette,* painted in 1876. Degas is represented by his paintings of racehorses and dancers; his 1876 cafe scene, *Absinthe,* also here, remains one of his most reproduced works. Paris-born Claude Monet was fascinated by the effect that changing light had on Rouen Cathedral, and in a series of five paintings displayed here, its stone bubbles to life.

One of the most celebrated works at the Orsay is by an American, Whistler's *Arrangement in Gray and Black: Portrait of the Painter's Mother,* better known as *Whistler's Mother.* It is said that this painting heralded the advent of modern art, although many critics denounced it at the time as "Whistler's Dead Mother" because of its funereal overtones. Today the painting has been hailed as a "veritable icon of our consciousness." Whistler was content to claim he made "Mummy just as nice as possible."

3 The Major Museums

Turn to "The Top Attractions," above, for a comprehensive look at the Louvre and the Musée d'Orsay.

Galerie Nationale du Jeu de Paume. Jardin des Tuileries/1 place de la Concorde, 1er. ☎ **01-42-60-69-69.** Admission 38 F ($6.45) adults, 28 F ($4.75) students, free for children 13 and under. Tues noon–9:30pm, Wed–Fri noon–7pm, Sat–Sun 10am–7pm. Métro: Concorde.

Bonjour to the New Pompidou

What has been called "the most avant-garde building in the world, the **Centre Pompidou,** place Georges-Pompidou or plateau Beaubourg (☎ **01-44-78-12-33**), closed in late 1997 for extensive renovations, but parts of it remain open. The entire complex is scheduled to be fully operational again sometime in spring 2000.

The dream of former president Georges Pompidou, this center for 20th-century art, designed by Richard Rogers and Renzo Piano, opened in 1977 and immediately became the focus of loud controversy. Its bold exoskeletal architecture and the brightly painted pipes and ducts crisscrossing its transparent facade (green for water, red for heat, blue for air, and yellow for electricity) were jarring in the old Beaubourg neighborhood. Perhaps the detractors were right all along—within 20 years the building began to deteriorate so badly that a major restoration was called for.

At this writing, the areas of the complex that remain open include the South Gallery (*la galerie sud,* site of such temporary exhibitions as a retrospective of the works of British painter David Hockney) and a re-creation of the jazz-age studio of Romanian sculptor Brancusi *(l'Atelier Brancusi),* which is configured as a minimuseum separate from the rest of the center. Both areas are open Monday and Wednesday through Friday from noon to 10pm, Saturday and Sunday from 10am to 10pm. A combined ticket to both costs 30 F ($5.10) for adults, 20 F ($3.40) for persons under 18.

To provide insight into the ambitious renovation of the complex, its administrators have erected a steel-and-polyester "information teepee" adjacent to the center. It's open Sunday, Monday, and Wednesday through Friday from 12:30 to 6pm, and Saturday from 2 to 6pm.

What can you expect to see when the Pompidou is going full blast again? It encompasses four separate attractions:

The **Musée National d'Art Moderne** (National Museum of Modern Art) offers a large collection of 20th-century art. With some 40,000 works, this is the big attraction, although only some 850 works can be displayed at one time. If you want to view some real charmers, see Alexander Calder's 1926 *Josephine Baker,* one of his earliest versions of the mobile, an art form he invented. Marcel Duchamp's *Valise* is a collection of miniature reproductions of his fabled Dada sculptures and drawings, displayed in a carrying case. Every time we visit Paris, we have to see Salvador Dalí's *Portrait of Lenin Dancing on Piano Keys*—it makes our day.

The **Public Information Library** offers free access to a million French and foreign books, periodicals, films, records, slides, and microfilms. The **Center for Industrial Design** emphasizes the contributions made in the fields of architecture, visual communications, publishing, and community planning. And the **Institute for Research and Coordination of Acoustics/Music** brings together musicians and composers interested in furthering the cause of music, both contemporary and traditional.

For years, the National Gallery in the Jeu de Paume, in the northeast corner of the Tuileries gardens, was one of the treasures of Paris, displaying some of the finest works of the Impressionists. To the regret of many, that collection was hauled off to the Musée d'Orsay in 1986. After a $12.6 million face-lift, the Second Empire building was transformed into a state-of-the-art gallery with a video screening room. No permanent

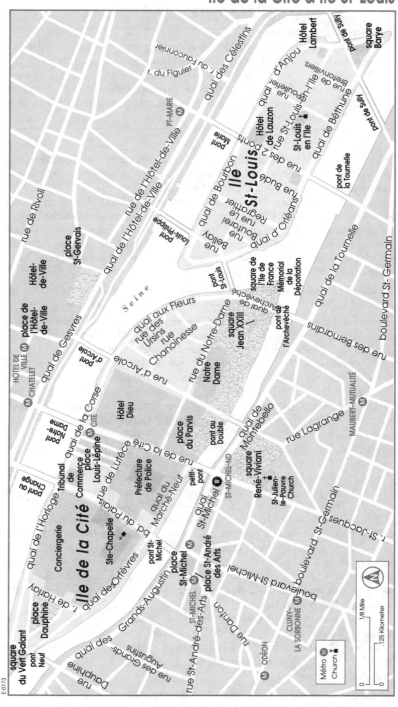

A Day at Giverny

If you've become entranced by Monet's spiritualism of light, consider making a day trip to his home and gardens at Giverny, where many of his paintings are displayed. We've given a full account of the trip in chapter 10.

Unfortunately, the charming **Musée de l'Orangerie** in the Jardin des Tuileries, home of Claude Monet's exquisite *Water Lillies,* closed in August 1999 for an estimated 2-year restoration.

collection is housed here, but every 2 or 3 months a new show is mounted. Sometimes the works of little-known contemporary artists are on display; at other times, an exhibit will feature unexplored aspects of established artists.

Originally, in this part of the gardens, Napoléon III built a ball court on which *jeu de paume,* an antecedent of tennis, was played—hence, the museum's name. The most infamous period in the National Gallery's history came during the Nazi occupation, when it served as an "evaluation center" for works of modern art. Paintings from all over France were shipped to the Jeu de Paume, and art condemned by the Nazis as "degenerate" was burned.

✪ **Musée Jacquemart-André**. 158 bd. Hausmann, 8e. ☎ **01-42-89-04-91.** Admission 48 F ($8.15). Daily 10am–6pm. Métro: Miromesnil or St-Philippe-du-Roule.

It's the finest museum of its type in Paris, an inspired 19th-century blend of taste and money, the treasure trove of a married couple devoted to 18th-century French paintings and furnishings, 17th-century Dutch and Flemish paintings, and works from the Italian Renaissance. The collection originally belonged to the André family, prominent French Protestants who made a fortune in banking and industry in the 19th century. The family's last scion, Edouard André, spent most of his life as an officer in the French army stationed abroad, returning later in his life to marry a well-known portraitist of French governmental figures and members of the aristocracy, Nélie Jacquemart. Together, they compiled a collection of rare French 18th-century decorative art and European paintings within an 1850s town house that was continually upgraded and redecorated according to the fashions of the times.

In 1912, Mme Jacquemart willed the house and its collection to the Institut de France, which paid for an extensive renovation and enlargement that was completed in 1996. The pride of the collection are works by Bellini, Carpaccio, and Uccelo, which are complemented by Houdon busts, Gobelins tapestries, Savonnerie carpets, della Robbia terra-cottas, an awesome collection of antiques, and works by Rembrandt *(The Pilgrim of Emmaus),* Van Dyck, Tiepolo, Rubens, Watteau, Fragonard, Boucher, and Mantegna. After a major restoration, one of the most outstanding exhibits consists of three 18th-century frescoes by Giambattista Tiepolo, depicting spectators on balconies viewing Henri III's arrival in Venice in 1574. Salons drip with gilt and the ultimate in fin-de-siècle style.

Take a break from the gilded age with a cup of tea in Mme Jacquemart's high-ceilinged dining room, adorned with 18th-century tapestries. Salads, tarts, tourtes (a round pastry filled with meat or fruit), and an assortment of Viennese pastries are served during the museum's opening hours and make a perfect light lunch or pick-me-up.

✪ **Musée Marmottan-Claude Monet**. 2 rue Louis-Boilly, 16e. ☎ **01-42-24-07-02.** Admission 40 F ($6.80) adults, 25 F ($4.25) ages 8–24, free for children 7 and under. Tues–Sun 10am–5:30pm. Métro: La Muette.

This collection has been hailed as "one of the great art treasures of the world," and that it is. In the past, a lone art historian would occasionally venture here to the edge of the Bois de Boulogne to see what Paul Marmottan had donated to the Académie des Beaux-Arts. Hardly anybody else did until 1966, when Michel Monet, son of Claude, died in a car crash, leaving what was then a $10 million bequest of his father's art to the little museum. The Académie des Beaux-Arts suddenly found itself with more than 130 paintings, watercolors, pastels, drawings, and a passel of Monet lovers, who can now trace the evolution of the great man's work in a single museum.

The collection includes more than 30 paintings of Monet's house at Giverny and many of water lilies, his everlasting fancy. The bequest also included *Willow* (1918), *House of Parliament* (1905), and a portrait by Renoir of the 32-year-old Monet. Ironically, the museum had always owned Monet's *Impression,* from which the movement got its name.

Paul Marmottan's original collection includes fig-leafed nudes, First Empire antiques, assorted objets d'art, bucolic paintings, and crystal chandeliers. Many tapestries date from the Renaissance, and you can also see an extensive collection of miniatures donated by Daniel Waldenstein.

Musée National du Moyen Age/Thermes de Cluny (Musée de Cluny). 6 place Paul-Painlevé, 5e. ☎ **01-53-73-78-00.** Admission 30 F ($5.10) adults, 20 F ($3.40) ages 18–25, free for age 17 and under. Wed–Mon 9:15am–5:45pm. Métro: Cluny-Sorbonne.

Along with the Hôtel de Sens in Le Marais, the Hôtel de Cluny is all that remains of domestic medieval architecture in Paris. You enter through the cobblestoned Court of Honor, where you can admire the flamboyant Gothic building with its clinging vines, turreted walls, gargoyles, and dormers with seashell motifs. Originally the Cluny was the mansion of a rich 15th-century abbot, built on top of and next to the ruins of a Roman bath. By 1515, it was the residence of Mary Tudor, teenage widow of Louis XII and daughter of Henry VII of England and Elizabeth of York.

Seized during the revolution, the Cluny was rented in 1833 to Alexandre du Sommerard, who adorned it with his collection of medieval works of art. Upon his death in 1842, both the building and the collection were bought back by the government.

The present-day collection of medieval arts and crafts is the finest in the world. Most people come primarily to see the *Unicorn Tapestries,* the most acclaimed tapestries of their kind. A beautiful princess and her handmaiden, beasts of prey, and just plain pets—all the romance of the age of chivalry lives on in these remarkable yet mysterious tapestries discovered only a century ago in Limousin's Château de Boussac. Five seem to deal with the five senses (one, for example, depicts a unicorn looking into a mirror held up by a dour-faced maiden). The sixth shows a woman under an elaborate tent with jewels, her pet dog resting on an embroidered cushion beside her, with the lovable unicorn and his friendly companion, a lion, holding back the flaps. The background in red and green forms a rich carpet of spring flowers, fruit-laden trees, birds, rabbits, donkeys, dogs, goats, lambs, and monkeys.

The other exhibits range widely, including several Flemish retables; a 14th-century Sienese (life-size) John the Baptist and other Italian sculptures; statues from Sainte-Chapelle, dating from 1243 to 1248; 12th- and 13th-century crosses, studded with gems; golden chalices, manuscripts, ivory carvings, vestments, leatherwork, jewelry, coins; a 13th-century Adam; and recently discovered heads and fragments of statues from Notre-Dame de Paris. In the fan-vaulted medieval chapel hang tapestries depicting scenes from the life of St. Stephen.

Downstairs are the ruins of the **Roman baths,** dating from around A.D. 200. Of these once-flourishing baths, the best-preserved section is seen in room X, the

---

A Timesaving Tip

Museums require that you check shopping bags and book bags, and sometimes lines for these can be longer than the ticket lines. Visitors who value their time should leave their bags behind: Some coat lines in Paris can take 30 minutes. Ask if a museum has more than one coat line, and, if so, go to the less frequented ones.

---

frigidarium. Once it measured 70 by 36 feet, rising to a height of 50 feet, with stone walls nearly 7 feet thick. The ribbed vaulting here rests on consoles that evoked ships' prows. Credit for this unusual motif goes to the builders of the baths, the boatmen of Paris. During the reign of Tiberius, a column to Jupiter was found beneath the chancel of Notre-Dame and is now on view in the court. Called "The Column of the Boatmen," it is now believed to be the oldest sculpture created in Paris.

Musée National Eugène Delacroix. 6 place de Furstenberg, 6e. ☎ **01-44-41-86-50.** Admission 22F ($4) adults, 15F ($2.70) ages 18–25 and over 60, free for age 17 and under. Wed–Mon 9:30am–5pm. Closed holidays. Métro: St-Germain-des-Prés.

This museum is only for serious Delacroix groupies, among whom we include ourselves. If you admire this artist and want to see where he lived, worked, and died, then this is worth at least an hour of your time. Delacroix (1798 to 1863) is something of an enigma to art historians. Even his parentage is a mystery. Many believe that Talleyrand had the privilege of fathering him. One biographer saw him "as an isolated and atypical individualist—one who respected traditional values, yet emerged as the embodiment of Romantic revolt." The poet Baudelaire called him "a volcanic crater artistically concealed beneath bouquets of flowers."

The museum is in one of the most charming squares on the Left Bank, with a highly romantic garden. A large arch on a stone courtyard leads to his studio, no poor artist's studio, but the tasteful creation of a solidly established man. Sketches, lithographs, watercolors, and oils are hung throughout, and a few mementos remain, including a lovely mahogany paint box.

♻ **Musée Picasso.** Hôtel Salé, 5 rue de Thorigny, 3e. ☎ **01-42-71-25-21.** www.paris.org/Musees/Picasso. Admission 30–38 F ($5.10–$6.45) adults, 20–28 F ($3.40–$4.75) ages 19–25 and over 60, free for age 18 and under. Apr–Sept Wed–Mon 9:30am–6pm; Oct–Mar Wed–Mon 9:30am–5pm. Métro: St-Paul, Filles-du-Calvaire, or Chemin-Vert.

When it opened at the beautifully restored **Hôtel Salé** (Salty Mansion), a state-owned property in Le Marais, the press hailed it as a "museum for Picasso's Picassos." And that's what it is. Almost overnight the museum became, and continues to be, one of the most popular attractions in Paris.

The state acquired the greatest Picasso collection in the world in lieu of a $50 million levy in inheritance taxes. The tax man claimed 203 paintings, 158 sculptures, 16 collages, 19 bas-reliefs, 88 ceramics, and more than 1,500 sketches and 1,600 engravings, along with 30 notebooks. These works span some 75 years of the artist's life and ever-changing style.

The range of paintings includes a remarkable self-portrait from 1901 and the masterpieces *Le Baiser (The Kiss), Reclining Nude,* and *Man with a Guitar,* all painted at Mougins on the Riviera in 1969 and 1970. It's easy to stroll through the handsome museum seeking your own favorite work—perhaps a wicked one: *Jeune Garçon à la Langouste (Young Man with a Lobster),* painted in Paris in 1941. The Paris museum owns several intriguing studies for *Les Demoiselles d'Avignon,* the painting that shocked the establishment and launched Cubism in 1907.

The Louvre, Tuileries & Les Halles (1e)

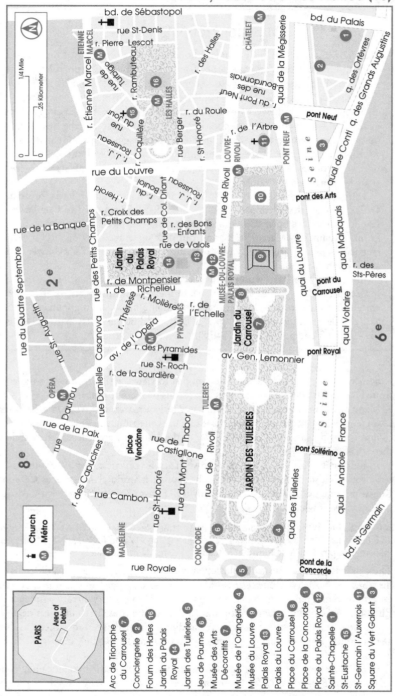

Arc de Triomphe du Carrousel 7
Conciergerie 2
Forum des Halles 16
Jardin du Palais Royal 14
Jardin des Tuileries 5
Jeu de Paume 6
Musée des Arts Décoratifs 7
Musée de l'Orangerie 4
Musée du Louvre 9
Palais Royal 13
Palais du Louvre 10
Place du Carrousel 8
Place de la Concorde 1
Place du Palais Royal 12
Sainte-Chapelle 1
St-Eustache 15
St-Germain l'Auxerrois 11
Square du Vert Galant 3

Museum Hopping in Paris

Museums in Paris have fairly standard hours. They are often closed on Tuesday and national holidays. Fees vary, but half-price tickets are usually provided to students, children ages 3 to 7, and extra-large families or groups. Sunday is the best day for serious museum-hopping, as most museums let you in for half price.

Whatever time of the year you come, Paris seems to be hosting an outstanding **exhibition**—keep your eyes open for huge, colorful posters hanging from lampposts. At least 15 special shows will be on during any given week, events such as a Chagall retrospective, a special exhibition of Giacometti sculptures, or a show on the Art of the Workers' Movement or the public life of Napoléon. The fees charged depend on the exhibit.

To find out what's showing while you're in town, stop at the **Paris Tourism Office,** 127 av. des Champs-Elysées (☎ **01-49-52-53-54;** Métro: Charles-de-Gaulle–Etoile). It's open daily from 9am to 8pm except May 1 (11am to 6pm from November to March). Here you can pick up a free copy of the English-language booklet "Paris Weekly Information," published by the Paris Convention and Visitors' Bureau.

You can buy **Le Pass-Musée (Museum and Monuments Pass)** at any of the museums that honor it, or at any branch of the Paris Tourist office. It offers free entrance to the permanent collections of 65 monuments and museums in Paris and the Ile-de-France. A 1-day pass is 80 F ($13.60); a 3-day pass is 160 F ($27.20); a 5-day pass is 240 F ($40.80).

Some visitors go to the Picasso Museum just to view the ribald paintings the artist turned out in his later years—perhaps just for his own erotic amusement.

Many of the major masterpieces, such as *The Crucifixion and Nude in a Red Armchair,* remain on permanent view. But because the collection is so vast, temporary exhibitions featuring such items as his studies of the Minotaur are held for the public at the rate of two each year.

In addition to Picasso's own treasure trove of art, his private collection of other masters' works is also displayed, including those of such world-class artists as Cézanne, Rousseau, Braque, André Derain, and Miró. Picasso was fascinated with African masks, many of which are on view.

Musée Rodin. In the Hôtel Biron, 77 rue de Varenne, 7e. ☎ **01-44-18-61-10.** Admission 28 F ($4.75) adults, 18 F ($3.05) ages 18–25, free for age 17 and under. Apr–Sept Tues–Sun 9:30am–5:45pm; Oct–Mar Tues–Sun 9:30am–4:45pm. Métro: Varenne.

These days Rodin is acclaimed as the father of modern sculpture, but in a different era his work was labeled obscene. The world's artistic taste changed, and in due course the government of France purchased the gray-stone 18th-century luxury residence in Faubourg St-Germain. The mansion was Rodin's studio from 1910 until his death in 1917. After the government bought the studio, it restored the rose gardens to their 18th-century splendor, making them a perfect setting for Rodin's most memorable works.

In the courtyard are three world-famous creations. Rodin's first major public commission, *The Burghers of Calais* commemorated the heroism of six citizens of the city of Calais who, in 1347, offered themselves as a ransom to Edward III in return for ending his siege of their port. Perhaps the single best-known work, *The Thinker,* in Rodin's own words, "thinks with every muscle of his arms, back, and legs, with his clenched fist and gripping toes." Not yet completed when Rodin died, *The Gate of Hell,* as he put it, is "where I lived for a whole year in Dante's *Inferno.*"

Inside the building, the sculpture, plaster casts, reproductions, originals, and sketches reveal the freshness and vitality of a remarkable artist. You can practically see many of his works emerging from marble into life. Everybody is attracted to *The Kiss,* of which one critic wrote, "the passion is timeless." Upstairs are two different versions of the celebrated and condemned nude of Balzac, his bulky torso rising from a tree trunk (Albert E. Elsen commented on the "glorious bulging" stomach). Included are many versions of his *Monument to Balzac* (a large one stands in the garden), which was Rodin's last major work and which caused a furor when it was first exhibited.

Other significant sculptures include Rodin's soaring *Prodigal Son, The Crouching Woman* (called the "embodiment of despair"), *and The Age of Bronze,* an 1876 study of a nude man, modeled by a Belgian soldier. (Rodin was falsely accused of making a cast from a living model.)

Generally overlooked is a room devoted to Camille Claudel, Rodin's mistress and a towering artist in her own right. She was his pupil, model, and lover, and created such works as *Maturity, Clotho,* and the recently donated *The Waltz* and *The Gossips.*

The little alley behind the mansion housing the Musée Rodin winds its way down to a pond with fountains and flower beds, even sandpits for children. It's one of the most idyllic hidden spots of Paris.

Petit Palais. Petit Palais, av. Winston-Churchill, 8e. ☎ **01-42-65-12-73.** Admission 27 F ($4.60) adults, 14.50 F ($2.45) under age 25, free on Sun. Special exhibitions 35–45 F ($5.95–$7.65) adults, as above for discounted rates. Tues–Sun 10am–5:40pm. Métro: Champs-Elysées.

Built by architect Charles Girault, this small palace faces the Grand Palais (housing special exhibitions); both were erected for the 1900 exhibition.

The Petit Palais contains a hodgepodge of art belonging to the city of Paris, and mainly interests the serious art lover who has more than a few days to spend in Paris. Most visitors come here for the temporary exhibitions, not the permanent collections. Of the latter, the most prominent are the **Dutuit** and **Tuck collections.** In the Dutuit collection are Egyptian, Greek, and Roman bronzes, rare ivory statues (the most prominent of which is of a Roman actor), and a series of ancient Greek porcelains. The collection also boasts enamels, sculpture, and hand-lettered and -painted manuscripts from the Middle Ages. A good collection of 17th-century Dutch and Flemish paintings are also on view, with representative artists including Breughel the Younger (*Wedding Pageant*), Rubens, Hobbema, Ruysdael, and others.

Edward Tuck donated the museum's other major collection in 1930. It's composed mainly of decorative artwork of the 18th century, including tapestries, heavily gilded furniture, wood-paneled salons, and porcelains, which give a good overview of French aesthetic sense at the time of the fall of the Ancien Régime.

A number of rooms are dedicated to 19th-century French painting, including a few works by major Impressionists. The collection contains canvases by Courbet, Daumier, Corot, Delacroix, Manet, Sisley, Mary Cassatt (*Le Bain*), Maurice Denis, Odilon Redon, a series of portraits (one by Clairin of Sarah Bernhardt), and art by Edouard Vuillard and Pierre Bonnard. The museum has a strong emphasis on the "academic school," especially the enormous compositions of Gustave Doré. Other important artists come from the symbolist school, including Osbert, whose *Soir Antique* is a cherished item. Notable paintings displayed include *The Death of Seneca* by David, the *Portrait of Lalande* by Fragonard, and the *Young Shepherd Holding a Flower* by Greuze. The museum also has sculptures by Rodin, Bourdelle, Maillol, and Carpeaux, and glassworks by Galle and Lalique.

4 Churches

Turn to "The Top Attractions," above, for a full look at Notre-Dame.

American Cathedral of the Holy Trinity. 23 avenue George V, 8e. ☎ **01-53-23-84-00.** Free admission. Daily 9am–5pm. Sun Holy Eucharist 9am and 11am. Métro: Alma-Marceau and George V.

The American Cathedral of Paris is one of the finest examples of Gothic Revival architecture in Europe, and a growing center for music and arts in Paris.

The cathedral building, consecrated in 1886, was designed by George Edmund Street, best known as the architect of the London Law Courts. An extraordinary series of pre-Raphaelite stained-glass windows illustrating the *Te Deum,* and other exceptional artworks, including an early- 15th-century triptych by the Roussillon Master, make the cathedral a worthy attraction. Americans particularly enjoy the 50 state flags flying in the nave and the remarkable needlepoint collection, including kneelers depicting the state flowers. A Memorial Cloister commemorates Americans who died in Europe during World War I and all the victims of World War II. Recently completed documentation, in several languages, clearly explains these and other highlights.

The cathedral is also a center of worship and community outreach. There is a regular schedule of Sunday and weekday services in English. There are study groups and service groups, including one that offers a weekly meal to the unemployed. A cultural organization, *Les Arts George V,* presents very reasonably priced choral concerts, lectures, and art shows.

✪ **Basilique du Sacré-Coeur.** Place St-Pierre, 18e. ☎ **01-53-41-89-00.** Free admission to basilica; joint ticket to dome and crypt 30 F ($5.10) adults, 16 F ($2.70) students and children. Apr–Sept daily 9am–7pm; Oct–Mar daily 9am–6pm. Métro: Abbesses; then take the elevator to the surface and follow the signs to the funiculaire, which goes up to the church for the price of 1 Métro ticket.

After the Eiffel Tower, Sacré-Coeur is the most characteristic landmark of the Parisian scene. Like the tower, it has always been the subject of much controversy. One Parisian called it "a lunatic's confectionery dream." An offended Zola declared it "the basilica of the ridiculous." Sacré-Coeur has had warm supporters as well, including the poet Max Jacob and the artist Maurice Utrillo. Utrillo never tired of drawing and painting it, and he and Jacob came here regularly to pray.

Its gleaming white domes and *campanile* (bell tower) tower over Paris like a 12th-century Byzantine church. But it's not that old. After France's defeat by the Prussians in 1870, the basilica was planned as a votive offering to cure France's misfortunes. Rich and poor alike contributed money to build it. Construction was begun on the church in 1876 and it was not consecrated until 1919, but perpetual prayers of adoration have been made here day and night since 1885. The interior of the basilica is brilliantly decorated with mosaics. The stained-glass windows were shattered during the struggle for Paris in 1944, but have been well replaced. Look for the striking mosaic of Christ on the ceiling, and also the mural of his Passion at the back of the altar. The crypt contains a relic of what some of the devout believe is Christ's sacred heart—hence, the name of the church.

Travel Tip

For a trip winding past three of the Left Bank's most historic churches, see our walking tour of the Latin Quarter in chapter 7.

The Opéra, Bourse & Grands Boulevards (2e, 9e & 10e)

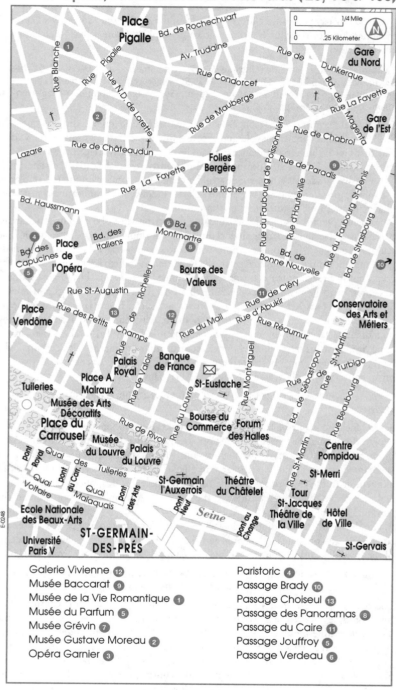

Galerie Vivienne ⑫
Musée Baccarat ⑨
Musée de la Vie Romantique ①
Musée du Parfum ⑤
Musée Grévin ⑦
Musée Gustave Moreau ②
Opéra Garnier ③

Paristoric ④
Passage Brady ⑩
Passage Choiseul ⑬
Passage des Panoramas ⑧
Passage du Caire ⑪
Passage Jouffroy ⑤
Passage Verdeau ⑥

On a clear day you can see for 35 miles from the dome. You can also walk around the inner dome of the church, peering down like a pigeon (one is likely to be keeping you company).

Basilique St-Denis. Place de l'Hotel-de-Ville, 2 rue de Strasbourg, St-Denis. ☎ **01-48-09-83-54.** Admission 32 F ($5.45) adults, 21 F ($3.55) seniors and students, free for children 11 and under. Apr–Sept Mon–Sat 10am–7:30pm, Sun noon–6:30pm; Oct–Mar Mon–Sat 10am–5pm, Sun noon–5pm. Métro: St-Denis Basilique.

In the 12th century, Abbot Suger placed an inscription on the bronze doors of St-Denis: "Marvel not at the gold and expense, but at the craftsmanship of the work." The first Gothic building in France that can be dated precisely, St-Denis was the "spiritual defender of the State" during the 12th-century reign of Louis VI ("The Fat"). The massive facade has a rose window and a crenellated parapet on the top similar to the fortifications of a castle. The stained-glass windows, in stunning mauve, purple, blue, and rose, were restored in the 19th century.

St-Denis, the first bishop of Paris, became the patron saint of the French monarchy. Royal burials began here in the sixth century and continued until the Revolution. The sculpture designed for tombs—some two stories high—span the country's artistic development from the Middle Ages to the Renaissance. (There are guided tours to the crypt, but in French only.) François I was entombed at St-Denis. His funeral statue is nude, although he demurely covers himself with his hand. Other kings and queens here include Louis XII and Anne of Brittany, as well as Henri II and Catherine de Médicis. Revolutionaries stormed through the basilica during the Terror, smashing many marble faces and dumping royal remains in a lime-filled ditch in the garden. (The royal remains were reburied under the main altar during the 19th century.) The basilica stands today in a busy northern suburb, but it is easily reached by Métro. Free organ concerts take place here on Sunday at 11:15am.

La Madeleine. Place de la Madeleine, 8e. ☎ **01-44-51-69-00.** Daily 7:30am–7pm. Métro: Madeleine.

The Madeleine is one of Paris's minor landmarks. Resembling a Roman temple, the church dominates the rue Royale, a short street designed by Gabriel that culminates in the place de la Concorde. Although its construction started in 1806, the Madeleine was consecrated as a church much later, in 1842. The building was originally intended as a temple to the glory of the Grande Armée (Napoléon's idea, of course). Later, several alternative uses were considered: the National Assembly, the Bourse, and the National Library.

Climb the 28 steps leading to the facade and look back: You will be able to see the rue Royale, the place de la Concorde and the obelisk, and, across the Seine, the dome of the Invalides. Inside, don't miss Rude's *Le Baptême du Christ,* to the left as you enter.

Mosquée de Paris. Place du Puits-de-l'Ermite, 5e. ☎ **01-45-35-97-33.** 15 F ($2.55) adults, 10 F ($1.70) students and children. Sat–Thurs 9am–noon and 2–6pm. Métro: Monge.

Located near the Jardin des Plantes, this Muslim place of worship is considered by many of its devotees to be one of the most beautiful structures of its kind in the world. The pink marble mosque was constructed in 1922 to honor the countries of North Africa who had given aid to France during World War I. Today, North Africans living in Paris gather on Friday, the Muslim holy day, or during Ramadan to pray to Allah. Short tours are given of the building, its central courtyard, and Moorish garden; guides present a brief history of the Islamic faith. However, you may just want to wander on your own, then join the students from nearby universities for couscous and sweet mint tea at **Le Restaurant de la Mosquée de Paris** (☎ **01-43-31-18-14**), the popular

Gregorians Unplugged

St-Germain-des-Prés stages the most wonderful concerts on the Left Bank; it has fantastic acoustics and a marvelous medieval atmosphere. The church was built to accommodate an age without microphones, and the sound effects will thrill you. For more information, call ☎ **01-43-25-41-71.** Arrive about 45 minutes before the performance if you'd like a front-row seat. Ticket prices range from 120 F to 250 F ($20.40 to $42.50).

Muslim restaurant that adjoins the grounds. Main courses range from 65 F to 110 F ($11.05 to $18.70); hours are daily from noon to 3pm and 7 to 10:30pm.

St-Germain-des-Prés. 3 place St-Germain-des-Prés, 6e. ☎ **01-43-25-41-71.** Daily 8am–8pm. Métro: St-Germain-des-Prés.

Outside it's an early- 17th-century town house, and handsome at that. But inside it's one of the oldest churches in Paris, dating from the 6th century when a Benedictine abbey was founded on the site by Childebert, son of Clovis, the "creator of France." Unfortunately, the marble columns in the triforium are all that remain from that period. At one time, the abbey was a pantheon for Merovingian kings. Restoration of the site of their tombs, St. Symphorien Chapel, began in 1981. During that work, unknown Romanesque paintings were discovered on the chapel's triumphal arch, making it one of the most interesting remains of old Christian Paris.

The Romanesque tower, topped by a 19th-century spire, is the most enduring landmark in the village of St-Germain-des-Prés. Its church bells, however, are hardly noticed by the patrons of Deux-Magots across the way.

The Normans nearly destroyed the abbey at least four times. The present building, the work of four centuries, has a Romanesque nave and a Gothic choir with fine capitals. Among the people interred at the church are **Descartes** (his heart at least) and **Jean-Casimir,** the king of Poland who abdicated his throne.

When you leave the church, turn right on rue de l'Abbaye and have a look at the 17th-century **Palais Abbatial,** a pink palace.

St-Sulpice. Rue St-Sulpice, 6e. ☎ **01-46-33-21-78.** Daily 7:30am–7:30pm. Métro: St-Sulpice.

Pause first outside quiet St-Sulpice. The 1844 fountain by Visconti displays the sculpted likenesses of four bishops of the Louis XIV era: Fenelon, Massillon, Bossuet, and Flechier. Work on the church, at one time Paris's largest, began in 1646 as part of the Catholic revival then occurring in France. Although laborers built the body by 1745, work on the bell towers continued until 1780 when one was finished, and the other left incomplete. One of the most priceless treasures inside is Servandoni's rococo **Chapel of the Madonna,** which contains a Pigalle statue of the Virgin. The church has one of the world's largest organs; it comprises 6,700 pipes and has been played by such musicians as Charles-Mari Widor and Marcel Dupre.

But the real reason to come to St-Sulpice is to see the Delacroix frescoes in the **Chapel of the Angels** (the first on your right as you enter). Seek out his muscular Jacob wrestling (or is he dancing?) with an effete angel. On the ceiling St. Michael is having some troubles with the Devil, and yet another mural depicts Heliodorus being driven from the temple. Painted in the final years of his life, the frescoes were a high point in the baffling career of Delacroix. If these impress you, you can pay the painter tribute by visiting the Delacroix museum, reviewed in "The Major Museums," above.

Insider Tip

To see the work that earned Delacroix his niche in art history, go to the Louvre for such passionate paintings as his *Liberty Leading the People on the Barricades,* or to the nearby **Church of St-Sulpice** (Métro: Mabillon) for the famed fresco *Jacob Wrestling with the Angel,* among others.

✪ **Sainte-Chapelle.** Palais de Justice, 4 bd. du Palais, 1er. ☎ **01-53-73-78-50.** Admission 35 F ($5.95) adults, 25 F ($4.25) students and ages 13–25, free for children 12 and under. Apr–Sept daily 9:30am–6:30pm; Oct–Mar daily 10am–5pm. Métro: Cité, St-Michel, or Châtelet–Les Halles. RER: St-Michel.

Countless travel writers have called this tiny chapel a jewel box. That hardly suffices. Nor will it do to call it "a light show." Go when the sun is shining and you'll need no one else's words to describe the remarkable effects of natural light on Sainte-Chapelle.

The church is approached through the Cour de la Sainte-Chapelle of the Palais de Justice. If it weren't for the chapel's 247-foot spire, the law courts here would almost swallow it up.

Built in 5 to 7 years, beginning in 1246, the chapel has two levels. It was constructed to house relics of the True Cross, including the Crown of Thorns acquired by St. Louis (the Crusader king, Louis IX) from the emperor of Constantinople. (In those days, cathedrals throughout Europe were busy acquiring relics for their treasuries, regardless of their authenticity. It was a seller's, perhaps a sucker's, market.) Louis IX is said to have paid heavily for his relics, raising the money through unscrupulous means. He died of the plague on a crusade and was canonized in 1297.

You enter through the lower chapel, supported by flying buttresses and ornamented with fleur-de-lys designs. The lower chapel was used by the servants of the palace, the upper chamber by the king and his courtiers. The latter is reached by ascending narrow spiral stairs.

Viewed on a bright day, the 15 stained-glass windows seem to glow with Chartres blue, and reds that have inspired the Parisian saying, "Wine the color of Sainte-Chapelle's windows." The walls consist almost entirely of the glass, which had to be removed for safekeeping during the Revolution and again during both world wars. In their biblical designs are embodied the hopes and dreams—and the pretensions—of the kings who ordered their construction.

Sainte-Chapelle stages concerts most nights in summer, with tickets ranging from 120 F to 150 F ($20.40 to $25.50). Call ☎ **01-42-77-65-65** for more details (daily from 11am to 6pm).

St-Etienne-du-Mont. Place St-Geneviève, 5e. ☎ **01-43-54-11-79.** Sept–June Mon–Sat 8:30am–noon and 2–7pm, Sun 8:30am–noon and 3–7:15pm; July–Aug Tues–Sun 10am–noon and 4–7pm. Métro: Cardinal-Lemoine or Luxembourg.

Once there was an abbey on this site, founded by Clovis and later dedicated to St. Geneviève, the patroness of Paris. Such was the fame of this popular saint that the abbey proved too small to accommodate the pilgrimage crowds. Now part of the Lycée Henri IV, the Tower of Clovis is all that remains of the ancient abbey (you can see the Tower from rue Clovis).

Today the task of keeping her cult alive has fallen on this church on place St. Geneviève, practically adjoining the Panthéon. The interior is Gothic, an unusual style for a 16th-century church. Construction on the present building began in 1492 and was plagued by delays until the structure was finished, 134 years later, in 1626.

The Marais, Beaubourg & Bastille (3e, 4e & 11e)

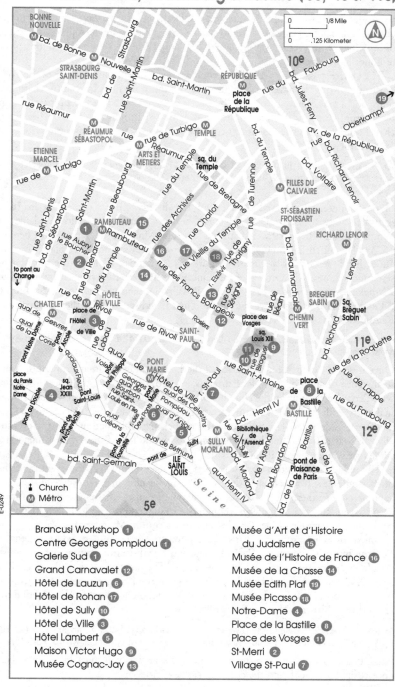

Brancusi Workshop 1
Centre Georges Pompidou 1
Galerie Sud 1
Grand Carnavalet 12
Hôtel de Lauzun 6
Hôtel de Rohan 17
Hôtel de Sully 10
Hôtel de Ville 3
Hôtel Lambert 5
Maison Victor Hugo 9
Musée Cognac-Jay 13

Musée d'Art et d'Histoire
   du Judaïsme 15
Musée de l'Histoire de France 16
Musée de la Chasse 14
Musée Edith Piaf 19
Musée Picasso 18
Notre-Dame 4
Place de la Bastille 8
Place des Vosges 11
St-Merri 2
Village St-Paul 7

E-0249

Besides the patroness of Paris, such men as Pascal and Racine were entombed in the church. Though St. Geneviève's tomb was destroyed during the Revolution, the stone on which her coffin rested was discovered later, and her relics were gathered for a place of honor at St. Etienne.

The church possesses a remarkable **rood screen,** built in the first part of the 16th century. Crossing the nave, it is unique in Paris—called spurious by some uncharitable souls, and a masterpiece by others. Another treasure is a wood-carved **pulpit,** held up by Samson, clutching a bone in one hand, with a slain lion at his feet. The fourth chapel on the right (when entering) contains impressive stained glass dating from the 16th century.

✪ **St-Eustache.** 2 rue du Jour, 1er. ☎ **01-42-36-31-05.** Apr–Sept daily 8am–8pm; Oct–Mar daily 9am–7pm. Sun mass 9:30am, 11am, and 6pm; Sun organ recitals 5:30pm. Métro: Les Halles.

In our opinion, this mixed Gothic and Renaissance church completed in 1637 is rivaled only by Notre-Dame. It took nearly a century to build. Madame de Pompadour and Richelieu were baptized here, and Molière's funeral was held here in 1673. The church has been known for organ recitals ever since Liszt played here in 1866. Inside rests the black-marble tomb of Jean-Baptiste Colbert, the minister of state under Louis XIV. On top of his tomb is his marble effigy flanked by statues of *Abundance* by Coysevox and *Fidelity* by J. B. Tuby. The church's most famous painting is Rembrandt's *The Pilgrimage to Emmaus.* There's a side entrance to the church on rue Rambuteau.

St-Germain l'Auxerrois. 2 place du Louvre, 1er. ☎ **01-42-60-13-96.** Daily 8am–8pm. Métro: Louvre.

Once it was the church for the Palace of the Louvre, drawing an assortment of courtesans, men of art and of law, local artisans, even royalty. Sharing the place du Louvre with Perrault's colonnade, the church contains only the foundation stones of its original belfry built in the 11th century. It was greatly enlarged in the 14th century by the addition of side aisles. The little primitive chapel that had stood on the spot eventually gave way to a great and beautiful church, with 260 feet of stained glass, including some rose windows from the Renaissance.

The saddest moment in its history was on August 24, 1572, the evening of the St. Bartholomew Massacre. On that night, the bells rang in the tower, signaling the supporters of Catherine de Médicis, Marguerite of Guise, Charles IX, and the future Henri III to launch a slaughter of thousands of Huguenots, who had been invited to celebrate the marriage of Henri of Navarre to his cousin, Marguerite of Valois.

The intricately carved **church-wardens' pews** are outstanding, based on designs by Le Brun in the 17th century. Behind the pew is a 15th-century triptych and Flemish retable, so badly lit you can hardly appreciate it. The organ was originally ordered by Louis XVI for the Sainte-Chapelle. In that architectural mélange, many famous men were entombed, including the sculptor Coysevox and the architect Le Vau. Around the chancel is an intricate 18th-century grille.

Val-de-Grâce. 1 place Alphonse-Laveran, 5e. ☎ **01-40-51-51-92.** Admission 30 F ($5.10) Tues–Wed noon–5pm, Sat 1–5pm, Sun 1:30–5pm (5pm is last entrance). Métro: Port-Royal.

According to an old proverb, to understand the French you must like Camembert cheese, the Pont-Neuf, and the dome of Val-de-Grâce.

After 23 years of a childless marriage to Louis XIII, Anne of Austria gave birth to a boy who would one day be known as the Sun King. In those days, if monarchs wanted to express gratitude, they built a church or monastery. On April 1, 1645, 7 years after his birth, the future Louis XIV laid the first stone of the church. At the time, Mansart was the architect. To him we owe the facade in the Jesuit style. Le Duc, however, designed the dome, and the painter Mignard decorated the church with frescoes. Le Mercier and Le Muet also had a hand in the church's fashioning.

Val-de-Grâce's origins go back even further, to 1050, when a Benedictine monastery was established on the grounds. In 1619, Marguerite Veni d'Arbouze was appointed abbess by Louis XIII. She petitioned Anne of Austria for a new monastery because the original one was decaying. Then came Louis XIV's church, which in 1793 was turned into a military hospital and in 1850 an army school.

5 Architectural & Historical Highlights

Arènes de Lutèce. Rues Monge and Navarre, 5e. No phone. Free admission. May–Sept daily 10am–10pm; Oct–Apr daily 10am–5:30pm. Métro: Jussieu.

Discovered and partially destroyed in 1869, this Roman amphitheater is Paris's second most important Roman ruin after the Roman Baths in the Musée de Cluny (see "The Major Museums," above). Today the site is home to a small arena, not so grand as the original, and pleasant gardens. You may feel as if you've discovered a private spot in the heart of the city, but don't be fooled. Your solitude is sure to be interrupted, if not by groups of students playing soccer then at least by parents pushing strollers down the walking paths. This is an ideal spot for a picnic. Bring a bottle of wine and fresh baguettes to enjoy in this vestige of the ancient city of Lutetia.

Bibliothèque Nationale de France (French National Library). Site Tolbiac/François Mitterand, Quai François Mauriac, 13e. ☎ **01-53-79-59-59.** Admission 20 F ($3.40). No one under 16 admitted. Tues–Sat 10am–8pm, Sun noon–7pm. Métro: Quai de la Gare.

Inaugurated in 1996, with a dramatic futuristic design that caused a flurry of speculation when it was first unveiled to the French public, this is the most recent of the *grand projets* inaugurated by former French president and master builder François Mitterrand. Conceived on the same grandiose scale and size as the *Cité de la Musique,* it houses the literary and historic archives of the French nation. As such, it's regarded as something akin to a repository of the soul of France, replacing outmoded, more cramped facilities on the rue des Archives in central Paris. Fully functional since 1998, it incorporates space for 3,600 readers at a time, many of whom enjoy views over two levels of a garden-style courtyard that seems very far removed from the urban congestion of Paris.

This is one of the most user-friendly and grandly accessorized academic facilities in Europe, a role model that will set academic and literary priorities well into the next century. The public has access to as many as 750,000 books and periodicals, with an additional 10 million historic (including medieval) documents that are shown only to qualified experts. There's an emphasis on computerized documentation and microfiche that's vastly more sophisticated than the charming but dusty and impossibly outmoded facilities that it replaced.

Although the appeal of this place extends mainly to serious scholars who are researching specific topics about French history and culture, there is a handful of special exhibits that might interest a casual tourist, as well as concerts and lectures. Concert tickets rarely exceed 100 F ($17) for adults, or 65 F ($11.05) for students, senior citizens, and children; a schedule is available at the library.

Conciergerie. 1 quai de l'Horloge, 1er. ☎ **01-53-73-78-50.** www.paris.org/Monuments/Conciergerie. Admission 35 F ($5.95) adults, 23 F ($3.90) ages 12–25 and over 60, free for children under 12. Apr–Sept daily 9:30am–6:30pm; Oct–Mar daily 10am–5pm. Métro: Cité, Châtelet, or St-Michel. RER: St-Michel.

London has its Tower, Paris its Conciergerie. Although the Conciergerie had a long and regal history before the Revolution, it was forever stained by the Reign of Terror and other horrors. It lives as an infamous symbol of the days when carts pulled up daily to haul off a fresh supply of victims to the guillotine.

On the Seine, the Conciergerie is approached through its landmark twin towers, the **Tour d'Argent** and the **Tour de César.** The vaulted 14th-century **Guard Room,** which dates from when the Capets made the Palace of the Cité a royal residence, is the actual entrance to the building. Also dating from the 14th century, and even more interesting, is the vast, dark, and foreboding Gothic *Salle des Gens d'Armes* (Room of People at Arms), utterly changed from the days when the king used it as a banquet hall.

But architecture plays a secondary role to the list of famous prisoners who spent their last miserable days here. Few in its history endured tortures as severe as Ravaillac's, who assassinated Henry IV in 1610. He got the full treatment—pincers in the flesh, and hot lead and boiling oil poured on him like bath water.

During the Revolution, the Conciergerie became a symbol of terror to the nobility and enemies of the State. Just a short walk from the prison, the Revolutionary Tribunal dispensed a skewed, hurried justice to the beat of the guillotine. If it's any consolation, the jurists of the Revolution did not believe in torturing their victims, only in decapitating them.

In failing health and shocked beyond grief, Marie Antoinette was brought here to await her trial. Only a small screen (and sometimes not even that) protected her modesty from the gaze of guards stationed in her cell. The Affair of the Carnation failed in its attempt to abduct her and secure her freedom. By accounts of the day, she was shy and stupid, although the evidence is that upon her death she displayed the nobility of a true queen. (What's more, the famous "Let them eat cake" she supposedly uttered when told the peasants had no bread is probably apocryphal.) It was shortly before noon on the morning of October 16, 1793, when her executioners came for her, grabbing her and cutting her hair, as was the custom for victims marked for the guillotine.

Later, the Conciergerie housed other noted prisoners, including Madame Elizabeth; Madame du Barry, mistress of Louis XV; Madame Roland ("O Liberty! Liberty! What crimes are committed in thy name!"); and Charlotte Corday, who killed Marat with a kitchen knife while he was taking a sulfur bath. In time the revolution consumed its own leaders, such as Danton and Robespierre. Finally, even one of the most hated men in Paris, the public prosecutor Fouquier-Tinville, faced the same guillotine to which he'd sent so many others.

Among the few interned here who lived to tell the tale was America's Thomas Paine, who reminisced about his chats in English with Danton.

Hôtel de Ville. 29 rue de Rivoli, 4e. ☎ **01-42-76-43-43.** Free admission. Information center open Mon–Sat 9am–6:30pm. Métro: Hôtel de Ville.

The Hôtel de Ville isn't a hotel at all, but the grandiose city hall of Paris. On a large square with fountains and turn-of-the-century lampposts, it is a 19th-century Cinderella's Palace. The medieval structure it replaced had witnessed countless municipally ordered executions. Henry IV's assassin, Ravaillac, was quartered alive on the square in 1610, his body tied to four horses that bolted in opposite directions. On May 24, 1871, the communards doused the city hall with petrol, creating a blaze that lasted for 8 days. The Third Republic ordered the structure rebuilt, with many changes, even creating a Hall of Mirrors evocative of Versailles. For security reasons, the major splendor of this building is closed to the general public. However, there is an on-site information center sponsoring exhibits on Paris in the main lobby.

Champs-Elysées (8e & 17e)

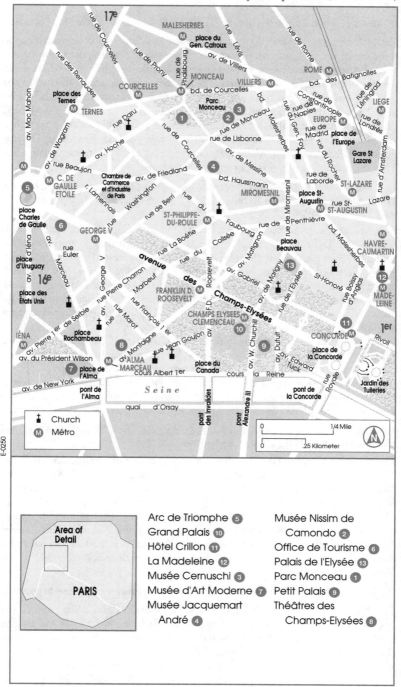

Church †
Métro Ⓜ

Area of
Detail

PARIS

Arc de Triomphe ⑤
Grand Palais ⑩
Hôtel Crillon ⑪
La Madeleine ⑫
Musée Cernuschi ③
Musée d'Art Moderne ⑦
Musée Jacquemart
André ④

Musée Nissim de
Camondo ②
Office de Tourisme ⑥
Palais de l'Elysée ⑬
Parc Monceau ①
Petit Palais ⑨
Théâtres des
Champs-Elysées ⑧

E-0250

Institut de France. 23 quai de Conti, 6e. ☎ **01-44-41-44-41.** Métro: Pont-Neuf or Odéon.

Designed by Louis Le Vau, this dramatic baroque building with an enormous cupola is the seat of all five Academies—Académie Francaise, des Sciences, des Inscriptions et Belles Lettres, des Beaux Arts, and des Sciences Morales et Politiques—which dominate the intellectual life of the country. The members of the Academy (limited to 40), the guardians of the French language who are referred to as "the immortals," gather here. Many of them are unfamiliar figures (though Jacques Cousteau and Marshall Pétain were members), and, indeed, the Academy is remarkable for the great writers and philosophers who have not been invited to join—Balzac, Baudelaire, Diderot, Flaubert, Descartes, Proust, Molière, Pascal, Rousseau, and Zola, to name only a few. The cenotaph was designed by Coysevox for Mazarin.

La Grande Arche de La Défense. 1 place du parvis de La Défense, Puteaux. ☎ **01-49-07-27-57.** Admission 40 F ($6.80) adults, 32 F ($5.45) ages 6–18, free for children 5 and under. Daily 10am–6pm (last ascent). RER: La Défense.

Designed as the architectural centerpiece of the sprawling and futuristic satellite suburb of La Défense, this massive steel-and-masonry arch rises 35 stories from the pavement. Built with the blessing of the late President François Mitterrand, the deliberately overscaled archway is the latest landmark to dot the Paris skyline. It extends that magnificently engineered straight line that links the Louvre, the Arc du Carrousel, the Champs-Elysées, the Arc de Triomphe, the avenue de la Grande Armée, and the place du Porte Maillot. The arch is ringed with a circular avenue patterned after the one that winds around the more famous Arc de Triomphe.

The monument is tall enough to shelter the Cathedral of Notre-Dame under its heavily trussed canopy. An elevator carries visitors to an observation platform, where they get a view of the carefully planned geometry of the surrounding streets.

You may notice nets rigged along the structure of the Grande Arche. When pieces of Mitterrand's grand project started falling to the ground, a mesh was erected to catch fragments before they hit people on the head. Would this were true for all politicians' follies.

Palais Bourbon/Assemblée Nationale. 33 Quai d'Orsay, 7e. ☎ **01-40-63-64-08.** Free admission. Hours vary. Métro: Assemblée Nationale.

The lower house of the French parliament, the Chamber of Deputies, meets at this 1722 mansion built by the Duchess of Bourbon, a daughter of Louis XIV. Reservations for one of two types of visits to the Palais can be made as early as 6 months in advance. Tours on art, architecture, and basic French government processes are given Monday, Friday, and Saturday. The tours are given in French (in English with advance booking). Guests may also observe sessions of the National Assembly, held Tuesday afternoon and all day Wednesday and Thursday beginning at 9:30am. Do remember that this is a working government building and therefore all visitors are subject to rigorous security checks.

Palais-Royal. Rue St-Honoré, 1er. Daily 8am–7pm. Métro: Palais-Royal–Musée-du-Louvre.

The Palais-Royal was originally known as the Palais-Cardinal, for it was the residence of Cardinal Richelieu, Louis XIII's prime minister. Richelieu had it built, and after his death it was inherited by the king, who died soon after. Louis XIV spent part of his childhood here with his mother, Anne of Austria, but later resided at the Louvre and Versailles. The palace was later owned by the duc de Chartres et Orléans (see "Parc Monceau," below), who encouraged the opening of cafes, gambling dens, and other public entertainments.

Although government offices occupy the Palais-Royal and they're not open to the public, do visit the **Jardin du Palais-Royal,** an enclosure bordered by arcades. Don't

The Arcades

Far from the crowds along the Grands Boulevards lie the iron and glass arcades that could be considered the Western world's first shopping malls. Most of them were built from the end of the 18th century to the middle of the 19th century. At the time, merchants were looking for innovative ways to display their wares to the growing middle class. Streets were crowded, dirty, unpaved, and badly lit. Glass-topped markets spared the stores' fashionable clientele the inconveniences of city life and launched a new pastime: window shopping. The covered arcades that remain today are still havens for strolling and shopping. They transport you to an era when Paris set the standard for urban style.

The arrondissement with the greatest concentration of these charming galleries is the 2e. Each has its own character. The **Passage du Caire,** 2 place du Caire (Métro: Sentier), was built in 1798 to commemorate Napoléon's triumphal entry into Cairo. The facade reflects the "Egyptomania" of the time. **Passage Choiseul,** at 44 rue des Petits-Champs (Métro: Quatre-Septembre), dates from 1827 and is the longest and most animated arcade. Discount shoes and clothing are piled outside the renovated stores. **Passage des Panoramas,** 11 bd. Montmartre and 10 rue Saint Marc (Métro: Montmartre), opened in 1800 and was enlarged with the addition of galleries Variétés, St-Marc, Montmartre, and Feydeau in 1834. This passage offers the largest choice of dining options—Korean food, a cafeteria, tea salons, bistros—as well as outlets for stamps, clothes, and knickknacks. Across the street is **Passage Jouffroy,** at 10 bd. Montmartre or 9 rue de la Grange-Batelière (Métro: Montmartre), built between 1845 and 1846. The richness of its decoration—as well as the fact that it was the first heated gallery in Paris—made Passage Jouffroy an immediate hit. The tile floors were restored in 1989, and the arcade now houses a wide variety of boutiques. The **Passage Verdeau,** 31 bis rue du Faubourg-Montmartre (Métro: Le Peletier), was built at about the same time as the Passage Jouffroy and has always suffered in comparison to its more glamorous neighbor. Not much appears to have changed in the last 150 years, including the old postcards and books that are the specialties here. By far the most sumptuous interior is that of **Galerie Vivienne,** 4 place des Petits-Champs, 5 rue de la Banque, and 6 rue Vivienne (Métro: Bourse), built in 1823. The neoclassical style of this arcade (a national monument) has attracted upscale art galleries, hair salons, and fashionable boutiques. The classical friezes, mosaic floors, and graceful arches have been beautifully restored and linked to the adjoining **Galerie Colbert,** which was built in 1826 to capitalize on the success of the Vivienne gallery. For a complete change of pace, head north on the rue St-Denis to the **Passage Brady,** 46 rue du Faubourg St-Denis (Métro: Strasbourg St-Denis), which has become an exotic bazaar. Indian restaurants and spice shops scent the air of this unusual passage, which opened in 1828.

miss the main courtyard, with the controversial 1986 sculpture by Buren: 280 prison-striped columns, oddly placed.

The Panthéon. Place du Panthéon, 5e. ☎ **01-44-32-18-00.** Admission 35 F ($5.95) adults, 23 F ($3.90) ages 12–25, free for children 11 and under. Apr–Sept daily 9:30am–6:30pm; Oct–Mar daily 10am–6:15pm (last entrance 45 minutes before closing). Métro: Cardinal-Lemoine or Maubert-Mutualité.

Some of the most famous men in the history of France (Victor Hugo, for one) are buried here in austere grandeur, on the crest of the mount of St. Geneviève. In 1744, Louis XV made a vow that if he recovered from a mysterious illness, he would build a church to replace the decayed Abbey of St. Geneviève.

Well, he recovered. In 1764, Madame de Pompadour's brother hired Soufflot to design a church in the form of a Greek cross with a dome reminiscent of St. Paul's Cathedral in London. When Soufflot died, his pupil Rondelet carried out the work, completing the structure 9 years after his master's death.

After the revolution, the church was converted into a "Temple of Fame"—ultimately a pantheon for the great men (and one woman: Marie Curie) of France. The body of Mirabeau was buried here, although his remains were later removed. Likewise, Marat was only a temporary tenant. Voltaire's body was exhumed and placed here—and allowed to remain.

In the 19th century, the building changed roles so many times—first a church, then a pantheon, then a church—that it was hard to keep its function straight. After Victor Hugo was buried here, it became a pantheon once again. Other notable men entombed within include Jean-Jacques Rousseau, Soufflot, Émile Zola, and Louis Braille.

Most recently, the ashes of André Malraux were transferred here because, according to President Jacques Chirac, "you lived your dreams and made them live in us." As Charles de Gaulle's culture minister, Malraux decreed that the arts should be part of the lives of all French people, not just Paris's elite.

The finest frescoes, the *Puvis de Chavannes,* line the end of the left wall before you enter the crypt. One illustrates St. Geneviève relieving victims of famine with supplies. The most outstanding of these depicts her white-draped head looking out over medieval Paris, the city whose patron she became.

6 Neighborhood Highlights

In Paris, the neighborhoods often turn out to be attractions unto themselves. The 1st arrondissement, for example, probably has a higher concentration of attractions per block than anywhere else in the world. Although all Paris's neighborhoods are worth wandering, some are more interesting than others. This is especially true of the Latin Quarter, Montmartre, the Grand Promenade, and the Marais, and we've featured them as independent walking tours in chapter 7. Some of our other favorites follow below.

ISLANDS IN THE STREAM: ILE DE LA CITÉ & ILE ST-LOUIS

ILE DE LA CITÉ: WHERE PARIS WAS BORN Medieval Paris, that blend of grotesquerie and Gothic beauty, bloomed on this island in the Seine (Métro: Cité). Ile de la Cité, which the Seine protects like a surrounding moat, has been known as "the cradle" of Paris ever since. As Sauval once observed, "The Island of the City is shaped like a great ship, sunk in the mud, lengthwise in the stream, in about the middle of the Seine."

Few have written more movingly about its heyday than Victor Hugo, who invited the reader "to observe the fantastic display of lights against the darkness of that gloomy labyrinth of buildings; cast upon it a ray of moonlight, showing the city in glimmering vagueness, with its towers lifting their great heads from that foggy sea." Medieval Paris was not only a city of legends and lovers, but also of blood-curdling tortures and brutalities. No story illustrates this better than the affair of Abélard and his charge Héloïse, whose jealous and unsettled uncle hired ruffians to castrate her lover. (The attack predictably quelled their ardor, and he became a monk, she an abbess.)

Don't miss the **Pont-Neuf,** or "New Bridge," at the opposite tip of the island from Notre-Dame. The span isn't new, of course; it's actually the oldest bridge in Paris, erected in 1604. In its day the bridge had two unique features: It was not flanked with houses and shops, and it was paved.

At the **Musée Carnavalet** in the Marais (see "History Museums" under "Specialty Museums," below), a painting called *Spectacle of Buffoons* shows what the bridge was like between 1665 and 1669. Duels were fought on the bridge; the nobility's great coaches crossed it; peddlers sold their wares on it; and entertainers such as Tabarin came here to seek a few coins from the gawkers. As public facilities were lacking, the bridge also served as a de facto outhouse.

Just past the Pont-Neuf is the "prow" of the island, the **Square du Vert Galant.** Pause to look at the equestrian statue of the beloved Henri IV, who was killed by an assassin. A true king of his people, Henry was also (to judge from accounts) regal in the boudoir. Hence the nickname "Vert Galant," or old spark. Gabrielle d'Estrées and Henriette d'Entragues were his best-known mistresses, but they had to share him with countless others, some of whom would casually catch his eye as he was riding along the streets of Paris.

In fond memory of the king, the little triangular park continues to attract lovers. If at first it appears to be a sunken garden, that's because it remains at its natural level; the rest of the Cité has been built up during the centuries.

ILE ST-LOUIS The little iron footbridge from the rear of Notre-Dame to the Ile St-Louis exposes visitors to a world of tree-shaded quays, aristocratic town houses with courtyards, restaurants, and antiques shops. (You can also take the Métro to Sully-Morland or Pont-Marie.) The fraternal twin of Ile de la Cité, Ile St-Louis is primarily residential; plaques on the facades of houses identify the former residences of the famous. **Marie Curie** lived at 36 quai de Béthune, near Pont de la Tournelle.

The most exciting mansion is the **Hôtel de Lauzun,** at 17 quai d'Anjou. It was the home of the duc de Lauzun, a favorite of Louis XIV, until his secret marriage angered the king, who had him tossed into the Bastille. Baudelaire lived here in the 19th century, squandering his family fortune and penning poetry that would be banned in France until 1949. Now the house belongs to the City of Paris and is used to house official guests.

Voltaire lived with his mistress in the **Hôtel Lambert,** at 2 quai d'Anjou, where their quarrels were legendary. The mansion also housed the Polish royal family for over a century.

Farther along, at **no. 9 quai d'Anjou,** stands the house where Honoré Daumier, the painter, sculptor, and lithographer, lived between 1846 and 1863. Here he produced hundreds of lithographs satirizing the bourgeoisie and attacking government corruption. His caricature of Louis-Philippe landed him in jail for 6 months.

RIGHT BANK HIGHLIGHTS

LES HALLES In the 19th century, Zola called it "the underbelly of Paris." For 8 centuries, **Les Halles** (Métro: Les Halles; RER: Châtelet–Les Halles) was the major wholesale fruit, meat, and vegetable market of the city. The smock-clad vendors, the carcasses of beef, the baskets of the best fresh vegetables in the world—all belong to the past. Today the action has moved to a steel-and-glass edifice at Rungis, a suburb near Orly Airport. The original market, Baltard's old zinc-roofed Second Empire "iron umbrellas," has been torn down.

Replacing these so-called umbrellas is **Les Forum des Halles,** which opened in 1979. This large complex, much of it underground, contains dozens of shops, plus several restaurants and movie theaters. Many of these shops are unattractive, but others contain a wide display of merchandise that has made the complex popular with both residents and visitors alike.

For many tourists a night on the town still ends in the wee hours with a bowl of onion soup at Les Halles, usually at **Au Pied de Cochon** (The Pig's Foot) or at **Au Chien Qui Fume** (The Smoking Dog). One of the most classic scenes of Paris was elegantly dressed Parisians (many fresh from Maxim's) standing at a bar drinking cognac with blood-smeared butchers. Some writers have suggested that one Gérard de Nerval introduced the custom of frequenting Les Halles at such an unearthly hour. (De Nerval was a 19th-century poet whose life was considered "irregular." He hanged himself in 1855.)

A newspaper correspondent described today's scene this way: "Les Halles is trying to stay alive as one of the few places in Paris where one can eat at any hour of the night."

BELLEVILLE & MÉNILMONTANT   The 20th arrondissement of Paris is often overlooked by sightseers who scurry to the most famous sights of the city and fail to explore its ethnic outskirts. This area, between the Père-Lachaise cemetery to the south and the rue de Belleville to the north, is comprised of two districts, each with its own personality and allure. Belleville and Ménilmontant began as pretty country villages but quickly became slums when Haussmann expelled many of Paris's workers from the city during his rebuilding projects.

Belleville (Métro: Belleville, Pyrénées) was the sight of some of the heaviest fighting during the uprising of the Paris Commune; today, different battles are being waged. The present fight centers on the explosion of urban renewal that has taken Paris by storm. Residents have formed a group known as the "Bellevilleuse," whose aim is to make sure that the redevelopment of Belleville doesn't sacrifice its international working-class atmosphere—no chi-chi boutiques or tapas bars here. Merchants are more likely to offer specialties from countries such as Greece, China, North Africa, and Eastern Europe.

The hill in the center of Belleville is a good place to start a tour. Narrow alleyways emerge to panoramic views near the top of the hill and cheap ethnic restaurants and fun shops at the base. You can also look out over Paris from the Jardin de Belleville, although development has seriously diminished the garden's tranquillity.

The **Parc des Buttes-Chaumont,** created by Baron Haussmann's designers, is one of the area's most appealing attractions. A small classical temple there provides a view westward toward Montmartre from its perch in the center of a small lake. Provincial houses and gardens line streets in the park's eastern range and seem a bit anachronistic in such a quickly expanding city.

In contrast to these quaint reminders of days gone by is the **Parc de la Villette,** an ultramodern science park that surrounds some of the newest housing developments in Paris. Playgrounds, fountains, and sculptures are all innovative creations of more modern city planners. Here, you'll also find **La Géode,** a geodesic dome in the midst of colorful gardens that houses a cinema and several surprising additions, including a real submarine.

Ménilmontant (Métro: Ménilmontant) is even more ethnically diverse than its sibling district. A perpetual influx of immigrants, including Russian Jews, Spanish Republicans, Poles, Armenians, North Africans, and Asians, keeps the area constantly changing. Its big attraction is **Père-Lachaise Cemetery** (see "Cemeteries," below). Famous for the many celebrities interred within its walls, the cemetery is also the sight of the Paris Commune's last stand against the French government. Here 147 Fédérés were lined up and shot against its eastern wall in revenge for the murder of the archbishop of Paris. A much less violent attraction is the **Musée Edith Piaf,** located at

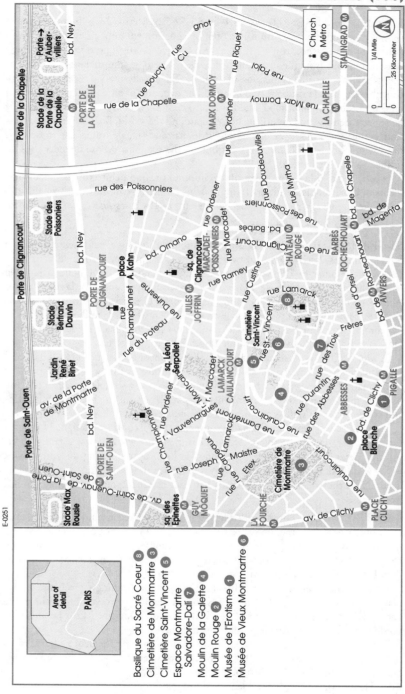

Montmartre (18e)

Church
Métro

Area of detail

PARIS

Basilique du Sacré Coeur (8)
Cimetière de Montmartre (3)
Cimetière Saint-Vincent (5)
Espace Montmartre
Salvadore-Dalí (7)
Moulin de la Galette (4)
Moulin Rouge (2)
Musée de l'Erotisme (1)
Musée de Vieux Montmartre (6)

E-0251

5 rue Crespin-du-Gast, 11e (☎ **01-43-55-52-72;** Métro: Ménilmontant), open Monday through Thursday from 1 to 6pm by appointment only. Be aware that if you don't phone in advance, you won't have the security code you'll need to buzz your way into the building from the street, and you're likely not to be admitted into the crowded site, which has become something of a shrine. Technically the visit is free, although contributions to the *caisse* are appreciated. The daughter of an acrobat, the great Piaf grew up in this neighborhood, and her songs, such as "La Vie en Rose" and "Non, je ne regrette rien," would eventually be heard around the world. Born as Giovanna Gassion, she assumed the name of Piaf, or "little sparrow." This privately run museum is filled with Piaf memorabilia and is a tribute to the songbird, whose memory lives on in the heart of the French.

Nearby is the **Villa Calte,** a beautiful example of the fine architecture that many residents of the arrondissement are trying to save. Fronted by an intricate wrought-iron fence, the house has a pleasant garden where parts of Truffaut's *Jules et Jim* were filmed.

LEFT BANK HIGHLIGHTS

ST-GERMAIN-DES-PRÉS   This neighborhood in the 6th arrondissement (Métro: St-Germain-des-Prés) was the postwar home of existentialism, associated with Jean-Paul Sartre, Simone de Beauvoir, Albert Camus, and an intellectual, bohemian crowd that gathered at the **Café de Flore,** the **Brasserie Lipp,** and **Les Deux-Magots.** Among them, the black-clad poet and singer Juliette Greco was known as *la muse de St-Germain-des-Prés,* and to Sartre she was the woman who had "millions of poems in her throat." Her long hair, black slacks, black sweater, and black sandals launched a fashion trend adopted by young women from Paris to California.

In the 1950s, new names appeared, like Françoise Sagan, Gore Vidal, and James Baldwin, but by the 1960s the tourists were just as firmly entrenched. Today St-Germain-des-Prés retains a bohemian and intellectually stimulating street life, full of many interesting bookshops, art galleries, cave (basement) nightclubs, and bistros and coffeehouses, as well as two historic churches.

Just a short walk from the Delacroix museum, **rue Visconti** was designed for pushcarts and is worth visiting today. At **no. 17** is the house where Balzac established his printing press in 1825. (The venture ended in bankruptcy, forcing the author back to his writing desk.) In the 17th century, the French dramatist Jean-Baptiste Racine lived across the street. Such celebrated actresses as Champmeslé and Clairon also lived here.

MONTPARNASSE   For the "lost generation," life centered around the literary cafes of Montparnasse, at the border of the 6th and 14th arrondissements (Métro: Montparnasse-Bienvenue). Hangouts such as the **Dôme,** the **Coupole,** the **Rotonde,** and the **Sélect** became legendary, as artists—especially American expatriates—turned their backs on Montmartre, dismissing it as too touristy.

Picasso, Modigliani, and Man Ray came this way, and Hemingway was also a popular figure. So was Fitzgerald when he was poor (when he wasn't, you'd find him at the Ritz). William Faulkner, Archibald MacLeish, Isadora Duncan, Miró, James Joyce, Ford Madox Ford, even Trotsky—all spent time here.

The most notable exception was Gertrude Stein, who never frequented the cafes. To see her, you would have to wait for an invitation to her salon at **27 rue de Fleurus.** She bestowed this favor on Sherwood Anderson, Elliot Paul, Ezra Pound, and, for a time, Hemingway. When Pound launched himself into a beloved chair and broke it, he incurred Stein's wrath, and Hemingway decided there wasn't "much future in men being friends with great women."

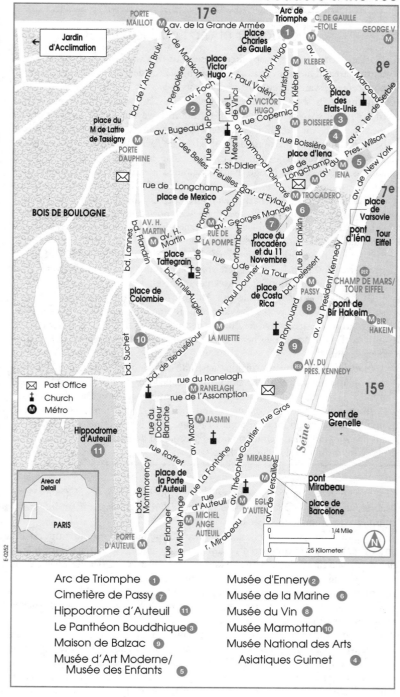

Arc de Triomphe ❶   Musée d'Ennery ❷

Cimetière de Passy ❼   Musée de la Marine ❻

Hippodrome d'Auteuil ⓫   Musée du Vin ❽

Le Panthéon Bouddhique ❸   Musée Marmottan ❿

Maison de Balzac ❾   Musée National des Arts

Musée d'Art Moderne/   Asiatiques Guimet ❹
    Musée des Enfants ❺

The Mother of the Lost Generation

"So Paris was the place that suited those of us that were to create the twentieth century art and literature, naturally enough." Gertrude Stein, who made this pronouncement, wasn't known for her modesty.

In the 1920s, she and her lover, Alice B. Toklas, became the most famous expatriates in Paris. To get an invitation to call on Lovey and Pussy (nicknames for Gertrude and Alice) at **27 rue de Fleurus,** in the heart of Montparnasse, was to be invited into the innermost circle of expatriate Paris. Although their former residence is in private hands and you can't go inside, literary fans flock to this fabled address to stare at the facade that once housed literature's two most celebrated female companions.

Though Gertrude didn't achieve popular success until the 1933 publication of her *Autobiography of Alice B. Toklas,* she was known and adored by many members of the Lost Generation—all except Ernest Hemingway, who tarred her in his posthumous memoir, *A Moveable Feast.*

But to many sensitive young men arriving from America in the 1920s, La Stein was "The Mother of Us All." These young fans hung onto her every word, while Alice baked her notorious hash brownies in the kitchen.

At rue de Fleurus, Gertrude and Alice surrounded themselves with modern paintings, including pieces by Vallotton, Toulouse-Lautrec, Picasso, Gauguin, and Matisse. Gertrude paid $1,000 for her first Matisse, $30 for her first Picasso. In fact, the two artists met here. The Saturday-night soirées became a Montparnasse legend.

Not all visitors came to worship. Gertrude was denounced by many, including avant-garde magazines of the time, which called her a "fraud, egomaniac, and publicity seeking." Braque called her claim to influence art in Paris "nonsense."

In spite of the attacks, the jokes, and the lurid speculation, Stein, at least in public, kept her ego intact. Bernard Fay once told her he'd met three people in his life who ranked as geniuses: Gide, Picasso, and herself.

"Why include Gide?" Stein asked.

When not receiving guests, Stein was busy buying the paintings of Cézanne, Renoir, Matisse, and Picasso. One writer said that her salon was engaged in an international conspiracy to promote modern art.

The grand salon of Natalie Barney is still at **20 rue Jacob.** This American expatriate and writer from Ohio conducted a salon here every Friday that attracted the literati of her day, including Djuna Barnes, Colette, Janet Flanner, Gertrude Stein, William Carlos Williams, and Sylvia Beach. The salon met on and off for half a century, interrupted only by two world wars. Near the place Furstenburg, Barney's former residence is landmarked but not open to the public. In the garden you can see a small Doric temple bearing the inscription *A l'Amitié,* "to friendship."

Aside from the literary legends, one of the most notable characters of the sector was Kiki de Montparnasse. Actually she was an artist's model and prostitute named Alice Prin. She sang at **Le Jockey** at 127 boulevard du Montparnasse, which no longer exists, although Hemingway called it the best nightclub "that ever was." In her black hose and garters, she captivated dozens of men, among them Frederick Kohner, who went so far as to entitle his memoirs *Kiki of Montparnasse.* Kiki would later write her own memoirs, with an introduction by Hemingway. Papa called her "a Queen," noting that that was "very different from being a lady."

Towering over the entire arrondissement is the **Tour Montparnasse** (☎ **01-45-38-52-56**), rising 688 feet above the Paris skyline. Like the Eiffel Tower, it's an instantly recognizable landmark. Completed in 1973, it was immediately denounced by some critics as "bringing Manhattan to Paris." The city soon passed an ordinance outlawing any further structures of this size in the heart of Paris. Today, the tower houses a mammoth underground shopping mall, as well as much of the infrastructure for the Gare de Montparnasse railway station, one of the city's biggest. You can ride an elevator up to the 56th floor, then climb three flights of stairs to the rooftop terrace. From the top, your view will include virtually every important monument of Paris, including Sacré-Coeur, Notre-Dame, and the hypermodern La Défense district along Paris's northwestern fringe. A bar and restaurant are on the 56th floor. Admission to the tower costs 46 F ($7.80) for adults, 38 F ($6.45) for seniors, 35 F ($5.95) for students, and 30 F ($5.10) for children 5 to 14 (children 4 and under enter free). From April through September, it's open daily from 9:30am to 11:30pm; October through March, Monday to Friday from 9:30am to 10:30pm. Metro: Montparnasse-Bienvenue.

The life of Montparnasse still centers around its cafes and exotic nightclubs, many only a shadow of what they used to be. Its heart is at the crossroads of the boulevard Raspail and the boulevard du Montparnasse, one of the settings of *The Sun Also Rises.* Hemingway wrote that "the boulevard Raspail always made dull riding." Rodin's controversial statue of Balzac swathed in a large cape stands guard over the prostitutes who cluster around the pedestal. Balzac seems to be the only one in Montparnasse who doesn't feel the weight of time.

7 Specialty Museums

Be sure to turn to "The Top Attractions" and "The Major Museums," above, for the cream of the crop. "Especially for Kids," below, includes lots of museums parents will love. The museums reviewed below represent the curious, fascinating, and sometimes arcane balance of Paris's offerings.

ART MUSEUMS

Le Panthéon Bouddhique. 19 av. d'Iéna, 16e. ☎ **01-40-73-88-11.** Admission 16 F ($2.70) adults, free for under age 18. Wed–Mon 9:45am–6pm. Métro: Iéna.

This museum retraces the religious pasts of China and Japan from the 4th to the 19th centuries. Approximately 250 Japanese works of art represent different Buddhist traditions and, along with 33 Chinese masterpieces, show the evolution of Buddhism as it passed from India to China and migrated to Japan, where it was embraced around A.D. 1000. Many of the pieces were acquired by Emile Guimet on his 1876 voyage to Japan. His booty included a large number of sculptures from the Kamakura period (1192 to 1333) and the Muromachi-Momoyama period (14th to 16th centuries). The museum's peaceful seasonally changing Japanese garden is an ideal place to meditate. The gift shop sells textiles, porcelain, jewelry, and reproductions of Buddhas and other divinities.

Musée Bourdelle. 18 rue Antoine-Bourdelle, 15e. ☎ **01-49-54-73-73.** Admission 17.50 F ($3) adults, 9 F ($1.55) students and children. Entrance to temporary exhibitions 30 F ($5.10) adults, 20 F ($3.40) students and children. Tues–Sun 10am–5:40pm. Métro: Falguière.

Here you can see works by the star pupil of Rodin, Antoine Bourdelle (1861 to 1929), who became a celebrated artist in his own right. The museum displays the artist's drawings, paintings, and sculptures, and lets you wander at will through his studio, garden, and the house where he lived. The most notable works are his 21 different studies of Beethoven. The original plaster casts of some of his greatest works are also on display. Although some of the exhibits are badly captioned, the impact of Bourdelle's genius is still felt.

Musée Cernuschi. 7 av. Velasquez, 8e. ☎ **01-45-63-50-75.** Admission 17.50–35 F ($3–$5.95) adults, 9–25 F ($1.55–$4.25) students and seniors, free for age 17 and under. Tues–Sun 10am–5:40pm. Métro: Monceau or Villiers. Bus: 30 or 94.

This small museum bordering the Parc Monceau is devoted to the arts of China. If you love art objects of the Far East, then head here for at least a cursory visit. The museum has a number of treasures, including a 3-ton bronze Japanese Buddha, although the treasure trove is no match for the Guimet (see below). The building is another one of those mansions whose owners stuffed with art objects, then bequeathed them to the city of Paris. The address was quite an exclusive one when the town house was built in 1885.

Inside, there is, of course, a bust of the founder Henri Cernuschi (1820 to 1896), a self-perpetuating memorial to a man whose generosity and interest in the East was legendary in his day. Now the collections include a fine assortment of Neolithic potteries, as well as bronzes from the 14th century B.C., the most famous being a tiger-shaped vase. The jades, ceramics, and funereal figures are exceptional, as are the pieces of Buddhist sculpture. Most admirable is a Bodhisattva from Yun-kang (A.D. 6th century). Rounding out the exhibits are some ancient paintings, the best known of which is *Horses with Grooms,* attributed to Han Kan (A.D. 8th century, Tang dynasty). The museum also houses a good collection of contemporary Chinese paintings.

Musée Cognacq-Jay. Hôtel Donon, 8 rue Elzévir, 3e. ☎ **01-40-27-07-21.** Admission 17.50 F ($3) adults, 9 F ($1.55) ages 18–25, free for age 17 and under. Tues–Sun 10am–5:40pm. Métro: St-Paul or Rambuteau.

The founders of the Samaritaine department store, Ernest Cognacq and his wife, Louise Jay, were fabled in Paris for their exquisite taste. To see what that long-ago excitement was all about, and also to view what they accumulated from around the world, head for this museum housed in the 16th-century Hôtel Denon, with its Louis XV and Louis XVI paneled rooms. Some of the most valuable decorative works of the 18th century are exhibited here, ranging from paintings and ceramics (or porcelain) to delicate cabinets. On view are paintings by Canaletto, Fragonard, Greuze, Chardin, Boucher, Watteau, and Tiepolo.

Musée d'Art Moderne de la Ville de Paris. 11 av. du Président Wilson, 16e. ☎ **01-53-67-40-00.** Admission 27 F ($4.60) adults, 14.50 F ($2.45) ages 18–24, free for under age 18 and over 60. Tues–Fri 10am–5:30pm, Sat–Sun 10am–6:45pm. Métro: Iéna or Alma-Marceau.

Next door to the Palais de Tokyo, this museum bordering the Seine displays a permanent collection of paintings and sculpture owned by the city of Paris. Come here only if repeated visits to the Musée d'Orsay and the Louvre have not satiated your need to see fine art in Paris. The museum presents ever-changing exhibitions on individual artists from all over the world or on trends in international art. The salons display works by such artists as Chagall, Matisse, Léger, Rothko, Braque, Picasso, Dufy, Utrillo, Delaunay, Rouault, and Modigliani.

See, in particular, Pierre Tal Coat's *Portrait of Gertrude Stein,* with Picasso's version of this difficult subject in mind. Other sections in the museum show work by young artists and new trends in contemporary art. The **Musée des Enfants** has exhibitions and shows for children.

Musée d'Arts d'Afrique et d'Océanie. 293 av. Daumesnil, 12e. ☎ **01-44-74-84-80.** Admission 30 F ($5.10) adults, free for under age 18. Fri–Wed 10am–5:30pm. Métro: Porte-Dorée.

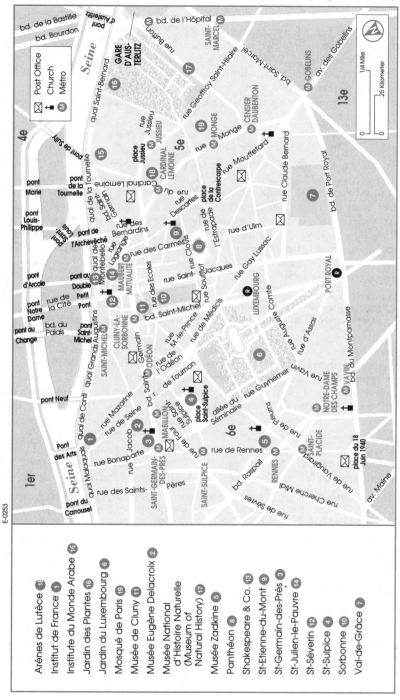

Arénes de Lutèce 18
Institut de France 1
Institute du Monde Arabe 16
Jardin des Plantes 16
Jardin du Luxembourg 6
Mosqué de Paris 19
Musée de Cluny 11
Musée Eugène Delacroix 2
Musée National
d'Histoire Naturelle
(Museum of
Natural History) 17
Musée Zadkine 5
Panthéon 8
Shakespeare & Co. 13
St-Etienne-du-Mont 9
St-Germain-des-Prés 3
St-Julien-le-Pauvre 14
St-Séverin 12
St-Sulpice 4
Sorbonne 10
Val-de-Grâce 7

E-0253

193

Within an art deco building originally conceived as part of the French Colonial exhibition of 1931, you'll find an extensive collection of ethnic art from central Africa that's especially rich in carved masks and carved statues, as well as some magnificent bronzes from Benin. Also represented is a series of Aboriginal bark paintings. To a lesser extent are art objects from the Pacific islands, and a somewhat limited collection of woven carpets and gold jewelry from the Magreb region of Arab-speaking North Africa. In the cellars is a group of aquariums and terrariums containing crocodiles, iguanas, and tortoises.

Musée d'Ennery. 59 av. Foch, 16e. ☎ **01-45-53-57-96.** Free admission. Thurs and Sun 2–5:45pm. Closed Aug. Métro: Porte Dauphine.

This is the result of the fierce passion and determination of Madame Clémence d'Ennery, who in 1876 began assembling more than 7,000 Japanese objets d'art, many of which she found in antiques shops and boutiques around Paris. Some of her more compelling finds include Kyoto ceramics from the 18th and 19th centuries; Namban art objects, a style resulting from the collision of Japanese and Portuguese cultures from 1543 to 1630; and Chinese furniture from the 17th to 19th centuries. The setting—the Ennery family's private home, erected in the 1870s—underwent a radical renovation in 1999. Exact details hadn't been settled yet at the time of this writing, so phone before your actual visit.

Musée des Arts Décoratifs. In the Palais du Louvre, 107 rue de Rivoli, 1er. ☎ **01-44-55-57-50.** Admission 30 F ($5.10) adults, 20 F ($3.40) ages 18–25, free for age 17 and under. Tues and Thurs–Fri 11am–6pm, Wed 11am–9pm, Sat–Sun 10am–6pm. Métro: Palais-Royal or Tuileries.

In the northwest wing of the Louvre's Pavillon de Marsan, this museum holds a treasury of furnishings, fabrics, wallpaper, objets d'art, and other items displaying living styles from the Middle Ages to the present. A visit here is recommended only if you have an abiding interest in the decorative arts of France, and take the kids only if one of them has expressed an interest in becoming a decorator. Notable on the first floor are the 1920s art deco boudoir, bath, and bedroom of couturier Jeanne Lanvin by designer Rateau. Decorative art from the Middle Ages to the Renaissance is on the second floor; rich collections from the 17th, 18th, and 19th centuries occupy the third and fourth floors. The fifth has specialized centers on wallpaper and drawings, and documentary centers detailing fashion, textiles, toys, crafts, and glass trends.

Musée Gustave Moreau. 14 rue de la Rochefoucault, 9e. ☎ **01-48-74-38-50.** Admission 22 F ($3.70) adults, 15 F ($2.55) students 18–25 and for adults on Sun, free for under age 18. Mon and Wed 11am–5:15pm, Thurs–Sun 10am–12:45pm and 2–5:15pm. Métro: St-Georges.

This house and studio display the works of the symbolist painter Gustave Moreau (1826 to 1898), who embraced the bizarre and painted mythological subjects and scenes in a sensuous, romantic style. Among the works displayed are *Orpheus by the Tomb of Eurydice* and *Jupiter and Semele*. Moreau taught at the Ecole des Beaux Arts, and his influence can be seen in the works of Rouault, who became the first curator of this museum. Matisse was also a student of his.

Musée National des Arts Asiatiques-Guimet. 6 place d'Iéna, 16e. ☎ **01-45-05-00-98.** Closed until spring of 2000. Métro: Iéna or Alma-Marceau.

Comprised of three museums devoted to the art and archaeology of the vast Asian region from Afghanistan to Japan, this museum was named after its founder, the research chemist and wealthy industrialist Emile Guimet. Originally established in Lyon, the Guimet was transferred to Paris in 1889. In 1931, it received the collections of the Musée Indochinois du Trocadéro and, after World War II, the Asian collections of the

Louvre. Today it's one of the richest museums of its kind in the world. The most interesting exhibits encompass Buddhas, heads of serpentine monsters, funereal figurines, and antiquities from the temple of Angkor Wat. Some galleries are devoted to Tibetan art: fascinating scenes of the Grand Lamas entwined with serpents and demons.

The main museum is currently undergoing extensive renovations, adding several new underground galleries, and will be closed until spring 2000. The only building that will remain open to the public during the renovations is **Le Panthéon Bouddhique,** 19 avenue d'Iéna, 16e. Admission is 16 F ($2.70) adults, 12 F ($2.05) students, free for under age 18. It's open Wednesday through Monday from 9:45am to 6pm.

Musée Nissim de Camondo. 63 rue de Monceau, 8e. ☎ **01-53-89-06-40.** Admission 25 F ($4.25) adults, 18 F ($3.05) under age 18 and over 60. Wed–Sun 10am–5pm. Closed Jan 1, Bastille Day (July 14), and Dec 25. Métro: Villiers.

This museum is a jewel box of elegance and refinement, evoking the days of Louis XVI and Marie Antoinette. Visit it for a keen insight into the decorative arts of the 18th-century, all in a town-house setting that brings these elements to life more than in most museums. The pre–World War I town house was donated to the Museum of Decorative Arts by Comte Moïse de Camondo (1860 to 1935) in memory of his son, Nissim, a French aviator killed in combat during World War I.

Entered through a courtyard, the museum is like the private home of an 18th-century aristocrat—richly furnished with needlepoint chairs, tapestries (many from Beauvais or Aubusson), antiques, paintings (inevitable Francesco Guardi scenes of Venice), bas-reliefs, silver, Chinese vases, crystal chandeliers, Sèvres porcelain, and Savonnerie carpets. And, of course, a Houdon bust (in an upstairs bedroom). The Blue Salon, overlooking the Parc Monceau, is impressive. You can wander unimpaired through the gilt and oyster-gray salons.

Musée Zadkine. 100 bis rue d'Assas, 6e. ☎ **01-43-26-91-90.** Admission 27 F ($4.60) adults, 19 F ($3.25) ages 7–26. Tues–Sun 10am–5:30pm. Métro: Notre-Dame des Champs.

This museum near the Luxembourg Gardens and boulevard St-Michel was once the private residence of the sculptor Ossip Zadkine (1890 to 1967). Now the famous artist's collection has been turned over to the city of Paris for public viewing. Included are some 300 pieces of sculpture, displayed both within the museum and in the garden, bringing a little rural charm to the city. Some drawings and tapestries are also exhibited. Chances are you won't be visiting here unless you've already seen some of Zadkine's works and want to know more about him and his work. At these headquarters where he worked from 1928 until his death, you can see how he moved from "left wing" Cubism extremism to a renewed appreciation of the classic era. You can visit his garden for free even if you don't want to go into the museum. In fact, it's one of the finest places to relax in Paris on a sunny day, sitting on a bench taking in the two-faced *Woman with the Bird.*

CRAFT & INDUSTRY MUSEUMS

Manufacture Nationale de Sèvres. 4 Grande rue, Sèvres. ☎ **01-45-34-34-00.** Free admission. Salesroom Mon–Sat 10am–5pm. Métro: Pont-de-Sèvres, then walk across the Seine to the Left Bank.

Madame de Pompadour loved Sèvres porcelain. She urged Louis XV to order as much as possible, thus ensuring its favor among the chic people of the 18th century. Two centuries later, it's still fashionable. If porcelain's your thing, you'll be awed by plate after plate; but if you'd rather see pork chops on your plate, you'll find far more intriguing diversions in Paris.

The state of France has owned the Sèvres factory for more than 2 centuries. It was founded originally in Vincennes, and moved to Sèvres, a riverside suburb on the western edge of Paris, in 1756. The factory's commercial service sells porcelain to the public Monday through Saturday (it's closed on holidays). Don't expect a tour of the factories, as they're closed to all except state visitors and industrial insiders. The showroom, however, is an intensely upscale testimonial to the acquisitive pleasures of the French-speaking world. Prices are high, as only 5,000 pieces of porcelain are produced every year.

There's a newer showroom in central Paris, at 4 place André-Malraux, 1er (☎ **01-47-03-40-20**); Métro: Palais-Royal.

Next door, the **Musée National de Céramique de Sèvres** (☎ **01-41-14-04-20**) boasts one of the finest collections of faience and porcelain in the world, some of which belonged to Madame du Barry, Pompadour's hand-picked successor. On view, for example, is the "Pompadour rose" (which the English insisted on calling the "rose du Barry"), a style much in vogue in the 1750s and 1760s. The painter Boucher made some of the designs used by the factory, as did the sculptor Pajou (he created the bas-reliefs for the Opéra at Versailles). The factory pioneered what became known in porcelain as the Louis Seize (Louis XVI) style—it's all here, plus lots more, including works from Sèvres's archrival, Meissen. This museum is open Wednesday through Monday from 10am to 5pm. Admission is 23 F ($3.90) adults, 15 F ($2.55) ages 18 to 25, free for age 17 and under.

Manufacture Nationale des Gobelins. 42 av. des Gobelins, 13e. ☎ **01-44-61-21-69.** Tours given in French (with English pamphlets) Tues–Thurs 2 and 2:45pm for 45 F ($7.65) adults, 35 F ($5.95) ages 7–24 and 65 or older, free for children under 7. Métro: Les Gobelins.

This is a museum for tapestry-lovers, and need not occupy much time for those not devoted to the subject. Sick of mass production? Take heart—a single tapestry can take well past 3 or 4 years to complete, employing as many as three to five full-time weavers. The founding father of this dynasty, Jehan Gobelin, came from a family of dyers and cloth-makers. In the 15th century, he discovered a scarlet dye that was to make him famous. By 1601, Henry IV had become interested, importing 200 weavers from Flanders whose full-time occupation was to make tapestries (many of which are now scattered across various museums and residences). Oddly enough, until this endeavor the Gobelin family had not made any tapestries, although the name would become synonymous with the art form.

Colbert, minister of Louis XIV, purchased the works, and under royal patronage the craftsmen set about executing designs by Le Brun. After the revolution, the industry was reactivated by Napoléon.

Les Gobelins is still going strong, and you can visit the studios *(ateliers)* of the craftspeople. Some of the antique high-warp looms are still in use. Weavers sit behind huge screens of thread, patiently inserting stitch after stitch.

Musée de Baccarat. 30 bis rue de Paradis, 10e. ☎ **01-47-70-64-30.** Admission 15 F ($2.55) adults, 10 F ($1.70) students, 7.50 F ($1.30) under age 17 and over 60. Mon–Sat 10am–6pm. Métro: Poissonnière or Château d'Eau.

This museum resembles an ice palace filled with crystal of all shapes and sizes. It's found in a Directoire building from the late 18th century, which houses Baccarat's headquarters. The museum contains some of the most impressive pieces produced by the company through the years. Czars, royalty, and oil-rich sheiks have numbered among the best patrons of the prestigious company, established in 1764. At the entrance to the museum stands "Lady Baccarat," a chandelier in the form and size of a woman.

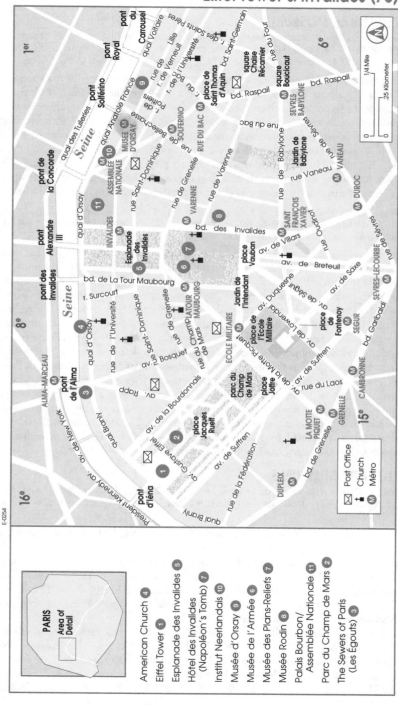

American Church ④
Eiffel Tower ①
Esplanade des Invalides ⑤
Hôtel des Invalides (Napoléon's Tomb) ⑦
Institut Neerlandais ⑩
Musée d'Orsay ⑨
Musée de l'Armée ⑥
Musée des Plans-Reliefs ⑦
Musée Rodin ⑧
Palais Bourbon/ Assemblée Nationale ⑪
Parc du Champ de Mars ②
The Sewers of Paris (Les Égouts) ③

Post Office ▨
Church ✝
Métro Ⓜ

CULTURAL MUSEUMS

Institut du Monde Arabe (Institute of the Arab World). 1 rue des Fossés-St-Bernard, 5e. ☎ **01-40-51-38-38.** Admission to permanent collections 25F ($4.50), to special exhibitions 45 F ($7.65). Combined ticket 55 F ($9.35). Tues–Sun 10am–6pm. Métro: Jussieu.

In a glass and aluminum structure built with funds from France and 20 Arab nations, Institut du Monde Arabe is much more than a museum. The building, which many consider to be one of the finest modern structures in Paris, houses a multimedia cultural center whose aim is to promote relations between France and the Arab world. The institute features art from three Arab regions, some dating from the 3rd century. There is also a massive library with literary works and periodicals in Arabic, French, and English, and an auditorium where Arab movies and plays are presented. If nothing else, come here to enjoy coffee or a light lunch at the center's 9th-floor restaurant/cafe while taking in the panoramic view of the city from the terrace that hangs out over the Seine.

Musée d'Art et d'Histoire du Judaïsm (Museum of Jewish History and Art). 71 rue du Temple, 3e. ☎ **01-53-01-86-60.** Admission 35 F ($5.95) adults, free for under age 18. Sun–Fri 10am–6pm. Métro: Rambuteau.

More Jews live in France than in any other European country except Russia, and now there is a museum to honor their history. President Chirac inaugurated the museum in 1998 in the Marais, the old Jewish quarter of Paris. Chirac was the first French president to apologize for the pro-Nazi Vichy regime's role in persecuting Jews in World War II. Unfortunately, the fate of the 78,000 French Jews deported during the war is hardly addressed here. A national, state-supported institution, the museum provides an overview of Jewish life in Europe since the Middle Ages. The collection includes religious objects and ancient manuscripts collected in the early 1800s by Isaac Strauss, as well as the holdings of a small Jewish Art Museum founded in Paris in 1948. Rooms deal with themes such as the role of Jews in the Italian Renaissance, and the Dreyfus affair, the late- 19th-century scandal over a Jewish army officer unjustly accused of treason. One entire room is dedicated to paintings and drawings by Marc Chagall, on loan from the Pompidou Center. The center also lent about two dozen paintings looted by Nazi occupiers and recovered after the war, including works by Utrillo, Léger, Matisse, Picasso, and Dufy.

HISTORY MUSEUMS

Musée Carnavalet. 23 rue de Sévigné, 3e. ☎ **01-42-72-21-13.** Admission 35 F ($5.95) adults, 25 F ($4.25) under age 25 and over 60. Tues–Sun 10am–5:40pm. Métro: St-Paul or Chemin-Vert.

If you like history but history books bore you, spend a couple of hours here for some insight into Paris's past. The comprehensive and lifelike exhibits are great for kids too. The history of Paris comes alive in intimate detail, right down to the chessmen Louis XVI used to distract his mind while waiting to go to the guillotine. The building, a renowned Renaissance palace, was built in 1544 by Pierre Lescot and Jean Goujon and later acquired by Madame de Carnavalet. The great François Mansart transformed it between 1655 and 1661.

But it's probably best known because one of history's most famous letter writers, Madame de Sévigné, moved here in 1677. Fanatically devoted to her daughter (she ended up moving in with her because she couldn't bear their separation), she poured out nearly every detail of her life in her letters, virtually ignoring her son. A native of the Marais district, she died at her daughter's château in 1696. It wasn't until 1866 that the city of Paris acquired the mansion, eventually turning it into a museum.

Several salons cover the Revolution, with a bust of Marat, a portrait of Danton, and a model of the Bastille (one painting shows its demolition). Another salon tells the

---

❓ Did You Know?

- The world's oldest "grocery store," Les Halles, moved in 1969, its first relocation in 8 centuries.
- Place Denfert-Rochereau, an old burial ground, was once called place d'Enfer, or "Hell Square"—it was stacked with millions of bones from old charnel houses to conserve space in 1785.
- On the narrow Seine island Allée des Cygnes stands a tiny Statue of Liberty.
- At the end of the 18th century, the place Charles-de-Gaulle–Etoile was the world's first organized traffic circle.
- Pont-Neuf (New Bridge) isn't so new. Dating from 1607, it's the oldest and most famous bridge in Paris.
- The Sorbonne began in 1253 as modest lodgings for 16 theology students who pursued their education on the site of the present-day University of Paris
- In 1938, workmen discovered 3,350 22-karat gold coins weighing 1.3 grams each while digging at 51 rue Mouffetard. An accompanying note said they belonged to Louis Nivelle, royal counselor to Louis XV, who mysteriously disappeared in 1757.

---

story of the captivity of the royal family at the Temple, including the bed in which Madame Elizabeth slept and the exercise book of the dauphin.

Exhibits continue at the Hôtel le Pelletier de St-Fargeau, across the courtyard. On display is furniture from the Louis XIV period to the early 20th century, including a replica of Marcel Proust's cork-lined bedroom with his actual furniture, including his brass bed.

Musée de l'Histoire de France. 60 rue des Francs-Bourgeois, 3e. ☎ **01-40-27-61-78.** Admission 20 F ($3.40) adults, 15 F ($2.55) children and seniors. Mon and Wed–Fri noon–5:45pm, Sat–Sun 1:45–5:45pm. Métro: Hôtel-de-Ville or Rambuteau.

This 18th-century palace, the Hotel de Soubise, has been steeped in French history since it was first conceived in 1371. The graceful baroque facade you see today dates from 1705, when the building's exterior was redesigned by the much underrated architect Delamair for the prince and princess of Soubise. In the early 1800s, Napoléon designated the building the official repository for his archives, and it's served that function for the French nation ever since. Exhibits range from the legacy of early medieval King Dagobert to the Nazi occupation.

You enter through the colonnaded Court of Honor. Before going inside, walk around the corner to 58 rue des Archives to the medieval turreted gateway of the original Clisson mansion. (The Clisson mansion gave way to the residence of the dukes of Guise, who owned the property until it was purchased by the Soubise family. Princess Soubise was once the mistress of Louis XIV, and apparently the Sun King was very generous, giving her the funds to remodel and redesign the palace.)

The archives contain documents that go back even farther than Charlemagne. The letter collection is highly valued, exhibiting the penmanship of Marie Antoinette (a farewell letter), Louis XVI (his will), Danton, Robespierre, Napoléon I, and Joan of Arc (the museum possesses the only known living sketch of her). Even the jailer's keys to the old Bastille are here.

One of the showcased rooms in the museum is the Salon de la Princesse (also known as the Salon Ovale), a richly decorated circular room one floor above street level. Sweeping expanses of gilt and crystal offset a series of ceiling frescoes painted by

Van Loo, Boucher, and Natoire. Occasionally, the nearby hotel de Rohan, around the corner on the rue Vieille du Temple, contains some of the overflow from this place, but only in the form of temporary exhibitions.

Paristoric. 11 bis rue Scribe, 9e. ☎ **01-42-66-62-06.** Admission 50 F ($8.50) adults, 30 F ($5.10) students and under age 18. Daily 9am–6pm (open until 9pm Apr–Oct). Shows begin every hour on the hour. Métro: Opéra. RER: Auber.

This unique multimedia show retraces the history of Paris in a state-of-the-art theater located in the heart of the city. The 2,000 years since Paris's birth unroll chronologically to the music of such varied musicians as Wagner and Edith Piaf. Maps, portraits, and scenes from dramatic times in the city's history are projected on the large screen as a running commentary (heard through headphones in one of 10 languages) gives details about the art, architecture, and events in the city's past. Many visitors come here first for a preview of what they want to see; others stop for a more in-depth look at what they've already visited. Although the show is sometimes hard to follow (and a bit expensive), it's worth the 45 minutes it takes to view it.

THE OFFBEAT

Musée de la Chasse (Hunting Museum). 60 rue des Archives, 3e. ☎ **01-53-01-92-40.** Admission 30 F ($5.10) adults, 15 F ($2.55) students and seniors, 5 F (85¢) ages 5–16, free for children 4 and under. Tues–Sun 11am–6pm. Métro: Rambuteau or Hôtel-de-Ville.

Near the Musée Carnavalet, the Hôtel Guénégaud, also built by François Mansart, has been restored and turned into the Musée de la Chasse by the Sommer Foundation. This museum, classified as one of the "eccentricities" of Paris, is obviously for the specialist—that is, those who like to hunt, like Hemingway, for sport. If that is your game, you'll find no better exhibition in all of Europe.

Mounted heads are plentiful, ranging from the antelope to the elephant, from the bushbuck to the waterbuck, from the moose to the bush pig. There's a Rembrandt sketch of a lion and a collection of wild-animal portraits by Desportes (1661 to 1743). The hunt tapestries are outstanding and often perversely amusing—one a cannibalistic romp, another showing a helmeted man standing eye to eye with a bear he is stabbing to death. The rifles, many dating from the 17th century, are exceptional, some inlaid with pearls, others engraved with ivory. The museum displays other historical weapons and a remarkable collection of paintings, including works by Rubens, Breughel, Oudry, Chardin, and Corot.

Musée de la Vie Romantique (Museum of Romanticism). 16 rue Chaptal, 9e. ☎ **01-48-74-95-38.** Admission 17.50 F ($2.95) adults, 9F ($1.50) students, free for children under 7. Tues–Sun 10am–5:40pm. Closed holidays. Métro: St-Georges.

This small museum is in a quarter that was called New Athens in the 19th century, when it was the center of literary and artistic life. Once the atelier of painter Ary Scheffer, the museum now displays the possessions and mementos of George Sand and holds temporary exhibits on the theme of romanticism.

Musée de l'Erotisme. 72 bd. de Clichy, 18e. ☎ **01-42-58-28-73.** Admission 40 F ($6.80). Daily 10am–2am. Métro: Blanche.

This tribute to the primal appeal of human sexuality was established by a private enterprise in 1997 in a 19th-century town house that was formerly a raunchy cabaret. Part art gallery, part museum, it presents a tasteful but appealingly risqué collection of art and artifacts that span the distances of time and space. Scattered over six floors, you'll find an oft-changing array of exhibitions that include erotic sculptures and drawings conceived to titillate, appeal, or convey the sense of awe and mystery invoked by the most talked-about human urge—sexuality. The oldest object in the collection is a palm-sized ancient Roman *tintinabulum* (bell), a phallus-shaped animal with the likeness of a nude woman riding astride it. Modern objects include resin, wood, and plaster sculptures by talented French artist Alain Rose, and works by American, Dutch, German, and French artists, including the evocative, free-form works of Robert Combas. Also look for everyday items with erotic themes from South America (terra-cotta pipes shaped like phalluses) and the United States (a belt buckle issued in the 1920s by affiliates of the Coca-Cola company that resembles a praying nun when it's fastened and a nude woman when it's open). There's a gift shop on the premises selling Asian amulets, African bronzes, and terra-cotta figurines from South America, with objects priced from 10 F to 1,500 F ($1.70 to $255). There's also an art gallery where serious works of art are sold at prices ranging from 1,000 F to 100,000 F ($170 to $17,000).

Musée du Parfum (Perfume Museum). 39 bd. des Capucines, 1e. ☎ **01-42-60-37-14.** Free admission. Mon–Sat 9am–6pm. Métro: Opéra.

The perfume museum is in a completely overhauled 19th-century theater on one of Paris's busiest thoroughfares. As you enter the lobby through a quiet courtyard, the lightly scented air reminds you why you're there—to appreciate perfume enough to buy a bottle in the ground-floor shop. But first, a short visit upstairs introduces you to the rudiments of perfume history. The copper containers with spouts and tubes were used in the distillation of perfume oils, and the exquisite collection of perfume bottles from the 17th to the 20th centuries is impressive. Even if perfume bores you, the air-conditioning is a welcome relief in the summer, and the rest rooms are spotless and free.

Musée du Vin (Wine Museum). 5 rue des Eaux, 16e. ☎ **01-45-25-63-26.** Admission (including glass of wine) 37 F ($6.25) adults, 31 F ($5.25) students, 32 F ($5.40) over age 60. Tues–Sun 10am–6pm. Métro: Passy.

This museum is in an ancient stone and clay quarry that was used by 15th-century monks as a wine cellar. It provides a good introduction to the art of wine-making, displaying various tools, beakers, cauldrons, and bottles in a series of exhibits. The quarry is right below Balzac's house (see below), and the ceiling contains a trap door he used to escape from his creditors.

8 Parks & Gardens

See "The Champs-Elysées: The Grand Promenade" in chapter 7 for a description of the **Jardin du Tuileries,** the most famous gardens in Paris. See "Right Bank Highlights" above for the **Buttes-Chaumont** and the **Parc de la Villette.**

JARDIN DU LUXEMBOURG Hemingway told a friend that these gardens (Métro: Odéon, RER: Luxembourg) "kept us from starvation." He related that in his poverty-stricken days in Paris, he wheeled a baby carriage (the vehicle was considered luxurious) and child through the gardens because it was known "for the classiness of its pigeons." When the gendarme went across the street for a glass of wine, the writer would eye his victim, preferably a plump one, then lure him with corn and "snatch him, wring his neck," and hide him under Bumby's blanket. "We got a little tired of pigeon that year," he confessed, "but they filled many a void."

Before it became a feeding ground for famished artists of the 1920s, Luxembourg knew greater days. Leon Daudet claimed, "There is nothing more charming, which invites one more enticingly to idleness, reverie, and young love, than a soft spring morning or a beautiful summer dusk at the Jardin du Luxembourg." It's always been associated with artists, although children, students from the Sorbonne, and tourists predominate nowadays. Watteau came this way, as did Verlaine. Balzac, however, didn't like the gardens at all. In 1905, Gertrude Stein would cross the gardens to catch the Batignolles-Clichy-Odéon omnibus pulled by three gray mares across Paris, to meet Picasso in his studio at Montmartre, where he painted her portrait.

Marie de Médicis, the much-neglected wife and later widow of the roving Henri IV, ordered a palace built on the site in 1612. She planned to live here with her "witch" friend, Leonora Galigal. A Florentine by birth, the regent wanted to create another Pitti Palace. The architect, Salomon de Brossee, wasn't entirely successful, although the overall effect is most often described as Italianate.

The queen didn't get to enjoy the palace for very long, as she was forced into exile by her son, Louis XIII, after it was discovered that she was plotting to overthrow him. Reportedly, she died in poverty in Cologne, quite a step down from the luxury she had once known in the Luxembourg. Incidentally, the 21 paintings she commissioned from Rubens that glorified her life were intended for her palace, but are now in the Louvre. You can only visit the palace the first Sunday of each month at 10:15am, for 45 F ($7.65). However, you must call (☎ **01-44-61-20-89**) to make a reservation.

But you don't come to the Luxembourg to visit the palace—not really. The gardens are the attraction. For the most part, they are in the classic French tradition: well groomed and formally laid out, the trees planted in patterns. A large water basin in the center is encircled by urns and statuary on pedestals, one honoring Paris's patroness St. Geneviève, with pigtails reaching to her thighs. Another memorial is dedicated to Stendhal.

Come here to soak in the atmosphere. It's a good place for kids: You can sail a toy boat, ride a pony, or attend an occasional grand guignol puppet show. Or even better, you can play boules with a group of elderly men who aren't ashamed to wear black berets and have Gauloises dangling from the corner of their mouths.

Crowds throng the park on May Day, when Parisians carry their traditional lilies of the valley. Birds sing, and all of Paris (those who didn't go to the country) celebrates the rebirth of spring.

BOIS DE BOULOGNE   One of the most spectacular parks in Europe is the Bois de Boulogne, Porte Dauphine, 16e (☎ **01-40-67-90-82;** Métro: Les-Sablons, Porte-Maillot, or Porte-Dauphine). The Bois is often called the "main lung" of Paris. Horse-drawn carriages traverse it, but you can also drive through. Its hidden pathways, however, can only be discovered by walking. You could spend days in the Bois de Boulogne and still not see everything.

Porte Dauphine is the main entrance, although you can take the Métro to Porte Maillot as well. West of Paris, the park was once a forest kept for royal hunts. It was in vogue in the late 19th century: Along the avenue Foch, carriages containing elegantly attired and coiffured Parisian damsels would rumble along with their foppish escorts. Nowadays, it's more likely to attract run-of-the-mill picnickers. (And at night, hookers and muggers are prominent, so be duly warned.)

When Emperor Napoléon III gave the grounds to the city of Paris in 1852, they were developed by Baron Haussmann. Separating Lac Inférieur from Lac Supérieur is the *Carrefour des Cascades* (you can stroll under its waterfall). The Lower Lake contains two islands connected by a footbridge. From the east bank, you can take a boat to these idyllically situated grounds, perhaps stopping off at the cafe-restaurant on one of them.

Restaurants in the Bois are numerous, elegant, and expensive. The Pré-Catelan contains a deluxe restaurant of the same name and a Shakespearean theater in a garden planted with trees mentioned in the bard's plays.

The *Jardin d'Acclimation* at the northern edge of the Bois is for children, with a small zoo, an amusement park, and a narrow-gauge railway. (See "Especially for Kids," below, for more details.)

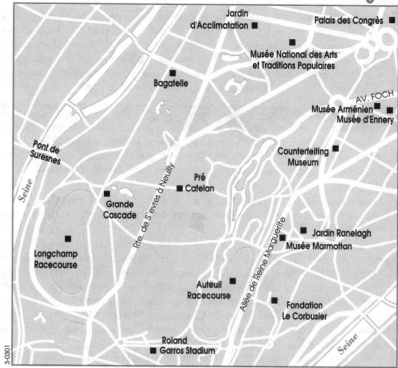

Two racetracks, **Longchamp** and **Auteuil,** are in the park. The annual Grand Prix is run in June at Longchamp (the site of a medieval abbey). Fashionable Parisians always turn out for this, the women in their finest haute couture. Directly to the north of Longchamp is the *Grand Cascade,* the artificial waterfall of the Bois de Boulogne.

In the western section of the Bois de Boulogne, the 60-acre **Bagatelle Park** owes it existence to a bet between the Comte d'Artois (later Charles X) and Marie Antoinette, his sister-in-law. The Comte wagered that he could erect a small palace in less than 3 months. He hired nearly 1,000 craftsmen and irritated the local populace by requisitioning all shipments of stone and plaster arriving through the west gates of Paris. He hired cabinetmakers, painters, and the Scottish landscape architect Thomas Blaikie—and he won his bet. If you're in Paris in late April, it's worth visiting the Bagatelle just for the **tulips.** In late May, one of the finest and best-known rose collections in all of Europe is in full bloom. For some reason, as the head gardener confides to us, "This is the major rendezvous point in Paris for illicit couples." In September the light is less harsh than summer or even in February; when stripped of much of its greenery, the park's true shape can be seen.

PARC MONCEAU   Much of the Parc Monceau, 8e (☎ **01-42-27-39-56;** Métro: Monceau or Villiers), is ringed with 18th- and 19th-century mansions, some evoking Proust's *Remembrance of Things Past.* The park was opened to the public in the days of Napoléon III's Second Empire. It was built in 1778 by the duke of Orléans, or Philippe-Egalité, as he became known. Carmontelle designed the park for the duke, who was at the time the richest man in France. "Philip Equality" was noted for his debauchery and pursuit of pleasure, so no ordinary park would do.

Monceau was laid out with an Egyptian-style obelisk, a medieval dungeon, a thatched alpine farmhouse, a Chinese pagoda, a Roman temple, an enchanted grotto, various chinoiseries, and, of course, a waterfall. These fairy-tale touches have largely disappeared, except for a pyramid and an oval naumachia fringed by a colonnade. Now the park is filled with solid statuary and monuments, one honoring Chopin. In spring, the red tulips and magnolias are worth the air ticket to Paris.

9 Cemeteries

The cemeteries of Paris are often viewed by sightseers as being somewhat like parks, suitable places for strolling. The graves of celebrities past also lure the sightseers. Père-Lachaise, for example, is a major sightseeing goal in Paris; the other cemeteries are of lesser interest.

✪ **Cimetière du Père-Lachaise.** 16 rue du Repos, 20e. ☎ **01-43-70-70-33.** Free admission. Mon–Fri 8am–6pm, Sat 8:30am–6pm, Sun 9am–6pm; closes at 5:30pm from early Nov to early Mar. Métro: Père-Lachaise.

When it comes to name-dropping, this cemetery knows no peer; it's been called the "grandest address in Paris." Everybody from Sarah Bernhardt to Oscar Wilde was buried here. So were Balzac, Delacroix, and Bizet. The body of Colette was taken here in 1954, and in time the little sparrow, Piaf, would follow. The lover of George Sand, the poet Alfred de Musset, was buried here under a weeping willow. Napoléon's marshals, Ney and Masséna, lie here, as do Chopin and Molière. Marcel Proust's black tombstone rarely lacks a tiny bunch of violets. Colette's black granite slab always sports flowers, and legend has it that cats replenish the red roses.

Some tombs are sentimental favorites: Lovetorn graffiti radiates a half-mile from the tomb of singer Jim Morrison. The great dancer Isadora Duncan came to rest in the columbarium where bodies have been cremated and "filed" away. If you search hard enough, you can find the tombs of that star-crossed pair Abélard and Héloïse, the ill-fated lovers of the 12th century. At Père-Lachaise they have found peace at last. Other famous lovers also rest here: A stone is marked "Alice B. Toklas" on one side, "Gertrude Stein" on the other. The grave site that attracted the most attention in 1998 was that of entertainer Yves Montand. His corpse was exhumed in the middle of the night for DNA testing in a paternity lawsuit.

Spreading over more than 110 acres, Père-Lachaise was acquired by the city of Paris in 1804. Nineteenth-century sculpture abounds, each family trying to outdo the other in ornamentation and cherubic ostentation. Frenchmen who died in the Resistance or in Nazi concentration camps are also honored by monuments here. Some French Socialists still pay tribute at the **Mur des Fédérés,** the anonymous grave site of the Communards who were executed in the cemetery on May 28, 1871. When these last-ditch fighters of the Paris Commune, the world's first anarchist republic, made their final desperate stand against the troops of the French government, they were overwhelmed, lined up against the wall, and shot in groups. A handful survived and lived hidden in the cememtery for years like wild animals, venturing into Paris at night to forage for food.

Map to Père-Lachaise

A free map of Père-Lachaise is available at the newsstand across from the main entrance. See also the map on page 206.

Impressions

Mrs. Allongby: They say, Lady Hunstanton, that when good Americans die they go to Paris.

Lady Hunstanton: Indeed? And when bad Americans die, where do they go?

Lord Illingworth: Oh, they go to America.

—Oscar Wilde, *A Woman of No Importance*, 1893

Cimetière du Montparnasse. 3 bd. Edgar-Quinet, 14e. ☎ **01-44-10-86-50.** Free admission. Mon–Sat 8am–5:45pm, Sun 9am–5:45pm; closes at 5:15pm Nov–Mar. Métro: Edgar-Quinet.

In the shadow of the Tour Montparnasse, this debris-littered cemetery is a burial ground of yesterday's celebrities. A map available to the left of the main gateway will direct you to the shared grave site of its most famous couple, Simone de Beauvoir and Jean-Paul Sartre. Others resting here include Samuel Beckett, Guy de Maupassant, editor Pierre Larousse (famous for his dictionary), and Alfred Dreyfus. The auto tycoon André Citroën is also interred here, as are sculptors Ossip Zadkine and Constantin Brancusi, composer Camille Saint-Saëns, Man Ray, the famous surrealist photographer and familiar figure in the cafes of Montparnasse, and Charles Baudelaire, who had already written about "plunging into the abyss, Heaven or Hell."

Cimetière St-Vincent. 6 rue Lucien-Gaulard, 18e. ☎ **01-46-06-29-78.** Free admission. Mar 16–Nov 5 daily 8am–6pm; Nov 6–Mar 15 daily 8am–5:30pm. Métro: Lamarck-Caulaincourt.

Along this street lies the modest burial ground of St-Vincent, with a view of Sacré-Coeur on the hill. Because of the artists and writers who have their final resting place here, it is sometimes called "the most intellectual cemetery of Paris," but that epithet seems more apt for other graveyards. The artists Maurice Utrillo (1883 to 1955) and Théopile-Alexandre Steinien (1859 to 1923) were buried here, as was the musician Arthur Honegger. The writer Marcel Aymé came to rest here, too. In theory, the cemetery is open all day, but if you try to disturb the caretaker's lunch—any time from noon to 2pm—you'll regret it.

Cimetière de Passy. 2 rue du Comandant-Schloesing, 16e. ☎ **01-47-27-51-42.** Free admission. Mar–Nov 8:30am–5:45pm; Dec–Feb 8:30am–5:15pm. Métro: Trocadéro.

This cemetery runs along the old northern walls of Paris, south and southwest of Trocadéro. It's a small graveyard, sheltered by a bower of chestnut trees, but it contains many grave sites of the famous—a concierge at the gate can guide you. The painter Edouard Manet was buried here, as was Claude Debussy. Many great literary figures since 1850 were interred here, including Tristan Bernard, Giraudoux, and Croisset. Also resting here are composer Gabriel Fauré, aviator Henry Farman, and actor Fernandel. Natalie Barney, high priestess of the city's most famous literary salon, is buried here, along with Renée Vivien, one of her many lovers, and the painter Romaine Brooks.

Cimetière de Montmartre. 20 av. Rachel, 18e. ☎ **01-43-87-64-24.** Free admission. Mon–Fri 8am–6pm, Sat 8:30am–6pm, Sun 8am–6pm; closes at 5:30pm in winter. Métro: Blanche or Place Clichy.

This cemetery, dating from 1795, lies west of Montmartre and north of the boulevard de Clichy. The Russian dancer Nijinsky and novelist Alexandre Dumas the Younger are

The Père-Lachaise Cemetery

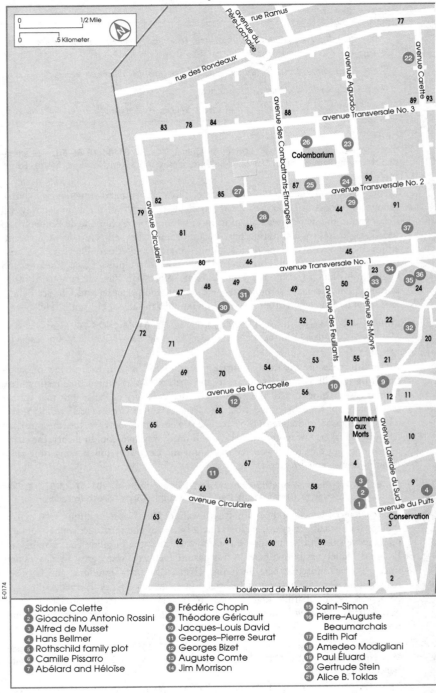

1. Sidonie Colette
2. Gioacchino Antonio Rossini
3. Alfred de Musset
4. Hans Bellmer
5. Rothschild family plot
6. Camille Pissarro
7. Abélard and Héloïse
8. Frédéric Chopin
9. Théodore Géricault
10. Jacques–Louis David
11. Georges–Pierre Seurat
12. Georges Bizet
13. Auguste Comte
14. Jim Morrison
15. Saint–Simon
16. Pierre–Auguste Beaumarchais
17. Edith Piaf
18. Amedeo Modigliani
19. Paul Éluard
20. Gertrude Stein
21. Alice B. Toklas

E-0174

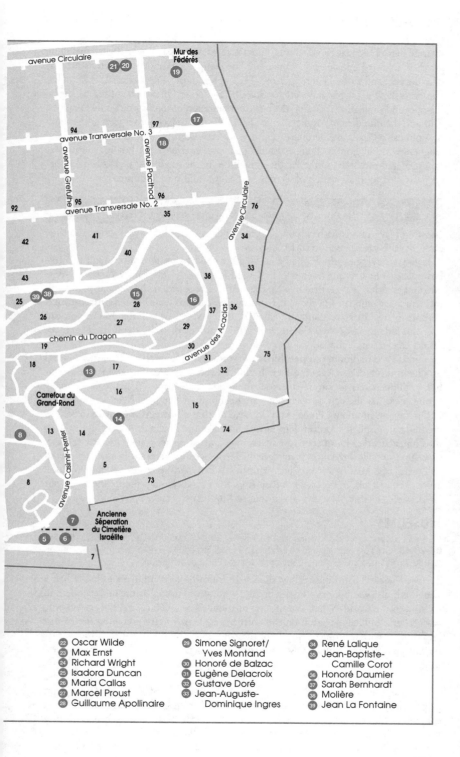

avenue Circulaire

Mur des Fédérés

avenue Transversale No. 3

avenue Gretuline

avenue Pacthod

avenue Circulaire

avenue Transversale No. 2

avenue des Acacias

chemin du Dragon

Carrefour du Grand-Rond

avenue Casimir-Perrier

Ancienne Séperation du Cimetière Israélite

22	Oscar Wilde	29	Simone Signoret/	34	René Lalique
23	Max Ernst		Yves Montand	35	Jean-Baptiste-
24	Richard Wright	30	Honoré de Balzac		Camille Corot
25	Isadora Duncan	31	Eugène Delacroix	36	Honoré Daumier
26	Maria Callas	32	Gustave Doré	37	Sarah Bernhardt
27	Marcel Proust	33	Jean-Auguste-	38	Molière
28	Guillaume Apollinaire		Dominique Ingres	39	Jean La Fontaine

interred here. The great Stendhal was buried here, as were lesser literary lights, including novelists Edmond and Jules de Goncourt. The composer Hector Berlioz rests here, as does the poet and writer Heinrich Heine. The impressionist painter Edgar Degas still has fans who show up at his grave site, as does the composer Offenbach. Alfred de Vigny, the poet and dramatist, is among the buried; a more recent tombstone honors François Truffaut, the film director of the *nouvelle vague.* We like to pay our respects at the tomb of Alphonsine Plessis, the heroine of *La dame aux camélias,* and Madame Récamier, who taught the world how to lounge. Émile Zola was interred here, but his corpse was exhumed and promoted to the Panthéon in 1908. In the tragic year of 1871, the cemetery was used for mass burials of victims of the Siege and the Commune.

10 Especially for Kids

Boasting playgrounds with tiny merry-go-rounds and gondola-style swings, the large parks of Paris are always a treat for kids.

If you're staying on the Right Bank, take the children for a stroll through the **Tuileries** (see "The Champs-Elysées: The Grand Promenade" in chapter 7), where there are donkey rides, ice-cream stands, and a marionette show; at the circular pond, you can rent a toy sailboat. On the Left Bank, similar delights exist in the **Jardin du Luxembourg** (see "Parks & Gardens," above). After a visit to the Eiffel Tower, you can take the kids for a donkey ride in the nearby gardens of the **Champ-de-Mars** (see "Parks & Gardens," above).

A great Paris tradition, **puppet shows** are worth seeing for their enthusiastic, colorful productions—they're a genuine French child's experience. At the Jardin du Luxembourg, puppets reenact sinister plots set in Gothic castles and Oriental palaces; many young critics say the best puppet shows are held in the Champ-de-Mars.

On Sunday afternoon, French families head up to the **Butte Montmartre** to bask in the fiesta atmosphere. You can join in the fun: Take the Métro to Anvers and walk to the Funiculaire de Montmartre (the silver cable car that carries you up to Sacré-Coeur). Once up top, follow the crowds to place du Tertre, where a Sergeant Pepper–style band will usually be blasting off-key and you can have the kids' pictures sketched by local artists. You can take in the views of Paris from the various vantage points and treat your children to ice cream. (For a walking tour of Montmartre, see chapter 7.)

MUSEUMS

Cité des Sciences et de l'Industrie. La Villette, 30 av. Corentine-Cariou, 19e. ☎ **01-40-05-70-48.** Cité Pass (entrance to all exhibits) 50 F ($8.50) adults, free to children 7 and under; Géode 25 F ($4.25). Tues–Sun 10am–6pm. Métro: Porte de la Villette.

A city of science and industry has risen here from the most unlikely ashes. When a slaughterhouse was built on the site in the 1960s, it was touted as the most modern of its kind in the world. When the site was abandoned as a failure in 1974, its echoing vastness and unlikely location on the northern edge of the city presented the French government with a problem. In 1986, the converted premises opened as the world's most expensive ($642 million) science complex, designed to "modernize mentalities" in the service of modernizing society.

The place is so vast, with so many exhibits, that a single visit gives only an idea of the scope of the Cité. Busts of Plato, Hippocrates, and a double-faced Janus gaze silently at a tube-filled, space-age riot of high-tech girders, glass, and lights— something like the way you might imagine the inside of an atomic generator or a futuristic airplane hangar. The sheer dimensions of the place pose a challenge to the curators of its constantly changing exhibits. Some exhibits are couched in Gallic humor—imagine using the comic-strip adventures of a jungle explorer to explain seismographic activity. **Explora,** a permanent exhibit, occupies the three upper levels of the building, examining four themes: the universe, life, matter, and communication.

The Cité also has a multimedia library, a planetarium, and an "inventorium" for children. The silver-skinned **geodesic dome** called the *Géode*—a 112-foot-high sphere with a 370-seat theater—projects the closest thing to a 3-D cinema in Europe.

The Cité is in **Parc de la Villette,** the city's largest park, with 136 acres of greenery—twice the size of the Tuileries. Here you'll find a belvedere, a video workshop for children, and information about exhibitions and events, along with a cafe and restaurant.

Musée de la Musique. 221 av. Jean-Jaurès, 19e. ☎ **01-44-84-45-00.** Admission 35 F ($5.95) adults, 25 F ($4.25) students and age 60 and over, 10 F ($1.70) age 17 and under. Visits with commentary, 60 F ($10.20) adults, 45 F ($7.65) students and age 60 and over, 20 F ($3.40) age 17 and under. Tues–Thurs noon–6pm, Fri–Sat 10am–7:30pm, Sun 10am–6pm. Métro: Porte-de-Pantin.

Situated within the $120 million stone-and-glass Cité de la Musique, this museum serves as a tribute and testament to music. Visitors can view 4,500 instruments primarily from the 17th century to the present as well as paintings, engravings, and sculptures that all relate to musical history. It's all here: cornets disguised as snakes, antique music boxes, even a postwar electric guitar. One especially appealing section covers the 16th century, with mandolins, lutes, and zithers. Models of the world's great concert halls and interactive display areas give visitors a chance to hear and better understand musical art and technology.

Musée Grévin. 10 bd. Montmartre, 9e. ☎ **01-47-70-85-05.** Admission 55 F ($9.35) adults, 36 F ($6.10) children 14 and under. Apr–Aug daily 1–7pm; Sept–Mar daily 1–6:30pm; school holidays daily 10am–7pm. Ticket office closes 1 hour before museum. Métro: Rue Montmartre.

Grévin is the number one waxworks of Paris. Comparisons to Madame Tussaud's of London are almost irresistible. It isn't all blood and gore, and doesn't shock as much as Tussaud's might. It presents a panorama of French history in a series of tableaux.

Depicted are the consecration of Charles VII in 1429 in the Cathedral of Reims (Joan of Arc, dressed in armor and carrying her standard, stands behind the king); Marguerite de Valois, first wife of Henri IV, meeting on a secret stairway with La Molle, who was soon to be decapitated; Catherine de Médicis with the Florentine alchemist Ruggieri; Louis XV and Mozart at the home of the marquise de Pompadour; and Napoléon on a rock at St. Helena, reviewing his victories and defeats.

There are also displays of contemporary sports and political figures, as well as 50 of the world's best-loved film stars. Two shows are staged frequently throughout the day. The first, called the **Palais des Mirages,** starts off as a sort of Temple of Brahma, and through magically distorting mirrors changes into an enchanted forest, then a fete at the Alhambra at Granada. A magician is the star of the second show, **Le Cabinet Fantastique;** he entertains children of all ages.

Musée de la Marine. In the Palais de Chaillot, place du Trocadéro, 16e. ☎ **01-53-65-69-69.** Admission 38 F ($6.45) adults, 25 F ($4.25) ages 8–25 and over 65, free for children 7 and under. Wed–Mon 10am–5:30pm. Métro: Trocadéro.

If your children have saltwater in their veins, you may want to take them to this museum. A lot here is pomp: gilded galleys and busts of stiff-necked admirals. Old ship models abound, including the big galley *La Réale,* the *Royal-Louis,* the rich ivory model *Ville de Dieppe,* the gorgeous *Valmy,* and a barge constructed in 1811 for Napoléon I, which was used to carry another Napoléon (the Third) and his empress, Eugénie, on their first visit to the port of Brest in about 1858. Winged cherubs hold up the imperial crown.

There are many documents and artifacts concerning merchant fishing and pleasure fleets, oceanography, and hydrography, with films illustrating the subjects. Thematic exhibits explain ancient wooden shipbuilding; the development of scientific instruments; merchant navy, fishing, steam, and sea traditions; and show some souvenirs of explorer Laperouse's wreck on Vanikoro Island in 1788. Important paintings include Joseph Vernet's *The Ports of France.*

Musée National d'Histoire Naturelle (Museum of Natural History). 57 rue Cuvier, 5e. ☎ **01-40-79-30-00.** Admission 30 F ($5.10) adults, 20 F ($3.40) children 4–16, free for children 3 and under. Apr–Sept Wed–Mon 10am–6pm; off-season Wed–Mon 10am–5pm. Métro: Jussieu or Gare d'Austerlitz.

This museum in the Jardin des Plantes has a wide range of science and nature exhibits that draw the children of Paris. It was founded in 1635 as a scientific research center by Guy de la Brosse, physician to Louis XIII. The museum's Grande Gallery of Evolution recently received a $90 million restoration. At the entrance, an 85-foot-long skeleton of a whale greets visitors. One display containing the skeletons of dinosaurs and mastodons is dedicated to endangered and vanished species. The museum also houses galleries that specialize in the fields of paleontology, anatomy, mineralogy, and botany. Within the museum's grounds are tropical hothouses containing thousands of species of unusual plant life and a menagerie with small animal life in simulated natural habitats.

AN AMUSEMENT PARK

Jardin d'Acclimation. Bois de Boulogne, 16e. ☎ **01-40-67-90-82.** Admission 13 F ($2.20), free for children 3 and under. Daily 10am–6pm. Métro: Sablons.

The definitive children's park in Paris is the Jardin d'Acclimation, a 25-acre amusement park in the northern part of the Bois de Boulogne. This is the kind of place that satisfies tykes and adults alike, but teenagers will dismiss. The visit starts with a ride from Porte Maillot to the Jardin entrance, through a stretch of wooded park, on a jaunty green-and-yellow narrow-gauge train. (The train operates only on Wednesday, Saturday, and Sunday from 1:30pm until the park closes. A one-way fare costs 6 F [$1].) En route you will discover a house of mirrors, an archery range, a miniature-golf course, zoo animals, an American-style bowling alley, a puppet theater (performances are only on Thursday, Saturday, Sunday, and holidays), a playground, a hurdle-racing course, and a whole conglomerate of junior-scale rides, shooting galleries, and waffle stalls. Inside the gate is an easy-to-follow layout map. The park is circular—follow the road in either direction and it will take you all the way around and bring you back to the train at the end.

You can trot the kids off on a pony or join them in a boat on a mill-stirred lagoon. Also fun to watch, and a superb idea, is **La Prévention Routière,** a miniature roadway operated by the Paris police. The youngsters drive through in small cars equipped to start and stop and are required by two genuine Parisian gendarmes to obey all street signs and light changes.

A ZOO

Parc Zoologique de Paris. Bois de Vincennes, 53 av. de St-Maurice, 12e. ☎ **01-44-75-20-00.** Admission 40 F ($6.80) adults, 30 F ($5.10) children 4–15, students 16–25, and over 60, free for chidren 3 and under. Daily 9am–6pm (until 5:30pm Dec–Mar). Métro: Porte Dorée or Château de Vincennes.

There's a modest zoo in the Jardin des Plantes, but without a doubt, the best zoo this city has to offer is in the Bois de Vincennes on the southeastern outskirts of Paris, quickly reachable by Métro. Many of this modern zoo's animals live in settings similar to their natural habitat, hemmed in by rock barriers, not bars or cages. Here you'll never see an animal in a cage too small for it. The lion has an entire veldt to himself, and you can lock eyes comfortably across a deep protective moat. On a cement mountain reminiscent of Disneyland's Matterhorn, exotic breeds of mountain goats and sheep leap from ledge to ledge or pose gracefully for hours watching the penguins in their pools at the mountain's foot. The animals seem happy and are playful. Keep well back from the bear pools or you might get wet.

11 Literary Landmarks

If there's a literary bone in your body, you'll feel a vicarious thrill on discovering the haunts of the famous writers and artists who have lived, worked, and played in Paris. Take the Métro to place St-Michel to begin your tour. As you wander away from the Seine, you'll encounter **rue de la Huchette,** one of the most famous streets on the Left Bank. Its inhabitants were immortalized in Eliot Paul's *The Last Time I Saw Paris.* Continuing into the Left Bank, you enter the territory of the Beat Generation, home to the **Café Gentilhomme,** described by Jack Kerouac in *Satori in Paris.* Allen Ginsberg's favorite, the **Hôtel du Vieux-Paris,** still attracts those in search of the Beats.

Stroll down **rue Monsieur-le-Prince,** the "Yankee alleyway," where Richard Wright, James McNeill Whistler, Henry Wadsworth Longfellow, and Oliver Wendell Holmes all lived at one time or another. During a famous visit in 1959, Martin Luther King Jr. came to call on Richard Wright, the Mississippi-born African American novelist famous for *Native Son.* King climbed to the third-floor apartment at no. 14, only to find that Wright's opinions on the civil rights movement conflicted with his own. Whistler rented a studio at no. 22, and, in 1826, Longfellow lived for a short time at no. 49. Oliver Wendell Holmes Sr. lived at no. 55. After strolling along this street, you can dine at the former haunts of Kerouac and Hemingway. (See our recommendation of **Crémerie-Restaurant Polidor,** 41 rue Monsieur-le-Prince, 6e, in chapter 5.) Or cross back over to the Right Bank for a drink at the famed **Hôtel de Crillon,** where heroine Brett Ashley broke her promise to rendezvous with Jake Barnes in Hemingway's *The Sun Also Rises.* Zelda and F. Scott Fitzgerald lifted their glasses here as well.

See also "Literary Haunts" in chapter 9.

Deux-Magots. 170 bd. St-Germain, 6e. ☎ **01-45-48-55-25.** Métro: St-Germain-des-Prés.

This long-established watering hole of St-Germain-des-Prés is where Jake Barnes meets Lady Brett in Hemingway's *The Sun Also Rises.* See "The Best Cafes" in chapter 5.

Harry's New York Bar. 5 rue Daunou, 2e. ☎ **01-42-61-71-14.** Métro: Opéra or Pyramides.

F. Scott Fitzgerald and Ernest Hemingway went on frequent benders here, Gloria Swanson gossiped about her affair with Joseph Kennedy, and even Gertrude Stein deigned to show herself from time to time. The place is still going strong (see chapter 9).

Maison de Balzac. 47 rue Raynouard, 16e. ☎ **01-42-24-56-38.** Admission 17.50 F ($3) adults, 9 F ($1.55) children and over age 60. Tues–Sun 10am–5:40pm. Métro: Passy or La Muette.

In the residential district of Passy, near the Bois de Boulogne, sits a modest house where the great Balzac lived for 7 years beginning in 1840. He fled here, cloaking

Impressions

And so I am an American and I have lived half my life in Paris, not the half that made me but the half in which I made what I made.

—Gertrude Stein, *An American and France,* 1936

himself in secrecy, after his possessions and furnishings were seized—to see him, you had to know a password. If a creditor knocked on the Raynouard door, Balzac was able to escape through the rue Berton exit.

The museum's most notable memento is Balzac's "screech-owl" (his nickname for his tea kettle), which he kept hot throughout the night as he wrote *La Comédie Humaine* to forestall his creditors. Also enshrined here are Balzac's writing desk and chair, and a library of special interest to scholars.

The little house is filled with reproduced caricatures of Balzac. A French biographer once wrote: "With his bulky baboon silhouette, his blue suit with gold buttons, his famous cane like a golden crowbar, and his abundant, disheveled hair, Balzac was a sight for caricature."

The house is built on the slope of a hill, with a small courtyard and garden.

Maison de Victor Hugo. 6 place des Vosges, 4e. ☎ **01-42-72-10-16.** Admission 17.50 F ($3) adults, 9 F ($1.55) ages 19–25, free for age 18 and under. Tues–Sun 10am–5:40pm. Closed national holidays. Métro: St-Paul, Bastille, or Chemin-Vert.

Today theater goers who saw *Les Misérables*, even those who haven't read anything by Paris's great 19th-century novelist, come to place des Vosges to see where he lived and wrote. Some thought Hugo (1802 to 1885) a genius, but Cocteau called him a madman, and an American composer discovered that in his old age he was carving furniture with his teeth! From 1832 to 1848, the novelist and poet lived on the second floor of the old Hôtel Rohan Guéménée, built in 1610 on what was then the place Royale. The museum owns some of Hugo's furniture as well as pieces that once belonged to Juliette Drouet, the mistress with whom he lived in exile on Guernsey, one of the Channel Islands.

Worth the visit are Hugo's drawings, more than 450, illustrating scenes from his own works. Mementos of the great writer abound, including samples of his handwriting, his inkwell, and first editions of his works. A painting of Hugo's funeral procession at the Arc de Triomphe in 1885 is on display, as are plentiful portraits and souvenirs of his family. Of the furnishings, a chinoiserie salon stands out. The collection even contains Daumier caricatures and a bust of Hugo by David d'Angers, which, compared to Rodin's, looks saccharine.

Le Procope. 13 rue de l'Ancienne-Comédie, 6e. ☎ **01-40-46-79-00.** Métro: Odéon.

Dating from 1686, this is the oldest cafe in Paris. It's located in St-Germain-des-Prés and was the restaurant of choice for such historical figures as Franklin and Jefferson. Writers from Diderot, Voltaire, George Sand, Victor Hugo, and Oscar Wilde all stopped by in their day as well (see chapter 5).

La Rotonde. 105 bd. Montparnasse, 6e. ☎ **01-43-26-68-84.** Métro: Raspail.

When they had money, Americans tended to drink on the Right Bank, notably in the Ritz Bar. When they didn't, they headed for one of the cafes of Montparnasse, which, according to Hemingway, usually meant La Rotonde. See "The Best Cafes" in chapter 5.

Shakespeare and Company. 37 rue de la Bûcherie, 5e. No phone. Daily 11am–midnight. Métro: St-Michel.

The most famous bookstore on the Left Bank was Shakespeare and Company, on rue de l'Odéon, home to the legendary Sylvia Beach, "mother confessor to the Lost Generation." Hemingway, Fitzgerald, and Gertrude Stein were all frequent patrons. Anaïs Nin, the diarist noted for her description of struggling American artists in 1930s Paris, also stopped in often. At one point, she helped her companion, Henry Miller, publish

Tropic of Cancer, a book so notorious in its day that returning Americans trying to slip a copy through Customs often had it confiscated as pornography. (When times were hard, Nin herself wrote pornography for a dollar a page.) Long ago, the shop moved to rue de la Bûcherie, a musty old place where expatriates still swap books and literary gossip, and foreign students work in exchange for modest lodgings. Check out the lending library upstairs.

12 Paris Underground

Les Catacombs. 1 place Denfert-Rochereau, 14e. ☎ **01-43-22-47-63.** Admission 27 F ($4.60) adults, 19 F ($3.25) ages 7–25 and students, free for children 6 and under. Tues–Fri 2–4pm, Sat–Sun 9–11am and 2–4pm. Métro: Denfert-Rochereau.

Every year an estimated 50,000 tourists explore some 1,000 yards of tunnel in these dank Catacombs to look at six million ghoulishly arranged skull-and-crossbones skeletons. First opened to the public in 1810, this "empire of the dead" is now illuminated with overhead electric lights over its entire length.

In the Middle Ages, the Catacombs were quarries, but by the end of the 18th century, overcrowded Parisian cemeteries were becoming a menace to the public health. City officials decided to use the Catacombs as a burial ground, and the bones of several million persons were transferred here. In 1830, the prefect of Paris closed the Catacombs to the viewing public, considering them obscene and indecent. He maintained that he could not understand the morbid curiosity of civilized people who wanted to gaze upon the bones of the dead. In World War II, the Catacombs were the headquarters of the French Resistance.

Les Egouts (The Sewers of Paris). Pont de l'Alma, 7e. ☎ **01-53-68-27-81.** Admission 25 F ($4.25) adults, 20 F ($3.40) students and seniors, 15 F ($2.55) children 5–12, free for children under 5. May–Oct Sat–Wed 11am–5pm; Nov–Apr Sat–Wed 11am–4pm. Closed 3 weeks in Jan for maintenance. Métro: Alma-Marceau. RER: Pont de l'Alma.

Some sociologists assert that the sophistication of a society can be judged by the way it disposes of waste. If that's the case, Paris receives good marks for its mostly invisible network of sewers. Victor Hugo is credited with making these sewers famous in *Les Misérables:* Jean Valjean takes flight through them, "All dripping with slime, his soul filled with a strange light." Hugo also wrote, "Paris has beneath it another Paris, a Paris of sewers, which has its own streets, squares, lanes, arteries, and circulation."

In the early Middle Ages, drinking water was taken directly from the Seine, and wastewater was poured onto fields or thrown onto the then-unpaved streets, transforming the urban landscape into a sea of rather smelly mud.

Around 1200, the streets of Paris were paved with cobblestones, with open sewers running down the center of each. These open sewers helped spread the Black Death, which devastated the city. In 1370, a vaulted sewer was built in the rue Montmartre, draining effluents directly into a tributary of the Seine. During the reign of Louis XIV, improvements were made, but the state of waste disposal in Paris remained deplorable.

In the early 1800s, under the reign of Napoléon I, 18½ miles of underground sewer were constructed beneath the Parisian landscape. By 1850, as the Industrial Revolution made the manufacture of iron pipe and steam-digging equipment more practical, Baron Haussmann developed a system that used separate underground channels for drinking water and sewage. By 1878, it was 360 miles long. Beginning in 1894, under the guidance of Belgrand, the network was enlarged, and new laws required that discharge of all waste and storm-water runoff be funneled into the sewers. Between 1914 and 1977, an additional 600 miles of sewers were added beneath the pavements of a burgeoning Paris.

Today, the network of sewers is 1,300 miles long. Within its cavities, it contains freshwater mains, compressed air pipes, telephone cables, and pneumatic tubes. Every day, 1.2 million cubic meters of wastewater are collected and processed by a plant in the Parisian suburb of Achères. One of the largest in Europe, it's capable of treating more than two million cubic meters of sewage per day.

The *égouts* of the city are constructed around four principal tunnels, one 18 feet wide and 15 feet high. As Hugo observed, it's like an underground city, with the street names clearly labeled. Further, each branch pipe bears the number of the building to which it is connected. These underground passages are truly mammoth.

Tours of the sewers begin at Pont de l'Alma on the Left Bank. A stairway here leads into the bowels of the city. However, you often have to wait in line as much as half an hour. Visiting times might change during bad weather, as a storm can make the sewers dangerous. The tour consists of a film on sewer history, a small museum visit, and then a short trip through the maze. Be warned that the smell is pretty bad, especially in the summer.

13 Organized Tours

BY BUS   Get-acquainted tours of Paris are offered by **Cityrama,** 147-149 rue Saint-Honoré, 1er (☎ **01-44-55-61-00;** Métro: Palais-Royal or Musée-du-Louvre). The company operates a fleet of double-decker red-and-yellow buses, each with oversized windows and a series of multilingual recorded commentaries that recite an overview of Paris's history and monuments. The most popular is a 2-hour tour that departs from the place des Pyramides, adjacent to the rue de Rivoli and the Tuileries Gardens, every day at 9:30am, 10:30am, 1:30pm, and 2:30pm. There are additional tours every Saturday and Sunday at 11:30am, and between March and October at 3:30 and 4:30pm daily. The price is 150 F ($25.50) per person. Other, more detailed tours are also available. They include a 3½-hour morning tour (Monday, Wednesday, Friday, and Saturday) to the interiors of Notre-Dame and the Louvre, priced at 295 F ($50.15) per person. There are 3½-hour morning tours to Versailles at 320 F ($54.40) per person and 3½-hour afternoon tours to Chartres at 275 F ($46.75) per person. You can buy tickets for both Versailles and Chartres for 500 F ($85). And if you're interested in a night tour of Paris to see how the City of Light got its name, tours depart every evening at 10pm in summer and at 7pm in winter, for 150 F ($25.50) per person.

CRUISES ON THE SEINE   A boat tour on the Seine provides sweeping vistas of the riverbanks and some of the best views of Notre-Dame. Many of the boats have open sundecks, bars, and restaurants. **Bateau-Mouche** cruises (☎ **01-42-25-96-10** for reservations, 01-40-76-99-99 for schedules; Métro: Alma-Marceau) depart from the Right Bank of the Seine, next to the Pont de l'Alma, and last about 75 minutes each. Tours leave every day at 20- to 30-minute intervals between May and October, beginning at 10am and ending at 11:30pm. Between November and April, there are at least nine departures every day between 11am and 9pm, with a schedule that changes frequently according to demand and the weather. Fares cost 40 F ($6.80) for adults and 20 F ($3.40) for children 5 to 15. Three-hour **dinner cruises** depart every evening at 8:30pm and cost between 500 F and 700 F ($85 and $119), depending on which of the set-price menus you order. Jackets and ties are required for men.

Some visitors prefer longer excursions along the Seine and its network of canals. The **Seine et le Canal Saint Martin** tour, offered by **Paris Canal, S.A.R.L.** (☎ **01-42-40-96-97**), requires advance reservations for 3-hour tours that begin at 9:30am at the quays in front of the Musée d'Orsay (Métro: Solférino) and at 2:30pm in front of the Cité des Sciences et de l'Industrie at Parc de la Villette (Métro: Porte de la Villette).

Excursions negotiate the waterways and canals of Paris, including the Seine, an underground tunnel below the place de la Bastille, and the Canal St-Martin. The cost is 100 F ($17) for adults, and free for children under 4. With the exception of excursions on Sunday and holidays, prices are usually reduced to 75 F ($12.75) for passengers ages 12 to 25 and over 60, and to 55 F ($9.35) for children 4 to 11. Tours are offered twice daily from mid-March to mid-November. The rest of the year, tours are offerd only on Sunday.

14 Special & Free Events in Paris

It won't cost you a franc to explore the streets of Paris. Walk along the quays of the Seine, and stop to browse through the shops and stalls. Each street opens onto a new vista.

If you're an early riser, a walk through Paris at dawn can be memorable; you'll see the city come to life. Storefronts are washed clean for the new day, cafes open, and vegetable vendors arrange their produce.

The spacious forecourt of the **Centre Georges Pompidou,** place Georges Pompidou, is a free "entertainment center" featuring mimes, fire-eaters, would-be circus performers, and sometimes first-rate musicians. Métro: Rambuteau or Hôtel-de-Ville.

In the corridors of the **Métro,** classical music students (often from the Conservatoire National) perform; a hat or violin case is passed for donations.

If you're in Paris during one of the major festivals, you can join in the fun on the streets for free. On **Summer Solstice** (June 21), during the **Fête de la Musique,** clowns, fire-eaters, and other performers roam the streets. On **Bastille Day** (July 14), the French traditionally drink wine and dance in the streets—fireworks are displayed, free concerts are given, and a parade of tanks heads down the Champs-Elysées.

For free Sunday-afternoon **organ concerts** in the city's old churches, check *Pariscope,* the guide to entertainment events.

Concerts featuring classical and contemporary music from the Netherlands are held at the **Institut Neerlandais,** 121 rue de Lille, 7e (☎ **01-53-59-12-40;** Métro: Assemblée-Nationale). The small-scale concerts are usually free, and rarely exceed 40 F ($6.80).

The **American Church,** 65 quai d'Orsay, 7e (☎ **01-40-62-05-00;** Métro: Invalides), presents free chamber-music concerts most Sundays at 6pm. Concerts are free, although there's a voluntary collection afterward to help defray costs.

15 A Day at the Races

Paris boasts an army of avid horse-racing fans who get to the city's eight racetracks whenever possible. Information on current races is available in such newspapers and magazines as *Tierce, Paris-Turf, France-Soir,* or *L'Equipe,* all sold at kiosks throughout the city.

The epicenter of Paris horse racing is the **Hippodrome de Longchamp,** Bois de Boulogne (☎ **01-44-30-75-00**). Established in 1855, during the autocratic but pleasure-loving reign of Napoléon III, it is the most prestigious, boasts the greatest number of promising thoroughbreds, and awards the largest purse in France. The most important events at Longchamp are **Le Grand Prix de Paris** in late June and the **Prix de l'Arc de Triomphe** in early October. Métro: Auteuil, then take one of the shuttle buses that operate on race days.

Another horse-racing venue is the **Hippodrome d'Auteuil,** also in the Bois de Boulogne (☎ **01-40-71-47-47**). Known for its steeplechases and obstacle courses, it sometimes attracts more than 50,000 Parisians at a time. Spectators appreciate the park's open-air promenades as much as they do the equestrian events. Established in 1870, the event is scattered over a sprawling 30 acres of parkland. It's designed to show to maximum advantage the skill and agility of both horses and riders. Races are conducted between early March and late December. Métro: Auteuil.

Also popular, though rough around the edges, is the **Hippodrome de Vincennes,** 12 route de la Ferme, Bois de Vincennes, 12e (☎ **01-49-77-17-17**). It holds most of its racing events under floodlights during evening hours in midwinter. Métro: Château de Vincennes.

Strolling Around Paris

The best way to discover Paris is on foot, using your own shoe leather. This chapter highlights the attractions of the Grand Promenade, Montmartre, the Latin Quarter, and the Marais.

Walking Tour 1
The Champs-Elysées:
The Grand Promenade of Paris

Start: Arc de Triomphe.
Finish: Place Vendôme.
Time: 3 leisurely hours; the distance is 2 miles.
Best Time: Sunday morning.
Worst Time: Rush hour.

In 1891, that "Innocent Abroad," Mark Twain, called the Champs-Elysées "the liveliest street in the world." It was designed for that favored pastime of Parisians, promenading. (It's perhaps a little too innocent to rank walking as Parisians' number one pastime, but surely it comes in second or third.) Nowadays, tourists follow the old Parisian tradition; Americans who would normally drive half a block to the drugstore are seen doing the sprint from place Charles-de-Gaulle–Etoile to place de la Concorde. You won't really know Paris until you've done it. (And it's even lovelier at night.)

In late 1995, after two hard, dusty, and expensive years of construction, Paris's most prominent triumphal promenade was reinaugurated with several important improvements. The contre-allées (constantly clogged side lanes) were removed, new lighting was added, pedestrian sidewalks widened, new trees planted, and underground parking garages built to rid the neighborhood of its curse: too many parked cars. The Grand Promenade is grand once again.

This is a lengthy walking tour, but it's the most popular walk in Paris. Start at the:

1. **Arc de Triomphe** (Métro: Charles-de-Gaulle–Etoile). To reach it, don't try to cross the square, the busiest traffic hub in Paris. Take the underground passage and live a little longer. For more on the long, vivid history of the Arc, turn to "The Top Attractions" in chapter 6.

Walking Tour 1: The Grand Promenade

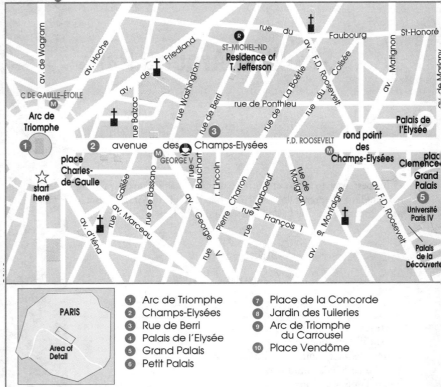

PARIS

Area of Detail

1. Arc de Triomphe
2. Champs-Elysées
3. Rue de Berri
4. Palais de l'Elysée
5. Grand Palais
6. Petit Palais
7. Place de la Concorde
8. Jardin des Tuileries
9. Arc de Triomphe du Carrousel
10. Place Vendôme

Stand here a moment (somewhere safe from traffic) and gaze down the long:

2. Champs-Elysées, which has been called "the highway of French grandeur." This avenue has witnessed some of the greatest moments in French history and some of the worst, such as when Hitler's army paraded down the street in 1940. Louis XIV ordered construction of the 1.1-mile avenue in 1667. Originally called the Grand-Cour and designed by Le Nôtre, it was renamed Champs-Elysées after the Elysian fields (the home of the virtuous dead) in 1709.

Stroll along the avenue. Along one stretch, it's a chestnut-lined park; on the other, a commercial avenue of sidewalk cafes, automobile showrooms, airline offices, cinemas, lingerie stores, and hamburger joints. To chronicle the people who have walked this broad avenue would be to tell the history of Paris through the last few centuries. Ever since the days of Thomas Jefferson and Benjamin Franklin, Americans have gravitated here, and even if the avenue has lost some of its turn-of-the-century elegance, it still hums like a hive.

☕ **TAKE A BREAK** Make it **Fouquet's,** 99 av. des Champs-Elysées (☎ **01-47-23-70-60**). Founded in 1901 and still serving coffee, wine, and food, this is an institution. In summer you can enjoy the flowers, and in winter the large glass windows will shelter you from the winds. Take plenty of money.

Head down the avenue toward place de la Concorde, staying on the left-hand side. When you reach:

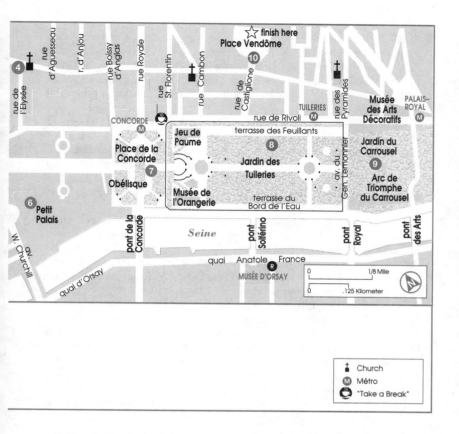

3. **Rue de Berri,** turn left to no. 20, site of Thomas Jefferson's residence from 1785 to 1789, when he was fledgling America's Minister to France. In its place today is a large apartment building. Back on the avenue again, continue to the Rond-Pont des Champs-Elysées, the dividing point between the avenue's park and commercial sections. Close by is a philatelist's delight, the best-known open-air stamp market in Europe, held Thursday and Sunday.

Continue down the avenue until you reach avenue Winston-Churchill on your right (from here there's a good panorama looking toward the Invalides). Ducking traffic and pausing for a view, cross back over to the other side of the Champs and turn down the avenue de Marigny. On your right will be the:

4. **Palais de l'Elysée,** France's presidential palace, whose main entrance is along fashionable Faubourg St-Honoré. Now occupied by the president of France, it cannot be visited without an invitation.

Built in 1718 for the Count d'Evreux, the palace had many owners before it was purchased by the Republic in 1873. One owner was Madame de Pompadour, who, when she "had the supreme delicacy to die discreetly at the age of 43," bequeathed it to the king. After her divorce from Napoléon, Josephine lived here, as did Napoléon III when he was president, beginning in 1848. When he became emperor in 1852, he moved to the Tuileries. Such celebrated English visitors as Queen Victoria and Wellington have spent nights here as well.

Now backtrack to the meeting of the Champs-Elysées and avenue Winston-Churchill, where you'll find the:

5. **Grand Palais,** which was constructed for the World Exhibition of 1900. When it's restored, the Grand Palais will be devoted to special exhibitions concerning Paris at the millennium. Also constructed for the 1900 World Exhibition was the:
6. **Petit Palais** (☎ 01-42-65-12-73), which contains a hodgepodge of works of art belonging to the city of Paris. (See "The Major Museums" in chapter 6 for a full description.)

    Postponing a visit for the moment, continue along the Champs-Elysées until you come to the landmark:
7. **Place de la Concorde,** an octagonal traffic hub built in 1757 to honor Louis XV. The statue of the king was torn down in 1792 and the name of the square changed to place de la Révolution. Floodlit at night, it is dominated nowadays by an Egyptian obelisk from Luxor, the oldest man-made object in Paris. It was carved circa 1200 B.C. and spirited out of French-dominated Egypt in 1829.

    In the Reign of Terror, the dreaded guillotine was erected on this spot, where it claimed the lives of thousands, everybody from Louis XVI, who died bravely, to Madame du Barry, who went screaming and kicking all the way. Marie Antoinette, Robespierre, Danton, Madame Roland, and Charlotte Corday were executed here in front of leering crowds. (You can still lose your life on the place de la Concorde if you chance the traffic and cross over.)

    For a spectacular sight, look down the Champs-Elysées, where the Marly horses frame the view. On the opposite side, the winged horses of Coysevox flank the gateway to the Tuileries. On each side of the obelisk are two fountains with bronze-tailed mermaids and bare-breasted sea nymphs. Gray-beige statues ring the square, honoring the cities of France. To symbolize the city's fall to Germany in 1871, the statue of Strasbourg was covered with a black drape that wasn't lifted until the end of World War I. Two of the palaces on the place de la Concorde are today the Ministry of the Marine and the deluxe Crillon Hotel, both designed in the 1760s by Ange-Jacques Gabriel.

    ☕ TAKE A BREAK The **Bar of the Hôtel de Crillon** (see chapter 4), 10 place de la Concorde (☎ 01-44-71-15-00), is one of the best places in the world to have a drink. Fashion designer Sonia Rykiel and sculptor "César" have given it new luster, and the drinks, the setting, the ambience, and the atmosphere have remained undiminished over the decades.

    From place de la Concorde, you can enter the:
8. **Jardin des Tuileries** (☎ 01-40-20-90-43), as much a part of Paris as the Seine. These statue-studded gardens were designed by Le Nôtre, the gardener to Louis XIV. About 100 years before that, a palace was built here by Catherine de Médicis. Connected to the Louvre, it was occupied by Louis XVI after he left Versailles; after the Revolution, Napoléon I called it home. Twice attacked by the people of Paris, it was burnt to the ground in 1871 and never rebuilt. But the gardens remain, the trees arranged geometrically along arrow-straight paths. Bubbling fountains soften the sense of order and formality.

    The neoclassic statuary is often insipid and is occasionally desecrated by rebellious "art critics." You'll find half of Paris in the Tuileries on a warm spring day, listening to the chirping birds and watching the daffodils and red tulips bloom. Fountains gurgle, and parents roll carriages over the grounds where 18th-century revolutionaries killed the king's Swiss guards.

At the other end of the Tuileries, pause at the:

9. Arc de Triomphe du Carrousel, at the Cour du Carrousel. Pierced with three walkways and supported by marble columns, the monument celebrates Napoléon and the Grand Armée's victory at Austerlitz on December 5, 1805. Surmounting the arch are statuary, a chariot, and four bronze horses. "Paris needs more monuments," Napoléon once proclaimed. He got his wish.

At this point, take avenue du Gal. Lemonnier to rue de Rivoli, away from the Seine. Take a left, then walk to the rue de Castiglione and turn right. You've reached the last stop on our tour, the:

10. Place Vendôme. Always aristocratic, sometimes royal, place Vendôme enjoyed its golden age in the heyday of the Second Empire. It has attracted such tenants as Chopin, who lived at no. 12 until his death in 1849. Louis Napoléon lived here, wooing his future empress, Eugénie de Montijo, at the Hôtel du Rhin. In its halcyon days, Strauss waltzes echoed across the plaza, before they were replaced by cannon fire.

There was a statue of the Sun King here until the Revolution, when it was replaced briefly by *Liberty*. Then came Napoléon, who ordered that a sort of Trajan's Column be erected in honor of the victor at Austerlitz. That Napoléon himself won the battle was "incidental." The column was made of bronze melted from captured Russian and Austrian cannons.

After Napoléon's downfall, the statue was replaced with one of Henri IV, everybody's favorite king and every woman's favorite man. Later Napoléon surmounted it once again, this time in uniform and without the pose of a Caesar.

The Communards of 1871, who detested royalty and its false promises, pulled down the statue, led by the artist Courbet. For his part in the drama, he was jailed and fined the cost of restoring the statue. He couldn't pay it, of course, and was forced into exile in Switzerland. Eventually Napoléon, wrapped in a Roman toga, won out.

To get to the nearest Métro stop, walk through the other end of place Vendôme on rue de la Paix until you reach rue Daunou and the Opéra station.

Walking Tour 2
Montmartre

Start: Place Pigalle.
Finish: Place Pigalle.
Time: 5 hours—more if you break for lunch. It's a 3-mile trek.
Best Time: Any day that it isn't raining. Set out by 10am at the latest.
Worst Time: After dark.

Soft white three-story houses, slender, barren trees sticking up from the ground like giant toothpicks—that's how Utrillo, befogged by absinthe, saw Montmartre. Toulouse-Lautrec brush-stroked it into a district of cabarets, circus freaks, and prostitutes. Today Montmartre remains truer to the dwarfish Toulouse Lautrec's conception than it does to Utrillo's.

Before all this, Montmartre was a sleepy farming community with windmills dotting the landscape. The name has always been the subject of disagreement, some maintaining that it originated from the "mount of Mars," a Roman temple that crowned the hill, others asserting that it means "mount of martyrs," a reference to the

Another Way to See Montmartre

Those finding the uphill climb to Paris's highest elevation too arduous can take a white-sided, diesel-powered train that rolls along the steep streets on a 35-minute guided tour. **Le Petit Train de Montmartre** carries 55 passengers and offers an English commentary as it takes you past major landmarks. You may board at either the place du Tertre (beside the Church of St-Pierre) or near the Moulin Rouge in the place Blanche. Trains run throughout the year, beginning at 10am and continuing until 10pm between June and September, and until 6pm the rest of the year. Depending on the season, departures are scheduled every 30 to 45 minutes. The round-trip cost is 30 F ($5.10) for adults, 18 F ($3.05) for children 3 to 12. For information, call **Promotrain,** 131 rue de Clignancourt, 18e (☎ **01-42-62-24-00**).

martyrdom of St. Denis, the patron saint of Paris, who was beheaded on the mountain along with his fellow saints Rusticus and Eleutherius.

The traditional way to explore Montmartre is on foot. Take the Métro to place Pigalle. Turn right after leaving the station and proceed down boulevard de Clichy, turn left at the Cirque Medrano, and begin the climb up rue des Martyrs. Upon reaching rue des Abbesses, turn left and walk along this street, crossing the place des Abbesses. Walk uphill along rue Ravignan, which leads directly to place Emile-Goudeau, a tree-studded square in the middle of rue Ravignan. At no. 13, across from the Timhôtel, stood the:

1. **Bateau-Lavoir** (Boat Washhouse), called the cradle of Cubism. Although gutted by fire in 1970, it has been reconstructed by the city of Paris. Picasso once lived here and, in the winter of 1905 to 1906, painted one of the world's most famous portraits, of Gertrude Stein. Other residents have included Kees van Dongen and Juan Gris. Modigliani had his studio nearby, as did Rousseau and Braque.

Rue Ravignan ends at place Jean-Baptiste-Clément. Go to the end of the street and cross it onto rue Norvins (which will be on your right). Here rues Norvins, St-Rustique, and des Saules collide at a point a few steps from the rue Poulbot, in a scene famously painted by Utrillo. Turn right and head down rue Poulbot. At no. 11, you'll come to the:

2. **Espace Montmartre Dalí,** 11 rue Poulbot (☎ **01-42-64-40-10**). This phantasmagorical world of Dalí features 300 original works by the artist, including his famous 1956 lithograph of Don Quixote. It is open daily from 10am to 6pm, charging 35 F ($5.95) for adults, 25 F ($4.25) for ages 8 to 25. Free for children under 8.

The rue Poulbot crosses the tiny:

3. **Place du Calvaire,** which offers a panoramic view of Paris. On this square (a plaque marks the house) lived artist, painter, and lithographer Maurice Neumont (1868 to 1930). From here, follow the sounds of an oompah band to the center point of Montmartre:

4. **Place du Tertre,** the old town square. All around the square run terrace restaurants with dance floors and colored lights. The Basilica of Sacré-Coeur gleams white through the trees. Here the cafes overflow with people, as do the indoor and outdoor art galleries. Some of the artists still wear berets, and the cafes bear such names as "La Bohème." So loaded with local color, applied as heavily as bad makeup, the square can seem somewhat gaudy and inauthentic.

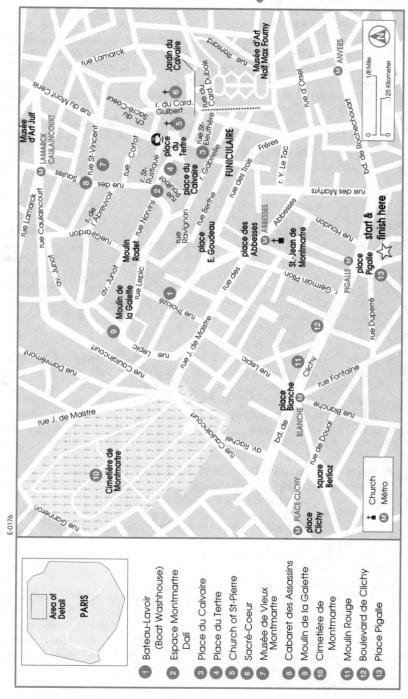

Walking Tour 2: Montmartre

Area of Detail

PARIS

1. Bateau-Lavoir (Boat Washhouse)
2. Espace Montmartre Dali
3. Place du Calvaire
4. Place du Terte
5. Church of St-Pierre
6. Sacré-Coeur
7. Musée de Vieux Montmartre
8. Cabaret des Assassins
9. Moulin de la Galette
10. Cimetière de Montmartre
11. Moulin Rouge
12. Boulevard de Clichy
13. Place Pigalle

Church
Métro

E-0176

☕ **TAKE A BREAK** Chances are, you'll be in Montmartre for lunch. Many restaurants, especially those around place du Tertre, are unabashed tourist traps. You'll be asked eight times if you want your portrait sketched in charcoal. The exception is **La Crémaillère 1900,** 15 place du Tertre, 18e (☎ **01-46-06-58-59**), a short distance from Sacré-Coeur. As its name suggests, this is a belle-epoque dining room, still retaining much of its original look, including paintings by Mucha. A terrace opens onto the square, or else you can retreat to the internal courtyard garden. A full menu is served throughout the day, including a standard array of French dishes—all the classics from sole meunière to mussels marinière. Go any time daily from noon to 12:30am.

Right off the square fronting rue du Mont-Cenis is:

5. St-Pierre. Originally a Benedictine abbey, it has played many roles—Temple of Reason during the French Revolution, food depot, clothing store, even a munitions factory. These days are calmer, and one of the oldest churches in Paris is back to being a church. Though it was consecrated in 1147, even older parts are in evidence: Two of the columns in the choir stall are the remains of a Roman temple. Among the sculptured works is a nun with the head of a pig, a symbol of sensual vice. At the entrance of the church are three bronze doors sculpted by Gismondi in 1980, of which the middle door depicts the life of St. Peter; the left door is dedicated to St. Denis, first bishop of Paris; and the right door honors the Holy Virgin.

Facing St-Pierre, turn right and follow rue Azaïs to:

6. Sacré-Coeur, overlooking square Willette, whose raindrop domes and bell tower loom above Paris and present a wide vista on sunny days. (For a complete description, see "Churches," chapter 6.) Behind the church and clinging to the hillside below are steep and crooked little streets that have survived the relentless march of progress. Facing the basilica, take the street on the left (rue du Cardinal Guibert), then go left onto rue du Chevalier-de-la-Barre and take a right when you reach rue du Mont-Cenis. Continue on this street to rue Cortot, then turn left. At no. 12 is the:

7. Musée de Vieux Montmartre (☎ **01-46-06-61-11**), with a wide collection of mementos of the neighborhood. Luminaries such as Dufy, van Gogh, and Renoir occupied this famous 17th-century house. Suzanne Valadon and her son, Utrillo, also lived here. It's open Tuesday through Sunday from 11am to 6pm. Admission is 25 F ($4.25) for adults, 20 F ($3.40) for students, free for children 10 and under.

From the museum, turn right heading up rue des Saules past a winery, a reminder of the days when Montmartre was a farming village on the outskirts of Paris. A grape-harvesting festival is held here every October.

The intersection of rue des Saules and rue St-Vincent is one of the most visited and photographed corners of the Butte. Here, on one corner, sits the famous old:

8. Cabaret des Assassins, long ago renamed **Au Lapin Agile** (see chapter 9 for details). Picasso and Utrillo once frequented this little cottage, which numerous artists have patronized and painted. On any given afternoon, French folk tunes, love ballads, army songs, sea chanteys, and music-hall ditties will stream out of the cafe and onto the street.

Turn left on rue St-Vincent, passing the Cimetière St-Vincent on your right. Utrillo is just one of the many famous artists buried here. Take a left onto rue

Girardon and climb the stairs. In a minute or two, you'll spot on your right two of the windmills *(moulins)* that used to dot the Butte. One of these:

9. Moulin de la Galette (entrance at 1 av. Junot), was immortalized by Renoir.

Turn right onto rue Lepic and walk past no. 54. In 1886, van Gogh lived here with his brother Guillaumin. Take a right turn onto rue Joseph-de-Maistre, then left again on rue Caulaincourt until you reach the:

10. Cimetière de Montmartre, second in fame only to Père-Lachaise and haunt of the mad Nijinsky, Dumas the Younger, Stendhal, Degas, and Truffaut, among others. See "Cemeteries" in chapter 6 for more information.

From the cemetery, take avenue Rachel, turn left onto boulevard de Clichy, and go to place Blanche, where an even better-known windmill than the one in Renoir's painting stands, the:

11. Moulin Rouge, one of the most talked-about nightclubs in the world. It was immortalized by Toulouse-Lautrec, but now exists in a much different form. The windmill is still here and so is the cancan. But the rest has become a superslick, outrageously expensive, gimmick-ridden variety show with a heavy emphasis on the undraped female form. (See chapter 9 for a full account.)

From place Blanche, you can begin a descent on:

12. Boulevard de Clichy, while fighting off the pornographers and hustlers trying to lure you into tawdry sex joints. With some rare exceptions, notably the citadels of the *chansonniers* (songwriters), boulevard de Clichy is one gigantic tourist trap. But everyone who comes to Paris invariably winds up here. The boulevard strips and peels its way down to:

13. Place Pigalle, center of nudity in Paris. The square is named after a French sculptor, Pigalle, whose closest brush with nudity was a depiction of Voltaire in the buff. Place Pigalle, of course, was the notorious "Pig Alley" of World War II. Toulouse-Lautrec had his studio right off Pigalle at 5 av. Frochot. When Edith Piaf was lonely and hungry, she sang in the alleyways, hoping to earn a few francs for the night.

Walking Tour 3
The Latin Quarter

Start: Place St-Michel.
Finish: The Panthéon.
Time: 3 hours, not counting stops.
Best Time: Any school day, Monday through Friday, from 9am to 4pm.
Worst Time: Sunday morning, when everybody is asleep.

This is the precinct of the Université de Paris (known for its most famous branch, the Sorbonne), where students meet and fall in love over café-crème and croissants. Rabelais named it the Quartier Latin after the students and the professors who spoke Latin in the classroom and on the streets. The sector teems with belly dancers, exotic restaurants, sidewalk cafes, bookstalls, *caveaux* (basement nightclubs), *clochards* (bums), *chiffonniers* (ragpickers), and gamin boys and girls.

A good starting point for your tour is:

1. Place St-Michel (Métro: Pont St-Michel), where Balzac used to draw water from the fountain when he was a youth. This was the scene of frequent skirmishes between the Germans and the Resistance in the summer of 1944.

☕ **TAKE A BREAK**   Open 24 hours a day, **Café le Départ St-Michel,** 1 place St-Michel (☎ **01-43-54-24-55**), lies on the banks of the Seine, within view of both the steeple of Sainte-Chapelle and the dragon statue of place St-Michel. The decor is warmly modern, with etched mirrors reflecting the faces of a diversified clientele, often Left Bank students. If you're hungry, opt for one of the warm or cold snacks, including sandwiches. Many patrons come here for a grilled *entrecôte* (steak) with french fries.

The quarter centers around:

2. **Boulevard St-Michel** to the south. From place St-Michel, with your back to the Seine, turn left down:

3. **Rue de la Huchette,** the setting of Elliot Paul's *The Last Time I Saw Paris.* Paul first wandered into this typical street "on a soft summer evening, and entirely by chance," in 1923. Although much has changed since his time, some of the buildings are so old that they have to be propped up by timbers. Paul captured the spirit of the street more evocatively than anyone, writing of "the delivery wagons, makeshift vehicles propelled by pedaling boys, pushcarts of itinerant vendors, knife-grinders, umbrella menders, a herd of milk goats, and the neighborhood pedestrians." (The local bordello has closed, however.)

Branching off from this street to your left is:

4. **Rue du Chat-qui-Pêche** (Street of the Cat Who Fishes), said to be the shortest, narrowest street in the world, containing not one door and only a handful of windows. It's usually filled with garbage or lovers, or both.

Now, retrace your steps toward place St-Michel and turn left at the intersection with rue de la Harpe, which leads to rue St-Séverin. At the intersection, take a left to see:

5. **St-Séverin.** This flamboyant Gothic church, named for a 6th-century recluse, lies just a short walk from the Seine. It was built from 1210 to 1230, and reconstructed in 1458, over the years adopting many of the features of Notre-Dame, located across the river. The tower was completed in 1487, the chapels between 1498 and 1520. Hardouin-Mansart designed the Chapel of the Communion in 1673 when he was 27 years old.

Before entering, walk around the church to examine the gargoyles, birds of prey, and reptilian monsters projecting from its roof. To the right, facing the church, is the 15th-century "garden of ossuaries." The stained glass inside St-Séverin is a stunning adornment.

After visiting this flamboyant Gothic church, go back to rue St-Séverin and follow it to rue Galande. Stay on rue Galande until you reach:

6. **St-Julien-le-Pauvre.** First stand at the gateway and look at the beginning of rue Galande, especially the old houses with the steeples of St-Séverin rising across the way—one of the most characteristic and most frequently painted scenes on the Left Bank. Enter the courtyard and you'll be in medieval Paris. The garden to the left of the entrance offers the best view of Notre-Dame.

Everyone from Rabelais to Thomas Aquinas has passed through the doors of this church. Before the 6th century, a chapel stood on this spot. The present structure goes back to the Longpont monks, who began work on it in 1170 (making it the oldest existing church in Paris). In 1655, it was given to the Hôtel Dieu, and in time it became a small warehouse for salt. In 1889, it was presented to the followers of the Melchite Greek rite, a branch of the Byzantine church.

Key to map:
1. Place St-Michel
2. Boulevard St-Michel
3. Rue de la Huchette
4. Rue du Chat-qui-Pêche
5. Church of St-Séverin
6. Church of St-Julien-le-Pauvre
7. Musée de Cluny
8. Sorbonne
9. Church of the Sorbonne
10. Panthéon

Return to rue Galande. Turn left at the intersection with rue St-Séverin. Continue on until you reach rue St-Jacques, then turn left and follow it to boulevard St-Germain. Turn right onto this boulevard and follow it until you reach rue de Cluny. Turn left and follow the street to the entrance to the:

7. **Musée de Cluny** (see "The Major Museums" in chapter 6 for details). Even if you're rushed, take time out to see *The Lady and the Unicorn* tapestry. After your visit to the Cluny Museum, exit onto boulevard St-Michel, but instead of heading back to place St-Michel, turn left, and walk down to place de la Sorbonne and the:

8. **Sorbonne,** one of the most famous academic institutions in the world. Founded in the 13th century, it had become the most prestigious university in the West by the 14th century, attracting such professors as Thomas Aquinas. Napoléon reorganized it in 1806.

   At first glance from place de la Sorbonne, the Sorbonne seems architecturally undistinguished. In truth, it was rather indiscriminately reconstructed at the turn of the century. A better fate lay in store for the:

9. **Church of the Sorbonne,** built in 1635 by Le Mercier. It contains the marble tomb of Cardinal Richelieu, a work by Girardon based on a design by Le Brun. At his feet is the remarkable statue *Learning in Tears.*

   From the church, go south on rue Victor Cousin and turn left when you reach rue Soufflot. At street's end lies the place du Panthéon and the:

10. Panthéon (see "Architectural & Historical Highlights" in chapter 6). Sitting atop Mont Ste-Geneviève, this nonreligious temple is the final resting place of such distinguished figures as Hugo, Zola, Rousseau, and Voltaire.

Walking Tour 4
The Marais

Start: Place de la Bastille.
Finish: Place de la Bastille.
Time: 4½ hours, with only cursory stops en route. The distance is about 2¾ miles.
Best Time: Monday through Saturday, when more buildings and shops are open. If interiors are open, often you can walk into courtyards.
Worst Time: Toward dusk, when shops and museums are closed and it's too dark to admire the architectural details.

When Paris began to overflow the confines of Ile de la Cité in the 13th century, the citizenry settled in Le Marais, the marsh that used to be flooded regularly by the high-rising Seine. By the 17th century, the Marais had become the center of aristocratic Paris. At that time, some of its great mansions, many now restored or still being spruced up today, were built by the finest craftsmen in France.

In the 18th and 19th centuries, fashion deserted the Marais for the expanding Faubourg St-Germain and Faubourg St-Honoré. Industry eventually took over, and once-elegant hotels deteriorated into tenements. There was talk of demolishing the blighted neighborhood, but in 1962 an alarmed community group banded together and saved the historic district.

Today the 17th-century mansions are fashionable once again. The *International Herald-Tribune* called this area the latest refuge of the Paris artisan fleeing from the tourist-trampled St-Germain-des-Prés. (Which is not to say that the area doesn't get its share of tourist traffic—quite the contrary.) The "marsh" sprawls across the 3rd and 4th arrondissements bounded by the Grands Boulevards, the rue du Temple, the place des Vosges, and the Seine.

The neighborhood has become the center of gay life in Paris, and is a great place for window-shopping in unconventional boutiques, up-and-coming galleries, and more.

Begin your tour at the site that spawned one of the most celebrated and abhorred revolutions in human history, the:

1. **Place de la Bastille.** Here, on July 14, 1789, a mob attacked the Bastille prison, igniting the French Revolution. Now nothing of this symbol of despotism remains. Built in 1369, its eight 100-foot towers once loomed over Paris. Within them, many prisoners, some sentenced by Louis XIV for "witchcraft," were kept, the best known being "The Man in the Iron Mask." And yet, when the revolutionary mob stormed the fortress, only seven prisoners were discovered. (The Marquis de Sade had been shipped to the madhouse 10 days earlier.) The authorities had discussed razing it anyway, so in itself, the attack meant nothing. But what it symbolized and what it unleashed will never be undone. Bastille Day is celebrated with great festivity each July 14.

Since the late 1980s, what had been scorned as a dull and grimy-looking traffic circle has become an artistic focal point of Europe, thanks to the construction of the Opéra Bastille on its eastern edge. (For details on the Opéra, see chapter 9).

It was probably easier to storm the Bastille in 1789 than it is to cross over to the center of the square for a close-up view of the:

Walking Tour 4: The Marais

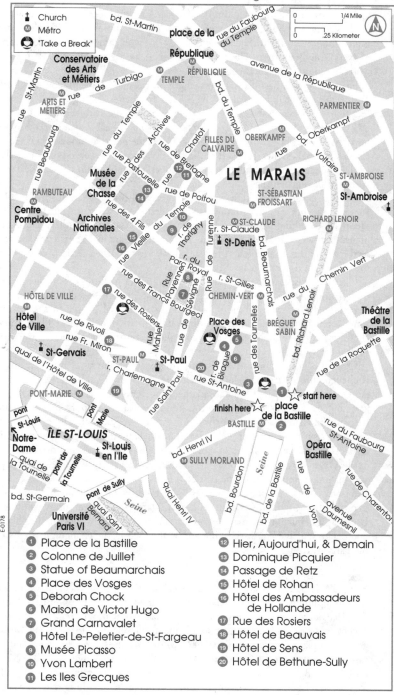

Legend:
- Church
- Métro
- "Take a Break"

Map labels:
bd. St-Martin • place de la République • rue du Faubourg du Temple • rue St-Martin • Conservatoire des Arts et Métiers • rue de Turbigo • TEMPLE • RÉPUBLIQUE • avenue de la République • ARTS ET MÉTIERS • PARMENTIER • rue Beaubourg • rue du Temple • rue des Archives • rue Pastourelle • rue de Bretagne • Chariot • FILLES DU CALVAIRE • OBERKAMPF • bd. Oberkampf • rue Voltaire • RAMBUTEAU • Musée de la Chasse • rue de Poitou • LE MARAIS • ST-SÉBASTIEN FROISSART • ST-AMBROISE • St-Ambroise • Centre Pompidou • Archives Nationales • rue des 4 Fils • rue Vieille du Temple • r. de Thorigny • ST-CLAUDE • r. St-Claude • St-Denis • RICHARD LENOIR • HÔTEL DE VILLE • rue des Francs Bourgeois • Parc Royal • Rue Payenne • rue de Sévigné • rue St-Gilles • CHEMIN-VERT • bd. Beaumarchais • rue du Chemin Vert • Théâtre de la Bastille • Hôtel de Ville • rue de Rivoli • rue des Rosiers • rue Mahler • Place des Vosges • rue de Turenne • BRÉGUET SABIN • rue Richard Lenoir • rue de la Roquette • St-Gervais • rue Fr. Miron • ST-PAUL • St-Paul • rue de Birague • rue des Tournelles • quai de l'Hôtel de Ville • r. Charlemagne • rue St-Antoine • BASTILLE • PONT-MARIE • rue saint Paul • finish here • place de la Bastille • start here • Opéra Bastille • rue du Faubourg St-Antoine • pont St-Louis • ÎLE ST-LOUIS • Notre-Dame • St-Louis en l'Île • pont Marie • SULLY MORLAND • Seine • rue de Charenton • quai de la Tournelle • pont de la Tournelle • bd. Henri IV • bd. Bourdon • bd. de la Bastille • rue de Lyon • avenue Daumesnil • bd. St-Germain • pont de Sully • Quai Henri IV • Seine • Université Paris VI • quai Saint Bernard • E-0178

Numbered list:
1. Place de la Bastille
2. Colonne de Juillet
3. Statue of Beaumarchais
4. Place des Vosges
5. Deborah Chock
6. Maison de Victor Hugo
7. Grand Carnavalet
8. Hôtel Le-Peletier-de-St-Fargeau
9. Musée Picasso
10. Yvon Lambert
11. Les Iles Grecques
12. Hier, Aujourd'hui, & Demain
13. Dominique Picquier
14. Passage de Retz
15. Hôtel de Rohan
16. Hôtel des Ambassadeurs de Hollande
17. Rue des Rosiers
18. Hôtel de Beauvais
19. Hôtel de Sens
20. Hôtel de Bethune-Sully

2. Colonne de Juillet (July Column). The July Column does not commemorate the Revolution, it honors the victims of the July Revolution of 1830, which put Louis-Philippe on the throne after the heady but wrenching victories and defeats of Napoléon Bonaparte. The tower is crowned by the winged *God of Liberty,* whose forehead bears an emerging star.

From place de la Bastille, walk west along the rue St-Antoine for about a block. Turn right, and walk north along the rue des Tournelles, noting the:

3. Statue of Beaumarchais. Erected in 1895, it honors the 18th-century author of *The Barber of Seville* and *The Marriage of Figaro,* which Rossini and Mozart respectively (and brilliantly) set to music. Continue north for a long block along rue des Tournelles, then turn left at the colorful, medieval-looking rue Pas-de-la-Mule (Footsteps of the Mule), which will open suddenly onto the northeastern corner of the enchanting:

4. Place des Vosges, the oldest square in Paris and once the most fashionable. Right in the heart of the Marais, it was called the Palais Royal in the days of Henri IV. The king planned to live here, but his assassin, Ravaillac, had other plans. Henry II was killed while jousting on the square in 1559, in the shadow of the Hôtel des Tournelles. Afterward, his widow, Catherine de Médicis, had the place torn down.

Place des Vosges, once the major dueling ground of Europe, was one of the first planned squares on the continent. Its 17th-century rosy-redbrick houses are ornamented with white stone. Covered arcades allowed people to shop at all times, even in the rain—quite an innovation in its day. In the 18th century, chestnut trees were added, sparking a continuing controversy: Critics say the trees spoil the perspective.

Over the years, fame often passed this way: Descartes, Pascal, Cardinal Richelieu, the courtesan Marion Delorme, Gautier, Daudet, and the most famous letter writer of all time, Madame de Sévigné, all lived here. But its best-known occupant was Victor Hugo (his home, now a museum, is the only house that can be visited without a private invitation—see below). The great writer could be seen rushing under the arcades of the square to assignations with his mistress. In the center of the square is a statue of Louis XIII on horseback.

Place des Vosges has become the centerpiece of many unusual, charming, and/or funky shops. One of the best of these is:

5. Deborah Chock, 24 place des Vosges (☎ 01-48-04-86-86), which inventories a constantly changing roster of unusual avant-garde and contemporary paintings. Use it as a debut for the many other art galleries that lie within the neighborhood. The staff is English-speaking and well versed in the changing currents of the Paris art scene.

☕ **TAKE A BREAK** Two separate cafes, each with loyal clients who have definite opinions about their relative merits, hold court from opposite sides of the place des Vosges. Both serve café au lait, glasses of wine and *eaux de vie,* sandwiches, pastries, and steaming pots of midafternoon tea. They are **Ma Bourgogne,** 19 place des Vosges (☎ 01-42-78-44-64), on the western edge, and its east-side competitor, **La Chope des Vosges,** 22 place des Vosges (☎ 01-42-72-64-04). Ma Bourgogne gets so crowded at lunchtime that getting a table is nearly impossible. La Chope gets more direct sunlight (something cherished by Parisians in midwinter) and is a bit less touristy. The debate is bitter and the caliber is even, but after circumnavigating the square, you'll be able to judge for yourself.

Near the square's southeastern corner, commemorating the life and times of a writer whose works were read with something approaching passion throughout the 19th century, is the:

6. Maison de Victor Hugo, 6 place des Vosges (☎ **01-42-72-10-16**). Now a museum and literary shrine that can be visited by the public, Hugo lived here from 1832 to 1848, when he went into voluntary exile on the Channel Islands after the rise to power of the despotic Napoléon III. "Literary Landmarks" in chapter 6 describes the museum in full.

Exit from the place des Vosges from its northwestern corner (a point directly opposite the Maison de Victor Hugo), and walk west along the rue des Francs-Bourgeois. At the intersection with rue de Sévigné, take a right turn. At no. 23 is the:

7. Le Musée Carnavalet (☎ **01-42-72-21-13;** for a full description, see "Specialty Museums" in chapter 6), a 16th-century mansion that is now a museum devoted to the history of Paris and the French Revolution. Here, among other things, you can see a model of the Bastille as it looked before it was torn down.

Continue to a point near the northern terminus of the rue de Sévigné, noting no. 29 (now part of the Carnavalet Museum). This is the:

8. Hôtel Le-Peletier-de-St-Fargeau, which bears the name of its former occupant, who was considered responsible for the death sentence of Louis XVI. It's used as offices and cannot be visited. At the end of the street you reach rue du Parc-Royal. Take a left onto this lovely street lined with 17th-century mansions. It leads to place de Thorigny, where the:

9. Musée Picasso is at no. 5 in the Hôtel Salé, originally built by a salt-tax collector (see "The Major Museums" in chapter 6 for a detailed description). You can visit the museum either now or come back at the end of the tour.

Next, walk northeast along the rue Thorigny and turn left onto rue Debelleyme. After a block, near the corner of the rue Vieille-du-Temple, is a worthwhile art gallery among the dozens in this neighborhood:

10. Yvon Lambert, 108 rue Vieille du Temple (☎ **01-42-71-09-33**). This gallery specializes in contemporary and sometimes radically avant-garde art from a spectrum of international artists that includes lots of cutting-edge Americans. Art is displayed in a cavernous main showroom, spilling over into an "annex" room on the side. An excellent primer for the local arts scene, it makes a nice contrast to the 17th-century trappings all around you.

Continue north for 2 short blocks along the rue Debelleyme until you reach the rue de Bretagne. Here, anyone who appreciates a really good deli will want to stop at:

11. Les Iles Grecques, 14 rue de Bretagne (☎ **01-42-71-00-56**). This is the most popular of the ethnic take-out restaurants in the neighborhood, a perfect starting point for anyone picnicking by the nearby Musée Picasso, the Square du Temple (just up rue de Bretagne), or the place des Vosges, all within 400 yards. You'll find flavorful Greek cuisine, including moussaka, stuffed eggplant, stuffed vine leaves, several varieties of olives, tarama—a savory paste made from fish roe—and both meatballs and vegetarian balls. Les Iles Grècques is open Monday from 3:30 to 8pm, and Tuesday through Sunday from 10am to 2pm and 3:30 to 8pm.

After you fill up on great food, head to:

12. Hier, Aujourd'hui, et Demain, at the same address (☎ **01-42-77-69-02**), is where France's great love affair with 1930s art deco can best be appreciated. Michel, the shop's alert owner, provides a tempting array of bibelots and fashionable art objects. Select from one of the widest arrays of colored glass in town, knowing in advance that works by such late 19th-century glassmakers as Daum, Gallé, and

Legras are avidly collected by enthusiasts around the world. Some items require special packing and great care in transport; others (many amusing) can be packed in a suitcase and carted home as a souvenir of your walk through the Marais.

After viewing Hier, Aujourd'hui, et Demain, walk southeast along the rue Charlot, to the corner of the rue Pastourelle. Here, you'll be tempted by the fabrics of:

13. **Dominique Picquier,** 10 rue Charlot (☎ **01-42-72-39-14**). Looking to redo your favorite settee? This stylish and well-established shop sells a wide roster of fabric (50% cotton, 50% linen) that stands up to rugged use. Virtually every pattern is based on some botanical inspiration, including ginko leaves, vanilla pods and vines, and magnolia branches. Everything inside costs the same: 380 F ($64.60) per meter, 346 F ($58.80) per yard—proof that the good life has come to the Marais.

Nearby, adjacent to the corner of rue Charlot and the rue du Perche, is the Marais's largest and most experimental art gallery:

14. **Passage de Retz,** 9 rue Charlot (☎ **01-48-04-37-99**). Established in 1994 in the heart of the Marais, this aggressively avant-garde gallery has about 2,100 square feet of floor space to show off its highly amusing exhibitions. The gallery has exhibited Japanese textiles, paintings by American abstract expressionists, modern Venetian glass, an occasional exposition of contemporary Haitian paintings, and selections from affiliated art galleries in Québec.

From here, walk 1 block farther along rue Charlot, turn left for a block onto the rue des 4 Fils, then go right on the rue Vieille-du-Temple, where you'll come across Delamair's:

15. **Hôtel de Rohan,** 87 rue Vieille-du-Temple, which was once occupied by the fourth Cardinal Rohan, the larcenous cardinal of the "diamond necklace scandal," which led to a flood of destructive publicity for the doomed Marie Antoinette. The first occupant of the hotel was reputed to be the son of Louis XVI. The interior is usually closed to the public, except during an occasional exhibition. In some cases, the courtyard can be visited.

Along the same street at no. 47 is the:

16. **Hôtel des Ambassadeurs de Hollande,** where Beaumarchais wrote *The Marriage of Figaro.* It is one of the most splendid mansions in Le Marais, and despite its name was never actually occupied by the Dutch embassy. It's not open to the public. Continue walking south along rue Vieille-du-Temple until you reach the:

17. **Rue des Rosiers** (Street of the Rosebushes), and turn left. It's one of the most colorful and typical streets remaining from Paris's old Jewish quarter, and you'll find an intriguing blend of living memorials to Ashkenazi and Sephardic traditions. The Star of David shines from some of the shop windows; Hebrew letters appear, sometimes in neon; couscous is sold from shops run by Moroccan, Tunisian, or Algerian Jews; restaurants serve strictly kosher food; and signs appeal for Jewish liberation. You'll come across many delicacies you might have read about but have never seen, such as savory sausage stuffed in a goose neck, roots of black horseradish, and pickled lemons.

☕ **TAKE A BREAK** The street offers a cornucopia of ethnic eateries that remain steadfast to their central European, Ashkenazi origins. **Chez Jo Goldenberg,** 7 rue des Rosiers (☎ **01-48-87-20-16**), has plenty of room to sit down and eat (see chapter 5 for more details).

Head down the rue des Rosiers to the rue Pavée, which gets its name from the fact that it was the first street in Paris, sometime during the 1300s, to have cobblestones placed over what had until then been an open sewer. At this "Paved Street," turn right and walk south until you reach the St-Paul Métro stop. Make a right turn along rue François-Miron. Although the facade at the 17th-century

18. **Hôtel de Beauvais,** 68 rue François-Miron, was badly damaged in the French Revolution, it remains one of the most charming in Paris. A plaque announces that, in 1763, Mozart lived here and played to the court of Versailles. (He was all of 7 years at the time.) Louis XIV presented the maison to Catherine Belier, wife of Pierre de Beauvais, who reportedly had the honor of introducing Louis, then 16, to the facts of life. To visit the interior, apply any afternoon to the **Association du Paris Historique,** on the ground floor.

Continue your walk along rue François-Miron until you come to a crossroads. At that point, take a sharp left along rue de Jouy. Continue along the street, cross rue Fourcy, and turn onto rue du Figuier. There you'll see the:

19. **Hôtel de Sens,** a Paris landmark at 1 rue de Figuier, built between the 1470s and 1519 for the archbishops of Sens. Along with the Cluny on the Left Bank, it is the only domestic architecture remaining from the 15th century. Long after the archbishops had departed in 1605, it was occupied by the scandalous Queen Margot, wife of Henri IV. Her new lover, "younger and more virile," slew the discarded one as she looked on in great amusement. The restoration of the Hôtel de Sens, as usual, was the subject of great controversy; nonetheless, today it houses the **Bibliothèque Forney** (☎ **01-42-78-14-60**). Leaded windows and turrets characterize the facade; you can go into the courtyard to see more of the ornate stone decoration—the gate is open Tuesday through Saturday from 1:30 to 8pm.

Retrace your steps to rue de Fourcy, turn right, and walk up the street until you reach the St-Paul Métro stop again. Turn right onto rue St-Antoine, the street where Henri II was fatally wounded in a jousting tournament in 1559. Walk along this street until you reach the:

20. **Hôtel de Bethune-Sully,** 62 rue St-Antoine. Work began on this mansion in 1625, on the order of Jean Androuet de Cerceau. In 1634, it was acquired by the duc de Sully, who had been Henri IV's minister of finance before the king was assassinated in 1610. After a straitlaced life as "the accountant of France," Sully broke loose in his declining years, adorning himself with diamonds and garish rings—and a young bride, who is said to have had a thing for very young men, whom she openly invited into their home.

The Hôtel de Sully was acquired by the French government just after World War II. It is now the seat of the National Office of Historical Monuments and Sites. Recently restored, the relief-studded facade is especially appealing. You can visit the interior of the hotel with a guide, on either Saturday or Sunday at 3pm, depending on the program. There is daily admittance to the courtyard and the garden that opens onto the place des Vosges. Frequent chamber music concerts are staged here. In the building there's an information center and a bookshop.

Continue walking along the street until you come to place de la Bastille and the Métro stop. If you feel like winding down with a meal, turn left onto the rue des Tournelles a block before the place de la Bastille, then take a quick right onto the rue de la Bastille.

☕ **WINDING DOWN**   Dating from 1864, **Bofinger,** 5-7 rue de la Bastille (☎ **01-42-72-87-82**), is a French/Alsatian brasserie, the most famous in Paris (see chapter 5 for details). Legend claims it was the first in Paris to pour draught beer. Go here for nostalgia, sauerkraut, and wines from the Côtes-du-Rhône.

8 Shopping

Shopping is a favorite pastime of the Parisians; some would even say it reflects the city's soul. The City of Light is one of the rare places in the world where you don't go anywhere to shop—shopping surrounds you instead. Each walk you take immerses you in uniquely French styles. The windows, stores, and people (even their dogs) brim with energy, creativity, and a sense of visual expression found in few other cities.

You don't have to buy anything to appreciate shopping in Paris—just soak up the art form the French have made of rampant consumerism. Peer in the *vitrines* (display windows), absorb cutting-edge ideas, witness new trends, and take home with you a whole new education in style.

1 The Shopping Scene

When you walk into a French store, it's traditional to greet the owner or sales clerk with a direct address, not a fey smile or even a weak bonjour. Only "Bonjour, madame" (or monsieur) will do.

BEST BUYS

PERFUMES, MAKEUP & BEAUTY TREATMENTS   A flat discount of 20% to 30% makes these items a great buy; qualify for a VAT refund (see below) and you'll save 40% to 45% off the Paris retail price, allowing you to bring home goods at half the U.S. price. Duty-free shops abound in Paris and are always less expensive than the ones at the airport.

For bargain cosmetics, try out French dime store and drugstore brands such as **Bourjois** (made in the Chanel factories), **Lierac,** and **Galenic. Vichy,** famous for its water, has a complete skin care and makeup line. The newest retail trend in Paris is the *parapharmacie,* a type of discount drugstore loaded with inexpensive brands, health cures, French beauty regimes, and diet plans. These usually offer a 20% discount.

FOODSTUFF   Nothing makes a better souvenir than a product of France brought home to savor later. Supermarkets are located in prime tourist neighborhoods; stock up on coffee, designer chocolates, mustards (try the Maille brand), and for the kids, perhaps American products in French packages.

FUN FASHION   Sure you can spend on couture or *prêt-à-porter,* but French teens and trendsetters have their own stores where the latest looks are affordable. Even the dime stores in Paris sell designer copies and hot-shot styles.

In the stalls in front of the department stores on bd. Haussmann, you'll find some of the latest fashion accessories, guaranteed for a week's worth of small talk once you get home.

VALUE-ADDED TAX (VAT) REFUNDS

French tax is now a hefty 20.6%, but you can get most of that back if you spend 2,000 F ($340) or more in any store that participates in the VAT refund program. Most stores participate.

Once you meet your required minimum purchase amount, you qualify for a tax refund. The amount of the refund varies with the way the refund is handled and the fee some stores charge you for processing it. So the refund at a department store may be 13%, whereas at a small shop it will be 15% or even 18%.

You will receive **VAT refund papers** in the shop; some stores, like Hermès, have their own; others provide a government form. Fill in the forms before you arrive at the airport, and expect to stand in line at the Customs desk for as long as half an hour. You are required by law to show the goods at the airport, so have them on you or visit the Customs office before you check your luggage. Once the papers have been mailed to the authorities, a credit will appear, often months later, on your credit-card bill.

All refunds are processed at the final point of departure from the **European Union (EU),** so if you are going to another EU country, don't apply for the refund in France.

Be sure to mark the paperwork to request that your refund be applied to your credit card so you aren't stuck with a check in francs that is hard to cash. This also ensures the best rate of exchange. In some airports you are offered the opportunity to get your refund back in cash, which is tempting. But if you accept cash in any currency other than francs, you will be losing money on the conversion rate. You'll do far better with a credit-card conversion.

DUTY-FREE BOUTIQUES

The advantage of duty-free shops is that you never have to pay the VAT tax, so you avoid the red tape of getting a refund. Both airports have shopping galore, but prices are often equal or better in the city. You'll find lots of duty-free shops on the avenues that branch out from the Opéra Garnier, in the 1e and 2e arrondissements. **Charles de Gaulle Airport** has a virtual shopping mall with crystal, cutlery, chocolates, luggage, wine, whisky, pipes and lighters, lingerie, silk scarves, perfume, knitwear, jewelry, cameras and equipment, cheeses, and even antiques.

BUSINESS HOURS

Shops are *usually* open Monday through Saturday from 10am to 7pm, but the hours vary greatly and Monday mornings in Paris do not run at full throttle. Small shops sometimes close for a 2-hour lunch break and may not even open until after lunch on Monday. Thursday is the best day for late-night shopping, with stores open until 9 or 10pm.

Sunday shopping is currently limited to tourist areas and flea markets, although there is growing demand for full-scale Sunday hours, as in the United States and the United Kingdom. The big department stores are now open on the five Sundays before Christmas. **Carrousel du Louvre,** a mall adjacent to the Louvre, is open and hopping on Sunday, but closed on Monday. The tourist shops that line the rue Rivoli across from the Louvre are all open on Sunday, as are the antiques villages, assorted flea markets, and specialty events. There are several good food markets in the streets on

Sunday. **Virgin Megastore** on the Champs-Elysées, a big teen hangout, pays a fine to stay open on Sunday.

CUSTOMS ALLOWANCES
See "Entry Requirements & Customs Regulations" in chapter 2.

SHIPPING IT HOME
Shipping charges will possibly double your cost on goods and you may have to pay duties on the items (see above). The good news: The VAT refund is automatically applied to all shipped items; no need to worry about the 2,000 F ($340) minimum. Some stores do have a $100 minimum for shipping, though. You can also walk into any post office and mail home a jiffy bag or small box of goodies. French do-it-yourself boxes cannot be reopened once closed, so pack carefully. The clerk at the post office will help you assemble the box (it's tricky), seal it, and send it off.

GREAT SHOPPING NEIGHBORHOODS
Paris neighborhoods are designated by **arrondissement** (see "City Layout" in chapter 3). When you are planning a day of combined sightseeing and shopping, check a map to see how the arrondissements connect so that you can maximize your efforts. Although Paris is made up of 20 arrondissements, only a handful are prime real estate for shopping.

The best of the shopping arrondissements include:

1st & 8th Arrondissements   These two *quartiers* adjoin each other (invisibly) and form the heart of Paris's best Right Bank shopping strip—together they're one big hunting ground. This area includes the famed **rue du Faubourg-St-Honoré,** where the big designer houses are, and the **Champs-Elysées,** where the mass market and teen scene are hot. At one end of the 1er is the **Palais-Royal,** one of the best shopping secrets in Paris, where an arcade of boutiques flanks each side of the garden of the former palace.

The 1er also contains the **avenue Montaigne,** the most glamorous shopping street in Paris, boasting 2 blocks of the fanciest shops in the world, where you simply float from big name to big name and in a few hours can see everything from Louis Vuitton to Ines de la Fressange, the model turned retailer. Avenue Montaigne is also the address of **Joseph,** a British design firm, and **Porthault,** makers of the fanciest sheets in the world.

2nd Arrondissement   Right behind the Palais Royal is the **Garment District** (Sentier), as well as a few very sophisticated shopping secrets such as **place des Victoires.** This area also hosts a few old-fashioned passageways, alleys filled with tiny stores, such as **Galerie Vivienne,** on rue Vivienne.

3rd & 4th Arrondissements   The border between these two arrondissements gets fuzzy, especially around the **place des Vosges,** center stage of the Marais. No matter. The districts offer several dramatically different shopping experiences.

On the surface, the shopping includes the "real people stretch" (where all the non-millionaires shop) of the **rue Rivoli** and **rue St-Antoine,** featuring everything from GAP and a branch of Marks and Spencer, to local discount stores and mass merchants. Two "real people" department stores are in this area, **Samaritaine** and **BHV;** there's also **Les Halles** and the **Beaubourg** neighborhood, which is anchored by the Centre Georges Pompidou.

Meanwhile, hidden away in the Marais is a medieval warren of tiny twisting streets chockablock with cutting-edge designers and up-to-the-minute fashions and trends. Start by walking around the place des Vosges for art galleries, designer shops, and special little finds, then dive in and lose yourself in the area leading to the Picasso Museum.

Finally, the 4e is also the home of the **Bastille,** an up-and-coming area for artists and galleries where the newest entry on the retail scene, **Viaduc des Arts** (which actually stretches into the 12e), is situated. It's a collection of about 30 stores occupying a series of narrow valuted niches under what used to be railroad tracks. They run parallel to the avenue Daumesnil, centered around the boulevard Diderot.

6th & 7th Arrondissements   Whereas the 6e is one of the most famous shopping districts in Paris—it is the soul of the Left Bank—a lot of the really good stuff is hidden in the zone that turns into the wealthy residential district of the seventh. **Rue du Bac,** stretching from the 6e to the 7e in a few blocks, stands for all that wealth and glamor can buy.

8th Arrondissement   See above, "1st & 8th Arrondissements."

9th Arrondissement   To add to the fun of shopping the Right Bank, the 9e sneaks in behind the 1er, so if you choose not to walk toward the Champs-Elysées and the 8e, you can instead head to the city's big department stores, all built in a row along the **boulevard Haussmann** in the 9e. Department stores here include not only the two big French icons, **Au Printemps** and **Galeries Lafayette,** but a large branch of Britain's **Marks and Spencer** and a branch of the Dutch answer to Kmart, the low-priced **C&A.**

2 Shopping A to Z

ANTIQUES

Le Louvre des Antiquaires. 2 place du Palais-Royal, 1er. ☎ **01-42-97-27-00.** Tues–Sun 11am–7pm. Closed Sun in July–Aug. Métro: Palais-Royal.

Located directly across from the Louvre, with three levels of fancy knickknacks and 250 separate vendors, Le Louvre des Antiquaires is just the place if you're looking for 30 matching Baccarat crystal champagne flutes from the 1930s, Sèvres tea service dated 1773, or maybe a small signed Jean Fouquet gold and diamond pin. Too stuffy? No problem. There's always the 1940 Rolex with the aubergine crocodile strap.

Prices can be high, but a few reasonable items are hidden here. What's more, the Sunday scene is fabulous, and there's a cafe with a variety of lunch menus beginning around 100 F ($17). Pick up a free map and brochure of the premises from the information desk.

Mlinaric, Henry, and Zervudachi. 54 Galerie de Montpensier, Palais-Royal, 1er. ☎ **01-42-96-08-62.** Mon–Fri 9:30am–1pm and 2–6:30pm (Fri until 5:30pm). Métro: Palais-Royal.

David Mlinaric, one of the three musketeers here, is the British interior designer who redecorated Spencer House—the late Princess Diana's ancestral manse in London—as well as all of Lord Jacob Rothschild's private residences. Tino Zervudachi is considered one of the hot young turks of Paris design. Hugh Henry, like Mlinaric, is English. Together they are the chicest antiques dealers on the Right Bank, specializing in museum-quality 18th-century items.

Village St. Paul. 23–27 rue St-Paul, 4e. No phone. Thurs–Mon 11am–7pm. Métro: St-Paul.

This isn't an antiques center but a cluster of dealers in their own hole-in-the-wall hideout. It's open, and hopping, on Sunday. Bring your camera, because inside the courtyards and alleys is a dream vision of hidden Paris: dealers in a courtyard selling furniture and other decorative items in French country and formal styles. The rest of the street, stretching from the river to the Marais, is also lined with dealers.

ART

✪ Galerie Adrien Maeght. 42 rue du Bac, 7e. ☎ **01-45-48-45-15.** Mon 10am–1pm and 2–7pm, Tues–Sat 9:30am–7pm. Métro: Bac.

This art house is among the most famous names in galleries, selling contemporary art on a very fancy Left Bank street that's far more chic and fashionable than the bohemian Left Bank Picasso knew.

Galerie 27. 27 rue de Seine, 6e. ☎ **01-43-54-78-54.** Tues–Sat 10am–1pm and 2:30–7pm. Métro: St-Germain-des-Prés.

This tiny closet of a store sells lithographs by some of the most famous artists of the early 20th century, including Picasso, Coll, Miró, and Léger.

Viaduc des Arts. 9–147 av. Daumesnil, 12e. ☎ **01-44-75-80-66.** Mon–Sat 11am–7pm. Métro: Bastille, Ledru-Rollin, Reuilly-Diderot, or Gare de Lyon.

This renovated establishment occupies a long 2-block stretch from the Bastille Opera to the Gare de Lyon, and features art galleries and artisans in individual boutiques created within the arches of an old train viaduct. You can start at one end and work your way to the other, or begin in the middle. It's nothing spectacular, but makes for interesting shopping.

BOOKS

See also the **Marché aux Livres** under "Markets," and **FNAC** and **Virgin Megastore** under "Music," below.

Brentano's. 37 av. de l'Opéra, 2e. ☎ **01-42-61-52-50.** Mon–Sat 10am–7:30pm. Métro: Opéra.

Brentano's is a large English-language bookstore selling guides, maps, novels, and non-fiction as well as greeting cards, postcards, holiday items, and gifts. It's located 1 block from the Garnier Opera.

Galignani. 224 rue de Rivoli, 1er. ☎ **01-42-60-76-07.** Mon–Sat 10am–7pm. Métro: Tuileries.

Sprawling over a very large street level, and supplemented with a mezzanine, this venerable wood-paneled bookstore has thrived in this location since its establishment in 1810. Enormous numbers of books are available in both French and English, with a special emphasis on French classics, modern fiction, sociology, and fine arts. Looking for English-language translations of works by Balzac, Flaubert, Zola, or Colette? Most of them are here; if not, they can be ordered.

Librairie La Bail-Weissert. 5 rue Lagrange, 5e. ☎ **01-43-29-72-59.** Mon–Sat 10am–12:30pm and 2–7pm. Métro: Maubert-Mutualité.

Paris is filled with rare bookshops, but this one has the best collection of atlases, rare maps, and engravings from the 15th to the 19th centuries. The shop sells original topographical maps of European and world cities, along with various regions of Europe. There is also a superb collection of architectural engravings.

Shakespeare and Company. 37 rue de la Bûcherie, 5e. No phone. Daily 11am–midnight. Métro: St-Michel.

See "Literary Landmarks" in chapter 6.

Tea and Tattered Pages. 24 rue Mayet, 6e. ☎ **01-40-65-94-35.** Daily 11am–7pm. Métro: Duroc.

At this largely English-language paperback bookshop, you can take a break from browsing to have tea at a little table. Though it's slightly out of the way, an extra dose of charm makes it worth the trip.

Village Voice Bookshop. 6 rue Princesse, 6e. ☎ **01-46-33-36-47.** Mon 2–8pm, Tues–Sat 10am–8pm. Métro: Mabillon.

On a side street in the heart of the best Left Bank shopping district, this is a favorite venue for expatriate Yankees. The location is in the vicinity of some of the Left Bank gathering places described in Gertrude Stein's *The Autobiography of Alice B. Toklas.* Established in 1981, the shop is a hangout for the literati. Its name has nothing to do with the countercultural New York newspaper.

W. H. Smith. 248 rue de Rivoli, 1er. ☎ **01-44-77-88-99.** Mon–Sat 9:30am–7pm, Sun 1–7pm. Métro: Concorde.

This bookstore provides books, magazines, and newspapers published in English (most titles are from Britain). You can get the *Times* of London, of course, and the Sunday *New York Times* is available every Monday. There's a fine selection of maps and travel guides, and a special children's section that includes comics.

CHILDREN: FASHION, SHOES & ASSORTED KID STUFF

Au Nain Bleu. 406 rue St-Honoré, 8e. ☎ **01-42-60-39-01.** Mon–Sat 9:45am–6:30pm. Métro: Concorde.

This is the largest, oldest, and most centrally located toy store in all of Paris. More importantly, it is probably the fanciest toy store in the world. But don't panic; in addition to the elaborate and expensive fancy stuff, there are rows of cheaper items (like penny candy) in jars on the first floor.

Bonpoint. 15 rue Royale, 8e. ☎ **01-47-42-52-63.** Mon–Sat 10am–7pm. Métro: Concorde.

Grandparent alert! Bonpoint is part of a well-known almost-haute-couture chain specializing in clothing for children and adolescents ages 1 week to 16 years. Clothing is well tailored, traditional—and extremely expensive. Drool over formal party and confirmation dresses, and the long and elegant baptismal robes, embroidered in France and edged in lace.

Dipaki. 18 rue Vignon, 9e. ☎ **01-42-66-24-74.** Mon–Sat 10am–7pm. Métro: Madeleine.

If you prefer clothes with hip, hot style and color, but that are wearable, washable, and affordable, forget Bonpoint and try this small shop—it's a representative of a truly sensational French line of clothes for toddlers. And it's only a block from the place de la Madeleine.

Natalys. 92 av. des Champs-Elysées, 8e. ☎ **01-43-59-17-65.** Mon–Sat 10am–7pm. Métro: F. D. Roosevelt.

Part of a French chain with a dozen stores in Paris and many elsewhere, Natalys sells upscale versions of children's (6 and under) and maternity wear. It has just enough French panache without going over the top in design or price.

Pom D'Api. 28 rue du Jour, 1er. ☎ **01-42-36-08-87.** Mon–Sat 10am–7pm. Métro: Les Halles.

This chain of kiddie shoe stores has other locations in Paris and all over France; it carries tiny gold woven sandals, patent leather high tops, and much more.

CHINA, CRYSTAL & PORCELAIN

✪ **Baccarat.** 11 place de la Madeleine, 8e. ☎ **01-42-65-36-26.** Tues–Fri 10am–7pm, Mon and Sat 10am–6:30pm. Métro: Madeleine. 30 bis rue de Paradis, 10e. ☎ **01-47-70-64-30.** Mon–Fri 9am–6:30pm, Sat 10am–noon and 2–5:30pm. Métro: Gare de l'Est.

Established in 1764, Baccarat is one of the leading purveyors of full-lead crystal in Europe, catering to a clientele that has included kings, oil emirs, presidents of France, and the merely affluent. Don't think that you'll be able to comparison-shop Baccarat crystal at its various branches—a central selling organization sets rigid prices. But if you're hunting for bargains, head for the rue de Paradis outlet and check out special sales or promotions on items discontinued from the company's catalogues. These sales are the biggest during 2 weeks in mid-January, although availability varies from year to year. While Baccarat's more prestigious outlet is on the place de la Madeleine, the rue de Paradis outlet is larger and contains the **Baccarat Museum** described in "Specialty Museums," chapter 6.

Lalique. 11 rue Royale, 8e. ☎ **01-53-05-12-12.** Mon 10am–6:30pm, Tues–Fri 9:30am–6:30pm, Sat 9:30am–7pm. Métro: Concorde.

Lalique is known around the world for its smoky frosted glass sculpture, art deco crystal, and unique perfume bottles. The shop sells a wide range of merchandise, including top-quality silk scarves, priced at around 1,000 F ($170) each, and designed to compete directly with those sold by Hermès, and leather belts with Lalique buckles.

✪ **Limoges-Unic/Madronet.** 34 & 58 rue de Paradis, 10e. ☎ **01-47-70-54-49** or 01-47-70-61-49. Mon–Sat 10am–6:30pm. Métro: Gare de l'Est.

Housed within two shops of more or less equal size, each within a 5-minute walk of the other, this store is crammed with Limoges china brands such as Daum, Baccarat, Lalique, Christofle, Haviland, and Bernardaud, as well as other table items: glass and crystal, silver, whatever your heart desires. They will ship your purchases, and English is widely spoken.

Manufacture Nationale de Sèvres. 4 place André-Malraux, 1er. ☎ **01-47-03-40-20.** Mon–Fri 11am–6pm. Métro: Palais-Royal.

This is one of only two official outlets in all of Paris for the very limited production of Sèvres porcelain. The other is in the western suburb of Sèvres, near the national museum of ceramics; see "Specialty Museums" in chapter 6. Since only about 5,000 pieces of the stuff are made every year, the porcelain is prized as one of the most celebrated names in French industry.

CHOCOLATE

Christian Constant. 37 rue d'Assas, 6e. ☎ **01-53-63-15-15.** Mon–Fri 8:30am–9pm, Sat–Sun 8am–8:30pm. Métro: St-Placide or Rennes.

Established in 1970, long after its grander and more history-bound competitors, Christian Constant sells some of the most delectable chocolates in Paris. Each is a blend of raw ingredients from Ecuador, Colombia, or Venezuela, usually mingled with scents of spices and flowers that include orange blossoms, jasmine, the Asian blossom ylang, and herbs usually made to brew tea, vetiver and verveine. Unpretentious and charming, the shop sells chocolates for take-away, priced at from 490 F ($83.30) per kilo (about $38 per pound). If you prefer to consume your chocolates on-site, they run a tearoom next door, at 18 rue de Fleurus (same phone), where cups of tea cost 27 F ($4.60); a pot of hot chocolate sells for 27 F ($4.60); and a simple cup of coffee costs 12 F ($2.05).

Debauve et Gallais. 30 rue des Saints Pères, 7e. ☎ **01-45-48-54-67.** Mon–Sat 9am–7pm. Métro: St-Germain-des-Prés.

Lose yourself in deep dark wood, deep dark chocolate, and one of Paris's best-known status brands. The counters are always lined with men buying chocolate for their significant others.

Jadis et Gourmande. 27 rue Boissy d'Anglas, 8e. ☎ **01-42-65-23-23.** Mon 1–7pm, Tues–Fri 9:30am–7pm, Sat 10:30am–7pm. Métro: Madeleine.

This small chain of Parisian chocolatiers has a less lofty rep than Christian Constant and much more reasonable prices. They are best known for their alphabetical chocolate blocks, which allow you to spell out any message you want, in any language. "Merci" comes prepackaged.

La Maison du Chocolat. 225 rue du Faubourg St-Honoré, 8e. ☎ **01-42-27-39-44.** Mon–Sat 9:30am–7:30pm. Métro: Ternes.

This chocolate shop has five other Paris locations. At each, racks and racks of chocolates are priced individually or by the kilo, at near or over 490 F ($83.30) for a kilo. (It's similar to Hermès when it comes to wrap, ribbon, and prices.) These stores offer a variety of chocolate-based products, including chocolate pastries, usually more affordable than the candy, and even chocolate milk!

DEPARTMENT STORES

In addition to the stores listed below, **Samaritaine,** 19 rue de la Monnaie, 1er (☎ **01-40-41-20-20;** Métro: Pont-Neuf or Châtelet–Les Halles), and **BHV,** 52 rue de Rivoli, 1er (☎ **01-42-74-90-00;** Métro: Hôtel de Ville), offer the department store experience at slightly lower prices. La Samaritaine has a fine inexpensive restaurant with a wonderful view of Paris on the fifth floor.

✪ **Au Printemps.** 64 bd. Haussmann, 9e. ☎ **01-42-82-50-00.** Mon–Wed and Fri–Sat 9:35am–7pm, Thurs 9:35am–10pm. Métro: Havre-Caumartin. RER: Auber.

This megastore is so richly associated with France's vision of the good life that it's been viewed as one of the city's tourist attractions since it was first established in the late 19th century. The setting is particularly beautiful—take a look at the facade for a reminder of the grandeur of Paris's gilded age. Inside, the merchandise is divided into housewares **(Printemps Maison),** women's fashion **(Printemps Mode),** and menswear **(Brummel).** As you enter from the street, you'll be assualted by a sea of cosmetics and perfume displays; upstairs, the merchandise is more diversified.

Check out the magnificent stained-glass dome, built in 1923, through which turquoise-colored light cascades into Café Flo on the 6th floor, where you can have a coffee or a full meal. Complete menus are available, with dishes and appetizers beginning around 65 F ($11.05); the menu is composed of pictures, so you needn't worry about your French.

Behind the store, there's a branch of the discount clothing/grocery store **Prisunic.**

Interpreters stationed at the Welcome Service in the basement will help you find what you're looking for, claim your VAT refund, and so on. Au Printemps also has a discount card for tourists, offering a flat 10% discount.

Bon Marché. 22 rue de Sèvres, 7e. ☎ **01-44-39-80-00.** Mon–Sat 9:30am–7pm. Métro: Sèvres-Babylone.

This two-part department store is on the Left Bank in the midst of all the cutie-pie boutiques. Don't be fooled by the name (literally, "low-budget" or "cheap"). For about 20 years now, it's worked hard to position itself in the luxury market, selling fashion for men, women, and children, furniture, upscale gift items, and housewares. There's also a gourmet grocery store. Some visitors compare it to Bloomingdale's with a stronger French accent. But mostly it's preferred by local residents of the Montparnasse district, who find it closer and more convenient to home than the more faraway stores on the Grands Boulevards.

Colette. 213 rue St-Honoré, 1er. ☎ **01-55-35-33-90.** Mon–Sat 10:30am–7:30pm. Métro: Palais-Royal.

Distinguishing the Giants

Galeries Lafayette and its neighbor, **Au Printemps,** have been competing for Parisian shoppers for nearly a century; you'll find the city firmly divided into GL types and Printemps types, although the differences between the two stores fade with global trends and international imports.

Right now, Galeries Lafayette is more old-fashioned in the way it does business and therefore feels a little more staid and French. Au Printemps seems more modern and American, especially now that the first floor of the main store has been renovated to match its housewares division, Printemps Maison.

Named after the great and still controversial French writer, Colette is Paris's store of the moment, a swank citadel for à la mode fashion. It has even made the elegant but staid rue St-Honoré less stuffy. For cutting-edge design in both fashion and home furnishings, this is the place to go. It is buzzing with excitement, displaying fashions by some of the city's most promising young talents, including Marni and Lucien Pellat-Fimet. Not to be overlooked are home furnishings by such designers as Tom Dixon, and even the zany Japanese accessories.

Even if you don't plan to buy any of the merchandise, patronize the **tea salon** downstairs, with its freshly made quiches, salads, cakes, and three dozen brands of bottled water—take your pick.

Galeries Lafayette. 40 bd. Haussmann, 9e. ☎ **01-42-82-34-56.** Mon–Wed and Fri–Sat 9:30am–6:45pm, Thurs 9:30am–9pm. Métro: Chaussée d'Antin or Opéra. RER: Auber.

Built in 1912, Galeries Lafayette, an almost legendary Paris department store, is now divided into several subdivisions: **Galfa** (which specializes in men's clothing), **Lafayette Sports** (sporting goods), and two other general merchandise stores, both known just as **GL,** though the larger one is often called *le magasin principal* (the main store).

Typically, the Galeries complements its vast selection with world-class service: There's a welcome desk, multilingual help, and a free shopping tote if you turn in receipts totaling 200 F ($34) or more. Be sure to pick up a tourist's discount card from your travel agent before you leave home, or from your hotel or the store itself after you arrive in Paris; the card provides a flat 10% discount for tourist shoppers that's separate from the VAT refund program.

Next door to GL there's a branch of the discount store **Prisunic,** which the chain also owns. This isn't the best Prisunic in town, but it's convenient and can give you a taste of French discount-store magic.

Within the complex is another affiliated store, **Lafayette Gourmet,** one of the fanciest grocery stores in Paris with prices that are less expensive than those offered at the famous Fauchon, Paris's "supermarket for millionaires" (see "Food," below). This store has its own entrance next to Prisunic, and has extended hours.

FASHION
CUTTING-EDGE CHIC

Azzadine Alaia. 7 rue de Moussy, 4e. ☎ **01-42-72-19-19.** Mon–Sat 10am–1pm and 2–7pm. Métro: Hôtel de Ville.

Alaia, who became the darling of French fashion in the 1970s, is the man who put the ooh-la-la body consciousness back into Paris chic. If you can't afford the current collection, try the stock shop around the corner at 18 rue de Verrerie (☎ **01-40-27-85-58**), where last year's leftovers are sold at serious discounts. Both outlets sell leather trenchcoats, knit dresses, pleated skirts, cigarette pants, belts, purses, and fashion accessories.

Claude Montana. 31 rue de Grenelle, 7e. ☎ **01-45-44-17-74.** Mon–Fri 10am–7pm, Sat 11am–7pm. Métro: Sèvres-Babylone.

"The State of Claude Montana," he calls it, making a lame pun and leaving you wondering just what state that could be. Confusion? Undress? Or merely deconstructed chic? For rock-and-roll stars and wannabes, Montana's is the place. Don't expect quite as much excess in recent collections as you would have found a few years ago; he's returned to softer, more "feminine" cuts within his women's line, and a renewed emphasis on modern but not particularly radical designs in his menswear.

Courrèges. 40 rue François 1er, 8e. ☎ **01-53-67-30-00.** Mon–Sat 9:45am–6:45pm. Métro: F. D. Roosevelt.

Don't look now: André Courrèges is hot again. Even those little white vinyl go-go boots and disco purses in silver metallic cloth are back. Courrèges's brings a humorous touch to '70s retro, with bold color, plastic, and fun. There's another branch of his store in the **Carrousel du Louvre** mall (☎ **01-40-15-05-85**).

Elle. 30 rue St-Sulpice, 6e. ☎ **01-43-26-46-10.** Mon–Sat 10:30am–7pm. Métro: Odéon.

Elle magazine runs its own boutique that sells specific items featured in the magazine, many of them hot, hip, and affordable. The store carries both housewares and clothing items, as well as costume jewelry.

Hervé Leger. 29 rue du Faubourg-St-Honoré, 8e. ☎ **01-44-51-57-17.** Mon–Sat 10am–7pm. Métro: Concorde.

This creator of the Band Aid Dress (La Robe à bandes), a tightly wrapped concoction of stretch materials and color, has opened his own shop for those with curves to flaunt and cash to burn.

Jean-Charles de Castelbajac. 6 place St-Sulpice, 6e. ☎ **01-46-33-87-32.** Mon–Sat 10am–7pm. Métro: Odéon or St-Sulpice.

Castelbajac is the bad boy of French fashion, known for flamboyant and amusing gear in primary colors, often with cryptic but evocative inscriptions scribbled artfully across the clothing. Examples include excerpts from novels and poems by Proust and Mallarmé, or autobiographical snippets ("in 1968, I created my first overcoat, using a fabric similar to this one you see here"). His store is located in a cluster of designer shops that's great for gawking.

Jean Paul Gaultier. 6 rue Vivienne, 2e. ☎ **01-42-86-05-05.** Mon–Fri 10am–7pm, Sat 11am–7pm. Métro: Bourse or Palais-Royal.

Tucked in one of Paris's most famous passageways, this large boutique features the typical fare of this master punk turned tailor: street fashion made high fashion for men and women. A slightly newer branch of the store, featuring exactly the same inventory, is at 30 rue du Faubourg St-Antoine, 12e (☎ **01-44-68-84-84;** Métro: Bastille).

Lolita Lempicka. 14 rue du Faubourg-St-Honoré, 8e. ☎ **01-49-24-94-01.** Mon–Sat 10:30am–7pm. Métro: Concorde.

Lolita, formerly of the hidden Marais and the underground fashion scene, has gone mainstream with her own shop, tiny but quite visible, on this street of streets. The clothes continue to be inventive and creative, and usually very sexy. And despite the new tony location, they're hardly mainstream. (Women's clothing only.)

DESIGNER BOUTIQUES & FASHION FLAGSHIPS

There are two primary fields of dreams in Paris when it comes to showcasing the international big names in design: the rue du Faubourg-St-Honoré and the avenue Montaigne. While the Left Bank is gaining in designer status with recent additions, including Christian Dior, Giorgio Armani, and Louis Vuitton, the heart of the international designer parade is on the Right Bank.

The **rue du Faubourg-St-Honoré** is so famously fancy that it is simply known as "the Faubourg." It was the traditional miracle mile until recent years, when the really exclusive shops shunned it for the wider and even more deluxe avenue Montaigne at the other end of the arrondissement. (It's a long but pleasant walk from one fashion strip to the other.)

While the **avenue Montaigne** is filled with almost unspeakably fancy shops, a few of them have affordable cafes (try Joseph at no. 14) and sales help is almost always cordial to the well dressed. (You needn't be decked in fur to play the game: A good handbag and pair of shoes are all that matter. Leave *les baskets*—running shoes—at home, s'il vous plait.)

The mix is quite international—from British (Joseph), to German (Jil Sander), to Italian (Krizia). Chanel, Christian Lacroix, Porthault, Nina Ricci, Christian Dior, and Ungaro are just a few of the French big names; also check out some of the lesser-known creative powers that be: The whimsical boutique run by Ines de la Fressange, former Chanel model, is a knockout. And don't miss a visit to Caron. Most of the designer shops sell men's and women's clothing.

The Faubourg hosts other traditional favorites: Hermès, Lanvin, Jaeger, Sonia Rykiel, and the upstart Façonnable, which sells preppy men's clothing in the United States through a business deal with Nordstroms. Note that Lanvin has its own men's shop (Lanvin Homme), which has a cafe downstairs—perfect for a light (and affordable) lunch.

✪ **Chanel.** 31 rue Cambon, 1er. ☎ **01-42-86-28-00.** Mon–Sat 10am–7pm. Métro: Concorde or Tuileries.

If you can't have the sun, the moon, and the stars, at least buy something with Coco Chanel's initials on it, either a serious fashion statement (drop-dead chic) or something fun and playful (tongue in chic). Karl Lagerfeld's designs come in all different flavors and have added a subtle twist to Chanel's classicism.

This store is adjacent to the Chanel couture house and behind the Ritz, where Mademoiselle Chanel once lived. Check out the beautiful staircase of the maison before you shop the two-floor boutique—it's well worth a peek.

Christian Dior. 26-32 av. Montaigne, 8e. ☎ **01-40-73-54-44.** Mon–Sat 10am–7pm. Métro: F. D. Roosevelt.

This famous couture house is set up like a small department store, selling men's, women's, and children's clothing, as well as affordable gift items, makeup, and perfume on the first floor as you enter. Unlike some of the other big-name fashion houses, Dior is very approachable.

✪ **Hermès.** 24 rue du Faubourg-St-Honoré, 8e. ☎ **01-40-17-47-17.** Mon–Sat 10am–6:30pm. Métro: Concorde.

The single most important status item in France is a scarf or tie from Hermès. Patterns on the illustrious scarves, which retail for around 1,500 F ($255) each, have recently included the galaxies, Africa, the sea, the sun, and the old standby, horse racing and horse breeding. But the choices don't stop there; this large flagship store has beach towels and accessories, dinner plates, clothing for men and women, a large collection of Hermès fragrances, and even a saddle shop; a package of postcards is the least expensive item sold.

Ask to see the private museum upstairs. And outside, note the horseman on the roof with his scarf-flag flying.

✪ **Louis Vuitton.** 6 place St-Germain-des-Prés, 6e. ☎ **01-45-49-62-32.** Mon–Sat 10am–7pm. Métro: St-Germain-des-Prés.

This Left Bank store is so gorgeous to look at that the famed merchandise becomes secondary. Not content to cover the world's luggage with his initials, Vuitton has branched into assorted colored leather goods, writing instruments, various travel products, and even publishing. Look for the traditional collection of leather, including Vuitton's highly visible monogrammed brown-on-brown bags in printed canvas, on the street level. The mezzanine showcases upscale pens, writing supplies, and stationery. And the top floor carries the company's newest line of goods—women's shoes and bags in shiny patent leather and nontraditional colors that include pink, blue, beige, and teal.

DISCOUNT & RESALE

Anna Lowe. 104 rue du Faubourg St-Honoré, 8e. ☎ **01-42-66-11-32.** Mon–Sat 10am–7pm. Métro: Miromesnil.

Anna Lowe is one of the premier boutiques in Paris for the discriminating woman who wishes to purchase a little Chanel, or perhaps a Versace, at discount. Many clothes are runway samples; some have been gently worn. The boutique is only half a block from rue du Faubourg-St-Honoré, where haute couture is much more expensive.

Mendès. 5 rue d'Uzès, 2e. ☎ **01-42-36-83-32.** Mon–Thurs 10am–7pm, Fri–Sat 10am–6pm. Métro: Grandes Boulevards.

In the center of the French garment district, this store mainly sells Yves Saint Laurent, Christian Lacroix, and Montana. Prices, though discounted, can be quite steep and you have to get lucky to find anything worth sighing over.

Réciproque. 88-123 rue de la Pompe, 16e. ☎ **01-47-04-30-28.** Tues–Sat 11am–7:30pm. Métro: Pompe.

Forget about serious bargains, but celebrate what could be your only opportunity to own designer clothing of this caliber; every major big name is carried here along with shoes, accessories, menswear, and wedding gifts. Everything has been worn, but some items only on fashion runways or during photography shoots.

MENSWEAR

Alain Figaret. 21 rue de la Paix, 2e. ☎ **01-42-65-04-99.** Mon–Sat 10am–7:30pm. Métro: Opéra.

Alain Figaret is one of France's foremost designers of men's shirts and women's blouses. Although this store has a broad range of fabrics, 100% cotton is its specialty. Also check out the silk neckties, which come in distinctively designed prints that can be quickly identified by the educated eye, and silk scarves for women. (If you are comparison shopping, Figaret and Charvet are a half block apart.)

Charvet. 28 place Vendôme, 8e. ☎ **01-42-60-30-70.** Mon–Sat 9:45am–6:30pm. Métro: Opéra.

The duke of Windsor made Charvet famous, but Frenchmen of distinction have been buying their shirts here for years. The store offers ties, pocket squares, underwear, and pajamas as well, and women's shirts are also available, all custom-tailored or straight off the peg.

Favourbrook. Le Village Royal, 25 rue Royale, 8e. ☎ **01-40-17-06-72.** Mon–Sat 10am–7pm. Métro: Concorde or Madeleine.

English taste and conservative style are the hallmarks of this upscale menswear store. Within a woodsy-looking enclave that might remind you of an exclusive men's club,

---

Food Markets

Outdoor food markets are plentiful in Paris. Some of the better-known ones include the **Marché Buci** (see listing under "Markets" in this chapter), the **rue Mouffetard** (6e; Métro: Monge or Censier-Daubenton), or the **rue Montorgueil,** just behind the St-Eustache church (1e; Métro: Les Halles).

---

you'll find a collection of vests, dinner jackets, ascots, neckties, shirts, bow ties, cummerbunds, and the kind of gift items you might want to present as a wedding present to a valued colleague. An equivalent inventory of nonessential but desirable fashion accessories for women is available at the establishment's sister store, **Violet,** also within Le Village Royal, 25 rue Royale, 8e (☎ **01-40-17-08-72**).

FOOD

Albert Ménès. 41 bd. Malesherbes, 8e. ☎ **01-42-66-95-63.** Mon 2–7pm, Tues–Sat 10am–7pm. Métro: St-Augustin or Madeleine.

One of the most prestigious small-scale purveyors of foodstuffs in Paris prides itself on selling only food that has been picked, processed, and packaged by hand. Consequently, you'll find food from obscure corners of France here whose small-scale production simply isn't available at supermarkets. The 45 producers whose goods are represented produce sugared almonds, sardines, exotic honeys, terrines and pâtés, and baked goods. It's all esoteric, even by French standards. Ménès prides itself, strangely enough, on being the first food store in France to import both Heinz Ketchup and Kellogg's Corn Flakes, both of which appeared on shelves for the first time here in the 1920s.

✪ **Fauchon.** 26-30 place de la Madeleine, 8e. ☎ **01-47-42-60-11.** Mon–Sat 9:40am–7pm. A "Mini-Fauchon" is open Mon–Sat 9:40am–8:30pm. Métro: Madeleine.

At the place de la Madeleine stands one of the most popular sights in the city—not the church, but Fauchon, now a three-part shop crammed with gastronomical goodies. One shop sells dry goods; one sells candy, pastry, and bread; and one sells fresh fruits and veggies. A cafeteria and coffee bar (Brasserie Fauchon) are nestled in the basement of one shop, and a full restaurant, **Le 30,** is located above (see chapter 5).

Even though prices are steep, it's easier than ever to pay for your goods: You are given an electronic card when you first enter the store and the value of each purchase is electronically encoded on it. When you finish shopping, head for the *caisse* (cash register), surrender the card, and pay the tally, then return to the counters to pick up your groceries.

Hediard. 21 place de la Madeleine, 8e. ☎ **01-43-12-88-77.** Mon–Sat 9am–11pm. Métro: Madeleine.

This 1850 temple of haute gastonomie has recently been completely renovated, perhaps to woo tourists away from Fauchon. The decor is now a series of salons filled with almost Disneyesque displays meant to give the store the look of a turn-of-the-century spice emporium. Upstairs, you can eat at the Restaurant de l'Epicerie.

La Maison du Miel. 24 rue Vignon, 9e. ☎ **01-47-42-26-70.** Tues–Sat 10am–7pm. Métro: Madeleine.

"The House of Honey" has been a family tradition since before World War I. The entire store is devoted to products made from honey: honey oil, honey soap, and, of course, various honeys to eat, including one made from heather. This store owes a tremendous debt to the busy bee.

Maison de la Truffe. 19 place de la Madeleine, 8e. ☎ **01-42-65-53-22.** Tues–Sat 9am–9pm, Mon 9am–8pm. Métro: Madeleine.

This tiny shop resembles a New York deli more than a Parisian boutique. It's your source not only for truffles but foie gras, caviar, and other gourmet foodstuffs. Gift food baskets are a house specialty. There are also a few tables and chairs so you can grab a quick bite.

Marks and Spencer. 35 bd. Haussmann, 9e. ☎ **01-47-42-42-91.** Mon–Sat 9am–8pm (Thurs until 9pm). Métro: Chausée-d'Antin. Also at 88 rue de Rivoli, 4e (☎ 01-44-61-08-00). Métro: Hôtel de Ville.

Okay, so it's a British department store specializing in clothing for men, women, and children. But the entire ground floor is a giant supermarket devoted to the St. Michael's brand of English foodstuff, and includes prepared foods for picnics.

Poilâne. 8 rue du Cherche-Midi, 6e. ☎ **01-45-48-42-59.** Mon–Sat 7:15am–8:15pm. Métro: St-Sulpice.

One of the most prestigious and best-loved bakeries in Paris, Poilâne hasn't changed much since it first opened its doors in 1932. Come here to taste and admire the beautiful loaves of bread decorated with simple designs of leaves and flowers that will make you yearn for an all-but-disappeared Paris. Specialties include apple tarts, butter cookies, and a chewy sourdough loaf cooked in a wood-burning oven. Breads can be specially wrapped to stay fresh during your journey home. If the line is too long on Saturday morning, visit their second location at 49 bd. de Grenelle, 15e (☎ **01-45-79-11-49**). Cash only.

JEWELRY

Cartier. 7 place Vendôme, 1er. ☎ **01-44-55-32-50.** Mon and Sat 10am–7pm, Tues–Fri 10am–6:30pm. Métro: Opéra or Tuileries.

One of the most famous jewelers in the world, Cartier has prohibitive prices to match its glamorous image. Go to gawk, and if your pockets are deep enough, pick up an expensive trinket.

Chaumet. 12 place Vendôme, 1er. ☎ **01-44-77-24-00.** Mon–Sat 10am–6:30pm. Métro: Opéra or Tuileries.

This decidedly French establishment has long catered to old money. It's the kind of place where distinguished-looking gentlemen buy jewels for their wives *and* mistresses and no one bats an eye.

✪ **Van Cleef and Arpels.** 22 place Vendôme, 1er. ☎ **01-53-45-45-45.** Mon–Sat 10am–6:30pm. Métro: Opéra or Tuileries.

This place sells jewels to the rich and famous. During the 1920s and '30s, a stopover here was *de rigueur* for Jazz Age millionaires. Later, its designers came up with an intricate technique that remains a vital part of its allure today—the invisible setting, wherein a band of sparkling gemstones, each cut to interlock with its neighbor, creates an uninterrupted flash of brilliance. Gemologists consider it one of the store's foremost achievements.

KITCHENWARE

A. Simon. 48 rue Montmartre, 2e. ☎ **01-42-33-71-65.** Mon–Sat 8:30am–6:30pm. Métro: Etienne Marcel.

This large kitchenware shop, not in Montmartre but near the Forum des Halles mall (half a block from Mendès, the Yves Saint Laurent outlet), supplies restaurants and professional kitchens. But it will also cover your table with everything from menu cards and wine tags to knives, copper pots, and pans. It also stocks white paper doilies and those funny little paper things they put on top of the tablecloth at bistros.

Dehillerin. 18 rue Coquillière, 1er. ☎ **01-42-36-53-13.** Tues–Sat 8am–6pm, Mon 8am–12:30pm and 2–6pm. Métro: Les Halles.

Dehillerin is the most famous cookware shop in Paris, located in the "kitchen corridor," alongside A. Simon and several other kitchenware stores. The shop has more of a professional feel to it than the beginner-friendly A. Simon, but don't be intimidated. Equipped with the right tools from Dehillerin, you too can learn to cook like a master chef.

LEATHER GOODS
Didier Lamarthe. 219 rue St. Honoré, 1er. ☎ **01-42-96-09-90.** Mon–Sat 10am–7pm. Métro: Tuileries.

A cult hero in France yet virtually unknown elsewhere, this designer is famous for his handbags and small leather goods in funky fashion shades like melon or mint. Sure, he does more conservative colors like navy and black, but if you want the world to know you've been to Paris and that you're totally *branché* (plugged in), spring for a risqué shade.

Longchamp. 390 rue St-Honoré, 1er. ☎ **01-42-60-00-00.** Mon–Sat 10am–7pm. Métro: Concorde.

Longchamp is a French brand known for high-quality leather and strong everyday durables that come in basic as well as fashion shades. Check out their pale pink or steel-colored patent leather for a touch of Paris. Their best bet is a series of nylon handbags attached to leather handles that fold for storage or travel and unfold for shopping. Items are priced according to size but begin at around $45.

Morabito. 55 rue François, Ier, 8e. ☎ **01-53-23-90-40.** Mon–Sat 10am–7pm. Métro: F. D. Roosevelt.

While Hermès has the international rep, Morabito is the secret insider's source for chicer-than-thou handbags that begin at a bare minimum of 2,000 F ($340), and quickly climb to as much as 35,000 F ($5,950) and more.

LINGERIE
Cadolle. 14 rue Cambon, 1er. ☎ **01-42-60-94-94.** Mon–Sat 9:30am–1pm and 2–6:30pm. Métro: Concorde.

Herminie Cadolle invented the brassiere in 1889. Today the store she founded is managed by her family, and they still make the specialty brassieres for the Crazy Horse Saloon. This is the place to go if you want made-to-order items or if you're hard to fit.

Marie-Claude Fremau. 16 rue de la Paix, 2e. ☎ **01-42-61-61-91.** Mon–Sat 10am–7pm. Métro: Opéra.

The French are big on shops that sell towels and bathrobes as well as underwear. Naturally, French bathroom wear has characteristic flair and style—we're talking about a yellow silk bathrobe with a ruffled collar for about $300. The newest store is at 104 rue de Rennes, 6e (☎ **01-45-48-82-76**).

Sabbia Rosa. 73 rue des Sts-Pères, 6e. ☎ **01-45-48-88-37.** Mon–Sat 10am–7pm. Métro: Sèvres-Babylone.

Madonna shops here for $400 silk panties. Doesn't everyone?

MALLS
Forum des Halles. 1-7 rue Pierre-Lescot, 1er. No general phone. Mon–Sat 10am–7:30pm. Métro: Etienne-Marcel, Les Halles, or Châtelet.

Once the site of Paris's great produce market, Les Halles is now a vast crater of modern metal with layers of boutiques built around a courtyard. There's one of everything here, but the feel is very sterile, without a hint of the famous French *joie de vivre*.

Le Carrousel du Louvre. 99 rue de Rivoli, 1er. No general phone. Tues–Sun 10am–8pm. Métro: Palais-Royal or Musée du Louvre.

If you want to combine an accessible location, a fun food court, handy boutiques, and plenty of museum gift shops with a touch of culture, don't miss Le Carrousel. Always mobbed with locals and visitors, this is one of the few venues allowed to open on Sunday. There's a Virgin Megastore, a branch of the Body Shop, and several other emporiums for conspicuous consumption. Check out Diane Claire for the fanciest souvenirs of Paris you've ever seen.

Les Trois Quartiers. 23 bd. de la Madeleine, 1e. ☎ **01-42-97-80-06.** Mon–Sat 10am–7pm. Métro: Madeleine.

This is a conveniently located modern mall with branch stores of many upscale designers and a large parfumerie, Silver Moon.

Marché Saint Germain. 14 rue Lobineau, 6e. No general phone. Mon–Sat 11am–7pm. Métro: Odéon.

Marché Saint Germain used to be an open-air food market until it was transformed into a modern shopping mall. Now only a few food and vegetable stalls remain in one corner—the rest of the market is dominated by low ceilings, neon lights, and mostly American and British chain stores. Examples include Kitchen Bazaar, Silver Moon, and Kenzo.

Montparnasse Shopping Centre. Between rue de l'Arrivée and 22 rue du Départ, 14e. No general phone. Mon–Sat 8:30am–10pm. Métro: Montparnasse-Bienvenue.

This shopping center is sort of a quick fix minimall in a business center and hotel (Le Meredien) complex, with a small branch of Galeries Lafayette and some inexpensive boutiques. Visiting it is really only worthwhile if you also take a trip across the street to Inno, with its deluxe supermarket in the basement. You may be tempted to play with the automatic train track for shopping carts.

Palais des Congrès de Paris Boutiques. 2 place de la Porte-Maillot, 17e. No general phone. Mon–Sat 10am–7pm. Métro: Porte Maillot.

A shopping center for convention-goers, located inside the Palais des Congrès building, this mall offers some 50 shops, including branch stores of many French big names. You'll also find a Japanese department store and hairdresser. Its anonymity and distance from most of touristic Paris has taken its toll on some of the shops here, but if you happen to be in the neighborhood, and are absolutely committed to shopping, it might be useful.

MARKETS

Marché aux Fleurs. Place Louis-Lépine, Ile-de-la-Cité, 4e. Daily 8:30am–4pm. Métro: Cité.

Artists and photographers love to capture the Flower Market on canvas or film. The stalls are ablaze with color, and each is a showcase of flowers, most of which escaped the perfume factories of Grasse in the French Riviera. The Flower Market is along the Seine, behind the Tribunal de Commerce. On Sunday it becomes a bird market.

Marché aux Livres. Square Georges Brancion, 15e. Sat–Sun 10am–4pm in winter, 10am–6pm in summer. Métro: Porte de Vanves.

This charming two-building market for used books, old books, rare books, and some ephemera is slightly in the middle of nowhere but nonetheless thronged by serious collectors. The market is covered but open, and doesn't close on a rainy day—the really valuable texts are draped in plastic.

And don't forget the ***bouquinistes*** along the left bank of the Seine, on the quai de Montebello.

✪ **Marché aux Puces de Clignancourt.** Av. de la Porte de Clignancourt, 18e. Daily 9am–6pm. Métro: Porte de Clignancourt; from there, turn left and cross bd. Ney, then walk north on av. de la Porte de Clignancourt. Bus: 56.

The most famous flea market in Paris is actually a grouping of more than a dozen different flea markets. This is a complex of 2,500 to 3,000 open stalls and shops on the northern fringe of Paris, selling everything from antiques to junk, from new to vintage clothing.

The market begins with stalls of cheap clothing along avenue de la Porte de Clignancourt. As you proceed, various streets will tempt you. Hold on until you get to the rue des Rosiers, then turn left. Vendors start bringing out their offerings around 9am and start taking them in around 6pm. Hours are a tad flexible depending on weather and crowds. Monday is traditionally the best day for bargain seekers, since the market is more sparsely attended and the merchants are more eager to sell.

First-timers at the flea market always want to know two things: "Will I get any real bargains?" and "Will I get fleeced?" Actually, it's all relative. Obviously, the best buys have been skimmed by dealers (who often have a prearrangement to have items held for them). And it's true that the same merchandise displayed here will sell for less in the provinces of France. But from the point of view of the visitor who has only a few days to spend in Paris—and only half a day for shopping—the flea market is worth the experience. Vintage French postcards, old buttons, and bistro ware are quite affordable; each market has its own personality and an aura of Parisian glamor that can't be found elsewhere.

Dress casually, and show your knowledge if you are a collector. The dealers in most of the markets are serious and only get into the spirit of things if you speak French or make it clear that you know what you are doing and have some expertise in their field. The longer you stay, the more you chat, the more you show your respect for the goods, the more room you'll have for negotiating the price.

Most of the markets have rest-room facilities; some have a central office to arrange shipping. There are cafes, pizza joints, and even a few real restaurants scattered throughout. Beware of pickpockets and teenage troublemakers.

Marché aux Puces de la Porte de Vanves. Av. Georges-Lafenestre, 14e. Sat–Mon 6:30am–4:30pm. Métro: Porte de Vanves.

This weekend event sprawls along two streets and is actually the best flea market in Paris; dealers swear by it. There's little in terms of formal antiques and few large pieces of furniture. You'll do better if you collect old linens, used Hermès scarves, toys, ephemera, costume jewelry, perfume bottles, and bad art. Asking prices tend to be high, as dealers prefer to sell to nontourists. On Sunday, there's a food market one street over.

Marché aux Timbres. Av. Matignon, off the Champs-Elysées at Rond-Point, 8e. Generally Thurs–Sun 10am–7pm. Métro: F. D. Roosevelt or Champs-Elysées–Clemenceau.

This is where Audrey Hepburn figured it out in *Charade*, remember? At this stamp collector's paradise, nearly two dozen stalls are set up on a permanent basis under shady trees on the eastern edge of the Rond-Point. The variety of stamps is almost unlimited—some common, some quite rare.

Marché Buci. Rue de Buci, 6e. Daily 9am–7pm. Métro: St-Germain-des-Prés.

This traditional French food market is held at the intersection of two streets and is only 1 block long, but what a block it is! Seasonal fruits and vegetables dance across tabletops as chickens spin on the rotisserie. One stall is entirely devoted to big bouquets of fresh flowers. Monday mornings are light.

MUSEUM SHOPS

La Boutique de la Comédie Française. 2 rue de Richelieu, 1er. ☎ **01-44-58-14-30.** Daily 11am–8:30pm. Métro: Palais-Royal.

This is the official gift and souvenir shop of the most historic and prestigious theater in France. The plays commemorated inside have elicited in the French as much emotion and loyalty as Shakespeare has in the British. Look for plates and cups depicting 18th-century misers, maidens, and faithful servants, as well as scarves, pens, drinking glasses, and napkins honoring the French theater. You might appreciate the beer mugs *(les chopes)* emblazoned with the frontispiece of Molière's original folio for *Le Bourgeois Gentilhomme.* The gift shop remains open in August, when the theater itself is closed.

La Boutique du Musée de la Monnaie. 11 quai de Conti (entrance at 2 rue Guénégaud), 6e. ☎ **01-40-46-55-35.** Mon–Fri 9am–5:30pm, Sat 10am–1pm and 2–5:30pm. Métro: Pont-Neuf or Odéon.

Jewelry made from coins and/or semiprecious stones, reproductions of antique coins, and medallions of every imaginable sort are sold here, sometimes to consumers who have little or no interest in touring the museum itself. If your tastes and interests involve small, cunning, and valuable objects, this might be the place for you.

La Boutique du Musée des Arts Decoratifs. 105 rue de Rivoli, 1er. ☎ **01-42-61-04-02.** Daily 10am–7pm. Métro: Palais-Royal or Tuileries.

This two-part boutique is divided by the entryway to the museum. On the right is a fabulous bookstore. On the left is a boutique selling reproductions of museum items: gifts, knickknacks, and even a custom-made Hermès scarf.

Musée et Compagnie. 49 rue Etienne-Marcel, 1er. ☎ **01-40-13-49-12.** Mon–Sat 10am–6:30pm. Métro: Etienne-Marcel.

This shop contains a selection of reproductions based on originals contained within the approximately 20 *Musées Nationaux* of France, including the Louvre, the Musée d'Orsay, the Grand Palais, and the Musée Picasso. Prices range from 100 F ($17) for a pair of ear clips to as much as 3,000 F ($510) for a reproduction of an object from Greek, Assyrian, or Roman antiquity. It's useful to check out the larger inventories of roughly equivalent merchandise at the establishment's sibling shop, **Musée-Halles,** Forum des Halls, Porte-Berger Niveau-2, 2e (☎ **01-40-39-92-21;** Métro: Halles), which maintains the same hours.

MUSIC

FNAC Montparnasse. 136 rue de Rennes, 6e. ☎ **01-49-54-30-00.** Mon–Wed and Fri–Sat 10am–7:30pm, Thurs 10am–9:30pm. Métro: St-Placide.

This is one of the busiest members of a large chain of music and bookstores known for its wide selection and discounted prices. There are eight other branches of the chain at other locations in Paris, including FNAC **St-Lazare,** 109 rue St-Lazare, 9e (☎ **01-55-31-20-00;** Métro: St-Lazare), which maintains the same hours as listed above; FNAC **Champs-Elysées,** 74 avenue des Champs-Elysées, 8e (☎ **01-53-53-64-64;**

Métro: F. D. Roosevelt), open daily from 10am to midnight; and FNAC in the **Forum des Halles,** 1-7 rue Pierre-Lescot, 1er (☎ **01-40-41-40-00;** Métro: Châtelet–Les Halles), open Monday through Saturday from 10am to 7:30pm.

Virgin Megastore. 52–60 av. des Champs-Elysées, 8e. ☎ **01-49-53-50-00.** Mon–Sat 10am–midnight, Sun noon–midnight. Métro: F. D. Roosevelt. Branch stores: Carrousel du Louvre; both airports; Gare Montparnasse.

This is the largest music store in Paris, in a landmark building that helped rejuvenate the Champs-Elysées. There's a bookstore and cafe located downstairs.

PERFUME & MAKEUP (DISCOUNT)

Catherine. 7 rue Castiglione, 1er. ☎ **01-42-60-48-17.** Mon–Sat 9:30am–7pm. Métro: Concorde.

This well-respected, family-owned shop carries an impressive stock of all the big-name perfumes and cosmetics, and sells them cheerfully and politely at discounts of between 20% and 25% off retail. In addition, their paperwork is usually extremely well organized, allowing refunds of the 15% value-added tax (VAT) to be cleared through French Customs efficiently and quickly. Many of the staff here speak English, and many have a refreshing sense of humor.

Michel Swiss. 16 rue de la Paix, 2e. ☎ **01-42-61-61-11.** Mon–Sat 10am–7pm. Métro: Opéra.

This is tricky for a first-timer. There's no storefront window; instead, you enter a courtyard and take an elevator to get upstairs to the shop. Once you're inside, you'll find the major brands of luxury perfumes, cosmetics, leather bags, pens, neckties, fashion accessories, and gifts. All items are discounted to varying degrees, with an additional VAT discount if you qualify. In summer, don't be surprised if there is a line of people waiting to use the elevator.

Parfumerie de La Madeleine. 9 place de la Madeleine, 8e. ☎ **01-42-66-52-20.** Mon–Sat 10:30am–7:30pm. Métro: Madeleine.

This shop offers good discounts, depending on the brand (10% on Chanel, 30% on Sisley). There are tons of fragrances and a few designer accessories in the bright, modern, chic shop. Discounts are included in the prices as marked.

SHOES

Maud Frizon. 81-83 rue des Sts-Pères, 6e. ☎ **01-45-49-20-59.** Mon–Sat 10:30am–7pm. Métro: Sèvres-Babylone.

The collection of women's shoes here is among the most unusual in the city. Virtually everything sold is made in France.

SOUVENIRS & GIFTS

Au Nom de la Rose. 46 rue du Bac, 7e. ☎ **01-42-22-22-12.** Mon–Sat 10am–7:30pm. Métro: rue du Bac.

Everything sold here is coming up roses. Inventories include home accessories, fashion accessories, perfumes, scented candles and soaps, and gift items that re-create the spirit of Valentine's Day year-round. Attached to the shop is a florist, open Monday through Saturday from 9am to 9pm.

Galerie Architecture Miniature Gault. 206 rue de Rivoli, 1er. ☎ **01-42-60-51-17.** Mon–Sat 10am–7pm, Sun 11am–7pm. Métro: Tuileries.

This store features Lilliputian town models complete with pint-sized houses, stores, and fountains—miniature versions of French country villages and Parisian neighbor-hoods, all built to scale. Collectors visit the Galerie to buy models and kits for their

The Scent of a Parisian

If there's one thing that international shoppers come to Paris for, it's cosmetics—after all, the City of Light is the world capital of fragrances and beauty supplies. These are a few of our favorite perfume and makeup shops:

While you can buy **Caron** scents in any duty-free or discount parfumerie, it's worth visiting the source of some of the world's most famous perfumes. The store is located at 34 av. Montaigne, 8e (☎ **01-47-23-40-82;** Métro: F. D. Roosevelt), and is a tiny shop with old-fashioned glass beakers filled with fragrances and a hint of yesteryear. *Fleur de Rocaille,* a Caron scent, was the featured perfume in the movie *Scent of a Woman.* Store hours are Monday through Saturday from 10am to 6:30pm.

While there are other branches of **Annick Goutal** (☎ **01-42-60-52-82;** Métro: Concorde) in Paris—and while you can test Goutal bath amenities at many of the upscale hotels—the mosaic tile on the sidewalk at the 14 rue Castiglione store in the 1st arrondissement, and its unique and unearthly scents, make it worth stopping by. Try Hadrien for a unisex splash of citrus and summer. Store hours are Monday through Saturday from 10am to 7pm.

Off a small courtyard halfway between the place de la Madeleine and the Champs-Elysées, **Makeup Forever,** 5 rue de la Boetie, 8e (☎ **01-42-66-01-60;** Métro: St-Augustin), is where French models and actors go for their makeup. They also have fashion sunglasses at reasonable prices. The outlet was created by French stylist and entrepreneur Dany Sanz in 1984, and now maintains branches in New York and throughout the world. Check out the accessories, including suitcases, purses, and small travel kits ranging in price from 100 F to 3,000 F ($17 to $510). Store hours are Monday through Saturday from 10am to 7pm.

If you think you've heard of every perfume and aromatherapy gimmick out there, this one will still impress you: At the very New-Age **Octée,** 18 rue des Quatre-Vents, 6e (☎ **01-46-33-18-77;** Métro: Odéon), the collection of fragrances is color coded to match your personality, skin type, and mood. There's perfume, sprays, soaps, and body lotion, and you test everything on colored ribbons. Store hours are Tuesday through Saturday from 11am to 7pm.

Salons du Palais Royal Shiseido, 142 Galerie de Valois, Palais Royal, 1er (☎ **01-49-27-09-09;** Métro: Palais Royal). Shiseido, the fourth-largest maker of cosmetics and skin-care goods in the world, has become more prominent thanks to the merchandising efforts of this store, one of the most beautiful in Paris. In addition to an awesome array of skin-care products and makeup, it stocks at least a dozen fragrances created by the company's artistic director, Serge Lutens, that are sold here exclusively. Don't be afraid to wander in and ask for some scent strips.

own villages and towns. A hand-painted ceramic depiction of a house or French national monument ranges in price from 65 F to 4,000 F ($11.05 to $680), depending on its size and intricacy. A hand-painted Limoges pillbox goes for around 350 F ($59.50).

La Boutique de l'Hotel de Crillon. 10 place de la Concorde, 8e. ☎ **01-49-24-00-52.** Mon–Sat 9am–9pm, Sun 10am–9pm. Métro: Concorde.

Set immediately to the left of the entrance to Paris's most famous hotel, this is a hyper-upscale boutique that trades on its association with prestige and glamor. About half of the merchandise bears the Crillon's logo. They sell porcelain dishes, Baccarat crystal, ashtrays, napkin rings, linens, bathrobes and nightgowns, umbrellas, leather gloves, and tasseled silk napkins.

La Tuile à Loup. 35 rue Daubenton, 5e. ☎ **01-47-07-28-90.** Mon 1–7pm, Tues–Sat 10:30am–7pm. Métro: Censier-Daubenton.

This emporium has been selling authentic examples of all-French handcrafts since around 1975, making a name for itself through its concentration of authentic, hand-produced woven baskets, cutlery, and wood carvings. Especially appealing are the hand-painted crockery and charming stonewear from traditional manufacturers such as Quimper and Lunéville, and from small-scale producers in the Savoie Alps and Alsace.

STATIONERY

✪ **Cassegrain.** 422 rue St-Honoré, 8e. ☎ **01-42-60-20-08.** Mon–Sat 10am–7pm. Métro: Concorde. Also at 81 rue des Sts-Pères, 6e. ☎ 01-42-22-04-76. Métro: Sèvres-Babylone.

Nothing says elegance more than thick French stationery and note cards. Cassegrain offers beautifully engraved stationery, most often in traditional patterns, and business cards engraved to order. Several other items for the desk, many suitable for gifts, are for sale as well; there are even affordable pencils and small desktop accessories.

TABLEWARE

Conran Shop. 117 rue du Bac, 7e. ☎ **01-42-84-10-01.** Tues–Sat 10am–7pm, Mon noon–7pm. Métro: Sèvres-Babylone.

This shop might remind you of an outpost of the British Empire, valiantly imposing British aesthetics and standards on the French-speaking world. Inside, you'll find articles for the home, for the kitchen and dining room, glass and crystal vases, fountain pens and stationery, reading material and postcards, and even a selection of chocolates, teas, and coffees to help warm up a foggy English day. It lies adjacent to the sprawling department-store racks of Bon Marché, at the top of a street known for its collection of charming shops.

Geneviève Lethu. 95 rue de Rennes, 6e. ☎ **01-45-44-40-35.** Mon–Sat 10am–7pm. Métro: St-Sulpice.

This Provençal designer has shops all over France, with several others in Paris, all selling her clever and colorful Pottery Barn meets French Mediterranean tableware. Newer designs stress influences from India, South America, and Africa as well. Energy, style, and verve are rampant here. Prices are moderate.

WINES

Les Caves Taillevent. 199 rue du Faubourg St-Honoré, 8e. ☎ **01-45-61-14-09.** Mon 2–8pm, Tues–Fri 9am–8pm, Sat 9am–7:30pm. Métro: Charles-de-Gaulle–Etoile or Ternes.

This is a temple to the art of making fine French wine. Associated with one of Paris's grandest restaurants, the nearby Taillevent, it occupies the street level and cellar of an antiques building in a neighborhood awash with memories of the French empire. Stored here are more than half a million bottles of wine, ranging in price from 26 F ($4.40) to exceptionally rare vintages such as a 1995 Romani-Conti Burgundy (Côtes de Nuit) priced at 22,000 F ($3,740)

Paris After Dark

9

After a long sleep, Paris nightlife has awakened. Late-night bars fill like gaudy aquariums, and French rap has flourished as a kind of hybrid of British, American, and North African influences. In this chapter we describe after-dark diversions that range from cafe concerts to "where the boys are."

Parisians start the serious part of their evenings just as Anglos stretch, yawn, and announce it's time for bed. Once a Paris workday is over, many people go straight to the cafe to meet up with friends; after a time, they proceed to a restaurant, bar, or theater; and much later, they grace a nightclub or late-night bar.

For the cafe scene, see chapter 5.

1 The Performing Arts

Announcements of shows, concerts, and operas are plastered on kiosks all over town. Listings can be found in *Pariscope,* a weekly entertainment guide with a section in English, or the English-language *Boulevard,* a bimonthly magazine. Performances start later in Paris than in London or New York—anywhere from 8 to 9pm—and Parisians tend to dine after the theater. You may not want to do the same, since many of the less-expensive restaurants close as early as 9pm.

A STATESIDE TICKET AGENCY For tickets and information to just about any show and entertainment in Paris, **Globaltickets,** from Edwards and Edwards, has a New York office if you'd like to arrange your schedule before you go. It's at 1270 Ave. of the Americas, Suite 2414, New York, NY 10020 (☎ **800/223-6108** or 914/328-2150). They also have an office in Paris for assistance while you are there: 19 rue des Mathurins, 9e (☎ **01-42-65-39-21;** Métro: Havre-Caumartin). A personal visit isn't necessary. Edwards and Edwards will mail tickets to your home, fax confirmation, or leave tickets at the box office in Paris. There is a markup of 10% to 20% (excluding opera and ballet) over box-office price plus a U.S. handling charge of $8. Hotel/theater packages are also available.

DISCOUNTS Several agencies sell tickets for cultural events and plays at discounts of up to 50%. One is the **Kiosque Théâtre,** 15 place de la Madeleine, 8e (no phone; Métro: Madeleine), offering leftover tickets for about half price on the day of the performance. Tickets for evening performances are sold Tuesday through Friday from 12:30 to 8pm and Saturday from 2 to 8pm. If you'd like to attend a matinee, buy your ticket Saturday from 12:30 to 2pm or Sunday from 12:30 to

There are many ticket agencies in Paris, most of them near the Right Bank hotels. *Avoid them if possible.* The cheapest tickets can be purchased at discount ticket kiosks (see "Discounts," under "The Performing Arts" in this chapter) or the box office of the theater itself. Remember to tip the usher who shows you to your seat in a theater or movie house around 3 F (50¢).

4pm. Other, possibly less crowded, branches are in the basement of the Châtelet–Les Halles Métro station and in front of the Gare Montparnasse.

Students with ID can often get last-minute tickets by applying at the box office an hour before curtain time.

For easy availability of tickets for festivals, concerts, and the theater, try one of two locations of the **FNAC** record store chain: 136 rue de Rennes, 6e (☎ **01-49-54-30-00;** Métro: Montparnasse-Bienvenue), or in the Forum des Halles, 1-7 rue Pierre-Lescot, 1er (☎ **01-40-41-40-00;** Métro: Châtelet–Les Halles).

THEATER

Comédie-Française. 2 rue de Richelieu, 1er. ☎ **01-44-58-15-15.** Tickets 70–190 F ($11.90–$32.30). Métro: Palais-Royal or Musée-du-Louvre.

Those with a modest understanding of French can still delight in a sparkling production of Molière at this national theater, established to keep the classics alive and promote the most important contemporary authors. Nowhere else will you see the works of Molière and Racine so beautifully staged. The box office is open daily from 11am to 6pm, but the hall is dark from July 21 to September 5. In 1993, a Left Bank annex was launched, **Comédie Française–Théâtre du Vieux Colombier,** 21 rue du Vieux-Colombier, 4e (☎ **01-44-39-87-00**). Although its repertoire varies, it's known for presenting some of the most serious French dramas in town. Tickets are 160 F ($27.20), 65 F ($11.05) for age 26 and under.

OPERA, DANCE & CLASSICAL CONCERTS

Cité de la Musique. 221 av. Jean-Jaurès, 19e. ☎ **01-44-84-45-00,** or 01-44-84-44-84 for tickets and information. Tickets 80–200 F ($13.60–$34) for 4:30 and 8pm concerts.

Of the half-dozen *grands travaux* (great projects) conceived by the Mitterrand administration, this testimony to the power of music has been the most widely applauded, the least criticized, and the most innovative. At the city's northeastern edge in what used to be a run-down and depressing neighborhood, this $120 million stone-and-glass structure incorporates a network of concert halls, a library and research center for the study of all kinds of music from around the world, and a museum, described fully in "Specialty Museums" in chapter 6. The complex hosts a rich variety of concerts, ranging from Renaissance through the 19th and 20th centuries, including jazz and traditional music from different nations around the world.

Maison de Radio France. 116 av. Président-Kennedy, 16e. ☎ **01-42-30-15-16.** Tickets 50–100 F ($8.50–$17). Métro: Passy-Ranelagh.

This is the site of many of the performances of the Orchestre Philharmonique de Radio-France and the somewhat more conservative Orchestre National de France. The concert hall's box office is open Monday through Saturday from 11am to 6pm.

✪ **Opéra Bastille.** Opera National de Paris. Place de la Bastille, 120 rue de Lyon, 75012 Paris. ☎ **01-43-43-96-96.** Tickets 60–660 F ($10.20–$112.20) opera, 60–650 F ($10.20–$110.50) dance. Métro: Bastille.

This controversial building—it's been called a "beached whale"—was designed by Canadian architect Carlos Ott, with curtains created by Japanese fashion designer Issey Miyake. Since its much-publicized opening in July 1989 (for the French Revolution's bicentennial), the opera house has presented masterworks such as Mozart's *Marriage of Figaro* and Tchaikovsky's *Queen of Spades*. The main hall is the largest of any French opera house, with 2,700 seats, but music critics have lambasted the acoustics. The building contains two additional concert halls, including an intimate 250-seat room that usually hosts chamber music. Both traditional opera performances and symphony concerts are presented here.

Several concerts are given for free in honor of certain French holidays. Write ahead for tickets.

Opéra-Comique. 5 rue Favart, 2e. ☎ **01-42-44-45-45.** Tickets 50–610 F ($8.50–$103.70). Métro: Richelieu-Drouot.

This is a particularly charming venue for light opera, on a smaller scale than Paris's major opera houses. Built in the late 1890s in an ornate style that might remind you of the Palais Garnier, it's the site of small productions of such operas as *Carmen, Don Giovanni, Tosca,* and *Palleas & Melisande*. There are no performances between mid-July and late August. The box office, however, is open year-round, every Monday through Saturday from 11am to 7pm.

✪ **Opéra Garnier (Palais Garnier).** Place de l'Opéra, 9e. ☎ **01-40-01-17-89.** Tickets 60–650 F ($10.20–$110.50) opera, 30–405 F ($5.10–$68.85) dance. Métro: Opéra.

Opéra Garnier is the premier stage for dance and, once again, for opera. Because of the competition from the Opéra Bastille, the original opera has made great efforts to present more up-to-date works, including choreography by Jerome Robbins, Twyla Tharp, Agnes de Mille, and George Balanchine. This rococo wonder was designed in a contest by young architect Charles Garnier at the heyday of the French Empire. The facade is adorned with marble and sculpture, including *The Dance* by Carpeaux. The world's great orchestral, operatic, and ballet companies have performed here. Now months of painstaking restorations have burnished the Garnier's former glory: In mid-1995, it reopened grandly with Mozart's *Cosí fan tutte*, its boxes and walls lined with flowing red and blue damask, gilt gleaming abundantly, its Chagall ceiling cleaned and air-conditioning added. The box office is open Monday through Saturday from 11am to 6:30pm.

Théâtre des Champs-Elysées. 15 av. Montaigne, 8e. ☎ **01-49-52-50-50.** Tickets 60–750 F ($10.20–$127.50). Métro: Alma-Marceau.

This art deco theater, which attracts the haute couture crowd, hosts both national and international orchestras as well as opera and ballet. If Brooke Astor were your date, you'd take her here, perhaps to a performance of the visiting Vienna Philharmonic. The box office is open Monday through Saturday from 11am to 7pm. Events are held year-round, except in August.

Théâtre National de Chaillot. 1 place du Trocadéro, 16e. ☎ **01-53-65-30-00.** Tickets 180 F ($30.60) adults, 120 F ($20.40) under age 25 and over 60. Métro: Trocadéro.

Designed as part of the architectural complex facing the Eiffel Tower, this is one of the city's largest concert halls, hosting a variety of cultural events that are announced on billboards in front. Sometimes (rarely) dance is staged here, or else you might see a brilliantly performed play by the great Marguerite Duras. The box office is open Monday through Saturday from 11am to 7pm and Sunday from 11am to 5pm.

2 The Club & Music Scene

Paris is still a late-night mecca, though some of the once-unique attractions now glut the market. The fame of Parisian nights was established in those distant days when the British and Americans still gasped at the sight of a bare bosom in a chorus line. The fact is that contemporary Paris has less vice than London, Hamburg, or San Francisco.

Nevertheless, both the quantity and the variety of Paris nightlife still exceed that of other cities. Nowhere else will you find such a huge and mixed array of nightclubs, bars, dance clubs, cabarets, jazz dives, music halls, and honky-tonks.

MUSIC HALLS

Olympia. 28 bd. des Capucines, 9e. ☎ **01-47-42-25-49.** Tickets 150–300 F ($25.50–$51). Métro: Opéra or Madeleine.

Charles Aznavour and other big names make frequent appearances in this cavernous hall. The late Yves Montand appeared once, and the performance was sold out 4 months in advance. Today you are more likely to catch Gloria Estefan. A typical lineup might include an English rock group, showy Italian acrobats, a well-known French singer, a dance troupe, juggling American comedians (doing much of their work in English), plus the featured star. A witty emcee and an on-stage band provide a smooth transition. Performances usually begin at 8:30pm Tuesday through Sunday; Saturday matinees start at 5pm.

CHANSONNIERS

Chansonniers (literally "songwriters") provide a bombastic musical satire of the day's events. This combination of parody and burlesque is a time-honored Gallic amusement and a Parisian institution. Songs are often created on the spot, inspired by the "disaster of the day."

Au Caveau de la Bolée. 25 rue de l'Hirondelle, 6e. ☎ **01-43-54-62-20.** Fixed-price dinner 260 F ($44.20) Mon–Fri, 300 F ($51) Sat. Cover 150 F ($25.50) Mon–Sat if you don't order dinner. Drinks 30–65 F ($5.10–$11.05) each. Dinner Mon–Sat 8:30pm; cabaret 10:30pm. Métro: St-Michel.

To enter this bawdy boîte, you descend into the catacombs of the early- 14th-century Abbey of St-André, once a famous cafe that attracted such personages as Verlaine and Oscar Wilde, who slowly snuffed out his life in absinthe here. The singing is loud and smutty, just the way the predominantly student audience likes it. Occasionally, the audience sings along. Frankly, you'll enjoy this place a lot more if you can follow the thread of the French-language jokes and satire, but even if you don't, there are enough visuals (magic acts and performances by singers) to amuse.

The fixed-price dinner is followed by a series of at least four entertainers, usually comedians. In lieu of paying admission for the cabaret, you can order dinner. If you've already had dinner, you can just order a drink.

✪ **Au Lapin Agile.** 22 rue des Saules, 18e. ☎ **01-46-06-85-87.** Cover (including the first drink) 130 F ($22.10). Tues–Sun 9:15pm–2am. No meals are served; drinks cost 30–40 F ($5.10–$6.80). Métro: Lamarck.

Picasso and Utrillo patronized this little cottage near the top of Montmartre, then known as the Cabaret des Assassins. It has been painted by numerous artists, including Utrillo. For many decades, the heart of French folk music has beat here. You'll sit at carved wooden tables in a dimly lit room with walls covered by bohemian memorabilia and listen to French folk tunes, love ballads, army songs, sea chanteys, and music-hall ditties. You're encouraged to sing along, even if it's only the "oui, oui, oui-non,

non, non" refrain of "Les Chevaliers de la Table Ronde." The best sing-alongs are on weeknights after tourist season ends.

Théâtre des Deux Anes. 100 bd. de Clichy, 18e. ☎ **01-46-06-10-26.** Tickets 220 F ($37.40). Performances Tues–Sat at 9pm, Sun matinee 3:30pm. Closed July–Sept. Métro: Blanche.

Since around 1920, this theater has staged humorous satires of the foibles, excesses, and stupidities of various French governments. Favorite targets include President Jacques Chirac and other mandarins and kingmakers of the *héxagone française*. Cultural icons, French and foreign, receive a grilling that is very funny and sometimes harshly caustic. Don't expect the setup of a nightclub: The place considers itself more of a theater than a cabaret, and does not serve drinks or refreshments. The 2½-hour show is conducted entirely in rapid-fire French slang, so if your syntax isn't up to par, you won't appreciate its charms.

NIGHTCLUBS & CABARETS

Decidedly expensive, these places give you your money's worth by providing some of the most lavishly spectacular floor shows anywhere.

Chez Michou. 80 rue des Martyrs, 18e. ☎ **01-46-06-16-04.** Cover including dinner, aperitif, wine, coffee, and show 550 F ($93.50). Dinner nightly at 8:30pm. Show begins nightly at 10:30pm. Métro: Pigalle.

The setting is blue, the emcee wears blue, and the spotlights shining on the stage bathe performers in yet another shade of blue. The creative force behind the color coordination and a hearty dollop of cross-genderism is Michou, veteran impresario whose 20-odd cross-dressing belles bear names like Hortensia and DuDuche, and who lip-synch in costumes from haute couture to haute concierge, reviving songs by anatomically accurate songstresses. Look for tributes to such American stars as Whitney Houston, Diana Ross, and Tina Turner, and such French luminaries as Mireille Mathieu, Sylvie Vartan, "Dorothée," and the immortal Brigitte Bardot. If you don't want dinner, you'll have to stand at the bar, paying a compulsory 200 F ($34) for the first drink, 110 F ($18.70) for each additional drink. Reservations are necessary for diners, but not for barflies.

✪ **Crazy Horse Saloon.** 12 av. George V, 8e. ☎ **01-47-23-32-32.** Reservations recommended. Cover 450–560 F ($76.50–$95.20) including two drinks at a table; 290 F ($49.30) including two drinks at the bar; dinner spectacle 750 F ($127.50). Shows Sun–Fri 8:30 and 11pm; Sat 7:30, 9:45, and 11:50pm. Métro: George V or Alma-Marceau.

Since it was established in 1951, this sophisticated strip joint has thrived as a staple on the Paris theatrical circuit thanks to good choreography and its sly, often coquettish celebration of the female form. The theme that binds each of the 5-minute dance numbers is *La Femme* in her various emotional states: temperamental, sad, dancing/bouncy, or joyful. The numbers feature gorgeous girls, girls, girls, outfitted in the kind of costumes that support Paris's image as one of the erotic capitals of Europe. Specific dance numbers that endure season after season include "The Itch" and "The Erotic Lesson," which might end up teaching you a thing or two. Dinner is a tasteful, well-prepared event served with flair at Chez Francis, a restaurant under separate management a few steps from the cabaret itself. Shows last just under 2 hours.

✪ **Folies-Bergère.** 32 rue Richer, 9e. ☎ **01-44-79-98-98.** Cover 160–320 F ($27.20–$54.40); dinner and show 660–740 F ($112.20–$125.80). Tues–Sat at 9pm, Sun at 3pm. Métro: Rue-Montmartre or Cadet.

The Folies-Bergère has been a Paris institution for foreigners since 1886. Josephine Baker, the African American singer who used to throw bananas into the audience, became "the toast of Paris" here. According to legend, the first GI to reach Paris at the 1944 Liberation asked for directions to the club.

Don't expect the naughty and slyly permissive skin-and-glitter revue that used to be the trademark of this place. In 1993, all of that ended with a radical restoration and reopening under new management. Today, the site is configured as a conventional 1,600-seat theater that focuses on musical revues permeated with a sense of nostalgia for old Paris. You're likely to witness an intriguing, often charming, but not particularly erotic repertoire of mostly French songs, interspersed with the banter of a master/mistress of ceremonies. A restaurant serves set-price dinners in an anteroom to the theater. Latecomers are not admitted.

L'Ane Rouge. 3 rue Laugier, 17e. ☎ **01-47-64-45-77.** Reservations recommended. Dinner and show 250 F ($42.50). Dinner 8pm; show 10pm–midnight. Open daily. Métro: Ternes.

This red-and-black minitheater has been a showcase for French satire and humor ever since it opened shortly after World War II. You'll enjoy an earthy, well-flavored dinner of conservative French specialties, followed by a 2-hour medley of French-language stand-up comedy, ribald stories, and sometimes politicized jokes. If your knowledge of French is zero, you won't enjoy this place, and if you hate being singled out by a comedian in front of a crowd, stay away. But if you're an advanced amateur with an appreciation of eternally earthy themes (the cuckolded husband, the lecherous priest, the incompetent bureaucrat), you'll find the place a rollicking insight into another culture's humor.

Le Canotier du Pied de la Butte. 62 bd. Rochechouart, 18e. ☎ **01-46-06-02-86.** Reservations required. Cover 210 F ($35.70) including the first drink. Performances daily between 7:30 and 10:30pm. Closed mid-Jan to mid-Feb. Métro: Anvers.

The worst thing you can say about this place is that it's touristy, but the visitors who show up share a genuine appreciation of the nuances, lyricism, and poetry of popular French songs. Each performance includes appearances by two men and two women, who interact on stage with their own versions of the hits made famous by Edith Piaf, Yves Montand, Jacques Brel, and Maurice Chevalier. The byword is nostalgia, unleashed by the bucketful within a cozy red, black, and white theater with room for no more than 70 occupants.

Le Paradis Latin. 28 rue Cardinal-Lemoine, 5e. ☎ **01-43-25-28-28.** Cover 465 F ($79.05) including a half bottle of champagne; or dinner and show 680–1,250 F ($115.60–$212.50). Dinner Wed–Mon 8pm, revue 9:30pm. Métro: Jussieu or Cardinal-Lemoine.

Built in 1889 by Alexandre-Gustave Eiffel, with the same metallic skeleton as the famous tower, Le Paradis Latin represents the architect's only venture into theater design. The place is credited with introducing vaudeville and musical theater to Paris. In 1903, the building functioned as a warehouse. In the 1970s, however, it was transformed into a successful cabaret whose singers, dancers, and special effects extol the fun, frivolity, and permissiveness of Paris. The master of ceremonies speaks in French and English.

✪ **Lido de Paris.** 116 bis av. des Champs-Elysées, 8e. ☎ **800/227-4884** or 01-40-76-56-10. Cover for 10pm or midnight show 450–660 F ($76.50–$112.20) including a half bottle of champagne; or 8pm dinner-dance, including a half bottle of champagne, and 10pm show 815–1,015 F ($138.55–$172.55). Métro: George V.

Impressions

Brothers, brothers, come quickly! I am drinking stars!

—Dom Pérignon

As it heads for the millennium, the Lido has changed its feathers and modernized. Its $15 million current production, *C'est Magique,* is a dramatic reworking of the classic Parisian cabaret show, with eye-popping special effects and bold new themes, both nostalgic and contemporary, including aerial and aquatic ballets that use more than 60,000 gallons of water per minute. The show, the most expensive ever produced in Europe, uses 80 performers, $4 million in costumes, and a $2 million lighting design with lasers. There's even an ice rink and swimming pool that magically appear and disappear. The Bluebell Girls, those legendary sensual showgirls, are still here, however. Now that the celebrated chef Paul Bocuse is a consultant, the cuisine is better than ever. The quality of the shows and the professionalism of the entertainers seem to justify the high prices charged.

Moulin Rouge. Place Blanche, 18e. ☎ **01-53-09-82-82.** Cover 490–550 F ($83.30–$93.50) including champagne; or dinner and show 770 F ($130.90). For seats at the bar, cover 360 F ($61.20) includes two drinks, additional drinks 90 F ($15.30) each. Dinner nightly at 7pm. Revues presented nightly at 9 and 11pm. Métro: Blanche.

The establishment that Toulouse-Lautrec immortalized in his paintings is still here, but the artist would probably have a hard time recognizing it today. Colette created a scandal here by giving an on-stage kiss to Madame de Morny, but its harder to shock today's audiences. Try to get a table, as the view is much better on the main floor than from the bar. The ongoing emphasis on the strip routines and saucy sexiness of *La Belle Époque,* and of permissive, promiscuous Paris between the world wars, keeps bringing people here. Handsome men and girls, girls, girls, virtually all of them topless, contribute to the enduring appeal that survives despite an increasing jadedness on the part of both audiences and staff. Dance finales usually include two dozen of the belles ripping loose with a topless cancan in a style that might have been appreciated by Gigi herself.

Villa d'Este. 4 rue Arsène-Houssaye, 8e. ☎ **01-42-56-14-65.** Cover 190 F ($32.30) including the first drink; or dinner (including wine) and show 330–720 F ($56.10–$122.40). Tues–Sat, doors open at 8pm, the orchestra plays from 8:30pm, the show begins at 9:50pm, and there's dancing after the show until 2am. Métro: Charles-de-Gaulle–Etoile.

In the past, this club booked Amalia Rodrigues, Portugal's leading fadista, and French chanteuse Juliette Greco. Today you're more likely to hear French singer François de Guelte or other top talent from Europe and America. Villa d'Este has been around for a long time, and the quality of its offerings remains high. You'll probably hear some of the greatest hits of such beloved French performers as Piaf, Aznavour, Brassens, and Brel.

LE COOL JAZZ

The great jazz revival that long ago swept America is still going strong here, with Dixieland or Chicago rhythms being pounded out in dozens of jazz cellars, mostly called caveaux. Most clubs are between rue Bonaparte and rue St-Jacques on the Left Bank, which makes things easy for seekers of syncopation.

Au Duc des Lombards. 42 rue des Lombards, 1er. ☎ **01-42-33-22-88.** Cover 80–100 F ($13.60–$17). Nightly 10pm–3am. Métro: Châtelet.

Popular, comfortable, and appealing, this jazz club replaced an earlier club 9 years ago, and has thrived in a low-key way ever since. Artists begin playing at 10pm and continue (with breaks) for 5 hours, touching on repertoires that include everything from "free jazz" to more traditional forms such as "hard bop." Unlike at many of its competitors, tables can be reserved here, and will usually be held until 10:30pm.

Baiser Salé. 58 rue des Lombards, 1er. ☎ **01-42-33-37-71.** Cover 60–80 F ($10.20–$13.60) Wed–Sun; free otherwise. Daily 6pm–6am, music daily 10:30pm–3am. Métro: Châtelet.

Set in a cellar that's lined with jazz-related paintings, with a large central bar and an ongoing roster of videos that show great jazz moments from the past, this is an appealing and musically varied jazz club. There's no food, or even any particular glamor—everything is very, very mellow and laid-back. Genres featured include Afro-Caribbean, Afro-Latino, salsa, merengue, rhythm and blues, and less frequently fusion.

Caveau de la Huchette. 5 rue de la Huchette, 5e. ☎ **01-43-26-65-05.** Cover 60 F ($10.20) Sun–Thurs, 70 F ($11.90) Fri–Sat; students, 50 F ($8.50) Sun–Thurs, 60F ($10.20) Fri–Sat. Sun–Thurs 9:30pm–2:30am, Fri–Sat and holidays 9:30pm–4am. Métro and RER: St-Michel.

This celebrated jazz caveau, reached by a winding staircase, draws a young crowd, mostly students, who dance to the music of well-known jazz combos. In prejazz days, Robespierre and Marat frequented the place. Drinks go for around 26 F ($4.40) each.

Jazz Club La Villa. In the Hôtel La Villa, 29 rue Jacob, 6e. ☎ **01-43-26-60-00.** Cover 120–150 F ($20.40–$25.50) including the first drink. Mon–Sat 10:30pm–2am. Closed in Aug. Métro: St-Germain-des-Prés.

This club is unusual because it lies in the red-velour cellar of a small but chic four-star hotel in the Latin Quarter. Don't expect backpackers or impoverished artists. It's elegant, and has a reputation for bringing in famous artists to please hard-core aficionados of styles from bebop to modern jazz. Artists rotate once a week. The venue includes a predictable array of tiny tables, banquettes, armchairs, and a stage that has welcomed such artists as Joe Lovano, Hank Jones, and Shirley Horn.

Jazz Club Lionel Hampton. In the Hôtel Méridien, 81 bd. Gouvion-St-Cyr, 17e. ☎ **01-40-68-30-42.** Cover 130–160 F ($22.10–$27.20) including the first drink. Additional drinks 65–100 F ($11.05–$17) each. Nightly 10:30pm–2am or later, depending on business. Bar opens at 6:30pm daily. Métro: Porte-Maillot.

Some of the world's jazz greats, including Lionel Hampton, have performed in the Hôtel Méridien's central courtyard. The hotel is near the Champs-Elysées and the Arc de Triomphe.

La Chapelle des Lombards. 19 rue de Lappe, 11e. ☎ **01-43-57-24-24.** Cover 100–125 F ($17–$21.25) including first drink. Women enter free Thurs before midnight. Thurs–Sat 10:30pm–dawn. Métro: Bastille.

Its proximity to the Opéra Bastille seems incongruous, considering the radically experimental African/Caribbean jazz and Brazilian salsa that's the norm here. It's a magnet for South American and African expatriates, and the rhythms and fire of the music propels everyone onto the dance floor.

L'Arbuci. 25-27 rue de Buci, 6e. ☎ **01-44-32-16-00.** No cover. Dinner 200–250 F ($34–$42.50). Wed–Sat dinner services at 7:30 and 10:30pm; live music begins at 10pm. Métro: Mabillon or St-Germain-des-Prés.

The artists who perform here are likely to be lesser-known jazz players, sometimes from Southeast Asia, Madagascar, or the Philippines. The venue is subterranean, smoky, and intimate, and the music and ambience are often more appealing than the entrance suggests. Clients who opt not to have dinner are charged from 60 to 75 F ($10.20 to $12.75) per drink. The bar is open until 3am.

Le Bilboquet/Club St-Germain. 13 rue St-Benoît, 6e. ☎ **01-45-48-81-84.** No cover. Le Bilboquet nightly 8pm–2:45am; jazz music 10:30pm–2:45am. Club St-Germain Tues–Sun 11pm–5am. Métro: St-Germain-des-Prés.

This restaurant/jazz club/piano bar, where the film *Paris Blues* was shot, offers some of the best music in Paris. Jazz is played on the upper level in the restaurant, Le Bilboquet, a wood-paneled room with a copper ceiling, brass-trimmed sunken bar, and Victorian candelabra. The menu is limited but classic French, specializing in lamb, fish, and beef. Dinner costs 180 F to 300 F ($30.60 to $51).

Under separate management is the downstairs Club St-Germain disco, where entrance is free but drinks cost 100 F ($17). You can walk from one club to the other but have to buy a new drink each time you change venues.

Le Petit Opportun. 15 rue des Lavandières-Ste-Opportune, 1er. ☎ **01-42-36-01-36.** Cover 80 F ($13.60). Tues–Sat 9pm–5am; live music 10:30pm–2:30am. Métro: Châtelet.

Cramped and convivial, with a lingering sense of the 13th-century masons who built the solid cellar around you, this is a jazz club seating no more than 45 patrons, many of whom are regular clients. Its specialty is the traditional back-to-basics "hard bop" that avoids the dissonance and irregular rhythms of "free jazz." Artists come from Europe and North America, and perform for 3-hour sessions. The rest of the time, the place functions as an arts-conscious cafe and pub.

Le Sunset. 60 rue des Lombards, 1er. ☎ **01-40-26-21-25.** Cover 50–100 F ($8.50–$17). Nightly 7:30pm–3am; music 10:30pm–3am. Métro: Châtelet.

Since 1976, this club has flourished within a two-story setting that includes a street-level restaurant, where set menus are 82 F ($15). In the smoky cellar, gloss-white tiles emulate a workaday Métro station. A roster of Italian, French, and American jazz artists including such names as Roy Haynes, Also Romano, and Richard Galliano play in sets until 3 or 4am, depending on the crowd.

New Morning. 7-9 rue des Petites-Ecuries, 10e. ☎ **01-45-23-51-41.** Cover 100–180 F ($17–$30.60). Call ahead, but the hours are generally Mon–Sat 8pm–1:30am. Métro: Château-d'Eau.

Jazz maniacs come to drink, talk, and dance at this long-enduring club, which is now in the same league as the Village Vanguard in New York's Greenwich Village. The club remains on the see-and-be-seen circuit, as exemplified by recent guests: Spike Lee and the artist formerly known as Prince. The high-ceilinged loft, previously a newspaper office, was turned into a nightclub in 1981. Many styles of music are played and performed. The club is especially popular with jazz groups from Central and South Africa. A phone call will let you know what's going on the night you plan to visit. Sometimes they're open on Sunday. No food is served.

Slow Club. 130 rue de Rivoli, 1er. ☎ **01-42-33-84-30.** Cover 80–100 F ($13.60–$17). Tues–Thurs 10pm–3am, Fri–Sat 10pm–4am. Métro: Châtelet.

One of the most famous jazz cellars in Europe, capped with medieval ceiling vaults that have been praised for their acoustic intimacy, this site is a venue for a revolving set of artists who tend to focus on New Orleans jazz. Clients, mostly in their 30s and early 40s, appreciate the cross-cultural diversity of the music.

DANCE CLUBS

The nightspots below are among hundreds of places where people go chiefly to dance—distinct from others where the main attraction is the music. The area around the **Eglise St-Germain-des-Prés** is full of dance clubs. They come and go so quickly that you could arrive in your club clothes to find a hardware store in the place of last year's disco—but, like all things in nature, the new springs up to take the place of the old. Check out *Time Out: Paris* or *Pariscope* to get a sense of current trends.

A Bar Crawl in Trendy Ménilmontant

If **rue Oberkampf** were any hotter, it would melt off the map. How did it all happen so fast? Longtime residents shake their heads in disbelief and worry that the quirky authenticity of the neighborhood may disappear under the swarms of night crawlers that have migrated north en masse from the Bastille. "Too many *ban-lieusards* go to the Bastille," the owner of Café Cannibale told me, referring to the well-known reluctance of trendy Parisians to socialize with the suburban crowd.

The success of the ultra-hip Café Charbon undoubtedly encouraged entrepreneurs to renovate abandoned factories and seedy bars for the artists who were flowing into the neighborhood, and for the restless crowd that was already tiring of the Bastille. Some of the new spots seem intentionally dilapidated, while others evoke the elegance of 19th-century watering holes. The walls often exhibit the work of local artists, and the music is kept fairly low-key to avoid attracting the troublemakers often drawn by aggressive music. Drinks are reasonably priced, and a glass of mint tea makes a refreshing alternative to alcohol. You can munch on inexpensive salads, snacks, or a hot *plat du jour,* but the food is definitely secondary to the ambience.

Starting from Métro Ménilmontant and heading down rue Oberkampf, your first stop is the divey **Le Scherkhan** at no. 144 (☎ 01-43-57-29-34). Sink into an easy chair under the fangs of a stuffed tiger, inhale the incense, and dream of equatorial Africa. Open daily 5pm to 2am. Stop in at the live music club **Le Cithéa** at no. 114 (☎ 01-40-21-70-95) if it's open, or continue on to **Café Mercerie** at no. 98 (☎ 01-43-38-81-30). At the end of the fashionably grungy bar is a tiny back room lined with long sofas. Open weekdays 5pm to 2am, weekends 3pm to 2am. Across the street at no. 109 is the popular **Café Charbon** (☎ 01-43-57-55-13), a relaxed place to hang out during the day and a crowded hotspot at night. It's set in a turn-of-the-century dance hall with a stunning art nouveau interior. Farther down on the same side of the street at no. 99 is the plush **Mecano Bar** (☎ 01-40-21-35-28). Mysterious old implements on the wall are left over from its days as a tool factory. The spacious back room has a palm tree, a skylight, and murals of seminude ladies lounging about in *fin de siècle* naughtiness. Open daily noon to 2am. Backtrack a few steps and turn left onto rue St. Maur to no. 111-113, the **Blue Billard** (☎ 01-43-55-87-21), a camera factory turned into an upscale bar and pool hall, with 22 blue tables under a mezzanine and skylight. Open daily 11am to 2am. A few steps farther on at no. 117 is a local favorite, **Les Couleurs** (☎ 01-43-57-95-61), outfitted with tacky posters, chrome-and-plastic chairs, and kitschy rec-room lamps. The campy decor is '70s, but the sounds are strictly '90s. Live bands regularly play "free jazz," alternative rock, and anything experimental. Open daily noon to 2am. Turn right at rue Jean-Pierre Timbaud and at no. 93 you'll find **Café Cannibale** (☎ 01-49-29-95-59), a softly lit beauty that shimmers with mirrors, chandeliers, and candles. The menu includes a good-value Sunday brunch for 80 F ($13.55). Open daily 8am to 2am.

Club Zed. 2 rue des Anglais, 5e. ☎ **01-43-54-93-78**. Cover 50–100 F ($8.50–$17) including the first drink. Wed–Thurs 10:30pm–3am, Fri–Sat 10:30pm–5am. Métro: Maubert-Mutualité.

This popular nightspot in a former bakery with a vaulted masonry ceiling may surprise you with its mix of musical offerings, including samba, rock-and-roll, 1960s pop, and jazz.

La Balajo. 9 rue de Lappe, 11e. ☎ **01-47-00-07-87.** Cover 50 F ($8.50) including first drink on Sun afternoon, 100 F ($17) evenings. Thurs–Sat 11:30pm–5am, Sun 1–11pm. Métro: Bastille.

Established in 1936, this dance club is best remembered as the venue where Edith Piaf first won the hearts of thousands of Parisian music lovers. Today, Le Balajo is hardly as fashionable, although it continues its big-band tradition on Sunday afternoon when patrons age 45 and up dance to World War II–era swing and bebop. Thursday to Saturday nights, they bring out the disco ball, or play reggae, salsa, rock-and-roll, and rap.

La Chapelle des Lombards. 19 rue de Lappe, 11e. ☎ **01-43-57-24-24.** Cover 100 F ($16.95) Thurs, 120 F ($20.30) Fri–Sat. Métro: Bastille.

A festive tropical ambience and diverse music—everything from salsa to raggae—attract a lively mixed crowd to this hip club near the Bastille. To really enjoy this place, you have to dress the part, which means no sneakers or jeans, but rather your sophisticated best.

La Coupole. 102 bd. Montparnasse, 14e. ☎ **01-43-20-14-20.** Ballroom cover 100 F ($17) for evening sessions, 60–80 F ($10.20–$13.60) for Sat and Sun matinees. Tues 9:30pm–4am, Fri–Sat 3–7pm and 9:30pm–4am, Sun 3–9pm. Métro: Vavin.

This landmark cafe has a basement ballroom that's a popular place to waltz and tango to orchestra music as well as bump and grind to "disco retro" (the best disco tunes of the 1960s, 1970s, and 1980s). The upstairs cafe is covered in chapter 5's "The Best Cafes."

La Java. 105 rue du Faubourg du Temple, 11e. ☎ **01-42-02-20-52.** Cover 80 F ($13.60) Thurs, 100 F ($17) Fri–Sat, 40 F ($6.80) Sun. Thurs–Sat 11pm–5am, Sunday 8pm–2am. Métro: Belleville.

Once this dance hall was one of the most frequented in Paris, and the great Piaf and Maurice Chevalier made their names here. Today, you can still dance the waltz, and perhaps even tango on a Sunday afternoon. Brazilian and Latin themes predominate on some nights.

Le New Riverside. 7 rue Grégoire-de-Tours, 6e. ☎ **01-43-54-46-33.** Cover for men 90 F ($15.30) including first drink, but women pay cover only after midnight Fri–Sat. Daily 11pm–6am. Métro: St-Michel or Odéon.

If thoughts of Woodstock fill you with nostalgia, and if you want to meet French people who feel the same, this is the place for you. The battered Left Bank cellar club attracts droves of people who appreciate the indestructible premises and nostalgic music. You'll hear a K-Tel range of 1970s electronic rock and pop, especially The Doors. The crowd is between 25 and 40.

Le Saint. 7 rue St-Severin, 5e. ☎ **01-43-25-50-04.** Cover 60–90 F ($10.20–$15.30) including first drink. Daily 11pm–6am. Métro: St-Michel.

Set in three medieval cellars deep within Paris's university area, this place lures 20- and 30-somethings who dance and drink and generally feel happy to be in a Left Bank student dive. The music melds New York, Los Angeles, and Europe, and often leads to episodes of "Young Love Beside the Seine" that many visitors remember in a kind of shameful reverie for months afterward.

Les Bains. 7 rue du Bourg-l'Abbé, 3e. ☎ **01-48-87-01-80.** Cover 100 F ($17) including first drink. Nightly midnight–6am. Métro: Réaumur.

This chic enclave has been pronounced "in" and "out," but lately it's very "in," attracting model types and growing a bit gayer, especially on Monday night. Customers dress more for show than for comfort. The name Les Bains comes from the place's old function as a Turkish bath attracting gay clients, none more notable than

After-Dark Diversions

On a Paris night, the cheapest entertainment, especially if you are young, is "**the show**" staged at the extreme southeasterly tip of the Ile de la Cité, behind Notre-Dame. Equivalent in many ways to a Gallic version of the Sundowner Festival in Key West, Florida, it spontaneously attracts just about everyone who ever wanted to try their hand at performance art. Entertainment is strictly spontaneous, and usually includes magicians, fire-eaters, jugglers, mimes, and musicmakers from all over the world, performing against the backdrop of the illuminated cathedral. Completely unchoreographed, the venue provides one of the greatest places in Paris to meet other young people in a sometimes moderately euphoric setting.

Another popular people's venue is a **walk along the Seine** after 10pm. Take a graveled pathway down to the Seine from the Left Bank side of the Pont de Sully, close to the Institut du Monde Arabe, and walk to the right, away from the cathedral of Notre-Dame. This walk, which comes to an end near place Valhubert, is the best place to see spontaneous Paris in action at night. Joggers and saxophone players come here, and many Parisians show up to take part in impromptu dance parties.

To quench your thirst, wander over to the **Café-Brasserie St-Regis**, 6 rue Jean du Bellay, 4e (☎ 01-43-54-59-41), for a take-out drink. It's on the Ile St-Louis, across the street from Pont St-Louis. If you want to linger inside, you can order a plat du jour, priced at around 60 F ($10.20), or a coffee at the bar. But if you're looking for maximum mobility, do as the Parisians do and order beer to go *(une bière à emporter)* in a plastic cup, priced at 13 F ($2.20), and take it with you on a stroll around Ile St-Louis, wandering more or less aimlessly in the balmy air of a Parisian summer. The little cafe is open daily from 7am to 2am. Métro: Musée-du-Louvre.

If you're caught waiting for the Métro to start running again at 5am, try **Sous-Bock Tavern,** 49 rue St-Honoré, 1er (☎ 01-40-26-46-61; Métro: Pont-Neuf), at the corner of rue du Pont-Neuf. A crowd of young drinkers gathers here to sample some 400 varieties of beer. If you want a shot of whisky to accompany your brew, you face a choice of 150 varieties. The tavern is open daily from 11am to 5am. The dish to order here is a platter of mussels—curried, with white wine, or with cream sauce. They go well with the brasserie-style french fries. Also appealing are tagliatelle with salmon, pavé of rump steak, and old-fashioned fish-and-chips.

If you're looking for some of the best (and most flamboyant) drag in Paris, head to **Madame Arthur,** 75 bis rue des Martyrs, 18e (☎ 01-42-54-40-21; Métro:

Marcel Proust. It may be hard to get in if the bouncer doesn't like your looks. A restaurant has been added.

Les Coulisses/La Bohème. 5 rue du Mont-Cenis, 18e. ☎ 01-42-62-89-99. Cover 100 F ($17) Fri–Sat, but free for patrons of either restaurant. Restaurants daily 8pm–5am; disco 11pm–5am. Métro: Abbesses.

Its premises combine a cellar-level disco with a street-level restaurant that bears two names. During the day, between 7:30am and around 8pm, it's known as La Bohème; from 8pm to 5:30am, it becomes a bit more formal and becomes Les Coulisses. The food remains the same, featuring a set-price menu at 160 F ($27.20), and platters from

Abbesses or Pigalle). It's the longest-running transvestite show in Paris, attracting both straight and gay people who find the revue funnier, and more tasteful, than they might have expected. The creative force behind the affair is Madame Arthur, who is no lady, and whose stage name during her shticks as mistress of ceremonies is Chantaline. This place has been here so long that, according to Pigalle lore, it used to welcome the invading armies of Julius Caesar. But despite its detractors (and very few people don't like the nightly ooh-la-la's) it's still going strong, thanks to between 9 and 11 artists whose campy personae bear names like Vungala, Lady Lune, and Miss Badabou. You can visit just to drink, or you can dine from an uncomplicated fixed-price menu. Reservations are strongly advised. The club is open daily from 9 to 10:30pm for dinner, with the show beginning at 10:30pm. Additional shows, according to demand, are on Friday and Saturday at 7pm, with dinner beginning at 6pm. After the last show, around 12:30am, the place is transformed into a disco. Cover (including the first drink) is 165 F ($28.05); or dinner and show 295 F ($50.15).

If drag shows aren't your cup of tea, how about *The Last Tango in Paris?* At **Le Tango,** 13 rue au Maire, 3e (☎ **01-42-72-17-78;** Métro: Arts-et-Métiers), memories of Evita and Argentina live on. This dive with a bordello decor features zouk music from the French Caribbean and Africa, as well as house, garage, and virtually every form of high-energy dance music known in New York and Los Angeles. Most patrons are in their 20s and 30s. The cover is 40 F ($6.80). It's open Thursday through Saturday from 10:30pm to 5am and Sunday from 5 to 11pm.

Another fun and trendy dance place is **La Guinguette Pirate,** Quai de la Gare, 13e (☎ **01-44-24-89-89;** Métro: Quai de la Gare), a Chinese junk moored off the banks of the Seine. This is the latest '90s version of the fabled *guinguette,* or river cafe, offering great jazz, zouk, and live salsa. Cover is 50 F ($8.50).

If you're looking for a sophisticated, laid-back venue without the high-energy exhibitionism of nightclubs, consider a drink at the **Sanz-Sans,** 49 rue du Faubourg St-Antoine, 4e (☎ **01-44-75-78-78;** Métro: Bastille). It's a multiethnic playground where the children of prominent Parisians mingle, testifying to the unifying power of jazz. Set in a richly upholstered, red-velvet duplex, many of the most important conversations seem to occur on the stairway or the back-room couches, where margaritas slide down silk-scarved throats. The later it gets, the sexier the scene. No cover.

70 F to 100 F ($11.90–$17). Most nighttime clients eventually filter down to the disco, whose decor is a cross between a feudal château and a scene from the Italian *Commedia dell'Arte.* The crowd ranges from 20 to around 45.

Rex Club. 5 bd. Poissonière, 2e. ☎ **01-42-36-83-98.** Cover 50–80 F ($8.50–$13.60) including the first drink. Wed–Sat 11:30pm–6am. Métro: Bonne-Nouvelle.

This echoing blue-and-orange space emulates the techno-grunge clubs of London, complete with an international, mood-altered clientele enjoying the kind of music only someone ages 18 to 28 could love. A revolving host of deejays is on hand, including regular appearances from a local techno-circuit celeb, Laurent Garnier.

ROCK-&-ROLL

Bus Palladium. 6 rue Fontaine, 9e. ☎ **01-53-21-07-33.** Cover 100 F ($17) for men, 100 F ($17) for women Fri–Sat only. Tues–Sat 11pm–6am. Métro: Blanche or Pigalle.

Set in a single room with a very long bar, this rock-and-roll temple has varnished hardwoods and fabric-covered walls that barely absorb the reverberations of nonstop recorded music. You won't find techno, punk-rock, jazz, blues, or soul here. It's rock-and-roll and nothing but rock-and-roll, for hard-core, mostly heterosexual, rock wannabes ages 25 to 35. Alcoholic drinks of any kind cost 80 F ($13.60), except for women on Tuesday, when they drink as much as they want for free.

SALSA

Les Étoiles. 61 rue du Château d'Eau, 10e. ☎ **01-47-70-60-56.** Cover 150 F ($25.50) including first drink. Métro: Château d'Eau.

Since 1856, this red-swabbed old-fashioned music hall has shaken with the sound of performers at work and patrons at play. Its newest incarnation is as a restaurant discothèque where the music is exclusively salsa and the food Cubano. Expect simple but hearty portions of fried fish, shredded pork or beef, white rice, beans, and flan as bands from Venezuela play salsa to a crowd that already knows or quickly learns how to dance to South American rhythms.

3 Bars, Pubs & Clubs

WINE BARS

Many Parisians now prefer the wine bar to the traditional cafe or bistro. The food is often better and the ambience more inviting. For cafes, see "The Best Cafes" in chapter 5.

✪ **Au Sauvignon.** 80 rue des Sts-Pères, 7e. ☎ **01-45-48-49-02.** Mon–Sat 8:30am–10:30pm. Métro: Sèvres-Babylone.

This tiny place has tables overflowing onto a covered terrace where wines range from the cheapest Beaujolais to the most expensive Saint Émilion Grand Cru. A glass of wine is 21 F to 30 F ($3.55 to $5.10), and it costs an additional 2 F (35¢) to consume it at a table. To accompany your wine, choose an Auvergne specialty, including goat cheese and terrines. The fresh Poilâne bread is ideal with ham, pâté, or goat cheese. The place is decorated with old ceramic tiles and frescoes done by Left Bank artists.

Aux Négociants. 27 rue Lambert, 18e. ☎ **01-46-06-15-11.** Mon and Fri noon–8pm, Tues–Thurs noon–10:30pm. Métro: Lamarck-Caulincourt or Château-Rouge.

Ten minutes downhill from the north facade of Sacré-Coeur, this bistro à vins has flourished since it was founded in 1980 as an outlet for wines produced in the Loire Valley. Artists, street vendors, and office workers all come here, linked only by an appreciation of wine and the allure of the simple but hearty plats du jour priced from 60 F to 70 F ($10.20 to $11.90). It's hearty and unpretentious, the kind of place you'd expect to find in the countryside. Wines range from 16 F to 28 F ($2.70 to $4.75) for a glass.

Juveniles. 47 rue de Richelieu, 1er. ☎ **01-42-97-46-49.** Mon–Sat noon–11pm. Métro: Palais-Royal.

This is a spin-off of one of Paris's most successful wine bars, Willi's, which lies a short distance away. Louder, less formal, less restrained, and, at least to wine lovers, more daring than its older sibling, it prides itself on experimenting with a wide roster of wines from "everywhere." There's no automatic allegiance to prestigious Bordeaux or high-profile Burgundies at this British-owned spot, where high-quality but lesser-known wines from Spain, France, California, and Australia decant for 19 F to 49 F

($3.25 to $8.35) a glass. Anything you like, including the "wine of the week," can be hauled away uncorked from a wine boutique on the premises. If you're hungry, Juveniles offers an assortment of tapas-inspired platters for 34 F to 62 F ($5.80 to $10.55) each. Examples include warm ratatouille with basil; a salad with strips of grilled quail; roasted codfish with onions and spices; and lasagna.

La Tartine. 24 rue de Rivoli, 4e. ☎ **01-42-72-76-85.** Thurs–Mon 8:30am–10pm and Wed noon–10pm. Métro: St-Paul.

Mirrors, brass detail, and frosted-globe chandeliers make La Tartine look like a movie set of Old Paris. At least 60 wines are offered at reasonable prices, including seven kinds of Beaujolais and a large selection of Bordeaux served by the glass. Glasses of wine cost 9 F to 16 F ($1.55 to $2.70), sandwiches 14 F to 45 F ($2.40 to $7.65), and the charcuterie platter is 45 F ($7.65). We recommend the light Sancerre wine and goat cheese from the Loire Valley.

Le Sancerre. 22 av. Rapp, 7e. ☎ **01-45-51-75-91.** Mon–Sat 8am–9pm. Métro: Alma Marceau.

Very few of the bars of Paris have allied themselves as closely to the wine of an individual region as this place. Produced in the Loire Valley in red, rosé, and the best-known version of all, white, Sancerre is known for its not-too-dry fruity aroma and legions of fans who believe it should be more celebrated than it already is. Don't even think of asking for a wine from more celebrated, and more expensive, wine-producing regions. Glasses of this aromatic wine cost 26 F ($4.40) each, derive from several different producers within the Sancerre district, and are consumed in rooms outfitted with wood paneling that's evocative of an auberge Sancerrois. Simple platters of food—chitterling sausages, or omelets studded with potatoes and chives or country ham—are the most popular accompaniments, and cost 42 F to 73 F ($7.15 to $12.40).

Les Bacchantes. 21 rue Caumartin, 9e. ☎ **01-42-65-25-35.** Mon–Sat noon–midnight. Métro: Havre-Caumartin or Opéra.

Les Bacchantes prides itself on offering more wines by the glass (at least 50) than any other wine bar in Paris. It also does a hefty restaurant trade, so much so that it's hard to decide whether it's a bistro specializing in wine, or a wine bar with a particular penchant for well-prepared cuisine bourgeoise. Amid massive exposed beams, old belle-epoque posters, and old-fashioned paneling, blackboards announce a great list of vintages and platters. Bacchantes attracts theatergoers before and after performances at the nearby Olympia Theatre, as well as anyone interested in esoteric and carefully chosen vintages from small-scale wine makers. The wines, which cost 13 F to 30 F ($2.20 to $5.10) per glass, are mainly French. Platters of food cost 62 F to 98 F ($10.55 to $16.65).

✪ **Willi's Wine Bar.** 13 rue des Petits-Champs, 1er. ☎ **01-42-61-05-09.** Mon–Sat noon–11pm. Métro: Bourse, Louvre, or Palais-Royal.

Journalists and stockbrokers patronize this increasingly popular wine bar in the center of the financial district, run by an Englishman, Mark Williamson. About 250 kinds of wine are offered, including a dozen wine specials you can taste by the glass for 20 F to 83 F ($3.40 to $14.10). Lunch is the busiest time—on quiet evenings you can better enjoy the warm ambience and 16th-century beams. Daily specials are likely to include lamb brochette with cumin or lyonnaise sausage in truffled vinaigrette, plus spectacular desserts such as chocolate terrine. Platters of food, each priced at 90 F ($15.30), include Scottish salmon baked in a salt crust, served with a fricassée of artichoke hearts, and filet of beef roasted with ginger.

Paris's bar scene is hopping, though bars here aren't as clearly defined as in other cities—they can be cafes and cafes can be bars, restaurants can be bars, and bars can also be clubs. It can get confusing. The best way to think about it is not to let the name give you any preconceived notions of what the place might be like. (Café Marly, for example, is much more than just a cafe, and Buddha-bar is known more for its food than its cocktails.)

BARS & PUBS

These "imported" establishments try to imitate American cocktail bars or masquerade as British pubs—most strike an alien chord. But that doesn't prevent fashionable Parisians from barhopping (not to be confused with cafe-sitting). In general, bars and pubs are open daily between 11am and 1:30am, though, of course, there are exceptions to the rule.

Bars and Salons of the Plaza Athénée. 25 av. Montaigne, 8e. ☎ **01-53-67-66-65.** Métro: Alma-Marceau.

Residents of the surrounding neighborhood have always enjoyed dropping into this hotel for a drink in cosseted, supremely well-upholstered circumstances. The drinking venue is set to move from the Bar Anglais, on the hotel's lower level, to one of the street-level salons. A pianist and singer usually perform between 10:30pm and 1:30am, and a prosperous, polyglot crowd of hotel guests and upscale locals amuse and entertain one another.

Bar du Crillon. In the Hôtel de Crillon, 10 place de la Concorde, 8e. ☎ **01-44-71-15-00.** Métro: Concorde.

Although some visitors consider the Bar du Crillon too stiff and self-consciously elegant to ever allow anyone to have a good time, its social and literary history is remarkable. Hemingway set a climactic scene of *The Sun Also Rises* here, and over the years it has attracted practically every upper-level staff member of the nearby American embassy—including the recently deceased U.S. ambassador to France and *femme formidable,* Pamela Harriman—as well as a gaggle of visiting heiresses, stars, starlets, and wannabes. Under its new owner, the Concorde Group, the bar has been redecorated by Sonia Rykiel and no longer basks in the 1950s glow so favored by past clients. If this particular bar doesn't appeal to you, there's another option just down the hall, the Edwardian-style **Jardin d'Hiver.** Here, amid potted palms and very upscale accessories, you can order tea, cocktails, or coffee.

China Club. 50 rue de Charenton, 12e. ☎ **01-43-43-82-02.** Métro: Bastille.

Designed to recall France's 19th-century colonies in Asia or a bordello in 1930s Shanghai (on the ground floor) and England's empire-building zeal in India (upstairs), the China Club will allow you to chitchat or flirt with the singles who crowd into the street-level bar, then escape to calmer, more contemplative climes upstairs. You'll see regulars from Paris's worlds of fashion and the arts, along with a pack of postshow celebrants from the nearby Opéra de la Bastille. There's a Chinese restaurant on the street level serving dinner every night from 7pm to 12:30am, a scattering of books, newspapers, and chess boards upstairs, and a more animated (and occasionally raucous) bar in the cellar, where live music is presented every Friday and Saturday between 10pm and 3am. There's never a cover charge. Beer costs 25 F ($4.25).

L'Académie de la Bière. 88 bis bd. du Port-Royal, 5e. ☎ **01-43-54-66-65.** Métro: Port-Royal.

The decor is paneled, woodsy, and rustic, an appropriate foil for an "academy" whose curriculum includes more than 150 kinds of beer, each from a microbrewery. Stella Artois, the best-selling beer in Belgium, isn't available, although more than half of the dozen on tap are from small-scale, not particularly famous breweries in Belgium that deserve to be better known. Mugs or bottles cost from 29 F to 43 F ($4.95 to $7.30) each, depending on how esoteric they are. Snack-style food is available, including platters of mussels, assorted cheeses, and sausages with mustard.

Le Bar l'Hôtel. In L'Hôtel, 13 rue des Beaux-Arts, 6e. ☎ **01-44-41-99-00.** Métro: St-Germain-des-Prés.

This is the hyper-artsy and theatrically overdecorated bar of a hotel that has wooed film-industry types who want to avoid the more mainstream luxury of Paris's palatial hotels. The rose-filter cheeriness is deceptive: This is the hotel where Oscar Wilde died, disgraced and impoverished, after his self-imposed exile from England. The staff is conscientiously straitlaced, but you'd expect a musical comedy to break out at any moment.

Le Floridita. 19 rue de Presbourg, 16e. ☎ **01-45-00-84-84.** Métro: Etoile.

Although the climate is colder, and the politics a lot more sedate, some aspects of this place might remind you of pre-Castro Cuba. Part of that derives from the macho brown and green decor that evokes a private men's club, and a namesake (Le Floridita) inspired by a long-gone bar in Havana. You can drink Cuba libres, cognac, or endless cups of coffee, or eat platters of food priced from 80 F to 130 F ($13.60 to $22.10). You can also do what many bars in the world expressly outlaw—puff away at any of the cigars that this place stockpiles for the smoking pleasure of its guests of either gender. Regular clients sometimes opt to store their cigars on-site, in a safe originally designed as a bank-style safety-deposit vault. Cafe and cigar service are every Monday through Saturday from 10:30am to 2am; meals are served Monday through Saturday from noon to 2pm and from 8 to 11:15pm.

Le Forum. 4 bd. Malesherbes, 8e. ☎ **01-42-65-37-86.** Métro: Madeleine.

Its clients, who include frequent business travelers to Paris from around the world, compare this place to a private club in London. Part of that comes from the carefully polished oak paneling and ornate stucco, and part from its store of single-malt whiskies, the widest selection in town. You can also try 150 different cocktails, including many that haven't been in popular circulation since the jazz age. Champagne by the glass is common, as is that high-octane social lubricant, the martini.

Le Fumoir. 6 rue de l'Amiral Coligny, 1er. ☎ **01-42-92-00-24.** Métro: Louvre-Rivoli.

Set within a neighborhood that's not otherwise known for particularly exotic nightlife, this bar provides a kind of classy raucousness from a worldly, well-traveled crowd that either lives or works within the district. The decor is a lot like that of an English library, with about 6,000 books providing an aesthetic backdrop to the schmoozing and kibbutzing. A Danish chef prepares an international menu featuring meal-sized salads (the one with scallops and lobster is particularly savory); roasted codfish with zucchini; and roasted beef in red wine sauce. Rack of lamb comes with a side portion of puréed green beans. More popular even than the food items, however, are the stiff mixed drinks, the medley of wines and beers, and the dozen or so types of cigars for sale. It's open daily from 11am to 2am.

Le Web Bar. 32 rue de Picardie, 3e. ☎ **01-42-72-57-47.** Métro: Temple.

Few other nightclubs seem to tap as gleefully into the computer age as Le Web Bar. It occupies a three-story space at the eastern edge of the Marais that echoes with the sound of people talking and schmoozing with each other and with silent computer-transmitted partners many thousands of miles away. The site consists of a restaurant on the street level, a battery of at least 25 computers one floor upstairs, and a top-floor art gallery. And to keep things perking, there's live music every night beginning around 7pm. Beer costs 18 F ($3.05); a plat du jour averages 50 F ($8.50), and use of the somewhat battered computers is free. Menu items stress comfort food, which in this case refers to such conservative French specialties as boeuf bourguignonne. If you want to check out the place ahead of time, it has a Web page at **www.ethernite.com**. It's open daily from 8am to 2am.

Pub St-Germain-des-Prés. 17 rue de l'Ancienne-Comédie, 6e. ☎ **01-43-29-38-70.** Métro: Odéon.

With 9 different rooms and 650 seats, this is the largest pub in France, offering 450 brands of beer, 26 of which are on draft. The deliberately tacky decor, which has seen a lot of beer swilled and spilled since its installation, consists of faded gilt-framed mirrors, hanging lamps, and a stuffed parrot in a gilded cage. Leather booths let you drink discreetly in an atmosphere that is usually quiet, relaxed, and posh. Featured beers change frequently, but usually include Amstel, many different Belgian brews (including both blonde and brunet versions of Belforth), Whitbread, and Pimm's No. 1. If frat houses turn you on, it gets really fun between 10:30pm and 4am, when above the chatter of live rock everything becomes loud, raucous, and sudsy.

Ritz Bars. In the Hôtel Ritz, 15 place Vendôme, 1er. ☎ **01-43-16-30-30.** Métro: Opéra.

In 1944, during the liberation of Paris, Ernest Hemingway made political and literary history by ordering a drink at the Ritz Bar while gunfire from retreating Nazi soldiers still rang in the streets outside. The Ritz commemorates this event with bookish memorabilia, rows of newspapers, and stiff drinks served within a setting reminiscent of a woodsy English club. Look for its entrance, and homage to other writers such as Proust, close to the rue Cambon entrance to the hotel. If you get thirsty during the daytime, when the Hemingway Bar isn't open, head for the hotel's Bar Vendôme instead, near the main (Place Vendôme) entrance. The setting is equally cozy and woodsy, albeit a bit more grand. During some peak hours, say between 5:30 and 8:30pm, it's wise to reserve a table in advance.

4 Gay & Lesbian Bars & Clubs

Gay life is centered around Les Halles and Le Marais, with the greatest concentration of gay and lesbian clubs, restaurants, bars, and shops between the Hôtel-de-Ville and Rambuteau Métro stops. Gay dance clubs come and go so fast that even the magazines devoted to their pursuit—*e.m@ale* and *Illico,* both distributed free in the gay bars and bookstores—have a hard time keeping up. For lesbians, the guide *Exes Femmes* publishes a free seasonal listing of bars and clubs. Also look for Gai Pied's *Guide Gai,* available at kiosks for 69 F ($11.75) and *Pariscope's* regularly featured English-language section, "A Week of Gay Outings."

The gay scene here is constantly exploding, although some clubs have the life span of butterflies. The neighboring **Open Café,** 17 rue des Archives, 4e (☎ **01-42-72-26-18**), and **Café Cox,** 15 rue des Archives, 4e (☎ **01-42-72-08-00**), Métro: Hôtel-de-Ville or Rambuteau, both get so busy in the early evening that the crowd stands out on the sidewalk. These places are where you'll find the most mixed gay crowd in

Paris—from hunky American tourists to sexy Parisian men. The mood is especially flirtatious on Saturday between 10pm and midnight, before the boys head to the dance clubs. **Le Quetzal,** 10 rue de la Verrerie, 4e (☎ **01-48-87-99-07;** Métro: Hôtel-de-Ville), attracts a lot of posers with a constant bored look (pleading to be entertained), but that's only early in the evening. Later on, the place gets fun and slightly cruisy. A new and successful place in Les Halles is **Le Tropic Café,** 66 rue des Lombards, 1er (☎ **01-40-13-92-62;** Métro: Châtelet–Les Halles). The trendy good-looking crowd here parties until dawn. For the most sedate and slightly intellectual gay bar in the city, head to **Le Duplex Bar,** 25 rue Michel-Le-Comte, 3e (☎ **01-42-72-80-86;** Métro: Rambuteau), where the men actually talk to one another (gasp!— cruising optional). A mixed techno club welcoming both gays and lesbians is **Mixer,** 23 rue St-Croix-de-la-Bretonnerie, 4e (☎ **01-48-87-55-44;** Métro: Hôtel-de-Ville), but there's not much dancing here.

If you're a gay male and in Paris on Sunday night, head to **Blockhaus,** 25 blvd. Poissonière, 2e (☎ **01-40-26-60-31;** Métro: Bonne Nouvelle), a male-only dance club with a military decor and a backroom that's so hot it might be called "steam heat" or "tropical heat wave." There's also a hot new dance club for men in the 18th arrondissement called **Le Gibus,** 18 rue du Faubourg du Temple 11e (☎ **08-36-68-78-81;** Métro: République), which rocks on Friday and Saturday nights with guest deejays from around the world. Some of the most drop-dead gorgeous men in Paris show up here, often to be entertained by drag shows, which the French do with such exquisite perfection. **Le Dépôt,** 10 rue aux Ours, 3e (☎ **01-44-54-96-96;** Métro: Etienne-Marcel or Rambuteau; open daily noon to 8am; admission 45F/$8, including one drink), is Paris's newest and largest sex club. It claims to be all one backroom (several levels, that is) of hardcore cruising, with morning parties and theme nights weekly.

A new restaurant with a bar fast becoming popular with women is **Okawa,** 40 rue Vieille-du-Temple, 4e (☎ **01-48-04-30-69;** Métro: Hôtel-de-Ville), where trendy lesbians (and some gay boys) sip drinks at happy hour. **Les Scandaleuses,** 26 rue des Ecouffes, 3e (☎ **01-48-97-39-26;** Métro: St-Paul), continues to be one of the city's most popular rendezvous spots for lesbians. With a video bar, it's open 7 nights a week. Chic Chanel dykes show up here on the arm of motorcycle matrons. Men are also welcome. On most weekends, there are special deejay nights. It's definitely a smoke-gets-in-your-eyes kind of place. Less smoky but also less hip, **L'Unity Bar,** 176 rue St. Martin, 3e (☎ **01-42-74-68-34;** Métro: Châtelet–Les Halles), is run by a Franco-American couple. Join the ladies in a game of hard-driving pool.

Recently acquired by a beautiful young woman, **L'Entr'acte,** 25 bd. Poissonnière, 2e (☎ **01-40-26-01-93;** Métro: Montmartre), attracts a crowd much like the owner.

More butch, **L'Enfer,** 34 rue du Départ, 14e (☎ **01-42-79-94-94;** Métro: Montparnasse), rocks with a huge crowd of trendy lesbians on Friday and Saturday; Thursday is more mixed, with gay men welcome.

Amnesia Café. 42 rue Vieille-du-Temple, 4e. ☎ **01-42-72-16-94.** Métro: Hôtel-de-Ville.

Its function and clientele changes throughout the course of the day, despite the constant presence of a local cadre of gay men. Combining aspects of a cafe, tearoom, bistro, and bar, it includes two beige bar and dining areas, a mezzanine, and a cellar-level bar that opens later in the evening. Beer and cocktails are the drinks of choice, with a specialty coffee (café amnesia) that combines caffeine with cognac and Chantilly cream. Deep armchairs and soft pillows combine with 1930s accents here, creating an ambience that's conducive to talk and a cheerfulness that's not always apparent in the more sexually charged bars nearby. Plats du jour cost 60 F to 80 F ($10.20 to $13.60) each and include surprisingly conservative food like Basque chicken and beef bourguignonne.

Banana Café. 13 rue de la Ferronnerie, 1er. ☎ **01-42-33-35-31.** Métro: Châtelet or Les Halles.

This popular gay bar is a ritualized stopover for anyone visiting or doing business in Paris. Occupying two floors of a 19th-century building, it has walls the color of an overripe banana, dim lighting, and a well-publicized policy of raising the price of drinks after 10pm, when things become really interesting. On theme nights such as Valentine's Day, expect the entire premises to be plastered with pink crepe paper. There's a street-level bar and a dance floor in the cellar that features a live pianist and recorded music—sometimes with dancing. On many nights, go-go dancers from all over perform from spotlit platforms in the cellar.

Bar Hotel Central. 33 rue Vieille-du-Temple, 4e. ☎ **01-48-87-99-33.** Métro: Hôtel-de-Ville.

Bar Hotel Central is one of the oldest bars for men in the Hôtel-de-Ville area. It's tacky and a bit drab but still gets its share of tourists. There is a small hotel upstairs (see "Gay-Friendly Hotels" in chapter 4). Both the bar and its hotel are in a 300-year-old building in the heart of the Marais.

La Champmeslé. 4 rue Chabanais, 2e. ☎ **01-42-96-85-20.** Métro: Pyramides or Bourse.

The leading lesbian bar in Paris. With dim lighting, background music, and comfortable banquettes, La Champmeslé offers a cozy meeting place for women, and to a much, much lesser extent for "well-behaved" men. The club is housed in a 300-year-old building heavy on exposed stone and ceiling beams, with retro 1950s-style furnishings. Every Thursday night, one of the premier lesbian events of Paris, a cabaret, begins at 10pm (but the price of cover and drinks doesn't rise); and every month there is a well-attended exhibition of paintings by mostly lesbian artists. The bar is named in honor of a celebrated 17th-century actress, La Champmeslé, who was instrumental in interpreting the then-fledgling dramatic efforts of the celebrated playwright Racine.

Le Bar. 5 rue de la Ferronnerie, 1er. ☎ **01-40-41-00-10.** Métro: Châtelet.

Covering the street level and the cellar of a sprawling building in a neighborhood long known for an availability of commercial sex, this is the largest gay bar in Paris. You'll find three bars on the premises, a mostly blue decor that incorporates lots of sinuous lines, and an ambience that's more sexually charged and explicit in the cellar than on the street level. The average age here is early 30s.

Le Pulp. 25 bd. Poissonnière, 2e. ☎ **01-40-26-01-93.** Métro: Rue Montmartre.

This is one of the most visible and popular lesbian discos in Paris. Outfitted like a burgundy-colored 19th-century French music hall, a new management has made its seedy past a distant memory. Today it's fun, trendy, and chic. It's best to show up before midnight. The venue, as the French like to say, is very cool, with all types of cutting-edge music played in a setting that just happens to discourage the presence of men. If you're gay and male and want to hang out with the girls, head for the establishment's side entrance, where a "separate but equal" facility, Le Scorp (same address), offers a roughly equivalent format that, alas, never manages to be as much fun as such other gay male bastions like Le Queen. Both Le Pulp and Le Scorp are open Wednesday through Saturday from midnight to at least 6am. Entrance to Le Scorp is 70 F ($11.90). Entrance to Le Pulp is free every Wednesday and Thursday, and costs 50 F ($8.50) every Friday and Saturday.

Le Queen. 102 av. des Champs-Elysées, 8e. ☎ **01-53-89-08-90.** Cover 50 F ($8.50) Mon, 100 F ($17) Fri–Sat. Métro: F. D. Roosevelt.

Should you miss gay life à la New York, follow the flashing purple sign on the "main street" of Paris, near the corner of avenue George-V. The place is often mobbed, primarily with gay men and, to a lesser degree, models, actresses, and the like. Look for go-go boys, drag shows, muscle shows, and everything from 1970s-style disco nights (Monday) to Tuesday-night foam parties (only in summer), when cascades of mousse descend onto the dance floor. Go very, very late, as the place is open daily from midnight to 6 or 7am.

5 Literary Haunts

See also "Literary Landmarks" in chapter 6.

✪ **Harry's New York Bar.** 5 rue Daunou, 2e. ☎ **01-42-61-71-14.** Métro: Opéra or Pyramides.

"Sank roo doe Noo," as the ads tell you to instruct your cab driver, is the most famous bar in Europe—quite possibly in the world. Opened Thanksgiving Day 1911, by a bearded Hemingway precursor by the name of MacElhone, it's sacred to Papa disciples as the spot where members of the ambulance corps drank themselves silly during World War I, and as the master's favorite place to snuff brain cells in Paris. The site is legendary for other reasons too: White Lady and Sidecar cocktails were invented here in 1919 and 1931, respectively. It's also the alleged birthplace of the Bloody Mary and the headquarters of a loosely organized fraternity of drinkers known as the International Bar Flies (IBF). Harry's New York Bar has stayed in the family: Duncan, MacElhone's bilingual grandson now owns and runs it.

The place's core is the street-level bar, where CEOs and office workers loosen their neckties on more or less equal footing. Daytime crowds draw from the neighborhood's insurance, banking, and travel industries; evening crowds include pre- and posttheater groupies and night owls who aren't bothered by the gritty setting and deliberately unflattering lighting. A softer ambience reigns in the cellar, where a pianist provides highly drinkable music every night from 10pm to 2am, accompanied by whatever patron feels uninhibited enough to join in.

La Closerie des Lilas. 171 bd. du Montparnasse, 6e. ☎ **01-40-51-34-50.** Métro: Port-Royal.

Hemingway, Picasso, Gershwin, and Modigliani all loved the Closerie, and ever since, Parisians and foreigners, literary or not, have flocked here. Even though the lilacs that gave the place its name only bloom in spring, the management strews bouquets of them throughout the bar all year long. Don't expect a reverent hush—on some nights the place is as energetic as a New York singles bar. Look for the brass nameplate of your favorite Lost Generation artist along the banquettes or at the bar.

Rosebud. 11 bis rue Delambre, 14e. ☎ **01-43-35-38-54.** Métro: Vavin.

The popularity of this place known for a bemused and indulgent attitude toward anyone looking for a drink and some talk hasn't diminished since the 1950s, when it attained its fame. The name refers to the beloved sled of Orson Welles's great *Citizen Kane*. Just around the corner from Montparnasse's famous cafes, and thick in associations with Jean-Paul Sartre and Simone de Beauvoir, Eugene Ionesco, and Marguerite Duras, Rosebud draws clients ages 35 to 65, though the staff has recently remarked upon the appearance of—gasp!—students. Drop in at night for a glass of wine, a shot of whisky, or a bite to eat, maybe a hamburger or chili con carne.

10

Side Trips from Paris

Paris, the city that began on an island, is itself the center of a curious landlocked island known as the **Ile de France.**

Shaped roughly like a saucer, it lies encircled by a thin ribbon of rivers: the **Epte, Aisne, Marne,** and **Yonne.** Fringing these rivers are mighty forests with famous names—**Rambouillet, St-Germain, Compiègne,** and **Fontainebleau.** The forests are said to be responsible for Paris's clear, gentle air, and the unusual length of its spring and fall. This may be debatable, but there's no argument that they provide the capital with a fine series of excursions, all within easy reach.

The forests surrounding Paris were the domain of kings and the ruling aristocracy, and they're still sprinkled with the magnificent *châteaux* (palaces) of their former masters. Together with ancient villages, glorious cathedrals, and little country inns, they turn Ile de France into a traveler's paradise. Because the region is comparatively small, almost everything is at your doorstep.

The difficult question is where to go. What we're offering in this chapter is merely a handful of the dozens of possibilities for 1-day jaunts. For a more extensive list of excursions in the Ile de France, consult *Frommer's France 2000.*

1 Versailles

13 miles SW of Paris, 44 miles NE of Chartres

For centuries, the name of this Parisian suburb resounded through the consciousness of every aristocratic family in Europe. The palace at Versailles outdazzled every other kingly residence in Europe; it was a horrendously expensive scandal and a symbol to later generations of a regime obsessed with prestige above all else.

Back in the *grand siécle* (17th), all you needed to enter was a sword, a hat, and a bribe for the guard at the gate. Providing you didn't have smallpox, you'd be admitted to the precincts of the château, to stroll through salon after glittering salon—to watch the Sun King at his banqueting table, to dance or flirt or even do something far more personal. Louis XIV had all the privacy of a bus station.

ESSENTIALS

GETTING THERE　To get to Versailles, 13 miles southwest of Paris, catch the RER line C at the Gare d'Austerlitz, St-Michel, Musée d'Orsay, Invalides, Ponte-de-l'Alma, Champ-de-Mars, or Javel station

A Weekend Trip to London

Regardless of how much you love Paris, too long a stint within the confines of the French capital might make you itch for the monumentality and cultural familiarity of London, at least for a weekend. So if the allure of Gallic charm and French *laissez-faire* has begun to pale, know that transit between Paris and London is easier than ever.

A giant boost for cross-channel commerce occurred in 1994, when Queen Elizabeth II and former French President François Mitterand jointly inaugurated the **Channel Tunnel** (the Chunnel), whose debut had been dreamed about since the military campaigns of Napoléon. Now the *Eurostar* train roars through it, reducing the travel time between Paris and London to a breathtakingly brief 3 hours, at prices that rival conventional train and ferryboat fares, and at a level of convenience (direct transit between Paris's Gare du Nord and London's Waterloo Station) never before imagined. One-way fares, with some restrictions, begin at $109 second class and $179 first class, with discounts for Eurail or Britrail passholders. Additional discounts are offered to youths under 18 and students. If you're willing to pay for it, you can opt for ultra-upscale service, enhanced cuisine, and such perks as limousine service to and from Waterloo Station and your hotel for a maximum of $299 each way, tax included.

Where should you lay your weary head for the 2 or 3 nights you spend in London? The folks at Eurostar can even set that up for you as part of a rail-and-hotel package at a highly discounted rate. For as little as $317 per person, you can buy a package that includes rail transport, 2 nights (double occupancy) in a convenient hotel, and a city sightseeing tour. The price is hard to beat and the sheer convenience of the routing makes the plan easier and faster than flying.

From North America, these packages can most easily be arranged by calling the **Eurostar** division of RailEurope (☎ **800/EUROSTAR**). For details about hotel packages, contact **EuroVacations** (☎ **888/281-EURO**). If you're already in Paris, contact any travel agency or talk to your hotel concierge, who should be able to arrange the same basic package, depending on seasonal promotions.

---

and take it to the Versailles Rive Gauche station, from which there's a shuttle bus to the château. The 35 F ($5.95) trip takes about 35 to 40 minutes; Eurailpass holders travel free on the train, but pay 20 F ($3.40) for a ride on the shuttle bus.

Regular SNCF trains also make the run from central Paris to Versailles: One train departs from the Gare St-Lazare for the Versailles Rive Droite RER station, a 15-minute walk from the château. If you can't or don't want to walk, you can take bus B from Versailles Chantiers to the château for 8 F ($1.35) each way.

As a last resort, you can get to Versailles using a combination of Métro and city bus. Travel to the Pont-de-Sèvres stop by Métro, then transfer to bus 171 for a westward trek that will take from 20 to 45 minutes, depending on traffic. The bus will cost you three Métro tickets and will deposit you near the gates of the château.

If you're driving, take route N-10, following the signs to Versailles, then along avenue de Géneral Leclerc. Park on the place d'Armes in front of the château.

ORIENTATION   The palace dominates the town. Three main avenues radiate from place d'Armes in front of the palace. The **tourist office** is at 7 rue des Réservoirs (☎ **01-39-50-36-22**).

✪ THE CHÂTEAU

The **Château de Versailles,** place d'Armes (☎ **01-30-84-74-00**), was conceived of as a glittering private world, far from the grime and noise and bustle of Paris. Seeing all of the château's rooms would take several days, although most visitors in a rush devote only a morning to the château. You should probably skip some of the rooms and save your energy for the park, which is the ultimate in French landscaping. Its makers disciplined every tree, shrub, flower, and hedge into a frozen ballet pattern and spread them among soaring fountains, sparkling pools, grandiose stairways, and hundreds of marble statues. It's like a colossal stage setting—even the view of the blue horizon seems like an ornately embroidered backdrop. The garden is an Eden for puppet people, a place where you expect the birds to sing coloratura soprano.

Inside, the **Grand Apartments,** the **Royal Chapel,** and the **Hall of Mirrors** (where the Treaty of Versailles was signed) can be visited without a guide. Other sections of the château may be visited only at specific hours or on special days. Some sections are temporarily closed as they undergo restoration. Try to save time to visit the **Grand Trianon,** which is a good walk across the park. In pink-and-white marble, it was designed by Hardouin-Mansart for Louis XIV in 1687 but is now mostly furnished with Empire pieces. You can also visit the **Petit Trianon,** built by Gabriel in 1768. This was the favorite residence of Marie Antoinette, who could escape the rigors of court here, and a retreat for Louis XV and his mistress, Madame du Barry.

The château is open May 2 through September 30, Tuesday through Sunday from 9am to 6:30pm; until 5:30pm the rest of the year. The grounds are open daily from 7am to dusk, which can be anytime between 5:30 and 9:30pm, depending on the time of year. The Trianons maintain the same hours as the château, but they open 1 hour later. Admission to the château is 45 F ($7.65) for adults, 35 F ($5.95) for ages 18 to 25, and free for under age 18 and over 60. Admission to the Grand Trianon is 25 F ($4.25) for adults, 15 F ($2.55) for ages 18 to 25, and free for under age 18. Admission to the Petit Trianon is 15 F ($2.55) for adults, 10 F ($1.70) for ages 18 to 25, and free for under age 18. Admission to both Trianons is 30 F ($5.10) for adults, 20 F ($3.40) for ages 18 to 25, and free for under age 18. Adults pay the reduced rates for all attractions after 3:30pm.

EVENING SPECTACLES The French government offers a program of evening fireworks and illuminated fountains throughout the summer called **Les Fêtes de Nuit de Versailles (Rêve de Roi).** These always capture the heightened sense of the glory of France's *ancien régime.* At scattered dates throughout the summer, 200 actors in period costume portray Louis XVI and members of his court. Between April and October, shows begin at 10:30pm (9:30pm during August and September). Spectators sit on bleachers clustered at the château's boulevard de la Reine entrance, adjacent to

---

Impressions

When Louis XIV had finished the Grand Trianon, he told [Mme de] Maintenon he had created a paradise for her, and asked if she could think of anything now to wish for. . . . She said she could think of but one thing—it was summer, and it was balmy France—yet she would like well to sleigh ride in the leafy avenues of Versailles! The next morning found miles and miles of grassy avenues spread thick with snowy salt and sugar, and a procession of those quaint sleighs waiting to receive the chief concubine of the gaiest and most unprincipled court that France has ever seen!

—Mark Twain, *The Innocents Abroad* (1869)

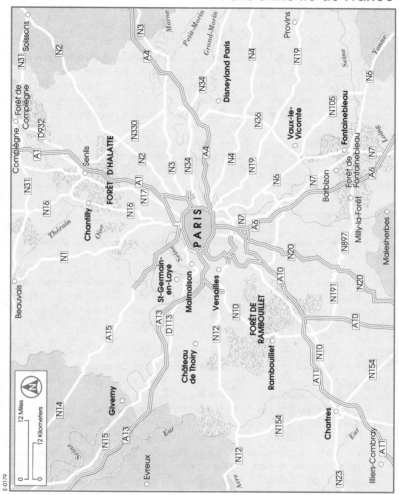

the Fountain (Bassin) of Neptune. The most desirable seats cost 250 F ($42.50), and standing room sells for 70 F ($11.90), with no discounts offered for either children or students. Gates that admit you into the bleacher area open 90 minutes before show-time, and the show itself lasts 90 minutes.

Tickets can be purchased in advance at the tourist office in Versailles—inquire by phone, fax, or mail—or in central Paris at any of the FNAC stores (☎ **02-49-87-50-50**; see chapter 8). You can also take your chances and buy tickets an hour prior to the event from a kiosk adjacent to the boulevard de la Reine entrance. Call ☎ **01-30-83-78-88** for general information about any of the nighttime or Sunday afternoon spectacles on the grounds surrounding the château.

SUNDAY AFTERNOON PROMENADES IN THE PARK Every Sunday between early April and mid-October, and every Saturday between early July and late August, between 11am and noon, and again between 3:30 and 5:30pm, classical music is broadcast throughout the park, and every fountain is turned on. The effect of these

Food Fit for a King

Between 1682 and 1789, the Versailles château housed a royal entourage whose population, except for 8 years during the minority of Louis XV, remained constant at 3,000. To feed them, the sprawling kitchens employed a permanent staff of 2,000. Without benefit of running water or electricity, they labored over banquets that became day-to-day rituals at the most glorious court since the collapse of ancient Rome.

The fruits and vegetables that appeared on the royal tables were produced onsite, in **Les Potagers du Roi** (the King's Kitchen Garden). Surprisingly, the gardens have survived and can be found a 10-minute walk south of the château's main entrance, at 6 rue du Hardy, behind an industrial-looking gate. Twenty-three acres of fertile earth are arranged into parterres and terraces as formal as the legendary showcases devoted to flowers, fountains, and statuary during the royal tenure.

Meals at Versailles were quite a ritual. The king almost always dined in state, alone at a table visible to hundreds of observers and, in some cases, other diners, who sat in order of rank. Fortunately for gastronomic historians, there are many detailed accounts about what Louis XIV enjoyed and how much he consumed: He was addicted to salads and ate prodigious amounts of basil, purslane, mint, and wood sorrel. He loved melons, figs, pears, and peaches. The real culinary rage at the court, however, was for peas, imported from Genoa for the first time in 1660.

Today, Les Potagers du Roi are maintained by about half a dozen gardeners under the direction of the École Nationale du Paysage. It manages to intersperse the fruits and vegetables once favored by the monarchs with experimental breeds and hundreds of splendidly espaliered fruit trees.

The kitchen gardens can be visited only between April and November, every Saturday and Sunday from 10am to 5pm. Adults pay 40 F ($6.80); persons under 18, 20 F ($3.40). Look for the entrance at 6 rue Hardy (☎ **01-39-24-62-00**), about a quarter-mile south of the château itself. Free guided tours of the garden, in French, each last an hour, and depart every hour on the hour. A kiosk on the premises sells the fruits and vegetables grown in the gardens.

Grandes Eaux Musicales is to duplicate the landscaping vision of the 18th-century architects who designed Versailles. They even allow you to walk freely around the park, enjoying the juxtapositions of grand architecture and lavish waterworks. The cost of admission to the park during these events is 25 F ($4.25) per person.

DINING

Le Potager du Roy. 1 rue du Maréchal Joffre. ☎ **01-39-50-35-34.** Reservations required. Fixed-price menu 130 F ($22.10) at lunch, 175 F ($29.75) at dinner. AE, V. Tues–Sat noon–2:30pm; Tues–Sun 7–10:30pm. FRENCH.

Philippe Letourneur cooks from the heart, preparing food one Parisian critic called soulful. He specializes in uncomplicated cuisine with robust flavors, adding a breath of novelty to Versailles's jaded and world-weary dining scene. His attractive restaurant occupies an 18th-century building in a neighborhood known during the days of the French monarchs as the *Parc des Cerfs* ("Stag Park"). Here any bored courtier could find paid companionship with B- and C-list courtesans. The skillfully prepared menu

Versailles

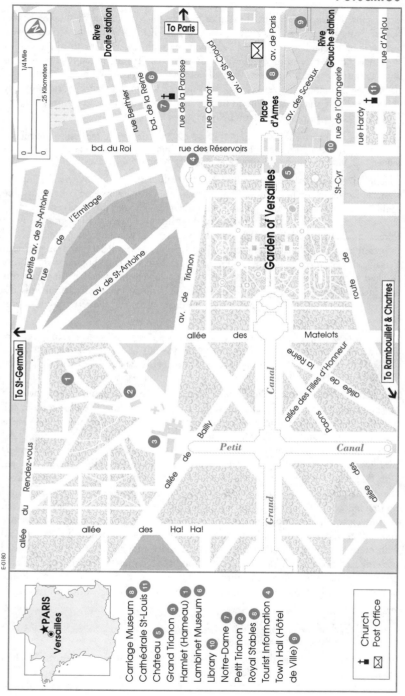

To Paris

Rive Droite station
Rive Gauche station

rue Berthier
bd. de la Reine
rue de la Paroisse
rue Carnot
av. de St-Cloud
av. de Paris
rue d'Anjou

bd. du Roi
rue des Réservoirs

Petite av. de St-Antoine
rue de l'Ermitage
av. de St-Antoine

Place d'Armes

av. des Sceaux
rue de l'Orangerie
rue Hardy

St-Cyr

Garden of Versailles

av. de Trianon

allée des Matelots

To St-Germain

du Rendez-vous
allée de Bailly

allée des Ha! Ha!

Petit Canal
Canal
Grand Canal

la Reine
allée des Filles d'Honneur
Paons
route de
allée des

To Rambouillet & Chartres

PARIS
Versailles

Carriage Museum 8
Cathédrale St-Louis 11
Château 5
Grand Trianon 3
Hamlet (Hameau) 1
Lambinet Museum 6
Library 10
Notre-Dame 7
Petit Trianon 2
Royal Stables 8
Tourist Information 4
Town Hall (Hôtel de Ville) 9

✝ Church
✉ Post Office

E-0180

281

is reinvented with the seasons. Examples include foie gras served with a vegetable-flavored vinaigrette; a ragout of macaroni with a persillade of snails; roasted duck with a navarin of vegetables; and roasted codfish served with roasted peppers in the style of Provence. Looking for something earthy and unusual? Try the fondant of pork jowls with a confit of fresh vegetables. If at all possible, save room for the chocolate cake, flavored with orange and served with coconut ice cream—it's oozing and intensely chocolatey. Note that this restaurant derives its name from the nearby King's Kitchen Gardens (see the box "Food Fit for a King," above).

Le Quai No. 1. 1 av. de St-Cloud. ☎ **01-39-50-42-26.** Reservations required. Main courses 85 F ($14.45); fixed-price menu 110 F ($18.70) at lunch, 140–185 F ($23.80–$31.45) at dinner. MC, V. Tues–Sat noon–2:30pm and 7:30–11pm; Sun noon–2:30pm. FRENCH.

This relatively informal seafood bistro is in an 18th-century building overlooking the western facade of France's most famous château. Lithographs and wood paneling spangle the dining room, and outside there's a terrace. Though the cuisine isn't as opulent, esoteric, or expensive as what's served within chef Gérard Vié's grander main restaurant, **Les Trois Marches** (see below), it's charming, very French, and dependable in presentation. The fixed-price menus make Le Quai a dining bargain in high-priced Versailles. Specialties include seafood sauerkraut, seafood paella, bouillabaisse, home-smoked salmon, and an enduringly popular upscale version of North American surf and turf, with grilled Breton lobster and sizzling sirloin. The chef recommends the seafood platter. Care and imagination go into the cuisine, and the service is both professional and polite.

✪ Les Trois Marches. In the Hôtel Trianon Palace, 1 bd. de la Reine. ☎ **01-30-84-38-40.** Reservations required. Fixed-price menu 350 F ($59.50) at lunch Mon–Fri, 610–750 F ($103.70–$127.50) at lunch Sat–Sun and at dinner. AE, DC, MC, V. Daily noon–2pm and 7:30–10pm. FRENCH.

Situated in a 5-acre garden, the Trianon hotel became world famous in 1919 when it served as headquarters for signatories to the Treaty of Versailles. The dining room still retains an old-world splendor in its crystal chandeliers and fluted columns. Gérard Vié is the most talented and creative chef in Versailles these days, attracting a discerning clientele that doesn't mind paying the high prices. His *cuisine moderne* is subtle, often daringly conceived and inventive, and the service is smooth. Begin with a lobster salad flavored with fresh herbs and served with an onion soufflé; a galette of potatoes with bacon, chardonnay, and sevruga caviar; or perhaps the citrus-flavored bisque of scallops. You'll understand why the chef is considered such an innovator when you taste his main courses, especially his pigeon roasted and flavored with rosé and accompanied by celeriac and truffles. If you arrive in late autumn, you might encounter penne-like pasta, tossed with morels, mushrooms, and Parmesan, and blended in a butter sauce deeply infused with the flavor of white Alba truffles. One dish that is absolutely deserving of a culinary prize is celeriac fashioned into ravioli, filled with foie gras, and topped with a thick slice of black truffle. It's too hard to choose a dessert, so opt for the signature assortment.

2 The Forest & Château of Rambouillet

34 miles SW of Paris, 26 miles NE of Chartres

Once known as La Forêt d'Yveline, the Forest of Rambouillet is one of the loveliest woods in France. More than 47,000 acres of greenery stretch from the valley of the Eure to the high valley of Chevreuse, the latter rich in medieval and royal abbeys. Lakes, copses of hiding deer, and even wild boar are some of the attractions of this "green lung." Most people, however, come here to see the château, which can be visited when it is not in use as a "Camp David" for French presidents.

ESSENTIALS

GETTING THERE It takes 2 hours to see the château at Rambouillet. **Trains** depart from Paris's Gare Montparnasse every 20 minutes throughout the day. One-way passage costs 41 F ($6.95) for about a 35-minute ride. Information and train schedules can be obtained by contacting **La Gare de Rambouillet,** place Prud'homme (☎ **01-53-90-20-20**). By car, take the N-10 southwest from Paris, passing Versailles along the way.

VISITOR INFORMATION The **tourist office** is at the Hôtel de Ville, place de la Libération (☎ **01-34-83-21-21**).

SEEING THE SIGHTS

Dating from 1375, the **Château de Rambouillet,** Parc du Château (☎ **01-34-83-00-25**), is surrounded by a park in one of the most famous forests in France. George Pompidou used to stay here, as did Louis XVI and Charles de Gaulle. Before the château became a royal residence, the marquise de Rambouillet kept house here; it is said she taught the cultured ladies and gentlemen of Paris how to talk, introducing them to a long, gaudy string of poets and painters.

François I, the Chevalier king, died of a fever at Rambouillet in 1547 at age 52. When the château was later occupied by the comte de Toulouse, Rambouillet was often visited by Louis XV, who was amused (in more ways than one) by the comte's witty and high-spirited wife. Louis XVI acquired the château, but his wife, Marie Antoinette, was bored with the place and called it "the toad." In his surprisingly modest boudoir are four panels representing the continents.

In 1814, Napoléon's second wife, Marie-Louise (daughter of Francis II, emperor of Austria), met at Rambouillet with her father, who convinced her to abandon Napoléon and France itself after her husband's humiliating defeats at Moscow and Leipzig. Afterward, she fled to her original home, the royal court in Vienna, with Napoléon's 3-year-old son, François-Charles-Joseph Bonaparte (also known as l'Aiglon, the young eagle, and, at least in title, the king of Rome). Later, before his death in Vienna at age 21, his claim on the Napoleonic legacy would be rejected by France's enemies, despite the fact that his father had had a special annex to the château at Rambouillet built especially for his use.

A year later, before his final exile to the remote island of St. Helena, a British colony in the south Atlantic, Napoléon insisted on spending one final night at Rambouillet, where he secluded himself with his meditations and memories.

In 1830, the elderly Charles X, Louis XVI's brother, abdicated the throne of France at Rambouillet as a Parisian mob marched on the château, and his troops began to desert him. From Rambouillet, he embarked for a safe, but politically controversial, haven in England.

Afterward, Rambouillet fell into private hands. At one time it was a fashionable restaurant that attracted Parisians by offering gondola rides. Napoléon III, however, returned it to the Crown. In 1897, it was designated as a residence for the presidents of the Republic. In 1944, Charles de Gaulle lived here briefly before giving the order for what was left of the French army to join the Americans in liberating Paris.

Superb woodwork is used throughout, and the walls are adorned with tapestries, many dating from the era of Louis XV.

The château is open Wednesday through Monday from 10 to 11:30am and 2 to 5:30pm, closing an hour early from October to March. Admission is 32 F ($5.45) for adults, 21 F ($3.55) for students 12 to 25, and free for children 11 and under.

DINING

La Poste. 101 av. du Général-de-Gaulle. ☎ **01-34-83-03-01.** Reservations recommended Sat–Sun. Main courses 119–156 F ($20.25–$26.50); fixed-price menu 119–156 F ($20.25–$26.50). AE, MC, V. Tues–Sun noon–2pm; Tues–Wed and Fri–Sat 7–10pm. FRENCH.

Set on a street corner in the town's historic center, across from the Sous-Préfecture de Police, this restaurant has been serving food since the mid–19th century, when it provided meals and shelter for the region's mail carriers. The two dining rooms are outfitted with rustic beams and old-fashioned accents that complement the flavorful, old-fashioned food that has been a staple since the beginning. Good-tasting menu items include homemade terrines of foie gras and freshly made pastries. A particularly flavorful two-fisted dish is a filet of beef served with a Perigueux sauce composed of Madeira wine and foie gras.

3 The Cathedral of Chartres

60 miles SW of Paris, 47 miles NW of Orléans

Many observers feel that the architectural aspirations of the Middle Ages reached their highest expression in the glorious Cathedral at Chartres. Come to see its soaring architecture, highly wrought sculpture, and, above all, its stained glass, which gave the world a new color, Chartres blue.

ESSENTIALS

GETTING THERE   It takes a full day to see Chartres. From Paris's Gare Montparnasse, trains run directly to Chartres, taking less than an hour and passing through a sea of wheat fields. **By car,** take A10/A11 southwest from the boulevard périphérique and follow the signs to Le Mans and Chartres (the Chartres exit is clearly marked).

VISITOR INFORMATION   The Office de Tourisme is on place de la Cathédrale (☎ 02-37-21-50-00).

SEEING THE SIGHTS

✪ **Cathédrale Notre-Dame de Chartres.** 16 Cloître Notre-Dame. ☎ **02-37-21-56-33.** Free admission. Mon–Sat 7:30am–7:15pm, Sun 8:30am–7:15pm (closes at 7pm Nov–Easter).

Reportedly, Rodin once sat for hours on the edge of the sidewalk, admiring this cathedral's Romanesque sculpture. His opinion: Chartres is the French Acropolis. When it began to rain, a kind soul offered him an umbrella, which he declined, so transfixed was he by the magic of this place.

The cathedral's origins are uncertain; some have suggested it grew up over an ancient Druid site that had later become a Roman temple. It is known that as early as the 4th century there was a Christian basilica here. A fire in 1194 destroyed most of what had then become a Romanesque cathedral, but spared the western facade and crypt. The cathedral you see today dates principally from the 13th century, when it was rebuilt with the efforts and contributions of kings, princes, churchmen,

Impressions

I am entirely absorbed by these plains of wheat on a vast expanse of hills like an ocean of tender yellow, pale green, and soft mauve, with a piece of worked land dotted with clusters of potato vines in bloom, and all this under a blue sky tinted with shades of white, pink, and violet.

—Vincent van Gogh (1890)

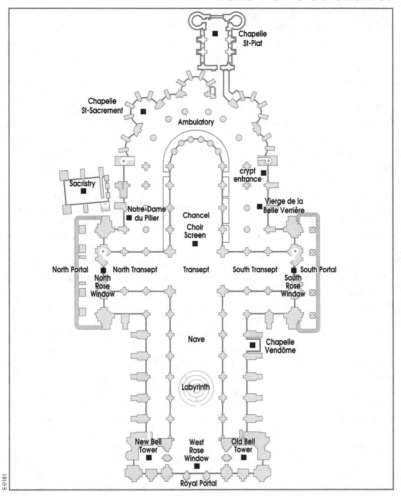

and pilgrims from all over Europe. One of the world's greatest high Gothic cathedrals, it was the first to use flying buttresses to support the soaring dimensions within.

French sculpture in the 12th century broke into full bloom when the **Royal Portal** was added. A landmark in Romanesque art, the sculptured bodies are elongated, often stylized, in their long flowing robes. But the faces are amazingly (for the time) lifelike, occasionally winking or smiling. In the central tympanum, Christ is shown at the Second Coming, with his descent depicted on the right, his ascent on the left. Before entering, walk around to both the **north and south portals,** each dating from the 13th century. They depict such biblical scenes as the expulsion of Adam and Eve from the Garden of Eden.

Inside is a celebrated **choir screen;** work on it began in the 16th century and lasted until 1714. The niches, 40 in all, contain statues illustrating scenes from the life of the Madonna and Christ—everything from the *Massacre of the Innocents* to the *Coronation of the Virgin.*

Music of the Spheres

If you're visiting Chartres on a Sunday afternoon, the cathedral features a free 1-hour organ concert beginning at 4:45pm, when the filtered light of the Ile de France sunset makes the western windows of the cathedral come thrillingly alive.

But few rushed visitors ever notice the screen: They're too transfixed by the light from the **stained glass.** Covering an expanse of more than 3,000 square yards, the glass is truly mystical, unlike anything else in the world. The stained glass, most of which dates from the 12th and 13th centuries, was spared in both world wars by painstakingly removing it piece by piece.

See the windows in the morning, at noon, in the afternoon, at sunset—as often as you can. Like the petals of a kaleidoscope, they constantly change. It's difficult to single out one panel or window above the others, but an exceptional one is the 12th-century *Vierge de la belle verrière* (Our Lady of the Beautiful Window) on the south side. Of course, there are three fiery rose windows, but you couldn't miss those if you tried.

The **nave,** the widest in France, still contains its ancient floor-maze, which formed a mobile channel of contemplation for monks. The wooden Virgin of the Pillar, to the left of the choir, dates from the 14th century. The crypt was built over two centuries, beginning in the 9th. Enshrined within is *Our Lady of the Crypt,* a 1976 Madonna that replaced one destroyed during the Revolution.

Try to take a **tour** conducted by **Malcolm Miller** (☎ 02-37-28-15-58; fax 02-37-28-33-03), an Englishman who has spent 3 decades studying the cathedral and giving tours in English with a rare blend of scholarship, enthusiasm, and humor. He usually conducts 75-minute tours at noon and 2:45pm Monday through Saturday for a fee of 30 F ($5.10) per person. Tours are canceled in the event of pilgrimages, religious celebrations, and large-scale funerals. French-language tours are conducted by other guides between Easter and late October at 10:30am and 3pm, and at 2:30pm the rest of the year, for a fee of 28 F ($4.75).

If you feel fit enough, don't miss the opportunity, especially in summer, to climb to the top of the **tower.** Open the same hours as the cathedral, except for a lunchtime closing between noon and 2pm, it costs 25 F ($4.25) for adults and 15 F ($2.55) for students. The **crypt,** gloomy and somber, but rich with a sense of medieval history, can be visited only as part of a French-speaking tour that's conducted whenever there's enough demand. The cost is 11 F ($1.85) per person.

After your visit, stroll through the **episcopal gardens** and enjoy yet another view of this remarkable cathedral.

EXPLORING THE OLD TOWN

If time remains, you may want to explore the medieval cobbled streets of the Vieux Quartier (Old Town). At the foot of the cathedral are lanes containing gabled houses and humped bridges spanning the Eure River. From the Bouju Bridge, you can see the lofty spires in the background. Try to find **rue Chantault,** which boasts houses with colorful facades, one 8 centuries old.

A highlight of your visit will be **Musée des Beaux-Arts de Chartres,** 29 Cloître Notre-Dame (☎ 02-37-36-41-39), open Wednesday through Monday, October 31 to May 2, from 10am to noon and 2 to 5pm, and the rest of the year Wednesday through Monday from 10am to noon and 2 to 6pm. Next door to the cathedral, this museum of fine arts charges 15 F ($2.55) for adults and 7.50 F ($1.30) for children. Installed in a former episcopal palace, the building at times competes with its exhibitions. One part

To Taste a Madeleine

And suddenly the memory returns. The taste was that of the little crumb of madeleine, which on Sunday mornings at Combray (because on those mornings I did not go out before church-time), when I went to say good day to her in her bedroom, my aunt Léonie used to give me, dipping it first in her own cup of real or of lime-flower tea.

—Marcel Proust, *Remembrance of Things Past*

Illiers-Combray, a small town 54 miles southwest of Paris and 15 miles southwest of Chartres, was once known simply as Illiers. Then Proust groupies started to come and signs were posted: ILLIERS, LE COMBRAY DE MARCEL PROUST. Illiers was and is a real town, but Marcel Proust in his masterpiece, *A la recherche du temps perdu (Remembrance of Things Past),* made it so famous as Combray that Life acknowledged fiction and the town officially changed its name to Illiers-Combray.

It was the taste of a luscious little madeleine that launched Proust on his immortal recollection. To this day, hundreds of his readers from all over the world flock to the pastry shops in Illiers-Combray to eat a madeleine or two dipped in lime-flower tea. Following the Proustian labyrinth, you can explore the gardens, streets, and houses he frequented until he was 13 and wrote about so richly later on. The town is centered around the **Eglise St-Jacques,** where Proust as a boy placed hawthorn on the altar.

Some members of Proust's family have lived in Illiers for centuries. His grandfather, François, was born here on rue du Cheval-Blanc. At **11 place du Marché,** just opposite the church, he ran a small candle shop. His daughter, Elisabeth, married Jules Amiot, who ran a shop a few doors away. Down from Paris, young Marcel would visit his aunt at 4 rue du St-Esprit, which has been renamed **rue du Docteur-Proust** in honor of Marcel's grandfather.

The **Musée Marcel Proust/Maison de Tante Léonie,** rue du Docteur-Proust (☎ 02-37-24-30-97), contains the world's most concentrated dose of memorabilia associated with the novelist, including objects that famously helped spark his creative vision. In his novels, this was Aunt Léonie's home, filled with antimacassars and antiques, all the typical bourgeois comforts of the day. Upstairs you can see the bedrooms where the young Marcel and his Aunt Léonie slept. Today, they contain souvenirs of key episodes in his novels. There is also a meticulously crafted re-creation of the Salon Rouge, which Proust maintained in his second-to-last residence, a site at 102 Bd. Haussmann, in Paris 8e, filled with furniture owned by his parents and grandparents. The museum can be visited only as part of French-language guided tours conducted at 2:30 and 4pm every Tuesday through Sunday. The cost is 30 F ($5.10) for adults, 20 F ($3.40) for students, free for children under 12.

In the center of town, a sign will guide you to further Proustian sights, each of which is open 24 hours a day without charge. They include the Église Saint-Hilaire and the Pré-Catalan, the garden maintained by Proust's Uncle Amiot.

dates from the 15th century and encompasses a courtyard. The permanent collection of paintings covers the 16th to the 20th centuries, and includes the work of such old masters as Zurbarán, Watteau, and Brosamer. Of particular interest is David Ténier's *Le Concert.* Special exhibitions are often mounted.

ACCOMMODATIONS

Hotel Châtelet. 6-8 av. Jehan-de-Beauce, 28000 Chartres. ☎ **02-37-21-78-00.** Fax 02-37-36-23-01. 48 units. TV TEL. 460–495 F ($78.20–$84.15) double. Third person 60 F ($10.20) extra. AE, DC, MC, V.

This relatively modern hotel has many traditional touches. Rooms are inviting and appealingly rustic, with reproductions of Louis XV and Louis XVI furniture. The larger, more expensive rooms face a garden, and thereby avoid noise from the street. Many windows along the front (street) side of the hotel open onto a view of the cathedral, but the more expensive rooms overlooking the garden have newer mattresses. Bathrooms are boxy, without a lot of shelf space, and have a tub and shower. In chilly weather, there's a log-burning fire in one of the salons. Breakfast is the only meal served, but there are numerous restaurants close by.

Hôtel de la Poste. 3 rue du Général-Koenig, 28003 Chartres. ☎ **02-37-21-04-27.** Fax 02-37-36-42-17. 57 units. TV TEL. 310–340 F ($52.70–$57.80) double. AE, DC, MC, V. In-house garage 40 F ($6.80).

This modest hotel is short on charm, but it offers one of the best values in Chartres. It's in the center of town, across from the main post office. The rooms are soundproof and well furnished, with wall-to-wall carpeting and acceptably comfortable mattresses. Bathrooms are cramped, with shower stalls and rather thin towels. The surprise here is the good, affordable food, backed up by one of the town's finest wine cellars. Set menus range in price from 82 F to 170 F ($13.95 to $28.90), and are served daily at both lunch and dinner. The worst thing about the hotel is the group tours.

Le Grand Monarque Best Western. 22 place des Epars, 28005 Chartres. ☎ **800/528-1234** in the U.S., or 02-37-21-00-72. Fax 02-37-36-34-18. 54 units. MINIBAR TV TEL. 600–720 F ($102–$122.40) double; 1,095–1,320 F ($186.15–224.40) suite. AE, DC, MC, V. Parking 50 F ($8.50).

Chartres's leading hotel is housed in a classical building enclosing a courtyard. Functioning as an inn almost since its original construction in the mid–19th century, and greatly expanded over the years, it still attracts guests who enjoy its old-world charm, with its art nouveau stained glass and Louis XV chairs in the dining room. The rooms are decorated with reproductions of antiques and most have sitting areas. Most accommodations are small to medium in size. Bathrooms are motel standard, with adequate shelf space and a shower and tub. The hotel also has an anachronistic restaurant; one local critic found the kitchen to be trapped in an "ancien régime time warp."

DINING

Le Buisson Ardent. 10 rue au Lait. ☎ **02-37-34-04-66.** Reservations recommended. Main courses 88–132 F ($14.95–$22.45); fixed-price menu 128–238 F ($21.75–$40.45). MC, V. Daily noon–2pm; Mon–Sat 7:30–9:30pm. FRENCH.

In a charming 300-year-old house in the most historic section of town, this restaurant is one floor above street level in the shadow of the cathedral. From its location you might expect it to be a tourist trap, but it isn't. The composition of the set-price menus changes with the seasons, and, like the à la carte dishes, are made with fresh meats, produce, and fish. Best-sellers include an escalope of warm foie gras prepared with apples and Calvados, or an émincée of roasted pigeon with sweetbreads and honey sauce. Other dishes are simpler, the kind you might have noticed in bistros: Codfish flavored with coriander and served with parsley flan as a main course is an especially good choice. A dessert specialty is crispy hot pineapples with an orange and passion-fruit salad.

4 Giverny—In the Footsteps of Claude Monet

50 miles NW o5f Paris

On the border between Normandy and the Ile de France, Giverny is home to the Claude Monet Foundation, in the house where the Impressionist painter lived for 43 years. The restored house and its gardens are open to the public.

ESSENTIALS

GETTING THERE   It takes a full morning to get to Giverny and to see its sights. Take the Paris-Rouen **train** from Paris–St-Lazare to the Vernon station, where a taxi can take you the 3 miles to Giverny. Perhaps the easiest way to enjoy Giverny and its association with the world's greatest Impressionists is on a full-day **bus tour** whose focal point is Monet's house and garden. You can arrange this through **Cityrama,** 2 rue des Pyramides, 1er (☎ **01-44-55-61-00;** Métro: Palais-Royal), or by contacting the outfit's most visible sales outlet, **American Express,** 11 rue Scribe, 9e (☎ **01-42-27-58-80;** Métro: Opéra).

By car, take the Autoroute de l'Ouest (Port de St-Cloud) toward Rouen. Leave the autoroute at Bonnières, then cross the Seine on the Bonnières Bridge. From here, a direct road with signs will bring you to Giverny. Expect about an hour of driving; try to avoid weekends.

Another way to get to Giverny is to leave the highway at the Bonnières exit and go toward Vernon. Once in Vernon, cross the bridge over the Seine and follow the signs to Giverny or Gasny (Giverny is before Gasny). This is easier than going through Bonnières, where there aren't many signs.

SEEING THE SIGHTS

✪ **Claude Monet Foundation.** rue Claude-Monet Parc Gasny ☎ **01-32-51-28-21.**

The French painter Claude Monet was a spiritualist of light, brilliantly translating its effects at different times of the day. In fact, some critics claim that he "invented light." His series of paintings of the cathedral at Rouen and of the water lilies, which one critic called "vertical interpretations of horizontal lines," are just a few of his masterpieces.

Monet came to Giverny in 1883, at age 43. While taking a small railway linking Vetheuil to Vernon, he discovered the village at a point where the Epte stream joined the Seine. Many of his friends used to visit him here at Le Pressoir, including Clemenceau, Cézanne, Rodin, Renoir, Degas, and Sisley. When Monet died in 1926, his son, Michel, inherited the house but left it abandoned until it decayed into ruins. The gardens became almost a jungle, inhabited by river rats. In 1966, Michel died and left the house to the Académie des Beaux-Arts. It wasn't until 1977 that Gerald van der Kemp, who restored Versailles, decided to work on Giverny. A large part of it was restored with gifts from American benefactors, especially the late Lila Acheson Wallace, former head of *Reader's Digest.*

You can stroll through the garden and view the thousands of flowers, including the famous *nymphéas* (water lilies). The Japanese bridge, hung with wisteria, leads to a dreamy setting of weeping willows and rhododendrons. Monet's studio barge was installed on the pond.

The foundation is open only April through October, Tuesday through Sunday from 10am to 6pm, charging 35 F ($5.95) for adults and 20 F ($3.40) for ages 7 to 18. Children under 7 enter free. The gardens may be visited for a discount of 10 F ($1.70) off each of the categories listed above. Advance reservations are important.

DINING

Auberge du Vieux Moulin. 21 rue de la Falaise. ☎ **02-32-51-46-15.** Main courses 72–95 F ($12.25–$16.15); fixed-price menu 98–158 F ($16.65–$26.85). MC, V. Tues–Sun noon–3pm and 7:30–10pm. Closed Jan. FRENCH.

Set within a stone-sided building that was originally a farmhouse in 1935, this is a convenient lunch stop for visitors at the Monet house. The Boudeau family maintains a series of cozy dining rooms filled with original Impressionist paintings. Since you can walk here from the museum in about 5 minutes, leave your car in the museum lot. Specialties include appetizers like snails in puff pastry with garlic-flavored butter sauce, guinea fowl braised in cider, chicken with shrimp, and escalope of salmon with sorrel sauce. Dessert might be a tarte Normande prepared with apple slices and Calvados. The kitchen doesn't pretend the food is any more than it is: good, hearty country fare with panache. The charm of the staff helps a lot, too. The stone building is ringed with lawns and has a pair of flowering terraces.

5 Saint-Germain-en-Laye

13 miles NW of Paris

Saint-Germain-en-Laye served as the seat of the royal court for centuries, and was even home to Louis XIV until he decided to build that little place in Versailles. Over the years, people have traditionally fled Paris for Saint-Germain-en-Laye in hopes of cooling off during the hot summer months, even though it is only 13 miles away. Today, this très riche bedroom community, with its fancy boutiques and rural environs, continues to maintain a certain allure for Parisians, especially on weekends. The forested areas that border the town provide the perfect place to walk, jog, or picnic. Saint-Germain-en-Laye is perhaps best known as the birthplace of béarnaise sauce, invented here in 1447 along with *pommes soufflés*, boiled and mashed potatoes dropped into hot oil, airier and crispier than french fried potatoes.

ESSENTIALS

GETTING THERE   Expect to spend a half day seeing Saint-Germain-en-Laye. **RER trains** (line A1) from the center of Paris take about 30 minutes. The St-Germain-en-Laye station is located just across the street from the château.

   By car, either take the N-13 west out of Paris (direction St-Germain-en-Laye) or get on the A-13 traveling west and take the St-Germain-en-Laye exit.

ORIENTATION   The town sits on the left bank of the Seine river. The large Parc St-Germaine is near the center of town and is bordered on its left side by the Château Vieux. Just across the street from the château is the RER station, and pedestrian and shopping streets fan out to the south and east.

VISITOR INFORMATION   The Office de Tourisme is at 38 rue Au-Pain (☎ 01-34-51-05-12).

SEEING THE SIGHTS

Just opposite the St-Germain-en-Laye RER station stands the **Château Vieux,** place du Château (☎ **01-39-10-13-00**), a brick and stone castle built in the 12th century by François I on a promontory overlooking the Seine. It served as a court in exile to the Stuart king of England, James II, who stayed here in the expectation that his supporters would wrest the throne from the Protestants William and Mary. (They never did.) Later Napoléon III ordered that the château be turned into a museum to display France's rich history, beginning with the cave dwellers from the last ice age through to the Carolingian era. His orders were carried out to the letter, and today two floors of the château are devoted to the **French Museum of National Antiquities** (Musée des Antiquités Nationales), where visitors can view exhaustive collections of stone and metal tools, weapons, and jewelry used or worn by the early settlers of Gaul. **La Chapelle** is the oldest part of the château, built by St. Louis in the 1230s. Although not actually part of the château proper, visitors can still walk through **Le Nôtre's Gardens** next door and admire the traditionally planned French landscape design. The building is open Wednesday through Monday from 9am to 5:15pm; the gardens are open daily from 7am to 8pm. Admission is 25 F ($4.25) for adults, 16 F ($2.70) on Sunday. Ages 18 to 25 pay 16 F ($2.70). Children under 18 enter free.

Built in 1678 by the marquise de Montespan, a paramour of Louis XIV, the building that houses **Le Musée Départmental Maurice Denis "Le Prieuré,"** 2 bis rue Maurice-Denis (☎ 01-39-73-77-87), was home to the painter Maurice Denis from World War I until his death in 1943. It was here that he befriended a group of artists known as the "Nabis." The museum has collections of works by Nabis masters such as Bonnard, Vuillard, and Paul Serusier, along with members of the Pont-Avon group, including Gauguin and Emile Bernard. Works by other artists, including Toulouse-Lautrec, are exhibited as well. You can also visit La Chapelle St-Louis, a chapel decorated by Denis, as well as his workshop. The museum is open Wednesday through Friday from 10am to 5:15pm, Saturday and Sunday from 10am to 6:30pm. Admission is 25 to 35 F ($4.25 to $5.95) for adults, 15 F to 25 F ($2.55 to $4.25) for students and seniors, and free for children under 12.

ACCOMMODATIONS & DINING

Cazaudehore. In the Hôtel La Forestière, 1 av. du Président Kennedy. ☎ **01-39-10-38-38.** Fax 01-39-73-73-88. Reservations required. Main courses 115–185 F ($19.55–$31.45); fixed-price menu 180–290 F ($30.60–$49.30) at lunch Tues–Fri; 370 F ($62.90) at lunch Sat–Sun and at dinner. AE, MC, V. Tues–Sun 12:30–2:30pm and 7:30–10:30pm. FRENCH.

Since its opening in 1982 by Jean-Baptiste Cazaudehore and his wife, Liliane, this restaurant has offered guests unpretentious but refined food. The dining rooms, with their large fireplaces, are filled with a unique collection of furniture and paintings from the past, creating a warm and inviting atmosphere. In the summer months, guests can dine in the English garden that surrounds the restaurant. The menu changes with the seasons and tends to have characteristic undertones from southwestern France. Typical main courses may include roasted lamb filet served with orange polenta, truffled duck with braised new potatoes, and escalope of fresh foie gras with gingerbread and corn galette.

In addition to taking over the restaurant, the Cazaudehores' son, Pierre, has transformed the family's country house into an auberge-style hotel, **La Forestière,** with 25 rooms and 5 suites. The bedrooms range from small to large, and furnishings range from classic Louis XIV to contemporary. Some rooms have a private balcony; others offer private terraces. A double costs 1,050 F ($178.50) and suites start at 1,450 F ($246.50). All rooms have minibar, TV, and telephone.

Le Pavillon Henri IV. 21 rue Thiers, 78100 St-Germain-en-Laye. ☎ **01-39-10-15-15.** Fax 01-39-73-93-73. 42 units. MINIBAR TV TEL. 980–1,280 F ($166.60–$217.60) double. AE, DC, MC, V.

This luxurious hotel dates from the 1500s, when Henri IV, possibly the most promiscuous French king of a very randy bunch, built the Château Neuf as a terraced hideaway for his illegitimate children. It was later bequeathed to the comte d'Artois, the brother of Louis XVI, who had it slated for demolition. Thanks to a little affair known today as the French Revolution, the château remained intact. Partially rebuilt in 1836, it now houses Le Pavillon Henri IV, where Dumas wrote *The Three Musketeers.* Standing at the edge of the belvedere gardens, originally laid out during the

Renaissance, it is still elegantly old-fashioned. A corner room has been set aside in remembrance of where the Sun King romped with Madame de Montespan. A chapel in one of the wings has beautifully preserved painted ceilings. The handsome guest rooms vary in size but are all classically outfitted with antiques from Louis XIV to Louis XVI; many rooms have a panoramic view of the Seine valley.

The refined atmosphere of the hotel carries through to its restaurant, which fills with sunlight on fair-weather days. The restaurant specializes in traditional French dishes like veal kidney dijonnaise, roast lamb, and *pommes soufflés* (invented here in 1447 along with sauce béarnaise), which is just the thing to top your châteaubriand. Most à la carte lunches and dinners cost between 300 and 400 F ($51 and $68) without wine; and the fixed-price menu is available daily for 240 F ($40.80).

6 Disneyland Paris

20 miles E of Paris

After provoking some of the most enthusiastic and controversial reactions in recent French history, the multimillion-dollar Euro Disney Resort opened in 1992 as one of the most lavish theme parks in the world. In 1994, it unofficially changed its name to "Disneyland Paris." Because the park was conceived on a scale rivaling that of Versailles, the earliest days of the project were not particularly happy. European journalists delighted in belittling it and accusing it of everything from cultural imperialism to the death knell of French culture. But after financial jitters, and goodly amounts of public relations and financial juggling, the resort is on track.

As Disneyland faces the millennium, it has become France's number-one tourist attraction, with 50 million annual visitors. MONSIEUR MICKEY TRIUMPHS! the French press headlined. Disney surpasses the Eiffel Tower and the Louvre in numbers of visitors and accounts for 4% of the French tourism industry's foreign currency sales. Forty percent of the visitors are French, half of these from Paris. Disneyland Paris looks, tastes, and feels like its parents in California and Florida—except for the $10 cheeseburgers "avec pommes frites."

Situated on a 5,000-acre site (about one-fifth the size of Paris) in the suburb of Marne-la-Vallée, the park incorporates the most successful elements of its Disney predecessors, but with a European flair. Allow a full day to see the park.

ESSENTIALS
GETTING THERE

BY TRAIN   The resort is linked to the RER commuter express rail network (Line A), which maintains a stop within walking distance of the theme park. Board the RER at such Paris stops as Charles-de-Gaulle–Etoile, Châtelet–Les Halles, or Nation. Get off at Line A's last stop, Marne-la-Vallée/Chessy, 45 minutes from central Paris. The round-trip fare from central Paris is 80 F ($13.60). Trains run every 10 to 20 minutes, depending on the time of day.

BY BUS   Each of the hotels in the resort connects by shuttle bus to both Orly Airport and Roissy–Charles de Gaulle. Buses depart from both airports at intervals of 45 minutes. One-way transportation to the park from either of the airports costs 85 F ($14.45) per person.

BY CAR   Take the A-4 highway east from Paris, getting off at exit 14, where it's marked PARC EURO DISNEYLAND. Guest parking at any of the thousands of parking spaces costs 40 F ($6.80) per day. An interconnected series of moving sidewalks speeds up pedestrian transit from the parking areas to the theme park's entrance. Parking for guests at any of the hotels within the resort is free.

INFORMATION

All hotels listed below provide general information about the theme park, but for specific theme-park information in all languages, contact the **Disneyland Paris Guest Relations office,** located in City Hall on Main Street, U.S.A. (☎ **01-60-30-60-53;** www.disneylandparis.com).

Coin-operated lockers can be rented for 10 F ($1.80), and larger bags can also be stored for 15 F ($2.55) per day. Children's strollers and wheelchairs can be rented for 30 F ($5.10) per day, with a 20 F ($3.40) deposit. Baby-sitting is available at any of the resort's hotels if 24-hour advance notice is given.

SEEING THE SIGHTS

The resort was designed as a total vacation package: Included within one enormous unit are the Disneyland Park with its five different entertainment "lands," six large hotels, a campground, an entertainment center (Village Disney), a 27-hole golf course, and dozens of restaurants, shows, and shops.

One of the attractions, **Main Street, U.S.A.,** features horse-drawn carriages and street-corner barbershop quartets. From the "Main Street Station," steam-powered railway cars leave for a trip through a Grand Canyon Diorama to Frontierland, with paddle-wheel steamers reminiscent of the Mississippi Valley described by Mark Twain.

The park's steam trains chug past **Adventureland**—with swashbuckling 18th-century pirates, the tree house of the Swiss Family Robinson, and reenacted legends from the Arabian Nights—to **Fantasyland.** Here, you can see the symbol of the theme park, he Sleeping Beauty Castle *(Le Château de la Belle au Bois Dormant),* whose soaring pinnacles and turrets are a spectacular idealized interpretation of the châteaux of France.

Visions of the future are displayed at **Discoveryland,** whose tributes to human invention and imagination are drawn from the works of Leonardo da Vinci, Jules Verne, H. G. Wells, the modern masters of science fiction, and the *Star Wars* series. Discoveryland has proven among the most popular of all the areas, and is one of the few that was enlarged (in 1995) after the park's original inauguration.

As Disney continues to churn out animated blockbusters, look for all its newest stars to appear in the theme park. The fact that the characters from such films as *Aladdin, The Lion King,* and *Pocahontas* are actually made of celluloid hasn't kept them out of the Ice Capades and it certainly won't keep them out of Disneyland Paris.

Disney also maintains an entertainment center, **Village Disney,** whose indoor/ outdoor layout is a cross between a California mall and the Coney Island boardwalk. Scattered on either side of a pedestrian walkway, illuminated by an overhead grid of spotlights, it's set just outside the boundaries of the fenced-in acreage containing the bulk of Disneyland's attractions. The complex accommodates dance clubs, snack bars, restaurants, souvenir shops, and bars for adults who want to escape from the children for a while. Unlike the rest of the park, admission to **Village Disney** is free, and consequently attracts night owls from Paris and its suburbs who wouldn't otherwise be particularly interested in the park itself.

Disneyland Paris is open July and August daily from 9am to 11pm; September through June, Monday through Friday from 10am to 6pm, Saturday and Sunday from 9am to 8pm. Opening and closing hours, however, vary with the weather and the season. It's usually a good idea to phone the information office (see above).

Admission to the park for 1 day, depending on the season, costs 160 F to 210 F ($27.20 to $35.70) for adults and 130 F to 165 F ($22.10 to $28.05) for children 3 to 12. Admission to the park for 2 days ranges from 310 F to 385 F ($52.70 to $65.45) for adults and from 250 F to 295 F ($42.50 to $50.15) for children. Children 2 and under are always admitted free. Peak season is from mid-June to mid-September, as well as Christmas and Easter weeks. Entrance to Village Disney is free, although there's usually a cover charge for the dance clubs.

Guided tours can be arranged for 50 F ($8.50) for adults and 35 F ($5.95) for children ages 3 to 11. They last 3½ hours and include 20 or more people. In view of the well-marked paths leading through the park, and the availability of ample printed information in virtually any language once you get there, guided tours are not really necessary.

ACCOMMODATIONS

The resort has six theme hotels that share a common reservation service. For more information, call ☎ **407/W-DISNEY** in North America. For information or reservations in France, contact the **Central Reservations Office,** Euro Disney Resort, S.C.A., B.P. 105, F-77777 Marne-la-Vallée Cedex 4 (☎ **01-60-30-60-30**).

EXPENSIVE

Disneyland Hotel. Disneyland Paris, B.P. 105, F-77777 Marne-la-Vallée Cedex 4. ☎ **01-60-45-65-00.** Fax 01-60-45-65-33. www.disneylandparis.com. 496 units. A/C MINIBAR·TV TEL. 1,600–2,390 F ($272–$406.30) for 1 to 4 persons; from 4,000 F ($680) suite. AE, DC, DISC, MC, V.

Located at the entrance to the park, this flagship hotel is Victorian in style, with red-tile turrets and jutting balconies; some observers have likened it to the town hall of a major European city. The bedrooms are plushly and conservatively furnished. The generously proportioned accommodations evoke the image of Disney, with cartoon depictions and a candy stripe decor. Beds are king, double, or twin. In some rooms, armchairs convert to day beds. Paneled closets, large mirrors, and private safes are found in some units. The luxury bathrooms have hair dryers, marble vanities, and twin basins, along with plush towels. On the Castle Club floor, there are free newspapers, all-day beverages, and access to a well-equipped private lounge.

Dining/Diversions: Three restaurants (The **California Grill** is recommended separately; see "Dining," below) and two bars.

Amenities: Health club with indoor/outdoor pool, whirlpool, sauna, private dining and banqueting rooms, room service, laundry, baby-sitting.

Hotel New York. Disneyland Paris, B.P. 100, F-77777 Marne-la-Vallée Cedex 4. ☎ **01-60-45-73-00.** Fax 01-60-45-73-33. www.disneylandparis.com. 563 units. A/C MINIBAR TV TEL. 970–1,690 F ($164.90–$287.30) for 1 to 4 persons; from 2,670–11,200 F ($453.90–$1,904) suite. AE, DC, DISC, MC, V.

Inspired by the Big Apple at its best, this hotel was designed around a nine-story central "skyscraper" flanked by the Gramercy Park Wing and the Brownstones Wing. (The exteriors of both of these wings resemble row houses.) The bedrooms are comfortably appointed with art deco accessories and New York–inspired memorabilia. Rooms contain private safes and paired double beds. Bathrooms are roomy, with hair dryers, twin basins, and fluffy towels. Some accommodations are set aside for non-smokers and others are wheelchair accessible.

Dining/Diversions: The hotel has a diner, one restaurant, a cocktail and wine bar, and an art deco bar.

Amenities: Indoor/outdoor pool, two outdoor tennis courts, health club, room service, laundry, baby-sitting.

MODERATE

Newport Bay Club. Disneyland Paris, B.P. 105, F-77777 Marne-la-Vallée Cedex 4. ☎ **01-60-45-55-00.** Fax 01-60-45-55-33. www.disneylandparis.com. 1,098 units. A/C MINIBAR TV TEL. 885–1,250 F ($150.45–$212.50) for 1 to 4 persons; from 1,850 F ($314.50) suite. AE, DC, DISC, MC, V.

This hotel was designed with a central cupola, jutting balconies, and a blue-and-cream color scheme, reminiscent of a harbor-front New England hotel from around 1900. Each nautically decorated bedroom offers closed-circuit TV information and movies. The layout is irregular, with guest rooms in various shapes and sizes. The most spacious rooms are the corner units. Amenities include private safes, phones with voice mail, and one king-size or two double beds. Some accommodations are reserved for nonsmokers, and others are equipped for those with disabilities. Bathrooms are roomy, with generous shelf space, deluxe toiletries, fluffy towels, and a tub and shower combination. The upscale **Yacht Club** and the less formal **Cape Cod** restaurants are the dining choices. Facilities include a lakeside promenade, a glassed-in pool pavilion, an outdoor pool, and a health club.

Sequoia Lodge. Disneyland Paris, B.P. 114, F-77777 Marne-la-Vallée Cedex 4. ☎ **01-60-45-51-00.** Fax 01-60-45-51-33. www.disneylandparis.com. 1,011 units. A/C MINIBAR TV TEL. 572–1,096 F ($97.25–$186.30) for 1 to 4 persons; from 1,350 F ($229.50) suite. AE, DC, DISC, MC, V.

Built of gray stone and roughly textured planking, and capped with a gently sloping green copper roof, this hotel resembles a rough-hewn, comfortable, and very large lodge in a remote section of the Rocky Mountains. The hotel consists of a large central building with five additional chalets nearby, each housing 100 bedrooms. The rooms are comfortably rustic. Bathrooms are tiled and fitted with shower and tub combinations and generous shelf space. Hair dryers are available upon request. The **Hunter's Grill** serves spit-roasted meats carved directly on your plate. Less formal is the **Beaver Creek Tavern.** Facilities include an indoor pool and health club.

INEXPENSIVE

Hotel Cheyenne and Hotel Santa Fe. Disneyland Paris, B.P. 115, F-77777 Marne-la-Vallée Cedex 4. ☎ **01-60-45-62-00** (Cheyenne) or 01-60-45-78-00 (Santa Fe). Fax 01-60-45-62-33 (Cheyenne) or 01-60-45-78-33 (Santa Fe). 2,000 units. TV TEL. Hotel Cheyenne 436–784 F ($74.10–$133.30) for 1 to 4 persons; Hotel Santa Fe 356–664 F ($60.50–$112.90) for 1 to 4 persons. AE, DC, DISC, MC, V.

Located next door to one another, these are the least expensive hotels at the resort. Both are situated near a re-creation of Texas's Rio Grande and evoke different aspects of the Old West. The Cheyenne accommodates visitors within 14 two-story buildings along "Desperado Street"; the Santa Fe, sporting a desert theme, encompasses four different "nature trails" winding among 42 adobe-style pueblos. This is the least accessorized and least elegant of all the Disney hotel properties, although the comfort level is still high. Bathrooms are medium in size, each with a tub and shower combination and adequate shelf space. The only disadvantage, according to some parents with children, is the absence of a swimming pool.

Tex-Mex specialties are offered at **La Cantina** (Hotel Santa Fe), and barbecue and smokehouse specialties predominate at the **Chuck Wagon Cafe** (Hotel Cheyenne).

DINING

Within the resort, there are at least 45 different restaurants and snack bars, each trying hard to please millions of European and North American palates. Here are a few recommendations:

Auberge de Cendrillon. Fantasyland. ☎ **01-64-74-24-02.** Reservations recommended. Main courses 105–140 F ($17.85–$23.80); fixed-price menu 175–210 F ($29.75–$35.70). AE, DC, DISC, MC, V. Thurs–Mon 11:30am to 90 minutes before closing of the park. FRENCH.

This is a fairy-tale version of Cinderella's sumptuous country inn, with a glass couch in the center. It is the major French restaurant at the resort. A master of ceremonies, in a plumed tricorne hat, wearing an embroidered tunic and lace ruffles, welcomes you. For an appetizer, try the warm goat-cheese salad with lardons or the smoked-salmon platter. If you don't choose one of the good fixed-price meals, you can order from the limited but excellent à la carte menu. Perhaps you'll settle happily for poultry in puff pastry, loin of lamb roasted with mustard, or sautéed medaillons of veal. Since the restaurant follows the park's seasonal schedules, lunches are usually easier to arrange than dinners.

California Grill. In the Disneyland Hotel. ☎ **01-60-45-65-00.** Reservations required. Main courses 55–205 F ($9.35–$34.85); children's menu 85 F ($14.45). AE, DC, MC, V. Sun–Fri 7–11pm, Sat 6–11pm. CALIFORNIAN/FRENCH.

Focusing on the lighter specialties for which the Golden State is famous, with many concessions to French palates, this airy and elegant restaurant manages to gracefully accommodate both adults and children. It features specialties such as oysters with leeks and salmon; foie gras with roasted red peppers; roasted pigeon with braised Chinese cabbage and black-rice vinegar; and salmon roasted over beechwood, served with walnut oil, sage sauce, asparagus, and a fricassée of mushrooms. Many items, such as "Mickie's pizzas," spaghetti Bolognese, and grilled ham with french fries, are conceived specifically for children. If you're looking for a quiet, mostly adult venue, go here as late as your hunger pangs will allow.

DISNEYLAND AFTER DARK

Buffalo Bill's Wild West Show. In the Festival Disney Building. ☎ **01-60-45-71-00.** 2 shows are staged nightly, at 6:30 and 9:30pm, costing (with dinner included) 325 F ($55.25) for adults, 195 F ($33.15) for children 3–11.

This is the premier theatrical venue of Disneyland Paris, a twice-per-night stampede of entertainment that recalls the show that once traveled the West with Buffalo Bill and Annie Oakley. You'll dine at tables that ring, amphitheater style, a dirt-floored riding rink where sharpshooters, runaway stage coaches, and dozens of horses and Indians ride very fast and perform some alarmingly realistic acrobatics. A Texas-style barbecue, served assembly-line style by waiters in 10-gallon hats, is part of the experience. Despite its corniness, it's not without charm and an almost mournful nostalgia for a way of life of another continent and another century. Wild Bill himself is dignified, and the Indians suitably brave.

7 Fontainebleau

37 miles S of Paris, 46 miles NE of Orléans

Set within the vestiges of a forest that bears its name (the Forêt de Fontainebleau), this suburb of Paris has offered refuge to French monarchs throughout the country's history. Kings from the Renaissance valued it because of its nearness to rich hunting grounds and its distance from the slums and smells of the city. Napoléon referred to the Palace of Fontainebleau, which he reembellished with his distinctive monogram and decorative style, as "the house of the centuries." Many pivotal and decisive events have occurred inside, perhaps none more memorable than when Napoléon stood on the horseshoe-shaped exterior stairway and bade farewell to his shattered army before departing to Elba.

ESSENTIALS

GETTING THERE   If you stay for lunch, a trip to Fontainebleau should last a half day. Trains to Fontainebleau, 37 miles south of Paris, depart from the Gare de Lyon in Paris. The trip takes between 45 and 60 minutes each way, and costs 94 ($16) round-trip. Fontainebleau's railway station lies 3 miles from the château, within the suburb of Avon. A local bus (it's marked simply CHÂTEAU) makes the trip to the château at 15-minute intervals every Monday through Saturday, and at 30-minute intervals every Sunday, for 10 F ($1.70) each way.

By car, take the A-6 south from Paris, exit onto N-191, and follow the signs.

ORIENTATION   Dominated by its château, the town is surrounded by the dense Forêt de Fontainebleau. The main squares are place du Général-de-Gaulle and place d'Armes. The **Office de Tourisme** is at Avon 4, rue Royale (☎ **01-60-74-99-99**).

✪ THE PALACE

Napoléon's affection for Fontainebleau was understandable. He was following the pattern of a succession of French kings in the pre-Versailles days who used Fontainebleau as a resort and hunted in its magnificent forests. François I, who tried to turn the hunting lodge into a royal palace in the Italian Renaissance style, brought along several artists, including Benvenuto Cellini, to work for him.

Under this patronage, the School of Fontainebleau gained prestige, led by the painters Rosso Fiorentino and Primaticcio. The artists adorned the 210-foot-long **Gallery of François I,** where stucco-framed panels depict such scenes as *The Rape of Europa,* and the monarch holding a pomegranate, a symbol of unity. The salamander, the symbol of the Chevalier king, is everywhere.

Sometimes called the Gallery of Henri II, the **Ballroom** displays the interlaced initials "H&D," referring to Henri and his mistress, Diane de Poitiers. Competing with this illicit tandem are the initials "H&C," symbolizing Henri and his ho-hum wife, Catherine de Médicis. At one end of the room is a monumental fireplace supported by two bronze satyrs, made in 1966 (the originals were melted down during the French Revolution). At the other side is the balcony of the musicians, with sculptured garlands. The ceiling displays octagonal coffering adorned with rosettes. Above the wainscoting is a series of frescoes, painted between 1550 and 1558, which depict such mythological subjects as *The Feast of Bacchus.*

An architectural curiosity is the richly and elegantly adorned **Louis XV Staircase.** The room above it was originally decorated by Primaticcio for the bedroom of the duchesse d'Etampes, but when an architect was designing the stairway, he simply ripped out her floor. Of the Italian frescoes that were preserved, one depicts the queen of the Amazons climbing into Alexander the Great's bed.

When Louis XIV ascended to the throne, he neglected Fontainebleau because of his preoccupation with Versailles. However, he wasn't opposed to using the palace for houseguests, specifically such unwanted ones as Queen Christina, who had abdicated the throne of Sweden in a fit of religious fervor. Under the assumption that she still had "divine right," she ordered the brutal murder of her companion Monaldeschi, who had ceased to please her.

Although Louis XV, and later Marie Antoinette, took an interest in Fontainebleau, the château found its renewed glory under Napoléon. You can wander around much of the palace on your own, visiting sites that evoke his 19th-century imperial heyday.

They include the **throne room** where he abdicated his rulership of France, his **offices,** his monumental **bedroom,** and his **bathroom.** Some of the smaller Napoleonic Rooms contain his personal mementos and artifacts.

After your long trek through the palace, visit the gardens and, especially, the carp pond; the gardens, however, are only a prelude to the Forest of Fontainebleau.

The **interior** (☎ **01-60-71-50-70**) is open September through June, Wednesday through Monday from 9:30am to 12:30pm and from 2 to 5pm. In July and August, it's open Wednesday through Monday from 9:30am to 6pm. A combination ticket allowing access to the *grands appartements* costs 35 F ($5.95) for adults and 23 F ($3.90) for students 18 to 25; free for under age 18. A ticket allowing access to the *petits appartements* and the Napoleonic Rooms is 16 F ($2.70) for adults and 12 F ($2.05) for students 18 to 25; free for under age 18.

ACCOMMODATIONS & DINING

Le Beauharnais. In the Grand Hôtel de l'Aigle Noir, 27 place Napoléon-Bonaparte. ☎ **01-60-74-60-00.** Fax 01-60-74-60-01. www.fontainebleau-online.com/aiglenoir.htm. E-mail: hotel-aiglenoir@fontainebleau-online.com. Reservations required. Main courses 150–280 F ($25.50–$47.60); fixed-price menu 195–450 F ($33.15–$76.50). AE, DC, MC, V. Daily noon–2pm and 7:30–9:30pm. Closed Dec 23–30. FRENCH.

This is the town's leading restaurant, which retains its old charm despite a complete renovation. Opposite the château, the building was once the home of the Cardinal de Retz. It dates from the 16th century and was converted into a hotel in 1720. The restaurant was installed in a former courtyard. The beautiful interior is filled with Empire furniture and potted palms. The refreshing menu includes such classics as Rouen roast duckling, but also dishes with more flair and subtlety, including sweetbreads with foie gras. The perfectly prepared grilled pigeon with pistachio nuts evokes Morocco. Dishes change according to season.

The **hotel** has 53 bedrooms and 3 suites, all with private baths and TVs, radios, minibars, direct-dial phones, double windows, and electric heating. The hotel also boasts a swimming pool, sauna, and fitness center. Each room is individually decorated, often with antiques and pleasantly tasteful colors. Doubles range in price from 990 F to 1,380 F ($168.30 to $234.60), suites from 2,400 F ($408).

Le Caveau des Ducs. 24 rue de Ferrare. ☎ **01-64-22-05-05.** Reservations recommended. Main courses 85–130 F ($14.45–$22.10); fixed-price menu 125–250 F ($21.25–$42.50). AE, MC, V. Daily noon–2pm and 7–10pm. FRENCH.

Deep beneath a series of 17th-century stone vaults built by the same masons who laid the cobblestones of the rue de Ferrare upstairs, this reasonably priced restaurant occupies what was once a storage cellar for the nearby château. Wood and flickering candles preserve the illusion. The restaurant isn't in the same league as Le Beauharnais, but offers simpler food in a more dramatic setting. Competently prepared, each dish could stand in a museum of French food of the 1950s: snails in garlic butter, roast leg of lamb with garlic-and-rosemary sauce, and virtually everything that can be done with the body of a duck. The filet of rump steak is quite tasty, especially when served in a brie sauce, as are the platter of sole, crayfish tails, and salmon on a bed of pasta. Expect good things from the strips of veal in a morel-studded cream sauce on a bed of fresh pasta.

Appendix A: Paris in Depth

IN THE BEGINNING Paris emerged at the crossroads of three major traffic arteries on the muddy island that today is known as the Ile de la Cité.

By around 2000 B.C., the island served as the fortified headquarters of the Parisii tribe, who referred to it as Lutetia. The pair of crude wooden bridges that connected the island to the left and right banks of the river were among the most strategically important in the region, and the settlement attracted the attention of the Roman Empire. In his *Commentaries,* Julius Caesar described the Roman conquest of Lutetia, recounting how its bridges were burned during the Gallic War of 52 B.C. and how the town on the island was pillaged, sacked, and transformed into a Roman-controlled stronghold.

Within a century, Lutetia had become a full-fledged Roman town, and some of the inhabitants abandoned the frequently flooded island in favor of higher ground on what is today the Left Bank. By A.D. 200, barbarian invasions increasingly threatened the stability of Roman Gaul, and the populace from the surrounding hills flocked to the fortified safety of the island.

Within about 50 years, a Christian community gained a tenuous foothold on the island. According to legend, St. Denis served as the city's first bishop (beginning around 250). Although the political power of the Roman Empire had begun to wane within the region by this time, the cultural and religious

Dateline

- **2000 B.C.** Paris (ancient Lutetia) thrives along a strategic crossing of the Seine, the fortified headquarters of the Parisii tribe.
- **52 B.C.** Julius Caesar conquers Paris during the Gallic Wars.
- **A.D. 150** Lutetia flourishes as a Roman colony, expanding to Paris's Left Bank.
- **200** Barbarian Gauls force Romans to retreat to the fortifications on Ile de la Cité.
- **300** "Paris" officially named as such. Roman power weakens in northern France.
- **350** Beginnings of Paris's Christianization.
- **400s** Frankish invasions of Paris, with social transformation from Roman to Gallo-Roman culture.
- **466** Birth of Clovis, founder of the Merovingian dynasty, first non-Roman ruler of Paris since the Parisii.
- **800** Coronation of Charlemagne, founder of the Carolingian dynasty and first Holy Roman Emperor, who rules from Aachen in modern Germany.
- **987** Hugh Capet, founder of France's foremost early medieval dynasty, rises to power. He and his heirs rule from Paris.

continues

- **1100** The Université de Paris attracts scholars from throughout Europe.
- **1200s** Paris's population and power grow, although frequently unsettled by plagues and feudal battles.
- **1422** England invades Paris during the Hundred Years' War.
- **1429** Joan of Arc tries unsuccessfully to regain Paris for the French. The Burgundians later capture and sell her to the English, who burn her at the stake in Rouen.
- **1500s** François I, considered first of the French Renaissance kings, embellishes Paris but chooses to maintain court in the Loire Valley.
- **1549** Henri II rules France from Paris. Construction of public and private residences begins, many of them in the Marais neighborhood.
- **1564** Construction of Catherine de Médicis's Tuileries Palace. Building facades in Paris move from half-timbered to more durable chiseled stonework.
- **1572** The Wars of Religion reach their climax with the massacre of Protestants on St. Bartholomew's Day.
- **1598** Henri IV, most eccentric and enlightened monarch of his era, endorses the Edict of Nantes, granting tolerance to Protestants, for which a crazed monk fatally stabs him 12 years later.
- **1615** Construction of the Luxembourg Palace by Henri IV's widow, Marie de Médicis.
- **1636** The Palais-Royal launched by Richelieu. Soon thereafter, two marshy islands

continues

attachment of the community to the Christian bishops of Rome grew even stronger.

During the 400s, with the great decline of the Roman armies, Germanic tribes from the east (the Salian Franks) were able to successfully invade the island, founding a Frankish dynasty here, and prompting a Frankish-Latin cultural fusion in the burgeoning town. The first of these Frankish kings, Clovis (466 to 511), founder of the Merovingian dynasty, embraced Christianity as his tribe's official religion, and spearheaded an explicit rejection of Roman cultural imperialism by encouraging the adoption of Parisii place names like "Paris," which came into common usage during this time.

The Merovingian dynasty was replaced by the Carolingians, whose heyday began with the coronation of Charlemagne in 800. The Carolingian Empire sprawled over western Germany and eastern France, but Paris was never its capital. The city remained a commercial and religious center, sacred to the memory of St. Geneviève, who reputedly protected Paris when it was repeatedly attacked by the Huns in the final days of the Roman Empire.

The Carolingian dynasty came to an end in 987, when the empire fragmented because of the growing regional, political, and linguistic divisions between what would eventually become modern France and modern Germany. Paris became the seat of a new dynasty, the Capetians, whose kings would rule France throughout the Middle Ages. Hugh Capet, the first of this line of kings, ruled as count of Paris and duke of France from 987 to 996.

THE MIDDLE AGES Around 1100, Paris began to emerge as a great city, with a university established on what is today known as the Left Bank that attracted scholars from all over Europe. Meanwhile, kings and bishops began building the towering Gothic cathedrals of France, one of the greatest of which became Paris's Notre-Dame, a soaring monument rising from the beating heart of the city. Paris's population increased greatly, as did the city's mercantile

Impressions

The French will only be united under the threat of danger. Nobody can simply bring together a country that has 265 kinds of cheese.

—Charles de Gaulle

activity. During the 1200s, a frenzy of building transformed the skyline with convents and churches (including the jewel-like Sainte-Chapelle, completed in 1249 after just 2 years of work). During the next century, the increasingly powerful French kings added dozens of monuments of their own.

As time passed, the fortunes of Paris became closely linked to the power struggles between the French monarchs in Paris and the various highly competitive feudal lords of the outlying provinces. Because of this tug-of-war, Paris was dogged by civil unrest, takeovers by one warring faction after another, and a dangerous alliance between the English and the powerful rulers of Burgundy during the Hundred Years' War. Around the same time, the city suffered a series of plagues, including the famous Black Death. To the everlasting humiliation of the French monarchs, the city was invaded by the English army in 1422. Joan of Arc (ca. 1412 to 1431) tried unsuccessfully to reconquer Paris in 1429, and 2 years later the English, supported by a tribunal of French ecclesiastics, burned her at the stake in Rouen (Normandy). Paris was reduced to poverty and economic stagnation, and its embittered and greatly reduced population turned to banditry and street crime to survive.

Despite Joan's ignominious end, the revolution she inspired continued in protracted form until Paris was finally taken from the English armies in 1436. During the several decades that followed, the English retreated to the channel port of Calais, abandoning their once-mighty territories in France. France, under the leadership of Louis XI, witnessed an accelerating rate of change that included the transformation of a feudal and medieval social system into the nascent beginnings of a modern state.

RENAISSANCE & REFORMATION The first of the Renaissance monarchs, François I, began an extensive enlargement of Paris's Louvre (which had begun its life as a warehouse storing the archives of Philippe Auguste before being transformed into a Gothic fortress by Louis IX in the 1100s) to make it suitable as a royal residence. Despite the building's embellishment, and the continued designation of Paris as the French capital, he spent much of his time at other châteaux amid the fertile hunting grounds of the Loire Valley. Many later monarchs would share his opinion that the narrow streets and teeming commercialism of Paris

in the Seine are interconnected and filled in to create the Ile St-Louis.

- **1643** Rise to power of Louis XIV, the "Sun King," the most powerful ruler since the Caesars. He moves his court to newly constructed Versailles.
- **1776** The American Declaration of Independence strikes a revolutionary chord in France.
- **1789** Outbreak of the French Revolution.
- **1793** Louis XVI and his Austrian-born queen, Marie Antoinette, are publicly guillotined.
- **1799** Napoléon Bonaparte crowns himself Master of France, and embellishes Paris further with neoclassical splendor.
- **1803** Napoléon abandons French overseas expansion and sells Louisiana to America.
- **1812** Defeat of Napoléon in the Russian winter campaign.
- **1814** Aided by a military coalition of France's enemies, especially England, the Bourbon monarchy, under Louis XVIII, is restored.
- **1821** Death of Napoléon Bonaparte.
- **1824** Death of Louis XVIII; Charles X accedes.
- **1830** Charles X is deposed; the more liberal Louis-Philippe is elected king. Paris prospers as it industrializes.
- **1848** Violent working-class revolution deposes Louis-Philippe, who is replaced by autocratic Napoléon III.
- **1853–70** Baron Haussmann forcibly redesigns Paris's landscapes.
- **1860s** The Impressionist style emerges.
- **1870** Franco-Prussian War ends in the defeat of France; Paris is threatened with bombardment by Prussian cannons placed on the outskirts of the city. A
continues

revolution in the aftermath of this defeat destroys the Tuileries Palace and overthrows the government. Rise of the Third Republic and its elected president, Marshal MacMahon.

- **1878–1937** A series of international expositions adds many enduring monuments to the Paris skyline, including the Eiffel Tower.
- **1914–18** World War I.
- **1940** German troops invade Paris. The official French government, under Pétain, evacuates to Vichy, while the French Resistance under de Gaulle maintains symbolic headquarters in London.
- **1944** U.S. troops liberate Paris. De Gaulle returns from London in triumph.
- **1948** Revolt in French colony of Madagascar costs 80,000 French lives. France's empire continues to collapse in Southeast Asia and equatorial Africa.
- **1954–62** War begins in Algeria and is eventually lost. Refugees flood Paris and the nation becomes bitterly divided over its North African policies.
- **1958** France's Fourth Republic collapses. General de Gaulle is called out of retirement to head the Fifth Republic.
- **1968** Paris's students and factory workers engage in a general revolt. The French government is overhauled in the aftermath.
- **1981** François Mitterrand is elected France's first socialist president since the 1940s. He is reelected in 1988.
- **1989** Paris celebrates the bicentennial of the French Revolution.
- **1992** Euro Disney opens on the outskirts of Paris.
- **1994** François Mitterrand and Queen Elizabeth II take

continues

were unhealthy and upsetting and would choose to reside elsewhere.

In 1549, however, Henri II triumphantly established his court in Paris and successfully ruled France from within the city's borders, solidifying Paris's role as the nation's undisputed capital. Following their ruler's lead, fashionable aristocrats quickly began to build private residences on the Right Bank, within a marshy low-lying area known as Le Marais (the swamp).

It was during this period that Paris as the world knows it today came into existence. The expansion of the Louvre continued, and Catherine de Médicis began building her Tuileries palace in 1564. From the shelter of dozens of elegant urban residences, the aristocracy of France imbued Paris with its sense of architectural and social style, as well as the mores and manners of the Renaissance. Stone quays were added to the banks of the Seine, defining their limits and preventing future flood damage, and royal decrees were passed establishing a series of building codes. To an increasing degree, Paris adopted the planned perspectives and visual grace worthy of the residence of a monarch.

During the late 1500s and 1600s, Protestants were brutally persecuted by the French kings. The bloodletting reached a high point under Henry III during the St. Bartholomew's Day massacre of 1572.

Henri III's tragic and eccentric successor, Henri IV, ended the Wars of Religion in 1598 by endorsing the Edict of Nantes, which offered religious freedom to the Protestants of France. Henry IV also laid out the lines for one of the memorable plazas of Paris: the Place des Vosges. As a reward for his leniency, Henry IV was stabbed in 1610 by a deranged monk who was infuriated by the king's support of religious tolerance.

After Henri IV's death, his second wife, Marie de Médicis (acting as regent), planned the Luxembourg Palace (1615), whose gardens have functioned ever since as a rendezvous for Parisians. In 1636, Cardinal Richelieu, who virtually ruled France during the minority of Louis XIII (the period in which the boy king was still too young to rule), built the sprawling premises of the Palais-Royal.

Under Louis XIII (1601 to 1643), two uninhabited islands in the Seine were joined together with landfill, connected to the Ile de la Cité and to the mainland with bridges, and renamed the

Ile St-Louis. Also laid out were the Jardin des Plantes, whose flowers and medicinal herbs were arranged according to their scientific and medical category.

THE SUN KING & THE FRENCH REVOLUTION

Louis XIV was crowned king of France when he was only 9 years old. Mazarin (1602 to 1661), Louis's Sicilian-born chief minister, dominated the government in Paris during the Sun King's minority.

This era marked the emergence of the French kings as absolute monarchs. As if to concretize their power, the face of Paris was embellished with many of the monuments that still serve as symbols of the city. These included new alterations to the Louvre, the construction of the Pont-Royal, the quai Peletier, the place des Victoires, the place Vendôme, the Champs Elysées, and the Hôtel des Invalides. Meanwhile, Louis XIV absented himself from the city center, constructing, at a staggering expense, the palace at Versailles, 13 miles southwest of Paris. Today, the palace stands as the single most visible monument to the most flamboyant and ostentatious era of French history.

Meanwhile, the rising power of England, particularly its navy, represented a serious threat to France, which was otherwise the most powerful nation in the world. One of the many theaters of the Anglo-French conflict was the American war for independence, during which the French kings supported American revolutionaries in their struggle against the Crown. Ironically, within 15 years the fervor that the French monarchs had nurtured crossed the Atlantic and destroyed them.

The spark that kindled the fire had come from Paris itself. For years before the outbreak of hostilities between the American revolutionaries and the British, the Enlightenment and its philosophers had fostered a new generation of thinkers who opposed absolutism, religious fanaticism, and superstition. Revolution had been brewing for almost 50 years, and after the French Revolution's explosive and world-shaking events, Europe was completely changed.

Though it began with moderate aims, the Revolution had soon turned the radical Jacobins into overlords, led by Robespierre.

On August 10, 1792, troops from Marseilles, aided by a Parisian mob, threw Louis XVI and his Austrian-born queen, Marie Antoinette, into prison. Several months later, after countless humiliations and a bogus trial, they were guillotined at the place de la Révolution (later renamed the place de la Concorde) on January 21, 1793. The Reign of Terror continued for another 18 months, with Parisians of all political persuasions fearing for their lives.

THE RISE OF NAPOLÉON

It required the militaristic fervor of Napoléon to unite France once again. Considered then and today a strategic genius with almost limitless ambition, he restored to Paris and to France a national pride that had been diminished during the Revolution's horror. After many impressive political and military victories, he entered Paris in 1799, at the age of 30, and crowned himself "First Consul and Master of France."

A brilliant politician, Napoléon moderated the atheistic rigidity of the early adherents of the Revolution by establishing peace with the Vatican. Soon

---

a ride together under the English Channel.

- **1995** Mitterrand dies; Chirac is elected. Paris is crippled by a general strike. Terrorists bomb the subway.
- **1997** Authorities enforce strict immigration laws, causing strife for African and Arab immigrants and dividing the country. French voters rebuff Chirac, electing Socialist Lionel Jospin as his new prime minister.
- **1998** Socialists triumph in local elections across France.
- **1999** The euro is introduced—at least in theory—as France prepares for the millennium

The New Parisians

The entire world continues to arrive on the city's doorstep. Some come to visit and leave money behind. (Parisians like that kind of visitor.) Friction, however, has accompanied another kind of visitor: the kind who comes to find a new life. A sizable number of Parisians have balked at the perceived drain on their resources brought about by immigration. Others are more welcoming, in the way they were to black artists like Josephine Baker in the 1920s or author James Baldwin in the 1950s, both of whom came to Paris to find an audience, acceptance, and honor.

Many Parisians view the immigrant population as a group that has diversified French society and has had an important impact on the country's culture. The impact is evident in the vast array of new restaurants opening in Paris, with cuisines as diverse as Vietnamese, Senegalese, and Martinique Creole. The immigrants have also changed Paris's nightlife; anything Cuban is in vogue, and you can find just as fine a salsa band in Paris today as you can in Havana.

African cuisine remains all the rage, and restaurants specializing in Senegalese fare are heavily patronized, even though you'll have to go to the less touristy arrondissements to find them.

Perhaps no one symbolizes the changing face of France more than Zinedine Zidane, who scored the goals that won France the World Cup in 1998. French kids voted this soccer hero, the son of Algerian immigrants, more popular than Michael Jordan, and French women find him sexier than Brad Pitt or Antonio Banderas. After France won the World Cup, anti-immigration fever cooled perceptibly, and the country experienced a feeling of generosity and goodwill unlike anything it had known since the liberation of World War II. No soccer fan, President Chirac pinned Legion of Honor ribbons on Zidane and his teammates. But to expect Zidane to lead France into its multicultural future is a bit much to ask, even for a World Cup hero. Anti-immigrant fever still remains a major social problem, not only in Paris, but throughout France.

thereafter, the legendary love of Parisians for their amusements began to revive; the boulevard des Italiens became the rendezvous point of the fashionable, while the boulevard du Temple, which housed many of the capital's vaudeville and cabaret theaters, became the favorite watering hole of the working class. In his self-appointed role as a French Caesar, Napoléon continued to alter the face of Paris with the construction of the neoclassical arcades of the rue de Rivoli (1801), the triumphal arches of the Arc du Carrousel and the place de l'Etoile, and the neoclassical grandeur of the Church of the Madeleine. On a less grandiose scale, the city's slaughterhouses and cemeteries were sanitized and moved away from the center of town, and new industries began to crowd workers from the countryside into the cramped slums of a newly industrialized Paris.

Napoléon's victories had made him the envy of Europe, but his infamous retreat from Moscow during the winter of 1812 reduced his formerly invincible army to tatters as 400,000 Frenchmen lost their lives. After a complicated series of events that included his return from exile, Napoléon was defeated at Waterloo by the combined armies of the English, the Dutch, and the Prussians. Exiled to the British-held island of St. Helena in the remote reaches of the South Atlantic, he died in 1821, probably the victim of an unknown poisoner. Some time later, his body was interred within a massive porphyry sarcophagus in Les Invalides, Louis XIV's monument to the ailing and fallen warriors of France.

In the power vacuum that followed the expulsion and death of Napoléon, Paris became the scene of intense lobbying over the future fate of France. The Bourbon monarchy was soon reestablished, but with reduced powers. In 1830, the regime was overthrown. Louis-Philippe, duke of Orléans and the son of a duke who had voted in 1793 for the death of Louis XVI, was elected king under a liberalized constitution. His calm, prosperous reign lasted for 18 years, during which England and France more or less collaborated on matters of foreign policy.

Paris reveled in its new prosperity, grateful for the money and glamor that had elevated it to one of the top cultural and commercial centers of the world. Moving into the modern age, Paris received its first railway line in 1837 (running from the center of town to a suburb near St-Germain), and shortly thereafter the first gas-fed streetlights. It was a time of wealth, grace, culture, and expansion for some French people, although the industrialization of certain working-class districts of Paris produced horrible poverty. The era also witnessed the development of French cuisine to the high form that still prevails, while a newly empowered bourgeoisie reveled in its attempts to create the good life.

THE SECOND EMPIRE   In 1848, a series of revolutions spread from one European capital to the next. The violent upheaval in Paris revealed the increasing dissatisfaction of many members of the working class. Fueled by a financial crash and scandals within the government, the revolt forced Louis-Philippe out of office. That year, on the dawn of the Second Republic, Emperor Napoléon's nephew, Napoléon III, was elected president by moderate and conservative elements. Appealing to the property-owning instinct of a nation that hadn't forgotten the violent revolution of less than a century before, he established a right-wing government and eventually assumed complete power as emperor in 1851.

In 1853, Napoléon III undertook the largest urban redevelopment project in the history of Europe. He commissioned Baron Haussmann (1809 to 1891) to redesign the city of Paris. Haussmann created a vast network of boulevards interconnected with a series of places (squares) that cut across old neighborhoods. While this reorganization process gave the capital the look for which it is famous today, screams of outrage sounded throughout the neighborhoods that construction split apart. By 1866, the entrepreneurs of an increasingly industrialized Paris began to regard the Second Empire as a hindrance to its development.

In 1870, during the Franco-Prussian War, the Prussians defeated Napoléon III at Sedan and held him prisoner along with 100,000 of his soldiers. Paris was threatened with bombardments from German cannons, by far the most advanced of their age, set up on the city's eastern periphery.

Although agitated diplomacy encouraged a Prussian withdrawal, international humiliation and perceived military incompetence sparked a revolt in Paris. One of the immediate effects of the revolt was the burning of one of Paris's historic landmarks, the Tuileries. Today, only the sprawling gardens of this once-great palace remain. The tumultuous events of 1870 ushered in the Third Republic and its elected president, Marshal MacMahon, in 1873.

Under the Third Republic, peace and prosperity gradually returned and Paris regained its glamor. A series of Universal Expositions held in 1878, 1889,

1900, and 1937 was the catalyst for the construction of such enduring Paris monuments as the Trocadéro, the Palais de Chaillot, the Eiffel Tower, both the Grand and the Petit Palais des Champs-Elysées, and the neo-Byzantine church of Sacré-Coeur in Montmartre. Simultaneously, the réseau métropolitain (the Métro, or Paris subway) was constructed, providing a model for subsequent subway systems throughout Europe.

WORLD WAR I International rivalries and conflicting alliances led to World War I, which, after decisive German victories for 2 years, degenerated into the mud-slogged horror of trench warfare. Industrialization during and after the war transformed Paris and its outlying boroughs into one vast interconnected whole, by now one of the largest metropolitan areas in Europe and undisputed ever since as the center of France's intellectual and commercial life.

Immediately after the Allied victory, grave economic problems, coupled with a populace demoralized from years of fighting, encouraged the rise of Socialism and the formation of a Communist Party, movements that were centered in Paris. Also from Paris, the French government, led by the almost obsessively vindictive Clemenceau, occupied Germany's Ruhr Valley, then and now one of the most profitable and industrialized regions of Germany, and demanded every centime of reparations it could wring from its humiliated neighbor, a policy that contributed to the outbreak of World War II.

THE 1920s—AMERICANS IN PARIS The so-called Lost Generation, led by American expatriates Gertrude Stein and her longtime companion, Alice B. Toklas, led the list of celebrities that would "occupy" Paris after the First World War, ushering in one of its most glamorous eras, the 1920s. The living was cheap in Paris. Two people could manage for about a year on a $1,000 (scholarship,) providing they could scrape up another $500 or so in extra earnings. Paris attracted the littérateur, the bon viveur, and the drifter, and such writers as Henry Miller, Ernest Hemingway, and F. Scott Fitzgerald all lived here. Even Cole Porter came, living first at the Ritz, then later at 13 rue de Monsieur (7e). James Joyce, half blind and led around by Ezra Pound, arrived in Paris and went to the salon of Natalie Barney, a leading exponent of Amazon Love. She became famous for pulling off such stunts as inviting Mata Hari to perform a Javanese dance, completely nude, at one of her parties, labeled "for women only, a lesbian orgy." Colette was barred, although she begged her husband to let her go. With the collapse of Wall Street, many Americans returned home, except some hard-core artists such as Henry Miller, who wandered around smoking Gauloise cigarettes and generating several pages a day of *Tropic of Cancer,* which would be banned in America for decades. "I have no money, no resources, no hopes. I am the happiest man alive," Miller said. Eventually, he met the narcissistic diary writer, Anaïs Nin, and they began to live a life that gave both of them material for their prose. But even such diehards as Miller and Nin eventually realized their Paris of the 1930s was collapsing as war clouds loomed. Gertrude and Alice remained in France, as other American expatriates fled to safer shores.

THE WINDS OF WAR Thanks to an array of alliances, when Germany invaded Poland in 1939, France had no choice but to declare war. Within only a few months, on June 14, 1940, Nazi armies marched arrogantly down the Champs-Elysées. Newsreel cameras recorded the French openly weeping at the sight. The city suffered little from the war materially, but for 4 years it survived in a kind of half-life, cold, dull, and drab, fostering scattered pockets of fighters who resisted sometimes passively, and sometimes with active sabotage.

During the Nazi occupation of Paris, the French government, under Marshal

The Euro

One thing that has Parisians more concerned than they are over the millennium is the abandonment of the long-cherished franc in favor of the euro. The new European currency has moved from being a theoretical unit of money to reality. France is among the first wave of the 11 countries participating in the United European monetary system. On January 1, 1999, the euro became a currency in its own right, but at this introductory stage there are no banknotes or coins in circulation. Banks and other financial institutions have begun trading in euros, but the French franc remains the only currency for cash transactions.

Pétain, moved to the quiet and isolated resort of Vichy and cooperated (or actually collaborated, depending on your point of view) with the Nazis. Tremendous internal dissension, the memory of which still simmers today, pitted many factions against one another. The Free French Resistance fled for its own safety to London, where it was headed by Charles de Gaulle (1880 to 1970), who became president of France's Fourth Republic after the war.

POSTWAR PARIS   Despite its gains in both prestige and prosperity after the end of World War II, Paris was rocked many times by internal dissent as domestic and international events embroiled the French government in dozens of controversies. In 1951, Paris forgot its cares by celebrating the 2,000th anniversary of the founding of the city, and poured much of its energy into rebuilding its image as a center of fashion, lifestyle, and glamor. Paris became internationally recognized as both a staple in the travel diets of many North Americans and as a beacon for art and artists.

The War of Algerian Independence (1954 to 1958), in which Algeria sought to go from being a French département (an integral extension of the French nation) to an independent country, was an anguishing event, more devastating than the earlier loss of France's colonies. The population of France (and Paris in particular) ballooned immediately as French citizens fled Algeria and returned home with few possessions and much bitterness. In 1958, as a result of the enormous loss of lives, money, and prestige in the Algerian affair, France's Fourth Republic collapsed, and de Gaulle was called out of retirement to form a new government: the Fifth Republic.

In 1962, the Algerian war of liberation ended with victory for Algeria, as France's colonies in central and equatorial Africa became independent one by one. The sun had finally set on the French Empire.

In 1968, a general revolt by students in Paris, whose activism mirrored that of their counterparts in the United States, turned the capital into an armed camp, causing a near-collapse of the national government and the very real possibility of total civil war. Though the crisis was averted, for several weeks it seemed as if French society was on the brink of anarchy.

CONTEMPORARY PARIS   In 1981, François Mitterrand (by a very close vote of 51%) was elected as the first Socialist president of France since World War II. Massive amounts of capital were taken out of the country, and although the drain slowed somewhat after initial jitters, many wealthy Parisians still prefer to invest their money elsewhere.

Paris today still struggles with social unrest in Corsica and from Muslim fundamentalists both in and outside of France. In the mid-1990s, racial tensions continued to nag at France, as the debate over immigration raged. Many right-wing political parties have created a racial backlash against North Africans and against "corruptive foreign influences" in general.

On his third try, Jacques Chirac, tenacious survivor of many terms as mayor of Paris, won the presidency of France in 1995 with 52% of the vote. Mitterrand turned over the reigns of government on May 17 and died shortly thereafter. France embarked on a new era, but Chirac's popularity soon faded in the wake of unrest caused by an 11.5% unemployment rate. In the spring of 1998, France ousted its Conservative parties in a powerful endorsement of Prime Minister Lionel Jospin and his Socialist-led government. The triumph of Jospin and his Communist and Green Party allies represented a fresh disavowal of the center-right Conservatives. This was a stunning blow to Chirac's Neo-Gaullists and the center-right parties led by Francois Leotard, and certainly to Jean-Marie Le Pen's often fanatical National Front.

By putting the Left back in charge, the French had voted against all the new ideas proposed to them for pushing their country into competitiveness and out of its economic doldrums. In spite of this resistance to change, Jospin is still ever so gently moving France toward the millennium. Without breaking the budget or losing public favor, the prime minister has picked his way through the minefields of French politics—militant unions, a public wedded to generous benefits, and widespread resistance to change. Jospin refers to his path as "leftist realism."

In 1999, France joined with other European Union countries in adopting the euro as its standard of currency, although the French franc will still be in circulation until 2002. The new currency will accelerate the creation of a single economy, comprising nearly 300 million Europeans, with a combined gross national product approaching, by some estimates, $9 trillion, larger than that of the United States.

Paris faced 1999 not only with a new currency but with a new century looming, as it rushed to brush off monuments and ready museums and hotels for a horde of visitors expected to number in the millions, perhaps toppling all previous figures.

2 City of the Arts

Paris is arguably the premier artistic capital of Europe. For centuries, the city has produced, and been home to, countless artists and artistic movements, and it is still a hotbed of creativity and an important center of the international art world.

Paris's true artistic flowering began around 1150, when the city's active trade, growing population, and struggles for political and ecclesiastic power added dozens of new buildings to the city's skyline, including Paris's everlasting architectural symbol, the Cathedral of Notre-Dame, and, to the north of the city, the Cathedral of St-Denis. In these and other Gothic buildings, the medieval sculptures on the facades and inside the buildings depended less upon the structures they adorned and became more fully developed as freer artistic expressions of their anonymous creators. Secondary crafts, such as the manufacture and installation of stained glass (as represented by the windows in Paris's Sainte-Chapelle), became art forms in their own right, and French glass of this age attained an intensity of blues and reds that has never been duplicated.

Gothic painters became adept at the miniaturization of religious and secular scenes that art lovers could richly appreciate close at hand. The most famous

Paris Under Siege

Headlines around the world testify to a rip tearing through Paris's cultural fabric. Gitanes. Gauloise. The mention of the names of these cigarettes—which in the minds of many are as intrinsic to the Parisian identity as the Louvre or the Seine—conjures images of cluttered cafes filled with passionate talk and a thick blue-gray haze.

So who would have ever imagined walking into a cafe, restaurant, or bistro and seeing a separate section for nonsmokers? Who would have believed that lawsuits would be brought against French tobacco companies? And, sacré bleu, the stiff, strong tobacco of Gauloise and Gitanes, is losing ground to American brands, with their weaker tobaccos and filters. Certainly there must be an internal conspiracy afoot.

Since 1991, France has had a law against smoking in public places. It made headlines back then. But like a story in the tabloid press, no one ever really took it seriously—after all, this was France. Yet the law really was a law, and it is beginning to be more strictly enforced throughout the country, swaying French public opinion along with it. Even great photos from the past of such untouchable icons as Jean Cocteau, Jean-Paul Sartre, or Coco Chanel pursing their lips for the lens with their ever-present Gauloise glued in place are not safe from the legislation. Recently, a stamp was printed by the French post office commemorating André Malraux, French writer and adventurer and all-around provocateur. However, because of the 1991 antismoking law, it is also now illegal to have "any propaganda or publicity, direct or indirect, in favor of tobacco." So, the actual photo used for the stamp was doctored to delete Malraux's cigarette.

Is nothing sacred anymore?

---

of these, **Pol de Limbourg's** *Les très riches heures du duc de Berri* and **Fouquet's** *Heures d'Etienne Chevalier,* showed occasional scenes of medieval Paris in a charmingly idealized celebration of the changing of the seasons. Around 1360, Paris provided the setting for the painting of what is usually credited by art historians as the first (known) portrait, of Jean le Bon (artist unknown), and the weaving of one of the most famous tapestries in history, the *Angers Apocalypse.*

A FRENCH RENAISSANCE The evolution of French art slowed during much of the 1400s. By the 1500s, however, Paris enjoyed a great artistic rebirth, thanks to a military campaign into Italy and a subsequent fascination with all things Italian. Two of that era's main sculptors, who embellished the facades and fountains of Paris, were **Jean Goujon** (1510 to 1585), whose inspirations melded ancient Greek forms and Renaissance themes, and **Germain Pilon** (1535 to 1590), whose carvings of the French kings at St-Denis kept to mostly religious, rather than neoclassical, themes. By the late 1500s, under the auspices of the Renaissance king François I, the royal château at Fontainebleau, 37 miles south of Paris, became a caldron of the arts, eventually producing a style of painting known later as the school of Fontainebleau.

The arts in and around Paris during the 1600s so permeated French culture that the century has been known ever since as *Le Grand Siècle* (the grand century). France's monarchy by now was entrenched and its society sufficiently stable and centralized that the arts were able to flourish, and Paris was embellished with hundreds of aristocratic mansions within Le Marais district. Important painters included **Philippe de Champaigne** (1602 to 1674), famous for his severe portraits; **Charles le Brun** (1619 to 1690), who painted the Galerie d'Apollon at the Louvre; and his rival **Pierre Mignard** (1610 to 1695), painter of the interior of the cupola in the church of Val-de-Grâce. Simultaneously, the art of tapestry weaving was given a tremendous boost thanks to the establishment and royal patronage of the Manufacture Royale des Gobelins.

THE SUN KING RISES During the early 1700s, the taste for the grandiose in France was profoundly influenced by the personality of the Sun King, Louis XIV. His construction and furnishing of Versailles called for mind-boggling quantities of art and decoration, affording lavish commissions for sculptors and craftsmen of every kind. In furnishing the thousands of salons and apartments within the palace, the techniques of fine cabinetry reached their apogee under such cabinetmakers as **André-Charles Boulle** (1642 to 1732). Boulle's writing tables, secretaries, and *bombé*-fronted chests, either ebonized or inlaid with tortoiseshell, mother-of-pearl, and gilded bronze ornaments (ormolu), are today among the finest pieces of cabinetry in European history, and command appropriately stratospheric prices. Boulle was supplanted by Crescent and Oeben, under Louis XV, who were themselves replaced by such neoclassically inspired masters as Weisweiler and Kiesner during the reign of Louis XVI.

Painters from the era of Louis XIV and XV include **Largilière** and **Rigaud** and the skilled portraitists **La Tour** (1704 to 1766) and **Perronneau** (1715 to 1788), whose coloring techniques have been likened to those used by the Impressionists more than a century later. Also noteworthy, both as an artist and as a sociological phenomenon, was the female artist **Elisabeth Vigée-Lebrun** (1755 to 1842), whose lavish but natural style won her a position as Marie Antoinette's preferred painter. Especially famous paintings from this era are those of **Fragonard** (1732 to 1806) and **Boucher** (1703 to 1770), whose canvases captured the sweetness and whimsy of aristocratic life during the Ancien Régime.

In sculpture, painting, and furniture, the 18th century in Paris began with an allegiance to the baroque curve and a robustly sensual kind of voluptuousness, and ended with a return to the straight line and the more rigid motifs of the classical age. Especially indicative of this return to sobriety was **Houdon** (1741 to 1828), who is remembered for his extraordinarily lifelike portrait busts such as that of Voltaire.

A DEFT POLITICAL ART The French Revolution, whose first violence had erupted in 1789, brought a new politicization to the arts. Noteworthy was **David** (1748 to 1825), whose painting *Oath of the Horatii* has been credited as a real revolutionary catalyst. To reward his zeal, David was appointed Director of the Arts of the Revolution, surely incentive for such richly idealized paintings as *The Murder of Marat*. Always in control of his own political destiny, David was later appointed court painter to Napoléon.

Meanwhile, as France grew wealthy from the fruits of the Industrial Revolution and the expansion of its Colonial Empire, Paris blossomed with the paintings of **Ingres** (1780 to 1867) and his bitter rival, **Delacroix** (1798 to 1863). Primary among their academic disputes were allegiances to the beauty of line (Ingres) versus the subtleties of color (Delacroix).

THE BIRTH OF IMPRESSIONISM The subtle colorings of the landscape artist **Corot** (1796 to 1875) were probably the first hints of what would later become known as Impressionism. The movement is commonly thought to have been born at the 1863 Salon des Refusés, where works of painters such as Manet, who had been rejected by the mainstream art establishment, were shown. One of the most memorable paintings on display was Manet's then-scandalous and still-riveting *Déjeuner sur l'herbe*. Soon after, such artists as Sisley, Pissarro, Degas, Renoir, and the immortal Monet painted in the open air, often evoking the everyday life and cityscapes of Paris and its surroundings.

Later, the best scenes ever painted of Paris would be credited to **Utrillo** (1883 to 1955) and, to a lesser degree, **Marquet** (1875 to 1947). Utrillo in particular concentrated on the unpretentious, often working-class neighborhoods (especially Montmartre) rather than the city's more famous monumental zones. Marquet, whose work helped define the fauve school of painting, often executed his stylized and brightly colored works from the balcony of his Paris apartment.

Though many of them never made a career out of painting Paris itself, other 20th-century painters who made Paris their home included Vlaminck, Derain, Vuillard, Bonnard, Braque, Picasso, Dufy, and Matisse. Many of these artists used their canvasses as rebellions against the restrictions of "official" art as defined at the time by the aesthetic hierarchies of the Academy. Several movements that emerged from this artistic rebellion have, since their origins, been classified among the most potent and evocative schools of art in the world. Included among them were **fauvism,** a technique that employed vivid and arbitrary use of color in a manner that paved the way for the nonfigurative movements that were to follow. **Cubism,** the favorite style of early Picasso and Braque, developed as a means of breaking the subject matter into a stylized version of its basic geometric forms. **Dadaism,** an elaboration of the avant-garde movements that developed out of Cubism and Fauvism, managed to permeate painting with some of the absurdist moral and political philosophies then pervasive in the arts scene of Paris. Most stylized of all was **surrealism,** a movement that carried realism to boundaries never before explored, twisting everyday objects into bizarre, sometimes terrifying permutations that only a slightly mad genius, such as Salvador Dalí, could have conceived of.

Among sculptors, Paris's greatest contribution to the art of the late 19th century was **Auguste Rodin** (1840 to 1917), whose figures added new dimensions to the human form. Especially famous was the raw power emanating from his rough-surfaced sculptures *The Thinker* and *The Kiss*.

FRENCH ART TODAY   French artists today struggle in the shadow of the great modernists who transformed the artistic perceptions of the world during the early decades of the 20th century. Although the oeuvre of these contemporary artists will doubtless not surpass the fame, notoriety, and market value of, say, Matisse, Braque, or Monet, they are enjoying popularity and even energetic biddings whenever their works are presented at expositions. **Oliver DeBré** (born in Paris in 1920), whose early studies in architecture and literature influenced his role as the most important abstract artist in France today, has garnered a significant reputation through a retrospective of his work at the Jeu de Paume. And there are many others. **Gérard Garouste** (born in Paris in 1926), who does much of his painting in a studio in the Normandy countryside, is one of Europe's contemporary masters of the postmodern still life.

Ernest Pignon-Ernest (born in Nice in 1942), on the other hand, has succeeded in taking contemporary art directly to the streets. Inspired by the canvasses of 17th-century Italian master Caravaggio, Pignon-Ernest executes "neo-Renaissance" serigraphs, produced cheaply and abundantly, which he then plasters over hundreds of buildings as an artistic statement. Although based in Paris throughout most of the year, his "decoration" of the walls of Naples was widely publicized in the art world and brought a new appreciation of Caravaggio even to Italy.

Detractors of **Pierre Soulages** (born in 1919) compare him to a Gallic version of Mark Rothko; his fans praise his all-black canvasses as "sumptuous" and claim that he can imbue shades of the color black with more meaning and subtlety than most artists can evoke with a full palette. He is the most controversial of France's contemporary artists, and possibly the most depressing.

Whatever the personal stylistic idiosyncrasies of this new generation of Paris artists, all of them are part of an artistic tradition that has endured in the City of Light for centuries. Art is, and has been, a vital and integral part of Parisian society since its humble beginnings, and Paris's current artistic sophistication is the product of centuries of development. The city's current art scene pays tribute to the legacy of all who came before, and is as diverse and volatile as ever. Whatever your artistic tastes, Paris offers something to suit them.

3 Architecture Through the Ages

Not only is Paris a world art capital, the city itself is art, an organic collection of beautifully designed and constructed buildings that represent diverse architectural styles and periods. Walking through Paris can be like excavating layers of sediment at an archaeological dig: Each edifice bears the characteristic signatures of the period in which it was constructed. Paris's buildings are not only ornate and elegant, they tell the tale of the city's long and impressive architectural history.

Despite its role as an outpost of ancient Rome, the development of Paris into a bustling community of traders, merchants, and clerics didn't really come to pass until the 1100s. Historians cite the abandonment of Romanesque building techniques within the Ile de France at around 1150. Because of that, the city has surprisingly few Romanesque buildings, good examples of which are more common in such French provinces as Burgundy. Identified by their thick walls, barrel vaults, and groined vaults, small windows, and minimal carvings, the city's most important Romanesque buildings include the churches of St-Germain-des-Prés, St-Pierre-de-Montmartre, St-Martin des Champs, and, in the suburbs, the Church of Morienval.

THE GENIUS OF THE GOTHIC AGE   The genius of Paris's architects, however, arrived during the Gothic age, which was signaled early in the 1200s with the construction of the cathedrals of St-Denis, in Paris's eastern suburbs; Chartres, 60 miles to the city's southwest; and Notre-Dame of Paris, situated on the Ile de la Cité. Before the mid–15th century, Gothic architecture would transform the skyline of Paris as dozens of new churches, chapels, and secular buildings outdid their neighbors in lavishness, beauty, and intricacy of design.

Although Gothic architecture was firmly rooted in the principles of the Romanesque, it differs from its predecessor in its penchant for complicated patterns of vaulting and columns, and walls that became increasingly thinner as the weight of ceilings and roofs were transferred onto newly developed systems of abutment piers (flying buttresses). Because of the thinner walls, larger openings became architecturally feasible. Churches became filled with light filtered through stained glass, and enormous rose windows awed their observers with the delicate tracery of their stonework.

A CLASSICAL RESURGENCE   During the Renaissance, beginning around 1500, influences from Italy rendered the Gothic style obsolete. In its place arose the yearning for a return to the aesthetics of ancient Greece and Rome. Massive arcades, often decorated with bas-relief sculpture of symbols of triumph, as well as Corinthian, Doric, and Ionic pediments, added grandeur to the Paris of the Renaissance kings. All links of royal residences to feudal fortresses vanished as the aristocrats of Paris competed with one another to construct elegant town houses and villas filled with sunlight, tapestries, paintings, music, and fine furniture.

During the early 17th century, many of Paris's distinctive Italianate baroque domes were created. Louis XIV employed such Italian-inspired architects as Le Vau, Perrault, both Mansarts, and Bruand for their buildings and Le Nôtre for the rigidly intelligent layouts of his gardens at Versailles. Paris and the surrounding region flourished with the construction of the lavishly expensive château of Vaux-le-Vicomte and the even more elaborate royal residence of Versailles. Meanwhile, wealthy entrepreneurs encouraged the development of new expressions of artistic and architectural beauty from the many salons sprouting up throughout the city.

By the early 19th century, a newly militaristic Paris, flushed with the titanic changes of the Revolution and the subsequent victories of Napoléon, returned to a restrained and dignified form of classicism. Modeling their urban landscape on an idealized interpretation of imperial Rome, buildings such as the Church of the Madeleine evoked the militaristic rigidity and grandeur of the classical age.

ART NOUVEAU & ART DECO By 1850, enjoying a cosmopolitan kind of prosperity, Paris grew bored with things Greek and Roman. After a brief flirtation with Egyptology (inspired by Napoléon's campaign in the Egyptian desert and the unraveling of the secrets of the Rosetta stone), a new school of eclecticism added controversial but often elegant touches to the Paris landscape. Among them were the voluptuous lines of the art nouveau movement, whose aesthetic was inspired by the surging curves of the botanical world. Stone, cast iron, glass, and wood were carved or molded into forms resembling orchids, vines, laurel branches, and tree trunks, each richly lyrical and based on new building techniques made possible by the Industrial Age. Youthful and creative architects began to specialize in the use of iron as the structural support of bridges, viaducts, and buildings, such as the National Library (1860). These techniques opened the way for Gustave Eiffel to design and erect the most slandered building of its day, the Eiffel Tower, for the Paris Exposition of 1889.

During the 1920s and 1930s, art deco, a streamlined, modernist style incorporating the newly developed materials and decorative techniques of the machine age, captured sophisticated sensibilities around the world. After Braque defined Cubism, the angular simplicity of the new artistic movement influenced architectural styles as well. Le Corbusier, a Swiss-born architect who settled in Paris in 1917, eventually developed his jutting, gently curved planes of concrete, opening the doors for a new, but often less talented, school of modern French architects.

ARCHITECTURE TODAY Critics haven't been kind to the rapidly rusting, exposed structural elements of Paris's notorious Centre Pompidou. In the 1980s, an obsolete railroad station beside the Seine was transformed into the truly exciting Musée d'Orsay and an expanse of dreary 19th-century slaughterhouses was refigured into a tourist-worthy site by the creation of a hypermodern science museum. In the 1990s, the Opéra Bastille brought new life to the decaying eastern edge of the Marais but, predictably, sparked a controversy over its iconoclastic design. And screams of outrage could be heard throughout France when I. M. Pei's glass pyramid was built as the postmodern centerpiece of one of the Louvre's most formal 17th-century courtyards.

Mitterrand inaugurated the Grande Arche de La Défense for France's bicentennial, on July 14, 1989. This 35-story office complex shaped like a hollow cube is the endpoint of the voie triomphale (triumphal way) begun in 1664 at the Tuileries Gardens. Its roof covers 2½ acres, and it's estimated that Notre-Dame could fit into its hollow core. One of the latest additions to the architectural scene (opened in 1995) is the Cité de la Musique, designed by architect Christian de Portzamparc as a complex of interconnected post-Cubist shapes.

Although the buildings of the Mitterrand presidency were "designed for eternity," critics are already pointing out flaws in the late president's "chance for immortality," his $5.8 billion architectural spending spree. Many of the Mitterrand buildings are suffering defects and mishaps, including stone slabs falling from the Opera at Bastille, fragments of the Grand Arche flaking into a net, and rain gushing into the orchestra pit at the City of Music. Paris's futuristic National Library was scheduled to open when the builders realized that the light bathing the building was going to destroy the fragile paper of the rare books it was to house. After much tinkering with tinted glass, the flaws were corrected. The pyramid at the Louvre remains trouble-free, so far.

The great French architect Paul Chametov said, "At the end of a decade (the 1980s) that was tipsy from competitions, drunk from media hype, and driven mad by the expectations of a real-estate boom, we inherit an architecture that is only new on the day it is inaugurated." Of course, the celebrated Pompidou Center, built in honor of former President George Pompidou, is in so much trouble that it has been shut and will host only jackhammers, leaky pipes, and time-whistles until the cusp of the millennium.

President Jacques Chirac can hardly match the cultural monuments of his predecessor, falling slabs of marble or not. In 1996, he announced his building plans: the creation of a major new museum for African, Oceanic, and pre-Columbian art. Assigned to the Passy Wing of the Palais de Chaillot in the Trocadero section of Paris, it will open, if plans go well, in late 2001, just months before the end of Chirac's 7-year term.

Appendix B: Useful Terms & Phrases

1 Glossary of French-Language Terms

A well-known character is the American or lapsed Canadian who returns from a trip to Paris and denounces the ever-so-rude French. "I asked for directions, and he glowered at me, muttered inaudibly, and turned his back." "She threw her baguette at me!" While Parisians often seem to carry upon their backs a burden of misery that they famously dole out to immigrants and foreigners, it is often amazing how a word or two of halting French will change their dispositions, and if not bring out the sun, at least put an end to the Gallic thunder and rain. At the very least, try to learn a few numbers, basic greetings, and—above all—the life-raft, *"Parlez-vous anglais?"* As it turns out, many Parisians do speak a passable English, and will use it liberally, if you demonstrate the basic courtesy of greeting them in their language. Go out, try our glossary on, and don't be bashful. *Bonne chance!*

BASICS

English	French	Pronunciation
Yes/No	**Oui/Non**	wee/nohn
Okay	**D'accord**	dah-*core*
Please	**S'il vous plaît**	seel voo *play*
Thank you	**Merci**	mair-*see*
You're welcome	**de rien**	duh ree-*ehn*
Hello (during daylight hours)	**Bonjour**	bohn-*jhoor*
Good evening	**Bonsoir**	bohn-*swahr*
Goodbye	**Au revoir**	o ruh-*vwahr*
What's your name?	**Comment vous appellez-vous?**	ko-mahn-voo-za-pell-ay-*voo?*
My name is . . .	**Je m'appelle . . .**	jhuh ma-*pell* . . .
Happy to meet you	**Enchanté(e)**	ohn-shahn-*tay*
Miss	**Mademoiselle**	mad mwa-*zel*
Mr.	**Monsieur**	muh-*syuh*
Mrs.	**Madame**	ma-*dam*
How are you?	**Comment allez-vous?**	kuh-mahn-tahl-ay-*voo?*
Fine, thank-you, and you?	**Très bien, merci, et vous?**	tray bee-ehn, mare-ci, ay *voo?*
Very well, thank-you	**Très bien, merci**	tray bee-ehn, mair-*see*

So-so	**Comme ci, comme ça**	kum-*see*, kum-*sah*
I'm sorry/excuse me	**pardon**	pahr-*dohn*
I'm so very sorry	**désolé(e)**	day-zoh-*lay*
That's all right	**il n'y a pas de quoi**	eel nee ah pah duh kwah

GETTING AROUND/STREET SMARTS

English	French	Pronunciation
Do you speak English?	**Parlez-vous anglais?**	par-lay-voo-ahn-*glay*?
I don't speak French	**Je ne parle pas francais**	jhuh ne parl pah frahn-*say*
I don't understand	**Je ne comprends pas**	jhuh ne kohm-*prahn* pas
Could you speak more loudly/more slowly?	**Pouvez-vous parler un peu plus fort/ plus lentement?**	Poo-*vay* voo par-lay un puh ploo for/ ploo lan-te-*ment*?
Could you repeat that?	**Répetez, s'il vous plait**	ray-pay-*tay*, seel voo *play*
What is it?	**Qu'est-ce que c'est?**	kess-kuh-*say*?
What time is it?	**Qu'elle heure est-il?**	kel uhr eh-*teel*?
What?	**Quoi?**	kwah?
How? *or* What did you say?	**Comment?**	ko-*mahn*?
When?	**Quand?**	kahn?
Where is . . . ?	**Où est . . . ?**	ooh-eh . . . ?
Who?	**Qui?**	kee?
Why?	**Pourquoi?**	poor-*kwah*?
Here/there	**ici/là**	ee-*see*/lah
Left/right	**à gauche/à droite**	a goash/a drwaht
Straight ahead	**tout droit**	too-drwah
I'm American/ Canadian/British	**Je suis américain(e)/ canadien(e)/anglais(e)**	jhe sweez a-may-ree-*kehn*/ can-ah-dee-*en*/ahn-glay (*glaise*)
Fill the tank (of a car), please	**Le plein, s'il vous plaît**	luh plan, seel-voo-*play*
I'm going to . . .	**Je vais à . . .**	jhe vay ah . . .
I want to get off at . . .	**Je voudrais descendre à . . .**	jhe voo-*dray* day-son drah-ah
I'm sick	**Je suis malade**	jhuh swee mal-*ahd*
airport	**l'aéroport**	lair-o-*por*
bank	**la banque**	lah bahnk
bridge	**pont**	pohn
bus station	**la gare routière**	lah gar roo-tee-*air*
bus stop	**l'arrêt de bus**	lah-*ray* duh boohss
by means of a bicycle	**en vélo/par bicyclette**	uh *vay*-low, par bee-see-*clet*
by means of a car	**en voiture**	ahn vwa-*toor*
cashier	**la caisse**	lah *kess*
cathedral	**cathédral**	ka-tay-*dral*
church	**église**	ay-*gleez*
dead end	**une impasse**	ewn am-*pass*
driver's license	**permis de conduire**	per-mee duh con-*dweer*
elevator	**l'ascenseur**	lah sahn *seuhr*
entrance (to a building or a city)	**une porte**	ewn port
exit (from a building or a freeway)	**une sortie**	ewn sor-*tee*
fortified castle or palace	**château**	sha-*tow*
garden	**jardin**	jhar-*dehn*

gasoline	**du pétrol/de l'essence**	duh pay-*troll* de lay-*sahns*
ground floor	**rez-de-chausée**	ray-de-show-*say*
highway to . . .	**la route pour**	la root por
hospital	**l'hôpital**	low-pee-*tahl*
insurance	**les assurances**	lez ah-sur-*ahns*
luggage storage	**consigne**	kohn-*seen*-yuh
museum	**le musée**	luh mew-*zay*
no entry	**sens interdit**	sehns ahn-ter-*dee*
no smoking	**défense de fumer**	day-*fahns* de fu-may
on foot	**à pied**	ah pee-*ay*
one-day pass	**ticket journalier**	tee-kay jhoor-nall-ee-*ay*
one-way ticket	**aller simple**	ah-*lay sam*-pluh
police	**la police**	lah po-*lees*
rented car	**voiture de location**	vwa-*toor* de low-ka-see-on
round-trip ticket	**aller-retour**	ah-*lay* re-*toor*
second floor	**premier étage**	prem-ee-*ehr* ay-*taj*
slow down	**ralentir**	rah-lahn-*teer*
store	**le magazin**	luh ma-ga-*zehn*
street	**rue**	roo
suburb	**banlieu, environs**	bahn-*liew,* en-veer-*ohns*
subway	**le métro**	le may-tro
telephone	**le téléphone**	luh tay-lay-*phone*
ticket	**un billet**	uh *bee*-yay
ticket office	**vente de billets**	vahnt duh bee-*yay*
toilets	**les toilettes/les WC**	lay twa-*lets*/les vay-*say*
tower	**tour**	toor

NECESSITIES

English	French	Pronunciation
I'd like . . .	**je voudrais . . .**	jhe voo-*dray* . . .
a room	**une chambre**	ewn *shahm*-bruh
the key	**la clé (la clef)**	la clay
I'd like to buy . . .	**Je voudrais acheter . . .**	jhe voo-dray ahsh-*tay* . . .
aspirin	**des aspirines/**	deyz ahs-peer-*eens*/
	des aspros	deyz ahs-*prohs*
cigarettes	**des cigarettes**	day see-ga-*ret*
condoms	**des préservatifs**	day pray-ser-va-*teefs*
dictionary	**un dictionnaire**	uh deek-see-oh-*nare*
dress	**une robe**	ewn robe
envelopes	**des envelopes**	days ahn-veh-*lope*
gift (for someone)	**un cadeau**	uh kah-*doe*
handbag	**un sac**	uh sahk
hat	**un chapeau**	uh shah-*poh*
magazine	**une revue**	ewn reh-*vu*
map of the city	**un plan de ville**	unh plahn de *veel*
matches	**des allumettes**	dayz a-loo-*met*
necktie	**une cravate**	uh cra-*vaht*
newspaper	**un journal**	uh zhoor-*nahl*
phone card	**une carte téléphonique**	uh cart tay-lay-fone-*eek*
postcard	**une carte postale**	ewn carte pos-*tahl*
road map	**une carte routière**	ewn cart roo-tee-*air*
shirt	**une chemise**	ewn che-*meez*
shoes	**des chaussures**	day show-*suhr*
skirt	**une jupe**	ewn jhoop

soap	**du savon**	dew sah-*vohn*
socks	**des chaussettes**	day show-*set*
stamp	**un timbre**	uh *tam*-bruh
trousers	**un pantalon**	uh pan-tah-*lohn*
writing paper	**du papier à lettres**	dew pap-pee-*ay* a *let*-ruh
How much does it cost?	**C'est combien?/ Ça coûte combien?**	say comb-bee-*ehn?/ sah coot comb-bee-*ehn?*
That's expensive	**C'est cher/chère**	say share
That's inexpensive	**C'est raisonnable/ C'est bon marché**	say ray-son-*ahb*-bluh/ ssay bohn mar-*shay*
Do you take credit cards?	**Est-ce que vous acceptez les cartes de credit?**	es-kuh voo zaksep-*tay* lay kart duh creh-*dee?*

IN YOUR HOTEL

English	French	Pronunciation
Are taxes included?	**Est-ce que les taxes sont comprises?**	ess-keh lay taks son com-*preez?*
balcony	**un balcon**	uh bahl-cohn
bathtub	**une baignoire**	ewn bayn-*nwar*
bedroom	**une chambre**	oon *shahm*-bruh
for two occupants	**pour deux personnes**	poor duh pair-*sunn*
hot and cold water	**l'eau chaude et froide**	low showed ay fwad
Is breakfast included?	**Petit déjeuner inclus?**	peh-*tee* day-jheun-ay ehn-*klu?*
room	**une chambre**	ewn *shawm*-bruh
shower	**une douche**	ewn dooch
sink	**un lavabo**	uh la-va-*bow*
suite	**une suite**	ewn sweet
We're staying for . . . days with	**On reste pour . . . jours avec**	ohn rest poor . . . jhoor ah-*vek*
with air-conditioning	**avec climatisation**	ah-*vek* clee-mah-tee-zah-sion
without	**sans**	sahn
youth hostel	**une auberge de jeunesse**	oon oh-bayrge-duh-jhe-ness

IN THE RESTAURANT

English	French	Pronunciation
I would like . . .	**Je voudrais**	jhe voo-*dray*
to eat	**manger**	mahn-*jhay*
to order	**commander**	ko-mahn-*day*
Please give me . . .	**Donnez-moi, s'il vous plaît . . .**	doe-nay-*mwah,* seel voo play . . .
a bottle of . . .	**une bouteille de . . .**	ewn boo-*tay* duh . .
a cup of . . .	**une tasse de . . .**	ewn tass duh . . .
a glass of . . .	**un verre de . . .**	uh vair duh . .
a plate of . . .	**une assiette de . . .**	ewn ass-ee-*et* duh . . .
an ashtray	**un cendrier**	uh sahn-dree-*ay*
bread	**du pain**	dew pan
breakfast	**le petit-déjeuner**	luh puh-*tee* day-zhuh-*nay*
butter	**du beurre**	dew burr
check/bill	**l'addition/ la note**	la-dee-see-*ohn*/la noat
Cheers!	**à votre santé**	ah vo-truh sahn-*tay*
Can I buy you a drink?	**Puis-je vous payer un verre?**	*pwee*-jhe voo pay-ay uh *vaihr?*

cocktail	un apéritif	uh ah-pay-ree-*teef*
coffee	du café	dew ka-*fay*
coffee—black	un café noir	uh ka-*fay* nwahr
coffee—with cream	un café-crème	uh ka-*fay* krem
coffee—with milk	un café au lait	uh ka-*fay* o lay
coffee—decaf	un café décaféiné	uh ka-*fay* day-kah-fay-*nay*
coffee—espresso	un café express	uh ka-*fay* ek-*sprehss*
dinner	le dîner	luh dee-*nay*
fixed-price menu	un menu	uh may-*new*
fork	une fourchette	ewn four-*shet*
Is the tip/ service included?	Est-ce que le service est compris?	ess-ke luh ser-vees eh com-*pree?*
knife	un couteau	uh koo-*toe*
napkin	une serviette	ewn sair-vee-*et*
pepper	du poivre	dew *pwah*-vruh
platter of the day	un plat du jour	uh plah dew jhoor
salt	du sel	dew sell
soup	une soupe/un potage	ewn soop/uh poh-*tahj*
spoon	une cuillère	ewn kwee-*air*
sugar	du sucre	dew *sook*-ruh
tea	un thé	uh tay
tea—with lemon	un thé au citron	uh tay o see-*tron*
tea—herbal	une tisane	ewn tee-*zahn*
Waiter!/Waitress!	Monsieur!/Mademoiselle!	mun-*syuh*/mad-mwa-*zel*
wine list	une carte des vins	ewn cart day *van*
appetizer	une entrée	ewn en-*tray*
main course	un plat principal	uh plah pran-see-*pahl*
tip included	service compris	sehr-*vees* cohm-*preez*
wide-range sample of the chef's best efforts	menu dégustation	may-*new* day-gus-ta-see-*on*
drinks not included	boissons non comprises	bwa-*sons* no com-*preez*
cheese tray	plâteau de fromage	plah-*tow* duh fro-*mahj*

SHOPPING

English	French	Pronunciation
antiques store	un magasin d'antiquités	uh maga-*zan* d'on-tee kee-*tay*
bakery	une boulangerie	ewn boo-lon-zhur-*ree*
bank	une banque	ewn bonk
bookstore	une librairie	ewn lee-brehr-*ree*
butcher	une boucherie	ewn boo-shehr-*ree*
cheese shop	une fromagerie	ewn fro-mazh-*ree*
dairy shop	une crémerie	ewn krem-*ree*
delicatessen	une charcuterie	ewn shar-koot-*ree*
department store	un grand magasin	uh grah maga-*zan*
drugstore	une pharmacie	ewn far-mah-*see*
fishmonger shop	une poissonerie	ewn pwas-son-*ree*
gift shop	un magasin de cadeaux	uh maga-*zan* duh ka-*doh*
greengrocer	un marchand de légumes	uh mar-*shon* duh lay-*goom*
hairdresser	un coiffeur	uh kwa-*fuhr*
market	un marché	uh mar-*shay*
pastry shop	une pâtisserie	ewn pa-tee-*sree*
supermarket	un supermarché	uh soo-pehr-mar-*shay*
tobacconist	un tabac	uh ta-*bah*
travel agency	une agence de voyages	ewn azh-ahns duh vwa *yazh*

COLORS, SHAPES, SIZES, ATTRIBUTES

English	French	Pronunciation
black	**noir**	nwahr
blue	**bleu**	bleuh
brown	**marron/brun**	mar-*rohn*/bruhn
green	**vert**	vaihr
orange	**orange**	o-*rahnj*
pink	**rose**	rose
purple	**violet**	vee-o-*lay*
red	**rouge**	rooj
white	**blanc**	blahnk
yellow	**jaune**	jhone
bad	**mauvais(e)**	moh-*veh*
big	**grand(e)**	gron/gronde
closed	**fermé(e)**	fer-*meh*
down	**en bas**	on *bah*
early	**de bonne heure**	duh bon *urr*
enough	**assez**	as-*say*
far	**loin**	lwan
free, unoccupied	**libre**	*lee*-bruh
free, without charge	**gratuit(e)**	grah-*twee*/grah-*tweet*
good	**bon/bonne**	boa/bun
hot	**chaud(e)**	show/shoad
near	**près**	preh
open (as in "museum")	**ouvert(e)**	oo-*ver*
small	**petit(e)**	puh-*teel*/puh-*teet*
up	**en haut**	on *oh*
well	**bien**	byehn

NUMBERS & ORDINALS

English	French	Pronunciation
zero	**zéro**	*zare*-oh
one	**un**	uh
two	**deux**	duh
three	**trois**	twah
four	**quatre**	*kaht*-ruh
five	**cinq**	sank
six	**six**	seess
seven	**sept**	set
eight	**huit**	wheat
nine	**neuf**	nuf
ten	**dix**	deess
eleven	**onze**	ohnz
twelve	**douze**	dooz
thirteen	**treize**	trehz
fourteen	**quatorze**	kah-*torz*
fifteen	**quinze**	kanz
sixteen	**seize**	sez
seventeen	**dix-sept**	deez-*set*
eighteen	**dix-huit**	deez-*wheat*
nineteen	**dix-neuf**	deez-*nuf*
twenty	**vingt**	vehn
twenty-one	**vingt-et-un**	vehnt-ay-*uh*
twenty-two	**vingt-deux**	vehnt-*duh*

thirty	**trente**	trahnt
forty	**quarante**	ka-*rahnt*
fifty	**cinquante**	sang-*kahnt*
sixty	**soixante**	swa-*sahnt*
sixty-one	**soixante-et-un**	swa-*sahnt*-et-*uh*
seventy	**soixante-dix**	swa-sahnt-*deess*
seventy-one	**soixante-et-onze**	swa-sahnt-et-*ohnze*
eighty	**quatre-vingts**	kaht-ruh-*vehn*
eighty-one	**quatre-vingt-un**	kaht-ruh-vehn-*uh*
ninety	**quatre-vingt-dix**	kaht-ruh-venh-*deess*
ninety-one	**quatre-vingt-onze**	kaht-ruh-venh-*ohnze*
one hundred	**cent**	sahn
one thousand	**mille**	meel
one hundred thousand	**cent mille**	sahn meel
first	**premier**	*preh*-mee-ay
second	**deuxième**	*duhz*-zee-em
third	**troisième**	*twa*-zee-em
fourth	**quatrième**	*kaht*-ree-em
fifth	**cinquième**	*sank*-ee-em
sixth	**sixième**	*sees*-ee-em
seventh	**septième**	*set*-ee-em
eighth	**huitième**	*wheat*-ee-em
ninth	**neuvième**	*neuv*-ee-em
tenth	**dixième**	*dees*-ee-em
eleventh	**onzième**	*ohnz*-ee-em
twelfth	**douzième**	*dooz*-ee-em
thirteenth	**treizième**	*trehz*-ee-em
fourteenth	**quatorzième**	kah-*torz*-ee-em
twentieth	**vingtième**	*vehnt*-ee-em
thirtieth	**trentième**	*trahnt*-ee-em
one-hundredth	**centième**	*sant*-ee-em

THE CALENDAR

English	French	Pronunciation
January	**janvier**	*jhan*-vee-ay
February	**février**	*feh*-vree-ay
March	**mars**	marce
April	**avril**	a-*vreel*
May	**mai**	meh
June	**juin**	jhwehn
July	**juillet**	*jhwee*-ay
August	**août**	oot
September	**septembre**	sep-*tahm*-bruh
October	**octobre**	ok-*to*-bruh
November	**novembre**	no-*vahm*-bruh
December	**decembre**	day-*sahm*-bruh
Sunday	**dimanche**	dee-*mahnsh*
Monday	**lundi**	*luhn*-dee
Tuesday	**mardi**	*mahr*-dee
Wednesday	**mercredi**	*mair*-kruh-dee
Thursday	**jeudi**	*jheu*-dee
Friday	**vendredi**	*vawn*-druh-dee
Saturday	**samedi**	*sahm*-dee
yesterday	**hier**	ee-*air*

today	**aujourd'hui**	o-jhord-*dwee*
this morning/	**ce matin/**	suh ma-*tan*/
this afternoon	**cet après-midi**	set ah-preh mee-*dee*
tonight	**ce soir**	suh *swahr*
tomorrow	**demain**	de-*man*

2 Glossary of Basic Menu Terms

Note: To order any of these items from a waiter, simply preface the French-language name with the phrase "Je voudrais" (jhe voo-*dray*), which means, "I would like . . ." *Bon Appetit!*

Useful Terms & Phrases

MEATS

English	French	Pronunciation
beef stew	**du pot au feu**	dew poht o *fhe*
marinated beef braised with red wine and served with vegetables	**du boeuf à la mode**	dew bewf ah lah *mhowd*
brains	**de la cervelle**	duh lah ser-*vel*
chicken	**du poulet**	*dew poo*-lay
rolls of pounded and baked chicken, veal, or fish, often pike, usually served warm	**des quenelles**	day ke-*nelle*
chicken, stewed with mushrooms and wine	**du coq au vin**	dew cock o vhaihn
chicken wings	**des ailes de poulet**	dayz ehl duh poo-lay
frogs' legs	**des cuisses de grenouilles**	day cweess duh gre *noo* yuh
ham	**du jambon**	dew jham-bohn
haunch or leg of an animal, especially that of a lamb or sheep	**du gigot**	dew *jhi*-goh
kidneys	**des rognons**	day *row*-nyon
lamb	**de l'agneau**	duh l'ahn-*nyo*
lamb chop	**une cotelette d'agneau**	ewn koh-te-lette duh l'ahn-*nyo*
rabbit	**du lapin**	dew lah-pan
sirloin	**de l'aloyau**	duh l'ahl-why-*yo*
steak	**du bifteck**	dew beef-*tek*
filet steak, embedded with fresh green or black peppercorns, flambéed and served with a cognac sauce	**un steak au poivre**	uh stake o *pwah*-vruh
double tenderloin, a long muscle from which filet steaks are cut	**du chateaubriand**	dew sha-tow-bree-*ahn*
stewed meat with white sauce, enriched with cream and eggs	**de la blanquette**	duh lah blon-*kette*
sweetbreads	**des ris de veau**	day *ree* duh voh
veal	**du veau**	dew *voh*

FISH

English	French	Pronunciation
fish (freshwater)	**du poisson de rivière,** *or* **du poisson d'eau douce/**	dew pwah-sson duh ree-vee-*aire*, dew pwah-sson d'o *dooss/*
fish (saltwater)	**du poisson de mer**	dew pwah-sson duh *mehr*
mediterranean fish soup or stew made with tomatoes, garlic, saffron, and olive oil	**de la bouillabaisse**	duh lah booh-ya-*besse*
eel	**de l'anguille**	duh l'ahn-*ghee*-uh
herring	**du hareng**	dew ahr-*rahn*
lobster	**du homard**	dew oh-*mahr*
mussels	**des moules**	day *moohl*
mussels in herb-flavored white wine with shallots	**des moules marinières**	day moohl mar-ee-nee-*air*
oysters	**des huîtres**	dayz hoo-*ee*-truhs
pike	**du brochet**	dew broh-*chay*
shrimp	**des crevettes**	day kreh-*vette*
smoked salmon	**du saumon fumé**	dew sow-mohn fu-*may*
tuna	**du thon**	dew tohn
trout	**de la truite**	duh lah tru-*eet*
wolffish, a mediterranean sea bass	**du loup de mer**	dew loo-duh-*mehr*

SIDES/APPETIZERS

English	French	Pronunciation
butter	**du beurre**	dew bhuhr
bread	**du pain**	dew pan
goose liver	**du foie gras**	dew fwah grah
liver	**du foie**	dew fwah
potted and minced pork and pork by-products, prepared as a roughly hopped pâté	**des rillettes**	day ree-*yett*
rice	**du riz**	dew ree
snails	**des escargots**	dayz ess-car-*goh*

FRUITS/VEGETABLES

English	French	Pronunciation
cabbage	**du choux**	dew *shoe*
eggplant	**de l'aubergine**	duh l'oh-ber-*jheen*
grapefruit	**un pamplemousse**	uh pahm-pluh-moose
grapes	**du raisin**	dew ray-*zhan*
green beans	**des haricots verts**	day ahr-ee-coh *vaire*
green peas	**des petits pois**	day puh-tee-*pwah*
lemon/lime	**du citron/du citron vert**	dew cee-*tron*/dew cee-tron *vaire*
orange	**une orange**	ewn or-*ahn*-jhe
pineapple	**de l'ananas**	duh l'ah-na-*nas*
potatoes	**des pommes de terre**	day puhm duh *tehr*
potatoes au gratin	**des pommes de terre dauphinois**	day puhm duh tehr doh-feen-*wah*
french fried potatoes	**des pommes frites**	day puhm *freet*
spinach	**des épinards**	dayz ay-pin-*ards*
strawberries	**des fraises**	day *frez*

SOUPS/SALADS

English	French	Pronunciation
cucumber salad	**une salade de concombres**	ewn sah-lahd duh con-*con*-bruh
fruit salad	**une salade de fruit/ une macédoine de fruits**	ewn sah-lahd duh *fweel* ewn mah-say-doine duh fwee
green salad	**une salade verte**	ewn sah-lahd *vairt*
lettuce salad	**une salade de laitue**	ewn sah-lahd duh lay-tew
onion soup	**de la soupe à l'oignon**	duh lah soop ah low-*ñon*
salad, native to Nice, composed of lettuce, tuna, anchovies, capers, tomatoes, olives, olive oil, wine vinegar, and herbs	**une salade niçoise**	ewn sah-lahd nee-*swaz*
sauerkraut	**de la choucroute**	duh lah chew-*kroot*
vegetable soup with basil	**soupe au pistou**	duh lah soop oh pees-tou

BEVERAGES

English	French	Pronunciation
beer	**de la bière**	duh lah bee-*aire*
milk	**du lait**	dew *lay*
orange juice	**du jus d'orange**	dew joo d'or-*ahn*-jhe
water	**de l'eau**	duh lo
red wine	**du vin rouge**	dew vhin *rooj*
white wine	**du vin blanc**	dew vhin *blahn*
coffee	**un café**	uh ka-*fay*
coffee (black)	**un café noir**	uh ka-fay *nwahr*
coffee (with cream)	**un café crème**	uh ka-fay *krem*
coffee (with milk)	**un café au lait**	uh ka-fay o *lay*
coffee (decaf)	**un café décaféiné** (slang: **un déca**)	un ka-fay day-kah-fay-*nay* (uh *day*-kah)
coffee (espresso)	**un espresso** (*un express*)	un ka-fay ek-*sprehss*-o (uh ek-*sprehss*)
tea	**du thé**	dew *tay*
herbal tea	**une tisane**	ewn tee-*zahn*
drinks not included	**boissons non compris**	bwa-sons nohn com-*pree*

DESSERTS

English	French	Pronunciation
cake	**du gâteau**	dew gha-tow
cheese	**du fromage**	dew fro *mahj*
thick custard dessert with a caramelized topping	**de la crème brulée**	duh lah krem bruh-*lay*
caramelized upside-down apple pie	**une tarte tatin**	ewn tart tah-*tihn*
tart	**une tarte**	ewn tart
vanilla ice cream	**de la glace à la vanille**	duh lah glass a lah vah-*nee*-yuh
fruit, especially cherries, cooked in batter	**du clafoutis**	dew kla-foo-*tee*

SPICES/CONDIMENTS

English	French	Pronunciation
mustard	**de la moutarde**	duh lah moo-*tard*-uh
pepper	**du poivre**	dew *pwah*-vruh
salt	**du sel**	dew *sel*
sour heavy cream	**de la crème fraîche**	duh lah krem *fresh*
sugar	**du sucre**	dew *sooh*-kruh

COOKING METHODS

English	French	Pronunciation
cooked in parchment paper	**en papillotte**	ehn pah-pee-*yott*
cooked over a wood fire	**cuit au feu de bois**	kwee oh fhe duh *bwoi*
minced and potted meat, seasoned and molded into a crock	**une terrine**	ewn tair-*een*
puff pastry shell	**vol-au-vent**	vhol-o-*vhen*
a method of food preparation native to Lyon and its region that usually includes wine sauce accented with shredded and sautéed onions	**à la lyonnaise**	ah lah lee-ohn-*nehz*
in the style of Burgundy, usually with red wine, mushrooms, bacon, and onions	**bourgignon/ à la bourguignonne**	boor-geehn-*nyon*/ a lah boor-geeh-ny-*uhn*
method of cooking whereby anything (including fish, meat, fruits, or vegetables) is simmered in a reduction of its own fat or juices	**un confit**	uh khon-*feeh*

MISCELLANEOUS

English	French	Pronunciation
I'm a vegetarian	**Je suis végétarien/ Je suis végétarienne**	Jhe swee vay-jhay-tar-e-en Jhe swee vay-jhay-tar-e-*enne*
a fixed-price, precomposed meal, usually offering a limited choice of the specific dishes that comprise it	**le menu/le prix fixe/ la formule/la table d'hôte**	le meh-noo/le pree-*feex*/ lah for-*muhl*/ lah tah-bluh *doht*
tasting menu	**le menu gastronomique/ le menu dégustation**	le meh-noo gah-stroh-noh-meek/le meh-noo day-goo-stah-sion

Frommer's Online Directory

by Michael Shapiro

Michael Shapiro is the author of *Internet Travel Planning*
(The Globe Pequot Press).
Bruce Gerstman compiled the Paris listings for this directory.

Frommer's Online Directory is a new feature designed to help you take advantage of the Internet to better plan your trip. Part 1 lists general Internet resources that can make any trip easier, such as sites for booking airline tickets. This is not meant to be a comprehensive list—it's a discriminating selection to get you started. In Part 2 you'll find some top online guides for Paris.

The Top Travel-Planning Web Sites

Among the most popular travel sites are online travel agencies. The top agencies, including Expedia, Preview Travel, and Travelocity, offer an array of tools that are valuable even if you don't book online. You can check flight schedules, hotel availability, car rental prices, or even get paged if your flight is delayed.

While online agencies have come a long way over the past few years, they don't always yield the best price. Unlike a travel agent, they're unlikely to tell you, for example, that you can save money by flying a day earlier or a day later. On the other hand, if you're looking for a bargain fare, you might find something online that an agent wouldn't take the time to dig up. Because airline commissions have been cut, a travel agent may not find it worthwhile to spend half an hour trying to find you the best deal. On the Net, you can be your own agent and take all the time you want.

Online booking sites aren't the only places to book airline tickets—all major airlines have their own Web sites and often offer incentives, such as bonus frequent flyer miles or Net-only discounts, for buying online. These incentives have helped airlines capture the majority of the online booking market. According to Jupiter Communications, online agencies such as Travelocity booked about 80 percent of tickets purchased online in 1996, but by 1999 airline sites were projected to own more than half of the online market, with online agencies' share of the pie dwindling each year.

Below are the Web sites for the major airlines serving Paris. These sites offer schedules and flight booking, and most have pages where you can sign up for e-mail alerts listing weekend deals and other late-breaking bargains.

Air Canada. **www.aircanada.ca**
Air France. **www.airfrance.com**
American Airlines. **www.aa.com**

British Airways. **www.british-airways.com**
Continental Airlines. **www.flycontinental.com**
Delta Air Lines. **www.delta-air.com**
Northwest Airlines. **www.nwa.com**
TWA. **www.twa.com**
USAirways. **www.usairways.com**

WHEN SHOULD YOU BOOK ONLINE?

Online booking is not for everyone. If you prefer to let others handle your travel arrangements, one call to an experienced travel agent should suffice. But if you want to know as much as possible about your options, the Net is a good place to start, especially for bargain hunters.

The most compelling reason to use online booking is to take advantage of last-minute specials, such as American Airlines' weekend deals or other Internet-only fares that must be purchased online. Another advantage is that you can cash in on incentives for booking online, such as rebates or bonus frequent flyer miles.

Online booking works best for trips within North America—for international tickets, it's usually cheaper and easier to use a travel agent or consolidator. Online booking is certainly not for those with a complex international itinerary. If you require follow-up services, such as itinerary changes, use a travel agent. Though Expedia and some other online agencies employ travel agents who are available by phone, these sites are geared primarily for self-service.

LEADING BOOKING SITES

Below are listings for the top travel booking sites. The starred selections are the most useful and best designed sites.

Cheap Tickets. **www.cheaptickets.com**
Essentials: Discounted rates on domestic and international airline tickets and hotel rooms. Sometimes discounters such as Cheap Tickets have exclusive deals that aren't available through more mainstream channels. Registration at Cheap Tickets requires inputting a credit card number before getting started, which is one reason many people elect to call the company's toll-free number rather than booking online. One of the most frustrating things about the Cheap Tickets site is that it will offer fare quotes for a route, then later show the fare as invalid for your dates of travel. Other Web sites, such as Preview Travel, consider your dates of travel before showing available fares. Despite its problems, Cheap Tickets can be worth the effort because its fares can be lower than those offered by its competitors.

✪ Expedia. **expedia.com**
Essentials: Domestic and international flight, hotel, and rental car booking; late-breaking travel news, destination features, and commentary from travel experts; deals on cruises and vacation packages. Free registration is required for booking.

Is it Safe?

Far more people look online than book online, partly due to fear of putting their credit cards through on the Net. Though secure encryption has made this fear less justified, there's no reason why you can't find a flight online and then book it by calling a toll-free number or contacting your travel agent. To be sure you're in secure mode when you book online, look for a key (in Netscape) or padlock (Internet Explorer) icon at the bottom of your Web browser.

Take a Look at Frommer's Site

We highly recommend Arthur Frommer's Budget Travel Online (**www. frommers.com**) as an excellent travel-planning resource. Of course, we're a little biased, but you will find indispensable travel tips, reviews, monthly vacation give-aways, and online booking on the site.

Subscribe to Arthur Frommer's Daily Newsletter (**www.frommers. com/newsletters**) to receive the latest travel bargains and inside travel secrets in your mailbox every day. You'll read daily headlines and articles from the dean of travel himself, highlighting last-minute deals on airfares, accommodations, cruises, and package vacations. You'll also find great travel advice by checking our Tip of the Day or Hot Spot of the Month.

Search our Destinations archive (**www.frommers.com/destinations**) of more than 200 domestic and international destinations for great places to stay, tips for traveling there, and what to do while you're there. Once you've researched your trip, you might try our online reservation system (**www.frommers.com/ booktravelnow**) to book your dream vacation at affordable prices.

Expedia makes it easy to handle flight, hotel, and car booking on one itinerary, so it's a good place for one-stop shopping. Expedia's hotel search offers crisp, zoomable maps to pinpoint most properties; click on the camera icon to see images of the rooms and facilities. But like many online databases, Expedia focuses on the major chains, such as Hilton and Hyatt, so don't expect to find too many one-of-a-kind resorts or B&Bs here.

Once you're registered (it's only necessary to do this once from each computer you use), you can start booking with the Roundtrip Fare Finder box on the home page, which expedites the process. After selecting a flight, you can reserve it until midnight the following day or purchase online. If you think you might do better through a travel agent, you'll have time to try to get a lower price. And you may do better with a travel agent because Expedia's computer reservation system does not include all airlines. Notably absent are some leading budget carriers, such as Southwest Airlines.

Expedia's World Guide, offering destination information, is a glaring weakness—it takes a lot of page views to get very little information. However, Expedia compensates by linking to other Microsoft Network services, such as its Sidewalk city guides, which offer entertainment and dining advice for many of the cities it covers.

Preview Travel. www.previewtravel.com
Essentials: Domestic and international flight, hotel, and rental car booking; Travel Newswire lists fare sales, deals on cruises, and vacation packages. Free (one-time) reg-istration is required for booking. Preview offers express booking for members, but at press time this feature was buried below the fold on Preview's reservation page.

Preview features the most inviting interface for booking trips, though the wealth of graphics involved can make the site somewhat slow to load. Use Farefinder to quickly find the lowest current fares on flights to dozens of major cities. Carfinder offers a sim-ilar service for rental cars, but you can only search airport locations, not city pickup sites. To see the lowest fare for your itinerary, input the dates and times for your route and see what Preview comes up with.

In recent years Preview and other leading booking services have added features such as Best Fare Finder: after it searches for the best deal on your itinerary, the fare finder will check flights that are a bit later or earlier to see if it might be cheaper to fly at a different time. While these searches have become quite sophisticated, they still occasionally overlook deals that might be uncovered by a top-notch travel agent. If you have the time, see what you can find online and then call an agent to see if you can get a better price.

With Preview's Fare Alert feature, you can set fares for up to three routes and you'll receive e-mail notices when the fare drops below your target amount.

Note to AOL Users: You can book flights, hotels, rental cars, and cruises on AOL at keyword: Travel. The booking software is provided by Preview Travel and is similar to Preview on the Web. Use the AOL "Travelers Advantage" program to earn a 5 percent rebate on flights, hotel rooms, and car rentals.

Priceline.com. www.priceline.com

Even people who aren't familiar with too many Web sites have heard about Priceline.com. Launched in 1998 with a $10 million ad campaign featuring William Shatner, Priceline lets you "name your price" for domestic and international airline tickets and hotel rooms. In other words, you select a route and dates, guarantee with a credit card, and make a bid for what you're willing to pay. If one of the airlines in Priceline's database has a fare that's lower than your bid, your credit card will automatically be charged for a ticket.

You can't say what time you want to fly—you have to accept any flight leaving between 6am and 10pm on the dates you choose, and you may have to make one stopover. No frequent flyer miles are awarded, and tickets are nonrefundable and can't be exchanged for another flight. So if your plans change, you're out of luck. Priceline can be good for travelers who have to take off on short notice (and who are thus unable to qualify for advance purchase discounts). But be sure to shop around first—if you overbid, you'll be required to purchase the ticket and Priceline will pocket the difference.

Travelocity. www.travelocity.com

Essentials: Domestic and international flight, hotel, and rental car booking; deals on cruises and vacation packages. Travel Headlines spotlights the latest bargain airfares. Free (one-time) registration is required for booking.

Travelocity almost got it right. Its Express Booking feature enables travelers to complete the booking process more quickly than they could at Expedia or Preview, but Travelocity gums up the works with a page called "Featured Airlines." Big placards of several featured airlines compete for your attention—if you want to see the fares for all available airlines, click the much smaller box at the bottom of the page labeled "Book a Flight."

Some have worried that Travelocity, which is owned by American Airlines' parent company, AMR, directs bookings to American. This doesn't seem to be the case; I've booked there dozens of times and have always been directed to the cheapest listed flight. But the "Featured Airlines" page seems to be Travelocity's way of trying to cash in with ads and incentives for booking certain airlines. (It's hard to blame these booking services for trying to generate some revenue; many airlines have slashed commissions to $10 per domestic booking for online transactions, so these virtual agencies are struggling.) There are rewards for choosing one of the featured airlines. You'll get 1,500 bonus frequent flyer miles if you book through United's site, for example, but the site doesn't tell you about other airlines that might be cheaper. If the United flight costs $150 more than the best deal on another airline, it's not worth spending the extra money.

On the plus side, Travelocity has some leading-edge techie tools for modern travelers. Exhibit A is Fare Watcher e-mail, an "intelligent agent" that keeps you informed of the best fares offered for the city pairs (round-trips) of your choice. Whenever the fare changes by $25 or more, Fare Watcher will alert you by e-mail. Exhibit B is Flight Paging: If you own an alphanumeric pager with national access that can receive e-mail, Travelocity's paging system can alert you if your flight is delayed. Finally, though Travelocity doesn't include every budget airline, it does include Southwest, the leading U.S. budget carrier.

FINDING LODGINGS ONLINE

While the services above offer hotel booking, sites devoted primarily to lodging may include properties that aren't listed on more general online travel agencies. Some lodging sites specialize in a particular type of accommodations, such as bed-and-breakfast inns, which you won't find on the more mainstream booking services. Other services, such as TravelWeb, offer weekend deals on major chain properties, which cater to business travelers and have more empty rooms on weekends.

All Hotels on the Web. www.all-hotels.com
Well, this site doesn't include all the hotels on the Web, but it does have tens of thousands of listings throughout the world. Bear in mind that each hotel listed has paid a small fee ($25 and up) for placement, so it's not an objective list, but more like a book of online brochures. Also see Hotels and Travel on the Net (**www.hotelstravel.com**) which claims to offer discount booking on more than 100,000 hotels and other lodgings in more than 120 countries.

Hotel Reservations Network. www.180096hotel.com
Bargain room rates at hotels in more than two dozen U.S. and international cities. HRN prebooks blocks of rooms in advance, so sometimes it has rooms—at discount rates—at hotels that are supposedly sold out. Select a city and input your dates, and you'll get a list of the best prices for a selection of hotels. Descriptions include an image of the property and a locator map; to book online click the "Book Now" button. HRN is notable for some deep discounts, even in cities where hotel rooms are expensive. The toll-free number is printed all over this site; call it if you want more options than are listed online.

Places to Stay. www.placestostay.com
Mostly one-of-a-kind places in the U.S. and abroad that you might not find in other directories, with a focus on resort accommodations. Again, listing is selective—this isn't a comprehensive directory, but it can give you a sense of what's available at different destinations.

✪ TravelWeb. www.travelweb.com
TravelWeb lists more than 16,000 hotels worldwide, focusing on chains such as Hyatt and Hilton, and you can book almost 90 percent of them online. TravelWeb's Click-It Weekends, updated each Monday, offers weekend deals at many leading hotel chains. TravelWeb is the online home for Pegasus Systems, which provides transaction processing systems for the hotel industry.

LAST-MINUTE DEALS AND OTHER ONLINE BARGAINS

There's nothing airlines hate more than flying with lots of empty seats. The Net has enabled airlines to offer last-minute bargains to entice travelers to fill those seats. Most of these are announced on Tuesday or Wednesday and are valid for travel the following weekend, but some can be booked weeks or months in advance. You can sign up for weekly e-mail alerts at airlines' sites (for airlines' Web site addresses, see above) or check sites (see below) that compile lists of these bargains and send them in one convenient weekly e-mail. But last-minute deals aren't the only online

A Handy Tip

While most people learn about last-minute air specials from e-mail dispatches, you can get a jump start by finding out precisely when these deals become available and check the airlines' Web sites at this time. Because these deals are limited, they can vanish within hours, sometimes even minutes, so it pays to log on as soon as they're available.

bargains—other sites can help you find values even if you can't wait until the eleventh hour.

✪ 1travel.com. www.1travel.com
Deals on domestic and international flights, cruises, hotels, and all-inclusive resorts such as Club Med. 1travel.com's Saving Alert compiles last-minute air deals so you don't have to scroll through multiple e-mail alerts. A feature called "Drive a little using low-fare airlines" helps map out strategies for using alternate airports to find lower fares. And Farebeater searches a database that includes published fares, consolidator bargains, and special deals exclusive to 1travel.com. *Note:* The travel agencies listed by 1travel.com have paid for placement.

BestFares. www.bestfares.com
Bargain-seeker Tom Parsons lists some great offers on airfares, hotels, rental cars, and cruises, but the site is poorly organized. News Desk is a long list of hundreds of bargains, but they're not broken down into cities or even countries, so it's not easy to find what you're looking for. If you have time to wade through it, you might find a good deal. Some material is available only to paid subscribers.

Go4less.com. www.go4less.com
Specializing in last-minute cruise and package deals, Go4less has some eye-popping offers. You can avoid sifting through all this material by using the Search box and entering vacation type, destination, month, and price.

LastMinuteTravel.com. www.lastminutetravel.com
Travel suppliers with excess inventory distribute unsold airline seats, hotel rooms, cruises, and vacation packages through this online agency.

Smarter Living. www.smarterliving.com
Best known for its e-mail dispatch of weekend deals on 20 airlines, Smarter Living also keeps you posted about last-minute bargains on everything from Windjammer Cruises to flights to Iceland.

✪ WebFlyer. www.webflyer.com
WebFlyer is the ultimate online resource for frequent flyers and also has an excellent listing of last-minute air deals. Click on "Deal Watch" for a roundup of weekend deals on flights, hotels, and rental cars from domestic and international suppliers.

TRAVELER'S TOOLKIT
Veteran travelers usually carry some essential items to make their trips easier. The following is a selection of online tools to smooth your journey.

✪ Foreign Languages for Travelers. www.travlang.com
Learn basic terms in more than 70 languages and click on any underlined phrase to hear what it sounds like. (*Note:* Free audio software and speakers are required.)

Intellicast. www.intellicast.com
Weather forecasts for all 50 states and cities around the world. Note that temperatures are in Celsius for many international destinations.

Check Your E-mail at Internet Cafes

Until a few years ago, most travelers who checked their e-mail while traveling carried a laptop, but this posed some problems. Not only are laptops expensive, but they can be difficult to configure, incur expensive connection charges, and are attractive to thieves. Thankfully, Web-based free e-mail programs have made it much easier to check your mail.

Just open an account at a free e-mail provider, such as Hotmail (hotmail.com) or Yahoo! Mail (mail.yahoo.com) and all you'll need to check your mail is a Web connection, easily available at Net cafes and copy shops around the world. After logging on, just point the browser to www.hotmail.com, enter your username and password, and you'll have access to your mail.

Internet cafes have become ubiquitous, so for a few dollars an hour you'll be able to check your mail and send messages back to colleagues, friends and family. If you already have a primary e-mail account, you can set it to forward mail to your freemail account while you're away. Freemail programs have become enormously popular (Hotmail claims more than 10 million members) because they enable everyone, even those who don't own a computer, to have an e-mail address they can check wherever they log on to the Web.

MasterCard. www.mastercard.com/atm

Visa. www.visa.com/pd/atm

Find ATMs in hundreds of cities in the U.S. and around the world. Both sites include maps for some locations and list airport ATM locations, some with maps. Remarkably, MasterCard lists ATMs on all seven continents (there's one at Antarctica's McMurdo Station). *Tip:* You'll usually get a better exchange rate using ATMs than exchanging traveler's checks at banks.

Net Café Guide. www.netcafeguide.com/mapindex.htm

Locate Internet cafes at hundreds of locations around the globe. Catch up on your e-mail, log on to the Web, and stay in touch with the home front, usually for just a few dollars per hour.

Tourism Offices Worldwide Directory. www.towd.com

An extensive listing of tourism offices, some with links to these offices' Web sites.

The Travelite FAQ. www.travelite.org

Tips on packing light, choosing luggage, and selecting appropriate travel wear.

Universal Currency Converter. www.xe.net/currency

See what your dollar or pound is worth in more than a hundred countries.

U.S. Customs Service Traveler Information.
www.customs.ustreas.gov/travel/index.htm

Wondering what you're allowed to bring back to the U.S.? Check at this thorough site, which includes maximum allowance and duty fees.

The Top Web Sites for Paris

Most of the following sites are in both English and French. Though many of them will first come up in French, follow the icons for English versions. If it's not evident at first, scroll down to find an American or British flag.

CITY & ACCOMMODATIONS GUIDES

Champs Elysees. **www.champselysees.org**
Click around the neighborhood map for shops, restaurants, and movies in the neighborhood. If you prefer to skip the crowds, check out the 360-degree views of the area on the site.

Digital City: Paris. Keyword: Paris (AOL). **digitalcity.aol.com/paris/webguide**
A well-organized guide to the city's Web sites, including night life, dining, attractions, performing arts, outdoor activities, transportation, lodging, and information relevant to locals.

❂ Jack's Inimitable Guide to Paris. **www.worldtable.com/Jack/Paris/Paris.toc.html**
Organized by arrondissement, Jack has put together dozens of walking tours of the city, combining history with his own opinions and vivid descriptions of the streets. Print out some of the pages and walk with Jack into museums and attractions, around the Latin Quarter, and through other neighborhoods. His Secret and Unexpected Paris section leads visitors to places he claims are tough to find.

Paris.Com. **www.paris.com**
This site's strength is the lodging section, consisting of uncritical reviews accompanying photos of the rooms. There's a little bit of information on attractions.

Paris Digest. **www.parisdigest.com**
This independent site contains articles that link visitors to restaurants, hotels, museums, monuments, parks, and activities. It includes city history and tips for getting around.

Paris France Guide. **www.parisfranceguide.com**
Though this magazine publisher claims that this guide offers everything you need to know about France, it actually concentrates on Paris. It's full of current articles and listings on nightlife, restaurants, events, theater, and music.

Paris Free Voice. **parisvoice.com**
An opinionated monthly magazine that caters to travelers. The calendar of events includes music, movies, and performance art listings.

❂ Paris Pages. **www.paris.org**
The lodging reviews are organized by area of the city and nearby monuments. The city guide includes an event calendar, shop listings, map of attractions with details about each, and photo tour.

Paris Tourist Office. **www.paris-touristoffice.com**
Includes contact information and the closest metro stops for museums, lodging, restaurants, and night life. For details on city events, click on the scrolling list.

Smartweb: Paris. **www.smartweb.fr/paris**
This city guide shows the big attractions, such as the Louvre and Eiffel Tower, and includes history, photos, admission fees, and hours. Navigate the shopping and gallery listings organized by district and preview the airports' terminals.

thinkparis.com. **www.thinkparis.com**
Teaming up with the monthly magazine *Paris Voice,* this guide offers a calendar of events and a small dining section where readers can submit their own reviews.

MUSEUMS

Louvre Museum Official Website. **mistral.culture.fr/louvre/louvrea.htm**
After checking out their descriptions of the guided tours, permanent collections, and temporary exhibitions, download the free QuickTime VR software to take a virtual stroll through the museum. Mona Lisa awaits.

Musée d'Orsay. www.musee-orsay.fr
Samples from the sculpture, architecture, painting, and photography collections accompany history and descriptions of the pieces and artists. Find information about events, guided tours, hours, admission, and directions. There's also a history of the museum, which was converted from a train station.

Musée de la Musique. www.cite-musique.fr
Hours, admission, and contact information make up only part of the site. Download a free version of Real Audio and listen to music as you peruse photos of the modern property as well as pianos, harps, and other instruments in the museum's collections.

Musee Rodin. www.musee-rodin.fr
Preview the grounds and collections of Rodin's sculptures, paintings, engravings, photos, and sketches. Read a bio of the artist, a history of the museum, and details of the garden. The operating hours, admission, directions, and address will help get you there.

Paris Museum Pass. www.intermusees.com
Don't care about the temporary exhibits and just want to see classic art? This budget pass gets visitors into permanent collections around the city.

Pompidou Center. www.cnac-gp.fr
Arguably the most architecturally wacky place in Paris, the Pompidou site posts a huge amount of information and pictures of its collections. Art buffs will have a field day searching through the museum's catalog of artwork in the Documentation section. They also present new media exhibits in their Works Online section.

OTHER MAJOR ATTRACTIONS

Catacombs of Paris. www.multimania.com/houze
If the spooky photos of skulls and bones don't scare you away, read the history about Paris's underground caverns.

Château de Versailles. www.chateauversailles.com
Before visiting the old digs of Louis the XIV, print out pages from this reference full of history, pictures of the grounds, and the works of art that hang on the palace walls.

Disneyland Paris. www.disneylandparis.com
This guide to the park includes videos that let you preview attractions such as Fantasyland, Frontierland, and Discoveryland. (Download the free QuickTime software to see them.) Dining and lodging guides describe each establishment with photos and more QuickTime videos. Answer some questions in the Holiday Planner section and get an idea of a travel package that fits your needs.

Eiffel Tower. www.tour-eiffel.fr
Read the history of the tower and download a free version of QuickTime VR software to get simulated views from the top.

DINING GUIDES

The French take their cuisine seriously. Photos on these Web sites occasionally portray the restaurants, but they usually concentrate on showing off the food.

Great Parisian Restaurants. www.blanc.net/en/frame.html
About a half-dozen ad-based restaurant reviews comprise this site. The photos and menu details give a good idea of what to expect.

Guide to Pubs and Bars in Paris. www.net-europa.com/gap
Parisian bars are organized by best ambience, worst ambience, cheapest, most expensive, and best for late night drinks. The editors describe and review each establishment and let readers submit comments.

Paris Inside Out. **www.paris-anglo.com/pio/chapters/eatdrink/restaurants.htm**
This guide for Americans living abroad offers an excellent dining section with reviews of restaurants and bars.

Paris Zagat. **www.zagat.com**
Choose Paris from the pull-down menu and see what other travelers have to say about the local cuisine and service. At press time it appeared that Zagat was preparing to impose membership fees to access parts of this site; other parts, such as summaries of reviews and rankings were expected to remain free.

GETTING AROUND

Aeroports de Paris. **www.paris-airports.com**
For the Charles de Gaulle and Orly airports, find listings of hotels, restaurants, and car-rental agencies. The parking map and accessibility information for disabled travelers might help out upon landing.

RATP. **www.ratp.fr/index.eng.html**
Métro and bus maps as well as street maps to the city will help get you around. Download a free version of Adobe Acrobat to view some of the street maps. RATP links to Subway Navigator, which shows you how to use the Métro from one point to another.

✪ Subway Navigator. **www.metro.ratp.fr:10001/bin/cities/english**
An amazing site with detailed subway route maps for Paris, Lyon, Marseilles, and some other French cities, as well as more than 60 cities around the world. Select a city and enter your departure and arrival points. Subway Navigator maps out your route and tells you how long the trip should take. It will even show your route on a subway map.

Index

FROMMER'S® COMPLETE TRAVEL GUIDES

Alaska
Amsterdam
Arizona
Atlanta
Australia
Austria
Bahamas
Barcelona, Madrid & Seville
Beijing
Belgium, Holland & Luxembourg
Bermuda
Boston
Budapest & the Best of Hungary
California
Canada
Cancún, Cozumel &
  the Yucatán
Cape Cod, Nantucket & Martha's Vineyard
Caribbean
Caribbean Cruises & Ports of Call
Caribbean Ports of Call
Carolinas & Georgia
Chicago
China
Colorado
Costa Rica
Denmark
Denver, Boulder & Colorado Springs
England
Europe
Florida
France
Germany
Greece
Greek Islands
Hawaii
Hong Kong
Honolulu, Waikiki & Oahu
Ireland
Israel
Italy
Jamaica & Barbados
Japan
Las Vegas
London
Los Angeles
Maryland & Delaware
Maui
Mexico
Miami & the Keys

Montana & Wyoming
Montréal & Québec City
Munich & the Bavarian Alps
Nashville & Memphis
Nepal
New England
New Mexico
New Orleans
New York City
Nova Scotia, New Brunswick &
  Prince Edward Island
Oregon
Paris
Philadelphia & the
  Amish Country
Portugal
Prague & the Best of the Czech Republic
Provence & the Riviera
Puerto Rico
Rome
San Antonio & Austin
San Diego
San Francisco
Santa Fe, Taos &
  Albuquerque
Scandinavia
Scotland
Seattle & Portland
Singapore & Malaysia
South Africa
Southeast Asia
South Pacific
Spain
Sweden
Switzerland
Thailand
Tokyo
Toronto
Tuscany & Umbria
USA
Utah
Vancouver & Victoria
Vermont, New Hampshire
  & Maine
Vienna & the Danube Valley
Virgin Islands
Virginia
Walt Disney World & Orlando
Washington, D.C.
Washington State

FROMMER'S® DOLLAR-A-DAY GUIDES

Australia from $50 a Day
California from $60 a Day
Caribbean from $70 a Day
England from $70 a Day
Europe from $60 a Day
Florida from $60 a Day

Hawaii from $70 a Day
Ireland from $50 a Day
Israel from $45 a Day
Italy from $70 a Day
London from $85 a Day
New York from $80 a Day

New Zealand from $50 a Day
Paris from $85 a Day
San Francisco from $60 a Day
Washington, D.C.,
  from $60 a Day

FROMMER'S® PORTABLE GUIDES

Acapulco, Ixtapa &
  Zihuatanejo
Alaska Cruises & Ports of Call
Bahamas
Baja & Los Cabos
Berlin
California Wine Country
Charleston & Savannah
Chicago

Dublin
Hawaii: The Big Island
Las Vegas
London
Maine Coast
Maui
New Orleans
New York City
Paris

Puerto Vallarta, Manzanillo
  & Guadalajara
San Diego
San Francisco
Sydney
Tampa & St. Petersburg
Venice
Washington, D.C.

FROMMER'S® NATIONAL PARK GUIDES

Family Vacations in the
  National Parks
Grand Canyon

National Parks of the
  American West
Rocky Mountain

Yellowstone & Grand Teton
Yosemite & Sequoia/
  Kings Canyon
Zion & Bryce Canyon

FROMMER'S® GREAT OUTDOOR GUIDES

New England
Northern California

Southern California & Baja
Washington & Oregon

FROMMER'S® MEMORABLE WALKS

Chicago
London

New York
Paris

San Francisco
Washington D.C.

FROMMER'S® IRREVERENT GUIDES

Amsterdam
Boston
Chicago
Las Vegas

London
Los Angeles
Manhattan

New Orleans
Paris
San Francisco

Seattle & Portland
Vancouver
Walt Disney World
Washington, D.C.

FROMMER'S® BEST-LOVED DRIVING TOURS

America
Britain
California

Florida
France
Germany

Ireland
Italy
New England

Scotland
Spain
Western Europe

WHEREVER YOU TRAVEL, *H*ELP IS NEVER FAR AWAY.

From planning your trip to providing travel assistance along the way, American Express® Travel Service Offices are always there to help you do more.

Paris

American Express Travel Service
11 Rue Scribe
(33) (1) 47777707/7928

Travel

www.americanexpress.com/travel

American Express Travel Service Offices are found in central locations throughout Paris.